PUBLIC ADMINISTRATION
Policy, Politics, and Practice

Second Edition

William C. Johnson
Bethel College

Boston, Massachusetts   Burr Ridge, Illinios   Dubuque, Iowa
Madison, Wisconsin   New York, New York   San Francisco, California   St. Louis, Missouri

McGraw·Hill
A Division of The **McGraw·Hill** Companies

Book Team

Publisher *Bevan O'Callaghan*
Sponsoring Editor *Irving E. Rockwood*
Managing Editor *John S. L. Holland*
Production Manager *Brenda S. Filley*
Managing Art Editor *Pamela Carley*
Editors *Ronald C. Harris, Catherine G. Leonard*
Designer *Charles Vitelli*
Permissions Coordinator *Janice M. Ward*
Typesetting Supervisor *Libra Ann Cusack*
Typesetter *Juliana Arbo*
Proofreader *Diane Barker*
Graphics *Shawn Callahan, Lara M. Johnson, Laura Levine*
Marketing Manager *Kirk Moen*

Vice President of Production and Business Development *Vickie Putman*
Vice President of Sales and Marketing *Bob McLaughlin*
Director of Marketing *John Finn*

Cover Photo *Fischer Bessi*
Cover design *Jennifer Smith*
Research by *Pamela Carley*

Library of Congress Catalog Card Number: 95-76521

ISBN 1-56134-425-7

Printed in the United States of America

10 9 8 7 6 5 4 3

William C. Johnson is Professor of Political Science at Bethel College, St. Paul, Minnesota, where he teaches a broad range of undergraduate courses, including public administration. In addition, he is a member of the Community Faculty of Metropolitan State University in St. Paul, where he directs independent studies in urban planning, and he serves on the Planning and Zoning Board of Lino Lakes, Minnesota. He is the coauthor (with John Harrigan) of *Governing the Twin Cities Region* (1978) and the author of *The Politics of Urban Planning* (1989) and numerous articles.

Public Administration: Politics, Policy, and Practice is the product of Professor Johnson's 29 years of classroom teaching, coupled with extensive experience in government at the grassroots level. The book also reflects Professor Johnson's strong belief in the link between accountability in government and an informed citizenry. The result is an exceptionally clear and dynamic text that combines a wealth of theoretical insights with practical observations culled from real-world experience.

Preface

As I wrote this book, I had in mind an image of the students whom I expected to read it. Although they vary in age and background, they are all students in an American college or university who are enrolled in an introductory course in public administration.

The course should enlighten them on the subject of how government goes about its business. More to the point, students need to know how they relate to the many components of government in this country (and in other nations as well). That is what this book is about.

I take neither a purely positive nor a purely negative view of the achievements of American public administration. Governments operate in an atmosphere of public distrust, which appears to be growing, and it is fashionable to criticize government agencies and their employees as bumbling at best and downright corrupt at worst. This book portrays public policy in a more balanced light. Public policy has had some remarkable successes and some dismal failures. Much more common are outcomes that delight neither a program's supporters nor its detractors, with plenty of ifs, buts, and on-the-other-hands. It is vital that students be able to identify and explain complex policy outcomes. From there, they can arrive at their own evaluations.

The major themes in this book are as follows:

Government's primary mission in society is to serve the public purposes as they have evolved from societal needs and popular expectations over the decades. Public administration consists of the means for accomplishing those purposes in a sustained and efficient manner, and the discipline must be evaluated by this criterion.

Public administration begins with public policy, government's choices of action to fulfill the public purposes. The vast complex of policies characteristic of modern societies ensures the need for administration. In this sense, public policy and public administration are inseparable, and neither can be fully understood without a working knowledge of the other.

Government in the United States is a complex network of organizations whose major components include not only federal agencies but those commonly labeled state and local. Without neglecting agencies of the federal government, this text gives much attention to administration in state and local governments, for they are, after all, the major employers of public personnel and the average citizen's most common point of contact with government.

Public administration is also carried on, in an important sense, by private organizations. Much of what governments do is paralleled or duplicated in the private sector. These public/private relationships are highlighted in Chapter 7.

Organization of the Book

In keeping with these themes, I have divided this book into five parts: Introduction, Structures, Policies, Operations, and Outcomes. This indicates one of its basic purposes: to portray public administration as the enterprise of carrying out the laws and policies that the people's representatives have enacted.

Part One consists of Chapter 1, which serves as an *Introduction* to the basic concepts used in the book and offers an overview of the discipline and profession of public administration.

Part Two, called *Structures,* sketches the government organizations through which Americans receive their goods and services, the general concepts of organization and bureaucracy by which these units of government are structured, and the relationships among the national, state, and local governments that are necessary to carry out most policies. Because public administration is an organized activity, it is essential to grasp the frameworks of these organizations early in the study.

Part Three gives attention to the *Policies* that administrators are charged to carry out. One must understand how public policies originate and how they acquire their forms, including the role that administrators play in policymaking and the exercise of power that produces one set of policies rather than another. A major policy area is regulation of business, which offers many examples of the dilemmas that must be resolved in the administrative process. Of growing importance are the cooperative relationships between governments and private sector organizations, the choice of which are policy alternatives in themselves. Governments must also concern themselves with their many impacts, for better or worse, on individuals and groups of citizens. These impacts may include the provision of services, citizens' participation in administrative decisions, and administrative actions that affect constitutional rights and liberties.

Part Four surveys *Operations,* the internal dynamics of administrative organizations. First, there is a survey of the issues of leadership and management by government executives. This is followed by an inquiry into planning and decision making by public agencies. The selection and management of government employees, amid such issues as employee organization and conflicts of interest, is a central task of many administrators. Finally, the control of spending and revenue determines both how much government is able to do and how efficiently it can achieve its purposes.

Part Five concludes the book by asking about the *Outcomes* of administration and how the public evaluates and responds to them. Many factors determine whether and how well policies are implemented, and it is also possible to learn why a given policy may not have been implemented well. A growing demand is that the outcomes of administration be evaluated systematically and objectively, in order to learn how to implement policy more successfully in the future. The final chapter examines the means by which American citizens, directly or indirectly through their representatives, hold administrators accountable for their actions or inactions.

Although there is a logical order in the topics and chapters, I realize that teaching priorities differ. Some instructors will prefer to discuss finance and personnel management earlier in the course, for instance. They should encounter no major problems in choosing a different order in their courses, since successive chapters do not depend heavily on the preceding ones.

I have provided five discussion questions and two analytical exercises at the end of each chapter, all designed to broaden students' thinking about the issues raised and help them identify differences of opinion. There is also an instructor's manual available, in which I provide a set of test questions for each chapter. These questions are also available on a microcomputer test-generator program, EZ-TEST.®

I am indebted to several persons for their contributions in bringing this book to print: Irving Rockwood, formerly of Brown & Benchmark's editorial staff; Catherine Leonard, a painstaking editor; and from the academic realm, George Agbango, Bloomsburg University; Buck Miller, Christopher Newport University; Stephen C. Brooks, University of Akron; martha Swann, Catawba College; Guisette Salazar, Central Connecticut State University; Lucinda McKinney, Southern Illinois University-Carbondale; Robert Cullins Jr., University of Nevada-Las Vegas; Robert R. Wiggins, Cedarwille College; Bradley Martin, university of Findlay, who offered criticism of the first edition. The few (I hope) errors in fact or judgment that remain are my own responsibility.

William C. Johnson

Contents

Part III. Policies

15. Administrative Accountability 431

Public Administration:
To Serve and Protect

Learning Objectives

After reading this chapter, you should be able to do the following:
1. Define politics and government, public policy, and public administration, and the connections among them.
2. Identify and define the seven essential public purposes.
3. Identify and define the tools for implementation.
4. Understand how public administration is both a discipline and a
   profession.
5. Describe the global dimensions of public administration.
6. Identify the central ethical demands on public administration.

Health, as a description of physical and mental well-being,
is intensely personal, but health *care,* as a way of preserving
or restoring that well-being, is markedly *social.* Since these
two areas are tightly intertwined, health inevitably becomes a
public concern and thus a political one.

We frequently read about families without medical insurance whose finances have been devastated by a critical illness.
A television program may portray a demonstration in front of
the White House by AIDS victims demanding more funds for
research. We might open a newsmagazine and read about a
genetic breakthrough at a state university that identifies a person's tendency to mental illness. And a medical student may

express her concern that her future income in family practice will be insufficient to repay her government-backed loan. In such ways the personal and public dimensions of health overlap.

Each of these personal situations is a piece of the very large picture of **public administration.** We can begin to define it simply as the activities of government that determine the supply of goods and services to the public. (We discuss this in more detail later in this chapter.) Public administration matters for health care and for many other issues that join personal and social concerns. The challenge is to decide how to organize and manage the health care system to best advantage, although no single structure may be best for all, since life circumstances vary widely. For this reason we can expect constant change in public health care, just as we do in such areas as social welfare, criminal justice, telecommunications, and education.

Health care management poses four kinds of dilemmas that are common to many areas of public administration today. The first is a political task: to reconcile the competition among citizens and organized interest groups to define *health* as a set of public goals. How personal is health, and how public? This was the basic conflict responsible for the failure of President Clinton's reform efforts of 1993–1994. Second, the nation must determine what role government should play in health care, versus the organized private players whose profits and professional aims are at stake, versus individuals whose own life choices go far to decide what care, if any, they need.

A third dilemma, once the role of government is chosen, is to distribute responsibilities among the national, state, and local authorities. Even before the Clinton program failed in Congress, many states devised reforms of their own. Oregon was a pioneer. Chapter 5 recounts its efforts. It is unclear which legal provisions must be national, and which can vary from state to state.

Finally, whatever "macrosystem" evolves, the problem remains of overseeing its overall impact. Does it meet everyone's needs fairly? Is its quality high enough? Does it incorporate innovations in technology and up-to-date medical knowledge? Above all, is its cost reasonable? Americans now spend about a trillion dollars a year on medical services (about 15 percent of the gross domestic product), and that figure is expected to rise at least 10 percent annually for the foreseeable future. Not even the national government may be able to coordinate it well, but the public demands some protection against lapses and abuses. This too comes under the topic of public administration.

From radar-evading warplanes and radar-aided weather forecasts to food stamps and food label requirements, the range of goods and services provided by government continues to grow, as does the requirement for more competent administration to ensure that citizens' needs are met at reasonable cost. In the 1790s the federal government had annual budgets of less than $10 million and employed fewer than 3,000 people as clerks, customs collectors, mail carriers, and diplomats. Today it has an annual operating budget of more than $1.5 trillion and directly employs about 3 million civilians, many of them "administrators." To this we must add the more than 86,000 state and local governments, which spend another $1 trillion and have more than 14 million employees. Big government, we may conclude, is largely big administration.

Two points stand out here. First, the scope of public administration is far broader than most people realize, even while they deplore "big government." Second, employees can be considered public administrators—not just tax collectors and social security clerks but state university professors, police officers, building inspectors, forest rangers, and bus drivers. For this reason public administration is hard to escape, nor would we want to escape most of it, since it provides goods and services on which we depend. To enlarge our understanding of public administration, we begin by examining several related concepts: government, politics, and public policy.

Government and Politics: The Publicness of Public Administration

As we commonly use the word, *government* has two general meanings: (1) "The legal entity that maintains order and provides the goods and services society requires." It has authority to enforce laws and to compel the payment of taxes. In the United States the term can refer to national, state, or local government or to all of them collectively. (2) "The process of maintaining social order and supplying goods and services." The word has its origin in the Greek term for the pilot of a ship, suggesting that to govern is to steer a society's development and to make choices that continually create its future.

Politics in Public Administration

We must distinguish government from politics. As government carries out its duties, it inevitably bestows benefits on some groups and denies them to others. For example, the elderly, who spend much time in hospitals or doctors' offices, receive extensive benefits under Medicare, but those confined to nursing homes or requiring expensive prescription drugs do not qualify. Those who live near airports enjoy more convenient access than those farther away, but if they live under the main takeoff route they suffer intolerable noise. Even attempts to benefit everyone (e.g., national defense or local police protection) can spread advantages unevenly. Some companies and communities prosper from weapons contracts and military bases; others do not. The young men thrust into combat in Korea and later in Vietnam by the draft bore a burden from which women and older males were exempt.

At its heart, *politics* is concerned with government's use of its legal authority to distribute benefits and costs among members of a society (Easton, 1953). Since citizens do not quickly agree on such distributions, conflict usually arises in which the contestants seek to influence the outcomes, and they use whatever power they can muster. Victims of AIDS and the disabled concluded that they deserve more than they currently receive and so have mobilized money, lawyers, and lobbying skills to alter that distribution. Politics, defined as "cooperation and conflict over the distribution of benefits and costs in society," thus pervades all public administration.

Let us examine more closely what government does and how politics affects it, with an example from another kind of health dilemma. "You can't order permethrin or captan at the local restaurant. Zineb does not come in a handy table dispenser. . . . But these agricultural pesticides are finding their way onto American dinner plates. And that's causing increasing public concern" (Belsie, 1989). These substances kill fungi and vermin infesting our fruits and vegetables, but they cling to our food and eventually reach our tables. Scientists suspect that many promote cancer, but they disagree on the risk. What disturbs many consumers is that they cannot weigh the risk, for no apple carries a label detailing its pesticide residue.

In 1985 the U.S. Environmental Protection Agency (EPA) proposed a ban on captan, a widely used fungicide. However, after sparring with fruit growers and chemical manufacturers, it backed off. Upon more study, it acted early in 1989, barring captan on forty-two crops but allowing it on twenty-four others. Future research data are likely to guide more changes, but the uncertainty will probably persist. That the EPA exists at all is due to public demand. President Richard M. Nixon established the agency in 1970, with the mandate that government protect citizens from health hazards that they are unable to detect or avoid themselves. But what EPA should do about pesticides remains open to political and scientific judgment.

Government in the United States has several essential **public purposes** (the broad tasks the public expects it to carry out). These encompass all the objectives for government's exercise of its vast power and authority and the beneficial impacts on society they are intended to have. The public goods may be supplied by a governmental agency (e.g., a pension check or access to a freeway), or a private source may provide it (e.g., a guaranteed student loan or nonflammable seats in an airliner).

(continued on p. 6)

Box 1.1

The Essential Public Purposes

Examples:

1. Protect lives, property, and rights of citizens.

National defense
Antidiscrimination regulations
Public health and disease control
Police and fire protection
Workplace safety regulation

2. Maintain/ensure supply of essential resources.

Protection of oil imports
Emergency food supplies
Energy aid for poor
Water supply

3. Support persons unable to care for themselves.

Pensions for retired persons
Homes/therapy for disabled
Foster homes for children
Unemployment compensation

4. Promote steady and balanced economic growth.

Interest rate regulation
Financing for new businesses
Stimuli to international trade
Employment skills training
Transportation facilities
Labor/management negotiations

5. Promote quality of life and personal opportunity to succeed.

Education, early childhood to adult
Housing assistance
Cultural amenities
Recreational facilities

6. Protect natural environment.

Conservation of soil and water resources
Wildlife protection
Pollution control
Wastes management

7. Promote scientific and technological advancement.

Subsidies to scientific research
Space exploration
Patents for inventions
Information dissemination

What Government Does: The Public Purposes

What national, state, and local governments aim to accomplish in American society could make an impossibly long list. That multitude of purposes is one problem for public administration, for to do each of those things, do them efficiently, and do them without hindering the flow of other benefits is beyond any mortal's comprehension. To gain some appreciation for this, let us survey seven major broad-range purposes of government. Box 1.1 provides a brief overview of these.

First, since ancient times governments have been expected to protect the lives and property of their citizens. The Declaration of Independence stated that "governments are instituted among men" to secure our rights to "Life, Liberty, and the pursuit of Happiness" and thereby added the protection of civil rights and liberties to this task. Threats to these basic rights may arise from a hostile nation, other citizens, natural disasters, the random nature of life, or within government itself. Life is risky for everyone, and although the risk of death or destruction cannot be eliminated, the authority and resources of government often can reduce it. Efforts of the National Cancer Institute have extended the lives of many cancer victims, and stricter building codes have improved the prospects of Californians for surviving the next major slip of the San Andreas Fault. Loss of opportunity or personal dignity can be harder to deal with, but governments seek to prevent racial and religious discrimination in the sale and rental of housing.

A second historic task has been to maintain or ensure the supply of such essential resources as water, food, medicine, shelter, and energy. Today governments and private enterprises share this responsibility in complex ways. Water, electricity, and natural gas are common commodities of municipal or regional urban governments. Food supply is usually left to private producers and distributors, although if a natural disaster were to cut these off suddenly, government would have to become the supplier or allocator of last resort. Through their regulatory roles, governments also oversee the prices, quality, and marketing of many foods and fuels.

Third, governments support those who cannot care for themselves and lack others to help them: neglected children, persons with mental or physical disabilities, the unemployed, and others who become dependent. Their needs are diverse and often complex. For example, an abused child may be given sanctuary in a foster home, but a mentally ill alcoholic living in a cardboard box on a Los Angeles sidewalk requires a combination of services. Guardians must respect the autonomy of each dependent person yet have the authority and competence to recognize and meet basic needs.

Governments at all levels have long accepted, as a fourth purpose, responsibility for promoting steady and balanced economic growth. The fully "free market" does not exist, and employment, domestic and international trade, availability of credit, and the value of the dollar are highly sensitive to whatever government does. Governments have long built canals, highways, and airports to stimulate business and now must contemplate linking everyone to the "information superhighway." Stimulation of private economic development, from Washington's sweeping budgetary and fiscal policies to a city's efforts to lure new employers, emerged in the 1980s as a central measuring rod of all governmental performance.

Fifth, governments have acquired a broad mission to promote the "quality of life" and personal opportunity to succeed. Education from early childhood to late in life is a centerpiece of this effort. This purpose took on special urgency during the 1960s, when lawmakers recognized that opportunities could be more equally distributed with public policies that compensated for racial, linguistic, and cultural disadvantages and physical disabilities. Such quality of life is not a luxury but a social (if not always legal) right in an affluent society.

As a sixth task, governments are responsible for protecting the natural environment from unthinking exploitation and ruin. From President Theodore Roosevelt's forest conservation efforts to present concerns over the greenhouse effect, we have come to recognize that wise environmental management guards the nation's material means of meeting its other goals. This has a global dimension: Amazon rain forests and the ozone layer over Antarctica are of great concern, and although they are outside the direct powers of American government, they require its participation in international policy and administrative action.

Finally, governments must promote scientific and technological advancement and disseminate the information gained from research so it can be applied throughout the society. The framers of the Constitution recognized this by providing for patent protection, but today's efforts extend to active governmental involvement in nuclear energy, computers, genetic engineering, and exploration of space. Much of this research and development takes place in private corporations, but governments fund a large share of it.

These purposes overlap and reinforce one another. For example, scientific research on disease also protects the lives of citizens. Good education expands individuals' employment prospects and society's economic innovation and productivity. For this reason, most public policies serve multiple goals.

These public purposes are not entirely compatible, however. First, they compete for limited funds. Support for inner-city schools, for example, must be weighed against AIDS research funds, subsidies for cotton growers, and submarines. Second, some purposes inherently contradict one another. For instance, the improvement of employment opportunities for women and people of color may diminish prospects for white males, and restricting the use of certain farm chemicals that pollute groundwater may reduce production of some foods and thus the well-being of their growers.

Moreover, popular attitudes toward these purposes often reflect a curious mixture of distrust and dependence. A benefit that one group claims as a basic right will be resisted by another that deems it a waste of public funds or an intrusion into one's privacy. Current debates about expensive school programs for children with disabilities or about government funding for public radio and television and the arts illustrate this. Public purposes therefore represent ideals we cannot fully or exclusively serve, and the compromises we must make become the "real" purposes.

How Government Organizes to Serve the Public Purposes To carry out its mandates, governments organize into departments and agencies with specific legal powers. The Environmental Protection Agency (EPA) has a mandate from Congress in the Toxic Substances Control Act of 1976 to test chemicals currently in use for their effects on human health and the natural environment. For these studies it employs a committee of scientists from several federal agencies to run whatever tests are necessary and to recommend action to the EPA administrator. The agency is then empowered to make rules that carry the force of law and that can restrict a chemical's use or ban it altogether. Perhaps 60,000 chemicals are now in use; the EPA can seriously examine only a tiny fraction of these.

What do the examples presented thus far tell us about the special responsibilities of government? Only government has the legal authority to determine that a pesticide or fungicide poses a health threat to humans and to prohibit its use. And only government can oversee the complex commercial medical system, approving new pharmaceuticals, licensing health professionals, and acting against such health risks as epidemics. These are mandates that public officials cannot ignore.

Failures of the Administrative Process Governments do not always succeed in fulfilling these purposes; we can see that for ourselves. Some failures attract wide publicity, which underlines the difficulties that many situations pose. On November 5, 1987, Lisa Launders Steinberg, aged 6, died at St. Vincent's Hospital in New York City as a result of a severe beating by her adoptive parents, who were charged with murder. Neighbors in their apartment building claimed they had called police and a child abuse hot line many times about the violence in her home, which was also directed at the mother, Hedda Nussbaum. Although this case drew unusual attention from the press, such situations are not rare. That same year in New York City alone 108 abused and neglected children died.

Forty-five of those deaths occurred in families previously known to the city child abuse agency (Roberts, 1988).

There are many reasons for governmental failures. One observer claimed of the New York child protection system as it worked in the Steinberg case, "Everyone has done their job. You find this person made the visit, this person made the referral, this person made the call and everyone is covered on paper and has done their minimal legal responsibilities" (Uhlig, 1987). But in the end, no one prevented Lisa's death. Mayor Edward I. Koch lamented a year later that his administration could not have prevented most of the child abuse deaths, even in situations of which the city was already aware (Levine, 1988). Administrative shortcomings are also apparent in examples ranging from bacterially or chemically contaminated drinking water to miscalculated unemployment benefits.

Yet we must put these failures in perspective. Local governments have removed countless children from abusive situations and have helped reduce violence in many families. Many chemicals already known to be toxic have been banned or controlled, from asbestos to DDT, and lives have certainly been saved as a result. And nearly all who receive benefit payments, from Social Security to unemployment compensation, do get their checks on time and in the correct amounts.

A major task of this book is to compare the accomplishments and the shortcomings, to evaluate how well governments fulfill their purposes, and to learn why they succeed or fail.

The Growth of Government: How and Why Big Government Got Big

Responding to public purposes, as served by the basic processes just described, has produced an ever larger **public sector** (that portion of the nation's resources that is obtained and allocated by national, state, and local governments). How can we account for this relentless growth in government throughout the nation's history? Each additional governmental purpose seems to have made the next one necessary or desirable. There are many possible explanations for this growth, not one of which is unanimously accepted by scholars.

Factors that make up one category of growth stimulants include industrialization, urbanization, and the rise of technologies that closely link widely dispersed areas. Cities need tighter control of land uses and more police and fire protection than rural areas, and industries require regulation to protect the public from harmful market practices. The invention of the automobile brought innumerable public services and regulations. Governmental expansion was unavoidable for a society that sought technological progress and the orderly application of that technology.

Another perspective on big government places the United States in a global context, competing with other nations for security and prosperity. In the twentieth century, we have faced the demands of preparing for and fighting war and the growing interdependence of national economies. Such intense competition, whether violent or peaceful, requires central mobilization and management of our resources, matching that of our partners and adversaries. The size of the military establishment and its budget greatly affects the domestic economy. Similarly, economic competitiveness has become a major public purpose for all levels of government. For example, when Mitsubishi of Japan located an automobile factory in Bloomington, Illinois, that city and state proclaimed a victory resulting from the financial incentives they offered.

The dynamics of the democratic process also add to the growth of government, for the public purposes become what citizens want. Demands for public health clinics, cancer research, and regulation of toxic chemicals are expressed through elections, opinion polls, interest groups, and the values of those in public office. Although many programs may benefit only a minority, those minorities have sufficient size and power to claim a share of some government's budget. Focusing their attention only on their preferred programs, these groups are unconcerned about the overall size of government. Citizens often view government as their "problem solver of last resort," ready to step in when they perceive that private institutions cannot cope with a problem. Public authority may not be able to restore their well-being completely, but people want at least some mitigation of the problem.

Government programs may also grow not from demands by groups that would directly benefit from them but from a sense of moral obligation to help the poor and the victims of discrimination. As the nation completed the decade of the 1950s, in which incomes grew steadily, it was confronted by books and television programs that portrayed those whom prosperity had bypassed. Coupled with the growing militancy of the civil rights movement, these media made the nation ready to back the legislation of the mid-1960s that expanded national programs for economic opportunity and equal rights. That wave is diminished in the 1990s but continues to spawn innovation in the state and local arenas.

These popular forces for government growth make it difficult to reduce public spending in the 1990s. Although polls show that a majority of the population favors balanced federal budgets and more modest state and local programs overall, they also show that a significant number favors maintaining or even increasing spending on the major domestic programs. Meeting a need is somehow divorced from how to pay for it, even in this era of loud complaints over taxes and government debt.

Another perspective blames the bigness of government on the ambitions of bureaucrats and legislators. In this view the very success of a program is a justification to extend it, and those who manage a department instinctively seek a larger budget and extended power. Even a program's failure can be an argument for growth if its partisans can convince others that it was not big enough to do the job. Legislators, wishing to serve constituents (and thus to retain their votes), are happy to oblige them. This service may then appear in the form of a highway, income subsidy, health program, or neighborhood park. If this growth is considered unnecessary, this reflects negatively on the forces behind it. Where necessity lies, however, is more a political than an administrative decision.

All these explanations appear to have some validity, although empirical studies have not found any one of them to be dominant. We do better to see these influences as interdependent, shaping one another as they shape government as a whole. One typical study focuses on a blend of the demands of key socioeconomic groups, the interests dependent on corporations and the military, the philosophical orientations of many officeholders, and the broad preferences of voters for social spending to reduce the risks of life (Lewis-Beck & Rice, 1985, pp. 26–27).

If these broad forces are impelling government to grow, then it is beyond the ability of individual political leaders, even presidents, to reduce. President Ronald Reagan came to office in 1981 determined to cut domestic spending and increase the military establishment. He succeeded in the latter but not in the former. Indeed, his administration oversaw an increase in federal spending in proportion to the entire economy. We can expect government to shrink only when permitted by the large-scale environmental and political conditions that spurred its growth in the first place. And that, short of a catastrophe of unimaginable size or a more radical change in the public philosophy than ever before seen, may be impossible. Even if Congress succeeds in reducing federal spending in the 1990s, the demands for growth may simply shift to the state capitals and city halls and swell their budgets instead.

This survey of public administration emphasizes a key perspective, the implementation of **public policies.** The task of administration is to carry out policies—government's choices of action—in an organized fashion in the service of the public purposes. Public administration springs from the relationship among three basic elements of the policy process.

Public Policy: The Objectives and Tools of Public Administration

Figure 1.1

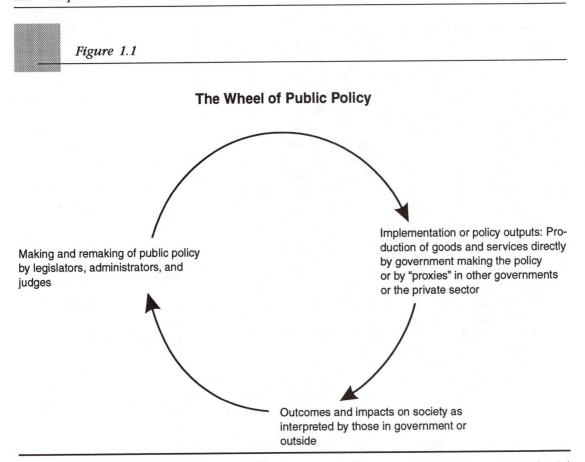

The Wheel of Public Policy

Making and remaking of public policy by legislators, administrators, and judges

Implementation or policy outputs: Production of goods and services directly by government making the policy or by "proxies" in other governments or the private sector

Outcomes and impacts on society as interpreted by those in government or outside

(The terms *public policy, implementation, outputs, outcomes,* and *impacts* are defined in this or succeeding chapters and in the glossary.)

The Cycle of Public Administration

The first element of public administration is the ongoing formulation of public policies–the initial choices to produce goods and services like health care and pollution control. The second element is the management of resources and authority by public agencies in the production of those goods and services. This takes place, for example, as a neighborhood nurse identifies a child in need of immunization and schedules it. The outcomes of these efforts for society constitute the third element: the extent to which the purposes are fulfilled and the public response to them. An aggressive regulatory program may reduce the level of pesticides in the environment, but people may well become even more sensitive to the remaining pollutants and demand stricter limits in the future.

Figure 1.1 shows how these three elements are closely interdependent. What happens in the second depends on the first, and

Box 1.2

The Policy Process in Housing

The history of governments' experiences in housing the poor illustrates well the wheel of public policy. Prior to the 1930s, local governments took only sporadic interest in the lack of decent and affordable homes for those at the lowest end of the income spectrum. Aside from safety and sanitary legislation, they viewed such problems as outside their jurisdiction.

The Depression sparked a national awareness of housing deficiencies. In 1937 Congress voted funds to assist cities in new home construction to replace slums and provide construction jobs to the unemployed. It increased aid in this area in legislation in 1949, 1954, and later. Larger cities responded by replacing substandard dwellings with high-rise apartment buildings for low-income households, and by 1960 these had become home to tens of thousands.

The outcomes of this effort demanded reformulation of housing policies. The high-rise projects were often plagued by crime, vandalism, and decay and proved to be poor living environments for children. St. Louis and Newark had to demolish some buildings that became intolerable. New legislation backed low-rise dwellings on scattered sites, subsidized home ownership for the poor, and supplied rent subsidies that enabled them to select their own places. For many these programs had positive results, but the rising costs of housing generally and the lack of decent low-cost dwellings limited what administrators could accomplish with public funds.

The next turn of the wheel obtained help from more sources. The 1980s witnessed innovative housing efforts by state and local agencies and new enterprises in the business and nonprofit sectors. Some of these targeted the homeless and the disabled in addition to the traditional poor. From Miami to Seattle, city authorities and community institutions are enlarging housing opportunities by whatever means that work for them. The federal government's role is gradually shifting toward a supportive rather than a leading one. As human needs, the housing market, and political tides change, society constantly redefines its policies, and the means of carrying them out must likewise change.

the third depends on the second. Each effort to reformulate policies grows out of the outcomes (successful or not) of previous programs. Although the "real" process is much more complex than this, with reverses, side paths, and delays, this figure helps us see public administration as a progression of cycles, constantly moving from policies to programs to outcomes and on to revised policies and programs. Every result of administration, whether "successful" or not, creates new situations that demand a response.

Public administration is thus as dynamic as the society it serves. The interplay among public policies, implementation, and outcomes in housing policy, as Box 1.2 shows, is typical of what happens in government. Rarely can goals be inscribed in concrete, nor can the programs that serve them, which operate in unstable environments. Outcomes are equally dynamic. For example, homes for poor people are affected not only by governments but by na-

(continued on p. 15)

Box 1.3

The Essential Tools of Implementation

Examples:

1. Cash payments to individuals

Pensions to retired and disabled persons
Support to low-income and unemployed
Subsidies to farmers
Home rental subsidies
Below-market-rate home and business loans
Food stamps (cash equivalents)

2. Construction and maintenance of infrastructures

Airports, harbors, highways, and streets
Mass transit facilities
Water and waste treatment facilities
Public schools, hospitals, prisons
Museums, libraries, sports facilities
Military bases and weapons

3. Provision of services

Teaching and counseling
Medical and nursing care
Delivering mail
Public transportation
Research and information distribution
Mediating and resolving conflicts
Promoting economic development

4. Regulation of individual and corporate behavior

Criminal apprehension and prosecution
Restricting use of harmful chemicals
Standards for professional practice
Land-use zoning and building controls
Controls on wages and workplace safety
Controls on financial transactions

5. Maintaining capacity to govern

Collecting taxes and fees
Maintaining own facilities
Internal spending controls
Hiring and managing personnel
Planning and decision making
Communication within government and to public
International diplomacy

tional and local economies, group cultural orientations, personal choices, and technologies of home construction.

The Tools of Implementation

Governments use many techniques and procedures in carrying out these programs; we can think of them as **tools of implementation.** These tools can be divided into four major categories, with a fifth supporting one, as highlighted in Box 1.3. A unique set of political and administrative choices distinguishes each category.

Cash Payments   First, a major share of the budgets of the national and state governments consists of cash payments to individuals. The U.S. Department of Health and Human Services and state departments of public assistance write checks to the elderly, poor, unemployed, and disabled. The U.S. Department of Agriculture provides payments to farmers and farm corporations. And local housing agencies subsidize the rent of low-income families. Such direct redistribution of income fulfills a variety of social and economic purposes, from providing a basic standard of living to promoting the health of a vital sector of the economy.

In determining how much to pay and to whom, governments must identify the beneficiaries. Laws specify in detail what qualifies a person for aid, but administrators select recipients. A local Social Security employee must decide whether an applicant is sufficiently disabled to draw payments. Thus, although printing and mailing out checks is routine, the decision making that must precede it may not be.

Construction and Maintenance of Infrastructures   The second tool is the construction and maintenance of public facilities—airports and harbors, streets and highways, water and sewage systems, parks and cultural facilities, schools, and hospitals—in short, the capital investments that serve all governmental activities. Included in this process are decisions to build and maintain a given facility, where to locate it, and how to design and manage it.

Any new infrastructure creates further possibilities for governments and businesses alike, and these multiply the choices they must make. When the nation chose, in the 1950s, to invest hundreds of billions of dollars in the interstate and urban freeway network, it committed itself to uncounted choices on location of routes and interchanges, standards of construction, and means of financing it. After the freeways were in place, governments faced many further decisions on land-use control, automobile safety, pollution abatement, and industrial location, not to mention the explosive development of metropolitan suburbs.

Provision of Services   The third tool for implementation is the provision of services. Government employees teach reading, deliver mail, place children in foster homes, transport people to workplaces, and forecast the weather. In most cases, the users do not pay directly for these services, or they pay only a fraction of the cost. These services can be provided outside of government, and many are, but because of their nature, legislatures have often chosen a public means of delivery for reasons of cost, fairness, and ease of control.

Administrative choices in this third category are as numerous as those in the first two. In initiating the particular service, an agency must select the recipients, the level and quality of the service, the means of delivery, and the charge, if any. What level of intelligence should a child with a mental disability have to benefit from reading instruction? With what frequency should the city run a bus through a certain neighborhood? These questions suggest that needs can vary widely among individuals and communities and that providers must be both sensitive and flexible in matching the service to the client.

Regulation of Behavior   Fourth, governments at all levels regulate individual and corporate behavior. They specify what conduct is required or prohibited and the means by which many actions must be taken. Some criminal laws ban actions that threaten life and property. Many more civil laws specify how chemicals are marketed, homes are built, people marry and divorce, doctors practice medicine, and tobacco is advertised. This process is more uniquely governmental than the previous ones, since only public authority can impose such regulations and enforce compliance. Only government, acting within the law, can execute a person for murder, and only government can prevent occupation of a building that lacks proper fire safety facilities.

Once a legislature chooses the regulation, an administrative organization must determine which actions comply with it and which do not. The U.S. Food and Drug Administration must certify all medicines before they can be prescribed or sold, and it can further restrict use of approved drugs. Since regulation prohibits certain actions, the agencies' challenge is to secure compliance without constant policing or the threat of imminent punishment.

The Capacity to Govern   Finally, governments devote considerable administrative effort to maintaining their own capacities to govern. This is not a tool in the same sense as the preceding four, since it does not directly forward the achievement of the public purposes. Yet it is essential to maintain the systems that can do those things well and consistently. This involves collecting revenue and managing spending, maintaining facilities, obtaining and using personnel and information resources, and communicating within and among agencies. For example, medical professionals who work with AIDS or tuberculosis patients must pass information about cases among themselves and record their treatments and findings for others to learn from. Medical advances depend heavily upon a sophisticated information system, which in turn requires investment in the means to generate, disseminate, and interpret data.

Public administration was defined earlier as the activities of government that determine the supply of goods and services to the public. Let us expand this, in view of the discussion so far in this chapter, into five essential features:

Public Administration: A Profession—And Many Professions

- First, lawmakers consider the goods and services supplied to be vital to the "common weal," or public purposes of the nation or community, and fear that their loss or mismanagement would gravely damage our lives and property and diminish our opportunities.
- Second, those who provide these goods and services are accountable to the public or its elected representatives and must answer for the outcomes of their activities, both positive and negative.
- Third, this accountability requires a capacity for management: obtaining and deploying money, personnel, information, and technology for producing these goods and services. The aim is to obtain the most or best products possible or to use the fewest resources to produce a level of service.
- Fourth, public administration is based on organizations, primarily governmental ones but also many private associations, from electric utilities to foster homes. Their organizational dynamics and interrelationships determine how well the goods and services are produced and whom they benefit.
- Fifth, because people disagree about how these essential goods and services are distributed, their complaints and demands spark conflict. Public administration thus becomes political when individuals or groups seek to win and when government organizations use power to apply and enforce their policies.

To supply medical services to all who need them, protect the nation from hazardous and fraudulent business practices, and maintain highways and water supplies, government must have superior powers: to collect taxes, command personal services, take private land, and deprive a person of property and liberty. But to ensure that officials do not exercise these powers arbitrarily or for private gain, they must answer to the citizens. For this **accountability**, the nation relies on such institutions as written constitutions and laws, popular elections, independent courts, and the mass media. We shall consider in Chapter 15 how well this system of accountability works in practice.

We can now more fully define **public administration** in a democratic political system as the process by which government organizations supply essential goods, services, and regulations, managing resources and resolving conflicts under a mandate of efficiency and fairness, while accounting to the public for both means and outcomes.

A History of the Profession

Public administration is like medicine and law in that it is both a profession and an object of study. Since it puts the choices of public policy into practice, its practitioners must act amid uncertainty about whether their acts will achieve the desired ends. Yet they have available to them a body of knowledge to guide them. Thus, the director of a county health department practices a profession to the extent that she applies recognized standards and takes a systematic approach to delivering services, selecting and supervising personnel, and organizing the office.

Early Years　The profession of public administration in the United States dates back at least to Benjamin Franklin's establishment of the Post Office in colonial days. But Alexander Hamilton, the first secretary of the treasury, could be called the founder of American public administration, for he took the lead in filling out the new executive branch in the early 1790s and specifying its procedures (Van Riper, 1987, pp. 10–12). It was not until the late nineteenth century, however, that the profession came to be recognized as such. The Pendleton Act of 1883 established the first formal merit system in the national government. Similar reforms in the states and cities soon followed. Economic regulation as a purpose of administration was instituted at the federal level with the founding of the Interstate Commerce Commission in 1887 (although the states and localities had always provided some consumer protection). This required government to determine rational prices for thousands of train trips for passengers and freight, and later to set standards for a great volume of other business practices.

The Twentieth Century　Many events and situations in the first half of the twentieth century promoted the self-awareness of public administrators as professionals rather than as clerks. The **scientific management** movement, identified with the industrial engineer Frederick Taylor, sought the "one best way" to organize and accomplish each task. It focused on improving productivity in menial, repetitive jobs in factories and offices, but the idea spread to programs of all kinds and found favor among administrators who wanted to reduce corruption and increase efficiency in government. The faith that correct administration could be taught led to instituting the first academic program for training public administrators at Syracuse University in 1911.

Innovations in government required new capacities for managerial expertise. City management by an appointed executive began to develop in 1907 in Staunton, Virginia. Central budgeting for the national government was mandated by Congress in 1921, establishing the predecessor for today's Office of Management and Budget. The New Deal era greatly expanded the public purposes and federal agencies entrusted with them. Provision of support payments to the unemployed and elderly was a key innovation of that decade, and the Housing Act of 1937 initiated a program of federal grants to cities for slum clearance and low-cost home construction, with all the problems resulting from joint management by several units of government.

The 1960s witnessed further expansion of federal, state, and local relations in efforts to improve the nation's quality of life. The civil rights movement and President Lyndon B. Johnson's War on Poverty reawakened the concern for the disadvantaged members of society. Innovative programs called for new administrative methods and philosophies, and for organizing services on a much larger scale than ever before. The mixed record of success achieved by these programs both deflated some of the initial optimism and compelled revision or reduction of many. Administrators accustomed to constant program expansion had to learn how to reduce them selectively.

The 1970s and 1980s expanded the role of the private sector (businesses, nonprofit institutions, and voluntary associations) in implementing public policy. Public resistance to rising taxes stimulated the search for new approaches to providing services, whether those for medical care, housing rehabilitation, or job creation. Thus, a government manager might no longer provide a service directly but was still forced to coordinate the actions of other providers. Administration found it necessary to concern itself with the performance of complex systems, ensuring that each part, whether governmental or private, played its assigned role. (The health care complex provides a good example. Because it has no central direction, keeping it focused on the broad needs of the public challenges the skills of administrators more than ever before.)

The past two decades have also experienced the growing complexity and sophistication of technologies for information processing and decision making. Whereas in the past administrators often had few facts to go on in reaching major decisions, now more data are available in libraries and storage banks than they can process.

Box 1.4

A Sampling of Professions in Government

Accountants audit financial records of federal, state, and local government agencies and examine private institutions such as banks.

Botanists maintain gardens in public parks, monitor endangered plant species, and experiment with corn genetics.

Clergy conduct religious services and counsel in prisons, hospitals, and the armed forces.

Engineers plan and oversee drainage systems, highway construction, airports, and space flights.

Geologists locate mineral deposits and seek to forecast earthquakes.

Historians maintain archives and direct museums.

International lawyers advise government on trade, immigration, and military issues.

Librarians research issues for Congress and help children pick out books they are able to read.

Mediators help to settle labor/management disputes.

Pediatricians care for children in public hospitals and clinics and do research on childhood diseases.

Reading specialists design public school programs for students with reading disabilities.

Systems analysts set up and manage complex computer and communications networks essential to all units of government.

Urban planners enforce zoning codes and design neighborhood housing rehabilitation programs.

Zoologists manage fish and wildlife sanctuaries and research cattle diseases.

Naturally, the faster flow of information also requires quicker decisions. For example, when the tanker *Exxon Valdez* began to spill its oil into Prince William Sound in Alaska on March 24, 1989, officials in Washington and Juneau had to act quickly to limit the spread of the floating oil yet needed to review information from many similar accidents. This is one illustration of the way in which public administration has become both an art and a science, requiring the generation, selection, and application of strategic information.

Public Administration Today: Specialization and Fragmentation

As a result of the widening of public purposes over two centuries, the nature of public administration has changed from clerkship, to profession, to cluster of professions. No longer concerned merely with organization and methods, it encompasses planning, policy execution, evaluation, information management, and relations among organizations engaged in public service. Many other professions have "gone public," as Box 1.4 indicates. Because of its composite character, public administration lacks the clear identity it had in 1930.

Despite this specializing and fragmenting of public management, the "generalist" administrator provides a common core, exercising responsibility for agencies and departments and making sure that all the specialties act together effectively for the public mission. People from many professions may serve as generalist administrators upon promotion from posts of their specialization, but they must transcend their specialty and comprehend the larger picture.

Public Administration: A Global Practice

International competition not only causes national governments to grow in size and scope, but also links their administrative structures and processes more closely, compelling them to become more alike. The distinction between domestic and foreign policies fades as their problems and programs converge. Public administration is thus being transformed by global demands and forces.

- Economic and technological competition among the North American, European, and Asian-Pacific blocs compels each nation to marshal its resources to increase efficiency and productivity.
- Each nation must manage its balance of imports and exports for maximum economic health and currency value.
- A global governance system of money flows and credit has gradually appeared, tightly linking the governments and private financial institutions of each nation.
- Governmental relations with multinational corporations and foreign-based investors have proliferated, both to regulate their activities and to provide incentives for desired investment and production.
- Public demands have grown for international action to guard the natural environment by controlling toxic wastes; limiting emission of acid-forming gases, carbon dioxide, and chlorofluorocarbons into the atmosphere; protecting rain forests and endangered species; and managing ocean resources.
- International movement of refugees and immigrants presents challenges of controlling entry and providing social services.
- Travel between nations for business, scientific, cultural, educational, and pleasure purposes further multiplies interpersonal contacts that require responses by American institutions of all kinds.
- Continued efforts by the affluent nations to promote development and relieve distress in the developing countries raise questions of allocation of funds among many worthy causes.

It is beyond the scope of this book to catalog in detail how these often conflicting demands from around the globe are being met within American public administration. But it is important to grasp their widespread impact on public decisions. For example, congressional actions to approve United States entry into the North American Free Trade Agreement and the World Trade Organization are affecting not only Congress's own policies on finance, trade, and labor, but also those of state and local governments on business regulation, economic development, and pollution control. As agreements with other nations expand, effects on internal policies grow at the same rate and often in unexpected ways.

A further consequence of this interdependence is that administrators of one nation increasingly learn from the experiences of others. Formal structures of government, with their frameworks of leadership and accountability, differ considerably, even among Western democracies. Americans sometimes ask whether an administrative system headed by a prime minister, who works in close harmony with a parliament, can implement policy more effectively than the American separation-of-powers system. They also look to Europe and Japan for policy reform options in such areas as waste management, energy conservation, and urban transportation to use in their own innovative efforts. This book will provide several instances of global and cross-national administration that offer insights for American choices.

Public Administration: A Discipline— And Many Disciplines

Public administration is linked with political science, sociology, psychology, business management, economics, and engineering. Its focus is the knowledge base that professionals use and the means of expanding it. For example, a student may do research on the outcomes of public health programs in Detroit and Seattle so that administrators and policymakers in New York and other cities can improve their effectiveness. Or a study of the regulation of one toxic chemical can yield valuable insights for controlling similar new substances. As such knowledge accumulates, it provides a base for further research and greater breadth and depth in professional education as well.

Public Administration as an Academic Discipline: Early History

Those who study and analyze public administration, unlike its practitioners, also act as critics. Rather than doing the job, they are concerned with how it is done, how well, and with what outcomes. The academic discipline of public administration has its historical landmarks, just as the profession does. In 1887 the young scholar (and future president) Woodrow Wilson published an essay, "The Study of Administration," that called for explicit attention to the field's principles. He argued that what administrative theory then existed originated in continental Europe, inspired by authoritarian regimes with which the United States had little in common. What the nation needed was a scientific concept of administration safely removed from the "hurry and strife of politics" (Wilson, 1941, p. 493). So enlightened, administrators would conduct the people's business more honestly, efficiently, and responsibly.

By the 1920s scholars of public administration had responded to Wilson's plea and given students their first textbooks in the field, a sign that the discipline had attained its adolescence. The principles and methods they taught were further elaborated in the 1930s, when a temporary orthodoxy of "best ways" was established (Gulick & Urwick, 1937). But as the scope of government continued to expand after World War II, the more diverse policy challenges and administrative means to meet them cast doubt on the principles that were so firmly held. Simon (1950 and 1957) more usefully portrayed public decision making in terms of the broader social and cultural environments that conditioned administrative choices in unique ways.

The New Public Administration

Further governmental reforms in the 1960s forced many scholars to rethink their premises. The civil rights movement and the antipoverty programs reawakened the concern for public administration's influence on individual opportunities. Younger scholars in the field gathered in the fall of 1968 for what came to be known as the Minnowbrook Conference. The simplistically named "new public administration" movement that stemmed from it called on the profession to shift from its historic emphasis on programmatic efficiency toward advocacy for the poor and the minorities and reform of the governmental structures that perpetuated their disadvantages (Marini, 1971). This spirit remains alive, albeit hampered by budget limitations and a conservative temper in the nation at large.

Concern for the outcomes of the antipoverty and equal opportunity programs of the 1960s spurred the "policy studies" movement among political scientists, economists, and those of many other disciplines. Basically, they sought more systematic approaches to designing public policies and means of implementation to replace the intuitive (and presumably less effective) methods that prevailed then. Several professional journals appeared (e.g., *Policy Studies Review*, *Public Policy*, *Journal of Policy Analysis and Management*, and *Policy Science*), and academic studies proliferated. Their many findings frequently disagreed, but they highlighted the complexities that administrators face when they seek to turn a policy into results, particularly when many agencies and units of government must cooperate. They also illustrate the difficulties of coping with the information flow mentioned earlier.

The professional and disciplinary streams of the field of public administration come together in the American Society for Public Administration, which is the only nationwide association that joins administrative generalists with specialists and practitioners with scholars. Although the purposes of those two streams diverge, the flow of information between them is considerable.

The Ethics Issue

The current literature of public administration is also marked by a strong concern for ethics and accountability (see Bowman, 1991). Because citizens both depend on and fear government, they insist that its actions be subject to normative standards—to what they understand to be beneficial, responsible, and legitimate. We fear amorality and are rightly offended when a government action appears arbitrary or violates an accepted ethical norm. As Box 1.5 indicates, many such questions will arise in the health care reform issue.

A democratic system depends on popular trust and confidence, not only by citizens toward government but also among public officials. To call something a public purpose and hold government accountable for fulfilling it implies that there are known standards and that all participants support them. Yet we lack generally accepted standards in such matters as those involving the beginning and end of life, intrusions on personal privacy, and genetic manipulation. Scholars continue to search for data, principles, and ethical standards that can be applied to emerging problems like these to guide and support the administrators, legislators, and judges who must make the day-to-day choices on them.

Ethics in the public arena have both negative and positive dimensions. The former involve behaviors to avoid, such as bribery, prejudice, dishonesty, and abuse of authority; these are in both the legal and the moral codes. But the line between "right" and "wrong"—the point at which a questionable act becomes punishable—is hard to define and to detect. Such acts are sometimes collective, shared by an entire office, agency, or unit of government. The misuse of public funds in the U.S. Department of Housing and Urban Development during the 1980s involved a network of employees. Seeing instances like this one, the public often suspects public servants of these negatives, and many believe they are more common today than ever before.

The positive ethical standards include a wide range of actions that increase the level of justice, quality of services, attention to clients' needs, efficiency in use of public resources, and so on. They consist of "what should be done," often going the second mile beyond the formal requirements of law or policy. This is a basic goal of the Total Quality Management movement, with its ethos of team-

Box 1.5

Ethical Issues in the Health Care Reform Debate

Reform of the health care system is not merely a question of organization and management, as the opening of this chapter may have suggested. We also face questions that touch basic ethical values of our society.

Some problems relate simply to honest compliance with the law. It has been easy for medical professionals to defraud the Medicaid and Medicare systems with false and inflated charges, and government administrators have been unable to prevent it (and have even abetted it at times). When so much money flows through many hands, some people cannot resist taking some.

At another level, reform raises questions of patient choice of medical providers. We have a long tradition of voluntary doctor/patient relationships. Reorganizations that seek more efficient use of resources would limit choices to those of a certain clinic or health maintenance organization. Many fear bureaucratic interference into what has been such an intimate matter.

The extent of government obligation to children raises another issue. Low-income mothers often fail to get adequate care both before and after they give birth, because of poverty, neglect, and/or substance addiction. How intrusive should public health agencies be, while respecting parental rights? Is there an obligation to enforce medical care on such people and their dependents?

Medical choices at the end of life also pose headaches for governments. When Oregon voters in 1994 approved a "right-to-die" initiative, they established procedures by which a person could commit what amounts to voluntary suicide. Oregon courts have overturned the statute, but their decision is likely to be appealed. Any such right-to-die procedure is fraught with ethical controversy, as the actions of Dr. Jack Kevorkian continue to be.

work, personal commitment, and customer service, which we discuss later. These standards too commonly depend on a group's choices, although in the end each individual in a work setting must decide on her or his commitments. Social service agencies that encounter clients with complex and difficult needs constantly face these open-ended ethical choices. In both the negative and positive dimensions, this attention to ethics responds to both the popular concerns about government and the overwhelming tasks that the public sector has assumed.

Entangled with the issue of administrative ethics—how well government is doing its job—is the much larger question of what it ought to be doing. To what degree the public sector should be responsible for "family values" or reconciling cultural conflicts or narrowing the gap between rich and poor complicates the "how to do it" debates over welfare reform, health care, and equal opportunity. The nation must discern what government can do well, what it must do even if it cannot do it to popular satisfaction, what it should do in cooperation with the private sector, and what it should not try to do at all. If we decide that poverty is a condition necessary to some people because of their own shortcomings, this dictates one direction of welfare reform. On the other hand, if we believe the poor can succeed with proper help, this defines the public obligation differently. Students of administration may prefer to avoid such "worldview" discussions, yet they would miss an essential dimension of their discipline.

Summary

The term *government* has two meanings: (1) the legal organization that maintains order and provides the goods and services its citizens require and (2) the process of governing, by which that organization maintains order and supplies goods and services. *Politics* consists of cooperation and conflict over the distribution of benefits and costs in society and thus pervades all government and public administration.

Governments exist to fulfill essential public purposes, which set the basic goals for policy and its implementation. Their major purposes include (1) protecting the lives, property, and liberty of their citizens; (2) maintaining or ensuring the supply of essential resources; (3) supporting those unable to care for themselves; (4) promoting steady and balanced economic growth; (5) promoting the "quality of life" and personal opportunity to succeed; (6) protecting the natural environment and its resources; and (7) promoting scientific and technological advancement.

The expenditures, employment, and powers of American governments have grown steadily. This reflects (1) the services and regulations necessary to order a complex urban, technological society and economy; (2) international competition in the military and economic spheres requiring mobilization of the nation's resources; (3) citizen demands for services and protections to which elected officials respond; and (4) ambitions of administrators and legislators for bigger agencies and budgets. These factors in combination are likely to sustain this growth.

Public administration can be portrayed as a "wheel of relationships" focused on the implementation of public policy. The formulation of specific policies, the production of goods and services and their delivery to constituents, and the outcomes of those policies and the responses that society makes to them affect each other continually.

Governments use several techniques and procedures for policy implementation: (1) cash payments to individuals, (2) construction and maintenance of infrastructures that serve the society, (3) provision of services, and (4) regulation of individual and corporate behavior. To wield these tools, governments must also maintain their own capacities as organizations to make these decisions and carry them out.

Public administration in a democratic political system is the process by which government organizations supply essential goods, services, and regulations, managing resources and resolving conflicts under a mandate to do so efficiently and fairly while accounting to the public for both means and outcomes.

Public administration is both a professional and an academic discipline. Its practice is as old as the nation itself but only began to take on a professional character toward the end of the nineteenth century. It has evolved into a cluster of professions, linked by the common concern for the public purposes and overseen by the generalist administrator with broad agency responsibilities.

The academic discipline of public administration developed to promote its professional character by analyzing its past performance and generating knowledge for more effective practice. Its current concerns range from the rational analysis of policy to the critique of public ethics and search for administrative accountability.

International cooperation and competition profoundly affect American public administration, interlinking nations' policy implementation and blurring the distinction between domestic and foreign policies. Administrators can learn much from other nations' experiences in dealing with common problems. The area of multinational public administration, which oversees joint action, is also growing.

Scholars and practitioners alike recognize ethics as a prime concern of the profession. The enormous impact of government on personal and social well-being leaves little room for mistakes and wrongdoing. However, the complexity of policy choices and lack of clear standards often render ethical choices highly problematic.

Discussion Questions

1. Why have governments been forced to intervene in such issues as health care, child protection, and chemical regulation? What would have happened if they had not?

2. What political conflicts are most likely in fulfilling each of the seven public purposes? How are they usually resolved?

3. In what ways do the successes and failures of policy implementation result in additional efforts at making new policies?

4. How does a democratic political process typically affect public administration—both what government does and how it does it? Consider again the examples of health care, abused children, and chemicals in the environment.

5. In what policy areas must American administrators have contact with their counterparts in foreign countries? How are our policies affected by their need to cooperate?

Analytical Exercises

1. We have long been aware of the "military/industrial complex" that has built and maintained our national defense system. From a survey of newspaper and magazine articles, identify the major components of the emerging "health/industrial" and "education/industrial" complexes. Determine the specific public policy interests for each and their contribution to political and administrative conflicts.

2. Survey recent press reports on alleged ethical lapses or controversial choices by public administrators at the national, state, and/or local levels. These are common in law enforcement, education, and medical services. Determine what dilemmas they posed for the direct participants and for their superiors. Describe how these may have affected the image of government.

For Further Reading

Annual Editions: Public Administration. Guilford, CT: The Dushkin Publishing Group. This annually revised anthology presents approximately forty current articles dealing with a broad spectrum of issues in public administration.

Bowman, James S. (Ed.). (1991). *Ethical Frontiers in Public Management: Seeking New Strategies for Resolving Ethical Dilemmas.* San Francisco: Jossey-Bass. Diverse viewpoints on applying ethical principles to dilemmas of management, organization, and policy.

Chandler, R. C. (Ed.). (1987). *A Centennial History of the American Administrative State.* New York: Free Press. Eight perceptive articles on the current state of the profession and the forces and values that produced it.

Fry, B. R. (1989). *Mastering Public Administration: From Max Weber to Dwight Waldo.* Chatham, NJ: Chatham House. Concise historical perspective on the major thinkers and ideas in the development of public administration as a discipline.

Gulick, L., & Urwick, L. (Eds.). (1937). *Papers on the Science of Administration.* New York: Institute of Public Administration. Frequently cited statements that represented the "orthodoxy" of administrative theory in the 1930s and remain influential today.

Marini, F. (Ed.). (1971). *Toward a New Public Administration: The Minnowbrook Perspective.* San Francisco: Chandler. These articles represent the drive to reform the agenda of the discipline and the profession alike to favor the least advantaged members of society—a change that gradually did take place to an important extent.

Simon, H. A. (1957). *Administrative Behavior* (2nd ed.). New York: Free Press. A major reformulation of thought on such key administrative issues as decision making, value judgments, and organization theory.

Stillman, R. J., II. (1991). *Preface to Public Administration.* New York: St. Martin's Press. A brief and very readable survey of the development of public administration theory and practice and the key intellectual issues confronting it today.

Wilson, W. (1941). The study of administration. *Political Science Quarterly, 56,* 486–506. Originally published in *Political Science Quarterly, 1* (1887), 197–222. A landmark document that gave American public administration its focus and sparked debates that go on today, calling for a "science of administration" and its separation from the corruption and partisanship of politics.

The Anatomy of Administration

Learning Objectives

After reading this chapter, you should be able to do the following:

1. Describe the overall organization of national, state, and local governments and the types of administrative structures within them.
2. Identify the constitutional principles for the organization of the executive branch.
3. Define cabinet department, noncabinet agency, government corporation, and independent regulatory commission.
4. Understand how these organizations have been shaped by political interests and pressures.
5. Explain the goals of past attempts to reorganize government and the results of those efforts.

On November 10, 1987, the day before Veterans Day, President Ronald Reagan surprised Washington observers by backing a bill in Congress that would elevate the Veterans Administration to a full cabinet department. He and his staff had opposed this move even though most veterans' groups and most members of Congress supported it. The president's change of heart removed all barriers. The bill passed easily and went to the Oval Office for signature early in 1988.

What explains this seeming formality of a change in bureaucratic labeling? The Veterans Administration (VA) had existed since 1930 as a noncabinet agency, answerable to the president but lacking the mystique of cabinet status. Actually larger than most cabinet departments, its budget in 1988 came to about $27 billion, and it employed 240,000 people. Approximately 27 million veterans and about twice that many dependents and survivors of veterans currently receive VA benefits. Does this size justify the change?

There is one simple explanation for the change to cabinet status and several deeper but related ones. First, 1988 was an election year, and many veterans and their dependents vote; thus, the change can easily be interpreted as an appeal to them. Of course, both Republicans and Democrats endorsed it, which appears to cancel out any partisan benefit. Yet no politician running for reelection could afford to oppose cabinet status for veterans.

Beyond the political motives a more significant debate took place. Proponents argued that part of the benefit was symbolic: Cabinet status would provide stronger recognition of the sacrifice that veterans made for their country. Furthermore, their secretary's presence in cabinet meetings would give veterans a stronger voice in presidential decision making. Veterans' organizations also believed that a department would be better able to protect itself from budget cuts than a noncabinet agency.

Many of the VA's critics (and no one in Washington defended the way in which it was then run) also asserted that as a department, it would be subject to more vigilant congressional and public scrutiny. Its conglomeration of programs—encompassing 172 medical centers, nursing care, pension and compensation payments, vocational rehabilitation, mortgage loan guaranties, and life insurance—presents a daunting administrative challenge, and although no one expected that department status would solve it alone, some hoped for modest improvement.

Many observers outside Congress had long claimed that the VA had no good administrative reason to exist. All its programs duplicated those in other departments for nonveterans. For example, its medical functions could well be performed by the Department of Health and Human Services. Furthermore, critics noted that many medical benefits were going to veterans for injuries not received in combat, a service for which nonveterans did not qualify, and that departmental status would freeze an overly generous package and thereby harm other programs. But their arguments failed to stop the bandwagon once President Reagan and most members of Congress tallied up the political benefits.

The organization of government is vital to its performance. It is equally vital to determining what jobs it does, for whom, and how much support each one gets. Whether the Department of Veterans Affairs is a "better" organization today is open to dispute, but no one claims that its political status has suffered. Where an agency stands in the hierarchy of its government, and with which other agencies it is connected, shapes its leadership, budgets, and accountability. This lesson applies to organization at all levels of government, from the largest federal benefit programs to county health services and municipal recreation offerings.

Public policy implementation is assigned to specific organizations with such names as *Department, Bureau, Agency, Office, Commission,* and *Administration.* We can study administrative actions only as they occur within and among such units. Whether large or small, public organizations respond distinctively to their tasks and constituents, which determine how well they ultimately serve the public.

The Complexity of Government

This organization of government is so complex that most citizens don't even try to comprehend it, even within their own communities. The complexity is due partly to the sheer number of separate agencies. The 1994 *United States Government Manual* takes 726 pages to describe briefly all major administrative units within the executive branch. In addition, many programs require the cooperation of two or more separate units to carry them out. Many states have veterans' affairs departments of their own that administer additional benefits and cooperate with the U.S. Department of Veterans Affairs. Whether this degree of complexity, this profusion of agencies with multiple and overlapping functions, can be simplified without reducing government performance of vital duties is an issue this chapter addresses after describing the "anatomy" of government.

The form of the American national government was at first quite simple. President Washington and the First Congress agreed to establish an executive structure consisting of three departments (State, War, and Treasury), whose heads answered to the president personally. Each department had assigned duties, and its secretary could easily monitor its performance. This structure was distinct from that of state government and excluded Congress from most administrative operations (Van Riper, 1987).

That national structure expanded during the nineteenth and early twentieth centuries as specific needs arose. Congress had no advance plan to create and enlarge departments, but it responded to needs that appeared and to constituents who wanted a particular service. Both world wars expanded some federal agencies enormously, but the return of peace often curtailed the expansion. More permanent growth spurts came in the 1930s and the 1960s to serve expanded concepts of public purposes in such areas as providing for the needy and protecting civil rights. This growth was obvious in the national government, but state and local structures and employment have expanded even more rapidly in the past 40 years with federal financial aid and public demand for more services.

Most administrative units have both a political and an administrative reason for their origin and growth, as the opening story on the Department of Veterans Affairs illustrated. That is, they enjoy the support of significant political interest groups that benefit from their services.

Urban mass transit provides another example. State and local governments are primarily responsible for it, and Congress participates largely by channeling financial aid to their agencies. Congress created the Urban Mass Transportation Administration (UMTA) in the Department of Transportation in 1968 for good administrative reasons—to allocate funds and account for their spending. But it was equally important for the Johnson administration and a Democratic Congress to demonstrate their concern for improved mobility for urban dwellers. The concern for good transit unites inner-city and suburban residents; therefore, the UMTA could attract broad political support. But Congress had to be careful to spread the funds widely to aid all forms of transit used by these constituents.

The Principles of the Constitution

The gentlemen who met in Philadelphia in the summer of 1787 to draw up a new constitution for the United States had two broad aims that were not entirely compatible: to construct a government that could effectively use its assigned powers (unlike the 10-year-old Confederation) and to prevent such a government from becoming tyrannical (as they perceived Britain's colonial regime to have been). They had to improvise on a large scale, since no government with the features they sought then existed. The constitution they devised made much theoretical sense, argued James Madison, Alexander Hamilton, and John Jay, authors of the New York newspaper articles that have come to be known as *The Federalist*. But whether it was workable could only be learned from experience.

The founders applied four basic constitutional principles. **Federalism** is the first: a system that allocates certain powers by a constitution to a national government and others to the governments of regions within the nation. It was an obvious choice; thirteen states already existed, and their authorities exercised most governing powers. The national government was to operate in the limited realm that the Constitution specified (most of it in Article I, Section 8, on the powers of Congress) and was expected to have very few dealings with the states. As we will see in Chapter 4, however, federalism has become a framework within which the levels of government interact intensively.

Separation of powers is the second principle. It divides the government into three branches: executive, legislative, and judicial. Each has distinct powers of its own and is designed to check and balance the other two. As Madison described it in *The Federalist* No. 51, the preservation of liberty required such a division of governmental powers, in which the "great security against a gradual concentration of the several powers in the same department [i.e., branch] consists in giving to those who administer each department the necessary constitutional means and personal motives to resist encroachments of the others" (Hamilton, Jay, & Madison, n.d.). This balancing of powers meant that major policy initiatives had to secure the support of all three branches (or at least not be opposed by the judiciary) in order to be implemented. It was actually a "government of separated institutions *sharing* powers" (Neustadt, 1980, p. 26). Because Congress dispenses both authority and money, it is a partner with the executive branch in the administration of policy.

It often seems that both principles—federalism and separation of powers—impede government action to meet public needs, although when the president and Congress agree that urgent action is needed, they can move quickly. At times state executives and courts have hindered the efforts of authorities at the federal level to reduce racial discrimination. Although the function of the executive branch is to carry out the laws and that of Congress is to make them, lack of cooperation between the two branches can stalemate action on urgent problems.

Third, the Constitution (with many of its subsequent amendments) guarantees citizens certain rights and liberties. In some cases, these are protections against government action—abridgment of free speech and religious worship, for example. Others are procedural limits; government cannot take away life, liberty, or property except by due process of law. Laws and court interpretations have broadened our concepts of rights to areas, such as education, medical care, privacy, and employment, that are central to personal survival and economic well-being. Since the federal and state courts are dominant in defining these, they play a major role in setting standards for administrative agencies to follow.

Finally, the Constitution prescribes means by which citizens can hold their government accountable, compelling officials to answer for their actions. Officials are elected for specified terms, and many incumbents' campaigns for reelection focus on their public policies in which voters are most interested. Citizens may also petition their government to act on grievances, a First Amendment right that protects interest group and individual expressions on matters of public policy. Extra-constitutional institutions, such as political parties and the news media, supplement these agencies of popular control. The need to be accountable and open to influence thus adds complexity to the administrative system as well. This has been called the "multiple crack" in the American system: the multitude of opportunities for individuals and groups to intervene at every step of the legislative and administrative processes (Grodzins, 1966, pp. 274–276).

The National Executive Branch

Five basic units compose the executive branch today: the Executive Office of the President, cabinet departments, noncabinet line and staff agencies, government corporations, and independent regulatory commissions. Unlike the simple cabinet departments of George Washington's day, they differ not only in their size and functions but also in their manner of control and supervision. The nature of a particular agency and its placement in the structure reflect a policy decision made at some point in the past and repeatedly confirmed by subsequent political forces.

The Executive Office of the President

The Executive Office of the President had its beginnings in the clerks and secretaries who worked directly under President Washington, writing letters, greeting visitors, and gathering information. Although the White House staff grew modestly over the years, the president's organization was not formalized until Franklin D. Roosevelt did so in 1939. Figure 2.2 on page 36 indicates its present components. Working most closely under the chief executive is the White House Office, which includes the president's chief of staff, assistant for national security affairs, legal counselors, and a host of assistants and deputy assistants with specialized functions. Most of these people work in the West Wing of the White House, in which the Oval Office is located.

Of great importance to the president is the Office of Management and Budget (OMB), which prepares the annual budget for his submission to Congress and coordinates the management of administrative and regulatory programs. Chapters 6 and 12 describe its role more fully.

An equally vital part of the Executive Office is the National Security Council, established in 1947 to bring together the perspectives of the Departments of Defense and State on questions affecting the nation's security overseas. The council consists of the president, the vice president, and the secretaries of those two departments and is formally advised by the director of Central Intelligence and the chairman of the Joint Chiefs of Staff (the highest military officer). The council's research is done by its staff, headed by the president's assistant for national security affairs.

The Executive Office of the President includes a variety of smaller units. The Office of the United States Trade Representative has become the nation's principal negotiator on overall foreign trade policy. This function has become so important to the nation's economic well-being that Congress chose to give the president direct responsibility for it rather than to place it under the Department of State or the Department of Commerce. Other units, such as the Council of Economic Advisers, advise the president and do not administer programs.

(continued on p. 36)

Figure 2.1

The Government of the United States

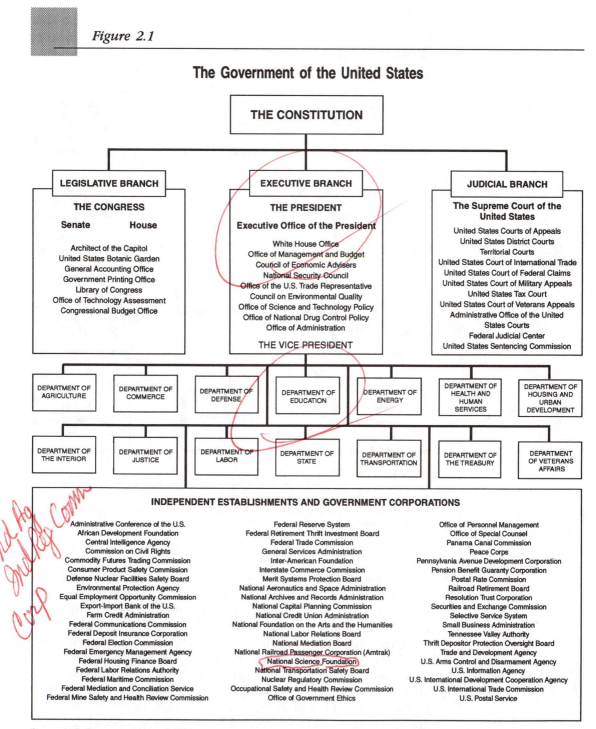

THE CONSTITUTION

LEGISLATIVE BRANCH

THE CONGRESS

Senate   **House**

Architect of the Capitol
United States Botanic Garden
General Accounting Office
Government Printing Office
Library of Congress
Office of Technology Assessment
Congressional Budget Office

EXECUTIVE BRANCH

THE PRESIDENT

Executive Office of the President

White House Office
Office of Management and Budget
Council of Economic Advisers
National Security Council
Office of the U.S. Trade Representative
Council on Environmental Quality
Office of Science and Technology Policy
Office of National Drug Control Policy
Office of Administration

THE VICE PRESIDENT

JUDICIAL BRANCH

The Supreme Court of the United States

United States Courts of Appeals
United States District Courts
Territorial Courts
United States Court of International Trade
United States Court of Federal Claims
United States Court of Military Appeals
United States Tax Court
United States Court of Veterans Appeals
Administrative Office of the United States Courts
Federal Judicial Center
United States Sentencing Commission

DEPARTMENT OF AGRICULTURE

DEPARTMENT OF COMMERCE

DEPARTMENT OF DEFENSE

DEPARTMENT OF EDUCATION

DEPARTMENT OF ENERGY

DEPARTMENT OF HEALTH AND HUMAN SERVICES

DEPARTMENT OF HOUSING AND URBAN DEVELOPMENT

DEPARTMENT OF THE INTERIOR

DEPARTMENT OF JUSTICE

DEPARTMENT OF LABOR

DEPARTMENT OF STATE

DEPARTMENT OF TRANSPORTATION

DEPARTMENT OF THE TREASURY

DEPARTMENT OF VETERANS AFFAIRS

INDEPENDENT ESTABLISHMENTS AND GOVERNMENT CORPORATIONS

Administrative Conference of the U.S.
African Development Foundation
Central Intelligence Agency
Commission on Civil Rights
Commodity Futures Trading Commission
Consumer Product Safety Commission
Defense Nuclear Facilities Safety Board
Environmental Protection Agency
Equal Employment Opportunity Commission
Export-Import Bank of the U.S.
Farm Credit Administration
Federal Communications Commission
Federal Deposit Insurance Corporation
Federal Election Commission
Federal Emergency Management Agency
Federal Housing Finance Board
Federal Labor Relations Authority
Federal Maritime Commission
Federal Mediation and Conciliation Service
Federal Mine Safety and Health Review Commission

Federal Reserve System
Federal Retirement Thrift Investment Board
Federal Trade Commission
General Services Administration
Inter-American Foundation
Interstate Commerce Commission
Merit Systems Protection Board
National Aeronautics and Space Administration
National Archives and Records Administration
National Capital Planning Commission
National Credit Union Administration
National Foundation on the Arts and the Humanities
National Labor Relations Board
National Mediation Board
National Railroad Passenger Corporation (Amtrak)
National Science Foundation
National Transportation Safety Board
Nuclear Regulatory Commission
Occupational Safety and Health Review Commission
Office of Government Ethics

Office of Personnel Management
Office of Special Counsel
Panama Canal Commission
Peace Corps
Pennsylvania Avenue Development Corporation
Pension Benefit Guaranty Corporation
Postal Rate Commission
Railroad Retirement Board
Resolution Trust Corporation
Securities and Exchange Commission
Selective Service System
Small Business Administration
Tennessee Valley Authority
Thrift Depositor Protection Oversight Board
Trade and Development Agency
U.S. Arms Control and Disarmament Agency
U.S. Information Agency
U.S. International Development Cooperation Agency
U.S. International Trade Commission
U.S. Postal Service

Source: U.S. Government Manual, 1994.

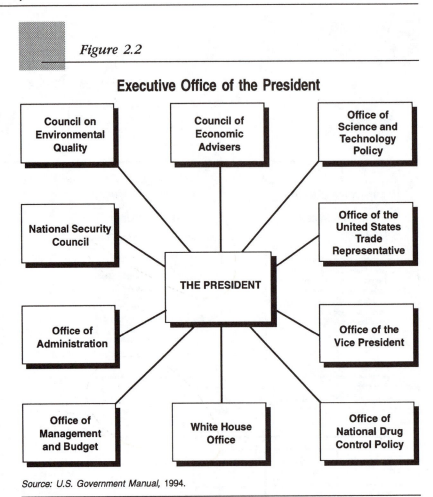

Figure 2.2

Executive Office of the President

| Council on Environmental Quality | Council of Economic Advisers | Office of Science and Technology Policy |

National Security Council

Office of the United States Trade Representative

THE PRESIDENT

Office of Administration

Office of the Vice President

Office of Management and Budget

White House Office

Office of National Drug Control Policy

Source: U.S. Government Manual, 1994.

The president relies on the components of his Executive Office for much of his information about the nation and world, advice on how to act, and means of carrying out his decisions. The text in this chapter describes the most important of these components.

To the limited extent that the president can control the executive branch as a whole, he does so through his Executive Office. President Richard M. Nixon reorganized the former Bureau of the Budget into the Office of Management and Budget in 1970 to strengthen his control of the far-flung departments, then populated mostly by Democrats whom he believed to be unsympathetic to his programs. President Ronald Reagan used the OMB to expand his influence over many regulatory agencies. However, the Executive Office remains limited in its managerial reach to the selected programs and agencies to which it chooses to devote special attention.

Another dilemma surrounds the Executive Office: To whom is it primarily responsible, the president or the public (including Congress)? Presidents have regarded the offices within it as theirs alone, providing advice untainted by the special interests of the departments. Yet the executive branch as a whole is accountable to Congress and the courts and must inform them of its activities. Criminal conduct by presidential staffers can be prosecuted; several participants in the planning and subsequent cover-up of the 1972 burglary of the Democratic Party offices in the Watergate building spent time behind bars. But it remains unclear how answerable staff members are to anyone but the president for their routine actions.

The Cabinet Departments

The fourteen **cabinet departments** are the major executive organizations of the national government. Each is headed by a secretary (except the Justice Department, over which the attorney general presides) appointed by the president and confirmed by a simple majority of the Senate. That person, along with top subordinates, may also be removed at the will of the president. Traditionally, these departments have been charged with the major functions of the national government: defense, foreign affairs, finance, law enforcement, management of federal lands and natural resources, and service to specific clienteles, such as farmers, business, labor, and urban dwellers. The four newest departments—Transportation (1967), Energy (1977), Education (1979), and Veterans Affairs (1989)—encompass major policy areas for which Congress deemed a separate department to be necessary and that focus attention on major interest groups.

No fully objective criteria dictate whether a cabinet-level department should exist for a given public purpose or function, particularly for those of twentieth-century origin. Political factors are often decisive. The creation of the Department of Education reflected President Carter's close relationship with the National Education Association and Congress's desire not only to court that powerful interest group but also to make education more visible than it was as a unit of the Department of Health, Education, and Welfare. President Reagan's effort to disestablish that department in 1981 received little support, even from Republicans in Congress, and Terrel Bell, whom he had appointed as its secretary, actively opposed it. No one wished to give the impression of downplaying education as a national priority or to alienate the large teachers' organizations.

Each department consists of separate divisions with various titles and often very diverse constituents. Figure 2.3 depicts the components of the Department of Justice. They include such high-visibility units as the Federal Bureau of Investigation, Drug Enforcement Administration, and the Immigration and Naturalization Service. Management posts in these departments have proliferated

Figure 2.3

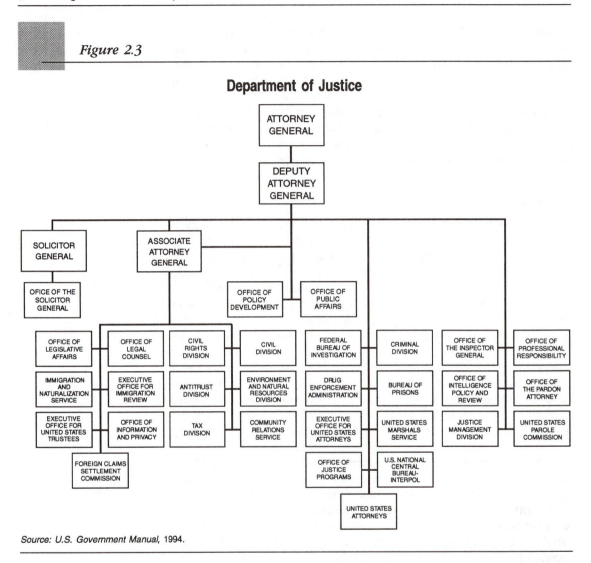

Department of Justice

in the past two decades and now include undersecretaries, deputy secretaries, assistant secretaries, and directors of the various subunits. Some departmental components are fairly autonomous. The Federal Bureau of Investigation and the Army Corps of Engineers (in the Defense Department) have long traditions of independence from their superiors, backed by Congress and constituencies outside government.

Other Arms of the Executive Branch

Noncabinet agencies are also directly responsible to the president but are not of cabinet rank. Most prominent are those that perform

Box 2.1

Declaration of Independence for Social Security

It is rare for a federal government unit to be removed from a cabinet level and put into the independent or noncabinet rank. But this happened to the Social Security Administration when, in March 1995, it was separated from its parent Department of Health and Human Services. It is a giant organization nevertheless, dispensing benefits of about $325 billion annually for more than 40 million elderly and disabled people.

There were several reasons for the shift, both political and administrative. One was to rebuild public confidence in Social Security, which had been shaken by forecasts that its retirement trust fund will be empty by 2029, before many of today's younger people begin to draw benefits. Another was to give the organization room to build its service capacity. Complaints were growing that the agency took too long to settle claims and allowed payments to ineligible applicants. As an independent unit, its chief executives are directly responsible to the president, who, if he is prudent, will monitor it more closely than he has been accustomed to.

a specialized function that does not fit well into a single department. The Environmental Protection Agency has regulatory responsibilities that Congress wanted to keep separate from cabinet departments because it feared that their many goals would dilute the EPA's commitment to enforcement. The National Aeronautics and Space Administration was established to carry out civilian missions clearly distinct from the military uses of space. Thus, it fit neither in the Defense Department nor in any other department. Other noncabinet agencies perform service functions to the government as a whole: The General Services Administration manages government buildings and supplies, and the Office of Personnel Management oversees recruiting and employee relations. In 1995 the Social Security Administration was reorganized as a noncabinet agency, as Box 2.1 describes.

Government corporations sell services to the public, just as private corporations do. Established by Congress, their charters permit a major degree of autonomy in their ordinary operations, and they may own property and borrow money in their own names. Some charge for their services and are financially self-supporting (e.g., the Tennessee Valley Authority [TVA] and the U.S. Postal Service [USPS]). Others, such as Amtrak (formally the National Railroad Passenger Corporation), receive a congressional subsidy for part of their operations. Ideally, this form of organization permits the corporation to operate at highest efficiency without undue intervention from outside authorities.

The Postal Service was created in 1970 from the former Post Office Department to reduce the political pressures upon its appointments and free it to make technological innovations that would improve mail delivery. Other corporations provide credit for home mortgages and student loans. Because each of these corporations sells a needed service, it has built up a constituency that exerts influence on its decisions. Thus, political pressures are as present in this group of organizations as in the previous ones, although they are more narrowly targeted (Tierney, 1984).

Finally, sixteen **independent regulatory commissions** oversee segments or activities of the private economy—railroads, radio and television, advertising, and the securities market, for example. They set and apply rules and standards for specific clients, which must be done in a relatively objective way. Thus, these commissions are relatively autonomous of the rest of the executive branch. They are headed by multimember boards or commissions appointed by the president (with Senate approval) but are insulated from his direct control by long and staggered terms. Congress sees them as accountable to itself as much as to the president, since they carry out its constitutional power to regulate interstate and foreign commerce. The most prominent of these agencies is the Federal Reserve System, the Board of Governors of which has broad powers over the money supply and interest rates and can thereby speed or slow the pace of economic activity. Chapter 6 covers these commissions more fully.

The regulatory commissions exist in an intensely political environment despite Congress's attempt to minimize partisan and presidential influences on them. Most new commissions were established only after lengthy legislative debate over whether such regulation was a proper function of government or would lead to excessive interference with the private market. The Consumer Product Safety Commission, for example, has a much broader mandate to investigate hazards to consumers than much of the business community prefers. It experiences strong pressures on its rule-making and adjudication processes to impose or relax standards on such products as clothing and toys.

The Political Bases of Executive Organization

The process that has established all five forms of executive organization has been highly political, and their administrative functions were essentially determined by influential interest groups that had the most to gain or lose by them. "Agencies must have strong political support from the community itself, whether from groups, political parties, or individuals, in order to become established and to survive" (Woll, 1977, p. 50). This fact need not hinder good administration, since the constituencies demand a satisfactory level of service. But it perpetuates duplication of services and facilities, such as the dual system of hospitals run by the Veterans Affairs and Health and Human Services Departments.

Congress multiplies this complexity by taking great interest in the details of administrative organization. "What may appear to be structural eccentricities and anomalies within the executive branch are often nothing but mirror images of jurisdictional conflicts within the Congress" (Seidman & Gilmour, 1986, p. 37). The separation-of-powers concept assigns to Congress the duty of administrative oversight to ensure that laws are implemented and money is spent as intended. It has divided this responsibility among committees and subcommittees that parallel the executive structures they must monitor. Each committee is relatively autonomous and can establish subcommittees it deems necessary to oversee the specialized areas of policy and implementation for which it is responsible. For example, eight committees in the Senate and ten in the House (some with one or more subcommittees) shared jurisdiction over the Department of Health and Human Services in the 1990 session. An army of congressional staff members gathers information on administrative operations and incorporates this knowledge into legislation. As a result, these agencies look as often to congressional committees for their political and financial support as to their own superiors in the hierarchy. Presidents and secretaries must then bargain with congressional committees for the control that is constitutionally assigned to their administrative organizations.

The federal and state courts deserve mention here for their role in setting and interpreting the mandates and limits for administration. Under the principle of *judicial review,* they may invalidate acts of all other parts of government when they are deemed to conflict with the Constitution. This applies not only to legislation but also to acts of executive agencies, from the president and federal departments to local police departments and school boards. In a series of recent rulings, including *Dolan v. City of Tigard* (1994), the U.S. Supreme Court clarified the rights of property owners vis-à-vis local and state land use control and reinterpreted or overturned several statutes.

The courts are also very much a part of the administrative process. It has often happened that, after a law is passed and an agency is charged with implementing it, someone files a lawsuit over how it is to be applied. A court judgment then becomes, in effect, part of the law. For example, a 1990 ruling of the U.S. Supreme Court forced states and the federal government to increase Medicaid payments for low-income people to a level sufficient to provide the "reasonable and adequate" compensation that the law mandates. That they had not fully budgeted for these payments was not deemed an adequate defense (Pear, 1991). We will return to the role of the courts in Chapter 15 in a fuller study of the accountability process.

The Organization of State Administration

The executive branches of the fifty states bear a marked resemblance to the national structure. State constitutions emulate the national one in their commitment to the separation of powers, checks and balances, civil rights and liberties, and accountability to the public. Those documents all prescribe elected governors and an administrative establishment responsible to them. The five types of organization that comprise the executive branch, described at the beginning of the last section, also exist in the states. Figure 2.4 displays the organization of California's executive branch. Although it is the largest of the states, its policy responsibilities are similar to those of the others.

The Executive Establishment at the State Level

First, all governors have some kind of executive office, although much smaller than the president's. It may consist of only a handful of secretaries, advisers, and public relations specialists, or it can encompass several offices responsible for budgeting, policy development, and management oversight. Most have a cabinet that coordinates the operations of administrative agencies.

The executive establishment of most states differs from the national one in one respect: Several officials are separately elected and so are legally independent of the governor. The offices of lieutenant governor, secretary of state, treasurer, controller or auditor, and attorney general are commonly filled in this way. This reflects the nineteenth-century popular suspicion that chief executives were likely to become corrupt and so needed checking by others whom they had not appointed. However, many of those posts are not central to state administration today, since legislatures have drained them of significant power.

State Administrative Units

Second, the major administrative departments reflect the primary areas of state responsibility: education, transportation, social services, public health and safety, employment and economic development, natural resources and recreation, and criminal justice. They also encompass such staff functions as revenue, financial administration, and personnel. These agencies have expanded steadily over recent years, reflecting the growing responsibilities of states in such fields as environmental protection, health care for low-income persons, child protection, and equal opportunity for minorities. Typically, governors appoint the heads of those departments with the approval of the state senate. Their internal organization resembles that of federal departments. California (as Figure 2.4 shows) has grouped many of its departments into four superagencies, respon-

(continued on p. 44)

Figure 2.4

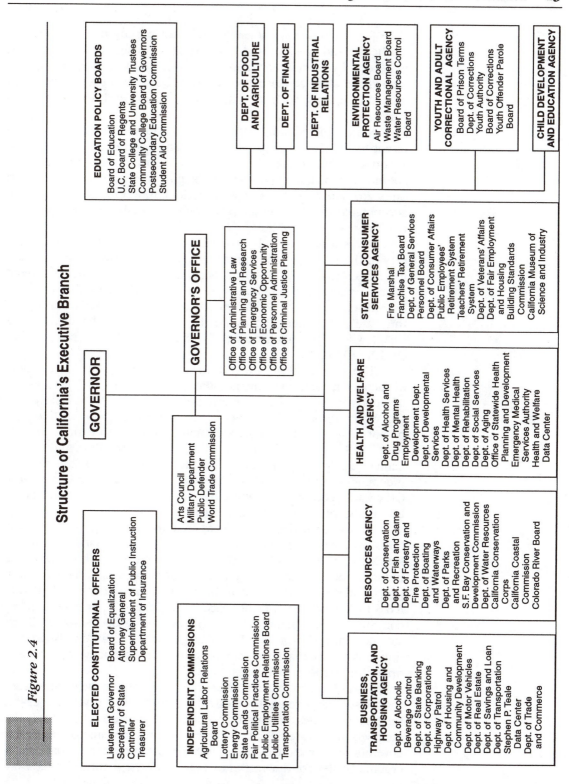

Structure of California's Executive Branch

GOVERNOR

GOVERNOR'S OFFICE
Office of Administrative Law
Office of Planning and Research
Office of Emergency Services
Office of Economic Opportunity
Office of Personnel Administration
Office of Criminal Justice Planning

ELECTED CONSTITUTIONAL OFFICERS
Lieutenant Governor
Secretary of State
Controller
Treasurer
Board of Equalization
Attorney General
Superintendent of Public Instruction
Department of Insurance

EDUCATION POLICY BOARDS
Board of Education
U.C. Board of Regents
State College and University Trustees
Community College Board of Governors
Postsecondary Education Commission
Student Aid Commission

INDEPENDENT COMMISSIONS
Agricultural Labor Relations
  Board
Lottery Commission
Energy Commission
State Lands Commission
Fair Political Practices Commission
Public Employment Relations Board
Public Utilities Commission
Transportation Commission

Arts Council
Military Department
Public Defender
World Trade Commission

DEPT. OF FOOD AND AGRICULTURE

DEPT. OF FINANCE

DEPT. OF INDUSTRIAL RELATIONS

ENVIRONMENTAL PROTECTION AGENCY
Air Resources Board
Waste Management Board
Water Resources Control
  Board

YOUTH AND ADULT CORRECTIONAL AGENCY
Board of Prison Terms
Dept. of Corrections
Youth Authority
Board of Corrections
Youth Offender Parole
  Board

CHILD DEVELOPMENT AND EDUCATION AGENCY

STATE AND CONSUMER SERVICES AGENCY
Fire Marshal
Franchise Tax Board
Dept. of General Services
Personnel Board
Dept. of Consumer Affairs
Public Employees'
  Retirement System
Teachers' Retirement
  System
Dept. of Veterans' Affairs
Dept. of Fair Employment
  and Housing
Building Standards
  Commission
California Museum of
  Science and Industry

HEALTH AND WELFARE AGENCY
Dept. of Alcohol and
  Drug Programs
Employment
  Development Dept.
Dept. of Developmental
  Services
Dept. of Health Services
Dept. of Mental Health
Dept. of Rehabilitation
Dept. of Social Services
Dept. of Aging
Office of Statewide Health
  Planning and Development
Emergency Medical
  Services Authority
Health and Welfare
  Data Center

RESOURCES AGENCY
Dept. of Conservation
Dept. of Fish and Game
Dept. of Forestry and
  Fire Protection
Dept. of Boating
  and Waterways
Dept. of Parks
  and Recreation
S.F. Bay Conservation and
  Development Commission
Dept. of Water Resources
California Conservation
  Corps
California Coastal
  Commission
Colorado River Board

BUSINESS, TRANSPORTATION, AND HOUSING AGENCY
Dept. of Alcoholic
  Beverage Control
Dept. of State Banking
Dept. of Corporations
Highway Patrol
Dept. of Housing and
  Community Development
Dept. of Motor Vehicles
Dept. of Real Estate
Dept. of Savings and Loan
Dept. of Transportation
Stephen P. Teale
  Data Center
Dept. of Trade
  and Commerce

sible for (1) business, housing, and transportation; (2) resources; (3) health and welfare; and (4) state and consumer services. Each is headed by a secretary, also appointed by the governor. This arrangement aims at close coordination between departments with related functions, such as Conservation, Parks and Recreation, and Forestry.

Noncabinet administrative units also abound but take many different forms. For example, California and several other states have a Lottery Commission. It and related agencies are controlled by autonomous boards appointed by the governor. Although most such units are small and have a very limited function, dozens may be accountable only to the governor and can easily be lost to his or her view and the public's.

States also have public corporations. Some are the sole property of the state government; others are jointly owned with private investors. More than 5,000 of these are to be found in the United States, operating throughout a state or within a local area. They have three features in common: a legal status distinct from that of the state government, access to the tax-exempt bond market (see Chapter 4 for the significance of this), and no direct taxing power (Walsh, 1978).

The Port Authority of New York and New Jersey is an example of such a corporation. It owns and operates billions of dollars' worth of public facilities: the Kennedy, LaGuardia, and Newark airports; the World Trade Center towers; bus terminals; a subway line; and harbor facilities. These generate enough revenue to finance maintenance and expansion. The governing board of the Port Authority is named jointly by the governors of the two states and so is entirely independent of the local governments in the New York City region. Other state corporations operate toll highways, finance home mortgages, and produce and sell electricity.

State universities and colleges are part of these governing structures but have a long tradition of autonomy, accountable only to the legislature or to a board of regents appointed by it. They contribute in major ways to the public purposes, from extending the education process through the life span to research on issues ranging from AIDS to the military uses of space. Occasionally, their output sparks controversy. For example, the Universities of Wisconsin and Minnesota developed hormones that greatly increase a cow's milk production, but small dairy farmers, who fear stiffer competition from large operators, oppose their use.

Finally, states have a wide range of independent regulatory agencies. They license businesses, set prices and levels of service for public utilities, and admit people to professions and trades. The members of a state's Public Utilities Commission are named by the governor and/or the legislature, but the nominees for professional licensing bodies are drawn from members of the regulated profession.

The complexity of administrative organizations is dictated by political factors as much at the state level as at the national. Their conflicts are on a geographically smaller scale, however, and the contestants are more likely to be personally acquainted. Each constituency and interest group prefers to relate to a clearly identifiable unit that responds to its needs. This is reinforced by the legislatures, which resemble Congress in their committee organization and concern for administrative details. Often they compete vigorously with their governors for "custody" of the agencies, a contest that is intensified when the governor is of a party different from that of one or both legislative majorities (Gormley, 1989a, p. 143).

The Organization of Local Governments

The more than 86,000 local jurisdictions vary widely in form and internal structure, which can make it difficult for a citizen to find out which government is responsible for neighborhood flooding or where to complain when a landlord does not provide enough heat. Several different patterns of local authority have developed. The ones used in a particular locality depend on the constitution and statutes of the state and the political choices of its citizens. All local authorities are under their state's legal jurisdiction and have only those powers specifically given them by their constitutions and legislatures.

General-Purpose Governments

First, local governments fall into either a general-purpose or a special-purpose category. The **general-purpose local government** includes counties, towns, and municipalities (cities or villages). These have broad powers: police and fire protection, public works, parks and recreation, land use regulation, housing, cultural facilities, mass transit, and industrial development, to name only the most obvious. As they prepare each year's budget, they must set priorities among these functions and coordinate their programs. Each purpose has a constituency interested in the quality of service, which applies political influence favoring it over others. Thus, a city or county must balance demands for better police protection for high-crime neighborhoods against replacement of a deteriorating bridge and enlargement of the public library.

Counties are active governing units in all states but Alaska, Connecticut, and Rhode Island. They are both administrative units of their state governments and self-governing authorities with their own elected officials. Their duties vary by state and by whether they are in urban or rural areas, but usually they include welfare services, law enforcement, and road maintenance. A major urban county is likely to have a wide range of responsibilities that dovetail

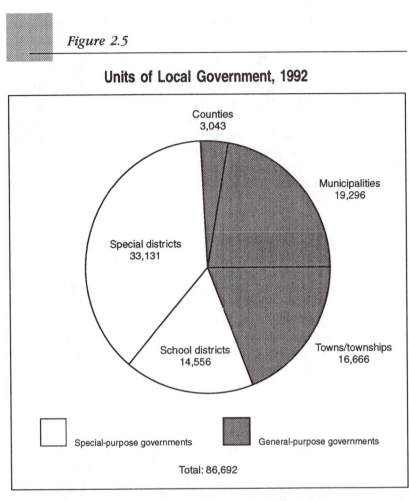

Figure 2.5

Units of Local Government, 1992

Total: 86,692

Source: U.S. Bureau of the Census, *Census of Governments,* 1992, Vol. 1, No. 1.

The forms of local government that are most familiar to many citizens—cities and counties—actually make up little more than one-fourth of all local units. There are more special districts than any other form, but most of them have little visibility.

with those of the municipalities within it. Some, such as Los Angeles County, California, provide municipal services to residents of areas that are not in any city and to incorporated cities by contract. Urban counties have been steadily expanding their activities, particularly in pollution control, waste management, health care, social services, and transportation (Schneider & Park, 1989).

Municipalities, unlike counties, are incorporated at the will of their residents, who may be able to choose their structure (the options are described beginning on page 48). They are the basic providers of police and fire protection, streets, sewers, water, parks, and land use controls. State law gives them some leeway on how they will perform their functions and which optional activities (perhaps industrial development or recreational programs) they engage in.

Towns and townships, which are legally distinct from cities and villages and exist in only twenty states, are harder to characterize. Most are governed by a board elected by their residents, although in some states the annual town meeting, in which all citizens may take part, is a major decision-making event. Although many governing boards in rural areas lack even one full-time employee and do little besides spread road gravel, urban towns function like municipalities in unincorporated areas, and some control public schools as well. In general, towns are strongest in states where county governments are least active.

A new form of local authority has emerged recently on the margins of government: the residential community association. This is the means by which the common property of townhouses, condominiums, and similar developments is controlled. Homeowners are required to belong to these associations and to pay fees or dues, which cover maintenance of buildings, streets, and recreational areas—functions for which local governments are normally responsible. The associations also restrict what residents can do with their homes, from exterior painting and landscaping to parking vehicles and keeping pets. An estimated 150,000 such associations exist around the country, and the housing related to them shelters about 32 million people. The trend toward such facilities has raised concern that local governments are not only abdicating their responsibilities for services but also allowing a new form of authority to control citizens' lives.

Special-Purpose Governments

Bodies that perform one or a few related functions are known as **special-purpose local governments**. School districts are the most common of these, responsible for elementary, secondary, vocational, and community college education. In most states, they are entirely autonomous from other local governments and are accountable only to the state departments of education and legislatures. They too are expanding their functions to encompass early childhood care, health maintenance, counseling, and job placement services.

Other special districts are responsible for such functions as airports, water supply, waste management, mass transit, hospitals, parks, fire protection, and drainage. (Their names differ; *district, commission, board,* and *authority* are the most common.) These districts have multiplied because they offer a flexible way to provide services without conforming to existing city and county boundaries. For example, a district charged with protecting water quality and preventing flooding on a stream can be created to cover an entire watershed, overlapping many other units' boundaries. An agency providing sewage service to a metropolitan region can take in the entire urbanized area, with its many cities and counties.

Special district administrators are usually appointed by their boards. They have the advantage of being able to concentrate only on the assigned function and need not balance widely differing constituent demands. They usually operate amid little publicity, which can be an advantage to them but also limits their accountability to the public. Many citizens do not realize that their local bus or sewage system is run not by their city but by a separate commission. These units are financed by fees for their services, property taxes, and/or subsidies from federal, state, or other local governments.

Local Forms of Organization

Internally, local governments exhibit three basic forms of administrative organization. Since each state authorizes various forms of local organization, each form can vary widely. Many states permit local citizens to adopt a "home rule" charter for their city or village that specifies the form of government they choose.

The Mayor/Council Form   The **mayor/council form** follows the national/state model in dividing powers between a single-chamber legislative body that makes the laws and a mayor who administers them and gives executive leadership to the city or county. The voters select both the council and the mayor for 2- or 4-year terms.

This model has two major variants: the "strong mayor" and the "weak mayor." In the former, the mayor is clearly the chief administrative officer and has extensive powers to appoint and dismiss department heads, prepare the budget, and oversee operations. The council's formal role is limited to legislating, and a strong mayor may be able to veto its actions. Neither is answerable to the other, and the risk of dissension, like that between the president and Congress, always exists. The council may inject itself into administrative matters, whereas the mayor and top department heads often exert policy leadership.

Structurally, a large city resembles the departmental scheme of the national and state governments, with units responsible for police, fire protection, social services, health, public works, and community development. In this form, their heads answer to the mayor, although the council may also exert informal political influence.

This strong mayor/council form is used in most large cities, some smaller ones, and a few counties. Since the mayors serve a fixed term of office, they cannot be removed for incompetence unless the state permits voters to recall them. Some mayors have built such strong political organizations that they have been able to exert power well beyond the formal description of their jobs. For example, Richard J. Daley of Chicago (late father of the current mayor, in office from 1955 to 1976) used his control of the county Demo-cratic Party organization to shape city policies and suppress conflict over controversial issues.

The "weak mayor" form is more common in smaller cities and towns, which have less complex administrative organization, and is widely used by county governments. This mayor may be directly elected first as a council member and then selected as mayor by fellow councillors. The council as a whole is likely to choose the staff and prepare the budget, with the mayor participating simply as presiding officer. Both also supervise the administration, although there may be a person with the title of clerk or coordinator with limited oversight powers. This kind of mayor can provide policy and administrative leadership by using his or her informal resources of persuasion and public relations (Svara & Associates, 1994).

The Council/Manager Form   The second type of local govern-ment organization centers on an appointed executive. When used in cities and counties, it is known as the **council/manager form** and is most popular in medium-sized communities. The elected council or board makes the policies and hires a professional manager to appoint all subordinate administrators, carry out policies, and be accountable for results. The manager has no secure tenure and can be dismissed at any time. There is usually a mayor in this system also, but that post has no administrative powers. A typical mayor would preside over council meetings, conduct public relations, and provide some policy leadership. Managers are expected to be non-partisan but are often active in recommending policy choices to the council or board. School districts and many other special-purpose governments also use the appointed-executive form. The governing board, typically a part-time body, selects a professional superintendent or director. The relationship is similar to that of the city manager.

The Commission Form   An elected body, usually composed of fewer than a dozen members, that both legislates and administers is the centerpiece of the **commission form** of local government. In those cities and counties, commissioners enact laws as a body, but as individuals they are assigned to head the administrative de-partments—one to public works, another to public safety, and a third to parks and recreation, for example. The commissioners are rarely specialists in their departments' functions, unless they have gained considerable experience on the job. There is a mayor in this system, but he or she usually lacks administrative powers. This form, once popular, is now less common because of its diffused pattern of ac-countability.

The internal management of cities and counties with all three types of organization is sometimes further fragmented by autono-mous boards that oversee the police, fire protection, housing, redevelopment, and other functions. The mayor and/or council appoints the boards' members, but the latter have wide discretion in internal policy and operations. Use of these boards decentralizes administrative control and reduces the accountability of elected officials to the general public for the given function. Instead, it can increase the power of agency employee organizations and specialized constituents (e.g., land developers or tenant unions, in the case of housing and redevelopment boards).

Native American Tribal Governments

Often ignored in the panorama of governments are the established Native American tribal authorities. The federal government formally recognizes 545 tribes, which have specific legal rights on their own territory. Since, under the U.S. Constitution, relations with "Indian tribes" are the responsibility of Congress, the states' jurisdiction over reservation lands is limited. This often leads to disputes that must be settled in court. The tribes are most visible as operators of gambling casinos (which provide substantial revenue), but they have expanded into education, health, job training, child care, and other services. Their authority is also relevant to non-Indians, who may find themselves subject to Indian judicial processes if they are charged with a crime on a reservation.

In 1987 Congress passed the Tribal Self-Government Demonstration Project Act. Implementation began in 1990. Thirty tribes were designated by the U.S. Bureau of Indian Affairs (BIA) to receive a package of federal funds for which they take substantial responsibility. Among them are the Mille Lacs Band of Ojibwe in Minnesota and the Cherokee Nation in Oklahoma, which have their own elected leaders and service agencies. These tribes had long been the wards of the BIA, with no autonomy whatever, so this represents a long overdue step toward recognizing them as local governing organizations in their own right.

Government Reorganizations: Hopes and Politics

We have seen how complex our governments' administrative structures are at the national, state, and local levels. It should be obvious why it is often difficult to understand who is responsible for what actions (or nonactions) and why separate agencies and units of government must cooperate constantly to make shared programs work. The distribution of food stamps to low-income households, for example, involves the U.S. Department of Agriculture with state and local social service agencies, all of which provide part of the funds and the rules by which the program is governed.

Complexity has several other drawbacks. Chief executives and department heads, who are accountable for administration, may have limited control of the programs under them. They may have too many units to supervise closely or may lack complete authority over them. Two agencies with overlapping responsibilities for services to troubled families may duplicate each other's efforts, or each may do nothing, assuming that the other will act. Or officials in separate agencies may have to spend time conferring on how to coordinate their efforts. Federal and state efforts to control air and water pollution offer many examples of this. Finally, it may be difficult to monitor the results of these programs when many hands are involved and to assign credit for success or blame for shortcomings.

We are not locked into this complex structure, however, for there is always the potential to rearrange it. Reorganization has been a dominant theme in the past 100 years of American public administration, and we have never lacked for proposals to gain greater economy, efficiency, responsiveness, or other virtues by moving bureaus and functions around. Some have been signal successes. The creation of the Bureau of the Budget (now the Office of Management and Budget) in 1921 was a landmark step, for it empowered the executive branch to prepare its own proposed spending and revenue plan before Congress made its fiscal decisions. Today a central executive budget is considered indispensable to proper financial management. But few such innovations have yielded benefits on this scale.

Arguments for Administrative Reform

Two broad arguments have guided the movements for government reorganization at the national, state, and local levels (March & Olsen, 1983). The first emphasizes the traditional goals of maximum efficiency in government operations and clear channels of executive authority and control. This language was embodied in the Reorganization Act of 1949, in which Congress required that any new structure be justified by the monetary savings and improved unity of control it would yield.

The second argument focuses on the political forces surrounding public organizations that provide essential services to specific constituencies like farmers, military veterans, and small businesses. When these interested parties are politically strong, they oppose any reorganization that appears to downgrade those agencies on which they depend. On the other hand, they may use their influence to upgrade a unit, as the National Education Association did on behalf of the Department of Education in the late 1970s. This form of rhetoric is power and service oriented rather than managerial and has been equally influential in shaping reorganization choices.

These two rhetorics compete with one another, but actual reorganizations embody both in some way. Today's Department of

Defense dates back only to 1949, when it was formed by a merger of the separate War and Navy Departments. Prior to that, interservice rivalry and lack of cooperation had long plagued military affairs. This forced Congress and the president to act. Although the Army, Navy, and Air Force remain separate subdepartments and have regular disputes, the Secretary of Defense is responsible for settling them. Under the preceding arrangement, only the president could mediate between War and Navy, and even his decisions did not always end the bickering. Internal reorganization of the Defense Department has continued, nevertheless, in search of more effective ways of structuring its tasks and resources.

Many other plans for government reorganization remain on library shelves, never having been adopted or even seriously considered. In general, they failed because they were not consistent with the political realities that created and sustained the structures that would have been altered. Since a particular structure provides more access and advantages to some interests than to others, prevailing political forces have an obvious stake in its reorganization.

A History of Administrative Reform

Local, state, and national governments in the late nineteenth century were shaped by the political parties that developed in the 1830s during the administration of President Andrew Jackson. Their minimal functions were expanding, though unsystematically, into such areas as road building, care for the poor, and railroad regulation. Legislators created agencies and offices as needed but were not guided by any overall design. Their personnel were chosen through the spoils system, in which the winners of each election replaced current administrators with their own supporters. Thus, tenure was short, there was minimal attention to qualifications other than political loyalty, and misuse of funds and authority was widespread.

Reform movements to reduce this party domination of administration and its attendant corruption arose sporadically after the Civil War and continued throughout the New Deal. Despite their diverse origins, these movements had two major aims. First, they aimed to increase the role of professionally and technically qualified people in the specialized functions of government. They had a close concern for police, public health, and education, which were growing responsibilities of local authorities.

Second, the reformers aimed to increase executives' ability to control administrators. Even an able mayor or governor could not manage most of these functions effectively because of the extreme fragmentation of their structures. Frequently, police departments were under an independent board of commissioners, not the mayor. Reformers sought these changes because they believed that the election of their favorites as governors and mayors would result in leadership that would make a difference in the operations of government.

A related reform was the grouping of government functions into organizations with clearly defined responsibilities. Many police departments around the turn of the twentieth century were operating ambulances, inspecting boilers, monitoring markets, and supervising elections. These "nonpolice" activities were natural targets of reorganization efforts (Knott & Miller, 1987, p. 42). Such restructuring, it was believed, would result in the skills of each professional being best employed and avoid duplication.

These two reforms implied, of course, less influence for political parties. In many states and localities, small, elite groups controlled party organizations and were only concerned with preserving their own power. The reformers—consisting of conservationists, urban merchants, professional groups, and those seeking new social policies—learned that if they organized, they could influence policy and administration outside of the traditional party machines. This became most obvious in the progressive electoral reforms that extended popular control over state and local governments, such as the initiative and referendum, nominations by primary elections, and the secret ballot (Knott & Miller, 1987, p. 80).

The Independent Regulatory Commission: A Legacy of the Reformers　The independent regulatory commission is a major inheritance from the reformers.

> One of the most effective political tactics of reformers was to remove certain aspects of policy-making from arenas where they could not compete effectively with political parties to arenas where they had a competitive advantage. The "politically independent" regulatory commission was a structural form that could be created in moments when public support was high, and then would remain an island of nonpartisan influence even when public support waned. (Knott & Miller, 1987, p. 51)

President Woodrow Wilson chose this form as the means to prevent industrial monopolies and restraints on trade when he succeeded in establishing the Federal Trade Commission (FTC) in 1914, which joined the Interstate Commerce Commission as the second of its kind.

At the state level, Governor Robert LaFollette of Wisconsin was instrumental in creating a railroad commission in 1905 to regulate rates and service. This was followed by many similar commissions in that and other states. The professional licensing boards appeared at this time, responding both to popular concerns about competent performance and to the rise of the associations of doctors, lawyers, and others. Often these independent units were used for purposes other than regulation. When Congress began to provide federal aid to road building in 1914, it required states to establish a separate administrative unit to handle these funds, and "highway commissions" were the most common response. Although these independent units contradicted the principle of direct executive control, they allowed specialized functions of government to be overseen by the professionals in those fields, which reformers deemed more important.

The City Manager Reform   The city manager form of government also originated in these progressive impulses. Dayton, Ohio, was the first large city to adopt it when an inept response to a flood in 1913 discredited the existing regime. A newly elected city council hired a politically nonpartisan civil engineer to control the entire administration. His success inspired imitations, and by 1928, 364 cities had followed Dayton's lead. This innovation was consistent with the unity-of-control theme, even though it removed the chief administrator from direct choice by the voters, since it placed one person in control who was continually accountable to the council and removable at any time.

Reform Movements in the National Government   Although reformers were concerned about the national government's structure as early as 1905, they paid close attention to it only after the great expansion of agencies in the 1930s. This bureaucratic sprawl multiplied noncabinet agencies, with which President Franklin D. Roosevelt, given his pragmatic management style, was comfortable. But it did become harder to manage from the White House. Consequently, in 1936 he appointed the President's Commission on Administrative Management, headed by Louis Brownlow, who had been one of the first city managers. After careful study, the commission recommended regrouping all functions of the national government into twelve executive departments. An outraged Congress flatly rejected that. The only real reform that resulted was the act that established the Executive Office of the President in 1939, which was described earlier.

Since World War II, reorganization movements have had more modest goals and have concentrated on clearer relationships among agencies with similar functions and increased roles for professionals in existing agencies. The establishment of the Defense Department, noted earlier, was most significant. Former president Herbert Hoover headed study commissions on the national government in the 1940s and 1950s, but their recommendations affected budgeting practices more than organization.

Most reorganizations in the national government resulted from its increased role in certain policy areas, such as energy and human services. In 1946 Congress created the Atomic Energy Commission as a noncabinet agency, both to promote and to regulate nonmilitary applications of nuclear energy after the atomic bomb ended World

War II. By 1974 it was clear that one agency could not be both an advocate for the private utilities generating electric power from nuclear reactors and a vigorous protector of public safety from its hazards. Congress thus divided those functions. The role of advocate for utilities was assumed by the Energy Research and Development Administration (which 3 years later became the core of the new Department of Energy). The independent Nuclear Regulatory Commission assumed the role of protector of the public safety.

Partial deregulation of the airlines was another source of reorganization. In 1978 Congress approved a plan for the gradual removal of federal controls over fares and routes, which was the province of the Civil Aeronautics Board (CAB). Another agency, the independent Federal Aviation Administration (FAA), had been created in 1958 to oversee safety of air travel. In 1986 the CAB's life expired, but the FAA, by then a key component of the Department of Transportation, was deeply enmeshed in public concerns over air traffic control and safety and had been charged with being too susceptible to the political power of the airlines. In 1988, a presidential commission on aviation safety called for its transfer to an independent regulatory agency with greater authority and autonomy. Six years later, President Clinton urged Congress to hand the FAA's air traffic control functions to a private corporation under government supervision, to upgrade its technology more quickly. Key members of Congress prevented action on both proposals.

Reorganization at the State and Local Levels

State executive branches have seen more reorganization in recent years. In the 1965–1978 period, twenty-one states undertook comprehensive restructuring. These reorganizations have been of two kinds: (1) grouping of multiple but related agencies into larger single-function units (e.g., public assistance) and (2) formation of "superdepartments" with broad missions, such as "human resources" and "natural resources" (Garnett & Levine, 1980). The purpose of both was to reduce the number of units answering directly to the governor, but there is no consensus on how large a department should be or on the proper breadth of its responsibilities. Legislatures also have defeated the purpose of these periodic reorganizations by creating new agencies not under the original umbrellas.

Reformers have also tried to reduce the number of local government units and the overlaps among them. To some, it makes sense to form a single municipal government for a metropolitan area that assumes the functions of all the cities, counties, and special districts. They argue that one chief executive, one budget, and one administrative hierarchy can be more efficient and accountable to the region's citizens. Some cities (Jacksonville, Indianapolis, and Nashville, to name the largest) consolidated their central city and county governments to achieve this goal. Many other plans to simplify the governance of metropolitan areas have been defeated by their voters when submitted to them in elections, however.

The logic of local consolidation has not appealed to most state legislators or voters who would have to approve such reorganization plans. Small local governments rest on a solid political base. The desire to keep them responsive and accountable to citizens resists such consolidations. They view large governments as bureaucratic, wasteful, and remote. As vigorously as constituent groups and legislative committees favor fragmentation in national and state executive branches to guard their special relationships, local citizens protect their small-community police and fire departments and zoning laws. To them, administrative efficiency is not measured simply in dollars.

The Outcomes of Reform: Goals vs. Realities

What shall we conclude about the results of these reorganizations? Advocates have foreseen greater economy and efficiency in government, assuming that no major policy changes take place. However, this has been a quest for a phantom. The actual costs of most governmental outputs are hard to measure, since they have no competition in the marketplace. Even if these costs were more easily calculated, the "aggregate sums available to be saved in the administration of government services are far smaller than commonly acknowledged" (Salamon, 1981, p. 481).

The reformers also sought to make policy more effective by arranging administrative units to secure maximum mutual cooperation, support from legislators and outside interests, and clear executive leadership. This is more realistic. An agency supporting urban mass transit may well find stronger backing in a department of transportation than in one of urban development, with its primary focus on housing and physical infrastructures.

Less exalted, though more common, is the third goal: to secure political advantages for elected officials. In many reorganizations, the aim is to "gain access, representation, visibility, and a secure institutional niche for a particular interest" (Salamon, 1981, p. 496). New political interests and movements rather than calculated administrative orthodoxy initiate these changes. When the Department of Housing and Urban Development was established in 1965, it was to be a signal of government's commitment to cities and to focus attention on their disadvantaged residents.

We can conclude this chapter with an essential political reality. As public agencies serve their constituents, a "structure of interests" wraps around each one, challenging the governmental hierarchy for the power to determine the agency's behavior. When we consider the wisdom and feasibility of potential organizational changes, we have to look at this structure and not just the agency itself (Long, 1949; Salamon, 1981). Thus, major reorganizations must obtain the active support of the dominant interest groups surrounding the organization to be changed. They can veto alterations they oppose, even when changes are sponsored by a determined chief executive.

When President Ronald Reagan asked Congress in 1985 to eliminate the Small Business Administration, an independent agency that provides loans and advice to operators of those enterprises, he proposed to consolidate its functions with those of the Commerce Department. But its constituents staunchly opposed him, preferring the smaller agency that was oriented exclusively to their interests. Congress listened to that enclosing interest structure and rejected the president's plea. Similarly, many small municipalities and school districts remain autonomous rather than merging with others, enjoying solid support from their residents, who value their "own" city hall and high school. To be successful, reorganizers must be able to transfer constituents' identities and loyalties to the new arrangement, a difficult social and political task.

Major reorganizations of government at any level are likely to take place only in response to the changing public purposes and methods of serving them and if supported by parallel shifts in the political forces benefiting from those efforts. For example, as health care occupies a larger share of public concern and government budgets, we are likely to see more agencies in national, state, and local structures that provide and regulate such care. This will probably increase complexity, but this issue is less important to these groups than whether the expected service is provided effectively.

What are we to conclude about the politics of government organization? No restructuring by itself, however logical or popular, can solve inadequate policy, uncommitted leadership, clumsy procedures, or miserly funding. How structures are arranged is important, but the most persistent problems cling tightly to any organization regardless of its location. Safety of air travel and nuclear reactors will not depend ultimately on regulatory structure, nor will a reorganized health care finance system easily overcome inflation of medical costs.

Summary

The national, state, and local administrative structures have grown in size and complexity over the years in response to the expansion of public purposes. They rest on a base of the constitutional principles of federalism, separation of powers, citizen rights and liberties, and accountability to the people.

The national and state governments are similar, for they encompass a chief executive's office, major departments that carry out their central functions, other line and staff agencies, government corporations, and independent regulatory agencies. Their specific shape depends on many political influences, not the least of which are rooted in Congress and the state legislatures.

Local governments show much more diversity. There are general-purpose (counties, towns, and municipalities) and special-purpose units (school districts and other single-function authorities). Internally, they can be organized on the mayor/council basis (as are the national and state governments), the council/manager form (centered on a professional city manager or superintendent), or a commission that both legislates and administers.

American history abounds with efforts to reorganize government for greater efficiency and executive control, but many failed to achieve their objectives. The independent regulatory commission and professional manager form of local government are among the most successful of these. Federal and state reorganizations have generally followed changes in functions and responsibilities, supported by the political forces most interested in the services that are rearranged thereby. Constituents of local governments have largely resisted consolidation, for they value the small units, which they can control.

Discussion Questions

1. What factors appear to promote complexity in American governmental organization (i.e., the number of agencies and units of government required to provide the services and regulations the public demands)?

2. The separation-of-powers system designed in 1787 still is supreme in the organization of the national, state, and many city governments. Many observers believe it unduly hinders them from making necessary decisions when they are needed. What other disadvantages does it have? What are its advantages?

3. Why are there so many units of local government, and why is their number growing? Is there any real public benefit to having so many?

4. Why have so many of the attempted reforms in government organization failed to meet the hopes of their sponsors?

5. The advocates of a governmental reorganization scheme are usually at a political disadvantage when compared with its opponents. Why?

Analytical Exercises

1. Identify all the units of local government that exercise authority in the community in which you live or attend school. Include their areas of responsibility, how they are held accountable to their residents, and their sources of revenue. Judge how visible each one is to its constituents and whether they are adequately informed on it. It may be easiest to begin with an interview of an official or a reporter for a local newspaper.

2. In the mid-1990s we are witnessing a debate over the need for several of the cabinet departments, including Commerce, Energy, Education, and Housing and Urban Development. Examine this debate to learn who stands on which side and for what reasons. Evaluate any reorganizations that result from it, in terms of the effects on policy, finance, and political power changes.

For Further Reading

Advisory Commission on Intergovernmental Relations. (1992). *Metropolitan Organization: The Allegheny County Case*. Washington, DC. Surveys the many units of local government in the Pittsburgh metropolitan area and the means by which they cooperate in providing public services.

Hamilton, A., Jay, J., & Madison, J. (n.d.). *The Federalist*. New York: Modern Library. The basic rationale for the American constitutional system, direct from its designers; Papers 10 and 51 are best known.

Knott, J. H., & Miller, G. J. (1987). *Reforming Bureaucracy: The Politics of Institutional Choice*. Englewood Cliffs, NJ: Prentice Hall. Surveys the many efforts at administrative reform and gives the key factors in their successes and failures.

Neustadt, R. E. (1980). *Presidential Power: The Politics of Leadership from FDR to Carter*. New York: Wiley. The classic statement on the actual boundaries of the power of presidents and how they can maximize it amid all the constraints.

Patterson, B. H. (1988). *The Ring of Power: The White House Staff and Its Expanding Role in Government*. New York: Basic Books. Surveys the people surrounding the president and describes how they extend his knowledge and power.

Radin, B. A., & Hawley, W. D. (1988). *The Politics of Federal Reorganization: Creating the U.S. Department of Education*. Elmsford, NY: Pergamon. Dramatizes the political process of federal reorganization that was completed in the late 1970s.

Seidman, H., & Gilmour, R. (1986). *Politics, Position and Power: The Dynamics of Federal Organization* (4th ed.). New York: Oxford University Press. Provides penetrating insights on why the national government is organized as it is and how its many parts relate to one another.

Wilson, J. Q. (1989). *Bureaucracy: What Government Agencies Do and Why They Do It*. New York: Basic Books. Sweeping and realistic survey of how federal departments and agencies operate and what motivates their managers and employees.

3

The Political Dynamics of Bureaucracy

Learning Objectives

After reading this chapter, you should be able to do the following:
1. Define organization, hierarchy, and bureaucracy.
2. Identify Weber's principles of bureaucracy.
3. Explain how bureaucracies have developed in American public administration.
4. Define organizational equilibrium and explain how it is maintained.
5. Identify the types of communications within and among government agencies and with the public.
6. Identify criteria and alternative forms for organizing government functions.
7. Explain the current reasons for dissatisfaction with public bureaucracy that has spurred the "reinventing government" movement and the major themes of that movement.

Vice President Albert Gore was handed a major challenge early in his term: to head the National Performance Review, a six-month study designed to create a "government that works better and costs less," in the words of its report title. He assembled a team of experienced federal employees to identify specific ways to improve services, increase efficiency, and simplify structure. The final report, issued in September 1993, foresaw savings of $108 billion over the next five years if all the recommendations were adopted.

The major fault with the federal organization, the commission decided, was that "Washington is filled with organizations designed for an environment that no longer exists—bureaucracies so big and wasteful they can no longer serve the American people" (National Performance Review, p. xxxii). In the drive to control these monsters, they were overlaid with layers of rules—detailed mandates and prohibitions for employees to follow. But these rules also stifle the initiative and innovation that could develop more productive administration. Thus, the commission called for a commitment to ongoing change, extending over a decade or more, not just a set of one-time reforms with quick payoffs.

Specific recommendations numbered in the hundreds. Among them were the closure of many field offices of the Department of Agriculture, consolidation of food safety programs into a single agency within the Department of Health and Human Services, sale of federally owned apartment buildings, and reform of the process by which the Department of Defense procures its weapons and other supplies from private contractors. Many others were matters of internal management that did not arouse opposition. Responses to the report varied from enthusiasm at the White House to great uncertainty and skepticism everywhere else. Some of the specific cost-cutting recommendations had been made before and Congress ignored them.

The skeptics probably had history on their side, as well as the logic of complexity. Large organized systems (what we later define more precisely as *bureaucracy*) seem to have inherently limited flexibility and productivity. They are harder for one person to comprehend and control, become defensive in the face of threats and demands for change, and resist "outside" scrutiny and evaluation. The Gore Commission succinctly diagnosed many of the ills, some of which are given in Box 3.1, but to cure them is another matter entirely. We will return to this issue and to the first year of experience with it at the end of this chapter.

The Logics of Organization and Bureaucracy

Organization is the assembly of knowledge, power, and will to accomplish certain purposes. If any of these are lacking, we cannot expect success in a group endeavor. The form of organization can vary widely, depending on the requirements for a given task. The U.S. Army differs radically from a community agency serving the elderly, although both are public agencies. Knowledge consists of the technical expertise and general experience necessary to carry out specialized tasks. Power, the central resource of politics, enables the organization to change social or environmental conditions in spite of others' resistance. Will embodies the dedication to a purpose, which directs the application of knowledge and power. To link these effectively and produce the desired result, whether a battle victory or aid to victims of Alzheimer's disease, is the test of any organization.

Box 3.1

Red Tape in the Federal Bureaucracy

Vice President Gore chose to emphasize the need for reform in the federal government by "horror stories" of excessive controls and sluggish action. The villain here is red tape, which actually consists of rules and restrictions designed to make everything happen in a precise and predictable way. Unfortunately, it also prevents desirable things from happening.

The federal government does at least one thing well: It generates red tape. But not one inch of that red tape appears by accident. In fact, the government creates it all with the best of intentions. . . .

Because we don't want politicians' families, friends, and supporters placed in "no-show" jobs, we have more than 100,000 pages of personnel rules and regulations defining in exquisite detail how to hire, promote, or fire federal employees. Because we don't want employees or private companies profiteering from federal contracts, we create procurement processes that require endless signatures and long months to buy almost anything. Because we don't want agencies using tax dollars for any unapproved purpose, we dictate precisely how much they can spend on everything from staff to telephones to travel. . . .

The district managers of Oregon's million-acre Ochoco National Forest have 53 separate budgets—one for fence maintenance, one for fence construction, one for brush burning—divided into 557 management codes and 1,769 accounting lines. To transfer money between accounts, they need approval from headquarters. They estimate the task of tracking spending in each account consumes at least 30 days of their time every year, days they could spend doing their real jobs. It also sends a message: You are not trusted with even the simplest responsibilities.

Or consider the federal employees who repair cars and trucks at naval bases. Each time they need a spare part, they order it through a central purchasing office—a procedure that can keep vehicles in the shop for a month. This keeps one-tenth of the fleet out of commission, so the Navy buys 10 percent more vehicles than it needs.

Or how about the new Energy Department petroleum engineer who requested a specific kind of calculator to do her job? Three months later, she received an adding machine. Six months after that, the procurement office got her a calculator—a tiny, handheld model that could not perform the complex calculations her work required. Disgusted, she bought her own.

—National Performance Review, 1993, pp. 1–2.

Each of the government organizations discussed in Chapter 2 can be called a **bureaucracy**. This term has been applied to private organizations from IBM to the Roman Catholic Church, but government organizations seem to be more bureaucratic than any others. We can understand bureaucracy as a form of organization that (1) is large enough that its top managers cannot have face-to-face relationships with all their subordinates, (2) is sufficiently specialized to require a precise division of labor, and (3) consists of offices arranged in a chain of command from the top executive to the lowest employee. It is the most widely used form in government and industry, since it structures the knowledge, power, and will needed to accomplish most complex tasks in modern society.

The organizations a society maintains, whether in government or in the private sector, reflect its overall values and purposes. Ancient Egypt and Sumeria first developed bureaucratic administrations to channel the waters of the Nile and the Euphrates Rivers through canals to irrigate fields. This required officials, scribes, records, and rules—all the features of what Max Weber later called a **bureau**. Demanding tasks calling for large numbers of people to work closely together require organizations with these features. A decentralized society that needs only minimal coordination of actions, on the other hand, can survive with small and loosely guided administrative units.

Classic Views of Organization

A basic principle of human organization is **hierarchy**, which is a system of persons holding authority over others with the ability to command behavior and punish lack of compliance. One may believe in this out of distrust in the ability of people to govern themselves, a fundamental assumption of most political systems in the history of the world. But even firm believers in democracy concede the need for some kind of hierarchical organization. After all, humans do need leadership to accomplish collective goals. Robert Michels, a European observer of socialist parties and labor unions in the first decade of the twentieth century, found that even organizations that most valued democracy could not pursue their goals without strong leadership. From this he proposed a general social law: "The majority of human beings . . . are predestined by tragic necessity, to submit to the dominion of a small minority, and must be content to constitute the pedestal of an oligarchy" (Michels, 1966, p. 390). No political system is immune to this "iron law," although there are means by which enlightened and determined followers can hold their leaders accountable to them.

The founders of the United States inherited hierarchical social principles from their European forebears but did not apply these principles as directly to governing as the Europeans had. The national executive branch created by President Washington and the First Congress did not penetrate deeply into national life. Forty years later, Alexis de Tocqueville observed that, although there was a degree of centralization in government and lawmaking in the nation and states, "there is no centralized administration and no hierarchy of public functionaries" ([1835] 1945, I, p. 91). The Constitution's principles of horizontally and vertically divided powers provided the young nation with its theory of administrative organization. When the national government issues a decree, "it must entrust the execution of its will to agents over whom it frequently has no control and whom it cannot perpetually direct. The townships, municipal bodies, and counties form so many concealed breakwaters, which check or part the tide of popular determination" ([1835] 1945, I, p. 282). As a result, the "authority which public men possess in America is so brief and they are so soon commingled with the ever changing population of the country that the acts of a community frequently leave fewer traces than events in a private family" ([1835] 1945, I, p. 219).

The Modern Era: Toward an American Science of Administration

Fifty-five years passed from de Tocqueville's tour of the United States to Woodrow Wilson's essay "The Study of Administration" in 1887. More than time had passed, however; demands on government were growing, requiring a new style of public management. Wilson called for a genuinely American "science of administration" that would "straighten the paths of government, to make its business less un-businesslike, to strengthen and purify its organization, and to crown its duties with dutifulness." Such a science already existed in Europe, but it was designed for centralized forms of government. If permitted to cross the Atlantic, it "must get the bureaucratic fever out of its veins; must inhale much free American air" (1941, pp. 485–486).

Wilson realized that democracies may find it harder than monarchies to administer their laws. Public opinion may not settle quickly on a single course of action, and a leader must compromise often and act slowly to build majority support. The public has the right to evaluate and criticize, but it also finds ways to hinder the lawful and efficient performance of government's duties. For this reason he favored separation of administration from politics. "The field of administration is a field of business. It is removed from the hurry and strife of politics. . . . Although politics sets the tasks for administration, it should not be suffered to manipulate its offices" (1941, pp. 493-494). Politics, in this sense, is the realm of debate and conflict that generates the laws, the arena in which the public reconciles its many differences. When it intrudes upon administration, it prevents efficient execution of the laws. Thus, administration serves democracy best when it stands apart to follow its own principles.

Bureaucracy: Weberian Theory in the American Context

European influences on the rapidly changing American administrative system were unavoidable. Americans went to England and Germany to study political science and law, and they returned eager to apply the principles they learned. Max Weber, a German social sci-

Box 3.2

Weber's Principles of Bureaucracy

(1) Bureaucracy rests on a body of law that grants authority to each employee within a limited sphere. The law describes the organization's powers and responsibilities, much as a democratic constitution does for a government as a whole.

(2) The agency establishes written rules that govern how it will act within that law. The rules specify how the agency will apply the law to particular cases, how it will proceed in enforcing its decisions, and what the duties and responsibilities of its personnel are. They prevent arbitrary and unpredictable treatment of clients and employees.

(3) The positions are arranged hierarchically; each is under a higher one and exercises supervision over lower ones. The highest person in this structure is accountable to one outside it, usually to the chief executive or a legislative body. No one may act independently or outside that legally defined authority.

(4) Employees of the bureaucracy are appointed on the basis of their competence to perform specific tasks, certified by experience, examination, or training. Their tenure depends solely on their seniority and achievement as judged by their superiors. This employment constitutes a full-time but voluntary career.

(5) Employees earn a monetary salary, the amount depending on rank in the hierarchy. This is their only compensation, and they have no other claim on the facilities or resources of the organization.

(6) All decisions and acts are recorded in writing. These records guide future actions and facilitate accountability to higher authority.

—Max Weber, *The Theory of Social and Economic Organization*. New York: Free Press, 1964.

entist who published his theory of bureaucracy early in the twentieth century, identified and analyzed some of those principles. His work deserves study here, not as a norm for American public organization but as a portrait of the imperatives that a technological society presents to any kind of government.

Weber asserted that only a structure based on law and a rational arrangement of competence and power could function in and regulate a capitalist industrial economy. Bureaucracy, as he described it, has the basic features presented in Box 3.2.

Weber's principles provide the foundation for the definition of bureaucracy given earlier in this chapter. It combines the French word *bure,* for the cloth covering of desks used by the king's financial clerks, with the Greek word *kratia* for *rule.* Rule by the regulations and records stored in desks, and above all by the knowledge and skills of those who sit at them, is the essence of bureaucracy. The paperwork that Vice President Gore lamented in the National Performance Review contains the organization's memory—its only guide to future decisions—which is necessary to any agency too large to rely on records kept within forgetful human minds.

This form of bureaucracy is **monocratic**, in which one person heads each unit. Thus it is, as Weber explained, "capable of attaining the highest degree of efficiency and is in this sense formally the most rational known means of carrying out imperative control over human beings. It is superior to any other form in precision, in stability, in the stringency of its discipline, and in its reliability. It thus makes possible a particularly high degree of calculability of results for the heads of the organization and for those acting in relation to it" (Weber [1922] 1964, p. 337).

Bureaucracy's superiority rests on its mastery (sometimes a monopoly) of technical knowledge. Modern industry and the professions have already built their power on this, and it is indispensable for any government that coexists with these centers of economic power. The control of bureaucratic machinery rests with the trained permanent official, who is more likely to get his or her way in the long run than the elected executives and legislators who are not specialists. Significantly, Weber warned that such organizations could use their power to become oppressive and self-serving if not kept accountable to the public. Viewing the political history of the twentieth century, we see that his concern was justified. This tendency naturally disturbs defenders of traditional democracy. Their concerns will be examined later.

Americans have long been familiar with many of Weber's norms. The original cabinet departments were created with a single head, fitting the ideal of unity of command. The civil service system that Congress created in the Pendleton Act of 1883 incorporated most of his principles of personnel management. It is ironic, in view of the negative meaning that bureaucracy has for most Americans today, that it was viewed by the end of the nineteenth century as a progressive innovation, one that would enhance government's ability to provide the goods and services that an industrial urban society demanded.

American Organizational Theory: A New Orthodoxy

Industrial engineering was an important American source of organizational theory, particularly the work of Frederick Taylor. Woodrow Wilson had called for an American science of administration, and Taylor offered just that in the first decade of this century. He sought to maximize the productivity of tools and workers and argued that scientific design and management of jobs could revolutionize industry and government alike. A popular movement sprang up to apply his concepts in all these realms. Public administration was deeply affected, not so much by Taylor's specific methods (which labor unions and members of Congress often opposed) as by the idea that there is a best way to organize any given job.

Box 3.3

Principles of Organizational Orthodoxy

(1) Employees should be assigned to tasks in conformance to the overall organizational design.

(2) Each agency should be headed by a single executive (and not by a board, as was common in many governments at that time).

(3) Each employee should normally have only one immediate superior—a unity of command.

(4) Top executives should have the advice and assistance of general staff members, to free them for their most important duties. These staffers act solely on behalf of the executive and under his supervision only. (This principle inspired the creation of the Executive Office of the President in 1939, as noted in Chapter 3.)

(5) The functions of a department should be assigned to its subunits according to one of the following principles: the purposes served by the unit, the implementation processes it uses, the clienteles it deals with, or the geographic area it covers.

(6) Duties should be delegated downward through the organization, and superiors should concern themselves only with the results of subordinates' efforts.

(7) Each official shall have sufficient authority to fulfill the assigned responsibilities.

(8) A supervisor shall have no more than six persons or units to oversee—the "span of control."

—L. Gulick and L. Urwick, eds., *Papers on the Science of Administration*. New York: Institute of Public Administration, 1937.

Influenced by these ideas, plus the experiences of such reforms as the city managership, American administrative scholars formulated an "orthodoxy" that dominated organizational thinking through the 1920s and 1930s and that reached a peak in *Papers on the Science of Administration* (Gulick & Urwick, 1937). Their major principles extended those of Weber and are summarized in Box 3.3.

These principles have been widely accepted and remain as ideals even where they are violated in practice. Some are so obvious as to be taken for granted (the delegation of duties from the head of an organization to subordinates, for example). Yet recent administrative theorists have challenged them, claiming they are contradictory and do not fit all types of organizations found in modern governments (Simon, 1957). Thus, they are no longer taught as unbreakable rules, but they still stand as points of departure for debates on ways to organize government.

The Human Relations Perspective: A Challenge to Orthodoxy

The most serious challenge to this orthodoxy addressed its treatment of employees as simply another resource, a means to an end, to be managed just as money, buildings, and machines would be. The alternative, loosely called the **human relations perspective**, takes account of social relationships in the workplace and their impact on productivity. It originated in the much-described Hawthorne experiments of the 1920s, in which researchers altered working conditions of a group of employees in the Hawthorne Works of the Western Electric Company to learn how to induce them to be more productive. Their output indeed improved, but after more inquiry the researchers learned that the gain was due more to the employees' social environment than to their physical working conditions. They had created an **informal organization** by their own choices that both reflected and conditioned their motives and behavior. As members, they might indeed seek to serve the organization's goals, but they also pursued goals of their own, which might have a higher priority for them. Whom they worked with and how their relationships formed created a group dynamic that might support or contradict the formal mandates of the organization.

Human relations theorists thus rejected the Weberian tenet that proper structural design is the only path to efficiency. They called for a sensitivity to what motivates people and to the interpersonal situations that either enhance or diminish the contributions they make. Thus, creating the conditions in which employees cooperate with superiors and one another is the central problem of organization.

The Expanding Role of Government: Another Challenge   The classic assumptions of administrative science also lost favor as a result of the public policy experiences of the 1930s and 1940s in which governments were called upon to undertake many more functions than before. Putting people back to work, restoring confidence in the financial system, replacing slums with livable homes, and allocating half the resources of an industrial society at war were not the kinds of activities that Wilson or Weber observed government doing or that Taylor could time with his stopwatch. The new era required innovative methods and structures, and no single approach could be proven "the best way."

Recent Thought: Two Streams   Recent thinking about public organizations has diverged into two broad and meandering streams on which the next two sections concentrate. One examines the position of government agencies in their political, social, and cultural contexts (their external characteristics). Their major challenges, from this perspective, come from outside as they search for resources and power to meet various constituencies' demands for services. The second stream focuses on the internal dynamics of bureaucracies, public and private alike. It analyzes the motives and behavior of leaders and members, the manner of their communication, the goals and interests of the whole organization and its parts, and the attitudes and norms that shape its response to its environment. Of course, evidence and concepts from one stream constantly cross over to enrich the other.

No generic government agency exists. Each one occupies a unique place in society that shapes both its internal and external identities. That place is first defined by the specific public purposes it serves through the programs assigned to it. Some such purposes are very narrow. The Internal Revenue Service and a local fire department, for example, have very specific missions. Others have more varied responsibilities, requiring greater flexibility and breadth of competence (witness the demands on the U.S. Immigration and Naturalization Service and state welfare departments). Their programs come from legislation and from the courts, which regularly revise and reinterpret them according to current demands.

An agency's place is also social, defined by its constituencies, who depend on it and demand its attention and service. Contrast a public library, hosting a typically literate and well-behaved clientele, with a prison, which must control society's least successful and most violent members. A large public school system covers a wide social spectrum and must create ways to cater to students who are gifted, disabled, or disruptive.

This place has an economic dimension as well. Each one has a budget, buys goods and services, and may compete in a marketplace with private businesses, as does the Postal Service for all but first-class letters. Many agencies, such as the Small Business Administration and state medical licensing boards, were placed in legally defined niches in the marketplace to regulate, subsidize, or otherwise alter some facet of the private economy. Some are also shapers of the national or municipal economy: The Federal Reserve is closely linked with the banking system, and a city's vocational education program prepares students to fill jobs in local industries.

Finally, each organization has a politically defined place determined by its visibility and influence with the general public and with executives and legislatures that oversee it. The Federal Bureau of Investigation acquired an aura under the leadership of J. Edgar Hoover as the nation's toughest and most successful law enforcement body. This led Congress and several presidents to show it great deference and to support it with ample funds. Moreover, Hoover was free to function autocratically, with little outside scrutiny. In contrast, the Postal Service has struggled with a poor public image that has not always been consistent with its achievements.

These diverse places that agencies occupy require a major qualification to Weber's concepts of bureaucracy. His ideal type assumed only a legal place for a bureau. That is, it performed a function assigned by law, such as collecting taxes or constructing roads. It was a **closed system** in that a relatively thick "shell" insulated it from external influences that might divert it from its mission. American public agencies, by contrast, are **open systems**, constantly vulnerable to outside influences at all levels of their hierar-

Government Organizations in Their Environments

chies. An open system must manage many, and often conflicting, forces from all directions that challenge its internal management. The public health and pollution control agencies cited in Chapter 1 are particularly open because of the political sensitivity of their missions.

Equilibrium: A Key to Organizational Survival

All organizations of whatever kind must maintain a long-term **equilibrium**, a balance of intake and output with their environments. Barnard (1938) and Simon (1957) posed this view of the demands that organizations must meet in order to survive and prosper. Basically, they take in sufficient resources (such as money, personal skills, legal power, and information) and, after utilizing them internally, produce outputs sufficient to satisfy those to whom they are accountable and to secure a continued flow of inputs.

This process is obvious in a business firm: Sale of the product or service earns money to purchase more materials and pay employees, which in turn supports additional production, sales, and income. If the firm is efficient in its operations, it earns more money than it pays out, which becomes its profit. If it does not earn a profit, this indicates that it is not in equilibrium and is on the road to bankruptcy. Its destiny thus rests with its management, both in devising effective responses to that market and in conducting internal operations at high efficiency.

We can also view government agencies in equilibrium situations, but the forces that act on them differ sharply. Dahl and Lindblom (1953, pp. 458–464) draw the major contrasts between them and typical private organizations in Box 3.4. The characteristics listed in the box are quite general; specific agencies can differ widely. For example, the tests that are useful to measure the efficiency of the National Aeronautics and Space Administration (NASA) and the U.S. Postal Service (USPS) are very different. NASA's most visible current outputs are launches of manned space vehicles, which take place only a few times a year at the most. One major failure clouds its image for years. By contrast, the USPS delivers billions of pieces of mail and must repeat its successes 6 days a week. One undelivered letter is much less important to it than is one NASA disaster to the space agency.

NASA and USPS must also search for equilibrium in their unique ways. For all public agencies, the immediate "customer" is the legislative body, which provides it with the powers and money necessary to attain its objectives. Beyond this are the constituent groups who receive the service or regulation from the agency and communicate their preferences and demands to the lawmakers. NASA has declined in relative size and funding over the past two decades because of reduced demand for space exploration and lack

Box 3.4

Characteristics of Government Organizations

In contrast to private enterprises, government organizations

(1) are controlled more by superiors or other political actors than they are by a price system;

(2) must cope with funding that is more highly contingent upon previous experience and perceptions of superiors;

(3) have more vaguely defined or multiple goals, among which cost reduction does not receive very high priority;

(4) are relatively insulated from automatic penalties and rewards of the price system;

(5) generally lack objective tests of efficiency in their operations;

(6) are able at times to shift their costs to other agencies rather than face them or go under; and

(7) are not generally provided by cost reduction with opportunity for growth.

—R. A. Dahl and C. E. Lindblom, *Politics, Economics, and Welfare.* New York: Harper & Row, 1953.

---

of dramatic goals for the future. Its product is not one from which people receive daily, tangible benefits. Once Neil A. Armstrong had beaten the Russians to the moon in 1969, many Americans concluded that we had won the space race and no longer needed to spend as much money. The agency was further wounded by the 1986 *Challenger* tragedy, which observers widely interpreted as a sign of internal mismanagement of a routine launch.

The USPS offers a different example of organizational equilibrium. Its efforts touch nearly every citizen directly. Some of its services, such as third-class mail and express delivery, compete in the market with private firms, whereas its first-class mail service is a monopoly (although fax and E-mail transmissions are reducing the importance of this). As its rates have increased, public perceptions of its service quality have not risen accordingly. This has spurred talk of privatizing its services, which would put it out of business as a public agency.

Factors of Organizational Success

An agency's management must provide for several crucial factors to achieve success. Lacking these, it will fail to satisfy the decision makers and constituents who support it with funds, authority, and political backing.

Goals and Purposes The first factor essential for success is that the organization must express its goals and purposes clearly and center its decisions on them. These goals and purposes have to draw constituent and legislative support and be achievable using the resources available. NASA scientists dream of a mission to Mars and argue that this vision could again ignite popular enthusiasm. But in the current tight budget situation, the agency lacks the funds to do any serious preparations for an expedition even if it abandoned all its other goals. Thus NASA must depend on more modest goals to preserve its current share of the budget.

Inducements   A second necessary factor is sufficient inducements for people to join the organization and, once hired, to work diligently for its goals. Some people join for monetary or other rewards not directly related to the organization's mission. Others join because of the mission itself, involvement in a prestigious or successful organization, or a general commitment to public service, and these are the incentives that are important to many government agencies, which cannot pay the high salaries that private companies pay for some skills. NASA, when it was at the forefront of space exploration, obtained the services of many talented people who had other attractive career options. To the extent that it lost its dynamic image, it became less inviting to the very people it needs to regain its equilibrium and growth.

Internal Efficiency   The third imperative for survival and effectiveness is internal efficiency in transforming resources into products. Government generation of electric power and local garbage collection can be compared readily for efficiency with their private counterparts. But that same quality is almost impossible to measure in an agency that does not sell a competitive product in the market. Agencies dealing with child protection services and regulation of toxic waste have no private counterparts, and their managers often rely on public and legislative satisfaction with their efforts as "efficient enough." They also know that there may be popular dissatisfaction even with well-run organizations that are wrestling with difficult social or technological problems. They must produce a steady stream of visible accomplishments with the resources they are given and avoid obvious failures.

The Structure of Interests   The fourth imperative for public agencies is to maintain links with supporting constituents and interest groups, the "structure of interests" identified in Chapter 2. This is essential if the agencies are to redefine their goals when necessary and to sustain the flow of personnel, money, and other resources needed to produce services. This structure of constituent interests includes the legislators and executives most related to the agency's functions, the beneficiaries of their services and those who would like to become such, and the suppliers of their purchases (such as military weapons contractors). (The Defense Department has been especially vigorous in stimulating its suppliers to exert political influence on behalf of its budget.)

This structure may also contain some "enemies" who want the agency's power reduced or its functions altered, or who want it eliminated altogether. The Environmental Protection Agency and similar state agencies face opposition from businesses that consider them overzealous. Such opposition was temporarily successful during the early years of the Reagan administration in cutting back the EPA's enforcement activity, but the pro-environment interests reasserted themselves. An agency may ignore weak opposition but must neutralize or convert that which threatens to disrupt the equilibrium. At times, it can do this only by altering its goals or methods of operation in the direction demanded by these opponents.

Why Administration Needs Politics It is necessary to cultivate these sources of political power because the American political system is so fragmented. It

> does not generate enough power at any focal point of leadership to provide the conditions for an even partially successful divorce of politics from administration. Subordinates cannot depend on the formal chain of command to deliver enough political power to permit them to do their jobs. . . . A major and most time-consuming aspect of administration consists of the wide range of activities designed to secure enough "customer" acceptance to survive and, if fortunate, develop a consensus adequate to program formulation and execution. (Long, 1949, p. 258)

The Tennessee Valley Authority provides a classic example of an agency compelled to alter its original goals because of its political environment. It was created by Congress in 1933 to bring not only flood control and electric power to an impoverished region but also regional planning, self-help cooperatives, and benefits to its poor white and black farmers. However, the political leaders in those states—conservative whites in government, business, and agriculture posts—prevented the TVA from threatening the region's hierarchical and racist social structure. As a result, the TVA had to limit its mission to building the dams, power stations, and fertilizer factories for which it is known today (Selznick, 1966).

Internal Dynamics of Public Organizations

The second main stream of thinking about public organizations focuses on their internal dynamics. Members of a bureaucracy have not one but several roles: civil servants, employees of an agency, members of a skill group or profession, and participants in one or more informal associations in the workplace. These provide employees with diverse identities and motives, which they carry to the job, thereby seeking to promote certain values through their positions: power within or outside the bureau, monetary income, prestige, convenience (the desire to minimize personal effort), security of any of the preceding for the foreseeable future, personal loyalty to one's agency or a higher entity, pride in good work, desire to serve some concept of the public interest, and commitment to a specific program of action (Downs, 1967, p. 84).

Most employees share every one of these motives, although their order of priorities can differ widely. Such a ranking in turn influences behavior, and when a cohesive work group agrees on its priorities, it can either support or frustrate the formal goals of the agency. The last four on the list are particularly relevant to the public purposes, and supervisors should give special attention to supporting these motives. Those in high-demand situations, such as public health workers, drug enforcement agents, and air traffic controllers, cannot function well for long without strong and positively reinforced motives for public service.

Public Officials and Their Motivations

We can categorize public officials according to their combined motivations (Downs, 1967, pp. 88–89). First, there are those who are purely self-interested, seeking only their own benefit. They fall into two types: **climbers** (who primarily seek power, income, and prestige) and **conservers** (who want to retain the advantages they currently have and who value convenience and security more than the climbers). They may or may not be serving the agency's goals at the same time, but those are not the highest aims.

A second group of officials has mixed motives, blending self-interests with loyalty to larger values. **Zealots** are loyal to narrow policies or concepts, such as AIDS research or pesticide regulation. They seek power both for its own sake and to obtain policies to which they are committed. **Advocates**, by contrast, are loyal to a broader set of functions or to a larger organization than zealots, perhaps pollution control or the Environmental Protection Agency in general. They also seek power because they want to influence policies concerning those functions or organizations. **Statesmen** strive for the power necessary to shape national policies, since they perceive themselves as loyal to the "general welfare" as they define it, whether it be promoting economic growth or protecting the interests of factory workers.

These types are abstract but useful yardsticks for comparing actual persons and groups. The Peace Corps offers examples of zealots, for the people attracted to it are not looking for security or convenience but for a dramatic cause to help the world. More stable agencies, such as the Postal Service, have the reputation of being secure career niches. Still other agencies offer the chance to use the contacts and skills gained in government employment as a stepping-stone to more money and power in a private position. The Defense Department and the regulatory agencies draw employees with this kind of ambition.

The Informal Structure of Organizations

Public officials, whatever their motives and ways of expressing them, interact with others in the organization in many ways. The Hawthorne study, mentioned earlier, demonstrated the informal character of an organization that coexists with the formal structures and influences their activities. This consists of the intricate network of associations, roles, influences, and norms that grow up in any organization, springing from the values and wills of those who make up the organization rather than from the rules and policies established by the management or lawmakers. The older the organization and the longer the tenure of its members, the more solidly established that informal structure will be.

Conflict: Individual Versus Organizational Goals Some social scientists assert that there is an inherent conflict between individuals and the organizations in which they work (Argyris, 1957). Normal adults achieve a certain level of competence and autonomy in life and are able to set priorities and make decisions. Yet they may be required to put those traits aside in taking a job and submitting to the organization's conditions and rules. While most are able to adjust for the sake of making a living and achieving other goals, this tension remains and may at times turn into public strife. Strikes and other labor actions display this open conflict on a large scale. Schoolteachers, transit workers, and garbage collectors have repeatedly struck their local employers, not just over money but also over status and work rules.

Managing Conflict Several means for resolving or managing conflicts among people and units within organizations exist (Hirschmann, 1970). First, those concerned can simply leave the organization; this is the "exit" option. A superior can also remove a person from a post, although this can be difficult if he or she is protected by civil service rules. This removal may terminate the conflict or exacerbate it, depending on the responses of those who remain or view it from the outside. The departure may be a "resignation in protest," by which a person publicizes his or her grievances. Attorney General Elliot Richardson resigned his post in 1973 rather than obey President Richard M. Nixon's order to fire Archibald Cox, the independent prosecutor investigating the Watergate scandal. Although Richardson's reputation was probably enhanced by his action, the president continued on the path that resulted in his own resignation less than a year later. Aside from a few celebrated cases, though, exit has little effect on public policy or management.

Another means of dealing with conflict is negotiation. If the conflict is deeply rooted, no simple "I win, you lose" resolution is possible. The contestants voice their positions and, in the interest of harmony, develop working agreements. As in any bargaining situation, both sides must be sensitive to what they can get and what they must give. Skilled mediators are often required where the differences are deep-seated and the parties have emotional stakes in the outcome. In other cases, people may redefine their grievances or submerge them in an expression of loyalty to the agency or to the larger public purposes it serves. Management, in turn, may provide additional incentives to resolve conflict, such as personal benefits or greater participation in decision making.

Bureaucratic Ideologies

From the combination of legal goals and missions, formal and informal structures, and personal roles, unique "ideologies" arise within agencies that give them character and condition their responses to their circumstances. A **bureaucratic ideology** consists of beliefs or statements of how the organization is valuable to society and the means by which it promotes those values (Downs, 1967, p. 237). It evolves, or is developed, to supply its managers and subordinates with a rationale for their efforts, a positive image to project to the political environment, an appeal to recruit personnel who are particularly desired, and criteria for making decisions in doubtful situations. Often the ideological content gives a unique style to the formal and informal messages. Organizations with very demanding or controversial missions, such as law enforcement, rely on an ideology to give their members unity and mutual trust as they face a common foe or task.

It is important, of course, that an agency's ideology support its assigned goals and public purposes, which are the baseline for effective accountability to the public. Formally, we assume that when the policymakers have created an organization and defined its mission, it acts according to that mission. However, the organization sometimes displaces the formal goals for others of its members' choosing. Often these alternatives are aimed at preserving the organization's stability and its employees' security amid change in its environment. Where many of the personnel are "conservers," as defined earlier, this tendency would be strong. In other situations, the agency may put a high priority on one of its goals and virtually neglect the others. It was common in the past for social service agencies, drawing on an informal ideology, to orient their care to white clients and ignore persons of color who had equal needs.

Two or more ideologies can compete for dominance in an agency, with one or another winning for a time. The U.S. Forest Service (USFS), with a public image of a strong commitment to protect the woodland resources of the nation, has also overseen large-scale cutting of forests on public lands. The Clinton administration has said that the agency has gone too far in the direction of timber cutting and has sought to change its policy by appointing as its head a top scientist who has been identified with protection of the spotted owl, an endangered species in the Northwest. However, the ideological debate will not die, since many of the agency's influential personnel support the timber sales programs (Cushman, 1994).

The communication process within and among government organizations and with the public shapes the choices and activities of individuals and groups with each other and with the leadership. Messages in a large organization travel on many paths. When we add the movement of information to and from sources external to it, we find that mapping this pattern is a major challenge.

Organizational Communication

Formal Communication in Public Bureaucracy

Messages that follow the hierarchical structure of the organization and relate to the exercise of authority and the duties of each member are called **formal communication**. Traditionally, they have been written and become part of the record on which the agency bases decisions. Such a communication may be a directive on a new procedure for enforcing environmental regulations, a report from a public works director to a city manager on the condition of the water mains, or a manual of instructions for state park rangers. More and more, these are transmitted by voice mail or electronic mail, which may or may not be printed for storage in a file.

Often there is a policy on what is to be communicated to whom, when, and in what form to ensure adequate distribution and precision in the message. A citizen who has had to file Form 4567-Z in quadruplicate begins to grasp such formality. When messages are initially sent electronically rather than on paper, there must be specific requirements as to who has access to them and how they will be stored. Administrative messages are often laden with specialized language—jargon—as Box 3.5 shows. Jargon permits communication in very precise ways for which "ordinary" language is not adequate. However, it also can confuse rather than enlighten those who are not initiated and can be deliberately used to obscure data that could be controversial or embarrassing.

(continued on p. 79)

Box 3.5

How Can You Communicate with the Natives in Washington?

The specialization and expertise that one finds in bureaucracies are always accompanied by unique languages that carry meanings important to these experts. Government bureaucrats use this "jargon" and add to it the tongues that originate in large public organizations. This can be frustrating to outsiders who want to know what their public servants are doing for (and to) them and, conversely, a source of pride to those who have mastered this unique language.

In the capital of the United States, the diplomats aren't the only people speaking a foreign language.

Within the federal bureaucracy, the mother tongue is "government-speak," says Lynn Bateman, president and publisher of Government Counseling Ltd.-Taurus, a Springfield-based firm that provides advice on how to sell to the government.

"There's no way to communicate in this community unless you know you need an APR to get the DPA from GSA so you can issue the RFP, so the case can go to the GSBCA."

Translation: an agency procurement request to get the delegation of procurement authority from the General Services Administration to issue the request for proposal so the case can be protested before the General Services Board of Contract Appeals.

In what other business can a person revel in the FAR (federal acquisition regulations), the FIRMR (federal information resources management regulations) and the CFR (code of federal regulations)? If the answer's not available in those documents, try the OIRM (Office of Information Resources Management) or the NTIS (National Technical Information Service) or the NIST (National Institute of Standards and Technology). If that doesn't work, ask the associate deputy assistant secretary or the principal dep-

uty assistant secretary or the associate director/assistant to the assistant secretary or the special assistant executive associate commissioner.

"People in the field think everyone in Washington is a joke," Bateman says. "We're not taken seriously. But that's why consultants make so much money. They're translators. Most of my clients would rather die than deal with regulations. So we're plumbers. They pay me lots of money for knowing which screw costs 5 cents."

Bateman is a part of a pervasive local industry that makes its living talking to itself and translating government-speak to the auslanders [outsiders]. The world of government-speak includes a vast printing establishment of federal government reports and hundreds of trade press and newsletter publications, topped by the Federal Register, the compendium of government rule-making that last year filled 53,841 pages.

Government-speak is inhabited by 356,583 federal employees in the Washington region plus thousands of private sector workers who are umbilically tied to the bureaucracy. In companies doing government business, a "government relations" group or a "federal systems" division is an absolute must.

And as long as the federal government is here, its special language will thrive. "You feel a little superior to those who don't understand the language," says Bob Dornan, vice president of Federal Sources, a Vienna, Va.–based consulting firm. "It's like being in an inside clique or fraternity with its own secret passwords. That feeling's definitely shared by everyone in the business."

—Willie Schatz, "Learning the Lingua Franca,"
Washington Post National Weekly Edition,
April 30–May 6, 1990.

Informal Communication and Feedback

A much greater volume of communication is informal. It deals with more subjects but lacks authority, although it may have considerable influence in some situations. Some informal messages flow along the lines of authority. For example, the public works director may have already quizzed the manager on how much money will be available to repair the water system before drawing up a request for the sum. Or the city manager may have learned in a conversation over coffee about a leak in a water main. Other informal information passes between personnel at the same level, from admonitions to new members of the organization on how to get along with the boss to observations on which rules are and are not enforced. Without this, conflicts could rarely be resolved or smooth working relationships established. Where members have to exercise much discretion on their own, as in a school, law enforcement agency, or scientific laboratory, this network is necessary to guide them. These messages can reinforce official communication, add to and interpret it, or contradict it. Also, informal communication is less likely to be in writing, as the originator may not want it preserved. An administrator must be sensitive to this flow, as must any constituent or legislator who deals with the organization.

Two-way communication is essential for management. At times, managers may be so deluged by information flowing into their offices that they cannot readily identify what is essential. However, an even harder problem for a top administrator in a large agency is obtaining feedback on the actions of subordinates. The higher the executives and the larger the organization, the less information typically reaches them about events "below" them. Compliance with their directives is far from automatic, and often it is hard to learn whether there has been any compliance. Where subordinates encounter diverse situations in the field and have a large amount of discretion, channels for such feedback will be uncertain (Kaufman, 1973). Social workers who spend much time in the homes of threatened children file reports, but those reports may not clearly describe the quality of services delivered or be timely enough to remedy mistakes.

Flow of data about misdeeds or conditions that could be embarrassing to the persons involved is most likely to be blocked. Top NASA officials knew nothing of the concerns of the engineers before the disastrous *Challenger* launch in January 1986.

> In any reasonably large government organization, there exists an elaborate system of information cutoffs . . . to prevent information, particularly of an unpleasant character, from rising to the top of the agency, where it may produce results unpleasant to the lower ranks. Thus, the executive at or near the top lives in constant danger of not knowing, until he reads it on Page

One some morning, that his department is hip-deep in disaster. (Peters, 1986, p. 27)

There is no ready way to prevent or dissolve blocks to feedback. Clearly, top administrators must convince their subordinates they are willing to listen to both bad and good news. Furthermore, they must keep their ears open to the informal networks, if only for clues of what needs additional inquiry. Much feedback on the agency's performance can come from the outside through interest and client groups who have regular contact with it, if those sources are cultivated.

Communication with the Outside: Public Organizations and Their Bases of Support

Communication between a public organization and the outside world is essential to an agency's efforts to achieve and maintain equilibrium. Governments produce great volumes of information and distribute it through many channels. Some messages are aimed at the general public and others at legislators, constituent groups, or other units of government. These also fall into formal and informal categories. In the formal class are press releases, reports, media interviews, and displays that are designed to account for and/or win support for its activities and supply information or instructions. Box 3.6 provides four examples.

Government communications to the public have several purposes. As in the first example in Box 3.6, they may aim to support and enlighten people in basically private activities (although if some avoided contracting AIDS as a result of reading the pamphlet, public health care costs would be reduced). A second purpose, illustrated by NASA but pursued by many agencies, is to publicize and win popular support for programs. This may include educational and economic benefits for certain publics, but the larger aim is to impress people with the importance of a service the agency performs.

Third, public agencies publicize benefits they make available and the means by which people may obtain them. Local governments engage in this constantly, as the third example in Box 3.6 shows. In some circumstances this is a challenge. Food stamps are distributed to low-income households through state and local welfare offices, and it is necessary to communicate this to all potential recipients. This is not thoroughly done, according to a Congressional Budget Office study that found that about 15 million of the 30 million eligible do not take part. Much of this shortfall is due to ignorance of the program or of how to apply for the aid (Tolchin, 1988). Communication must overcome such barriers as inability to read English, lack of access to the mass media, and transience.

Box 3.6

Government Messages to the Public

- In the summer of 1988, the U.S. Public Health Service mailed the eight-page pamphlet "Understanding AIDS" to every postal customer in the nation. Surgeon General C. Everett Koop's picture and message were on the cover. Its purpose was to provide brief and accurate information on how the disease spreads and how to avoid it. A Spanish translation was available upon request to a toll-free telephone number. This pamphlet is one example of public information services that range from instructions for canning vegetables to Central Intelligence Agency maps of Afghanistan.

- Visitors to the Kennedy Space Center in Florida are treated to elaborate demonstrations and displays of the National Aeronautics and Space Administration's accomplishments and ambitions, from John Glenn's *Mercury* orbits to manned voyages to Mars. Young people can even spend a week at Space Camp at the Marshall Space Center in Huntsville, Alabama. Similar to public relations campaigns of major corporations, these efforts are designed to win public support for NASA as an agency and for its budgets in years to come.

- Many local governments mail regular brochures to their residents to inform them of what these bodies are doing and what benefits are available. A typical flyer might list the recreational programs sponsored by the parks department, explain that Main Street will be torn up for repaving for the next month, and profile the city's newly hired finance director. The general purpose here is to build an awareness of community and an information base in addition to the specific purposes of each message.

- When the Census Bureau began to count the nation's heads by mail-in forms in the spring of 1990, it made a strong media appeal based on the importance of an accurate count. It enlisted clergy and other leaders in minority communities to explain why members of these groups in particular should respond. The message was, in effect, "Please cooperate—an accurate count benefits all of us!" Many government messages ask citizens to cooperate with public activities. Without citizen cooperation, many public efforts would fail.

Governments must also communicate their laws and regulations if they are to secure compliance, as the Census Bureau grasped in the fourth example in Box 3.6. Now that automobile drivers and passengers must use safety belts, states not only have had to publish notices of the legal requirement but have been forced to remind and motivate citizens constantly to buckle up. They have used media advertisements, billboards, and other means of promotion. Although ignorance of the law is no excuse, in the old legal dictum, police have a lighter enforcement load when citizens comply voluntarily.

Information flow becomes especially sensitive politically when serious risks to life and health exist. Many factories and outdoor environments are heavily laden with chemicals that threaten human health and life itself. Although some of these are on government property, many more are privately controlled. In 1986 Congress determined that citizens have the right to know what chemicals are manufactured, used, or stored in their communities and workplaces. This action obligates all levels of government to disclose what is on their premises and to require private enterprises to do the same. Yet the mandate has often been ineffective, since many steps are involved in getting the information to the public and it may not be provided in a timely or understandable form (Hadden, 1989).

Information from Without: The Influence of the Environment

Public agencies also obtain formal messages from outside: from legislators in the form of laws and budgets, citizen complaints, directives from higher executives, court decisions, and information from other agencies at national, state, and local levels. Some are sought but many others come unsolicited. Most call for response, and the urgency of the action often depends on the originator of the message. For example, constituent complaints are said to get a quicker response if they are routed through a member of Congress than if they are sent to the agency directly.

The informal message flow across the organization's borders is likewise busy. An agency constantly takes in information from its environment through many channels (e.g., a police officer hearing from a street contact about drug dealing in a certain house, or a public health service doctor learning from a foreign colleague about a promising new treatment for AIDS). It also sends messages out (e.g., when a police officer tells a state environmental inspector about a midnight dumping of toxic waste in a river, or a state employee informs a news reporter about excess spending on a new highway). In neither direction can this informal communication system be "managed," but supportive members of the organization and outside interest groups, with adequate incentives, can use the system to help fulfill the agency's mission rather than frustrate it.

The communication system of a public agency can appear to an outsider to be inefficient or difficult to penetrate. A letter to an official may never get a response, or the answer may come in a form letter that ignores the problem raised. Agencies differ widely in their means of handling public concerns. Some put high priority on promptness and satisfaction when they are sensitive to outside estimations of their performance. Others see no need to respond or are selective about whom they respond to, and they may answer out of a sense of their "place" in the political order. This lapse was addressed in the National Performance Review, which committed the federal government to "active listening" to its "customers."

Some local governments use new information technologies to reach citizens for all these purposes. Computers with terminals in public locations, cable television programs, and videotapes provide information about services, regulations, and job openings. Santa

Monica, California, has an interactive system, with which any resident with a home computer and modem can link up, that offers electronic mail, conferencing, and bulletin boards. Many other cities have followed its lead, so that their citizens have less reason to complain of being left "in the dark." Even so, many do not realize such information, which can affect their lives, is available, nor are they confident they can understand or believe "official" language.

For all these purposes, governments employ public relations and information specialists to channel the information flow to the public and the news media. Their function is to coordinate the total outgoing flow of information to make sure it serves the policies of the government. Specialists may also help interpret policies or actions, hold press conferences and arrange for television coverage, and answer questions from all sources. They seek to present the information in the most favorable light and for this reason are tempted to use it for image building. When a mayor's public information office reports that the crime rate is down one month before his or her honor seeks reelection, the line between "informing" and "puffing" may be hard to draw.

What has the study of bureaucracies produced to help a policymaker or administrator design or redesign a specific agency? The principles put forth in the 1920s and 1930s rested on a one-dimensional view of bureaucracy as a formal tool for carrying out known functions in the most efficient way possible. That is, once the mission was defined, this view dictated the structure that should carry it out. Later analysts rejected that "orthodoxy," not because the principles were wrong but because they did not readily apply to the increasingly complex missions of many public agencies. The best way to regulate the use of atomic energy and deliver health services must be learned by experimentation, not by mechanically applying principles. Organizational architects today must be flexible in their vision and sensitive to policy and social environments. The following section sets forth key points for them to consider, not absolute rules.

New public organizations are most often reincarnations of predecessors. When a local government unit is created, such as a newly incorporated city, it is likely to be a near clone of its neighbors, since that model is familiar and has a record of reasonable success. Thus, the real problem of organization design is to make ongoing adjustments to fit changing tasks, constituencies, and environments. Chapter 2 surveyed experiences with reorganizing governments to reduce complexity, gain efficiency, or achieve political objectives. In general, that experience demonstrates that although some reorganizations have been beneficial, there is no single ideal generic structure.

The Design of Organizations

Issues of Organizational Design

An organization's design should begin with what it is doing, for whom, and where. If its mission is fairly routine and consistency of operation is important, as with a motor vehicle licensing agency, it can resemble Weber's model of bureaucracy, with its written rules and its priority on a vertical hierarchy. But a scientific research organization, which employs creative and independent people for whom innovation is a high priority, should avoid a rigid hierarchy and rely on broad performance criteria rather than on precise rules.

The degree of **centralization** (the extent to which operations in every part of the organization are controlled by its chief executive and/or detailed rules) is a second issue. If the task is performed in one location, such as mailing benefit checks, no geographic decentralization is necessary. On the other hand, if the organization must decide on clients' eligibility for aid, many field offices are necessary for the close contacts that enable agents to make fair judgments. With such decentralization, however, the central office must pay rigorous attention to the fairness and consistency of decisions made in the field.

The task also determines the appropriate **span of control**. This is the number of persons or offices that a supervisor must oversee. Where close supervision is required or leaders and subordinates must interact frequently, five or less is desirable. Work that requires little oversight or that can be checked quickly permits a much wider span of control.

Another issue is the balance between specialists, who are highly skilled in a narrow range of competence, and generalists, who have broader management responsibilities and must integrate many activities and viewpoints. Some division of labor is necessary, but certain people must be able to maintain the cooperation among specialists. It is easy for an engineer, medical researcher, or accountant to view the task from a narrow standpoint and lose sight of the agency's larger mission. The generalist (who may have a specialist's background) has to keep the overall priorities in order and yet keep the specialized staff contributing to them.

Criteria for Organizational Design

However the organization is put together, certain criteria appear to be necessary. First, the organizational design should be as simple as possible, so that members and outsiders alike understand who performs what functions. Second, each person must be accountable to a higher authority, so that no decision or action goes without review and possible correction. Third, the structure should permit ready communication among those who need to be informed, especially when they are physically separate. Finally, it should be flexible enough to take on new responsibilities and methods and incorporate new members with different specialties.

Political criteria are necessary for the organization to exert control over its environment and itself. It must have units that can perceive and respond to external threats and opportunities, obtain needed resources, and reach clients with its services and regulations. Internally, it must resolve ongoing disagreements over priorities and methods and preserve order and consistency in its procedures. The difficulty in achieving both kinds of political capacity is illustrated by Florida's Department of Health and Rehabilitative Services. With an annual budget of $4.7 billion, it is the largest state agency in the nation. Its responsibilities encompass health care, children's services, and criminal offender rehabilitation. It was created in 1969, but legislators and constituents are still questioning whether its design is most appropriate for the toughest missions of any government (Mahtesian, 1994b). Its structure fits the textbook criteria for administrative integration. However, it will be seen as a failure if it cannot overcome the internal conflicts that hinder it from responding to its clients' needs.

Alternatives to Bureaucracy

From the discussion to this point, one might assume that bureaucracy, suitably adapted to the demands and limits of the democratic process, is the most workable form of organization to serve the public purposes on a large scale. But there are alternatives that can and do succeed in specialized contexts. The simplest is the **leader/follower organization** format, in which there is one superior (or a small number) and a cluster of followers (although there will be intermediate cadres in large structures). A new and somewhat experimental public agency with a few strong leaders, such as the scientific research and development team that developed the atomic bomb during World War II, illustrates this form (Rhodes, 1988). This structure depends too much on central figures to have widespread or long-term usefulness, however.

The **mosaic organization** is a loosely joined collection of autonomous organizations able to make some decisions jointly. The European Union is a large-scale example of this: Having grown haltingly since its inception in 1958, it has the potential to create a genuinely continental economy. Within American administration, the best examples are the councils of governments that help coordinate the planning and policymaking for metropolitan areas and the interstate compacts that oversee river basins. The key drawback, which hinders the European Union and the metropolitan councils equally, is that they have no authoritative decision maker, so any action requires the consensus of most, if not all, members. Like the

U.S. government under the Confederation (1777–1789), such agencies cannot accomplish much in highly divisive situations.

The **conglomerate** is a system of hierarchies united at the top by a single directorate. Although the separate units fit the bureaucratic model, the system allows them some autonomy and is flexible enough to add units and alter their relationships as needed. The Defense Department is such a conglomerate, consisting of three civilian departments for the Army, Navy, and Air Force; the four military commands (Army, Navy, Air Force, and Marine Corps); and other civilian divisions, all under the secretary of defense (see Figure 3.1, p. 87). The complexity of this system is a drawback, although it can provide a unifying link between organizations that would otherwise be entirely separate (as were the War and Navy departments before 1949).

Harder to classify are the many intergovernmental networks that implement many domestic programs. For example, state and county agencies that administer Medicaid for low-income people have a close financial and management relationship with the U.S. Department of Health and Human Services (DHHS). The DHHS imposes rules on their use of federal funds, yet it must depend on them to implement the program successfully. Such organizations are open enough to political influences to permit a flexible working relationship, with frequent intervention by federal and local lawmakers.

The Weberian system did not envision sharing power among organizations, but the American ideal of separation of powers maintains the bureaucratic forms while limiting the power that each agency can exercise on its own. Such networking of hierarchies may be the least noticed but most significant alternative that the American administrative system offers to the body of organization theory. Chapter 4 focuses on intergovernmental networking, and Chapter 7 adds the growing relationships with private organizations.

Bureaucracy as Disease and the Search for a Cure	The two key words of this chapter, *organization* and *bureaucracy,* are labels for the same thing, but our culture has attached very different values to them. In the debates over President Clinton's reform of the health care system, people said they wanted it to be better organized but didn't want it to be bureaucratic. They usually meant by this government bureaucracy and overlooked the large structures of health insurance companies and other private organizations in that industry. We need to understand, then, why bureaucracy is regarded as a disease and what cures are possible.

Bureaucracies seem to suffer from defects inherent in their virtues. They operate under rules designed to ensure efficient operation and fair treatment of clients, but those rules are often rigidly

(continued on p. 88)

Figure 3.1

Structure of the U.S. Department of Defense

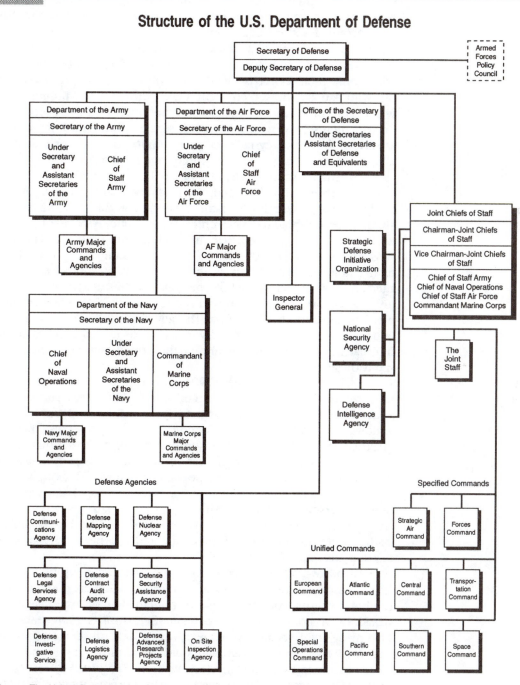

Source: The United States Government Manual, 1994.

applied, with no deviation for exceptional situations. Moreover, because they are oriented to what was done in the past, they stifle innovation, which is precisely what changing conditions demand. Bureaucracies are hierarchical so that they can be managed properly and account for their deeds and misdeeds, but this renders subordinates passive, unable to make full use of their own talents and initiative. Finally, bureaucracies are divided into units of specialists who apply their expertise to the complex problems of governing but who can also be secretive and unresponsive to the public. They wrap their procedures and decisions in paperwork, seemingly to protect themselves, while they confuse the citizens they serve. Just as serious, bureaucracy has a taint of authoritarianism, for it seldom allows citizens the opportunity to correct its abuses.

Are the basic purposes and rationales for bureaucracy consistent with those of a democratic polity? There are opposing views on this. First, there is the familiar argument that bureaucracy is antidemocratic, placing hierarchical, rule-bound systems of authority in control of society. These hierarchies influence legislators to pass laws and budgets that expand their programs and power. They treat employees and clients as things, objects of control and management, rather than as whole persons. Technical efficiency takes precedence over personal growth and fulfillment. This alienates people from one another and from the government, which should be under their control. Nearly everyone who has had to cope with the Internal Revenue Service or one of the armed services can understand these complaints.

A sharp debate in the 1790s on the place of administrative organization in a democracy pitted Thomas Jefferson against Alexander Hamilton. The latter argued for a strong and centralized national executive branch, reflecting the Federalists' trust in well-qualified men who take full responsibility for their actions. They were to act as trustees for the nation, serving its broad, long-term interests rather than fluctuating popular demands. Jefferson, by contrast, believed that each citizen should have the opportunity to participate personally in administration so as to gain the knowledge and skill to do it well. Thus, government should be highly decentralized but with its base in local communities, where citizens could develop this skill.

Woodrow Wilson offered one approach to solving both problems by distinguishing politics from administration, as noted earlier. If administrators operated solely in their realms of expertise, they would exert no undue influence on the people's representatives who made the laws and would give advice only on technical means and feasibility. Implementation could then proceed by the best means available, with no interference from "politics." Bureaucracy would be harnessed like a strong team of horses to pull the stagecoach without determining where it would go. As we have seen,

Box 3.7

Keys to Reinventing Government

It is hard to imagine a book about public administration becoming a big seller. But David Osborne and Ted Gaebler achieved just that with *Reinventing Government* (1992). Written in a breezy style with plenty of examples, it caught the attention of those who sought to cure an assortment of bureaucratic ills. Because it was so widely read and quoted, it deserves mention here—perhaps more for the direction in which it pointed than for the specific guidance it offered would-be reformers. The table of contents summarizes its message well:

1. Catalytic Government: Steering Rather than Rowing
2. Community-Owned Government: Empowering Rather than Serving
3. Competitive Government: Injecting Competition into Service Delivery
4. Mission-Driven Government: Transforming Rule-Driven Organizations
5. Results-Oriented Government: Funding Outcomes, Not Inputs
6. Customer-Driven Government: Meeting the Needs of the Customer, Not the Bureaucracy
7. Enterprising Government: Earning Rather than Spending
8. Anticipatory Government: Prevention Rather than Cure
9. Decentralized Government: From Hierarchy to Participation and Teamwork
10. Market-Oriented Government: Leveraging Change through the Market
11. Putting It All Together

---

however, this separation has never been possible because of the influence that the legislative, executive, and judicial authorities exert on one another and because of the assertive interest groups that do not leave administrators alone.

Max Weber, viewing the social consequences of the industrial revolution, understood the basic conflict as one not between bureaucracy and democracy but between industrialization and democracy. Running a modern society efficiently, Weber argued, requires rational decisions by experts, according to technical criteria. After a nation chose to industrialize, this method of organization followed logically for its government as well as business. In that respect, Jefferson was far-sighted in opposing industrialization, for he envisioned (and dreaded) the rigorous social and governmental organization that would inevitably accompany it.

This issue has been constantly revisited in the twentieth century, most recently in the "reinventing government" theme of the 1990s. Osborne and Gaebler (1992) attained near-bestseller status for their *Reinventing Government* (see its table of contents in Box 3.7). The term itself is so broad that it can be given nearly any meaning one chooses. A theme that had been developed earlier for industry use—Total Quality Management—began to penetrate the public sector as well, with equally ambiguous results. It was probably inevitable that these gave birth to the National Performance Review in 1993, as the opening story of this chapter highlighted.

These critics of bureaucracy usually agree on three general "cures" for its ills. First, they seek flexibility and innovation in place of rigidity and devotion to precedent. Many rules and procedures were laid down decades ago, before the telecommunications revolution, when government programs were more focused on routine tasks. The National Performance Review found that it has taken agencies up to a year to acquire personal computers for their offices, when they were already likely to be out of date. Rather, the broad mission of the organization should predominate over the rules.

Second, employees at all levels should be empowered and not pigeonholed in a strict hierarchy. Osborne and Gaebler (pp. 255–259) showed how "flattening" the pyramid and delegating more decisions to working-level employees increased both productivity and morale among aircraft maintenance workers in the Air Force's Tactical Air Command. At all levels of government, they found that problems are best solved and opportunities most often grasped by those at the working level.

Third, customer service and genuine accountability to citizens are the proper antidotes to the "specialist mentality" that bureaucracy fosters. This is not the kind of formal accountability that will be discussed in Chapter 15, which focuses on the overall performance of an agency or government. Rather, it is a responsiveness to the needs of each individual seeking a driver's license, building permit, or library card. We have all been put down by the behavior of some official who seems to radiate a sense of superiority, as if we are not worthy of the service we ask for. To some extent the rules should be changed, but more important, the attitudes and cultures of whole organizations need modification.

A skeptic would naturally ask whether government organizations are likely to adopt this new culture. No single answer is possible, since the "whole system" cannot change monolithically. What has happened is that bits and pieces have changed—an agency here, an office there, a bureau in the next state. There is no single key to change; uncounted factors can either promote or prevent it. Levin and Sanger (1994, pp. 70–75) identify the incentives that public managers face as the major variable. Most legal controls are oriented to prevent misuse of power and resources, and thus managers observe that taking risks is more dangerous than not taking them. Innovation is inherently risky, and lacking incentives to try it, prudent managers find every reason to prefer the status quo. Reinventing government must be a process of shifting rewards and penalties for all personnel to make full use of their ability to grasp the opportunities for beneficial change.

This controversy underscores how different most American public bureaucracies are from those in Weber's model. Although they are often described as rigid and rule-bound, they are less so than many in the world and probably less so than they were two decades ago or more. Because the politics/administration dichotomy has rarely been achieved, the rigid features of bureaucracy have been tempered by the political process at the same time that the tenets of democracy were reshaped by administrative organization. Even the Internal Revenue Service, an archetype of rule-bound bureaucracy, is a partially open system that must placate and at times yield to its many constituencies. The organizational imperative for order will inevitably clash with the democratic impulse for service and flexibility.

Summary

Organization is the assembly of knowledge, power, and will to accomplish certain purposes. *Bureaucracy* is a form of organization that (1) is large enough that its top managers cannot have face-to-face relationships with all their subordinates, (2) is sufficiently specialized to require a precise division of labor, and (3) consists of offices arranged in a chain of command from the top executive to the lowest employee. Complex societies maintain bureaucratic organizations designed to accomplish those unique purposes that require a high degree of technical knowledge and political power.

Hierarchy is a basic principle of human organization in which people are arranged in order of the authority they wield over others. As the United States grew in population and governmental responsibilities, its simple and decentralized forms of administration evolved into those that Max Weber labeled bureaucracies. Further development of organization theory produced a set of "principles" of sound organization. These were later challenged by those who emphasized the importance of human relations to the conduct of administration.

Each government organization occupies a unique place in the social, economic, and political life of the nation that conditions its internal organization and manner of operation. Each must maintain a long-run equilibrium with its environment by taking in such resources as money, personal skills, legal power, and information and producing the goods and services expected of it to the satisfaction of the public and policymakers.

Internally, public organizations are populated by officials with diverse identities and motives that may promote or hinder achievement of the collective mission. Conflict often arises because of incompatibility of these motives. Means of resolving or managing these conflicts range from removing certain persons from the organization to redefining interests and goals. Organizations depend upon formal and informal communications, both internal and external, to obtain needed information and secure cooperative efforts to achieve their missions. Formal communications follow the hierarchical structure and relate to the exercise of authority. Informal communications are less confined but can either support or hinder the organization's efforts in the messages they carry. Organizations communicate extensively to the public to promote their own missions. Information flow can be distorted or blocked, which results in supervisors who are unaware of conditions and in subordinates who lack proper instructions.

The design of an organization must be closely attuned to the mission, constituencies, and environments of that body. Design criteria include an appropriate hierarchy, proper degree of centralization, span of control, balance of authority between specialists and generalists, simplicity of structure, accountability, flexibility, and political competence. Alternatives to bureaucratic modes of organization include the leader/follower relationship, mosaic, conglomerate, and intergovernmental forms.

Bureaucracy and democracy are interdependent. Although their principles can conflict, an industrialized democracy requires bureaucratic forms of organization to manage many public purposes. The United States has synthesized the two, making its bureaucracies relatively accountable and compromising its nineteenth-century commitment to decentralized governance.

Discussion Questions

1. Why has *bureaucracy* become an epithet in modern society? Can a "good bureaucrat" also be a good public servant? Why or why not?

2. Why does Weber argue that bureaucracy is the superior form of organization for an industrialized society? To what extent does it contradict the ideals of democracy?

3. In what ways can informal communications within organizations differ from formal ones? How can they carry messages differently?

4. What happens to a government agency that doesn't fit the place in its environment that others intend it to fill?

5. How can government agencies best manage the conflicts that arise among their personnel while keeping them on task and providing their public services?

Analytical Exercises

1. Survey recent sources to learn how many of the recommendations of the Gore Commission, stated in the report of the National Performance Review, have been put into practice by Congress or the executive branch and what their results are to date. If any were specifically rejected, learn why.

2. It may be easiest to view open systems of administration in local government. Interview a city manager, chief of police, school superintendent, or county health director to learn how many other public agencies and private organizations he or she must interact with on the job. Determine what kinds of relationships exist with each of these other contacts and how that influences the choices your interviewee must make in that position.

For Further Reading

Barnard, C. (1938). *The Functions of the Executive.* Cambridge, MA: Harvard University Press. Classic statement on the essential responsibilities of an executive in any large organization.

Downs, A. (1967). *Inside Bureaucracy.* Boston: Little, Brown. Comprehensive and realistic survey of how people behave in modern bureaucratic organizations and the limits on the control that executives can exercise over them.

Garvey, G. (1993). *Facing the Bureaucracy: Living and Dying in a Public Agency.* San Francisco: Jossey-Bass. A memoir of an academic's adventures as a consultant in a federal agency.

Goodsell, C. T. (1994). *The Case for Bureaucracy: A Public Administration Polemic* (3rd ed.). Chatham, NJ: Chatham House. A self-styled "polemic" that defends the American administrative system as more productive and public serving than any other in the world.

Hummel, R. (1972). *The Bureaucratic Experience.* New York: St. Martin's Press. In a more negative view than Goodsell's, the author argues that bureaucracies force people to think and behave differently than they would otherwise, and thus they must learn how to adapt to them.

Kaufman, H. (1960). *The Forest Ranger: A Study in Administrative Behavior.* Baltimore: Johns Hopkins University Press. A well-known account of how the U.S. Forest Service integrated employees into its philosophy and methods.

National Performance Review. (1993). *Creating a Government That Works Better and Costs Less.* New York: Penguin Books. The much-hyped report of the commission headed by Vice President Gore, which began to show results in parts of President Clinton's federal establishment.

Weber, M. (1964). *The Theory of Social and Economic Organization.* (A. M. Henderson & T. Parsons, Trans.). New York: Free Press. (Originally published in 1922.) Pages 329–341 provide a concise statement of Weber's concept of bureaucracy, the point of departure for all subsequent studies of this type of organization.

4

Administration in the Intergovernmental Net

Learning Objectives

After reading this chapter, you should be able to do the following:
1. Define *federalism* and *intergovernmental relations.*
2. Define *dual federalism, cooperative federalism,* and *centralized federalism.*
3. Describe the evolution of the American federal system.
4. Define fiscal federalism and identify the major financial relationships between the national, state, and local governments.
5. Define mandates and identify the reasons for using them.
6. Identify the four groups of influential participants in intergovernmental policymaking and administration.

President Clinton came to the White House vowing to "end welfare as we know it." But what we "know" as welfare is a many-sided thing with favorable and negative images for nearly all of us. The national government and the states have wrestled with the problems of poverty and unemployment since the 1930s without solving them (which may be impossible) or satisfying citizens that they were making their best efforts. Although their programs have helped many become self-sufficient, a large number of people remain on public assistance today.

Conservatives and liberals disagree on many antipoverty approaches, but in 1988 congressional members of both persuasions joined to approve a reform package that emphasizes opportunities for the poor to work. In passing the Family Support Act, they created a comprehensive program that requires every state to set up a Job Opportunities and Basic Skills (JOBS) program to provide whatever services will aid the least employable to enter stable careers. This includes basic education, training in specific skills, help in finding jobs, and care for children. When Congress mandates that states undertake a program, it typically pays part of the new costs that they incur, but not all. Since 1991 its aid to JOBS has come to about $1 billion annually. The states must match the federal contribution with funds that they raise from their own taxes.

The JOBS program evolved from efforts that California, Florida, and Massachusetts had already undertaken to find work for welfare recipients and that had experienced some success. Just as important, policymakers at both levels of government wanted education, job training, and welfare officials to work more closely together in delivering services, which was often difficult because they are located in different state agencies.

JOBS has fallen short of expectations (which may have been unrealistic), but some results suggest that it is on the right track. Several states, most notably California and Florida, have had massive programs and largely positive results. Others report mixed outcomes from smaller experiments. Two factors seem to be responsible for the shortcomings. First, states have been hard-pressed financially to match the federal contribution and exceed it where necessary. The fiscal pressures of the economic recession of the early 1990s and the sharply rising costs of Medicaid and other benefit programs have meant that only about one-sixth of eligible people have been able to participate. Welfare reform of the scope envisioned by JOBS is simply more expensive in the short run than current programs.

A second reason is that state and county welfare agencies are not well prepared for the new focus on job preparation and placement. The organizational culture of their personnel is changing only slowly away from the simple distribution of benefits to a more holistic approach to life management of their clients. Often they must find or develop jobs for their clients, which requires contacting employers. Those with limited skills need considerable preparation for employment, and that can be expensive. They need jobs that can lead to rewarding careers and that pay enough to support a family, not just dead-end positions at the minimum wage. Yet many rural communities and inner-city neighborhoods lack enough of these opportunities. The burden of making these efforts work falls on each state and the resources it can muster and on the talents of its administrators (Stanfield, 1994).

Welfare reform, although a national issue, is basically a task for state and local governments. The national government participates largely through setting national standards, sharing in the funding, and perhaps focusing public attention on the need for change. The Family Support Act of 1988 thus adds further detail to the picture of governmental complexity drawn in Chapter 2. These separate

Box 4.1

Canada's Experience with Federalism

Canada was established as a federal system in 1867 with a stronger central government than its southern neighbor had then. Now, its 10 provinces have constitutionally guaranteed powers and rights, and Quebec enjoys special legal protection against discrimination toward its French-speaking population. Those provinces have actively used their powers as well, and their policy and administrative roles are now broader than those of American states, particularly in the area of natural resources regulation.

Canada has worked out unique means of resolving the policy and administrative issues that chronically arise between the national government in Ottawa and the provinces, which have their own elected parliaments and premiers. Whereas American intergovernmental relations are managed through Congress and the counterpart state and federal administrative agencies, Canada relies on regular meetings of the federal prime minister and the provincial premiers along with their close advisers. Through this means of "executive federalism," they set the shifting bounds of their authority and iron out whatever disagreements appear. Over 400 federal-provincial administrative committees that meet more or less regularly on such subjects as health, social assistance, environment, and regional development devise means to implement those executive agreements.

The best known of these "summit meetings" occurred at Meech Lake, Quebec, in 1987, in which those officials worked out agreements on some divisive constitutional issues, including admission of new provinces (Yukon and the Northwest Territories lack that status), reform of the Senate (the upper house of Parliament), and the special status of Quebec and the French language. In 1990 these agreements collapsed when two English-speaking provinces rejected proposals to increase Quebec's autonomy in the federal union. A 1994 election in that province returned to power the Parti Québecois, which has been advocating complete independence from Canada. Voters confronted the question of Quebec's separation on October 30, 1995, defeating it by a narrow margin. However uneasily, Canadian federalism thus survives.

governments—national, state, and local—work together on nearly all issues of domestic public policy and an increasing number of international ones as well. Whether its task is immunizing children, building highways, or permanently burying toxic wastes, no unit of government is an island unto itself. Moreover administration does not consist simply of running one agency. It also involves helping to keep an entire system of cooperation in order.

Federalism and Intergovernmental Relations

The term **federalism** denotes a system in which the powers of government are divided among one authority that governs the whole nation and several that govern its political subdivisions. The U.S. Constitution delegates powers to the national government, with the implication that those not mentioned are reserved to the states. This leaves the latter with a broad and undefined realm for action. Each state has a constitution that specifies its powers and limits. It is subordinate to the national government only on matters in the latter's constitutional domain. Yet the two levels are closely interdependent on most matters of domestic policy, a development not envisioned by the authors of the U.S. Constitution.

Federal Systems in Canada and Mexico

Canada and Mexico provide examples of federal systems with unique national/regional relationships. The Canadian provinces exercise independent authority in many policy areas, but the unique culture and identity of Quebec do not sit easily in a union dominated by English-speaking people. Box 4.1 illustrates both the difficulties posed by such a cultural mixture and the benefits that can be achieved from federal/provincial cooperation on health insurance. In Mexico, on the other hand, state policymakers and administrators have little autonomy. The central government, dominated by the Institutional Revolutionary Party, decides all matters of substance in spite of the powers granted the states by the nation's constitution.

The political rationale of federalism is that it prevents all governmental powers from accumulating at the top level and thereby safeguards against a national dictatorship and protects the power of local communities and citizens to govern themselves. In this sense, its logic resembles the separation-of-powers principle discussed in Chapter 2. But this rationale is effective only if the regional and local units have the political vitality, decision-making ability, and money to carry out their own choices. If they have no other alternative than to carry out mandates from the national capital, as in Mexico, then having their own formal governments means little.

The term *federal* is commonly used in two ways. One is the meaning just discussed, in which **federal system** refers to the combined national and state authorities and the norms that guide their many relationships. But *federal government* can also be a synonym for the national government as distinct from those of the states. The context of its use makes clear which meaning is intended.

Intergovernmental Relations: Conflict and Diplomacy

The concept of **intergovernmental relations** refers to the dynamics of a federal system in operation. It encompasses all the national, state, and local interactions in making and implementing their shared policies, financing their activities, and settling the conflicts that arise in that process. We can categorize them broadly as federal/state, federal/local, state/local, interstate, and interlocal relationships. These all require that officials be able to conduct "diplomacy" just as independent nations to advance their own interests. Thus, a city mayor may find it necessary to meet with federal pollution

Box 4.2

The Governmental Maze at Denver International Airport

The people of Denver, Colorado, decided in 1989 that they needed a new airport, voting to acquire 53 square miles of land and approve more than $2 billion in bonds to finance the project. Officials began construction almost immediately and promised it would open late in 1993. It didn't—not until February 1995.

A major international airport like Denver's is intricately woven into the federal system. The U.S. Department of Transportation committed about $500 million in federal support toward the total cost of $3.2 billion, spurred by key members of Congress who were heavily lobbied by Denver business interests. As with all airports, the Federal Aviation Administration specifies every detail that concerns navigation and safety. International flights serving that airport also come under the authority of other countries' aviation regulators and the International Civil Aviation Organization.

At the same time, the airport challenges the capacities of state and local governments. As a ground traffic hub, it requires high-volume road access, and Denver International's remote location, which is more than 20 miles farther from downtown than the existing airport, calls for an entirely new network. Water, sewage, and solid-waste facilities had to be constructed from scratch. Environmental regulations from state and federal authorities concern exhaust emissions, fuel storage, waste management, and noise abatement. Each agency's rules and procedures have to be applied or adapted to Denver's conditions by patient negotiations between the administrators concerned.

control officials one day, with the state transportation director the next, and with fellow mayors on the third to discuss plans for job development.

Put in another way, intergovernmental relations consist of contacts among the officials of the various governments who must ordinarily negotiate over their common concerns rather than issue commands. Thus, when there is a dispute about allowing a truck to carry nuclear wastes from a reactor in one state to a storage center in another, executives and administrators at the federal, state, and local levels must determine when, by what route, and under what safeguards it travels. Box 4.2 illustrates the intergovernmental complex that surrounds a major airport, from the city that actually owns and operates it to the Federal Aviation Administration that oversees its safety and navigation, to other units responsible for highways, utilities, and land use control in its vicinity. The outcomes of these negotiations vary with the legal, financial, and political power of each contestant.

How the Federal System Evolved   Policy implementation by many governments evolved with the steady expansion of the public purposes, the tools chosen to implement them, and the deep-seated popular preferences for locally controlled services. Americans have historically distrusted centralized power, and as the responsibilities of government expanded, they have preferred to keep control over services as localized as possible. In the 1960s, when public school districts needed additional financing, Congress devised an aid system that preserved their separate identities and at least some of their decision-making autonomy.

No one intentionally designed the federal system to operate as it does today. It evolved in an understandable response to several factors. First, Congress's power to levy an income tax (granted by the Sixteenth Amendment in 1913), together with its unlimited borrowing ability, gave the national government great fiscal flexibility. Most states and localities, by contrast, cannot legally run a deficit on current operating expenses. Thus, when state and local resources were inadequate to meet pressing needs, as in the 1930s and 1960s, Congress filled the gaps with federal revenues and borrowing. The grant system was a straightforward way both to transfer resources and to target them to specific ends. Since 1981, on the other hand, we have seen how huge federal deficits have forced cuts in those grants.

A second dynamic is the growing social and technological interdependence of the nation. For example, what was largely intrastate commerce in the early years (and thus subject only to state regulation) has become mostly interstate and global under the jurisdiction of Congress. Moreover, we cannot permit states to have varying standards for the testing of medicines and inspection of airliners, nor do we want a person to grow up with an inadequate education in one state and then move to another and become a burden on its welfare system. Thus, laws and regulations must follow problems across state lines, and the national government is best able to ensure the needed uniformity.

Third, articulate and well-financed interest groups have pressed the national government for aid. They strongly back grant programs in education, health, transportation, urban development, and environment protection, and Congress has been ready to oblige them within the limits of its fiscal capacity. Their demands have been supported by an evolving public ideology that assigns to the national government ultimate responsibility for these functions. These groups have little interest in how the federal system as a whole evolves as long as their benefits flow steadily.

Federalism before 1860

The framers of the U.S. Constitution designed a system to perform the relatively simple tasks of government in their day. By 1787 the thirteen states already had functioning governments and jealously protected their individual powers. They sought a national authority to govern only on those matters that transcended state lines: foreign affairs, national defense, and monetary and commercial regulation, to name the three most important. Thus, they specified that Congress (acting for the whole government) would have only those powers delegated to it; all others were reserved to the states.

James Madison defended this arrangement most eloquently a few months after the convention in *The Federalist* No. 45.

> The powers delegated by the proposed Constitution to the federal government are few and defined. Those which are to remain in the State governments are numerous and indefinite. The former will be exercised principally on external objects, as war, peace, negotiation, and foreign commerce. . . . The powers reserved to the several states will extend to all objects which, in the ordinary course of affairs, concern the lives, liberties, and properties of the people, and the internal order, improvement, and prosperity of the State. (Hamilton, Jay, & Madison, n.d.)

He and the other founders did not expect that the two levels would need to interact on any significant policy matters, nor could they foresee how the industrial revolution, just beginning across the Atlantic, would rearrange the governmental powers they had wrapped up so tidily.

Scholars often label the system prevailing in the nation's first 70 years, from 1789 to 1860, as **dual federalism**. That is, the policy realms of the nation and states remained small and largely separate from one another, approximately as the constitutional founders intended. Congress did provide grants of land to the states during that period to support schools and the building of canals and roads, but this did not involve continuing administrative relationships. At the same time, state responsibilities for education, health, social services, and transportation expanded steadily.

Cooperative Federalism

After 1860, the outlines of **cooperative federalism**, in which the national and state levels shared many of their responsibilities, gradually became apparent. The Civil War put to rest the idea that a state could secede from the Union or block enforcement of a federal law. The year 1862 saw the passage of the Morrill Act, which provided land grants for the establishment of state agricultural colleges. After 1887 Congress added cash grants for agricultural experimentation, highways, forestry, vocational education, and maternal and child health. In each case it set controls on the states' use of the funds. Yet the total amount of money transferred remained small ($232 million in 1932, the last year before the New Deal era began [Hale & Palley, 1981, p. 10]). Responding to challenges to the grant system on constitutional grounds, the Supreme Court decided in *Massachu-*

setts v. Mellon (1923) that no state's sovereignty was violated, since it was free to refuse the grants.

The Depression of the 1930s spurred intergovernmental cooperation. State and local funds for aiding the unemployed quickly ran out, and Congress devised new programs to fill the gaps. Grants were provided for school lunches, public works construction, distribution of surplus farm products, and slum clearance and housing. This expansion continued in the 1940s and 1950s under both Democratic and Republican administrations. By 1959 the annual volume of grants exceeded $6 billion. During that time the nation and states also expanded their joint regulation of many areas of the economy, such as banking, transportation, communication, food quality, and drugs. This also required cooperation to prevent conflicts and gaps in the regulations.

The basic concept of cooperative federalism in the 1950s remained unchanged, however: The national government was to help the states (and their localities) meet what were still defined as the latter's responsibilities and to do so largely by means of their own choosing. Such federal agencies as the Department of Health, Education, and Welfare had a major role in intergovernmental relations, primarily by mailing checks to the states and collecting information on what the grants accomplished. Counterparts of that agency in the states and counties actually provided the aid to the clients. In 1936 the Supreme Court ruled in *U.S. v. Butler* that Congress could spend money on anything it deemed to be in the general welfare, not limited to the specific powers delegated in the Constitution. Thus, it permitted Congress to aid (though not take over completely) any state government function.

The Impetus to Centralization

Two major developments in the 1960s launched the federal system in new directions: the "discovery" of poverty as a widespread condition (and policymakers' sense of obligation to remedy it) and the related triumph of the civil rights movement for African Americans, other minorities, and women in redefining the guarantees of the Bill of Rights. From Washington, the states and local governments were viewed as out of touch with, if not biased against, those citizens in greatest need. Congress saw these deficiencies as most serious in the areas of education, voting rights, housing, economic opportunity, and environmental protection. It thus enacted sweeping new programs that not only expanded the grant pool but also created new requirements and incentives for the states. These in turn created many complex administrative relationships.

For example, the Economic Opportunity Act of 1964 was an administrative as well as a policy innovation. It not only channeled grants to state and local agencies but also mandated the establishment of community action agencies to remedy the many conditions that were believed to cause poverty. These agencies were required to involve the recipients themselves in planning and advising on the program's implementation. Whereas the purpose of earlier grants had been to build homes, pave highways, or furnish educational supplies, the newer ones sought to change the lives of the recipients in holistic ways. This was both harder to do and harder to monitor to be sure it was being done.

This most recent period in the development of intergovernmental relations has no widely accepted name. Many elements of the cooperative period linger, since most federal aid is still oriented toward helping fulfill the state and local governments' responsibilities. In other respects, however, it is more centralized. When Congress passed the Education of All Handicapped Children Act in 1975, it mandated that the states prepare individualized education plans for pupils with disabilities that would place them in classes with nondisabled students to the extent that their capacities permitted. This has penetrated to every school district in the nation and has greatly expanded their special education endeavors. Congressional and court stipulations on civil rights in housing and employment likewise have centralized much policymaking for these matters in Washington.

The decade of the 1980s saw conflicting trends in the evolution of intergovernmental relations. President Reagan entered the White House determined both to reduce national controls over state and local governments and to cut back on financial aid. Over time, the aid level did drop, and some of the regulations attached to the surviving grants were deleted. But Congress, which holds the purse strings, was more responsive to the many constituent groups that benefited from existing programs and wanted them to continue. In 1984 the lawmakers, with Reagan's support, mandated a minimum alcohol-drinking age of 21 for all states, on pain of withdrawal of up to 10 percent of highway aid funds for states that did not comply. That action better fit a concept of **centralized federalism**, in which state policy and administration are mobilized to serve nationally defined goals.

As federal funds for many programs, such as housing, were cut substantially during the 1980s, state and local governments were forced to find other means of providing needed services. A burst of fiscal and managerial creativity has ensued as those authorities sought to replace the aid on which they depended. They have also initiated new policies in many fields, seeing that the innovativeness of Congress and the executive branch has been curtailed by the federal budget deficits.

The preceding historical survey shows the importance of financial relationships in the evolution of the system. **Fiscal federalism** encompasses the flow of money among the national, state, and local levels of government, and the intergovernmental aspects of federal taxation.

Fiscal Federalism

The Grant-in-Aid

The major feature of fiscal federalism is the **grant-in-aid**, a transfer of money from one government to another, generally national to state, national to local, and state to local. It is nearly always conditional: It must be spent for the purposes and by the procedures specified in law or the rules of the granting agency. The recipient is accountable to the grantor and must report afterward on use of the funds. Grants can be withdrawn if the terms are not followed. During the late 1970s and early 1980s, about 500 separately funded federal grant programs existed; the Reagan administration ended or consolidated about 100 of those.

The volume of grants-in-aid in constant dollars (adjusted to allow for inflation) peaked in fiscal year 1978 at $77.9 billion. In that year 17 percent of the federal budget supported state and local programs and provided 26.5 percent of total state and local spending. During the 1980s the percentages declined modestly, but many programs of aid to the states and local governments survived and a few have even expanded. In fiscal year 1994, these grants totaled an estimated $217 billion (adjusted for inflation) and made up 14.9 percent of total federal spending. Allowing for the loss of buying power due to inflation, the decline from 1978 to 1989 was close to 16 percent. After 1989, grant levels rose modestly, primarily for the Medicaid and Aid to Families with Dependent Children programs. The cutbacks in real dollar aid put severe pressure on some state and local treasuries. Although the Reagan administration and Congress were able to hold the net federal tax burden almost constant, steady increases in state and local taxes were necessary to maintain services.

Congress has five general objectives for the grant-in-aid. First, it seeks minimum national standards of service or protection where uniformity is necessary. For example, it set standards for air and water pollution control with which all states had to comply, although a state could impose stricter standards. If some were to fail to enforce these, the health of residents of adjoining states could be impaired.

Second, Congress seeks greater equality among states with respect to essential services such as education and health. Thus, it confers higher benefits on states with less affluent economies and lower tax potential. The logic is that citizens in poorer states are

Figure 4.1

Selected Federal Grants-in-Aid to State and Local Governments, 1994, by Function

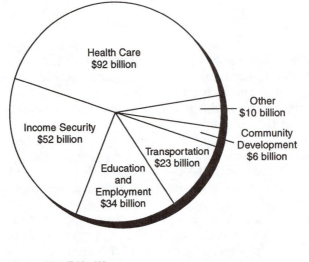

Source: *Statistical Abstract of the United States,* 1994, Table 468.

Transfers of funds from the federal government to states and localities are dominated by those for Medicaid, in the Health Care category, and Aid to Families with Dependent Children, in the Income Security category.

entitled to the same level of public services as those of wealthier states, consistent with the Fourteenth Amendment to the Constitution, which prescribes that no state may deprive any person of equal protection of the laws. In practice, however, this "premium" for the poorer states has been small.

Third, Congress wants to raise the quality level of state and local services. This was obvious in the Family Support Act of 1988, described at the opening of this chapter. Lawmakers had long complained that public funds should not be spent merely to keep people dependent on aid, and this program was designed to enhance their opportunities. Since this requires states to match the grants, it also spurs them to raise their own levels of support for family services.

Fourth, the national government wants to promote research and disseminate the knowledge resulting from it. Environmental protection and economic opportunity were two innovative policy areas for the 1960s, and much needed to be learned about how to do them well. Federally financed research projects in such fields as medicine, education, and energy generated information that proved useful to the states and localities in designing and operating their own programs.

Finally, Congress expects that financial aid will enable the receiving governments to upgrade their own administrative capacities. To secure a more professional civil service, many grants require participating state agencies to use personnel hired on the merit system rather than political appointees. Some grants provide explicitly for personnel training. The "701" grants, for example, subsidized local governments' land use planning staffs and studies with more than $1 billion during the 27-year life of the program, which ended in 1981.

Categorical and Block Grants

The grants are provided in two basic forms, depending on the strictness of the provisions regulating their use: categorical and block. The first named are designated for specific purposes and leave little room for discretion by either grantor or grantee. For example, a city expanding its recreational facilities in the late 1960s had to apply to several different agencies in order to buy land for use as a park, build a swimming pool on it, operate an activity center for senior citizens, plant trees and shrubbery, and purchase sports equipment. Administrators at both levels had to commit considerable time to grant management, especially in confining spending within each category.

Allocation of Categorical Grants Categorical grants can be allocated either by formula or by project. A federal agency distributes formula grants according to a predetermined scheme that leaves it with no discretion. For example, Congress may give each state equal amounts per capita in one program and in another skew the formula to favor the states suffering from economic decline. A recipient government thus has a legal right to a certain share.

Project grants are made to meet more specific needs that are not spread evenly throughout the population. Therefore, the state or local governments must request them. The granting agency examines each application for its general merit and conformity to its guidelines and uses its discretion in making the awards. Therefore, states and cities have found that it pays to develop their grantsmanship skills. For example, urban renewal programs were individually funded, and the cities that put in the earliest and best-written applications usually received the most money.

State and local agencies must match most categorical and project grants with their own funds or at least demonstrate that the aid is not being used to replace dollars from their own resources. In the Interstate Highway program, for example, the states supply 10 percent of the construction costs, whereas their share of other highway programs is usually 50 percent. The trend has been to reduce matching requirements, which have been unpopular with state and local officials because of the constraints placed on their own budgets.

Allocation of Block Grants   Block grants differ from categorical grants in that they place fewer restrictions on how the money can be used, and they allow more discretion to the recipients. These grants are allocated mostly by formula, although they may also require an application describing the would-be recipient's plans for the funds. In 1990 Congress enacted the Child Care and Development Block Grant to help working families afford good-quality day care. To qualify, a state must submit a plan to the federal government showing how it intends to use its share of the $2.5 billion that Congress provided for a 3-year period. With the funds states may support day-care centers directly or give vouchers to parents who then pass them on to day-care providers of their own choice. A state may spend up to 25 percent of the grant on developing new programs to meet special needs. There is more freedom to make choices than if this were a categorical grant, yet it has obvious legal boundaries.

Related Federal Support Programs

Revenue sharing—the broadest grant program of all—had the shortest life. Begun in 1972 as the nation was withdrawing from the Vietnam War, it provided about $83 billion to state and general-purpose local governments (see definition in Chapter 2) for an almost unlimited array of objectives over its lifetime. Revenue sharing was originally advocated as a way for the national government to share its broader revenue base with the states and localities, which were more restricted. Grants under this program made up only a small percentage of all federal grants, however, and had no significant impact on any single policy area. Political support for revenue sharing in Congress waned as time went on; grants to states were ended in 1980 and those to local units ceased in 1986.

Another important aspect of fiscal federalism lies in the federal tax-exempt status of interest earned from state and local bonds. This congressional provision is a valued supplement to the grants described earlier. A state may borrow money to build highways or a school district may borrow to enlarge its high school. The bondholder, who lent money for such projects, does not have to pay federal income tax on the interest earned and will therefore accept a rate that is several percentage points lower than a high-grade corporate borrower would pay. This "loophole" cost the federal treasury about $18 billion in 1987 and amounts to an indirect subsidy to the borrowing governments. Although the U.S. Supreme Court ruled in 1988 (*South Carolina v. Baker*) that Congress has the constitutional power to tax that interest, this benefit has strong support from members of Congress, who are sensitive to the concerns of the state and local officials they represent. In 1986 Congress cut back on the use of such bonds to subsidize private development, but their status for public projects remains intact.

Limitations and Problems of the Grant System

Several administrative problems clog the grant system and have drawn efforts to resolve them. First, many programs have numerous requirements that cause unintended difficulties. For example, seventeen different regulations on welfare and food stamps apply to a single client. Although each has a purpose, their combination hampers local caseworkers. Arkansas officials related an incident that may be fairly typical. Welfare mothers were willing to take jobs as a part of that state's innovative program to get people off welfare dependency. But they found that they would lose their children's health insurance under Medicaid, the federal program for the poor, before their new employers began covering them. Arkansas applied three times for permission to extend Medicaid coverage for 5 months but was turned down (Stevens, 1988). The Clinton administration, however, has waived many such regulations to permit states to try new approaches.

Some requirements that accompany grants apply to many or all federally financed programs (nondiscrimination or payment of prevailing wage rates on construction projects, for example). Many of these go beyond the immediate purpose of the grant and constitute mandates to state and local governments generally. They will be discussed in the next section.

Another problem stemming from the large number of grants that a unit of government receives is that there is no clear way to coordinate their combined impact. Dozens of similar programs may operate in a major metropolitan area with little or no communication among the agencies administering them. For example, joint planning for highways and mass transit has often been lacking. The Federal Highway Administration and the Urban Mass Transportation Administration are both in the Department of Transportation but may fail to coordinate the impacts of their programs at the local level. During the 1970s the Office of Management and Budget required that a local planning agency review all grant applications from its region and comment on their suitability. This offered the opportunity, at least, for federal and local officials to coordinate their efforts. But this provision was deleted by the Reagan administration, and no similar means for review now exists.

The largest problem of all may be the difficulty of accounting for the outcomes and impacts of the grants. No one agency has full control: The rule-setting, funding, spending, and reporting responsibilities are divided among many bureaucracies. This problem is not serious for established programs with accepted standards. The food stamp program, for example, is well routinized: Washington provides the partial aid and basic rules; state welfare departments add more rules and pay the administrative costs; and county or city agencies determine eligibility and distribute the stamps. But the procedures for other programs are less established, such as the efforts to curtail trade and abuse of illegal drugs, and there is no assurance that the separate implementers orchestrate their efforts well. It is rarely clear whom to praise or blame for the result or what should be done to remedy a problem.

Governments Sharing Regulation and Services

A complex network of **mandates** (legal requirements that the national government imposes on the states and localities or that the states impose on their local units) links administrators. Some of these are part of the grant system, but many are independent of the cash flow. In addition, they interact constantly in the everyday process of providing services and regulating individual and corporate behavior. In some cases, their responsibilities and actions are so intertwined that citizens cannot easily learn who is responsible for a given program.

Federal Mandates: Tools of Centralized Control

The number of mandates that Washington has imposed on the state and local governments has grown steadily over the years and has become a major concern. They stem from the national policy goals that Congress has identified for all governments in the United States to meet. These take several forms (Advisory Commission on Intergovernmental Relations, 1984).

Direct Orders   First, state and local governments must comply with certain direct orders imposed by Congress or the federal courts under threat of civil or criminal penalties. For example, the Equal Employment Opportunity Act of 1972 bars discrimination in hiring on the basis of race, color, religion, sex, and national origin. In 1985 the U.S. Supreme Court held that state and local employees are covered by federal minimum wage and hour standards, from which they had previously been judged exempt (*Garcia v. San Antonio Metropolitan Transit Authority*). That ruling also discredited the long-held conviction that states are somehow protected from such national mandates and appeared to open the door to further congressional intrusions on their spheres of action. Box 4.3 offers another example of a direct order, one that ensures safe drinking water for the nation.

Box 4.3

Drinking Water: How Clean?

Congress began to take interest in the purity of the nation's drinking water when data showed that many municipal and rural water systems were seriously polluted. Since this can no longer be regarded as a "local" problem, Congress mandated inspection and correction where contamination exceeded safe levels. But correction has proven to be both complex and expensive, as Massachusetts's experience shows.

What looks, tastes, and smells clean enough to drink, but isn't?

Boston's water, and the water of thousands of communities across the United States, including New York City, San Francisco, Seattle, Scranton, Pa., and Portland, Maine, according to federal standards. For Bostonians familiar with the pristine woods surrounding the sparkling blue water of the reservoirs that supply the city, the news is hard to swallow.

. . . Boston and other cities are scrambling to come up with ways to meet the standards set by the federal Safe Drinking Water Act.

Amendments to the act in 1986 require communities that get water from surface sources—lakes, streams, and reservoirs—to filter it before supplying consumers, or to file an "avoidance" plan if the town's water is so clean it doesn't need filtering.

Authorities in Boston ha[d] . . . planned to file such an "avoidance" plan with the U.S. Environmental Protection Agency (EPA) and work to protect the watershed surrounding the Quabbin and Wachusett reservoirs.

However, . . . the Massachusetts Water Resources Authority (MWRA), which regulates water and sewer systems in the state, voted to scrap protection plans and build a filtration plant instead.

The cost of the plant is expected to exceed $350 million—$30 a year per user for 10 years—more than triple the cost of watershed protection.

Environmentalists charge this is a shortsighted "technical fix" of a pollution problem that will only worsen. Without protection of delicate watershed lands, they say, the door is wide open for residential and industrial developments to move in, spoiling natural areas. . . .

"The board has tried and tried to find a way to avoid building a filtration plant. All the incentives are there to find an alternative," says [MWRA] board chairwoman Susan Tierney, recently appointed as state secretary of environmental affairs. . . . "But the readings on coliform counts look as though this is the last straw that will prevent [the MWRA] getting a waiver from federal law. As long as the law is on the books, we will have to comply."

Coliform is bacteria from human and animal waste. In more than 25 percent of the water samples taken over the past six months, the coliform levels exceeded federally set legal limits, says MWRA project director Allen Adelman. "And the counts weren't just close. They were often much higher."

But environmentalists contend that filtration will come at the expense of the longer-range solution of watershed protection. "The MWRA is being pound-foolish," says Paul Wingle of the Massachusetts Audubon Society. "This betrays a real end-of-the-pipe solution, a philosophy that is more expensive to maintain, and fails to prevent contaminants from working their way into the water in the first place.". . .

Stig Regli, the environmental engineer with the EPA who set the standards for safe water, says communities should not think of filtration and watershed protection as "either-or" propositions. "What we would like is for provisions in place to maintain protected watersheds, regardless of whether there is filtration. . . . It's a good strategy for controlling new contaminants. It's an investment in the future."

—Elizabeth A. Brown, "New U.S. Standards Squeeze Cities, States," *Christian Science Monitor,* February 5, 1991

Cross-Cutting Requirements   Second, cross-cutting requirements are mandates imposed on most or all grant programs to achieve policy goals not central to the particular grant. Thirty-six of these dealing with socioeconomic matters alone were identified in 1980 by the Office of Management and Budget. Many involved environmental protection, including the mandate of environmental impact statements for many construction projects. Moreover, no state or local government can discriminate according to race, ethnic origin, age, sex, or physical handicap in providing a service that receives any federal financial support. Thus, a public library that benefited from a grant, for example, must provide wheelchair access to its buildings.

Crossover Sanctions   A third regulatory tool is crossover sanctions, which impose a requirement on one program to influence state or local policy in another. Failure to comply with it may lead the federal agency to reduce or cut off funds even if the given program is administered properly. In 1974 Congress prohibited the secretary of transportation from granting any highway construction funds to states with a maximum speed limit over 55 miles per hour (later raised to 65 for rural interstate highways). The central purpose, as everyone realized, was to reduce oil consumption. Every state complied within two months, although not always happily. The 1984 mandate of a minimum drinking age of 21 for every state was a similar move.

Partial Preemption   Last, the national government may use partial preemption of state authority to regulate some aspect of the economy or the environment. Under the U.S. Constitution, Congress has the power to regulate interstate commerce, and few industries today do not have transactions across state lines. Congress may choose to control a particular activity completely or to select a partial takeover that leaves the states with significant responsibilities. In the latter case, it typically sets the basic policies and regulations but delegates to the states the authority to enforce them. Under the Occupational Safety and Health Act, states can operate their own programs to protect workers if they are at least as effective as the federal standards. If a state fails to do this, the U.S. Department of Labor can assume the regulatory power. The number of federal laws that require states to regulate an activity (at their own expense) has grown rapidly in the past 25 years, most dramatically in the areas of health, safety, and environmental protection.

Congress often requires state and local governments to spend money to comply with its mandates but provides little or no financial assistance for these costs. The Education for All Handicapped Children Act of 1975 required an expensive individualized procedure to identify and accommodate students' learning needs, and this was reinforced by the Americans with Disabilities Act. Yet federal grants have fallen far short of these extra costs, and an increasing portion of state and school district funds must now be devoted to such services.

The total cost of meeting these mandates is impossible to quantify, but some individual programs have been priced. Federally mandated health care programs consumed 14 percent of the states' budgets in 1990, and the percentage is projected to reach 28 percent by 1995 (Hinds, 1992). Ohio reported that it expected to spend $389 million of its own funds to comply with all federal mandates in 1995, about 2.5 percent of its own revenues. The city of Chicago spent $191 million from its own funds to meet unfunded federal mandates in 1991 (Dearborn, 1994). Governors and mayors are increasingly resisting new federal programs that would add to this burden and Congress pledged not to add new unfunded mandates in 1995 legislation.

These mandates are an important departure from earlier provisions in grant programs.

> The requirements traditionally attached to assistance programs may be viewed as part of a contractual agreement between two independent, coequal levels of government. . . . In contrast, the policies which the new intergovernmental regulation imposes on state and local governments are more nearly mandatory. They cannot be avoided, without incurring some federal sanction, by the simple expedient of refusing to participate in a single federal assistance program. (Beam, 1981, p. 10)

Intense debate has focused on this intrusion on state policymaking authority, which has reshaped the administrative environments of national as well as state and local agencies. Understandably, state and local officials resent the pressures this puts on their budgets. Nationally oriented interests emphasize the benefits that the mandated programs provide to their constituencies, such as people with disabilities.

Cooperative Regulation: Dealing with Overlapping Authority

The three levels of government also cooperate in regulating sectors of the economy in which Congress has not preempted state authority. National and state agencies regulate banking, consumer product safety, energy production, and highway safety, among others. Over the years they have come to agree on most issues where conflicts can arise. However, many differences seem to be chronic, such as the shared responsibilities for clean air and water. The large number of players in this realm certainly complicates the game: In 1992, eighteen federal agencies dealt with twenty-five separate water resources programs, interacting with more than 100,000 state and local water agencies. Even the staff time required to interact effectively slows decision making when consensus does exist (Advisory Commission on Intergovernmental Relations, 1992a, Ch. 3).

Local Authorities and Federal Agencies   Cities and counties must obey federal as well as state rules in planning the use of their land. The Army Corps of Engineers and the Environmental Protection Agency can veto the filling of a wetland or river shore by a developer. For example, the corps denied permission to construct a shopping mall in Attleboro, Massachusetts, because it would have destroyed a swamp (Bachmann, 1987). Another example is provided by the Federal Housing Authority, which has long set building standards for homes on which it would issue mortgages. As a result, local and state codes had to incorporate those standards.

Regulatory Activism at the State Level   The 1980s witnessed growing efforts by state governments to supplement federal regulations they believed to be inadequate. Led by the National Association of State Attorneys General, they have imposed limits on or won lawsuits over airline advertising, insurance coverage, corporate mergers, and consumer fraud. This has concerned such agencies as the U.S. Department of Transportation, which has its own guidelines for airline fare advertising. Debates rage over how much interstate diversity in rules is acceptable and what kind of protection consumers really need.

Box 4.4 illustrates well this trend toward state initiative. Although policymakers in Washington take a nationwide perspective on such issues, they may lack the sensitivity to local and regional problems that state leaders must have. The political momentum for environmental protection that peaked in Washington in the early 1970s changed course in the 1980s and now dominates many state capitals and such metropolitan areas as Los Angeles. Exactly which issues require uniform national rules and which can tolerate state-by-state diversity will be determined largely by the political strengths and strategies of the contending forces.

Joint Services   Governments at all levels also provide services jointly. The nation's recreation system is a blend of national, state, and local parks, forests, reservoirs, beaches, boat landings, and campgrounds (Grodzins, 1966). Administrative conflicts may arise when, for example, the National Park Service wants to keep a scenic riverway unspoiled and a state department of natural resources favors motorboat use and resort development to attract tourists.

The nation's law enforcement system is likewise a blend of governmental agencies. In keeping with the localist preferences of Americans for protection that is closely accountable to them, most

Box 4.4

The Next Step on Automobile Pollution Controls

In 1960 California became the first state to require pollution control devices on cars sold there. This action was a logical response to the smog that plagued the Los Angeles metropolitan area, the worst in the nation. When Congress set standards for all cars several years later, they were not as stringent, but California was allowed to retain its tighter restrictions. No other state, however, was permitted to deviate.

By the early 1990s the air quality in many urban centers had gotten worse, which led Congress to allow other states to adopt stricter auto pollution standards. As of 1994, New York and Massachusetts had followed California's lead, and other northeastern states were examining that option as well. But policymakers realized that gasoline-burning cars could be made only so "clean." Further cleaning of urban air could only come with "zero-emission vehicles" (powered by electricity). California again took the initiative when its Air Resources Board required the auto industry to begin selling such cars in 1998. New York and Massachusetts joined that mandate, and if the U.S. Environmental Protection Agency extends tougher emission standards throughout the Northeast, ten other states would also join the electric car market (Fulton & Newman, 1994).

This is one example of the states' taking the lead in regulation to protect public health. It is a clear departure from the past three decades, when Congress had to take on that task if it were to happen at all. These developments raise the question of how many different paths that states may follow in their policies. State and federal lawmakers must weigh the advantages and costs of both national uniformity, which may overlook important local differences in needs, and state independence, which may confuse the regulatory scene and drive up the costs of businesses that must comply with several different standards. It also poses challenges to automobile manufacturers around the world, either to make their fossil-fueled vehicles much cleaner or to produce an electric car with a price and performance that meets market demands.

policing is done by city officers and county sheriffs. However, these officials frequently interact with state police and investigative agencies, the Federal Bureau of Investigation, and Treasury agents. These higher agencies provide necessary crime laboratory work and fingerprint data to local police forces that lack such resources. In the effort to control organized crime and narcotics traffic that operates on an international scale, close teamwork and continual exchange of information are vital.

These interdependencies make it impossible for any state or local agency to ignore for long the rules, aid, or information that comes (or could come) from the national government. Similarly, most federal agencies must heed the impact of their programs around the country and seek the cooperative responses of the state and local governments and their constituents. Administrators require a keen sensitivity to such relationships, with a readiness both to speak up for their units' missions and interests and to negotiate with their counterparts.

Interstate, State/Local, and Interlocal Relations

The more than 86,000 state and local units often depend more on one another than on the national government. State, county, and city boundaries have little relevance to air and water quality, pursuit of criminal suspects, and highway planning. The resulting relationships may be horizontal (interstate or interlocal) or vertical (state/local).

Interstate Diplomacy

The states have developed many ties to one another, both with and without the federal government involved. With the approval of Congress, two or more states may join in a compact, which resembles a treaty between two sovereign nations. There are 123 interstate compacts that cover water, bridges, ports, and environment protection. The Port Authority of New York and New Jersey, mentioned in Chapter 2 as the special district governing many of the New York City region's transportation facilities, was formed in 1921 by such a compact. Many other agreements are informal—to share prison facilities, for example, or allow residents of one state to attend public universities in another at the resident tuition rate. States continually exchange information with one another through the Council of State Governments and the National Governors' Association.

On some issues, the federal government specifically promotes interstate cooperation. For example, in the Low-Level Radioactive Waste Policy Act of 1980, Congress mandated that states either join in compacts to maintain disposal sites or take the ownership and liability themselves for commercially generated wastes. This act covers not highly radioactive fuel rods from power plants, but less dangerous articles from medical and scientific laboratories. Over time, nine regional compacts were formed involving most of the states. The states were about to choose sites. This mandate was very controversial, not only because it would put a site in one member state rather than in another but also because it involved finding locations sufficiently safe to store materials that would remain dangerous to health for thousands of years. But several states balked. Michigan was expelled from the Midwest Compact in 1991 for refusing to permit a site within its borders. (It was the largest waste producer in the group.)

State and Local Relations

Each of the fifty states has an average of 1,600 local governments, with as many lines of interaction among them. The resulting relationships are as complex as federal/state and federal/local relations, and it is no easier to generalize about them. While the national and state governments are constitutionally autonomous, the counties, municipalities, and special-purpose districts are creatures of their states, with no inherent right to exist. Their powers are solely what their states' constitutions or lawmakers give them. State and local relations are thus more tightly controlled than national and state relations, although their outcomes also depend on political bargaining in the legislatures and executive agencies.

Most state and local relationships are conducted through the major state administrative departments. The state department of health oversees municipal hospitals and public health programs, the state department of welfare supervises the work of its counterparts in each county, and the state education department is responsible for the actions of local school districts. Each state agency enforces a body of rules determined by it or by the state legislature. State statutes determine local power to control land zoning, establish speed limits, and permit liquor sales.

State financial aid to local units is more extensive than that provided by Washington. The states' tax bases are broader and stronger than those of the localities, which depend largely on real estate taxes. Local units vary widely in their wealth. Affluent bedroom and industrialized communities have many times the per capita resources of a rural county or of a decaying inner city. In 1992 the total volume of state aid to local governments was $201 billion (*Statistical Abstract,* 1994, Table 463). Most of the grants are earmarked to support education, highways, and welfare, although many states also provide general local government aid, which permits the recipients more discretion. A formula set by the legislature or by the administering department allocates nearly all such aid.

State aid is also provided through sharing of tax revenues. For example, several states collect sales tax and return a percentage of it to the local jurisdictions in which it was paid. It is obviously more efficient for one governmental body to collect a tax than for two to collect it. This grant-and-tax system evolved over the years, just as the federal one did, and is at least as complex. The formulas and rules for expenditure are constant sources of legislative controversy as advocates for central cities, suburban and rural towns, school districts, and other units contend for a larger slice of the fiscal pie. Many state courts have heightened this controversy with rulings on the inequity of aid to schools, as Box 4.5 describes.

Interlocal Conflict and Cooperation

Local governments, under state supervision, enter into agreements with one another just as states do for purchase and sharing of services. Called **joint powers agreements**, such arrangements allow

Box 4.5

State Aid to Schools: How Equal?

Public schools have long relied for their support on local property taxes and varying amounts of aid from their state governments. This often results in wide spending disparities per pupil, since some school districts have much more valuable property to tax than others. Courts in many states (but not the U.S. Supreme Court) have ruled that such gaps violate constitutional guarantees of equal opportunity in education.

The most obvious solution to this disparity is for the state to fund schools entirely, as Hawaii does. A more commonly used option, which Michigan voters approved in 1994, is to increase state funding of elementary and secondary education to the level at which each district's spending per pupil is the same. The districts still tax property, but at a uniform rate, and state aid, funded by increased sales and cigarette taxes, fills whatever gap remains. Texas lawmakers, however, balked at this solu-

tion when faced with a court order to equalize school spending.

School funding is complicated, however, by disparities in students' needs from one area to another. Schools with a high proportion of students who live in poverty need more support to give them an equal chance. More than that, many argue that they need different forms of education from what state regulations permit. State legislatures and education departments have historically kept tight control of schools, and this control has increased with the level of state financial aid. If local teachers and schools are to design programs that better suit their unique settings, they will need more freedom from those rules even while they rely on the financial aid. This dilemma has spurred interest in the charter school movement described at the opening of Chapter 7.

two or more units to share what they have power to do individually. Two adjoining cities, for example, may establish a joint fire protection agency, and another may contract with its county sheriff for police protection. School districts commonly share purchasing and computer services and may jointly run a high school. These bring some degree of order to the jumble of local government relationships found especially in large metropolitan areas.

Administrative Conflict and Confusion at the Local Level

Pittsburgh's governmental network, described in Box 4.6, suggests that large numbers of adjacent and overlapping local governments in large metropolitan areas pose major challenges to policy and administrative coordination. Most major metropolises encompass hundreds of governments, each responsible for one or more public purposes in its geographic area, and conflicts can arise along their boundaries. For example, a large development project in one city can cause drainage and traffic problems for another nearby. Overlapping can also create situations in which cooperation is required to solve a problem. For instance, a dangerous intersection of a state

---

Box 4.6

Too Many Governments in Metropolitan Pittsburgh?

Those who live in or have visited Pittsburgh know that the city and its suburbs are spread over three river valleys and the surrounding hills. Steep hillsides and deep ravines often fragment the landscape. What is less well known is that its governance is also fragmented among hundreds of local units. Allegheny County, in which the region is located, has about 1.5 million people and 323 local governments (by the 1982 Census of Governments). There are 130 municipalities (including the city of Pittsburgh), 43 independent public school districts, and 149 "municipal authorities" (special districts that provide water, sewer, transit, parking space, and health services). In addition, there are about 250 volunteer firefighting companies that provide an essential service but are not classified as governments (Advisory Commission on Intergovernmental Relations, 1992b).

---

highway, county road, and city street cannot be corrected by one unit alone; all three must coordinate their capital budgets and construction plans to rebuild the intersection.

Another situation that results from overlapping is confusion about where responsibility lies. Where parks, roads, and drainage are controlled by more than one unit of government, for example, a citizen may have difficulty learning whom to turn to for the resolution of a problem.

The most common means of dealing with administrative conflicts among local governments is a combination of voluntary collaboration and joint-powers agreements. On occasion, a state agency steps in to settle a dispute or the conflict is brought into court. It is rare to find a metropolitan-level agency with any planning or policymaking powers. Metropolitan councils in Portland, Oregon, and Minneapolis/Saint Paul play significant but limited roles in controlling physical service systems and major land developments but have not reduced the governmental complexity in their regions. In other metropolitan areas, governmental units interact as little as they must, and a spirit of suspicion and rivalry often hinders communication.

In its study of Pittsburgh and Allegheny County, Pennsylvania, the Advisory Commission on Intergovernmental Relations (1992b) found that the county's municipalities and school and special districts had sought to overcome the fragmentation described in Box 4.6 through cooperative agreements to reduce conflicts and minimize costs of policing, firefighting, street improvement, and educational services. In the commission's view, small local authorities are inherently more accountable to the public, and when properly coordinated, their services need not be inefficient. Another positive feature was the role played by the Allegheny County authorities in supporting these relationships. Yet the report notes that political mistrust and conflict between some communities make needed cooperation very difficult to attain. The barriers to formal reorganization of governments also appear to hinder less formal cooperation.

There is no doubt that informal cooperation can make many public functions more effective. A study of mass transit services in the metropolitan area encompassing San Francisco, Oakland, and San Jose, California, showed that the region's seven public transit agencies had coordinated their services, transfers, and joint use of facilities quite well. The author of the study argued that when autonomous agencies are uncertain about each other's actions, they have a strong incentive to coordinate them voluntarily and that if they were under a single administrator, the resulting organization might be too unwieldy (Chisholm, 1989).

Others dispute the "many-is-good" view of local government espoused by the Advisory Commission on Intergovernmental Relations and by Chisholm. They argue that larger unified authorities are necessary for some urban regulations and services. LA 2000, a citizen organization in the Los Angeles metropolitan area, asserted that air pollution and traffic management can be dealt with only by strong agencies that cover the entire region. The 157 municipalities there are totally unable to agree on remedial policies, because they fear that such measures will be both expensive and restrictive to residents' liberties (Peirce, 1988).

Each viewpoint in the debate over interlocal cooperation has merit. Coordination of street-paving plans by adjacent cities or of mass transit schedules by special districts is much simpler than reducing vehicular traffic and its polluting emissions over thousands of square miles. Local governments collaborate readily when the dimensions of the problems are limited, there are standard solutions, and no one who is politically influential will suffer seriously. It is unclear whether such governments can mobilize resources and make difficult choices on the larger issues that confront entire urban regions. On the other hand, there is no assurance that a government at any level can accomplish this without overriding many local interests.

Political Relationships in the Federal System

Many political interests and organizations drive intergovernmental relations. Most public policy decisions result from shifting coalitions of economic and social interests. No single group has enough resources to dominate the major realms of policy. Administrators can maximize their power and influence when they ally themselves with those who benefit from the programs they implement.

Clusters of Influence

Four clusters of influential persons face each other in some degree of tension. To the extent that they agree on a program that spreads benefits among them, they determine how the federal system develops.

Members of Congress   The first group consists of members of Congress. They are constantly under pressure both to serve their constituents with federal programs but without excessive intrusion into local autonomy and to assert national interests and budget priorities (in which one aircraft carrier, for example, may be judged more worthy than a hundred local sewage plants). As a result, they send mixed signals through the federal system: more freedom for the states in one matter and a new mandate on another. They intervene in constituents' complaints over a Medicaid problem or river flooding and so render the administrators' environment less predictable. They definitely have the dominant power in the federal system but do not use it in a consistent direction.

State and Local Officials   The second cluster is made up of state and local elected officials. Governors, state legislators, mayors, city and county councils, and school boards try to obtain as much federal money as they can to support their programs yet retain enough independence to protect their political power. They struggle to control the uses and effects of the federal grants, mandates, and regulations that descend on them.

These officials exert influence in Washington through several organizations that do research, exchange information, and develop policy proposals. The most prominent of these are the National Governors Association, the National Conference of State Legislatures, the U.S. Conference of Mayors, the National League of Cities, and National Association of Counties. Their policy stances are not identical, but they share a common interest in seeking to retain control for themselves and deny it to the bureaucrats in their employ. Many cities and states maintain their own lobbying offices in Washington to influence legislation and secure grants.

Administrators   The third influential group—administrators in national, state, and local agencies who actually conduct most of the intergovernmental relations—is more diverse than the preceding two, but in many respects it is more powerful. In many policy areas these administrators have formed "self-governing professional guilds" that make and interpret the rules and standards by which states and localities must operate and exercise whatever discretion a program allows (Seidman & Gilmour, 1986, p. 197). These guilds operate more or less cohesively in many policy areas, including health, education, highways, social services, housing, and pollution control.

Broad-based associations of professionals in government administration speak for many of their concerns. These include the American Association of State Highway and Transportation Officials, the American Public Transit Association, the International Association of Chiefs of Police, and the American Public Health Association. Although these are private groups, they link government officials for mutual support, information, and advocacy. They maintain close relations with members of Congress on committees that touch their interests.

Administrators' power in the system tends to increase with the complexity of the policies they carry out. The 400-plus grant programs and the intergovernmental regulatory actions are so specialized that they tend to prevent outsiders from understanding them, let alone exerting much influence. Each cluster, or guild, has claimed its turf and the right to develop its policies. As early as 1963, Senator Edmund S. Muskie realized this, describing intergovernmental relations as "almost a fourth branch of government [which] has no direct electorate, operates from no set perspective, is under no special control, and moves in no particular direction" (cited in Seidman & Gilmour, 1986, p. 198). The changes of the 1980s curtailed some of those bureaucratic power centers and injected new blood into others, but Senator Muskie's generalization still holds true.

Private Interest Groups   The fourth group in these coalitions is that serving private interests. Such groups express more specialized concerns. The "highway lobby," for example, is well known as a supporter of federal aid for state road building. It encompasses truckers, construction firms and unions, automobile clubs, rural communities, and businesses that depend on good highway transportation. An alliance of land developers, labor unions, mortgage bankers, and civil rights organizations dating back to the 1940s backs housing and redevelopment officials in seeking federal housing aid (though with declining success since 1981). These private groups also exert influence by filing lawsuits that seek to change policies and practices and by appealing to sympathetic chief executives.

The States vs. the Federal Government: How Real Is the Conflict?

This overview of the politically powerful forces omits the states or the local governments as whole units. This is significant because one line of modern thinking poses a deep and continuous conflict between the national government, on the side of centralization, and the states, which defend the constitutional principles of federalism. Indeed, a great deal of rhetoric, particularly in election campaigns, denounces Washington's ambitions to "subvert" the states. President Reagan expressed this theme often when he sought to reduce federal controls on state policies and spending of grant funds.

But the political battle lines often run along other fronts. The dispute over the minimum drinking age, for example, pitted some states against Congress (which itself was divided), but since other states had already raised their drinking age, many of those that had not done so favored the increase to reduce problems near their borders. Interest groups also divided according to their various perspectives.

Rarely do the government and constituents of a state or a large city speak to Washington with one voice. The issue that currently unites state and local officials in opposition to the federal government better than any other is that of the burden caused by the mandates described earlier in this chapter. Even that pressure varies from one mandate to another, however.

Current intergovernmental debates often revolve around which level of government has enough money to respond to a given problem. The late 1980s witnessed a rising debate over the need to rebuild or expand the nation's roads, bridges, dams, airports, water and sewage systems, and other public works. In February 1988 a congressionally sponsored study by the National Council on Public Works Improvement recommended that governments at all levels budget $90 billion per year for such projects—twice the level at that time. Failing that, the study maintained, more bridges would collapse, more water supplies would be contaminated, and air travel would be curtailed.

Where could this extra money come from? Haunted by the deficit, congressional leaders stress that they cannot supply much without substantial cuts in other federal spending. (They do have two trust funds, fed by user fees and taxes, for aviation, highways, and mass transit; these totaled $28.7 billion in 1989. But those in Congress oppose rapid depletions of them, if only because these funds help compensate for the larger deficit.) Thus the national government is not a likely source for the foreseeable future.

But, because of rising costs in other areas and the loss of federal grants, state and local lawmakers have limited capacity for increased spending on infrastructures. If they do not raise taxes to fill the gaps, they must turn to user fees, such as higher sewer and water charges, park and museum admissions, and road tolls. They may also turn some of these facilities over to private owners and let them find the financing and charge customers accordingly. A third option, which some have adopted, is to create revolving funds from which loans can be made to local units for high-priority improvements. Chapter 12 addresses this issue of financing alternatives further.

What Directions for Intergovernmental Administration?

The politicking over who should pay for the repair of the nation's infrastructures might lead some to conclude that there are really no boundary lines in the federal system. In the 1960s Morton Grodzins used a metaphor of a marble cake to express that theme. In contrast to the dual federalism era, in which the realms of the national and state authorities were separated like the upper and lower halves of a layer cake, their responsibilities are now swirled together almost at random. As he expressed it, "No important activity of government in the United States is the exclusive province of one of the levels, not even what may be regarded as the most national of national functions, such as foreign relations; not even the most local of local functions, such as police protection and park maintenance" (Grodzins, 1966, p. 8).

The marble cake image is misleading, however, since the dark and light swirls are not spread randomly. Local park maintenance is not a concern of the U.S. Department of Interior, and it is rarely the province of any state agency. The Social Security insurance programs are exclusively federal. These regularities lead some observers to suggest that it is possible to establish criteria for distributing the functions of government and thereby sort out the tangled lines of responsibility that make the federal system hard for citizens to understand.

Decision Making: How Can Resources and Responsibilities Be Shared?

In 1982 the Advisory Commission on Intergovernmental Relations (ACIR) suggested criteria for the intergovernmental distribution of functions, as outlined in Box 4.7. Although they are not definitive guidelines, they can help in the consideration of some alternatives.

State and local officials are frustrated by the uncertainties and costs that accompany the package of federal grants, mandates, and shared regulations with which they must cope. There is also no doubt that the system could be simplified by using even these conflicting criteria. Most suggested reforms would end duplication of effort by giving one level exclusive or controlling responsibility for a function. For example, the national government might assume full control of food stamps and cash payments to the needy, with the states taking over financing of housing and urban redevelopment. Yet this is unlikely to happen, and for the same reason that the control of these programs was originally split. Let us look more closely at the ACIR's standards.

The public finance criterion regarding fiscal capacity (I-D) holds that financing responsibility should be assigned to the government(s) with adequate fiscal capacity. But *adequacy* is subject to political definition, and at present all levels struggle with many com-

(continued on p. 124)

Box 4.7

Which Level of Government Should Do What: Criteria for Decision Making

How you make a decision is sometimes as important as what you decide. In answering the question of which level of government should do what, the way the decision is made—meaning what criteria are used to make it—is extremely important. Is it based on political factors, fiscal concerns, regard for equity, practical administrative concerns, or a combination thereof? Unfortunately for policymakers, the four major criteria are likely to conflict on any given service.

The four major criteria for sorting out who should do what and elements of each follow.

In spite of the difficulties in applying all the criteria for assigning responsibility, it is clear that those who favor more diversity, less redistribution, administrative efficiency, and more fiscal accountability will favor assignment of greater financing and service responsibilities to the state and local levels. Those who emphasize uniform services, redistributive taxes and services, or a guarantee that special government services should at least be minimally available to all will emphasize service and financing at the federal level.

Our intergovernmental system, as it was conceived and now operates through grants-in-aid, seemingly reconciles competing centralist and decentralist approaches to the accountability questions. Grants have been created in order to avoid making the difficult trade-offs involved in completely separating out responsibilities level by level. Yet assessments of political accountability, governmental efficiency, political effectiveness, or equity criteria in the American federal system are mixed, at best. The political responsibility for intergovernmental program operations is divided and confused. The price of eliminating such confusion is the difficulty of making harder, more clear-cut choices on what levels of government should be responsible for what.

I. Public Finance Criteria

A. **Production Efficiency:** Assign functions to jurisdictions that are large enough to realize economies of scale.

B. **Trade-Offs among Complimentary Services:** Assign a function to a level of multipurpose jurisdictions that can choose among the variety of service alternatives for meeting similar objectives.

C. **Optimum Levels of Service:** Assign functions to governments geographically large enough to encompass the geographic scope of benefits received and costs incurred from a public policy. If the jurisdiction is too small for the extended benefits, the service will be under-provided; if the jurisdiction is too small to encompass the full costs or adverse side effects of the program, the program will be too large. If scope of benefits and costs match, the government responsible for the service should be fully responsible for financing for it—i.e., fiscal accountability.

D. **Fiscal Capacity:** Given an assignment of taxing authority—constitutional, statutory, or de facto—assign service financing responsibility to a level with adequate taxing authority and taxing capacity.

II. Political Criteria

A. **Political Accountability:** Functions should be assigned to jurisdictions that are controllable by, accessible to, and accountable to their residents, to jurisdictions that maximize the conditions and opportunities for active and productive citizen involvement, including full representation for minorities.

B. **Matching Desired Services to Public Preferences:** Functions should be assigned to a level that will provide diversity and a tailoring of services to community preferences. Under these circumstances, individuals will be able to pick among jurisdictions so as to best match their preferences to service and tax levels.

C. **Responsiveness:** Assign functions to levels that respond readily to changes in public preferences among types of services or taxes and their levels.

D. **Individual Freedoms:** Assign functions so that checks and balances on the power of government will operate.

III. Equity Criteria

A. **Redistribution of Income:** To redistribute income successfully by means of an expenditure program or tax instrument, the jurisdiction must be large enough to prevent those from whom resources would be taken from leaving and outsiders to whom resources might flow from immigrating.

B. **Minimizing Tax or Service Disparities:** Assign a function to a level and among jurisdictions so that disparities in resources with which public services can be financed will either be minimal or have minimal effects on the level of service provided.

IV. Administrative Efficiency Criteria

A. **Capacity:** Assign functions to levels that articulate program goals, evaluate programs, assess needs, and have adequate legal authority and management capability.

B. **Effectiveness:** Assign functions to levels that can effectively carry out the program with the least overhead and with the least amount of fraud, waste, and abuse.

—*Intergovernmental Perspective,* 8, Spring 1982, p. 7.

---

peting demands they cannot meet. A fluid system of burden sharing can be adjusted annually as resources flow in one direction or the other. The equity criteria (III) usually call for wider national participation (or state support of local programs), but political criteria II-B and II-C demand significant decision making at the lowest levels. Thus, to use the example of rebuilding infrastructures in a state, its cities and counties want to choose which roads and bridges to rebuild each year but, in view of the many nonresidents who use them, insist that the costs be shared by the state and the nation.

Localism and Pragmatism

Judged by the administrative principle of unified control and responsibility, the federal system is irrational and inefficient. But when measured against its guiding political principles—localism and pragmatism—it is hard to imagine it becoming anything else. Localism is the view that a service or regulation should be based in as small a jurisdiction as possible to make it most controllable by the people it affects. Whether it concerns police protection, zoning for land use, or waste processing, localism dictates that municipal or state officials serve the interests of their constituents. Power that is distant, in far-off Washington or even a metropolitan agency, is less accountable. This view is understandably common among state and local elected officials and reflects a general sentiment of their voters.

President Reagan reaffirmed the principle of localism in October 1987 with Executive Order 12612, which President Bush renewed in 1990. It asks federal administrative agencies to distinguish "between problems of national scope (which may justify federal action) and problems that are merely common to the states (which will not justify federal action because individual states, acting individually or together, can effectively deal with them)." Federal action should occur only when its constitutional authority is clear, and regulators should "refrain, to the maximum state possible from establishing uniform, national standards for programs and, when possible, defer to the states to establish standards." The order also requires federal agencies to show what effects any proposed new regulations will have on the costs or administrative operations of state and local governments (W. John Moore, 1988).

The complementary principle of pragmatism asserts that a needed service or regulation should be provided in the most effective manner possible. It will conflict with localism when a city cannot afford to build a needed sewage treatment plant and so demands that the state or Washington pay for it. A pragmatic perspective may also indicate national involvement when a state is lax in preventing chemical contamination of groundwaters or in sheltering the homeless. Members of Congress and most constituent organizations often adopt this perspective. Many administrators, even at state and local levels, are also pragmatic in this sense when they prefer increased funding or uniform national standards over local control when these may conflict. Time has shown that Executive Order 12612 is largely symbolic, since Congress and administrators claim considerable leeway for their own judgment on each program.

Most intergovernmental arrangements blend the values of localism and pragmatism in practical ways. The tension between them requires frequent negotiations and adjustments, however. Localism often dominates in programs with limited geographic scope, such as urban transit services. But when administrators struggle with potentially expensive problems that cross governmental boundaries—air pollution, notably—they seek help wherever it can be found.

Facing these diverse issues, administrators at all levels are pressed to achieve more with less to build better cooperative relationships and to devise creative solutions. The decade of the 1980s was described as a period of competitive, "fend-for-yourself" federalism, in which states and localities were left more to their own devices to raise money and solve problems than in the previous decade (Shannon, 1988). In the 1990s they can still draw on the federal treasury for some programs, but they must develop other sources of funds, particularly private businesses and nonprofit organizations. As they have greater freedom to develop new policies of their own, they bear the burden of digging up the resources to support them. Chapter 12 develops this issue more fully.

Summary

The term *federalism* denotes a system in which the total powers of government are constitutionally divided among one authority that governs the whole nation and several that govern its geographic subdivisions. These governments not only have their own policy responsibilities but also interact continually in implementing most domestic public policies. Intergovernmental relations encompass all these interactions, which are carried on through constant negotiation over specific programs and actions.

The American federal system evolved from dual federalism, in which the realms of the national and state governments were largely separate, to cooperative federalism, which involves the high degree of interaction that exists today. In the past three decades, the system has become more centralized as the states have been required to meet more policy mandates of the national government.

Fiscal federalism consists of the flow of money among the national, state, and local governments and the intergovernmental effects of federal taxation. Congress provides large sums to the state and local units to support their programs in many policy areas and ties specific administrative requirements to these grants in order to promote national policy objectives. Although these grants are major sources of funds, state and local officials are concerned about the difficulties of administering them and about their own diminished decision-making autonomy.

National and state governments also share in regulating sectors of the economy and providing services to the public. State and local governments must comply with many mandates imposed by Congress and the federal courts on their policy and administrative choices. These mandates put mounting pressures on their own financial resources. State and local governments jointly regulate many businesses and must work at coordinating their rules.

States cooperate with one another in many ways, often under formal compacts approved by Congress or joint-powers agreements. They also exercise detailed supervision over their local governments, granting them such powers as they have and giving them extensive financial aid. Local units may also contract with one another to share services and exercise their powers.

The political relationships in the American federal system are dominated by four clusters of influential people: members of Congress; state and local elected officials; administrators in national, state, and local agencies; and private interest groups with a stake in intergovernmental relationships. These contend for authority and money, seeking to advance their own concerns. In so doing, they steer the evolution of the federal system.

It may be possible to simplify the intergovernmental system and to clarify the tangled lines of responsibility. However, the system's evolution has been dominated by the principles of localism and pragmatism, which fail to support most restructuring proposals. This appears to be a period of competitive or "fend-for-yourself" federalism, in which state and local units must act aggressively to obtain resources even while they are constrained by numerous national policies and mandates.

Discussion Questions

1. Why has so much decision making for the federal system become centralized in Washington in recent years? Has this gone too far? Why or why not?

2. What factors prevent the American federal system from becoming as centralized as that in Mexico?

3. How would the federal system be different if the states received no financial aid from the national government and had to raise all their funds themselves?

4. How different would the implementation of policies be if, instead of using the state and local governments to administer family support, airports, and pollution control (among many others), the national government did it all through its own departments?

5. By what means do the states and local governments exercise as much power as they do in national government policy making? What are the limits to their power?

Analytical Exercises

1. Compile a list of the federal grants received by your state, county, or city, and their purposes. List each granting federal agency and each agency that receives and administers the grants. Learn as much as you can about the challenges of implementing the grants within federal rules and local needs and demands.

2. The 104th Congress, controlled by the Republicans, pledged to transfer power from Washington to the states and localities to enable them to meet their distinct needs in their own ways. Examine the extent to which this was actually done through legislation and budgets. Why did some proposals pass and others fail? What political and fiscal pressures were at work in these outcomes?

For Further Reading

Grodzins, M. (1966). *The American System.* Chicago: Rand McNally. Presents a systemic perspective on the close interdependence of federal, state, and local governments and the means by which they cooperate.

Howitt, A. M. (1984). *Managing Federalism: Studies in Intergovernmental Relations.* Congressional Quarterly Press (Washington, DC). Portrays the experiences of the 1970s and early 1980s in federal, state, and local grant management, focusing on the stresses and means of coping that have evolved.

Jones, C. O. (1975). *Clean Air: The Policies and Politics of Pollution Control.* Pittsburgh: University of Pittsburgh Press. Surveys the extensive intergovernmental cooperation (and the frequent lack of it) in efforts to improve Pennsylvania's air quality.

Kettl, D. F. (1983). *The Regulation of American Federalism.* Baton Rouge: Louisiana State University Press. Analyzes the patterns of regulations imposed by the federal government on the states as conditions of financial aid, particularly the Community Development Block Grants.

Peterson, P. E., Rabe, B. G., & Wong, K. K. (1986). *When Federalism Works.* Washington, DC: Brookings Institution. The management and impact of federal grants for health, housing, and education in four urban areas.

Seidman, H., & Gilmour, R. (1986). *Politics, Position and Power: The Dynamics of Federal Organization* (4th ed.). New York: Oxford University Press. See note in Chapter 2; also provides insights into federal/state relations.

Wright, D. S. (1988). *Understanding Intergovernmental Relations* (3rd ed.). Pacific Grove, CA : Brooks/Cole. Surveys the dynamics of American federalism.

The Sources of Public Policy

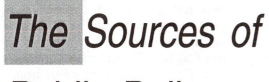

Learning Objectives

After reading this chapter, you should be able to do the following:

1. Identify the types and sources of public policy.
2. Define the popular and institutional agendas.
3. Define the policy cycle and describe its eight stages.
4. Explain how administrators participate in the making of public policies.
5. Explain the role of political power in the making of public policies.
6. Distinguish the four types of political power structures.
7. Explain how policymaking, implementing, and remaking are interdependent.
8. Identify the sources of political power used by participants in policymaking.

Should a government ration the types of medical care it provides at public expense to lower-income people? That is, should it tell them it will pay for treatment of pneumonia and crooked teeth but not for a liver transplant or therapy for chronic back pain? Or does the public purpose of protecting the lives of citizens qualify them for treatment of any disorder that threatens their well-being? Questions such as these are on the agendas of many state and local governments today, squeezed as they are between the rising costs of medical care for the poor and the limited funds to pay for it.

The state of Oregon participates, as do other states, in the Medicaid program, which covers about 240,000 of its low-income citizens who lack health insurance. In 1988 its legislators decided to curtail some kinds of expensive treatments, such as organ transplants, so that they could stretch their limited dollars to provide routine care to more people. But the media played up the plight of Donna Arneson, who needed a liver transplant, could not afford one on her own, and could not get it under Medicaid. Nevertheless, the state legislature, led by John Kitzhaber, president of the state senate and a practicing physician, reiterated to the public its strong desire for balanced medical care for the poor.

The Oregon Health Services Commission, a panel of health professionals and consumer advocates, responded by listing all the different medical procedures that are currently done. Then it held more than fifty community meetings around the state in 1989–1990 to get citizens' opinions on which treatments should have the highest priority. In 1991 the commission made public the ranking of 808 medical problems, from pneumonia and tuberculosis in the highest-priority category to brain deformities and terminal AIDS in the lowest. Its judgments were based on the threat to life of each problem, the cost of correction, and the likelihood of a treatment's success. Next, the list was sent to the state legislature, to determine the treatments that would be funded by Medicaid and those that would not be.

The scene shifted later in 1991 from Salem, Oregon's capital, to Washington, D.C. The plan did not conform to the federal regulations for administering Medicaid. A specific exemption from the Department of Health and Human Services was needed. Serious opposition to this move appeared among some members of Congress, who were concerned that it would result in further cuts in all forms of medical service to the poor. More telling yet, groups representing the disabled, such as those with cerebral palsy, opposed it, claiming that it would violate the Americans with Disabilities Act, which became law in 1990. The Bush administration then rejected the Oregon plan.

Oregon officials returned to the drawing board and altered the features that drew the federal objections. It resubmitted the plan to Washington early in 1993, after the Clinton administration took office. On March 19 it was approved, although the state was required to revise further its ranking of services for which it pays to eliminate any possibility of bias against persons with disabilities. The program will be tried over a 5-year period. The number of people aided will increase to 360,000; this is all who are believed to be eligible. The exact number of services paid for is subject to change with the funds available, but generally the state will not pay for treatments judged to be ineffective or for illnesses that are likely to clear up anyway. Since it could well set a precedent for other states and for federal policy, this program has been watched closely by medical policymakers nationwide.

Rationing medical care is a very touchy subject, but it is done informally every day. Many low- and middle-income people lack health insurance and could not afford an expensive treatment if it were needed. The best care is given to those with money enough to pay for it or with good insurance plans paid for by employers. With the costs of health care increasing much faster than the rate of inflation, major changes in public policy will be needed either to make this care available to those in need or to deny some kinds of care to some people. Oregon sought to make these choices a matter of public debate and record, and other governments are likely to follow its example.

Public policy consists of government's choices of actions intended to serve the public purposes. It is the bridge that connects the statements about the public purposes in Chapter 1 with the intended results for which administrators are responsible. Policies give government agencies authority and direction to spend money, supply personal services, restrict business practices, and carry on all governmental activities. One policy that emerged from Oregon's deliberations to deny payment for expensive organ transplants to Medicaid recipients is the provision of more thorough prenatal care, which would reduce the number of problems of birth. This choice gave new direction to the state's medical care administrators.

From Public Purposes to Public Policies

Policy Sources

Public policy takes several forms. Its most fundamental principles are expressed in the U.S. and state constitutions, which also govern the procedures by which policies are adopted. The most familiar policy form, and the focus of this chapter, is **statutory law**, enacted by Congress, state legislatures, and local boards and councils. Court decisions interpreting statutes and constitutions also become policy and are binding on legislators and executives. The rules and orders issued by executives and administrative agencies are also policy, for they extend and apply the statutory law in greater detail. Budgets of all governments are also policy, for they set the levels and objectives of spending as well as the amounts and sources of revenue.

Another key source of public policy is international relations: Some policies cross national borders, taking the form of treaties and less formal working agreements between and among governments. These accords structure American relations with other countries and with private foreign enterprises. Making and adjusting such policies require ongoing negotiations with those governments and such international agencies as the World Trade Organization and the European Union. The many agreements that the United States made with Canada and Mexico in the North American Free Trade Agreement will shape domestic policies in such realms as labor relations and environmental protection.

Policy in a more general sense also incorporates the informal statements and intentions of key decision makers in government. A congressional committee may express to a cabinet secretary its preference that a program be conducted in a certain way and that secretary, if prudent, will pay close heed. On the other hand, the secretary might give a law a somewhat different interpretation from what its authors in Congress intended, and that view guides its implementation.

Administrators play a crucial role in formulating public policy because of their specialized knowledge and experience in implementing current policies. In general, the higher the administrator's stand in the government hierarchy, the greater will be his or her influence over the substance of its policy. On the other hand, many high-level administrators lack expertise in their given policy area and may not remain in their posts long enough to sustain their influence. Every action of an agency can contribute to subsequent policies, and nearly all policymaking, for that reason, involves remaking existing policy. The ultimate success or failure of a policy is difficult to define, but such judgments constantly float through policy debates and incline decisions in one direction or another. Commonly, agencies offer such judgments either to justify a plea for more money or to press for desired legislative changes.

The Policy Cycle Begins: Setting the Agenda, Defining Problems and Objectives

Students of the policy process often use an abstract model that features several stages, from the first conceptions of a policy to its implementation and feedback. The model in Figure 5.1 is too simple to portray any actual decision sequence. The steps need not be taken consciously or in this order, and several can happen simultaneously. Nor is the movement in only one direction. Action in each stage depends both on those that follow and on those that precede it. The model has only the virtue of identifying, explicitly or implicitly, the key choices that must be made at some point.

Agenda Setting

Three events mark the beginning of the cycle: agenda setting, problem definition, and statement of public objectives. The first, setting the **agenda**, involves choosing the issues that warrant serious consideration for making or remaking policy (Cobb & Elder, 1972; Kingdon, 1984). We distinguish between two kinds of agendas. The **popular agenda** is the list of problems and issues in which the general public is most interested. Opinion polls regularly report that unemployment, crime, or lack of medical insurance heads the list

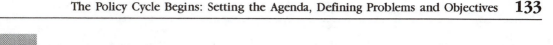

Figure 5.1

Stages of Public Policy

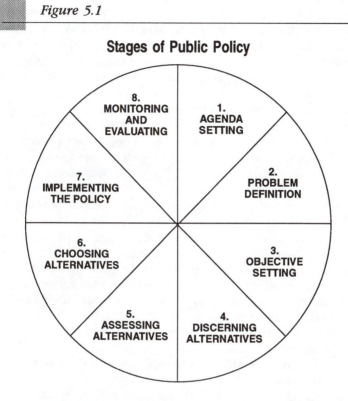

1. AGENDA SETTING: listing the issues that warrant serious consideration for the making or remaking of policy.

2. PROBLEM DEFINITION: determining the gap between the reality of a current situation and the ideal.

3. OBJECTIVE SETTING: choosing specific goals to be achieved by the policy to be formulated.

4. DISCERNING ALTERNATIVES: identifying potential courses of action that could achieve the designated objective.

5. ASSESSING ALTERNATIVES: forecasting the likely outcomes of each alternative, including benefits and costs.

6. CHOOSING ALTERNATIVES: enacting into law a specific package of programs and means of implementing them.

7. IMPLEMENTING THE POLICY: applying one or more of the implementation processes to achieve the objectives for which the policy was enacted.

8. MONITORING AND EVALUATING: learning the results of the policy as implemented and making judgments on whether it achieved its objectives. This activity usually leads back to Stage 1 to begin remaking of the policy.

The progress of policymaking can be likened (with some oversimplification) to the turning of a wheel. Just as a wheel makes many revolutions, policies have to be revised or remade at varying intervals.

of concerns in a given month. Issues rise and fall on this agenda because of such factors as media publicity, widespread public experiences, or the efforts of a president to publicize them. Nearly always, they reflect what government is already doing—well or badly. These issues can also vary regionally or locally; illegal immigration into California or a high crime rate in Atlanta may dominate the public agendas in those places.

Many issues have gone through an issue-attention cycle, from "alarmed discovery" of a problem and "euphoric enthusiasm" that it will be solved to "realizing the cost of significant progress" and "gradual decline of intense public interest" (Downs, 1972). Only a limited number of issues can hold the public's attention at any one time, and as a new one rises, an old one must fall, whether or not it has been resolved. Both success and failure of the action can be the cause of its removal from the agenda. For example, popular concern about environmental pollution has passed through several such cycles since its rise to prominence in the late 1960s. After publicity on the contamination of Lake Erie and the health threat of California smog, demand was widespread that action be taken. Several major laws followed, after which public attention shifted to other matters. However, such "crises" as toxic wastes and global warming have stimulated further upswings in public concern about the environment.

Institutional agendas, in contrast, consist of those items that government bodies or leaders, such as Congress or a city mayor, rank as high priorities for action. These concerns reflect the popular agendas but emphasize specific matters on which some agreement is possible. Thus, at a time when the public is worried about crime, legislators' agendas may include proposals to put more police on the streets or increase prison terms for violent offenders. If an issue does not hold the potential for new action, it will not be taken seriously. Agendas of national, state, and local governments frequently interlock, as with joint efforts on water quality or prevention of drug abuse. The rulings of courts in such areas as prisons and public education add issues for legislators and executives at all levels to wrestle with.

Administrative departments and agencies also have internal agendas that develop from assigned missions. A municipal housing and redevelopment authority sets priorities for its actions, perhaps to renew a neighborhood or rehabilitate older dwellings. Its director then seeks support from the city council and other sources of funds and authority.

Admission of an item to an institutional agenda is controlled by "gatekeepers," such as chief executives and legislative leaders, who decide not only that it is potentially soluble but also that it is sufficiently urgent and politically attractive to claim scarce legislative time. Oregon's state senator Kitzhaber was the key figure in focusing the lawmakers' attention on the health rationing issue, even though he aroused great antagonism by his opposition to the transplant funds (Specter, 1988).

Many factors shape institutions' agendas (Kingdon, 1984, pp. 17–18). A widely publicized event, particularly one that the news media label a crisis, can spur irresistible demand for action. The publicity in Oregon over Donna Arneson's liver disease set her apart from other, equally tragic victims. A jump in the unemployment rate can give more attention to proposals to stimulate the economy. The development of new technology or the accumulation of knowledge about the outcomes of an existing policy also help to set agendas. That the Oregon lawmakers had to deal with transplants at all is a result of the success of the medical profession in saving lives by that technology.

Ideologies, dominant personalities, and the tides of electoral politics are the key "filters" of agenda possibilities, since all such developments must be perceived and selected by politicians. President Reagan's election in 1980 significantly restructured not only the agenda of the executive branch but that of Congress toward tax cuts, increased military spending, and reduced government regulation of business. When President Clinton took office in 1993, he put universal health insurance and investments to spur economic growth on the congressional agenda. Yet his minority in the popular vote indicated that the nation was not necessarily committed to strong action on these complicated and expensive proposals. With the Republican victory in the congressional elections of 1994, the spotlight shifted to the reform agenda that House Speaker Newt Gingrich expressed in the "Contract with America."

Defining Problems

While they are setting the agenda, policymakers must also define the problem that confronts them. A "problem" is essentially a gap between a current and a preferred situation. "Every disparity between the actual and the desired is defined as a problem and is widely assumed to have a solution and one demonstrably better than any other alternative" (Vickers, 1980–1981, p. 553). "The solution is part of defining the problem. . . . Creativity consists of finding a problem about which something can and ought to be done" (Wildavsky, 1979, p. 3). All medical problems have objective measures, such as blood counts and the presence of the HIV virus, but they still require human judgments on what should be done for each person in his or her situation.

In politics, no problem is "given" in the sense that everyone will regard it in exactly the same terms. "There is no objective description of a situation; there can only be portrayals of people's experiences and interpretations" (Stone, 1988, p. 106). One participant chooses definitions of problems to convince others that her concept of the issue is the most accurate and thus her proposed solution is the best. Whichever definition is accepted inevitably shapes the policies devised to meet it. The Oregon leaders concluded that the problem with state health programs was the lack of basic care for many lower-income persons rather than the shortage of funds for costly transplants for a few, and the legislative outcome thus conformed to this conclusion.

Most issues that appear on popular and institutional agendas are familiar ones. "There are no permanent solutions, but only permanent problems" (Wildavsky, 1979, pp. 22–23). They are there because they haven't yet been "solved"—not because the earlier attempts have failed so much as because they have been replaced by new versions of the problem or new causes. Unemployment, for example, has dominated public agendas since the 1930s. During the Depression, the key cause was the slowdown in business activity, and World War II and the postwar global expansion in American markets did create many new jobs. During the 1980s, however, technological changes and the loss of those overseas markets created a new class of unemployed persons lacking essential skills. Detroit has long suffered from the decline of its automobile industry and its well-paying jobs. Its generous commitment to General Motors to keep some of those jobs is described in Box 5.1. Whether the price it paid for them was a fair one is a judgment call by those who gained or lost from the Poletown affair. The old definitions of the problem, although relevant, no longer suffice.

Other problems are familiar but call for radical redefinition because of the failure of current policy. Policymakers have generally viewed drug abuse narrowly: Drugs are either manufactured in the United States or smuggled in and sold to people who become addicted to them and commit crimes to support their habits. Solutions based on this view of the problem have not blocked the drug traffic. If the problem were redefined to focus on the dependence on chemicals of all kinds by young people for whom drugs provide a needed boost of personal self-esteem or an outlet for frustration, remedial efforts would take an entirely different course. The drug trade has an international dimension also, for it provides a livelihood for poor people in many countries. To interdict the influx of drugs requires careful coordination of administrative actions with foreign nations so as to respect their sovereignty. Until these larger contexts are defined, no realistic courses of action can appear.

A third group of problems is much smaller: the genuinely new ones that are so unlike others as to call for unique definitions. The federal government has been spearheading research to map the entire human gene structure, with steadily growing results. Concerned scientists, ethicists, and policymakers are asking if we know how to use this new knowledge most beneficially. It is unlikely that we will soon clone persons or create pseudo-human organisms, but

Box 5.1

A Cadillac Plant for Poletown: A Fair Trade?

Agenda setting and problem and objective definition are often fused together when officials are suddenly confronted with a pressing problem to solve. This happened in Detroit in 1980, when one of its biggest employers, General Motors Corporation (GMC), asked the city to help it find a site for a new plant to replace two obsolete facilities. If such a site were not available in Detroit, GMC could certainly find it in another city, but 6,000 jobs would also be relocated.

Mayor Coleman Young and the Community Economic Development Department did not want to lose either those jobs or GMC's tax payments and so set the objective of finding a site acceptable to the corporation. They chose the site of a vacant Dodge plant, but since it lacked the number of acres that GMC wanted, they further chose to acquire by legal condemnation 460 acres in the adjoining residential neighborhood known as Poletown. Detroit's policymakers

had to overcome the vigorous resistance of the more than 3,000 residents and 140 businesses and institutions in Poletown that were forced to move, and their lawsuits reached the Michigan Supreme Court before being rejected. In the end, the parcels of land were cleared and turned over to GMC without charge. In 1985 the new plant's 5,000 workers (note the loss of 1,000) began to roll Cadillacs, Buicks, and Oldsmobiles off the new plant's assembly lines (Jones & Bachelor, 1986).

Not only were the problems and objectives well defined for Detroit officials by General Motors, but it defined the alternatives for them: If they wanted to have the factory in the city, they had to find a place for it. They felt they had little choice, given the precarious financial situation Detroit faced. In many such cases, policy is strongly steered in certain directions by the circumstances.

there are many other applications from which to choose, such as correcting birth defects. Any policy must incorporate values of human health and well-being, and these cannot be quickly decided in a congressional committee session.

Many agenda issues return for reconsideration on a schedule that is determined either by the legislated life of a program (e.g., federal farm subsidy programs have typically been enacted for 5-year periods) or by the rapidly changing character of the problem (e.g., the costs of nursing care for a growing number of elderly persons). Policymakers must remain ready with current information and suitable tactics for these predictable returns.

Setting Objectives

A typical problem statement points to some potential objectives for solution, each attractive to specific persons and groups and each attainable in some degree but not fully compatible with one another. Such statements are most effective when expressed in concrete terms (e.g., to reduce the incidence of death due to kidney disease by 50 percent in 2 years). Yet when there is a legislative struggle over which objectives will dominate, the final statement that goes into the policy is usually vague enough to encompass most of the favored ones. The Oregon lawmakers had a natural political incentive to meet the medical needs of as many people as possible. Thus, they preferred to reach some of the 360,000 low-income people who lack health insurance with "bare-essential" care rather than to finance a handful of high-cost transplants.

Objectives can have many sources. The ethical values of our society, such as the obligation to preserve life, are quite compelling. Oregon legislators were pained to witness anyone's preventable death, let alone to appear to have caused it. Legal and professional standards interpret and expand these values and lay specific obligations on responsible people, particularly in government. We characteristically state our ethical values in absolute terms—rights and wrongs—but this focuses attention on our inevitable shortcomings in addition to stimulating improvement.

Advocates also call on society's available resources: "If we are rich enough to put a man on the moon, we can afford to. . . ." No matter what its current achievements are, an affluent technological society always feels obligated to set its goals beyond them. Although such thinking is an engine of progress, it also multiplies ethical dilemmas as more and more life-extending medical advancements appear.

Often a third source of objectives, citizens' demands, draws upon the first two. Those who see or experience the deficiencies most directly also advocate objectives that provide the most advantages for them. Many Oregonians want to believe that the state can pay for all transplants as well as cover other medical needs. But citizens' demands are not necessarily tied to their willingness to pay or to the realism of what can be done with given resources.

The Policy Cycle Continues: Discerning, Assessing, and Choosing the Alternatives

The objectives selected directly guide the choice of alternative policies. All choices flow in a continuous stream of decisions from the indefinite past to the uncertain future. They involve selecting one course of action from several options with the expectation that the selections will serve the policymakers' purposes. Government bodies often make it a messy and confusing process, and for good reason. A problem arrives on the public agenda only if it has not been solved by individuals or private organizations, and controversy often rages over what the options, purposes, and expectations really are. Medical care became a major public issue when its cost rose much faster than the ability of most people to pay for it. However, the problem was delivered to the lawmakers without remedies on which influential people and organizations could agree.

Discerning the Alternatives

In searching for alternative courses of action, policymakers usually begin with the "short list" of ideas with which they are familiar. Generally, each of these ideas is suggested or mandated by the definition that influential people have already given the problem or by the ideological stance they hold toward the general issue. Conservatives and liberals are often distinguished by the contrasting solutions they habitually consider for such matters as unemployment and social assistance.

If time is short or political pressures dictate, policymakers often "satisfice" with the information they have (Simon, 1957). This word, which is Herbert Simon's composite of *satisfy* and *suffice,* indicates that they end the search before they analyze every alternative and decide on the basis of what they do know. But where the known solutions do not suffice for politically significant people, the search will continue. The futile efforts to control the illegal drug trade currently are stimulating this kind of effort.

The search for alternatives has political boundaries like those of the previous stages. Since politicians are likely to have already defined the problem and set the objectives, they have also thought about which alternatives are preferred, which can be mentioned, and which must be excluded. "Controlling the number and kinds of alternatives considered is the essence of the political game" (Stone, 1988, p. 196). The Oregon debate over transplants would have fallen into chaos if other legislators had demanded consideration of equal treatment for sufferers from AIDS, for example. The state must deal with that affliction on its priority list, of course, but without appearing to draw resources away from prenatal care and other high-priority services.

Government administrators frequently suggest policy alternatives in the fields of their expertise. This is particularly common for the top executives of federal and state agencies who share a policy agenda with their president or governor. "Through feedback from the operation of programs . . . implementation can lead to innovation. If bureaucrats find a program is not going well in some particular, that recognition might feed into a policy change" (Kingdon, 1984, p. 34). Wherever the agenda includes remaking current policy, this influence is likely to be strongest. In the Oregon case, Freddye Webb-Petett, administrator of the Adult and Family Services Department, was a key participant through her initial decision to alter the funding and provision of statistics on transplant costs (Specter, 1988).

"New" ideas can come from governments other than the one deciding. Often a state or city adopts an idea that others have found successful. In 1987 Minnesota began to permit elementary and high school students to attend any public school of their choice (not limited to the one in their attendance area) if space was available. By 1990 six states had followed suit, and President Bush was advocating parental choice and interschool competition as a means of educational reform. Innovations in low-income housing, corrections reform, and environmental regulation have also spread among policymakers open to new solutions. European countries, and recently Japan, have also been the source of policy ideas in health care, education, waste management, and housing, although policy transfer across national and cultural boundaries is not always feasible.

Similar to the international transfer of ideas is the exchange from one policy realm to another. Some of the innovations incorporated in the community action programs in the Economic Opportunity Act of 1964 had first been tried with some success in efforts of the 1950s to control juvenile delinquency. For transfers of both types to succeed, those familiar with the issues must perceive how the idea must be adapted to the new situation.

Scientific and technological research and development often produce new policy alternatives. Scientists and engineers enjoy considerable prestige in a culture committed to the innovation they promote; to label a proposal as scientific is to endow it with unmatched credibility. Human organ transplants became much more feasible and thus more likely to enter the realm of policy during the 1980s because of the development of cyclosporine, a drug that helps prevent the body from rejecting the transplanted tissues.

On many issues, demands of new members of the policy community have enriched the stock of alternatives. Since the early 1960s, women, Hispanics, African Americans, and other groups that had not been included in policymaking succeeded both in making their demands heard and in joining the ranks of those who consider alternatives. Programs in employment, education, and many other realms have been broadened as a result. The "comparable worth" claim that jobs requiring equal skill and responsibility should pay the same salary regardless of who holds them—men or women, whites or persons of color—resulted from the efforts of disadvantaged groups.

These sources of policy alternatives also contribute to the definitions of problems and objectives. The influence of a proposed solution depends on its fit with the prevailing concept of the problem. A proposal to expand "parenting" education in a large city school system would be workable to the extent that the community sees the problem of child abuse and neglect as due to incompetent and poorly informed parents.

The source of an alternative obviously influences its chance of getting a serious hearing. Those who advocate legalizing the voluntary adult use of marijuana and cocaine are ordinarily dismissed (whether fairly or not) as users who want to avoid legal penalties for their pursuits. On the other hand, proposals for combating drug abuse that come from a respected public agency, such as the Federal Bureau of Investigation or the Public Health Service, invariably receive serious consideration.

Assessing the Alternatives

Basically, an assessment of alternatives is a forecast: If policy A is chosen, its likely outcome, B, will (or will not) close the gap between the present situation and the goal that was set. Also implicit is the expectation that unwanted situation C will not result from policy A. The data supporting that forecast may be extensive or sketchy and thus may be presented with confidence or hesitation. Policymakers do this assessment for each alternative; at the end, they ideally choose the one offering the greatest margin of expected benefits (given the objectives) over the costs or harms it would entail. In the real world of politics, all these judgments are complex and subjective. Even when there are "hard" data, participants can interpret and value them differently. Thus, as with defining problems and setting objectives, many judgmental criteria enter these deliberations. The issue of justice for juvenile offenders, highlighted in Box 5.2, provides such a policy challenge.

Benefits as Criteria for Assessment   First, what benefits are anticipated from each alternative? For whom? When? How much are they valued or needed? Which are measurable in dollars or other numbers, and which are not? How do these benefits compare with those provided to other groups in other policies? Who would be denied benefits? Answers to such questions require calculation of the value of each set of benefits for each group of recipients. The way that recipients respond to those possibilities clearly shapes that calculation. The Oregon legislature had to weigh the benefit of life-saving transplants for a few against basic care for many more low-income citizens. The former group could gain more immediate publicity for its cause, but the latter might exert more influence over the long run, particularly in votes, if all the beneficiaries were informed of the options.

Costs   The second criterion mirrors the benefits: costs incurred by each alternative. Again, policymakers must ask, "What costs?" "For whom?" "What would it cost the government?" "Who might be harmed as a result?" "What are the opportunity costs—that is, what other benefits could be gained with the funds if this alternative were not chosen?" Costs, like benefits, cannot be fully measured in dollars. Pain, fear, and lost opportunities lack an agreed-upon calculus. To ponder an action that even indirectly increases the pros-

Box 5.2

Which Approach to Juvenile Justice?

Policy analysis is most frustrating when none of the alternatives being assessed seems to promise success. The hard choices in juvenile criminal justice dramatize this well. Since 1988, violent crime by those under 18 has risen sharply, spurred by the illegal drug trade and availability of guns. It apparently caught by surprise the judges and corrections officers who were implementing a relatively lenient policy that stressed rehabilitation rather than punishment.

Now two major options face policymakers and there is no clear consensus for either. Advocates of one stress that with proper treatment, young offenders need not become career criminals. They point to treatment centers with counseling, education, and job skills development as having potential to turn teenagers' lives around and keep them out of the "crime schools" that adult prisons often are. Indeed, the lower recidivism rate of some juvenile institutions that practice such treatment support this claim.

But such "soft treatment" does not work for many hard-core young offenders, argue those on the other side. We simply don't know how to rehabilitate them, they conclude from other evidence. Since that is the case, we must set as a first priority protecting society from them. This requires long prison terms for homicides and rapes, for only in this way will offenders learn that society will not tolerate their behavior.

How should analysts, perhaps employed by a state department of corrections, who are not committed in advance to either approach, look at this? Can they design a corrections plan that is realistic in terms of experience and offers a better chance of success than what the state is doing now? Sifting through mountains of research data might lead to some conclusions but could also be confusing. Listening to passionate advocates of both sides may only bring frustration. The most likely plan would call for different kinds of treatment for diverse groups of offenders, abandoning the faith in "one best way." Even then, they must experiment continually, realizing that in a changing nation, all targets for public policy are moving and the policies themselves must respond flexibly to new conditions and information.

---

pect of early death, the Oregon lawmakers and administrators needed more than a list of monetary costs.

Feasibility   The third factor to consider is feasibility: How well is the alternative likely to work when assigned to a specific agency? Among the many questions one must ask are the following: Is there an agency with the will, skills, and resources to carry out this policy? Can the policy meet legal and constitutional tests if someone files a lawsuit over it? Do the knowledge and technology exist to enable its implementation? Is enough money available to fund it adequately? Unfortunately, such questions may not be answerable at the beginning. Many of the techniques for preventing air pollution were not feasible initially but were developed because of the legal mandates to reduce emissions levels to certain points.

Mutual Effects   Fourth, each policy relates in countless ways to other things that governments and private organizations do, and their success and failure are intertwined. Those who make policy should thus foresee these mutual effects. While the national government is formulating a health care policy, several states have gone ahead with programs of their own, interacting with health maintenance organizations, insurance companies, and hospitals. A system is gradually evolving in which each actor's choice interacts with policies of all the others.

Political Acceptability   The fifth criterion, political acceptability, is often the overriding one that puts all the alternatives in perspective. A policy is never made simply because it is "right" or "best." It emerges because it is judged right or best by legislators and executives who see that it fits the expectations that they and influential others hold of their jobs and of the government as a whole. This is not to say that they make inferior choices for that reason or that they are corrupt or irresponsible. Rather, because democracy is a process of shared decision making, a choice must fit the aims of those who join in making that decision. When there is widespread disagreement over an issue, the policy may be chosen only after long deliberation and might well be changed shortly thereafter.

This occurred with the catastrophic health care financing program for the elderly that Congress enacted in 1988 as part of the Medicare program. It was repealed a year later after well-orchestrated complaints from the more affluent retirees, who had to pay a surtax for it. Similarly, Oregon's ranking of the 808 forms of medical treatment could well change in each legislative session as their perceived urgency rises and falls.

Choosing the Alternatives

In the final step, policymakers choose one alternative (or a combination) to become official policy and add the "tools" with which to implement it. Where there is clear agreement on the law, the means of its administration can be equally clear. In 1961 President John F. Kennedy and Congress set the specific goal that an American was to set foot on the moon by the end of the decade. But the typical policy is a composite of several objectives, embodying many compromises among partisans of opposing views. American legislative bodies put a premium on reaching agreement, not only to secure the simple majority vote to pass a bill but also to preserve the ongoing working relationships that enable them to reach agreements on bill after bill. The price of that consensus is often ambiguity, which, although not pleasing all participants, permits closure on an issue.

Figure 5.2

The Legislative Process

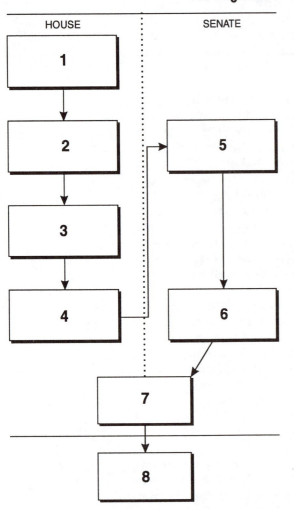

HOUSE   SENATE

1. Introduction of bill by one or more members. The idea and text of the bill often originate in the executive branch; presidents and governors present their own legislative programs under the authorship of members of their party.

2. Consideration by House committee and subcommittee. A bill is immediately referred to one or more committees for study. They hold hearings at which representatives from the executive branch and interest groups present their views. Members then may alter the text of the bill as they choose or simply not act on it at all. When finished, they report the bill to the House membership for passage.

3. The House Rules Committee determines (for most bills) when it will be considered by the whole House, for how much time the bill will be debated, and whether amendments to it will be accepted. (This step is not common in state legislatures.)

4. The House debates and votes on the bill. If it passes, it is sent to the Senate.

5. One or more Senate committees or subcommittees consider the House-passed bill and may repeat the actions of the House committee. The bill may be changed in any way and is then sent to the Senate membership.

6. The Senate majority leadership determines when the bill will be considered. The U.S. Senate has no limit on amendments from the floor and no limit on debate unless 60 senators vote for it.

7. If the Senate's version of the bill differs from the House text, it asks the House to concur in its changes. If the House refuses, a conference committee is called, with members from both houses, to work out a common text. That text is voted on by both houses, and if it passes, it is sent to the president or governor.

8. With executive branch advisers, the president or governor determines whether to sign or veto the bill. In the former case, the bill becomes law. If there is a veto and the legislators are still in session, they may override the veto by a two-thirds majority and the bill becomes law.

Congress and state legislatures follow similar procedures in enacting laws. For illustration purposes, the bill portrayed here will go first through the House of Representatives and then the Senate, although the reverse can be true and they can pass through both at about the same time.

Congress and state legislatures have an elaborate process through which a bill must pass to become law. Figure 5.2 outlines only the major steps that Congress takes. Realistically, laws are not designed so much as they evolve. Each participant responds to the initiatives and reactions of the others, and the enacted policy may deviate from the intention of its original author. Many laws blend aims and expectations that no one person would have selected at the beginning. The Tax Reform Act of 1986 was intended to simplify the Internal Revenue Code but accumulated many complex provisions demanded by those who had a share in its passage.

Each new policy alters and supplements existing policies and so must be carefully fitted into that context. The Oregon transplant decision is just one element of the state's health care financing policies, and administrators must work it into all the procedures and rules they currently follow and avoid new conflicts among them.

Tools of Implementation   The "tools" of implementation are an integral part of the policy choice. Basically, a tool is a method or approach used by government to achieve a specific objective. This concept first appeared in Chapter 1 with four major examples: cash payments to individuals, construction and maintenance of infrastructures, provision of services, and regulation of individual and corporate behavior. Many policies could be implemented by any or all of these tools. When a government seeks to increase the access of working parents to day care for their children, it can choose, first, to operate day-care centers directly with its own personnel. Or, second, it can give grants to community organizations to provide the service. A third alternative would be to give a tax credit or rebate to parents to cover their out-of-pocket child-care costs for whatever facilities they use. Less likely is use of the fourth tool: requiring employers to operate day-care centers for their workers. The policy goal and the tool used are interdependent, and political controversies are motivated by both choices. Nevertheless, legislators often fail to specify the tools to be used, because of neglect or lack of agreement, and expect the administrators to select them within broad limits.

Policymakers do not expect that their choice packages will completely solve the problem. No problem remains the same while it is being dealt with. If, by a happy circumstance, the targeted problem is minimized by the program, new problems are likely to appear that require different actions. As more people live longer as a result of advances in medicine and better sanitation, the number of victims of Alzheimer's disease and other maladies affecting the very old increases, which in turn calls for more research and long-term care.

In other instances, the "solutions" did not solve much and often created new problems, as with measures aimed at drug abuse. In either situation, no choice can be seen as permanent. Even when a long-term commitment is made, as with expensive facilities for airports and urban rapid transit, policymakers must expect to adjust to new realities in years to come.

**The Policy
Cycle
Concludes:
Implementation,
Monitoring, and
Evaluation**

The final two stages of the policy process are the "home territory" of administrators, for which they are directly responsible. Their performance here determines the success or failure of the policy and will shape its probable revisions.

Implementing the Policy

With the passage of a law or the selection of a policy by other means, the scene of action shifts to the agencies assigned to carry it out. Policy, before this point, is only an intention, a possibility. What it actually becomes happens at this stage. **Implementation** is the process of realizing public policy, thereby achieving the public purposes for which the policy was made.

Earlier students of public administration argued that implementation is primarily a "technical" task, clearly removed from the political controversies in which the policy was decided. In this view, there should be no uncertainty about how to implement a properly written law. Agencies must devise procedures, marshal resources, and monitor activities to make sure there is no dishonesty or waste. A hierarchical structure conveys the instructions of the top executives down through the organization and thereafter monitors the results. To claim that administration was not political was to believe that some realm of American government could be free from the pressures that corrupted elected officials at the turn of the twentieth century.

A more realistic view of implementation emerged after scholars examined what actually happened in the controversial programs that governments administered. Studies of social programs enacted in the 1960s showed that policies produced by legislative bargaining were often ambiguous or excessively optimistic, required extensive intergovernmental cooperation, and were inadequately funded. They had to attack genuinely difficult problems, from poverty to racial discrimination, for which there were no obvious solutions. It should have surprised no one that the political controversies and pressures that attended legislative action continued into the implementation stage, violating that hallowed neutral ground.

The implementation stage begins as a task assigned to one or more agencies, along with the authority to spend money, hire personnel, and obtain other resources necessary. Next, those agencies make rules and procedures by which to operate. Some degree of discretion is always permitted with regard to means, guidelines, and dates for action. When Congress passed the Child Care and Development block grant program in 1990, it scheduled a start in September 1991. Before the states could begin to implement the program, the Family Support Administration of the Department of

Health and Human Services had to write detailed regulations for who would be eligible, what standards the day-care facilities were to follow, and how the many state agencies were to coordinate their services. But delays in Washington set back by many months the starting date of the program.

These rules put to work the tools chosen to implement the policy. If it provides cash payments to individuals, for example, the rule determines the eligibility of each applicant and how much that person is to receive. Each of the tools can run into implementation problems if the goal is uncertain, difficult to attain, or wrapped in political controversy. However, those policies that provide direct services or apply regulations to persons who differ in their needs and requirements appear to present the greatest challenges. It is hard enough for Oregon to decide which medical procedures will be subsidized, but the harder task falls to the doctors and other caregivers who must determine what kind of aid each individual gets.

Monitoring and Evaluation

When administrators learn what happens as a result of implementing a policy and evaluate its success, they are moving from the end of one policy cycle to the beginning of a new one. Ideally, this begins as soon as results begin to flow in during the administration of a program. If administrators monitor and evaluate them sensitively, they are better able to correct the policy and the means they use to implement it. All new policies should be understood as opportunities for learning, and data collection is an essential part of the implementive effort. Mistakes are a natural feature of implementation, to be deplored only if one does not learn from them how to do better the next time.

At this point, the policy cycle can return to the beginning: agenda setting and redefinition of the problem and goals. The same political process that began the previous cycle—demands from powerful groups both inside and outside government—may initiate the next one. Failure (as these groups define it) in a significant program is most likely to stimulate its return to the agenda. The ongoing quest for means to deal with drug trade and abuse reflects the nation's persistent failure on this issue. There is no "normal" time limit on this cycle, and each stage can take from a few months to many years to complete.

Success can also reshape policy, particularly if the service provided appeals to constituency groups not currently benefiting from it. The Social Security program was enacted on a small scale in 1935, with modest payments to persons over 65 financed by an equally modest payroll tax. Over the years the Social Security Administration itself and the growing constituency groups to which it was responsive induced Congress to expand it to nearly universal coverage, including persons under 65 with disabilities that prevent them from working. This image of success continues to protect the program from erosion in the 1990s, even as other benefits are threatened with cutbacks.

In either event, the administrative experience with the policy provides the point of departure for future decisions. The problem is likely to have changed in the meantime, and the goal could become more ambitious or more modest. In extreme cases, the response could be to terminate the program. More likely, it has had enough success to preserve it in some form, but pressures arise to add or subtract features that appear likely to meet the current year's problems. The successes and failures of 30 years of space exploration have been highly publicized, and Congress's action on NASA's budget depends on how it perceives the current projects. The early successes of the shuttle program signaled its value to many, but the *Challenger* disaster of 1986 spurred calls for radical reform such as turning the space shuttle into a private business venture instead.

An International Perspective on Policymaking

When we view the American policymaking system compared to those of other nations, we realize how complex it is. The separation of the executive from the legislative authority; the bicameral Congress, with equal authority for both houses; and the further division of each house's authority among relatively autonomous committees all contribute to this. In addition, many important policies emerge from fifty state governments that are internally divided in the same fashion. The 80,000 or so local governments compound this even more. Observers often question whether the policies they produce are sufficiently coherent and consistent for all governments to implement them effectively.

Policies in other democracies emerge from a much less complex system (although not necessarily more effective for that reason). The typical parliamentary form of government, as found in Great Britain, Canada, Japan, and Germany, is centered on an elected legislature, the majority party of which chooses a prime minister and cabinet as its executive. The latter prepare budgets and bills that express their policy commitments. Parliament nearly always passes this legislation, since its party majority is committed in advance to support its chosen leaders. All four nations have bicameral parliaments, but none of the "second houses" exerts much independent influence on legislation.

Thus, policy in those nations emerges from one source of leadership (albeit with sensitivity to the preferences of legislators) rather than from the prolonged bargaining typical of the U.S. Congress. The stages of policymaking outlined in this chapter still apply to parliamentary nations, but participation in them is more narrowly confined once the agendas are set. Interest groups must exert their influence through the prime minister and cabinet and the top civil servants rather than through individual legislators, as in the United States. The circle of bargainers is much smaller, and their negotiations are not as open to public scrutiny.

For this reason also, top career administrators in other industrialized nations exert more influence on most policies than do their counterparts in the United States. High-ranking civil servants in Great Britain and Japan are intimately and continuously involved in policy formulation at the cabinet level. Their participation ensures that the policies that are ultimately enacted are realistic and workable. In Japan "once a policy decision is made it is carried out close to intent and with relative ease" (Cothran, 1987).

By contrast, American career civil servants are often excluded from the highest policymaking circles, which center on the White House. The common practice is to rely on presidential appointees, such as cabinet secretaries and undersecretaries and White House staff, for such advice. The policy proposals that emerge are further modified in congressional bargaining, so that they come to embody conflicting goals and are for that reason harder to implement. The result is likely to be less workable public policy compared with Japan's. However, the general trend in Japan as well as in the United States is toward more "political" (as opposed to bureaucratic) influence on public policies (Cothran, 1987).

Who Has the Power in Policymaking?

The essence of **power** is the ability to prevail in social conflicts, to secure one's goals in the face of opposition. Power is a central theme in policymaking and administration because it determines how governments distribute advantages and disadvantages among members of society. It is the dynamic that causes the policy cycle to turn, from putting a matter of concern on the agenda all the way to the evaluation of a policy's impacts. Power is unevenly distributed among individuals and groups in society; those Oregonians who wanted a wider distribution of health benefits prevailed over the transplant supporters. Administrators must be sensitive to who has how much power at what time, including individuals and groups in their own agencies and constituencies. They must also know how to preserve or increase their own power to maximize their impact on public policy. This is not a light demand, since power can be very "slippery," shifting with each change in circumstance.

Perspectives on Political Power

Power can be viewed from several perspectives, as Figure 5.3 summarizes. In one, it consists of the ability to define a problem and

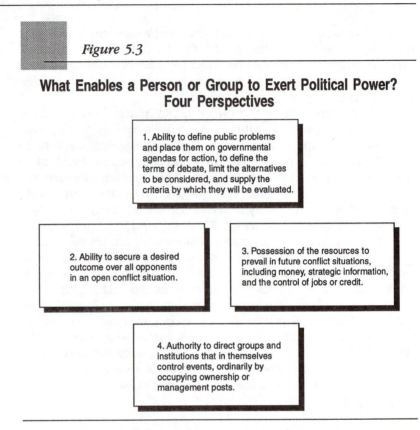

Figure 5.3

What Enables a Person or Group to Exert Political Power? Four Perspectives

1. Ability to define public problems and place them on governmental agendas for action, to define the terms of debate, limit the alternatives to be considered, and supply the criteria by which they will be evaluated.

2. Ability to secure a desired outcome over all opponents in an open conflict situation.

3. Possession of the resources to prevail in future conflict situations, including money, strategic information, and the control of jobs or credit.

4. Authority to direct groups and institutions that in themselves control events, ordinarily by occupying ownership or management posts.

A person or group can possess political power in any one or more of these ways. Which type of power is most effective depends on the goals one pursues and the situation in which it is exerted.

determine whether it is to have a place on the agenda of some unit of government (Bachrach & Baratz, 1963). For example, the harmful effects of some pesticides on the natural environment were eloquently publicized by the biologist Rachel L. Carson (1962). But the agricultural and chemical interests, allied with the U.S. Department of Agriculture, were able to prevent Congress from expanding the minimal regulation of pesticides for another decade. Only by securing enough publicity did the environmental groups gain the power to raise the issue to a high point on the public agenda and initiate practical steps for regulating the chemicals (Bosso, 1986).

This form of power extends to the ability to define the terms of debate, limit the alternatives to be considered, and supply the criteria by which they are evaluated. Those with specialized expertise can often do this on issues with which they are concerned (see Box 5.3 on the preparation for the expected swine flu epidemic in 1976).

A second perspective assumes an open-conflict situation, in which the most powerful player is the one who can secure a desired outcome over all opponents. Power exists when "(a) there is a con-

Box 5.3

Avoidance of a Nonepidemic

In February 1976 medical specialists in the Centers for Disease Control (CDC), a unit of the Department of Health, Education and Welfare, investigated the death of a soldier at Fort Dix, New Jersey. They found that his fatal virus was a strain of influenza believed to have caused an epidemic in 1918–1919 that killed about 20 million people worldwide. It was known as swine flu because it was usually confined to pigs but could be communicated to humans. Concerned that the nation was on the verge of another epidemic, Dr. David Sencer, CDC's director, organized a study that recommended a massive nationwide immunization program. A forceful leader with a dedicated staff of medical specialists, Sencer was convinced both of the danger of an epidemic and the effectiveness of preventive medicine.

Marshaling his evidence skillfully, Sencer secured the support first of the secretary of Health, Education and Welfare, then of President Ford. Ford realized that in an election year, the political as well as medical risks of an epidemic were too great to discount. After hearing no serious objection from medical professionals, he asked Congress to appropriate $135 million to buy enough vaccine to inoculate every person in the United States. Congress took only 3 weeks to provide the funds, and the program was on its way. Pharmaceutical companies immediately geared up for a high-speed program to produce 200 million doses of the vaccine.

One hitch soon appeared: The insurance companies that underwrite the liability of the drug manufacturers for their products declared that there were too many uncertainties about the swine flu program and the vaccine itself and refused to cover it. The president and Congress quickly responded by taking all risks on the government itself, which was the only way to keep the program alive.

Most of the immunizations were done by state and local health authorities, funded by a share of the $135 million. First priority was given to children and older persons, but they expected that nearly everyone would ultimately be vaccinated. The first shots were given on October 1, 1976, just in time for the winter "flu season." In the following weeks, several persons died afterward, but there was no evidence that the vaccine was the cause.

More sinister was the onset in vaccinees of Guillain-Barre Syndrome, a form of paralysis, which did appear to be a side effect of the serum. As the number of cases multiplied through November and December, CDC became concerned and called for a suspension in the program, which the president approved on December 16. Jimmy Carter moved into the White House on January 20 and called for a thorough review of the evidence. The inoculation program died a quiet death on March 11, 1977, when an advisory panel to the new secretary of Health, Education and Welfare recommended against further use of the vaccine (Neustadt & Fineberg, 1983).

flict over values or a course of action between A and B; (b) B complies with A's wishes; and (c) he does so because he is fearful that A will deprive him of a value or values which he, B, regards more highly than those which would have been achieved by noncompliance" (Bachrach & Baratz, 1963, p. 635). The victory need not be "total"; it may suffice to design the terms of compromise in one's favor. For example, a city department of community development may be reluctant to subsidize a new plant for a local industry. But if the company announces it will move its entire operation out of the city if it does not get the subsidy, it backs the government into a corner. Prudent officials usually yield to this show of power rather than lose the company's jobs and tax revenue. The company management then negotiates a deal with the city from which both reap benefits.

We can view power in a third way: the resources to prevail in a future conflict situation. The potential resources may consist of money, strategic information, or the control of jobs or credit. Research in Atlanta showed that a "law of anticipated reactions" often applies to community decisions. If a company is a major employer or investor, others will conform to its plans because they expect it will use its resources to induce them to act in that way. In this perspective, expectations readily translate into plans and concrete action. The Atlanta corporate power elite dominated decisions to construct major public projects because it provided the leadership for public officials who lacked adequate money to act on their own (Hunter, 1953).

A final form of power rests in the ability that individuals have to direct groups and institutions that control events. This type of power is personal but exerted through an organization. The president of a major bank or foundation that makes development loans in an area can affect the direction and success of a state's economic development program. In the same way, a city welfare director can apply the agency's influence on the council to revise a child protection program. The one with the most power in the group need not be the formal head; a determined city council member may be able to override a mayor's wishes on key issues. The Atlanta power structure described earlier was built on such major corporations as Coca-Cola and the city's leading banks.

Many factors can render a person or group powerful in political situations. The preceding definition from Bachrach and Baratz states that B complies to avoid being deprived by A of something he values. Rarely in domestic politics does this involve direct physical force. The "currency" is most likely to be money or credit, campaign contributions, votes, or jobs. Box 5.4 suggests that political as well as scientific and economic criteria were at work in the Environmental Protection Agency's choice of a clean-air gasoline additive. That a court intervened in this contest reminds us that politics has many arenas of activity, and even the judicial system may not pronounce the final word on this issue.

Beyond Conflicts: Indirect Sources of Power

Decisions are also made that do not involve "A depriving B," at least not of tangible values. An important source of power in policymaking and administration is legal **authority** that inheres in an elective

Box 5.4

Why Ethanol?

In the search for cleaner-burning gasoline to conform to the Clean Air Act amendments of 1990, scientists have identified several chemicals as possible additives. One of them is MTBE, a derivative of methanol produced from natural gas. Another is ethanol, or grain alcohol, which can be made from many plants (mostly from corn today). If either becomes the required additive, the industries that produce it can expect handsome profits.

In June 1994 the Environmental Protection Agency (EPA) chose to require refiners to use ethanol. (Opposing industries immediately filed a suit against that choice, and in 1995 a federal appeals court blocked EPA's mandate, ruling that the agency lacked authority to require a specific additive.) The industry expects that about 650 million gallons of it will be needed in 1996. The major producer is Archer-Daniels-Midland of Decatur, Illinois, which uses corn from midwestern farmers. Just 8 days before the EPA announcement, Dwayne Andreas, Archer-Daniels-Midland's chief executive officer, donated $100,000 to the Democratic Party at a fund-raising dinner. Andreas had once been a top source of campaign money for the Republicans, but after Clinton took office, the Democrats enjoyed most of that generosity, including substantial gifts that preceded the June dinner. Needless to say, the White House strongly supported the EPA decision, which was also applauded by farm belt interests. Methanol, on the other hand, was vigorously backed by the oil industry and by many environmental group leaders, an uncommon alliance (Dillin, 1994).

Did Andreas's cash tilt the decision? There is no way of proving or disproving that. Campaign contributions have long been suspect influences on major legislative and executive decisions by Democrats and Republicans alike. We can reasonably draw a picture of two political and industrial alliances competing for their favored products, with the outcome determined not by "neutral scientific criteria" (which are never neutral in their effects) but by a package of politically significant currencies. Andreas may not be able to wield power in every situation in which he is interested, but when policy choices are relatively open and he chooses effective allies, he and others like him can have their way.

---

or appointive office. A person in that office has been vested by federal, state, or local law with the right and duty to act on the public's behalf. A social worker who chooses to remove an endangered child from the home is backed by the full power of the state. In the stages of final policy choice and implementation, this is the crucial use of power. However, it is bounded by more restrictions than the other kinds; a public official who acts *ultra vires* (outside the law) in goals or methods forfeits that authority.

The term **influence** is often applied to a situation in which A prevails in a conflict without direct legal sanction or threatening to deprive B of anything. One may have a gift of persuasiveness, have special information that others respect, or make a plea for aid that draws others' sympathy. For example, a group seeking benefits from a county welfare agency for homeless children might succeed when it illustrates their plight in a poignant way and presents believable statistics on the number of children in need.

This power can be exercised in any of the policy cycle steps outlined earlier. Some participants' power, influence, or authority will be broad and exercised at every step; the president or strong big-city mayor might have this. The director of an administrative department, by contrast, might be influential at only one or two points. But success at one step can increase one's power in later stages when it enhances a reputation that others respect.

Administrators' Sources of Power

The power that public administrators can exert on the policy cycle depends on three major factors. First, the more intensively a government agency is already involved in the issue when it reaches the public agenda, the greater its administrators' role is likely to be. In the Oregon transplant issue, the experiences of the state Adult and Family Services Department set the stage for the legislature's choice. Remaking policy depends heavily on how the previous experience is interpreted, and those who have managed that experience often do so most compellingly.

Second, administrators have greater power when the issue to be decided is technologically, financially, or organizationally complex. The details of telecommunications networks and reimbursement for medical procedures bewilder most policymakers, who readily defer to those who can speak with expertise on those details. When most of the experts are outside of government, as is common, the private sector exerts the dominant influence.

Third, government administrators can exert power by forming coalitions with private interests. Every current and prospective public program has beneficiaries, and when they are mobilized, they can augment the influence administrators bring to bear. The Department of Veterans Affairs has long enjoyed close relations with the American Legion, Veterans of Foreign Wars, and Disabled American Veterans. Together they have undeniably greater influence on Congress than any would separately. There is thus no clear line between the power of a private interest group and a public agency when they mutually press for a certain policy decision. Scholars use the "**iron triangle**" model to denote this close three-way relationship among an administrative agency, one or more private interest groups, and the legislative committees responsible for their concerns. Each exerts power or influence on the other two through their regular communications, and each simultaneously provides services or political support that the others need.

Box 5.5

Concepts of Political Power Structure

1. Elitist: a cohesive grouping of persons in government agencies, corporations, financial institutions, information media, and/or foundations who dominate public policymaking and select the top governmental leaders.
2. Pluralist: regular and relatively balanced competition among groups representing business, finance, labor, agriculture, environmentalists, and many other interests, who bargain over policy choices and distribute the benefits among themselves.
3. Bureaucratic/technocratic: control of policy decisions by narrow professional specialists inside government and in private organizations, who enjoy a power advantage over all others in areas of their expertise.
4. Coalitional: control by open and shifting groupings of persons and organizations with interest in a given issue: government agencies, private interest groups, corporations, legislators, and news media.

The Nature of Power Structures

Besides studying power use in specific policymaking situations, scholars identify **power structures**–groups that consistently exercise power in a social system over a period of time. Box 5.5 summarizes four simplified types of power relationships that can apply to the national, state, or local levels.

Elites One model portrays a cohesive socioeconomic elite, a closely allied group with a common core of essential interests. Usually these represent major corporations, banks, information media, and foundations. Using their social positions and financial control, they consistently secure government decisions in their favor. Business interests have a privileged position in capitalist nations' policymaking processes and intervene as needed. However, direct or frequent involvement may be unnecessary to the extent that the policymakers are already sympathetic to them.

In the elitist view, elected officials and government administrators secure their posts only with the elite's approval; consequently, these governmental personnel are "reliable." This elite structure has been most often identified by researchers in local government (Hunter, 1953). However, C. Wright Mills (1956) portrayed the entire nation as dominated by this kind of structure, to which he added the top military leadership. Policies desired by the poor and any other "nonelites" would be enacted only to the extent that they would also benefit the elites. Since major business interests often maintain close relationships with government regulators, in this model the latter would be very much subject to their influence.

Pluralism   The second model paints a more competitive picture of the American political system. Pluralism envisions many groups contending for power, not just major corporations and financiers but also labor unions, farm organizations, environmental associations, small businesses, civil rights groups, and foreign nations. State and local public officials also join national decision-making contests to claim a share of benefits. The competitors' resources are sufficiently balanced over the long run that no single actor can completely dominate policymaking. What emerges are policies that provide some benefits to each participant. More important, elected public officials and top administrators are sufficiently independent of the contestants to mediate among them: They are free to uphold broad public interests. Dahl (1958) analyzed the New Haven political system in this way, and Rose (1967) extended this perspective to the nation as a whole.

Bureaucrats and Technocrats   A bureaucratic or technocratic perspective holds that as government has become more complex, power has shifted away from "generalist" elected officials and broad-based popular organizations toward the narrow professional specialists inside government and in private organizations who employ them. As in the elitist structure, there is little competition among large social groups to determine the content of policy. Only a handful of specialists really understand the complexities of regulating banks, controlling international trade, or choosing military weapons; therefore, they hold the real power over them.

However, this bureaucratic/technocratic view of power differs from the elitist model in that its members do not exert broad control over many government choices. A medical specialist can direct policy on immunization against an influenza epidemic but plays no role in any other realm where a different circle of experts reigns. There is little communication among specialists in different fields. On an issue, such as drug abuse, that involves many professions, it can be hard to secure their cooperation. This model finds the power centers largely within governmental bureaucracies but with allies in the private sector. The chief executives and legislators, being generalists, have formal authority over them but lack their expertise and must defer to their judgments on matters they do not fully understand. The effort to forestall a swine flu epidemic, as described in Box 5.3, illustrates this well. Only when the experts disagree publicly, as they have on the use of nuclear reactors to produce electricity, can the generalists assert their dominance.

Coalitions   The fourth, or coalitional, model is eclectic enough to incorporate the previous models' most useful features. It views power as exercised through various and shifting alliances, or **issue networks** (Heclo, 1978). In this view any significant policy issue is broad enough to involve a cluster of informed and interested people in private groups; governmental agencies at the national, state, and/or local levels; legislators who are customarily attentive to it; and others from the news media, universities, and research organizations. Interests with international connections often come into play: The major trading partners of the United States and multinational corporations employ lobbyists to express their demands. This network is broader in membership than the iron triangle defined earlier and is more likely to have internal disagreements.

These clusters are relatively open. People move into and out of them and can rise or fall in influence. Media publicity and information flow can attract more participants and so widen the scope of conflict (Schattschneider, 1960). Yet they are not quite pluralist systems, since a different coalition arises for each type of issue, and there is no assurance that it will represent all affected parties or that there will be significant competition among them. It is recognizable as a network because only a limited number of participants have sufficient interest and knowledge to devote energies to the issue. Although there may be some overlapping among related issues, each cluster has a unique membership.

Decision-making coalitions can vary in their membership from one issue to the next, in their internal consensus, and in their ability to distribute benefits among their members (Wirt, 1974, pp. 47–48). The larger the government making the decision, the broader and more diverse the coalitions are likely to be. Smaller units of local government may involve only a handful of people in their processes, while most national government controversies attract so many as to require extensive negotiation and adjustment of conflicting demands. The network that formed in 1993 to influence national policy on health insurance was larger than most but had intense internal conflicts over various features of President Clinton's plan and its rivals.

Including the Excluded   Whatever model best describes a given episode of policymaking, it is important to recognize who is not involved in it. We are increasingly sensitive to the nonparticipation of groups affected by public policy: the poor, the transient, people with physical and mental disabilities, children, and racial and non-English-speaking minorities. When decision makers design policies for child protection or medical aid, it is vital to include representatives of these groups, which are statistically most at risk to abuse, poverty, and discrimination. Some administrative agencies, in cooperation with voluntary groups, seek the views of those who would otherwise be excluded to make sure they are heard. As officials in Saint Paul, Minnesota, designed a comprehensive program to benefit families with small children, they held meetings with more than 900 parents in all parts of the city. The Children's Initiative, as the program is known, is obligated to use the insights and demands of these parents in establishing service centers to meet the needs of each neighborhood in the city.

Summary

Public policy consists of government's choices of actions that are intended to serve the public purposes. It provides government agencies with authority and direction to spend money, supply personal services, restrict business practices, and carry on all government activities. Policies are expressed in constitutions, statutory law, court decisions, administrative rules and orders, budgets, international agreements, and to some degree, the statements and intentions of powerful government decision makers. Public administrators play a crucial role in policymaking because of their expertise and central responsibility for implementing the policies made.

Policymaking can be briefly portrayed as a cycle with eight key stages: setting the agenda, defining the problem, setting objectives, discerning alternative actions, assessing the alternatives, choosing the alternatives to enact into law, implementing the chosen policy, and monitoring and evaluating the results. Agendas may be public (i.e., popular) or institutional. A problem is a perceived gap between a current and a preferred situation and creates an opportunity for disagreement about its precise definition. Objectives are likewise subject to political conflict, since the values and preferences of participants usually differ.

Policymakers must identify some acceptable alternative courses of action and evaluate and compare them to determine how well they will solve the problem at hand and meet policy objectives.

The choice of the final package of alternatives is made by legislators, who must also select the tools by which it will be implemented.

Implementing, monitoring, and evaluating the policy is the realm of administrators, who must make many decisions and judgments in this process. The outcomes of this stage typically feed back to the first when it becomes apparent that the policy needs revision.

The complexity of the American policymaking system becomes obvious when it is compared with those of parliamentary democracies. In the latter, there are fewer major participants, and policy emerges more quickly and often more coherently. High-level administrators play a more powerful role in policymaking there than in the United States.

Administrators must be sensitive to the means of obtaining and using power, using their involvement in the ongoing activity of implementation, technical expertise, and alliances with private interest groups. Political power is a central resource in policymaking. There are many ways to view it, and it can be structured in elitist, pluralist, bureaucratic/technocratic, and coalitional forms.

Discussion Questions

1. How did the Medicaid issue get on Oregon's public agenda? How difficult was it for the lawmakers and health officials to define the problems and objectives?

2. Why is it necessary to have some concept of the problems and objectives in an issue before discerning and assessing the alternative solutions?

3. What major factors can cause delays in moving through each stage of the policy cycle?

4. What kinds of issues are most likely to draw widespread public participation in policymaking? Which are least likely?

5. What advantages does the policymaking system in parliamentary democracies have over that of the United States, with all of its complexity? What disadvantages does it have?

Analytical Exercises

1. Identify an innovative policy that was recently passed in your city or state, perhaps in the field of health care, education, crime prevention, or social welfare. Interview key legislators, administrators, or journalists to learn who originated the idea, who was influential in processing and modifying it, and why it passed at the time that it did.

2. Over the years, the "tobacco lobby"—an alliance of farmers, manufacturers, and related interests from tobacco-producing states—has exercised strong influence over public policy. As its impact on policy has declined, its voice has remained strong. Trace the history of this lobby's successes and failures, perhaps using *Congressional Quarterly* and *National Journal,* and explain this change of fortunes in the policymaking arena.

For Further Reading

Cobb, R. W., & Elder, C. D. (1972). *Participation in American Politics: The Dynamics of Agenda-Building*. Boston: Allyn & Bacon. Explores how public and institutional agendas emerge from the many demands and alternatives for policy choices.

Dahl, R. A. (1958). *Who Governs?* New Haven, CT: Yale University Press. Classic study of decision making for the city of New Haven, demonstrating the pluralist perspective that no one elite dominates urban politics.

Hunter, F. (1953). *Community Power Structure*. Garden City, NY: Doubleday. Study of Atlanta's business elite, more politically powerful even than the city's political leaders.

Kingdon, J. W. (1984). *Agendas, Alternatives, and Public Policies*. Boston: Little, Brown. Insightful analysis of how decision makers match problems with solutions and come up with policies.

Light, P. (1995). *Still Artful Work: The Continuing Politics of Social Security Reform* (2d ed.). New York: McGraw-Hill. The ongoing struggle within Capitol Hill and the White House to make the trade-offs necessary to keep the Social Security system solvent in the future.

Lindblom, C. E. (1980). *The Policy-Making Process* (2nd ed.). Englewood Cliffs, NJ: Prentice Hall. Overview that stresses the limits and partisan character of policy analysis and the dominance of governmental and business managers in shaping agendas and outcomes.

Neustadt, R. E., & Fineberg, H. (1983). *The Epidemic that Never Was: Policy-Making and the Swine Flu Affair*. New York: Vintage Books. Well-documented report on the decision making that led up to a vaccination program and how the government handled its consequences.

Schattschneider, E. E. (1960). *The Semi-Sovereign People*. New York: Holt, Rinehart & Winston. Frequently referred-to analysis of why the content of policies depends on those who participate in making them and why so few participate.

Stone, D. (1988). *Policy Paradox and Political Reason*. Glenview, IL: Scott, Foresman. Penetrating analysis of how policymakers' values and perceptions interact with situations to generate governmental choices.

Business Regulation by Government

Learning Objectives

After reading this chapter, you should be able to do the following:

1. Define *regulation* and explain its purposes as applied to corporate business activity.
2. Define *market failure* in its several forms.
3. Identify the major regulatory agencies of government.
4. Define *adjudication* and *rule making*.
5. Identify the procedures for *rule making*.
6. Describe the major political influences on regulation.
7. Describe the deregulation trend of the past two decades and its outcomes.
8. Describe the international dimensions of business regulation and its political influences.

Kettleman City is a small community on the west side of California's San Joaquin Valley, populated mainly by Hispanic farm workers and their families. It is also the site of a hazardous waste landfill, operated by Chemical Waste Management, Inc. In 1990 the company requested a permit from Kings County to add an incinerator on its site, about 4 miles from the nearest homes. The county planning department and later the Board of Supervisors approved the permit, but the Kettleman City residents sued to overturn that decision. A year later, a state superior court judge blocked the project because, first, the county failed to examine its environmental impacts adequately, and second, residents had been excluded from the decision-making process. The county had not even provided the relevant information in Spanish, which many required to grasp what was to happen. As of 1994 the project remained blocked and appeals were pending.

Kettleman City is only one of many sites in the "environmental racism" controversy, based on claims that national, state, and local governments allow polluting and health-endangering facilities most often in areas inhabited by the poor and people of color. Such facilities include not only waste treatment plants and landfills but also large factories that produce significant amounts of pollution. Because such people have relatively little political power, governments often fail to control environmental effects where they live and are more ready to allow new sources of pollution to be located there. This raises the issue of the fairness of the nation's environmental regulation process.

One could cite parallels to Kettleman City in many parts of the nation: the lower Mississippi River valley between Baton Rouge and New Orleans, with its array of chemical plants; the soup of toxic wastes in the industrial southeast fringe of Chicago; and an incinerator and solid waste dump in Sunland Park, New Mexico. The controversies are not usually clear-cut, since the hazards also mean jobs for people who have few other places to work (Arrandale, 1993).

Environmental regulation is always controversial, since it puts large industrial profits and jobs in conflict with the health and safety of people who live in the shadows of such facilities. Government at some level—and often more than one—determines whether the pollution is excessive and what should be done to reduce it. It also issues permits for all new facilities. For a smaller-scale project, city or county approval may be sufficient, as was originally the case in Kettleman City. Increasingly, though, state and federal authorities become involved because of their regulations, and many choices are ultimately made in federal and state courts after a lawsuit by the side that lost in the administrative process.

That environmental regulation can often be a civil rights issue was admitted by the U.S. Environmental Protection Agency in 1993. Its office of civil rights began to investigate charges by African Americans in Louisiana and Mississippi that their states' permit procedures for waste treatment plants were biased and exposed them to more toxic pollution than that to which white people were exposed. Federal environmental laws do not directly address discrimination, so the plaintiffs base their claims on the Civil Rights Act of 1964, which outlaws discrimination on a much wider front. There is no doubt that the nation needs places to process its wastes and that this process cannot be made entirely "clean," but where it is to be done will be a much more complex regulatory question than it has been.

Government decisions are often most visible when they involve telling someone no. Yet, although government may say no to a company that would prefer to dump mercury-laden wastes into a river, it is at the same time saying yes to downstream residents who take their drinking water from it and seek to prevent that contamination. Although each regulation is a restriction of some kind, it is also a service to those who would have a lower quality of life (or perhaps no life at all) without it. Although a large body of regulation applies to individual citizens, much of it in the criminal realm, this chapter focuses on the regulations that apply to business activity.

Regulation is the process by which government requires or prohibits certain actions by individuals and institutions, mostly private but sometimes governmental, through the efforts of specially designated regulatory agencies (adapted from Reagan, 1987, p. 15). This process entails both deciding what actions will be covered and making sure that the rules are complied with. The agencies derive their powers to make and enforce these rules from their legislative bodies, which have constitutional authority to regulate commerce and protect the population's health, safety, and welfare.

Most of the specific controls over economic and occupational activities originate in administrative agencies rather than in legislatures. These agencies also decide how the rules will be interpreted and enforced for individual people and businesses. While many of their activities go virtually unnoticed by the public, some burst into political controversy from time to time, as in the instances of locating hazardous waste facilities.

Regulation and the Public Purposes

How people earn and spend money has long generated conflicts that governments cannot ignore. In 1787 James Madison observed in *The Federalist* No. 10 that the "various and unequal distribution of property" had always divided nations into groups with distinct interests. "The regulation of these various and interfering interests forms the principal task of modern legislation, and involves the spirit of party and faction in the necessary and ordinary operations of government" (Hamilton, Jay, & Madison, n.d.).

Madison wrote those words in support of a Constitution that allocated to Congress the power to "regulate Commerce with foreign Nations, and among the several States, and with the Indian Tribes" and "coin Money [and] regulate the value thereof" (Article I, Section 8). This regulatory power steadily expanded as the economy grew. The U.S. Supreme Court has affirmed that the national government has the police power to protect the public health, welfare, and safety against threats posed by improper business practices (*United States v. Darby Lumber Co.*, 1941). The states had long had that police power, and this ruling ratified the national government's ability to share in it.

Rationales for Regulation

Market Failure as the Basis of Economic Regulation

Regulation of business activity has been justified from both economic and political perspectives. Six major economic rationales stand out. All reflect a concept of **market failure**: undesirable social impacts of the workings of a freely operating economy (Reagan, 1987, p. 36).

Protect Competition The first justification for regulation is that the free market cannot always maintain the competition necessary to its success. The 1980s saw massive acquisitions of one company by another across the industrial board, which have the general effect of reducing competitiveness and creating near-monopolies. If one airline, for example, operates 80 to 90 percent of the flights from a particular city, it need not offer the competitive fares it would have to offer if it had more rivals. Competitors may also engage in unfair practices, such as agreeing among themselves to fix prices of their products or services at a high level and so deprive consumers of the advantage of a free market. Thus, regulation can be justified as a way of protecting competition against the market's own destructive tendencies.

Supervise Natural Monopolies Second, regulation is deemed necessary when a particular enterprise has a natural monopoly of business in its service area. Public utilities marketing electricity, gas, and cable TV (as well as telephone service and many railroads in past decades) have been allowed to operate without competition. It would not make economic sense to have competing companies run parallel sets of electric lines to serve the same areas. If left unsupervised, however, utilities could charge whatever rates they pleased or reduce service quality. For this reason, state and national government rules allow them to be monopolies but prevent them from abusing their position.

Inform and Protect Consumers A third concern is that consumers have inadequate information to judge many products on the market. They lack the means to determine the safety of medicines, the soundness of banks, or the competence of attorneys. Government must act as a "superconsumer" on their behalf by testing those goods and services and either providing information the public needs to choose intelligently, requiring companies and professionals to act responsibly, or banning from the market what it deems unsafe.

Minimize Negative Externalities The fourth economic rationale for regulation is that businesses often produce **negative externalities**: costs of transactions that fall upon people not participating in them. Consider a chemical company that sells a product to a customer for a certain price and disposes of its toxic wastes by dumping them in a nearby river instead of paying to reprocess them. A city downstream that takes its drinking water from the river must then pay extra to purify it, a cost that is not included in the chemical's price to its buyers. Regulation mandates that producers internalize such costs, typically by paying for the safe disposal or treatment of wastes.

Protect Employees   Fifth, the market has historically taken advantage of industrial employees, seeking to pay them as little as possible and providing working conditions that were often dangerous. As these employees organized into unions, they secured contractual and legal protection against such abuses. Today employment law ranges from arbitration of labor and management disputes and antidiscrimination statutes to inspection of workplaces for hazardous conditions.

Promote Steady Economic Growth   Finally, the free market has experienced boom and bust cycles, times of high unemployment and times of high inflation. Since neither extreme is socially and politically desirable, governments have sought to level these cycles. When there is little or no growth, the Federal Reserve Board lowers interest rates to stimulate investment. When growth is fast enough to threaten inflation (a situation that developed in 1994), the board raises the costs of borrowing and thus discourages businesses from expanding. This policy assumes that a complex economy cannot pace itself and so needs some degree of central guidance.

The Political Justification for Regulation

The major political rationale shaping the regulatory landscape is the popular fear of the immense power of business enterprises. With the maturing of the industrial revolution and emergence of large banks, railroads, and manufacturers by the turn of the twentieth century, government's power was seen as necessary to equalize the balance and enable the public to hold such large companies accountable. Factory workers, for example, were at the mercy of their employers in their wages, hours, and working conditions. Protective legislation and, above all, the right to form unions, as guaranteed by Congress in 1935, redistributed that power in the workers' direction. Similarly, consumer advocates, fearing the irresponsible marketing of unsafe products, led efforts to establish the Consumer Product Safety Commission as a counterweight to business power.

Economic Regulation   Regulation has developed along two distinct paths. First came **economic regulation**, concerned with preserving competition in industries and maintaining fair prices for products and services. (This type of regulation rests directly on the concept of market failure discussed in the previous section.) The first major federal regulatory program was initiated by Congress in 1887, when it created the Interstate Commerce Commission to monitor interstate railroad pricing. This was occasioned by the U.S. Supreme Court's decision (*Wabash, St. Louis, and Pacific Railway Co. v. Illinois,* 1886) that a state could not set fares or freight rates for any portion of a train trip that crossed a state line. Rail transportation was so vital to the nation's production that a reasonable and uniform rate structure was essential. Congress realized that it could not make thousands of rate decisions itself and so assigned this task to the new commission, which was to be both expert and nonpartisan. Subsequent laws restricted the formation of monopolies and imposed controls on energy, securities trading, airlines, and trucking. These regulations are very specific to each sector of the economy.

Social Regulation   Protecting or promoting the health, safety, and opportunities of individuals who may be harmed by business practices is the concern of **social regulation**. It has an undeniable economic impact, but the benefits are targeted at the general public rather than at specific segments of the market, and the authority of the regulatory agencies thus extends to a wide range of industries. The states and local governments had long used their police powers on behalf of the public health and safety, as with building regulations. Nineteenth-century towns inspected such marketed products as hay, vinegar, and cordwood to protect consumers from fraud. An early example of federal social regulation was the Food and Drug Act of 1906, which prohibited the manufacture or interstate trade of adulterated foods.

Today the body of social regulations guarantees the safety and worth of many consumer products, oversees workplace conditions, restricts pollution of the environment, and prevents discrimination by many enterprises on the basis of race, disability, religion, age, and gender. It is concerned not with the internal structure of the industries or the prices charged for the products but with the effects of products and services on the public. The goals are broader and the means more far-reaching than with economic regulation; consequently, social regulation is more politically controversial.

Regulatory Agencies   The task of making and enforcing regulations is scattered widely throughout the national and state governments. At the federal level, the major distinction is between the regulatory agencies that are subject to direct presidential supervision (whether in the cabinet or not) and the independent regulatory commissions. Box 6.1 lists the most prominent of these federal agencies.

(continued on p. 168)

Box 6.1

Major Federal Regulatory Agencies
(with organizational position and prominent current responsibilities)

Consumer Product Safety Commission	Independent. Makes and enforces rules on the safety of selected consumer products and may ban unsafe products from sale.
Employment Standards Administration	Unit of Department of Labor. Enforces federal laws on minimum wages and maximum hours.
Environmental Protection Agency	Noncabinet agency. Enforces air and water quality laws, controls toxic substances such as pesticides, oversees cleanup of toxic waste sites.
Equal Employment Opportunity Commission	Independent. Prohibits discrimination in employment on basis of race, color, religion, gender, national origin, or disability. Investigates complaints and seeks resolution through negotiation or litigation.
Federal Aviation Administration	Unit of Department of Transportation. Makes and enforces rules on manufacture, operation, and maintenance of aircraft and use of airspace.
Federal Communications Commission	Independent. Oversees use of interstate communications by radio, television, wire, and cable. Licenses broadcasting stations.
Federal Reserve System	Independent. Oversees lending and investing activities of commercial banks and determines the cost and availability of credit. Shares bank supervision powers with Comptroller of the Currency.
Federal Trade Commission	Independent. Prevents unfair competitive business practices and mergers that would unduly restrict competition. Prevents false advertising and misleading labeling of consumer products. Requires lenders to inform borrowers of full costs of loans.
Food and Drug Administration	Unit of Department of Health and Human Services. Evaluates and approves drugs and vaccines for public use. Sets standards for food additives. Oversees safety of blood used in transfusions.
Food Safety and Inspection Service	Unit of Department of Agriculture. Inspects meat and poultry shipped in interstate commerce.
Interstate Commerce Commission	Independent. Certifies rail, highway, and water carriers in interstate transportation.
Nuclear Regulatory Commission	Independent. Makes and enforces rules on nuclear power plants and other uses of radioactive materials.
Occupational Safety and Health Administration	Unit of Department of Labor. Sets safety and health standards for workplaces and inspects them for compliance.
Office of the Comptroller of the Currency	Unit of Department of the Treasury. Supervises operations of nationally chartered banks, including establishments and mergers.
Securities and Exchange Commission	Independent. Regulates marketing of securities, including dealers and exchanges, to prevent fraud and provide investors with adequate information.

Federal Agencies

Major units directly responsible to the president include the Food and Drug Administration (in the Department of Health and Human Services), Occupational Safety and Health Administration (Labor), Federal Aviation Administration (Transportation), Food Safety and Inspection Service (Agriculture), Comptroller of the Currency (Treasury), Army Corps of Engineers (Defense), and Environmental Protection Agency (a noncabinet unit). Each is headed by a single executive who is nominated by the president and confirmed by the Senate. This executive has no set tenure and may be removed at the will of the president or the department secretary.

Each of the fifteen independent regulatory commissions (IRCs) consists of five members (except the Federal Reserve Board of Governors), also appointed by the president with Senate approval. But they serve for set terms (ranging from 5 to 14 years, depending on the agency) that expire on a staggered schedule. Thus, a president can only replace the members gradually. Furthermore, the commission must be bipartisan; no more than a simple majority can belong to one political party. A member serves as its chair at the president's pleasure (except for the chair of the Federal Reserve Board, whose term is 4 years). These features are intended to insulate the commissions' decisions from political pressures that the White House might exert. However, a president who is in office for 8 years, as Ronald Reagan was, can significantly redirect a commission with his appointments.

The Federal Reserve Board of Governors is unique among these agencies in several ways and is arguably the most powerful economic regulator. It is actually the nation's central bank, with power to expand or contract the money supply, which in turn affects business activity and the rate of growth in the overall economy. The Federal Reserve System includes twelve regional Federal Reserve banks, which function as the central banks for all the private banks in their areas. Its Board of Governors (which has seven members) sets the policies for the system, including the interest rate that member banks pay for loans from it. That rate in turn affects the interest charged for all business and personal loans. The board thereby controls the accelerator and brake pedals of the nation's economy (although these controls are by no means total).

A major issue is how independent the IRCs ought to be of political pressures from Congress and the president. Most of them are oriented to economic rather than social regulation (the Consumer Product Safety Commission is an exception), which is generally more suited to decisions made by scientific and economic data and analysis. For example, the Federal Trade Commission uses relatively objective rules to determine when a company has practiced unfair competition. On those occasions when political influ-

Box 6.2

Reinventing the Federal Aviation Administration—But How?

Many of the federal regulatory agencies are targets of strong criticism, and the Federal Aviation Administration (FAA) has taken as many hits as any. Operator of the air traffic control system, its technology is obsolete and its management style is described as unresponsive, charges coming most often from the large commercial airlines. It has had four chief administrators from 1987 through 1994, and periods of vacancies between them. As a result, the career administrators just below them have assumed real control.

The National Performance Review recommended that FAA's air traffic control functions be transferred to a government corporation. With considerable independence from the congressional budget process and detailed rules for procurement, it would be free to invest in the latest control technologies. President Clinton endorsed the change and urged Congress to adopt it. However, key lawmakers objected, fearing that a corporation would be even less responsive and that the big airlines would pressure it to cut corners on safety. Private pilots are also suspicious that their interests would be ignored by a corporation that will pay little heed to their lobbyists.

This is another episode in the continual "custody battle" over regulatory agencies between executive and legislative branches in the national government and states. It is also a contest between those advocating "professional management" of regulatory choices and those who value political oversight and accessibility of the regulators to constituent pressures.

ences shape the commissions' decisions, Congress wants its own policies to have equal weight with the president's. By contrast, the agencies charged with social regulation are largely under the president's immediate control and usually apply his policy choices more directly. Box 6.2 recounts the recent efforts to transfer the air traffic control system to a new and more independent status, as a result of political pressures from those expecting to gain or lose by it.

State and Local Agencies

The states have a similar array of regulatory agencies, with a wide variety of responsibilities. (See Box 6.3 for some typical ones.) Their regulatory power is residual, formally limited to commerce confined within their borders and such interstate trade as Congress does not choose to preempt. Yet their general police power to protect the public health, safety, and welfare gives them a great deal of room, and they are generally expanding their roles. Each state regulates the prices for electricity, natural gas, cable television, and local telephone services within its borders through a public service or commerce commission. Each has an agency to make and enforce regulations on environmental protection. During the 1980s states with politically strong consumer movements expanded their roles in such matters as sales and loan regulation, landlord/tenant rela-

---

Box 6.3

Typical State and Local Regulatory Agencies

- *California Air Resources Board.* Enforces state clean air policies and cooperates with EPA on federal Clean Air Act. (Recall its role, described in Chapter 4, in mandating electric vehicles.) Cooperates with *South Coast Air Quality Management District,* which covers the Los Angeles metropolitan area and proposed a variety of restrictions on travel and use of polluting chemicals in that basin (many of which were successfully opposed by businesses and motorists).
- *Chicago Department of Inspectional Services.* Inspects commercial and residential buildings for compliance with municipal and state codes and may bring violators into court.

- *Delaware Office of Child Care Licensing.* Not only licenses day-care centers (as do similar agencies in every other state) but also conducts required training for caregivers.
- *Minnesota Environmental Quality Board.* In 1992 adopted strict rules on the release of food products modified by genetic splicing.
- *New York City Department of Consumer Affairs.* Licenses seventy-two different kinds of businesses or operators, including video games, children's rides, sightseeing buses, motion picture projectionists, and used-car dealers, and enforces rules of conduct for licensees.

---

tions, and innovative energy pricing, as the Reagan administration reduced its activity on consumer protection (Meier, 1985, pp. 113–116). State attorneys general have been particularly active in investigating and prosecuting consumer fraud and coordinating interstate policies on it. Cities and counties have major responsibilities for regulating the use of private land and buildings, liquor sales, and restaurants.

States also regulate the entry into and practice of many occupations. This is a form of consumer protection; it assures the public that a recognized member of a profession has demonstrated a legally defined level of competence. All states regulate health professionals, accountants, attorneys, barbers and cosmetologists, real estate agents, and engineers. The most restrictive form of regulation is licensing, by which the state permits only approved persons to practice a profession. These choices are made in most states by separate commissions for each specialty, composed of members of the profession (and often chosen or nominated by the private professional association of the state). Some add "public members" to the boards to provide a consumer's perspective. California and Florida, however, have consolidated professional licensing into a single department, which is less likely to be dominated by the associations (Meier, 1985, Chapter 7).

Although this regulatory activity pervades the American economy, it does not occupy a large share of federal or state budgets.

Figure 6.1

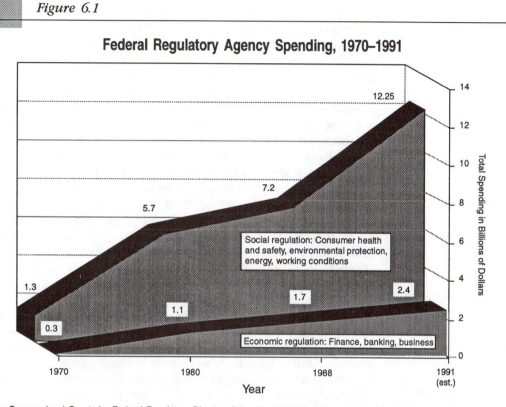

Federal Regulatory Agency Spending, 1970–1991

Social regulation: Consumer health and safety, environmental protection, energy, working conditions

Economic regulation: Finance, banking, business

Total Spending in Billions of Dollars

Year

Source: Congressional Quarterly, *Federal Regulatory Directory* (5th ed.), 1990, Washington, D.C.: CQ Publications.

Estimated spending by federal regulatory agencies in Fiscal Year 1991 was $12.25 billion. While the costs of economic regulation have not risen significantly since 1970, when the effects of inflation are cancelled out, social regulation programs grew substantially during this period.

In fiscal year 1986, an estimated 112,000 federal employees were engaged in such operations, a reduction from the 131,000 so employed in 1980. Estimated spending by federal regulatory agencies in fiscal year 1991 was $12.25 billion (see Figure 6.1). Although the costs of economic regulation have not risen significantly since 1970, when the effects of inflation are canceled out, social regulation programs grew substantially during this period.

Regulatory policymaking is intricately shared among legislators and administrators. Legislation states the purposes of the regulations and criteria to be followed, sometimes in great detail but more often in general terms. The agencies then generate the rules and standards in the necessary level of detail. The latter also have a legislative

Rule-Making Procedures

process by which they make policy decisions. Such rules have the force of law but vary in their effects. They may merely set out procedures for implementing a law already stated in sufficient detail. They are also necessary to interpret the law when new, unforeseen circumstances arise. Rules have even more effect when they prescribe how a generally stated policy will be put into effect. Often laws contain the words *reasonable, safe,* and *healthy* but give no criteria for them (Kerwin, 1994, pp. 5–6). Rule making sometimes has large spaces to fill in; after Congress passed the Americans with Disabilities Act in 1990, hundreds of rules had to be written to define compliance by employers, schools, health care facilities, and many other organizations that serve the disabled.

The rules that constitute economic and social regulation are so numerous and the publicity focused on them is so scant that there is danger that they could be made arbitrarily and be unfair to many. In some years federal agencies have issued as many as 7,000 new rules; this compares with about 300 annual acts of Congress (Bryner, 1987, p. 10). States, counties, and cities add substantial numbers of regulations for their own jurisdictions.

If regulatory activity is to be accountable to the public, accountability procedures must be open and recognized. Congress mandated such a means in the Administrative Procedures Act (APA) of 1946 and has amended this act several times. All states have enacted similar legislation, and so the following procedures, except for review by the Office of Management and Budget, are observed in broad outline there as well (Renfrow & Houston, 1987). Since rule making is an extension of legislative activity, the lawmakers naturally want to maintain some controls on it.

Under the APA, agencies may take regulatory action by two means. First, **adjudication** is a proceeding in which an agency makes a distinct ruling on each case before it. This is used more for economic than for social regulation, as these types were defined earlier in the chapter. Adjudication occurs when the Federal Communications Commission considers renewing the license of a radio or television station or when the Federal Trade Commission alleges that a company used deceptive advertising. The proceeding may be informal if the company involved does not dispute the facts of the case. But if the agency's decision is challenged, the proceeding is conducted like a court trial, with evidence presented by the parties to the case, and is presided over by an administrative law judge. The judge provides findings and conclusions to the commission, which issues a final order to resolve the dispute.

The Rule-Making Process

Of increasing importance today is the second means, **rule making**, which is the formulation of general regulations applicable to many

(continued on p. 174)

Figure 6.2

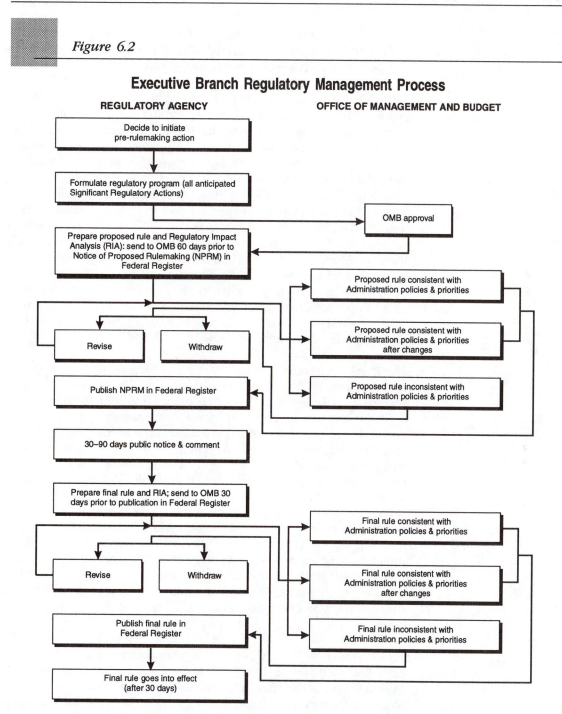

Executive Branch Regulatory Management Process

REGULATORY AGENCY **OFFICE OF MANAGEMENT AND BUDGET**

Decide to initiate
pre-rulemaking action

↓

Formulate regulatory program (all anticipated
Significant Regulatory Actions)

OMB approval

↓

Prepare proposed rule and Regulatory Impact
Analysis (RIA): send to OMB 60 days prior to
Notice of Proposed Rulemaking (NPRM) in
Federal Register

Proposed rule consistent with
Administration policies & priorities

Revise   Withdraw

Proposed rule consistent with
Administration policies & priorities
after changes

Publish NPRM in Federal Register

Proposed rule inconsistent with
Administration policies & priorities

↓

30–90 days public notice & comment

↓

Prepare final rule and RIA; send to OMB 30
days prior to publication in Federal Register

Final rule consistent with
Administration policies & priorities

Revise   Withdraw

Final rule consistent with
Administration policies & priorities
after changes

Publish final rule in
Federal Register

Final rule inconsistent with
Administration policies & priorities

↓

Final rule goes into effect
(after 30 days)

Source: U.S. General Accounting Office, *Regulatory Review: Information on OMB's Review Process,* 1989.

Federal agencies are required by the Administrative Procedures Act and recent executive orders to follow a detailed schedule for many kinds of rule making.

similar situations. The basic path of federal rule making consists of a number of waypoints as mandated by the APA and recent executive orders, which are summarized in Figure 6.2.

Setting the Agenda   The current procedures are set forth in Executive Order 12866, issued by President Clinton in 1993. First, each regulatory agency under the president's direct control (this does not include the independent commissions) must submit to the Office of Management and Budget a regulatory program listing actions that are either under way or planned. Intended to increase the president's oversight powers, this procedure also allows him to speed or block a process of special concern to him. This agenda is published in the *Federal Register* as the Unified Agenda of Federal Regulations. The independent commissions have chosen to publish their agendas there as well. The *Federal Register,* a daily publication of the federal government, lists all proposed and final rules issued by agencies as well as general notices on many subjects. It is sent to all depositories of government documents around the country, and many law offices and government agencies subscribe to it. It is also available on the Internet.

The Draft Regulation   Second, the administrators draft a proposed rule and publish it in the *Federal Register*. The typical rule is in precise legal language and is often quite long, which makes it difficult for any but specialists to grasp its meaning. The notice must also state the legal basis of the regulation, the issues that require it, and opportunities for people to gain more information about it and to comment on it. Often a public hearing is scheduled at which individuals can respond. The notice must list its place, date, and time.

Prior to publishing this proposed rule, agencies under the president's control must send the text to the Office of Information and Regulatory Affairs of the Office of Management and Budget. Agencies must show, after a cost/benefit analysis of major rules, that the rule will yield benefits that exceed its costs to the government and the private sector. Depending on its judgment of the cost/benefit analysis, the OMB may order a delay in publication to seek revisions.

Public Hearings   The third step is a waiting period of at least 30 days. During this time, interested parties may submit written or oral evidence and arguments. If there is serious opposition, it is likely to emerge at this time. Public hearings are required by law for some categories of rules. These are ordinarily attended only by attorneys and other specialists representing the regulated businesses, although outside groups can legally obtain public documents pertaining to the rule making. News reports on hearings are rare, although cer-

(continued on p. 176)

Box 6.4

Concluding Section of Final Rule on Definition of "Healthy" in Food Labeling

PART 101—FOOD LABELING

Section 101.65 is amended by adding new paragraphs (d)(2) through (d)(4) to read as follows:

§ 101.65 Implied nutrient content claims and related label statements.

(d) (2) The term "healthy" or any derivative of the term "healthy," such as "health," "healthful," "healthfully," "healthfulness," "healthier," healthiest," "healthily," and "healthiness" may be used on the label or in labeling of a food, other than raw single ingredient seafood or game meat products, main dish products as defined in § 101.13(m), and meal products as defined in § 101.13(l), as an implied nutrient content claim to denote foods that are useful in constructing a diet that is consistent with dietary recommendations provided that:

(i) The food meets the definition of "low" for fat and saturated fat;

(ii)(A) The food has a reference amount customarily consumed greater than 30 grams (g) or greater than 2 tablespoons and, before January 1, 1998, contains 480 milligrams (mg) sodium or less per reference amount customarily consumed, per labeled serving; or

(B) The food has a reference amount customarily consumed of 30 g or less or 2 tablespoons or less and, before January 1, 1998, contains 480 mg sodium or less per 50 g (for dehydrated foods that must be reconstituted before typical consumption with water or a diluent containing an insignificant amount as defined in §101.9 (f)(1), of all nutrients per reference amount customarily consumed, the per 50 g criterion refers to the "as prepared" form):

(C)(1) The food has a reference amount customarily consumed greater than 30 g or greater than 2 tablespoons and, after January 1, 1998, contains 360 mg sodium or less per reference amount customarily consumed, per labeled serving; or

(2) The food has a reference amount customarily consumed of 30 g or less or 2 tablespoons or less and, after January 1, 1998, contains 360

mg sodium or less per 50 g (for dehydrated foods that must be reconstituted before typical consumption with water or a diluent containing an insignificant amount as defined in §101.9 (f)(1), of all nutrients per reference amount customarily consumed, the per 50 g criterion refers to the "as prepared" form);

(iii) Cholesterol is not present at a level exceeding the disclosure level as described in § 101.13(h);

(iv) The food, other than a raw fruit or vegetable, contains at least 10 percent of the Reference Daily Intake (RDI) or Daily Reference Value (DRV) per reference amount customarily consumed, per labeled serving of vitamin A, vitamin C, calcium, iron, protein, or fiber;

(v) Where compliance with paragraph (d)(2)(iv) of this section is based on a nutrient that has been added to the food, that fortification is in accordance with the policy on fortification of foods in § 104.20 of this chapter; and

(vi) The food complies with definitions and declaration requirements established in part 101 of this chapter for any specific nutrient content claim on the label or in labeling.

(3) The term "healthy" or its derivatives may be used on the label or in labeling of raw, single ingredient seafood or game meat as an implied nutrient content claim provided that:

(i) The food contains less than 5 g total fat, less than 2 g saturated fat, and less than 95 mg cholesterol per reference amount customarily consumed and per 100 g;

(ii)(A) The food has a reference amount customarily consumed greater than 30 g or greater than 2 tablespoons and, before January 1, 1998, contains 480 mg sodium or less per reference amount customarily consumed, per labeled serving; or

(B) The food has a reference amount customarily consumed of 30 g or less or 2 tablespoons or less and, before January 1, 1998, contains 480 mg sodium or less per 50 g (for dehydrated foods that must be reconstituted before typical consumption with water or a diluent containing an insignificant amount as defined in § 101.9(f)(1), of all nutrients per reference amount customarily consumed, the per 50 g criterion refers to the "as prepared" form);

(C)(*1*) The food has a reference amount customarily consumed greater than 30 g or greater than 2 tablespoons and, after January 1, 1998, contains 360 mg sodium or less per reference amount customarily consumed, per labeled serving; or

(*2*) The food has a reference amount customarily consumed of 30 g or less or 2 tablespoons or less and, after January 1, 1998, contains 360 mg sodium or less per 50 g (for dehydrated foods that must be reconstituted before typical consumption with water or a diluent containing an insignificant amount as defined in § 101.9(f)(1), of all nutrients per reference amount customarily consumed, the per 50 g criterion refers to the "as prepared" form);

(iii) The food contains at least 10 percent of the RDI or DRV per reference amount customarily consumed, per labeled serving of vitamin A, vitamin C, calcium, iron, protein, or fiber;

(iv) Where compliance with paragraph (d)(3)(iii) of this section is based on a nutrient that has been added to the food, that fortification is in accordance with the policy on fortification of foods in § 104.20 of this chapter; and

(v) The food complies with definitions and declaration requirements established in this part for any specific nutrient content claim on the label or in labeling.

(4) The term "healthy" or its derivatives may be used on the label or in labeling of main dish products, as defined in § 101.13(m), and meal products, as defined in § 101.13(l) as an implied nutrient content claim provided that:

(i) The food meets the definition of "low" for fat and saturated fat;

(ii)(A) Before January 1, 1998, sodium is not present at a level exceeding 600 mg per labeled serving, or

(B) After January 1, 1998, sodium is not present at a level exceeding 480 mg per labeled serving;

(iii) Cholesterol is not present at a level exceeding 90 mg per labeled serving;

(iv) The food contains at least 10 percent of the RDI or DRV per labeled serving of two (for main dish products) or three (for meal products) of the following nutrients—vitamin A, vitamin C, calcium, iron, protein, or fiber;

(v) Where compliance with paragraph (d)(4)(iv) of this section is based on a nutrient that has been added to the food, that fortification is in accordance with the policy on fortification of foods in § 104.20 of this chapter; and

(vi) The food complies with definitions and declaration requirements established in this part for any specific nutrient content claim on the label or in labeling.

Dated: April 29, 1994.

David A. Kessler,
Commissioner of Food and Drugs
Donna E. Shalala,
Secretary of Health and Human Services
Federal Register, May 10, 1994

---

tain interest groups may publicize them to their members when they have a special concern.

At the end of this waiting period, the agency decides whether it will adopt the rule as drafted, modify its proposal, or delay further action. In the second alternative, it repeats the second and third steps. If the opposition is strong enough or if sufficient new problems arise with the rule, delay may be necessary for further research and/or negotiation. These steps often consume 3 to 4 years in producing major rules, because of their complexity and lack of agreement among influential interests. In several cases, agencies have allowed the contending parties to arrive at rules by negotiation among themselves, a practice that probably shortened the time required and increased their acceptance (Perritt, 1986).

Publishing the Rule   Only when the agency finally agrees on the proposed rule does it take the fourth step: The rule is published again in the *Federal Register*, along with a summary of its basis and purpose and the agency's response to the issues raised during the public participation stage. Box 6.4 contains the concluding section of a long rule in which the Food and Drug Administration clarified the standards that food products must meet before they can be advertised as "healthy." It was a response to companies' widespread use of that term to attract buyers seeking lower fat or lower sodium. Since there were no accepted standards for these substances, consumers could be misled by some labels.

A total of 30 days must elapse before the new rule goes into effect, unless its urgency requires that it be put into effect immediately. This is intended to allow time for all parties to be informed and to get answers to last-minute questions. At some point in the following year, the rule is added to the *Code of Federal Regulations,* a compilation of all current rules of federal agencies, published in fifty separate titles according to subject.

Advance notice of the final rule must also be sent to the Office of Management and Budget (OMB), which can recommend delay or withdrawal. The OMB has actually delayed or modified very few proposed or final rules, but agencies have taken care to comply with its views in the earlier stages. As a result, the OMB's influence over making regulations has grown steadily over the years, reducing the effects of the APA provisions for public access.

Enforcement: Procedures and Conflicts

After the regulation is decided, the agency must enforce its provisions. If it finds evidence of criminal wrongdoing, it must rely on the Department of Justice to prosecute the suspected offender. Since regulations are intended to prohibit conduct that would otherwise take place, this is a particularly challenging task, especially when the number of businesses regulated is large and the rules may be evaded easily. For example, the Food and Drug Administration is responsible for inspecting many thousands of food processing companies to ensure the safety of their products. However, it performed fewer than 20,000 inspections in 1988, compared with almost 33,000 in 1980. The General Accounting Office found that, as of late 1989, the FDA was visually checking only 9 percent of the foods imported into the U.S. and testing only 1 percent of them for contamination. Budget cuts in the 1980s reduced the number of inspectors while the demands on them rose (Hilts, 1989).

A party that chooses to contest a rule, order, or enforcement action may, unless Congress has specified otherwise in the agency's statutes, remove the dispute to a federal district court. Agencies assume that a controversial rule will not be final until full approval by the courts is granted. The application of the rule may even be deferred until final rulings are in hand. Courts are increasingly willing to take such cases and to examine both the substance of the decision and the fairness of the procedure by which it was reached. This means of holding the adjudication and rule-making processes accountable to the courts is of major importance to a society that is concerned about arbitrary use of administrative power and invasion of personal rights. Yet there is no guarantee that scattered court decisions will provide greater rationality or order to the regulatory process. The criteria that judges use in these cases may conflict with those employed by the agencies. Thus, those regulatory policies on which courts have issued rulings may lack internal consistency.

These regulatory proceedings assume that decisions can be made according to objective standards with no yielding to personal or political bias. In an effort to minimize regulators' arbitrariness, Congress often mandates decision criteria that include medical, technological, and economic data. Some laws require participation by scientific advisory bodies and review committees. For example, before it can issue any rule on a product suspected of causing cancer, birth defects, or genetic mutations, the Consumer Product Safety Commission must submit its evidence to a Chronic Hazard Advisory Panel made up of scientists.

Some requirements for scientific support of rules are very stringent. Congress, in its 1958 Delaney Amendment to the Food, Drug, and Cosmetic Act, ordered the FDA to ban any food additive that causes cancer in humans or animals, no matter how slight the statistical risk appears to be. This, of course, is an unrealistic standard, since proof of "zero risk" is scientifically impossible. Many other laws simply call for the agency to avoid "unreasonable adverse effects" or balance the risks against the costs of reducing them. Some of the delay in rule making is due to the time required to obtain evidence for credible scientific and economic judgments. These evaluations are often not as objective as they appear, since reliable data may be unavailable and the facts can be interpreted in differing ways. The causes of cancer are still in dispute among those best acquainted with it, and experts may disagree strongly over whether to label a given chemical, used at a particular concentration, as carcinogenic. This opens the door to personal biases and interest group pressures to resolve the uncertainty, despite the fact that inaction on a difficult issue is often politically safest.

Rule making and adjudication often become adversarial processes, focused on who wins and loses, rather than a mutual search for the greatest net public advantage. To determine whether a particular health or safety risk should be taken and by whom is unavoidably a political choice. Several issues are central to the politics of regulation: the relative power of groups that influence regulation, including average citizens; the oversight exercised by chief executives and legislators; relationships among national, state, and local governments; and the efforts needed to maximize compliance with the rules.

The Politics of
Regulation

Public Notice: Secrecy vs. Participation

Despite the legal requirements of public notice, hearings, and response time, most rules are made behind closed doors with scant input from those they will affect. "Some administrative officials seem to have a natural instinct to protect agency operations from public view by unnecessarily classifying material and functions from public scrutiny, thereby avoiding uninvited headaches" (Warren, 1988, p. 271). A 1979 U.S. Senate study of participants in rule-making hearings indicated very infrequent presence of organized public interest representatives (cited by Bryner, 1987, p. 38). In general, participation is lowest when issues are complex and have little apparent impact on the general public; regulations on banking, insurance, and securities trading are in this category.

This low participation rate is due partly to the fact that the Administrative Procedures Act permits many proceedings considered "informal" to be conducted privately. The rule makers consult only with certain representatives but do not allow the same access to others who are also affected by the rules. To follow all the public participation standards adds costs and time to an already complex and expensive process, and rule makers may wish to avoid them. One of the few federal agencies to promote major involvement by citizens is the Federal Communications Commission. Community organizations, particularly those with religious and civil rights interests, have shaped many decisions on the award and renewal of radio and television station licenses (Longley, Terry, & Krasnow, 1983).

The cost of participation for outside groups is also high. Some level of legal or technical expertise is usually necessary for effective participation. To refute the claims of an agency or another party to the proceedings requires evidence that is not readily obtainable—for example, about the carcinogenic properties of a chemical or the profits of a telephone company. The time of attorneys and scientific consultants must ordinarily be bought, and such services are expensive. On the other hand, the industries, professional groups, and trade associations with considerable profit at stake can readily invest the sums necessary for representation. A few public agencies have subsidized the appearance of groups that could not afford these costs, believing their evidence essential to represent important constituencies.

Government Regulation and Business Interests

The business interests that are subject to regulation have long exerted influence on the agencies. The strongest expression of this is the "capture" theory, which holds that an industry can exert so much influence on the agency regulating it that it prevents imposition of any rule that it opposes. After World War I, the railroads put aside their antagonism toward the Interstate Commerce Commission and developed a close relationship with it. In return for their political support, which helped maintain its independence from other parts of the government, the commission shifted to a more benign regulatory posture. This compromised its objectivity so much that, in the judgment of some scholars, it forfeited its right to exist as a separate agency (Huntington, 1952). The Nuclear Regulatory Commission has been investigated numerous times by Congress for giving favored treatment to the nuclear power industry. Often the commission members are appointed from the very companies they regulate and to which they expect to return after their terms expire. Capture is less likely in those agencies within cabinet departments, however, since their hierarchies are responsible to a broader array of interests. President Reagan was compelled by public pressures to alter the passive stance toward polluters that he had ordered the Environmental Protection Agency to take early in his administration.

Since regulatory issues have increased in political importance in the 1980s, presidents have taken more interest in the content of rules. President Reagan, who had promised in his election campaign to reduce the regulatory burden on business, directed (in Executive Order 12291) that new rules be subject to rigorous analysis to ensure that they would not impose excessive costs or have an adverse effect on the economy. Executive Order 12498 (January 1985) first mandated the review of proposed rules by the Office of Management and Budget. By 1988 one could conclude that OMB review had reinforced a long-term trend toward increased presidential power (Cooper & West, 1988). This is a clear response to the growth of administrative discretion, in which the president has reasserted his constitutional power as chief executive.

President Clinton continued this central monitoring of rule making, modified only in minor details by Executive Order 12866. The experience with it to date suggests that the regulatory agencies have been given greater discretion, as fewer rules have actually been reviewed by OMB. However, the White House retains the ability

■ *Box 6.5*

How Do We Warn Smokers?

Although information on the health hazards of tobacco was first published in 1939, the federal government did not take any action to warn smokers until 1964. In that year, relying on convincing data from the Surgeon General's Advisory Committee on Smoking and Health, the Federal Trade Commission (FTC) issued a rule requiring all cigarette packages and advertising to carry a clear warning of danger. Congress, prodded by an outraged tobacco industry and its own sense that this action went beyond FTC's authority, immediately asked it to delay the implementation date, to which it agreed. In 1965 Congress enacted its own requirement of a less obvious and threatening warning on cigarette packages only and temporarily revoked FTC's authority to make rules for tobacco.

Evidence on the risks of smoking continued to accumulate, along with pressures to provide more than a tiny warning label. In 1970, after the Federal Communications Commission proposed to ban cigarette advertising from radio and television, Congress enacted that ban itself. The FTC pressed the lawmakers to extend the health warning to printed advertising, but in 1971 most tobacco companies voluntarily agreed to add the warning labels. When the FTC concluded that the first labels were not sufficiently "clear and conspicuous," it ordered a revision, with which the companies complied in 1972 (Fritschler, 1989).

Antismoking laws and regulations multiplied in the ensuing years as the political resistance of the tobacco industry was overcome by health interests and the concerns of the general public. Although the regulatory commissions often took the lead in proposing rules, Congress guarded its own right to set the pace of this development. This is too sensitive an area of regulation to leave to an appointed agency.

(and the political incentives) to intervene in any regulatory choices that could cause serious controversy (Cushman, 1993).

Congress, concerned that agencies do not exceed the authority given them and that rules do not conflict with legislators' unwritten intentions, pays close attention to regulatory actions. It can immediately reverse any action by legislation and reduce an agency's rulemaking authority as long as the president does not successfully veto it. Box 6.5 illustrates Congress's role well. Since the 1970s it has increasingly written detailed requirements into regulatory legislation. It has also imposed tight deadlines on agencies for their rule making, which make it difficult for them to do necessary research, analysis, and coordination on technical issues.

The Regulatory Tangle: Agencies with Overlapping Powers

Regulatory choices are greatly complicated by the involvement of two or more agencies or levels of government. Under the Constitution, Congress has power to regulate interstate commerce, and there is little commercial activity today that is not potentially subject to such oversights. Thus, Congress can preempt state regulation over any issue it judges to be "interstate" and displace existing state rules. However, it has often turned back part of its authority to the states. In the Occupational Safety and Health Act, Congress permits a state to take control of inspection and enforcement of workplaces if it submits a plan for doing so and maintains federal standards. This poses important problems for both levels: The states must enforce rules they did not enact, and the federal Occupational Safety and Health Administration (OSHA) cannot completely control the programs entrusted to it. Moreover, OSHA may be unable to detect quickly or remedy lapses in state implementation.

Compliance with Rules: The Enforcement Dilemma

The final political issue is the extent to which the regulated businesses comply with the rules. The earlier discussion of the Food and Drug Administration's inability to inspect food processing companies with any frequency highlights a basic fact of life for regulators: They must rely on a high degree of voluntary compliance. If food processors relaxed their cleanliness standards the minute after the inspector's annual visit, the entire effort would fail.

Regulators must take care to communicate the rules clearly to affected parties. State and local agencies monitoring child care centers in large cities have hundreds of caregivers under their authority. When a standard is changed (perhaps regarding some feature of the facility's bathrooms), each center's operator must be informed. Because facilities differ, one caregiver's action to comply will not be the same as another's. The agency must give clear answers to questions and must sometimes inspect a facility to determine whether the rule is understood.

Strict enforcement of a rule in one situation can be a salutary warning to others of the cost of noncompliance. But in another situation it may arouse political opposition that appeals to the head(s) of the agency or to higher authority and results in changing the rule. One small firm, fined for mishandling toxic chemicals, is no threat to a federal or state pollution control agency. But a large company can easily enlist allies and fight back with a good chance of reducing or avoiding the penalty.

This is not to say that "good" regulations are simply those that will be observed and that unenforceable ones are "bad." But the strategies and costs of enforcement must be built into the agency's plan of operations. If some manufacturers choose to dump their wastes illegally rather than to pay the high costs of legal disposal, the regulation can become a dead letter. If the penalty for violations is low, even getting caught is no deterrent. A company will prefer to pay a $1,000 fine rather than to pay a $10,000 processing fee. If the inspection staff is inadequate to monitor disposal sites or unable to gather evidence on "midnight dumpers," these facts must shape the rule making in some way. If an agency cannot devote adequate resources to enforcement, the regulation itself may not be justified.

Political favoritism is a frequent cause of uneven enforcement. City and county building inspectors must certify that a home, office, or factory is fit for occupancy and that its plumbing, electrical, and other systems are safe. If not, the owner is ordered to make improvements to comply with the building code. Such building inspection in many cities is closely intertwined with the city's political structure. For example, Department of Inspectional Services personnel in Chicago are responsible for enforcing the standards written in state and municipal law and may take violators to court. Not surprisingly, they have been repeatedly accused of lax and biased enforcement and of outright bribe taking from politically favored constituents (Jones, 1984). This means that homes and workplaces are less safe than the lawmakers intended. Local regulation of this nature is often more susceptible to personal influence than at national and state levels because of inspectors' continuous face-to-face relationships within communities.

Governments are legally bound by their own regulations but do not always follow them. The Defense and Energy Departments are the nation's largest polluters in their handling of radioactive and toxic materials but have resisted efforts of the Environmental Protection Agency to inspect their facilities and secure their compliance with the standards that industry must follow. Moreover, state and local regulators have had no success with them, since they cannot sue the federal government without its consent. However, 1989 saw several enforcement actions begun after a steady buildup of congressional and environmentalist pressure. Three managers at the Army Proving Ground in Aberdeen, Maryland, were sentenced to probation for illegal handling of hazardous wastes. The Nuclear Regulatory Commission fined the Air Force $102,500 for mishandling radioactive materials at its Wright-Patterson base in Ohio. The Pentagon argues that such controls by federal and state agencies could hamper its national security mission, although it has changed many of its chemical-handling procedures to comply with the laws (Morrison, 1989).

The governmental decisions described in this chapter pose difficult problems for the average citizen who is concerned about what those decisions are and how they are made. Public access to this information is guaranteed only at certain stages of rule making, and even this presents major obstacles to those without skilled legal and technical advice. Most other decisions are simply part of administrative routines, and the public learns about them only when it happens to feel their effects. To be sure, these actions are probably taken under proper legal authority 99 percent of the time, yet their high level of detail can at times determine whether or not a business survives. A marginally profitable small business may find that its fate depends on rules its managers never heard of and cannot afford to comply with. While citizens have many means by which to participate in the policymaking described in Chapter 5, they have few opportunities where regulation is concerned, and the tools available are harder to use.

Deregulation and Its Consequences

Deregulation dominated the regulatory agenda of the 1980s. The list of administrative rules and regulations had grown rapidly in the previous two decades, particularly the social regulation described earlier. But as inflation worsened in the mid-1970s and the economy slumped, a growing number of observers blamed these rules. Business interests complained of paperwork and compliance costs for which they could see no compensating benefits. The Ford administration studied reductions of regulations in the airline, trucking, and railroad industries, all of which Congress later enacted with President Carter's support. The lawmakers also planted a time bomb in the form of the 1980 and 1982 legislation that lifted many of the rules under which savings and loan institutions operated.

The Reagan administration had two principal aims with regard to regulation. First, it promoted regulatory reform by centralizing rule-making review in the White House and applying economic standards to determining the rules' desirability. Second, it sought to reduce existing regulations deemed unnecessary or burdensome; this is the deregulation thrust (Eisner, 1993, p. 170). This second purpose also was evident in relaxed enforcement of existing regulations. Reduction of the inspection resources of the Food and Drug Administration has already been mentioned in this chapter. Fewer new rules were adopted because of the additional screening they received from the Office of Management and Budget. The number of published rules in the first 40 months of President Reagan's term was 33,364, contrasted with 43,247 in the last 40 months of the Carter administration (West & Cooper, 1985, p. 206). This was in part due to stronger encouragement of self-regulation in industries to avoid government imposition of standards.

The results of the reform and deregulation efforts satisfied neither their advocates nor their opponents. Public pressure compelled the Reagan administration to enforce the workplace safety and environmental protection rules more diligently after the news media publicized lapses in enforcement. The most successful deregulation, perhaps, has been the removal of restrictions on fares and service of airlines, trucking, and railroads. No major company now favors their restoration. The Civil Aeronautics Board, which was responsible for airline market rules, ceased to exist. Competition is strong in some markets, although limited in others because of mergers of previously competing carriers (Gerston, Fraleigh, & Schwab, 1988). Concerns about air travel safety continue, but rules in that area have become more stringent and have continued under the authority of the Federal Aviation Administration.

Deregulation has also been blamed for the disasters in the savings and loan industry that began in 1989. In 1980 and 1982 Congress gave these "thrift" institutions freedom to raise the interest rates they could pay depositors and to choose investments they could make with their funds. Historically, they had placed their depositors' savings in home mortgages, which were reasonably safe. But to pay the higher interest that would lure more deposits, many invested in speculative real estate ventures and high-interest (and high-risk) "junk bonds."

The real estate and junk bond markets slumped in the late 1980s. Many thrifts found that their investments were worth less than their deposits and so went into default. Deposits under $100,000 were insured by the Federal Savings and Loan Insurance Corporation, so the federal government had to take control of them and make good the savers' money. Although many operators of savings and loans were irresponsible and some violated criminal statutes, there was also a lapse by federal and state regulators in detecting and stopping such risky choices. It was to many observers a symbol of the failure of deregulation.

The Bush administration kept the Reagan reforms but presented a contradictory face on regulation. On the one hand, the president signed several bills that greatly increased the regulatory burden, notably the Americans with Disabilities, the Clean Air, and the Nutrition Labeling and Education Acts. The volume of new rules increased sharply. On the other hand, he established the Competitiveness Council, headed by Vice President Quayle, to extend his authority over rule making. In its short life, it blocked or eased a number of proposed rules that major business interests opposed.

President Clinton's modification of the Reagan/Bush procedures in 1993 gave the federal agencies more autonomy in rule making. He eliminated the Competitiveness Council but gave Vice President Gore broad responsibility for the rule-making process. The Office of Management and Budget may still review proposed regulations but is not expected to intervene as often as it had before. This was a reaction to the practice under his predecessor, in which secret business lobbying through the Competitiveness Council apparently reversed agency actions. Agency rule making requires that such lobbying be on the public record in order to reduce secrecy and improper pressure (Cushman, 1993).

Deregulation of some sectors of the economy is still under way. For example, the steady growth in telecommunications technology opens doors to many corporations to participate. Rules issued decades ago by the Federal Communications Commission and other agencies restricted telephone companies from expanding into new markets. However, this is changing: Old limits are being dropped, and this industry is increasingly free to transform its organization and business methods to match its new technological opportunities.

Regulation on the International Scale

The growing volume of international trade and global environmental effects of industrial development has put cooperative regulation on the agendas of all nations. When Congress agreed in 1994 to U.S. membership in the World Trade Organization, it committed the nation to an extensive body of rules, many of them still to be developed. The North American Free Trade Agreement (NAFTA) embodies yet more regulations. Many federal agencies participate in these actions, and state governments have a share.

The issue of child labor poses unique dilemmas for American regulators. Much of that was eliminated in this country early in the twentieth century, but such nations as India, Colombia, and China export carpets and clothing made by children as young as seven. Congress has considered both barring the import of products made with child labor and pressuring those nations to enforce their own child protection laws. This issue is made more difficult by mislabeling of products and by the fact that children who are prevented from working may well be forced into begging, if not starvation.

The U.S. border with Mexico also is the scene of regulatory issues. NAFTA created two joint agencies to deal with cross-border pollution: the North American Development Bank and the Border Environmental Cooperation Commission. One focus of concern is coal-fired power plants on the Mexican side of the border that emit much more sulfur dioxide than U.S. rules permit. Federal, state, and local officials of both nations also formed a regional air quality management authority to reduce the pollution that plagues Ciudad Juarez, Mexico, and its neighbor, El Paso, Texas. The nearly 2 million residents of this metropolitan area breathe some of the dirtiest air in North America, much of it from factories that operate under lenient and poorly enforced Mexican laws. Large investments in new technologies and diligent enforcement will be necessary on both sides of the border to achieve much progress (Bryce, 1994).

Summary

Regulation is defined as the process by which government requires or prohibits certain actions by individuals and institutions, mostly private but sometimes governmental, through the efforts of specially designated regulatory agencies. Governments undertake regulation to serve specific public purposes, which require that some activities by businesses be limited to protect the markets and well-being of other businesses and citizens in general. Several concepts of "market failure" are used to justify most regulations, joined with the political motivation to limit the exercise of economic power by large private enterprises. We can distinguish economic regulation, oriented to fair competition and pricing in the market, from social regulation, which is intended to protect the health, safety, and opportunities of citizens in general.

Many federal and state agencies make and enforce rules on various segments of the economy. Those directly under the control of the chief executive constitute one form, which emphasizes social regulation. The second form is the regulatory commission or board, which functions with some degree of independence from the executive and acts primarily in the realm of economic regulation.

Agencies regulate either by adjudicating, in which they apply standards on a case-by-case basis in a similar manner to courts, or by making rules that apply to many similar cases. In rule making, they follow a procedure designed to give the public advance notice of the action and an opportunity to express its views. Both procedures must be conducted in public, and the results of either can be appealed in the courts in case of disagreement.

Political power and influence shape regulatory outcomes. The extent of public participation and influence is generally small compared with that of the businesses that are directly affected, which raises questions of fairness and balance. Both executives and legislators seek to oversee and occasionally check the work of regulators, injecting their policy and political agendas. Separate governments often share regulatory tasks, posing additional problems of coordination. It is also necessary to plan carefully for enforcement, since the regulated businesses usually have motives and incentives for avoiding compliance with the rules.

The federal regulatory burden was reduced somewhat during the 1980s, particularly in transportation and financial institutions. Although the former has been fairly well received, the deregulation of savings and loan associations has proved a fiscal disaster.

Demands are increasing for the United States to coordinate its regulatory activities with those of other nations, particularly in the fields of trade and environmental protection. This requires a political process that is open to international influences and a global perspective.

Discussion Questions

1. To what extent can the placement of polluting and hazardous facilities in areas inhabited by the poor and people of color be blamed on government regulators? What could these residents have done to prevent it?

2. If the market can fail to operate properly, as regulators assume, can government also fail in its remedies of those shortcomings? Explain how this can happen.

3. Why does social regulation generally encounter more political conflict than economic regulation?

4. In what ways do businesses benefit from government regulation?

5. What conflicts are likely to arise when two or more agencies or units of government share regulation over a particular activity?

Analytical Exercises

1. An important regulatory process at the local level controls buildings and the use of land. Building codes, land use plans, and zoning maps specify the rules and are readily obtainable in city and county offices. Some cities are very strict on what they will allow to be built. Others have only lenient regulation. Summarize these rules for the place in which you live or attend school.

2. Choose a typical occupation with which you are familiar, such as restaurant operator, bank manager, dairy farmer, realtor, building contractor, health professional, or child caregiver. Identify the rules of federal, state, and local government with which an individual must comply in that occupation. Note also any conflicts and ambiguities in these regulations.

For Further Reading

Bryner, G. C. (1987). *Bureaucratic Discretion: Law and Policy in Federal Regulatory Agencies.* New York: Pergamon. Analysis of the use of discretion by federal regulatory officials, with case studies of four agencies.

Eisner, M. A. (1993). *Regulatory Politics in Transition.* Baltimore: Johns Hopkins University Press. Describes how U.S. regulatory policy developed in response to changing demands of the economy and society.

Fritschler, A. L. (1989). *Smoking and Politics: Policy-Making and the Federal Bureaucracy* (4th ed.). Englewood Cliffs, NJ: Prentice Hall. Very readable exploration of the interdependence of Congress and federal regulatory agencies regarding the touchy issues of regulating tobacco advertising and warning the public of the hazards of smoking.

Gerston, L. N., Fraleigh, C., & Schwab, R. (1988). *The Deregulated Society.* Belmont, CA: Brooks/Cole. Surveys the mixed results from the deregulation efforts of the late 1970s and 1980s, with several case studies.

Kerwin, C. (1994). *Rulemaking: How Government Agencies Write Law and Make Policy.* Washington, DC: CQ Press. The intricate process of writing and interpreting the rules that govern business activity.

7

Public/Private Administrative Relationships

Learning Objectives

After reading this chapter, you should be able to do the following:
1. Explain why privatization has attracted so much interest in the 1990s.
2. Identify and define the several forms of public/private cooperation and the reasons for using each.
3. Describe the procedure for contracting for goods and services.
4. Describe the arguments for and against increased use of private-sector organizations in providing public services.

American public schools are in the forefront of the "reinvention" movement. Parents and employers alike are unhappy with lower achievement test scores, increasing disorder, and resistance to change among professional school administrators. Many are convinced that the direction to go is to provide many alternative choices among schools, which must then compete for students and so will improve their offerings. Public education would thus become part of the market economy.

Private schooling is deeply rooted in American culture, dating from the years when the only schools were operated by churches, parents, and voluntary associations. Government-run education was an innovation of the nineteenth century, when industry needed literate workers and the nation had to Americanize its new immigrants. Now public schools have a near-monopoly on education in most communities and are the only realistic choice for most low-income and rural families.

One current movement is to expand elementary and secondary schooling choices for all students, using a combination of public and private options. Ten states (as of 1994) allow parents and teachers to establish "charter schools," with more freedom to experiment with management and curriculums than other public schools have. In a way this creates a public network of schools that would otherwise be private in character. The schools get state aid in proportion to the number of students who enroll, as well as start-up funds and technical assistance. The Goals 2000 legislation passed by Congress in 1994 provides federal endorsement of such schools as well.

Public school management is also a fertile field for privatization. For example, Educational Alternatives, Inc., a for-profit firm, operates public schools in Baltimore, Hartford, and Miami Beach; in 1989 Boston University undertook to renew the school system in Chelsea, Massachusetts, and has had a marked impact to date; and the Minneapolis School District hired as its superintendent the head of the Public Strategies Group, with a contract to achieve specified goals within a 3-year period. All these moves have been controversial and are too recent to evaluate fully, but they illustrate the demand for creativity that traditional government appears unable to supply.

Rationales for Privatization

The current wave of interest in public/private-sector relationships is less than 20 years old. At the state level, it grew out of the tax limitation movements that triumphed in California, Massachusetts, and other states in the late 1970s, which forced state and local governments to find new ways of funding public services. President Reagan's arrival in the White House gave new prominence to the Heritage Foundation and other groups that advocated reducing the size of government and delivering public services through alternative channels. Four distinct lines of thought are behind this movement, and their rationales have produced a variety of policy recommendations (Savas, 1987).

One group favors, for ideological reasons, sharp reductions in the size of government and maximum freedom for individual enterprise. Its members believe that a large public sector hampers individuals' liberty to pursue their chosen ends. They further see the marketplace as able to allocate money, natural resources, and human talent more efficiently than any government agency, because the marketplace seeks its own profits. Thus, they want private enterprises to assume many of the current functions of government, from delivering mail to educating children. They would exclude public agencies from all but a limited oversight role.

A second group (overlapping with the first to some extent) favors transferring to business enterprises those functions of government that can be conducted profitably. This group contends that there is no reason for governments to operate hospitals, prisons, recreational facilities, and waste treatment plants when private tax-paying companies can run them just as well. Some argue that education and housing for low-income households are also good areas for privatization. Because the success of business enterprises has to be measured by the bottom line of profit, proponents assert, they must be more efficient than government, which faces no such requirement.

A third group, whose members form a "populist" movement for privatization, would allow citizens more choices in the providers of the services they consume. Rather than having to depend on a large, distant bureaucracy for education or family counseling, these advocates want to empower neighborhood, religious, ethnic, and other voluntary associations to offer these services in ways of their choosing. Then people could select those that best meet their needs. Not fully comfortable with the two preceding positions, supporters of this approach suspect that a large corporation would be no more responsive to people's needs than a large government agency. They prefer community-based enterprises and nonprofit organizations controlled by those they serve.

The fourth group, and perhaps the largest, consists of pragmatists who want to deliver public services with the highest possible responsiveness and efficiency. They recognize that private enterprises have inherent advantages for some functions and that government should draw on them. Less committed to pure privatization, they favor government retention of functions that are essential to the public purposes, but they would look for the arrangements that best fit each case. They have no commitments to either business or nonprofit organizations as such but would choose whichever one best serves the purpose.

People in all four positions agree that government is often less efficient than the private sector. Large government agencies, which are dominated by bureaucratic hierarchies and inflexible rules, are less able to function with flexibility, speed, and responsiveness than private organizations (Seidman & Gilmour, 1986, p. 122). Furthermore, private entities are already carrying on functions that governments need not duplicate, such as building maintenance, data-processing services, and job training.

The preceding groups often agree that government agencies cannot objectively evaluate the costs and quality of their own services if they are the sole providers in their areas. Competitors provide a yardstick that may show that a given service can be done more efficiently. Thus, when one city saves money with private refuse collection, that experience can provide useful information to other cities.

The Uncertain Line between Public and Private

The potential relationships for public school reform with which this chapter opened highlight another class of complexity within the American administrative system. Not only are there many agencies within a single unit of government (as Chapter 2 described) and intricate relationships among units of government at the national, state, and local levels (covered in Chapter 4), but nearly all units of government have formal connections with private-sector organizations. In addition, many have transferred functions and services that they previously performed to private businesses. A major paradox of government in the 1990s is that the provision of public goods and services by organizations outside government has grown at the same time that the public purposes have expanded. Governments have acquired so many such relationships that their boundaries with the rest of society are often obscured. In this situation lie many consequences for public administration.

The American legal and constitutional tradition draws a clear line between government and organizations outside it. Governments are accountable to their citizens through formal processes of selecting their personnel; they can make laws that are binding on those citizens; and they must follow due process in making and enforcing those laws. Although private corporations may be "public" in the sense that they are legally chartered and their stock may be held by any person, they are not part of a government, nor can they exercise governmental powers. However, they are substituting to some extent for governments in serving essential public purposes.

The United States has a long history of voluntary group participation in serving the public purposes. In the 1830s Alexis de Tocqueville ([1835] 1945, I, p. 114) was struck by the American propensity to form voluntary associations to provide mutual benefits. He wrote, "If it is proposed to inculcate some truth or foster some feeling by the encouragement of a great example, they form a society. Wherever at the head of some new undertaking, you see the government in France or a man of rank in England, in the United States you will be sure to find an association." This movement was strongest in social services, education, and health care, where people already held a concept of a public purpose but no government agencies had yet taken them on as their specific responsibilities.

In local communities the line of separation between the public and private sectors has been particularly blurred. Chambers of commerce promote industrial development, United Way associations channel aid to the needy, churches operate hospitals and shelters for the homeless, and garden clubs plant flowers in city parks. In general, the "public activities of civic groups and business firms strengthen the position of . . . small local governments vis-à-vis the

Box 7.1

Dimensions of Privatization

1. Government divestment of function (pure privatization)	Sale of Conrail to private railroad Sale of public hospital Free-market local refuse collection
2. Voucher system	Consumer purchases private service with government funds
3. Coprovision and coproduction: private contribution to public functions	Donations by foundations Nonprofit enterprises in housing Nonprofit social service organizations Volunteers in public schools Neighborhood crime prevention Volunteer firefighting
4. Contracting and franchising for public services	Weapons and military services Building maintenance and cleaning Mass transportation Foster and nursing care Health and counseling services Highway and street construction
5. Government/private sector partnerships	Economic and industrial development Housing and urban renewal Education and job training

state and federal governments. As the local government's equivalent of a professional, specialized civil service, the firms-for-profit play the principal role" (Grodzins, 1966, p. 245).

What has been popularly called privatization actually has five variants, as Box 7.1 indicates. First, there is pure **privatization**, in which a government transfers a function completely or partially from its own administration to the private sector. This variant includes the sale of government-owned assets to a private holder. In the second form, government provides **vouchers**, or certificates, representing the prices of given goods or services to people who give them to private providers as payment. The third form consists of **private contributions** to public enterprises, by which individuals and organizations voluntarily provide funds and services either to government agencies or to programs that government would otherwise support. The fourth variant consists of **contracting**, in which a government purchases goods or services from a business or nonprofit association for its own use or for a third party. This form includes franchising, by which a government formally permits a private organization to provide a service but the latter charges customers directly. The last form consists of **partnerships**, in which governments and private entities enter into long-term cooperative relations for projects and share both resources and control.

Reducing the Size of Government: Pure Privatization

Pure privatization, also called load shedding, occurs when government turns a function over to a single private organization or to the market in general with no continuing control. Box 7.2 describes how this has taken place in Great Britain under the Conservative government. This is relatively rare in the United States and has taken place only when a reliable alternate provider stood ready to assume the function

For example, some cities and counties have sold their public hospitals to national profit-making companies because they were burdened with deteriorating buildings, obsolete equipment, declining occupancy, and reduced federal and state funding, and their constituents resisted higher taxes to pay for improvements. If they could not sell or lease the hospitals, their only alternative was to close them. These transfers raise questions, however, about how medical care for the poor will be affected and about whether new owners will keep the hospitals open if they lose money. Of course, governments continue to pay much of the cost of health care for lower-income people, and legal and professional standards control many of the choices the hospitals make. At present, the evidence from the transfers fails to give strong support to either proponents or opponents of such actions.

One of the Reagan administration's major privatization accomplishments came in 1986, when the national government sold its 85 percent stake in Conrail, a railroad network serving much of the Northeast, to private enterprise. The government had acquired its share in 1976 after the Penn Central Corporation went bankrupt, and it was politically unacceptable to allow that system to fall apart. Under government management and with massive public investments, the railroad was returned to profitability in 1981, so that the original intention to return it to private ownership could be carried out.

Several of President Reagan's advisers mapped out a major program of load shedding for the federal government. In March 1988 the Presidential Commission on Privatization, chaired by David Linowes, presented a blueprint for transferring the Postal Service, prisons, and the air traffic control system, among many other entities, to the private sector. Its rationale was that the federal agencies responsible for these areas had become "muscle-bound to the point

Box 7.2

How Far Can the British Carry Privatization?

The European approach to privatization differs greatly from that in the United States, and Great Britain offers the best example. In past decades, the British government had nationalized many key industries, such as railroads, steelmaking, telecommunications, motor vehicles, and airlines. This followed from the Labour Party's commitment to public ownership, but Conservative governments generally accepted this practice as well. Until Margaret Thatcher, that is. After she moved into 10 Downing Street in 1979, she began a steady process of "denationalization," which most observers believe has achieved considerable success.

Following her free-market philosophy, Britain privatized completely or sold its controlling interest in forty-seven large firms and dozens of smaller ones, through selling shares to individuals or existing private companies. This enabled the enterprises to make decisions more quickly, modernize their facilities, and shed unneeded workers and plants. Thus, British Airways has become a profit maker while expanding its world coverage. British Steel is the only large steelmaker in Europe that is profitable. And British Telecom, which operates the telephone system, has had to pay more attention to customers' demands than it did as a government enterprise, since it needs to win their patronage in a competitive market. It has even bought a 20 percent stake in MCI, the American telecommunications firm. Further privatization is likely. The targets most often discussed are the ailing coal industry and British Rail—and perhaps even the Post Office (Stevenson, 1994).

This form of privatization did not need to occur in the United States, since the nation never went the nationalization route to begin with. The other forms of public/private cooperation discussed in this chapter also are common in Britain. For example, government authorities have worked in partnership with business to redevelop a large area of the London docklands on the east side of the city, abandoned after maritime traffic migrated down the Thames to more modern facilities. Indeed, there is a steady exchange of information and experiences between the two nations, as each searches for workable approaches to chronic problems.

---

of paralysis," according to Linowes. He wrote, "The Government with its checks and balances does not lend itself to managing high technology. Government entities have injected themselves well beyond the realm of government into business, to the detriment of both business and government" (1988).

The desired realm of government is not the same for every observer, however. Many members of Congress disagreed with the president's privatizers, since large-scale load shedding raised too many uncertainties among their constituents to be immediately appealing. If delivery of first-class mail were done only by private companies, they feared that it would cost more, not less, to mail a letter to or from many rural communities. Other critics foresaw a loss of opportunity for citizens to influence or participate in decision making on the service if it left the public realm (Morgan & England, 1988). If a city's bus service becomes the sole responsibility of a private owner, residents could lose influence over its routes, schedules, and fares, except as they choose or refuse to ride.

Vouchers

The Linowes Commission also urged greater use of vouchers as a means of enhancing consumer choice in a privatization plan. These certificates have a specified value when used to purchase particular goods or services. A person receives a voucher from the government and gives it to a provider (whether it be a public or a private agency) of the goods or services. The provider then turns in the voucher for reimbursement. Consumers with several providers to choose from enjoy the freedom to select the one that best meets their needs. For example, the federal/state food stamp program operates on this principle. Instead of government giving out food directly, recipients take the stamps to grocery stores and make their own choices.

State and local governments have made limited use of vouchers, primarily for child care, housing, health services, and transportation. This concept has the potential for much wider use, however, where there are competent private providers of an essential service. Most imaginative is the proposal that parents be given education vouchers, which they would bring to any elementary or high school, public or private, to buy the kind of education they choose for their children. College students who get federal or state scholarships already have this opportunity, but to extend this to lower levels of education would induce competition among schools for students, with unpredictable results for both the public and private institutions. It could well stimulate the charter school movement, described at the opening of this chapter, as well as alternative schemes of school management.

A simple voucher program for a specific service would require five basic administrative steps. First, an agency would identify those eligible for vouchers, perhaps according to income level. Second, it would set the subsidy level. Next, the level and quality of the service would be set, along with eligible suppliers. Fourth, the program would be publicized and the vouchers distributed. Finally, the agency would redeem the vouchers after verifying that the services had been delivered at the level agreed upon. Such a program can be successful only if there are several competent providers and the government personnel continually monitor the operations to prevent fraud and substandard services (Valente & Manchester, 1984). The food stamp program has had difficulty ensuring that only those eligible receive benefits, but at least it can rely on the resources of many competing grocery stores. These administrative challenges have been great enough to deter most governments from experimenting with vouchers.

Box 7.3

Why Does Jubilee Enterprise Succeed where HUD Fails?

The Trenton Park Apartment complex on the southeast side of Washington, D.C., had a bad reputation. Crime was common in and around its deteriorating buildings, home to 259 low-income households. Its landlord was the U.S. Department of Housing and Urban Development (HUD), which took over the complex after its private owner went bankrupt—a common occurrence around the nation. But HUD's management left much to be desired.

Late in 1993 HUD sold the complex for one dollar to Jubilee Enterprise, a nonprofit group that had already enabled tenants to buy and improve apartment buildings elsewhere in Washington. Jubilee set up a board of three residents and two real estate specialists to run the complex and immediately began to make improvements. Its philosophy stresses building a sense of community and mutual responsibility among residents and giving them access to job training,

education, child care, and health services, a goal that public agencies find harder to accomplish. Although much remains to be done at Trenton Park, crime rates have fallen and community events have begun to build needed solidarity among residents.

Jubilee and similar efforts in other cities are now seen by federal officials as models for the many other housing projects that HUD owns but would rather not. The Enterprise Foundation, a national organization that finances community renewal efforts, is publicizing this potential. It offers a workable "middle way" between direct government ownership and management and profit-seeking private enterprise, both of which have inherent limitations in the lower-income housing field (Jacobson, 1994). This is in part an example of pure privatization, but it also places Jubilee Enterprise in the role of co-provider of a public service.

Coprovision and Coproduction

Closely related forms of public/private cooperation are **coprovision** (private contributions of money or expertise to public services) and **coproduction** (participation of private individuals, who provide those services). The contributors may be individuals, voluntary associations, or profit-making businesses. These are what President Bush apparently had in mind when he referred to the "thousand points of light" in his acceptance speech at the 1988 Republican National Convention. They encompass the volunteer who serves coffee and sandwiches at a shelter for the homeless and the business that contributes computers to the local high schools. Box 7.3 describes the role of Jubilee Enterprise in public housing in Washington, D.C., which is a bridge between pure privatization and coproduction.

Corporations and foundations devoted to public service are a major source of cash contributions. Although most are oriented to private charities, some support public functions when they can initiate a unique project or fulfill a special obligation to the community in which they operate. They have been major backers of housing and urban redevelopment efforts, often channeling funds through nonprofit associations that also receive government assistance. The Ford Foundation, with assets of $5.25 billion, is the largest of these benefactors. Community foundations, based in and committed to specific states or cities, have also grown. These draw funds from local sources and target needs in their areas, ranging from social services and education to medicine and the arts.

Examples of coproduction are equally numerous. Citizens who participate in neighborhood crime-watch programs and patrols supplement the efforts of police (and possibly put more pressure on them for prompt responses). A 1988 estimate by the National Sheriffs' Association put the number of volunteers in crime-watch groups at 10 million (Thomas, 1988). Most controversial of these have been the Guardian Angels, who patrol areas with large minority populations and have been particularly aggressive in their campaign against illegal drug dealers. Other coproducers volunteer in hospitals, schools, and prisons, doing what government personnel would otherwise be paid for, or, perhaps more important, giving service that would not otherwise be provided. Those who counsel criminal offenders and help them adjust after their release from prison ease the workload of probation officers and may reduce recidivism. Such volunteers may enable public programs to work better.

How well coprovision and coproduction succeed depends to an important extent on government agencies' use of the contributors and volunteers. First, if agencies are to be successful in attracting volunteer aid, they must show how it will make a difference in the community's quality of life. When volunteers fill specialized roles, agencies must recruit and carefully place those with the needed skills. A neighborhood anticrime patrol needs training by the police if it is to be more a help than a hindrance. Retaining volunteers over a period of time may call for special recognition, since people can get tired of the work, feel unappreciated, or have conflicts with co-workers.

The use of coproviders cannot be programmed as readily as the work of public employees. Volunteers may be effective in one endeavor but not in another. Administrators must be flexible, ready to enlist and use volunteers when available but not entirely dependent on them. Upper-income communities may have these contributors in greatest abundance, since their residents are most likely to have the leadership skills and self-confidence necessary, and this poses a problem of equity. Poorer areas can generate this activity with the help of neighborhood organizations and outside stimuli. However, if a city's economy is extremely depressed, the very magnitude of needs is more likely to discourage citizens and government personnel alike.

Government by Contract

Public/private relationships that retain government in the role of a customer are familiar to nearly every administrator. Contracting is the oldest kind of formal public/private relationship. Government has bought goods and services from private suppliers since George Washington's administration. Essentially, a vendor agrees to supply a naval ship, janitorial service, or management of a national park hotel according to certain standards for a price paid by the agency and/or a fee charged to individual customers. The contract may be open-ended or for a set term, and the vendor can be replaced by another, creating the potential for competition and thus better terms for the government. In some cases, government contracts with a private provider to serve members of the public directly; this is often called a *proxy service*. When government authorizes a private enterprise to supply a service and charge the public directly, this is called *franchising*. Cable television and mass transit are examples of this.

Contracting has proved to be preferable to "in-house" action when an agency can (1) get a job done at a lower cost and/or with higher quality than through its own personnel, (2) obtain special skills or expertise it does not currently have, or (3) avoid making heavy initial investments in facilities or equipment. Contracts can be with nonprofit organizations as well as with businesses. For example, Ramsey County, Minnesota, employs Volunteers of America, which is experienced with halfway houses for released prisoners, to operate its minimum-security correctional facility for women. The move to contracting may be spurred by a budget deficit, a well-publicized failure of the service, or the need to provide a new service.

Extent of Contracting   No governmental units of any size lack such contractual relationships. Of 1,086 cities and counties that responded to a 1987 survey, 99 percent reported some degree of contracting for services in the previous 5 years. The main reasons they gave for this were financial pressures (David, 1988). Box 7.4 lists the services most often contracted for. These units constantly face the choices of entering into new contracts, terminating others, changing vendors, and renegotiating terms. School districts must decide whether to operate their own buses or purchase transportation from a private bus company, and a city may retain its own street repair crews or contract for that work. Thus, administrators must acquire skill at contract management to ensure that they obtain the best possible terms and performance. Box 7.5 points to the current controversy over private management of state prisons.

Contracting is commonplace in the federal government as well. The Office of Management and Budget reported that it spent $210

(continued on p. 201)

Box 7.4

City and County Services Provided Contractually by Private Firms

Service

Adoption, air-pollution abatement, airport operation, airport services, alarm-system maintenance, ambulance, animal control, appraisals, architectural, auditorium management, auditing

Beach management, billing and collection, bridge (construction, inspection, and maintenance), building demolition, building rehabilitation, buildings and grounds (janitorial, maintenance, security), building and mechanical inspection, burial of indigents, bus operation, bus-shelter maintenance

Cafeteria and restaurant operation, catch-basin cleaning, cemetery administration, child protection, civil defense communication, clerical, communication maintenance, community center operation, computer operations, consultant services, convention center management, crime laboratory, crime prevention and patrol, custodial

Data entry, data processing, day care, document preparation, drug and alcohol programs

Economic development, election administration, electrical inspection, electric power, elevator inspection, emergency maintenance, environmental services

Family counseling, financial services, fire communication, fire-hydrant maintenance, fire prevention and suppression, flood-control planning, foster-home care

Golf-course operation, graphic arts, guard service

Health inspection, health services, homemaker service, hospital management, hospital services, housing inspection and code enforcement, housing management

Industrial development, insect and rodent control, institutional care, insurance administration, irrigation

Jail and detention, janitorial, juvenile delinquency programs

Labor relations, laboratory, landscaping, laundry, lawn maintenance, leaf collection, legal, legal aid, library operation, licensing

Management consulting, mapping, marina services, median-strip maintenance, mosquito control, moving and storage, museum and cultural

Noise abatement, nursing, nutrition

Office-machine maintenance, opinion polling

Paratransit system operation, park maintenance, parking enforcement, parking lot and garage operation, parking lot cleaning, parking meter servicing, parking ticket processing, patrol, payroll processing, personal services, photographic services, physician services, planning, plumbing inspection, police communication, port and harbor management, printing, prisoner transportation, probation, property acquisition, public administrator services, public health, public relations and information, public works

Records maintenance, recreation services and facility operation, rehabilitation, resource recovery, risk management

School bus, secretarial, security, sewage treatment, sewer maintenance, sidewalk repair, snow (plowing, sanding, removal), social services, soil conservation, solid waste (collection, transfer, disposal), street services (construction, maintenance, sweeping), street lighting (construction and maintenance), surveying

Tax collection (assessing, bill processing, receipt), tennis-court maintenance, test scoring, traffic control (markings, signs, and signal installation and maintenance), training (of government employees), transit management, transportation of elderly and disabled, treasury functions, tree services (planting, pruning, removal)

Utility billing, utility meter reading

Vehicle fleet management, vehicle maintenance, vehicle towing and storage, voter registration

Water-meter reading and maintenance, water-pollution abatement, water supply and distribution, water treatment, weed abatement, welfare

Zoning and subdivision control

—E. S. Savas, *Privatization: The Key to Better Government,* 1981, Chatham, NJ: Chatham House

Box 7.5

Should Prisons Be Run for Profit?

The nation's prison population is rising sharply, with convicted drug offenders the largest single group being locked up. Hard pressed to find cells for them, states have begun to contract with private companies to build and operate prisons. Since such firms spread the costs over the life of the facility, they do not have to burden their budgets for construction and equipment. The first private prison opened in Kentucky in 1989 for 450 inmates.

The major company in the prison business is Corrections Corporation of America, which in 1993 managed more than 8,000 beds. Overall, there were more than fifty private prisons in that year, and the number was increasing at about five per year. These are low- and medium-security facilities for the most part. In addition, many state-owned prisons were contracting for such services as health care, meals, education, and rehabilitation. Private prisons are not necessarily cheaper to operate, however, although personnel salaries tend to be lower and a contractor may achieve economies that are impossible for a state.

Several controversies surround this trend. Some observers are concerned that private companies will show less respect for prisoners' rights and that pressures to economize will reduce necessary services and security. Organized labor has also opposed privatization, having observed that privately employed prison personnel are paid less and tend not to join unions. A third argument was voiced by Pennsylvania's corrections commissioner, Joseph Lehman. He fears that profit-making prison operators will lobby strongly for locking up more and more offenders, hindering states from seeking community-based means of rehabilitation for those who would be better served by them (Lemov, 1993). These disagreements will not be quickly settled.

---

billion in fiscal year 1992 on contracts for goods and services. The proportion of payments to vendors in the entire budget rose sharply in the 1980s (Schneider, 1992). The Defense Department is the most publicized user, relying on private suppliers for everything from weapons systems to soldiers' boots. In the late 1980s it was awarding 15 million contracts annually to 60,000 or so companies (Halloran, 1989). The combined value of these contracts in fiscal year 1993 was $116 billion (*Statistical Abstract of the United States,* 1994, Table 542). The Department of Energy relies on contractors for an even larger share of its work. Private corporations operate its major nuclear weapons plants and provide consultant services that fill in for lack of expertise or sufficient staff in its own ranks. In 1989 it reported to Congress that it had a contract workforce of more than 100,000, compared with only 16,000 on its own staff (U.S. Senate Committee on Governmental Affairs, 1989).

Federal policy on contracting is stated in Circular A-76, issued and periodically revised by the Office of Management and Budget. It states that it is proper to contract for "commercial activities" but not for those that are "so intimately related to the public interest as to mandate performance by Government employees." The latter functions are those that "require either the exercise of discretion in applying Government authority or the use of value judgment in making decisions. . . ." Since these definitions are not precise, they leave much room for interpretation, on which the Office of Management and Budget has the final word.

In 1985 the Reagan administration identified 11,000 "commercial activities," ranging from movie making to fire protection, that could be performed by private contractors. The National Performance Review (1993, Chapter 2) renewed this call, though for a shorter list of activities that included printing, property management, and information technology. Congress has been reluctant to allow much additional contracting because of opposition from constituents and federal employees and its own uncertainty as to how the changes would affect its oversight of services.

How Contracts Are Made   The administrative procedure for entering into a contract can be complex, and managers must prepare carefully for a new relationship. An agency first decides on specifications for the goods or services it seeks, such as a specially equipped police vehicle, school bus service on a defined schedule, or cleanup of a toxic waste dump. It must be careful to state the requirements accurately and precisely to avoid later disputes.

Next, it advertises the request for bids, seeking at least two from qualified suppliers. Competitive bidding is mandatory for most government contracts unless there is only one source for an item. Some laws require special efforts to get bids from companies owned by women or people of color, although the U.S. Supreme Court ruled in January 1989 that such preferential treatment was permissible only to remedy explicit past discrimination.

Third, after a sufficient interval for companies to submit their bids, the agency examines the proposals. Ideally, it selects the lowest bid from a responsible supplier that meets the specifications. If there are problems at this stage, such as all bids being higher than the budgeted amount or none meeting the criteria, it may be necessary to repeat the process. Political pressures on behalf of a given contender may appear if the amount is significant. When bidders have personal, party, or financial links with officials or lobby extensively (as is common among major contractors with the Defense Department), there is a temptation to bend the laws, and the contract may be given to a contender that does not merit it.

Then the agency announces the award publicly and the parties formally ratify the contract. During the life of the agreement, the agency must continue to monitor the vendor's performance. Usually, there is a schedule of checks or inspections; outside complaints may also be heard. Staff members may have to be trained to do this monitoring. If there is failure to comply, the agency takes remedial action as the terms of the contract provide, including termination and, in extreme cases, legal penalties.

Methods of Payment   Several methods of payment can be used. Most common are fixed-price contracts, in which the vendor bids a certain sum to build a highway, for instance, or to perform 100 hours of consulting. The vendor keeps the difference if the cost of fulfilling the contract is lower than the compensation but must absorb any cost overrun. Thus, it must be careful to make the bid financially realistic yet low enough to win the contract. This provides a strong incentive for cost control.

Another method of payment, which is used when the costs cannot be easily foreseen, as in developing weapons that extend the state of the art, is the cost reimbursement contract. Government agrees to pay the contractor's actual costs of meeting the specifications plus a percentage for overhead and profit. This may lead to unexpectedly high costs and waste, although the terms can also include incentives for contractor efficiency.

Contract Management   The task of federal contract management is truly massive. Only a few such contracts raise serious problems, but those can draw intense publicity. When the army sought a high-performance antiaircraft gun in the late 1970s, it provided only performance specifications and called for prototypes. Ford Aerospace won the contract; the gun, first called *Divad* and later named after Sergeant York, went into production in 1982. However, after it failed numerous tests and proved to be much more expensive than expected, the army canceled the contract (Kettl, 1988, Chapter 2). The fault apparently lay in a combination of the army's unrealistic specifications and Ford's inept design and manufacturing. This sort of contract, for an innovative product, is highly vulnerable to mistakes. Administrators on both sides must be sensitive to each ongoing development and be willing to change course when necessary and pay the financial or psychological costs entailed by such risks. Box 7.6 offers an example of poor communications compounding the technical challenges of agency/contractor relations.

Contracting can raise personnel choices as well. Governments do not have the same obligations to employees of a contractor that they do to their own employees; no union contract or civil service rules control hiring, compensation, and firing. But if a new arrangement terminates an existing government service, the unneeded employees must be somehow placed elsewhere. Civil service rules may require their transfer to other agencies if possible. They may also be hired by a contractor who needs an expanded workforce.

Although a well-drawn contract can free the public administrator from management details, frequent meetings with the con-

Box 7.6

Was the *Challenger* Disaster a Contractor's Fault?

After the space shuttle *Challenger* exploded on January 28, 1986, an investigation focused on the intricate relationship between the National Aeronautics and Space Administration (NASA) and Morton Thiokol, the private company contracted to supply much of the equipment. Several engineers at the company had expressed the concern months earlier that the O-rings that sealed the joints in the booster rockets would fail to hold under some conditions, particularly in temperatures near the freezing point.

As the fateful *Challenger* launch of January 1986 approached, Thiokol engineers again voiced their misgivings. But their supervisors did not consider the risk high enough to mention in their Certification of Flight Readiness. On January 27, the day before the launch actually took place, Roger Boisjoly, a Thiokol engineer, was dismayed by the low temperature forecast for Cape Canaveral the next morning, and he again showed evidence that the O-rings might not seal. His supervisors and NASA project personnel declined to put off the launch, which had already been delayed three times. This was the shuttle flight that had the teacher Christa McAuliffe on board, so an unusual amount of publicity was focused on it. NASA personnel be-

lieved that a successful flight was necessary for the agency's public image and that each delay eroded that image a little more.

It is now history that the O-rings did fail and caused the tragedy, just as Boisjoly and his colleagues had warned their Thiokol supervisors during the six months prior to the launch. The commission that investigated the disaster found that these concerns had never been communicated to the higher-level NASA officials who actually made the decision to launch. Their relationship with Thiokol, crossing the boundary between government and private business, made it even harder to determine who was actually responsible for the failure than it would have been if the entire operation had been under NASA control: This way blame for the lapse could fall either on the private company's managers or on NASA administrators for failing to ferret out the crucial information they needed to make the correct decision. Of course, there is no assurance that the latter would have heeded the warning had they known of it, since the data load that accompanies one shuttle mission is enormous and the O-rings constituted only one of many calculated risks (Presidential Commission on the Space Shuttle *Challenger* Accident, 1986).

tractor may be necessary, as may adjustments to the terms if conditions change. A contract administrator can use the carrot (or stick) of future relations to bargain with. When performance is less than satisfactory but does not violate the contract terms, he or she must know how to exert effective pressure.

Fraud and poor performance have been recurring problems with contractors, the most publicized instances of which have been in the Defense Department. In fiscal year 1988 the department barred future contracting within varying time periods for 1,028 companies. Those firms' misdeeds included actual or suspected bribery of Defense officials, conspiracy with other companies to rig their bids, failure to fulfill terms of a contract, and delivery of shoddy goods. More than 22,000 auditors and inspectors were monitoring their performance in the late 1980s at a cost of more than $1 billion annually (Halloran, 1989).

Political pressures and personal favoritism can distort the award of contracts and evaluation of vendors' performance. Contractors have sometimes conspired with agencies to make sure that they got a job regardless of competitors' bids and competence. The companies have then shown their gratitude to the officials in "appropriate" ways. An agency may also overlook a vendor's excessive costs or failure to deliver the required service.

Public Service by Proxy   The proxy service is a form of contracting in which the purchase goes directly to the clients. The provider may be either a nonprofit organization or a profit-making firm. Proxy contracts play a major role in health care, housing, counseling, child protection, aid to the disabled, and employment training. State and local service agencies depend most heavily on them. In 1989, fourteen Massachusetts state agencies spent more than $800 million to purchase social services from more than 1,150 nonprofit contractors. In New York City several municipal agencies depend completely on nonprofit organizations to supply the human services for which they are responsible, at a cost of more than $1 billion. The providers range from foster homes, on the smallest scale, to large charitable organizations with thousands of clients. An increasing number of such groups were founded specifically as service agents for government and derive most or all of their revenue from their contracts. Their relationship with government is clearly one of mutual dependence (Smith & Lipsky, 1993, pp. 4-5).

The procedures that government must follow for establishing these proxy-service contracts are similar to those described earlier, but the monitoring task differs. The government must keep in close contact with the constituents to ensure that the terms are complied with. A public social worker must inspect workshops that train the disabled and visit foster homes regularly to verify the quality of care. If a contractor has a good record on a routine service, this monitoring can be infrequent, but new programs and inexperienced providers require close watching. Citizen relations with contractors are also important in services with high public contact. If the private trash collectors are late in their pickups or allow refuse to blow around, residents must know how to find a remedy. Usually they expect their city government to act on such problems, but they need to understand that the chain of accountability is longer than it would be if the city itself collected the waste.

Contracts for human services contain detailed rules to ensure fairness, quality of treatment, and efficient use of funds, probably as much as if government agencies were acting themselves. These organizations lose much of their "privateness" when they sign a contract and may become government entities in fact if not in law.

In the view of Smith and Lipsky (1993, p. 204), such contracting "has resulted in unprecedented involvement of government in the affairs of nonprofit organizations. Instead of shrinking the role of government and making the provision of public services subject to market discipline, contracting has actually diminished and constrained the community sector." The scope of public administration widens as a consequence.

Government in Partnerships

The most complex form of public/private cooperation is the partnership, a formal relationship in which one or more governmental units and nongovernmental entities jointly provide resources and maintain control over a project. These have proliferated especially in urban areas in the past decade. The rationale is that a joint effort can accomplish what neither partner could do as well by itself. Partnerships generate the most administratively complex relationships and have a mixed record of accomplishment.

The rationale for this cooperation rests on the perception that governments lack the efficiency and expertise to solve urban problems alone. At the same time, the private profit-making sector, though innovative and skilled, must show positive financial results from the service it renders to the community. What needs to be done is to harness private capabilities to serve the public interest by means of formal partnerships of the two parties. Thereby, "business will develop a sense of civic responsibility in this process, recognizing that their own interests coincide with having a healthy, viable city, with adequate services and a satisfied population. Government will learn to be more entrepreneurial" (de Neufville & Barton, 1987, p. 194).

Such partnerships are widely used in large-scale physical and social renewal of cities. Box 7.7 describes one of the most ambitious of them, the Atlanta Project. Many operate at the neighborhood level. Between 3,000 and 5,000 community development corporations are active around the nation in residential and commercial projects, with the backing of city officials, foundations, lenders, and their own residents.

State and local governments also enter partnerships for business expansion and job development. The University City Science Center in Philadelphia is a joint project of city planners, Drexel University, and scientist-entrepreneurs to provide space for small start-up companies in a deteriorating neighborhood (Steffens, 1992). These are clearly public subsidies for the favored companies, but advocates justify them in terms of the jobs retained or created in the state and tax revenue yielded over the long run. Critics are uncomfortable with the political influences that are inevitable in

Box 7.7

The Atlanta Project: Can a Partnership Meet the Challenge?

Atlanta is reveling in world attention as it prepares to host the 1996 Summer Olympics. But it is getting more negative attention too: It has plunged to the bottom of some "urban life" rating scales, with its high crime, drug abuse, homelessness, and poverty rates. This gap has disturbed civic leaders enough to spur them to launch a massive project to combat these ills. Former president Jimmy Carter has been its chief publicist and fundraiser, but the energy comes from city and school officials, corporate volunteers, foundations, and grassroots organizations of residents. In the project's first 18 months it received $18 million in cash and another $14 million in services (Knack, 1993).

The Atlanta Project also illustrates the pitfalls of large-scale enterprises that attack even larger-scale problems. With so many partners there is no assurance that each one will continue its support. A complicated decision-making structure can easily exclude some who want to participate or make suggestions. Racial tensions, chronic to Atlanta's politics, have left their mark too. Finally, there is the danger that the ambitious publicity needed to draw partner support is raising popular expectations above the level that can be achieved. Volunteers need some successes to reward their efforts and quickly drop out if they are discouraged. Planners must have a sense of realism in the midst of their optimism.

such partnerships and charge that private interests too often drain the public treasury to serve their own profits.

The federal government joined the network of urban partnerships in 1994 when the Department of Housing and Urban Development committed $20 million to the National Community Development Initiative, established 3 years earlier to make loans to community development corporations. The private partners are several major foundations, insurance companies, and financial enterprises. Together the contributions total $88 million and are intended to stimulate another $750 million in investments by states, cities, and private sources. Secretary Henry Cisneros, in announcing the grant, pledged that his department would give more attention to assembling such partnerships in the future (DeParle, 1994).

Public and private partnerships, though potentially rewarding, are also administratively challenging. Forming them is more complex than making a simple contract, since they continuously share authority and resources. Although the partnership is limited by law in how it can use public funds, it exercises considerable discretion in how it assembles its total financing package. Each partner must be able to make commitments and honor them. An administrator who depends on choices by a legislative body or federal department must lobby diligently for approvals and walk softly until they are granted. Where the partnership was formed to overcome a serious problem, such as a deteriorating urban neighborhood, a member may drop out because of discouragement or costs that are higher than expected.

Another dilemma is the extent of public involvement and publicity in the formation of these partnerships. Certainly, the citizens need to know of the plans and commitments being made, but the different interests of political, community, and business leaders may also spark disagreement that, if made known, would reduce the likelihood of cooperation. On the other hand, it would be unwise to exclude an active neighborhood organization from a community development corporation, for example, since residents' choices to live, shop, and invest have such a strong influence on its success.

Obviously, such partnerships blur the distinction between what is public and what is private. This cooperation can be beneficial if the projects could not have been completed otherwise. But some major urban renewal efforts, for example, have yielded large profits for developers and landowners and forced some low-income residents out of their homes. Occasional projects have been financial failures, with the city or state government bearing the financial brunt. Citizens who seek to fix responsibility for those outcomes may encounter only frustration.

Benefits, Costs, and Administrative Challenges

The central concern of this chapter is when and how units of government can cooperate with the private sector to best advantage to fulfill their public purposes. Whether a smaller government is preferable to a larger one is ultimately a matter for political judgment, not to be settled by administrative analyses.

The Advantage of Reduced Costs

First, cooperative schemes have reduced the costs of some public services. The city of Phoenix, Arizona, forced its sanitation department to compete against private companies for garbage collection contracts. After several years in which vendors won the bids, the city department increased its efficiency so much that it was able to undercut all the bids of the private companies. At the other end of the governmental scale, the Defense Department reduced some weapons production costs in the late 1980s by having several companies bid competitively for some or all of the number to be procured. Design and development of weapons had previously been competitive, but the winner got to produce what it developed at a price it determined. Now such monopoly awards are less common (Stevenson, 1988).

Yet cost reductions have not been the universal experience. In other transfers, there was little or no saving. A study of four experiences of privatization in New York City—commercial refuse collection, proprietary vocational education, school transportation, and management of sports facilities—found no clear advantage in cost or service quality in the new arrangements (Bailey, 1987).

Possible efficiencies can be easily offset by less visible drawbacks. "Government will still need to regulate a delivered service even though it has been privatized, since privatizing a service does not leave government without responsibilities" (Bailey, 1987, p. 148). Extra administrative costs arise, which are labeled by economists as "transaction costs"; these include research into providers, negotiation with them before and after signing, and monitoring of performance. If performance is substandard, the costs to government and the public multiply (Kettl, 1993, p. 194).

Furthermore, the savings that do result are often due to lower wages and benefits paid by the private providers. Public employees who are laid off or reduced to part-time status as a result also impose costs on society and government, but these do not appear on the balance sheets of the agencies involved in the privatizing. New York City learned in 1987 that the private nonprofit agencies it relies on for more than a billion dollars in social services had trouble recruiting qualified workers because of the lower salaries offered. Government employees in similar positions can earn up to 42 percent more than those in the nonprofit organizations (Blair, 1987).

Expanded Choices for Constituents

Another advantage cited of public/private cooperation is that it expands choices of constituents for types of service. This prospect is especially important for the most disadvantaged people, who lack the money to buy what they want in the marketplace. The plethora of rental housing programs in the 1970s and 1980s has certainly broadened opportunities for low-income people in most cities where a tight market has not driven up costs. Yet other transfers have been simply from a public monopoly to a private one, with no expansion of choice. For example, public health clinics in low-income areas have been replaced by private ones under contract, but clients have no more choice after the change than before. Government cannot assume that new opportunities will automatically open up with privatization. Instead, it must plan to ensure that they do appear if the private providers fail to take the necessary action. Government is itself an important means of providing alternatives, especially those unavailable in the marketplace, as it responds to voter demand and group pressures (Starr, 1987).

Efficiency of the Private Sector

The presumed higher efficiency of the private sector is another advantage claimed for privatization. But one cannot assume without question that any business enterprise or nonprofit association will operate a service more efficiently than a public agency. Most examples of cost savings on a constant level of service are in such operations as refuse collection, transportation, package delivery, and other routine functions in which inputs and outputs can be quantified. Efficiency in providing human services with a subjective quality, such as assistance for the homeless and education for students with special needs, cannot be so easily measured. "The very nature of social services, with their fuzzy objectives and uncertain technologies, makes it difficult for governments to write crisp, enforceable contracts" (Kettl, 1993, p. 173).

Those who assert that government is chronically inefficient claim that bureaucrats, employees' unions, and constituents press constantly to raise spending and avoid careful accounting for costs. The fact that the Phoenix sanitation department was able to cut costs by adopting the same equipment and methods that its private competitors used gives some credence to this claim. However, other examples, such as weapons contracting, raise doubts that greater efficiency occurs uniformly.

The virtues of competition among private providers have also been confirmed on occasion. But administrators must be alert to situations where competition is likely to be absent. It is not difficult in most places to find several firms that pave streets and clean buildings. But finding qualified nonprofit organizations to supply social services is difficult; studies in several states found that most agencies get only one bid (Kettl, 1993, p. 171). If a city does not want to be at the mercy of a sole contractor for a service, it could divide the field and allocate portions to several companies. These would then compete with one another and so protect the government's options. However, competition among providers may not reduce costs if they are all constrained by the same market forces or their employees all belong to one union (Bailey, 1987). Dividing the field of service among several providers may reduce any economies of scale that could be obtained. Also, the competitors may collaborate to divide that market and fix prices at a higher level.

Finally, public/private-sector relationships offer attractive opportunities to involve citizens in their own governance and add their resources to the public realm (Morgan & England, 1988). Although self-seeking motives often accompany this involvement—improving a corporate image or making one's own neighborhood safer—these need not conflict with the common good. The community development corporations described earlier have the potential to achieve such common good. Medoff and Sklar (1994) describe the Dudley

Street Neighborhood Initiative in Boston as a resident-initiated partnership that could draw in outside support for the plans it generated by itself. An estimated 1,800 are involved in its activities in education, job creation, and land redevelopment. However, its success hinges on the willingness of its "big" partners in government and business to give support without dictating their own priorities.

Challenges of Public/Private Cooperation

Public/private cooperation presents major challenges to policymakers and administrators. First, they need to set the terms of their collaboration with care. The profit-seeking or altruistic motives of an organization may not be fully aligned with the public purposes at the beginning. Public managers must ensure that corporate job training programs, for example, reach those most in need of help in preparing for employment and not cater only to those who are easiest to train. A religious organization that receives federal grants to counsel pregnant teenagers must not be permitted to pressure them to act according to its beliefs.

Second, the choice of how much to pay for the service remains with government, and when it is not a standard market item, such as cleaning a public building, it calls for careful estimation. There are few public functions on which a profit can be made without government payment or subsidy. Thus, if a city wants to shed its unprofitable bus service, it must decide what service levels it wants a private provider to maintain and what subsidy, if any, it will provide. This raises the question of how much profit a contractor should be permitted.

A third demand on administrators is to obtain sufficient performance information on the service. A private organization has no legal obligation to disclose operating data such as actual costs of providing a given item except as required by a contract. If a city supports a large network of private health clinics, for example, its health department must arrange to get prompt and thorough reports on what is happening and where any deficiencies may be. These monitoring costs reduce any savings gained from the transfer.

Governments generally devote little effort to monitoring contracts and often rely on providers' own reports (Kettl, 1993, pp. 174–175). When such oversight does not take place, the agency risks major service lapses and lawsuits as a result. In 1992 the U.S. Office of Management and Budget reported that federal agencies lose large sums of money each year because they fail to supervise their contractors' spending. For example, a company that supervises cleanup of toxic waste sites for the Environmental Protection Agency and the Department of Energy billed the government for country club fees and similar illegal charges. The major problem is

Box 7.8

Could the Postal Service be Privatized?

A favorite target of advocates for the privatization of government is the U.S. Postal Service. Although Congress did not respond, the Linowes Commission urged in 1985 that mail delivery be turned over to private business. The Postal Service had taken a step in that direction in 1970, when Congress converted it from a cabinet department to a government corporation that had to pay its own way through charges to its customers. It has a legal monopoly on first-class mail service and on the use of patrons' mailboxes, which at that time enabled it to dominate all but the parcel delivery market.

The Postal Service's market in 1995 is very different. It has efficient and aggressive competitors, such as United Parcel Service and Federal Express, for its package and letter delivery. Its first-class mail business has been eroded by the telephone companies that transmit fax messages and the networks that carry electronic mail. Does the nation still need a government agency in that market?

Congress has several rationales for keeping the Postal Service public. First, its uniform first-class postage rate enables residents of Hawaii and Alaska to communicate with the rest of the nation at no price disadvantage. Second, rural residents value their small (and inefficient) local post offices and fear that a firm like Federal Express would close them immediately. Third, non-profit mailers and periodical publishers get a price break from the Postal Service for the social benefit they provide, and a private postal business would have no incentive to continue this.

The options for a privatized postal service are many. Congress could simply abolish the Postal Service and open up an entirely free market. Or it could franchise several firms to deliver the mail, setting certain conditions for levels of service and prices. Less likely, it could give one private company a monopoly. Much depends on how the nation (and particularly its big mailers) define the means of moving information and goods as a public utility and how the technologies for it develop in years to come.

---

that the government lacks enough auditors to supervise contracts, and the number of auditors declined steadily during the Reagan and Bush administrations (Schneider, 1992).

Fourth, since government agencies remain accountable to the citizens for the privatized service, they must manage the political relationships involved. Box 7.8 surveys a few of many questions that Congress must answer as it considers privatizing the Postal Service. When a change is first proposed, constituents may be uncertain about their future benefits and therefore resist it. Government employees, whether unionized or not, will ask hard questions and probably oppose change. They are likely to argue that "privatized" employees have inherently less commitment to public service than those in civil service. Often they have spurred enough opposition among legislators to defeat or substantially alter such changes. When administrators consider a change toward private-sector participation, they must let constituents know what to expect and make appropriate provisions for public employees who may be displaced.

Kettl (1993) argues that government can be a "smart buyer" of goods and services only if it knows what it wants to buy, who can sell it, and how to judge what it has bought—not unlike the demands on individual consumers. It can do this only if it hires and trains enough competent personnel who can make these choices. Public officials cannot assume that the private market will competently fill gaps in government functioning without oversight.

"Smart-buying" administrators and policymakers should anticipate both opportunities and conflicts that could arise in the future. A debate has begun in many states over services to preschool children. Public schools increasingly offer optional early childhood education to give youngsters a head start and have pressured state legislatures to fund this expansion. They are especially targeting at-risk children who might have trouble succeeding later because of personal or family disadvantages. However, the organized private day-care network of businesses and nonprofit groups asserts that it can meet most needs at little or no cost to government. At stake is not only the issue of public versus private costs but also the kind of care and preparation for school that will be provided. If such care is furnished by public schools, it may broaden the choice for low-income parents who cannot afford the typical private preschool. The choices demanded here are not simply a few regulations and contracts but also the components of a flexible system that can respond to changing social needs, means of financing, and educational philosophies.

Average citizens who use this mix of public and private goods and services carry a special burden of evaluating their outcomes sensitively and comparing their quality and efficiency. Although they naturally would concentrate on how well the work is done as it affects them personally, they should be alert to who the provider is. They should know whether the hospital they use is under their county government, for example, or is owned by a profit-making company. The feedback to government they provide through their individual choices, their elected officials, and the interest groups they belong to is vital in shaping the future of these services.

Paul Starr's observations offer an appropriate closure to this discussion:

> In adjusting the public-private balance, we need to be attentive, sphere by sphere, to the special practical and moral considerations that arise in each. No single remedy is appropriate to the vastly different problems that distinguish collecting taxes from collecting trash, running schools from running railroads, managing prisons from managing shipyards. Nor ought we reduce our choices to a simple public-private dichotomy. We have a more extensive repertoire of intermediate options in organiza-

tional forms and modes of ownership, control, and finance. (1987, p. 136)

All these options add to, rather than subtract from, the complexity of the system by which we serve our public purposes.

Summary

Privatization concerns the formal relationships and agreements between units of government and private organizations. It has five dimensions: (1) pure privatization, in which a government transfers a function completely or partially from its own administration to the private sector or sells its assets to a private holder; (2) provision of vouchers (certificates for the price of given goods or services) to people who give them to a private provider as payment; (3) private contributions to public enterprises, by which individuals and organizations voluntarily provide funds and services either to government agencies or to programs that government would otherwise support; (4) purchase of goods or services, under contract, from a business or nonprofit association; and (5) formation of partnerships between governments and private entities for projects in which both share resources and control.

These arrangements are said to reduce the size of government, allow the private sector to conduct profit-making enterprises, increase the choices of constituents for service providers, and improve the efficiency of public services.

Each mode of privatization has proved to yield certain benefits, but there is no consistent pattern from one type of enterprise to another. Functions that are routine and can be easily prescribed by rules are easiest to manage in this way. Each has serious management challenges, since control of the privatized function is less direct and more open to dispute. Government administrators must pay close attention to setting the terms of the relationships and monitoring the results.

Discussion Questions

1. Which of the four rationales for privatization is most persuasive? Why?

2. Which of the present functions of national, state, or local governments is/are

most likely to be privatized in the near future? Which is/are least likely?

3. What is necessary to induce individuals, private organizations, and businesses to

contribute more of their money and efforts to public services?

4. How can government officials ensure that their partnerships with private companies

yield benefits to the whole public and not just to the companies?

5. Why is the provision of housing particularly appropriate for privatization?

Analytical Exercises

1. Assume there is a proposal to sell your city or county hospital to a private profit-making company. Identify the pros and cons of this move, taking the perspective of several different stakeholders, such as taxpayers, low-income and upper-income patients, and health professionals. Under what conditions would you support it?

2. You are the head of a nonprofit organization founded to serve the elderly. You have an opportunity to obtain a contract with your county government to expand

your services. The terms would apply tight restrictions with which you are uncomfortable but supply most of the funds you need to fulfill your mission. Without that contract, you must work hard to get voluntary contributions. You believe that your organization would serve elderly people more sensitively than the county welfare agency. And if you don't take the contract, another group will and could displace yours in the charitable "market." What choice would you make and why?

For Further Reading

Donahue, J. D. (1989). *The Privatization Decision.* New York: Basic Books. Broad-ranging inquiry into all aspects of privatization and public/private cooperation, with its pros and cons and political and administrative implications.

Eisinger, P. K. (1988). *The Rise of the Entrepreneurial State: State and Local Economic Development Policy in the United States.* Madison: University of Wisconsin Press. Surveys policies and programs of state and local government involving investments and subsidies to encourage business enterprises.

Kettl, D. F. (1988). *Government by Proxy: (Mis?)Managing Federal Programs.* Washington, DC: CQ Press. A series of cases on federal programs run by contractors, state and local governments, and other nonfederal agencies, raising questions of how well "proxy government" really works.

Kettl, D. F. (1993). *Sharing Power: Public Governance and Private Markets.* Washington, DC: Brookings Institution. Advances view that government has not done well in purchasing goods and services from the private sector and must learn to be a "smart buyer."

Savas, E. S. (1987). *Privatization: The Key to Better Government.* Chatham, NJ: Chatham House. Strong advocacy of privatization in all its forms by one of its best-known proponents, with emphasis on state and local governments.

Smith, S. R., & Lipsky, M. (1993). *Nonprofits for Hire: The Welfare State in the Age of Contracting.* Cambridge, MA: Harvard University Press. Examines the extensive role that private nonprofit organizations play in delivering government's services to citizens.

8

Public Administration and Its Publics

Learning Objectives

After reading this chapter, you should be able to do the following:

1. Identify the roles that governments can play toward individuals and groups in their publics.
2. Define citizen participation and the methods by which it is conducted.
3. Identify the major constitutional rights and liberties that are affected in the operations of public administration and the standards that administrators must follow.
4. Identify the central political issues in relations between citizens and public administrators.

The United States has always had porous borders. It takes time and paperwork to be admitted legally to this country, but millions have avoided that bureaucratic hassle and simply entered. As a result, some 4 million people are here illegally, a number that steadily increases, along with the legally admitted aliens. Illegal aliens are concentrated in six states: California, New York, Texas, Florida, Illinois, and New Jersey. Although some come to be united with family members already here, most are seeking work and a better living standard than they could find in their native countries.

All immigrants, legal or not, are entitled to federal nutritional and medical benefits, public education, and assistance from some state programs. Since some commit crimes, the cost of their trials and imprisonment adds to this burden. California reports that its state and local governments spent $2.3 billion just on the illegal (officially labeled *undocumented*) aliens in 1993, and Florida estimates its costs at $884 million. These states joined in a suit against the federal government to force Congress to provide more money to pay these bills, claiming that lax enforcement by the U.S. Immigration and Naturalization Service is the cause of this burden.

A further response is to curtail benefits to illegal immigrants and in other ways discourage them from staying in the United States. Governor Pete Wilson of California proposed a constitutional amendment that denies citizenship to children born of undocumented parents and asked the federal government to end the mandate to provide them with medical care. His state will also require all first-time applicants for a driver's license to show proof of legal residency (Mahtesian, 1994a). In November 1994, Californians voted to deny all but emergency services to undocumented aliens, although a federal judge blocked enforcement of most of these restrictions on constitutional grounds.

The question is, "What does government owe to those it has not admitted?" We make important distinctions between citizens and aliens, but should undocumented aliens be a third category and be treated as outcasts? There is a serious conflict between the ideal of meeting basic human needs of all people in our midst (not penalizing these immigrants' children for the sins of their parents, for example) and the policy of regulating the rate of immigration for the overall well-being of the nation. That nearly all aliens are people of color, poor, and non-English-speaking makes this a racial and ethnic issue as well. Many Americans of color identify with this issue. Moreover, diplomatic conflicts may arise with some nations from which the immigrants come, notably Mexico.

Who Are the Publics?

So far this book has focused on the organizations and policies that serve the public purposes outlined in Chapter 1. Those purposes, stated abstractly (to "protect lives and property"), are oriented toward the shared needs of large groups rather than toward the unique characteristics of individuals who face many specific threats to their lives and property. But how the public purposes are ultimately served is determined by their impact on one person at a time. Thus, to balance that impersonality, this chapter addresses administrative concerns for individuals and their diverse needs.

Policies wrap citizens in webs of benefits and restrictions that they often find hard to understand. These linkages have a deep impact on how they view authorities and on how much trust and confidence they place in them. Each person's contact with a public schoolteacher, police officer, immigration inspector, or driver's license examiner shapes those feelings.

We can break down those citizen/government relationships into several types, representing linkages that can differ widely from one to another. No government connects in exactly the same manner to every person at the same time, despite its best efforts to provide equal treatment. This is so even with national defense, which provides a "protective umbrella" for every person. The Department of Defense relates to some people as a military or civilian employer, to others as a purchaser of missiles or beans, and to still others as a disturber of their peace when C-5As take off from a base near their homes.

We can discern three segments of **publics** for the purposes of this chapter. First, we think of *individuals* in their direct contacts with government agencies. People do not perceive government as affecting "us" as much as "me." Although it may aim to treat members of large groups uniformly, such as postal customers or people whose houses are on fire, the effects inevitably differ according to individual circumstances. For example, one person's package may be damaged in the mail while another's arrives intact, or one person's home may be closer to a fire station and therefore suffer less damage than another home farther away.

A public can also be a *geographic community,* a cluster of people who are similarly affected by a policy according to where they reside or work. These may be residents of an urban neighborhood demolished for construction of a freeway or automobile plant, the people who live downwind from a nuclear weapons plant and receive repeated doses of radioactive fallout, or citizens of a town that gets a new sewage treatment plant with a federal grant. Such people can share their reactions to that impact and collectively decide how to respond. Their ability to organize politically and speak through a legislator and a unit of local government adds to their influence.

A third kind of public consists of people with a *common interest* that is relevant to public policy and who are affected alike in that relationship. Farmers, Hispanic Americans, airline passengers, children with mental disabilities, and licensed drivers are subjects of specific public policies that treat them in that narrowly functional sense. Each of us belongs to many such publics, whether formally organized or not, and through them we experience varying degrees of government support. A wheat farmer, for example, may be quite satisfied with the crop supports provided by the Department of Agriculture, but his son who has Down's syndrome may be poorly served by the public school he attends.

Interest groups often try to shape those collective relationships. For example, parents of children with disabilities are organized on the national, state, and local levels to influence policies affecting them. A geographic public may also organize formally when its interests are specific and widely shared. Neighborhood organizations in many large cities express their concerns over such matters as crime and housing deterioration. These groups differ in size and power, yet even small associations can find ways to shape policies or administrative actions affecting them.

Government-to-Public Roles

Government agencies and officials can assume several alternative **roles** (consistent relationships and forms of behavior suited to given settings) in relating to these individuals and publics. Some are inherent in the public purpose an action is intended to fulfill; others depend on more individual circumstances. Box 8.1 provides an overview of these roles.

The Benefactor Role

First, government can approach the public as a benefactor, supplying aid or services that meet a legally defined need, usually in response to citizen demands or expectations. The millions of elderly people who receive old-age, survivors, disability, and Medicare payments provide an obvious example, as do the farmers who qualify for crop subsidies. This category extends to state college and university students and to those in private institutions who have a government scholarship or reduced-interest loan. It includes children who choose to play in a city park and nature lovers who are happy that Yellowstone National Park exists, even if they never visit it. The key feature of a benefactor relationship is that the service matches the recipients' needs as they define them. Where the benefit is vital but its quality does not meet expectations, this relationship is strained and citizens may demand that it be expanded or upgraded.

Government is a benefactor to many economic and social interests as well. It has stimulated the growth of aviation, atomic energy, space technology, agriculture, and medical research and development. High-quality schools supply competent employees to local businesses, which is why companies join partnerships for education and job training. The justification is that such benefits to specific enterprises spread to the entire society; various miniaturized electronic components developed for space vehicles are now also used in consumer products, for example. However, we should carefully examine how much public good actually results from each "private" benefit.

Government agencies also act as benefactors when they sell goods and services to the public. In some cases they are the only providers to a given set of consumers. Many cities sell water and electricity to constituents and collect their refuse, charging fees that cover costs and occasionally return a "profit" to the treasury. In

Box 8.1

Relationships between Government and Citizens: Roles That Government Can Play

1. Benefactor

Support income of needy, elderly, and students
Educate persons from early childhood up
Provide cultural and recreational services
Supply housing to low-income households
Sell transportation, deliver mail
Subsidize scientific research and development

2. Regulator

Define and enforce criminal law
Regulate business for economic and social purposes
Limit use of private property

3. Custodian

Require school attendance for certain age groups
Care for persons with physical and mental disabilities
Care for children whose homes are unsuitable
Restrain and rehabilitate criminal offenders

4. Mediator/Advocate

Mediate civil and domestic disputes
Mediate labor–management conflicts
Settle landlord–tenant disagreements
Intervene on behalf of victims of discrimination
Provide legal counsel and representation

5. Employer

Provide jobs and pensions in public employment

6. Victimizer (normally unintentional)

Discriminate against certain classes of persons
Cause harm to health and well-being
Deprive persons of income and property

other situations they compete with private business; some cities sell liquor in competition with private retailers, for example. On the national scale, Amtrak offers transportation to people who could otherwise travel by bus or air, and it advertises heavily to increase its ridership. It is subsidized by Congress, which responds to strong political support from the cities that enjoy its rail service. There is no consistent pattern to such "retail" activities, and they exist only where there is sufficient demand from constituents.

The Regulator Role

Second, government acts as a regulator, controlling or restraining individual action to protect the larger public interest. Much of this is in the realm of business regulation, which is described in Chapter 6. Criminal law, which defines and outlaws acts by individuals and groups that harm or endanger other people and property, constitutes another major category. A regulatory role to one person (e.g., a banker who must follow legally prescribed management practices) is a benefactor role to another (e.g., a depositor in the bank). This situation complicates administrative choices where one action affects people in contrasting ways.

The Custodial Role

Third, government is a custodian, controlling and making choices for those unable to take full responsibility for themselves. In requiring school attendance (or some kind of education, even if at home) for children up to the age of 16, a state does not simply act as a benefactor. It says, in effect, "We know what is best for you, and you must attend school even if you or your parents would rather you did not." It also safeguards the welfare of children whose parents cannot or do not give them proper care and can place them in a foster home of the city or county's choosing. States also play a custodial role for those with mental and physical disabilities who lack adequate private care, and the mentally ill may be forcibly restrained for their own good and that of others.

A different kind of custodial relationship develops from a criminal conviction. A person who is judged likely to repeat an offense or who is otherwise a danger to society must spend a term in the county workhouse or state penitentiary or on probation with limits on activities. The state has the power to control nearly all aspects of an offender's existence. Whether and how the authorities can "correct" or rehabilitate an offender is often in doubt, however.

The central problem of both kinds of custodial relationship is to fit the quasi-parental requirement to individual and societal needs. Many legal battles have been fought over prison environments, therapy for the mentally ill, and standards for foster homes. City officials have debated whether they are legally responsible for the homeless, particularly those with marginal mental disabilities who resist using shelters and other forms of care.

The Mediator and Advocate Role

Fourth, government serves as a mediator or advocate, intervening in private relationships for the good of one or both parties. The courts do this frequently in resolving civil disputes, but many administrative units act similarly. A housing agency may secure a settlement between a landlord and tenant regarding the condition of an apartment, and a social worker may assist in a child custody dispute. The national and state governments have offices that mediate labor/management disputes to avoid strikes and violence. Generally, the aim is to secure a resolution to which the parties voluntarily agree.

Further, state and federal attorneys have intervened to protect the rights of minorities in voting, employment, housing, and other situations in which discrimination occurs. People who cannot afford to hire a lawyer in criminal trials are provided with defense counsel, often from the local public defender's office. Public advocates assist the elderly and disabled in coping with government agencies and private businesses. This form of advocacy has been controversial, since it places a government official in someone's "corner" in opposition to a private party or another part of government. The Legal Services Corporation, a federal agency, has provided free legal assistance to about 1.4 million low-income persons annually.

The Employer Role

Governments also act as employer (or former employer in the case of retirement benefits) for several million citizens. In so doing, governments may also be a benefactor (supplying or financing health care) and regulator (banning smoking in the workplace). Many other workers' jobs depend on government contracts, from aircraft assemblers in defense industries to family counselors in nonprofit organizations. A government job is a benefit to which some may believe themselves entitled. This subject is treated more fully in Chapter 11.

The Role as Victimizer of Citizens

A final role of government must also be discussed, that which turns some citizens into victims. In one sense, they are a "nameless mass whose destiny is subject to forces created by policy implementation. . . . Those in our midst who cannot obtain minimal education, employment, food, or shelter are essentially bereft of resources, and their inability to obtain these resources is to some greater or lesser extent a result of governmental activity" (Lewis, 1977, p. 21). A significant number of homeless people have mental illnesses but have been denied the therapeutic care they need to function outside of institutions. Lacking this, they barely survive in cardboard boxes and lack adequate nutrition and medical attention. These are the systematic victims whose condition results from long-term neglect or biases in public policy. Racial or gender discrimination, which

Box 8.2

Love Canal: Home or Death Trap?

A few hundred people have recently moved into homes on the fringes of Love Canal, on the east side of Niagara Falls, NY. They are willing to risk the unknown threats to health remaining after an expensive cleanup project. Are they victims? Perhaps, but nothing like the previous homeowners in that neighborhood.

As is common with unintended victimization, no single official or agency was fully responsible. Love Canal was originally dug to carry water from the Niagara River to a hydroelectric plant, but was turned into a disposal site by the Hooker Electrochemical Company in the 1940s and 1950s. After filling it with chemical wastes and covering it with a thin layer of soil, Hooker sold part of the site to the Niagara Falls Board of Education, which built an elementary school there. The company warned of potential dangers in the ground, but the effects of such chemicals were not well understood in those days. The rest of the area was sold for homesites after the city approved the subdivisions and built streets and sewers.

The residents began to complain, usually to the city government, of health problems and corrosive seepages from the ground soon after they moved in. No one seriously investigated their concerns until 1976, when state officials began to identify the toxic chemicals left by Hooker. City and school officials refused to act, concerned about legal liability and costs of remedies, and claimed that no solid evidence linked the chemicals with the birth defects and cancers that were common in the neighborhood.

Political action by residents finally resulted in state and federal action in 1978. Most of the residents moved out of the area after the state purchased their homes. The federal Superfund program dug up and destroyed the most hazardous substances, and the school property was buried under a clay cap to seal in the toxins. In 1988 most of the area was declared safe to live in, and abandoned homes were sold to new residents. In a 1994 court settlement, Occidental Chemical Corporation, which had earlier acquired Hooker, agreed to reimburse New York State for $98 million and continue to pump out and treat contaminated water draining the area. Critics argue that much waste remains in the area, however, and that testing of hazards is not adequate.

The new residents are taking a chance. They got their homes at bargain prices, but whether they will prove to be beneficiaries or victims of government's ventures at Love Canal is yet to be seen.

---

many governments have practiced, is another obvious form of victimization.

There are also people who are harmed or disadvantaged by an isolated action or inaction of a government. This group includes people who must put up with noise because their homes are near the flight path of a major airport or a needy person from whom a payment is withheld because of a clerical error. Some of these victims may suffer only from a nuisance or a situation that can be easily corrected, but sometimes life and health may be threatened, as in the Love Canal disaster described in Box 8.2.

Whether or not a person has been victimized in a given situation is often subject to political dispute. Whenever the political or judicial process places a "victim" label on a person or group, it creates an obligation on the part of government to remedy the situation or compensate the person(s). In 1988 the U.S. Supreme Court ruled in *Berkovitz v. United States* that a federal agency may be sued when it negligently approves an unsafe product. In that case, an infant contracted polio from a vaccine that had been approved by the Food and Drug Administration. Obviously, government cannot protect citizens from all hazards to life, and the boundary line between the avoidable and unavoidable is often blurred.

Constituents and Clients: How Citizens Relate to Government Roles

Not everyone is entirely satisfied with the ways in which government relates to them. This is obvious for victims but can be true for others as well. Citizens might want to alter the role relationship, but they differ widely in their ability to influence a government agency. We can distinguish between "constituents" and "clients" in this respect (Lewis, 1977). Constituents are those who, individually and collectively, have significant political influence over bureaucracies that relate to them, whether as benefactors, regulators, or others. They range from large industries that can soften the impact of antipollution regulations to a prominent urban homeowner who gets an otherwise unavailable city public works crew to remove a dead tree.

Clients, by contrast, are those who cannot alter an agency's behavior or decisions. The bureaucracy applies its rules impersonally, which it is expected to do, but it is not set up to make allowances for individual problems. Students in a large state university may find that the school goes by the book in processing registration and financial aid and may find it impossible to get special consideration for their unique circumstances (in contrast, perhaps, to the son or daughter of a state legislator). Even though clients may not be treated unfairly in a legal sense, when they lack a voice, they may gain fewer advantages than constituents.

Citizen Participation in Administrative Decisions

Citizen participation as used here denotes the formal roles played by people who are not elected or full-time appointed government officials in advising or making binding decisions on implementing public policies. These roles, and the powers vested in them, can vary widely. Often they take the form of boards and committees that meet regularly and are entitled to receive official information and to be consulted on given issues. Typically, their input can be reversed or ignored by officials, but they can sometimes exert significant influence.

Participation and the Democratic Process

Citizen participation is foreign to classic bureaucratic theory. Max Weber and Woodrow Wilson alike envisioned that once public servants were entrusted with their tasks and authority, they were to fulfill them without hindrance from the citizenry, who lacked the expertise to instruct or correct them. If citizens wanted to influence those actions, the democratic process demanded that they use the election of legislators and chief executives and the channels of free expression and petition.

Such a limited concept of democracy has been rejected by many politically aware people today. It is felt that many well-educated citizens, experts in their own fields, are qualified to evaluate their government's actions. Others, although they do not call themselves experts, see public programs as more relevant than ever to their lives and opportunities, with as much potential for personal harm as good. Taking the ancient tenets of democracy seriously, they try to influence directly not only legislators' policy decisions but also the means of implementing those decisions. The community development corporations and neighborhood councils described in Chapter 7, as well as a host of voluntary and professional organizations, bring such people together and amplify their voices.

The Advisory Commission on Intergovernmental Relations (1979, pp. 61–62) identified two major purposes of citizen participation: (1) to change government behavior so that it responds better to citizens' needs and desires and refrains from arbitrary, insensitive, or oppressive use of power; (2) to promote participation to help change citizen behavior by providing therapy to alienated and socially disturbed citizens, enabling people to exercise and enhance their vigilance over government, and helping people to develop their leadership capabilities. These aims are not necessarily consistent, so any practical system must emphasize some purposes over others.

Many levels of citizen participation are possible, depending on the influence people can exert (Arnstein, 1969). At the lowest level are *manipulation* and *therapy*, used by the real power wielders to make ordinary citizens feel better about their situations without actually having influence. Above that is *tokenism*—simply being informed of decisions, being consulted, or otherwise placated, which permits a person only to be heard. Involving more significant but less common participation are the top three levels: *partnership*, *delegated power*, and *citizen control*. Where these last three have been used, groups of citizens have exerted enough power to become involved in high-stakes political struggles over the distribution of money, services, and jobs. In public school reform, major contention concerns the amount of power that parents and community leaders have vis-à-vis school boards and administrators. Box 8.3 identifies the most widely used means of citizen participation in administrative decisions.

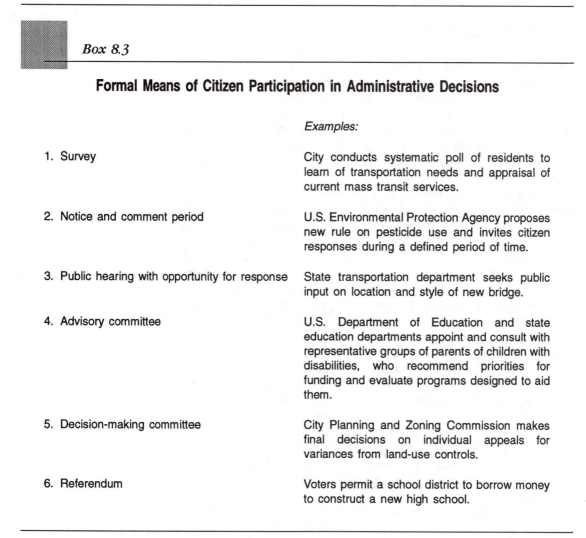

Box 8.3

Formal Means of Citizen Participation in Administrative Decisions

Examples:

1. Survey

City conducts systematic poll of residents to learn of transportation needs and appraisal of current mass transit services.

2. Notice and comment period

U.S. Environmental Protection Agency proposes new rule on pesticide use and invites citizen responses during a defined period of time.

3. Public hearing with opportunity for response

State transportation department seeks public input on location and style of new bridge.

4. Advisory committee

U.S. Department of Education and state education departments appoint and consult with representative groups of parents of children with disabilities, who recommend priorities for funding and evaluate programs designed to aid them.

5. Decision-making committee

City Planning and Zoning Commission makes final decisions on individual appeals for variances from land-use controls.

6. Referendum

Voters permit a school district to borrow money to construct a new high school.

Mandated Participation at the Local Level   Congress first took citizen participation seriously in the Economic Opportunity Act of 1964. It mandated that antipoverty programs in each city provide means by which residents of the neighborhoods served would have "maximum feasible participation" in their design, implementation, and evaluation. Officials were to make special efforts to include on advisory boards diverse racial, ethnic, age, and income groups, both genders, and the disabled and otherwise disadvantaged (Langton, 1981). Similar provisos accompanied other legislation, some of it still in effect.

To meet the mandates, cities formed committees by neighborhood election or appointment by elected officials, or established links with existing citizen organizations. But mayors, council members, and administrators were reluctant to give up their decision-making prerogatives unless they could gain political support or program efficiency in return. As a result, the committees had little influence in many cities in which their views were either not sought or ignored. In other cases, small cliques, which were not representative of a neighborhood, gained power to promote their narrow interests. These experiences initially gave citizen participation a bad name and only increased popular alienation from the programs and their administrators.

Nevertheless, some cities devised formal means for regular citizen input into key decisions affecting their neighborhoods. St. Paul, Minnesota, established a district council system in 1975 that was composed of members elected by the residents of each district. The councils regularly advise the mayor, city council, and planners on zoning choices and public investments, and their views are generally taken quite seriously. Other large and medium-sized cities have variants of this network; their success generally depends on the assertiveness and quality of each group's advice and advocacy and on the openness of the political climate (Scavo, 1993; Peirce, 1994).

Participation in Agency Regulation   The regulatory process, discussed in Chapter 6, has been opened in small ways to formal citizen participation. As of 1981, fourteen states required some "public" or consumer membership on boards that oversee a sector of business or professional activity.

Previously, only qualified specialists or members of the profession served on them (Scholz, 1981). Some federal regulatory proceedings allow individuals and citizen organizations to play a formal role in reviewing agency actions. For example, the Office of Surface Mining (OSM) in the Interior Department is open to citizen input at several points in the implementation of the Surface Mining Control and Reclamation Act. When a company wants to begin surface mining of coal, it must obtain a permit, which is given only after a waiting period in which anyone can express opposition or request a public hearing. After the mining begins, citizens can also file complaints that the terms of the permit are being violated, and the OSM must investigate them. There has been modest but significant participation in the permit decisions, and more in the enforcement process. More than one-third of these citizen complaints triggered mine inspections by the agency. People are most likely to participate when they can see actual events and effects of government decisions (Desai, 1989).

Governments must prepare citizens for intelligent participation by supplying them with information and settings in which they can express themselves. With careful efforts officials can encourage more extensive involvement. For example, Tampa held a "neighborhood convention" in the spring of 1994 at which officials from all city departments met with citizens and neighborhood organizations. Communication went in both directions—information on services was provided and there was public feedback—and personal acquaintances were made (Peirce, 1994). Truly interactive politics, which is now technologically possible through computer linkages, will be gradually introduced as officials see its advantages and budget for the systems.

Outcomes and Limits of Participation

Citizen participation in political and administrative decisions has been widely advocated as a counterweight to the biases of organized interests, a democratic expression of "the people" as opposed to the rich and powerful. But when someone speaks of participation by the people, we must always ask, "Which people?"

Citizen participants are often not "typical" citizens. Members of planning commissions, widely used to study land-use and development decisions and to recommend action to professional planners and city or county councils, are typically of middle to upper income, have above-average education, and are in business or professional occupations. They are likely to be homeowners and long-time community residents. There are relatively fewer women, members of minority racial and ethnic groups, and people under 30 and over 65. The willingness to participate and the capacity to do it effectively depend on personal qualities and skills that are cultivated by and lead to success in higher education and prestigious occupations. Citizens who lack these accomplishments often believe they can have no influence and so do not even try to participate. Knowing this, administrators who seek the sense of the public must be alert to who is not participating (Johnson, 1989).

Citizen influence can also be hampered if there are many clashing voices on an issue. State and local governments turn to advisory groups for guidance on choices involving economic development promotion—groups that often include business owners, labor leaders, and minority group representatives. Disagreement among them is common. This interplay can be beneficial if they speak for the full range of interests at stake. However, when citizen groups fail to convey a clear message, administrators may feel free to ignore them.

Citizen participation can also delay decision making and block necessary choices. Governments have to place airports, penal institutions, and waste-processing facilities somewhere. Such "LULUs" (locally unwanted land uses) produce major negative externalities such as loud noises, noxious smells, and personal danger and can impose health and monetary costs on their neighbors. Determined groups of influential citizens can veto site after site, and the final choice may depend more on the political weakness of the opponents of a facility than on rational judgments about a location's suitability. The environmental justice movement, introduced in Chapter 6, is a response to this power imbalance. The perception of whether citizen vetoes are beneficial depends heavily on one's location and perspective.

Administrators can readily prevent a well-designed participation system from working because of their fear, distrust, or professional pride. "Bureaucrats can often establish the structures for citizen participation by writing rules to govern it. For example, by creating boards composed of disinterested citizens or specifying that participation is to be 'advisory' only, bureaucrats can significantly decrease the potential for citizen impact" (Kweit & Kweit, 1981, p. 73). Through their words and attitudes, administrators can either encourage or discourage persons who are hesitant about their involvement.

Citizen Rights and Liberties

Government/citizen relationships are shaped by the mandates and limits imposed by the legal rights of citizens. In performing their routine functions, administrators may not think about those standards, but a society that is increasingly conscious of its rights and seeking to expand them will not let public servants violate them casually. The basic rights of citizens are defined by national and state constitutions, statutes, administrative rules, and court decisions and are surrounded by a protective shield of public opinion. Box 8.4 presents the basic guarantees of personal rights stated in the U.S. Constitution.

The area of citizen rights is complex and its standards are subject to change with each court decision, so this section can touch on only a few highlights. However, administrators must be aware of the potential for litigation in every action they take, and any case gives a court the opportunity to alter or refine established precedents. It is essential that administrators have a clear legal rationale behind their choices, if only so that they can defend them effectively in court.

The Declaration of Independence framed the basic tenet, "We hold these truths to be self-evident, that all men are created equal, that they are endowed by their Creator with certain unalienable Rights. . . . That, to secure these rights, Governments are instituted among Men, deriving their just powers from the consent of the governed,—That whenever any Form of Government becomes destructive of these ends, it is the Right of the People to alter or to abolish it." On the one hand, government has the mission of securing or protecting the rights of its citizens; on the other, we are reminded that it can violate them. A government that is strong enough to do the former can also do the latter unless its citizens are vigilant in their own protection.

Box 8.4

Selected U.S. Constitutional Guarantees

Amendment 1: Congress shall make no law respecting an establishment of religion, or prohibiting the free exercise thereof; or abridging the freedom of speech, or of the press; or the right of the people peaceably to assemble, and to petition the Government for a redress of grievances.

Amendment 4: The right of the people to be secure in their persons, houses, papers, and effects, against unreasonable searches and seizures, shall not be violated. . . .

Amendment 5: No person shall be . . . deprived of life, liberty, or property, without due process of law; nor shall private property be taken for public use without just compensation.

Amendment 14: All persons born or naturalized in the United States, and subject to the jurisdiction thereof, are citizens of the United States and of the State wherein they reside. No State shall make or enforce any law which shall abridge the privileges or immunities of citizens of the United States; nor shall any State deprive any person of life, liberty, or property, without due process of law; nor deny to any person within its jurisdiction the equal protection of the laws.

The most difficult task for administrators, especially those with enough discretionary power to make major policy choices, is to balance fairly the rights of persons or organizations with the rights and apparent needs of society. Local governments regulate the use of private land, for example, in the interest of public health, welfare, and safety. But when homeowners' defense of their quiet residential neighborhood clashes with an adjoining landowner's intention to construct a shopping center, the outcome cannot maximize everyone's rights or well-being.

Administrative Power and the Rule of Law

Four broad categories of administrative standards related to civil rights and liberties present the most pressing current controversies. First, administrative regulations and procedures that serve legitimate public purposes must be confined by due process of law or they can encroach on civil rights through malice, negligence, or lack of clear definition. Second, public goods and services must be provided in a fair and equitable manner as mandated by the Fourteenth Amendment. Third, positive administrative actions are often necessary to protect the public from violations of rights by units of government or private entities. Fourth, an agency may be obligated to refrain from acting in certain ways because of a person's right not to be interfered with by government.

Due Process of Law   The procedures that government must follow in acting toward a person, what we understand as **due process of law**, have steadily increased in significance within the administrative process. The Fifth and Fourteenth Amendments to the U.S. Constitution forbid the national government and the states from depriving a person of life, liberty, or property without due process. Most people identify due process with the requirement for a fair trial for one accused of a crime, but it applies with almost equal strictness to noncriminal matters. Persons who are subject to some administrative action–granting or denial of benefits, taking of property, or imposition of a penalty–are entitled to adequate notice and a fair hearing before resolution of their case. Many authoritative statements on such matters are decisions of the U.S. Supreme Court, having been occasioned by lawsuits in an atmosphere of legal ambiguity.

Persons who receive public assistance, whether through the Social Security system or state-operated aid programs, depend heavily on the checks they receive each month. An agency action to eliminate or reduce that support could be arbitrary or mistaken and have dire consequences for them. In *Goldberg v. Kelly* (1970), the U.S. Supreme Court ruled that such benefits cannot be terminated before the recipient has had a fair hearing. Justice William J. Brennan, delivering the majority opinion, stated, "When welfare is discontinued, only a predetermination evidentiary hearing provides the recipient with procedural due process. . . . The same governmental interests which counsel the provision of welfare, counsel as well its uninterrupted provision to those eligible to receive it." The opportunity to be heard must be suited to the recipient's ability and circumstances, such as the physical capacity to travel. However, later decisions have added some exceptions to that rule, so administrators must pay attention to the standards that pertain to their particular situation.

Another example of due process concerns the taking of private property for a public purpose, which must be done properly and with "just compensation" (Fifth Amendment). A city redevelopment agency that acquires land for a renewal project or a state that is routing a highway must compensate the owner as deemed fair by a court. Even when a government restricts the use of private land but does not acquire it, it may have to pay compensation. In 1988 the South Carolina Coastal Commission prevented David Lucas from building on his beachfront property in order to protect endangered species and prevent beach erosion. Lucas sued, claiming that his property had been essentially taken without compensation. The U.S. Supreme Court agreed with him in *Lucas v. South Carolina Coastal Commission* (1992), and the state had to buy the lots.

Equitable Provision of Public Goods and Services   A second realm of public rights is defined by the clause in the Fourteenth Amendment covering equal protection of the laws. What this broad dictum means in practice is in constant flux as new controversies arise. As a result, we must rely on a host of court decisions that apply to specific situations. Perhaps the most sweeping is *Brown et al. v. Board of Education of Topeka, Kansas* (1954 and 1955). Faced with the widespread practice of requiring children to attend separate schools because of their race, the justices ruled unanimously that it violated the equal protection clause: "Separate educational facilities are inherently unequal," for they place the stamp of inferiority on the excluded black children and thereby reduce their motivation and ability to learn. Since education is one of the most important functions of state and local governments, the opportunity to learn, "where the state has undertaken to provide it, is a right that must be made available to all on equal terms." The 1955 decision mandated that federal district courts issue such orders as necessary to eliminate discrimination "with all deliberate speed."

In education, efforts were first concentrated on eliminating *de jure* segregation (required by law). After steady but conflict-ridden progress had been made on that, courts and school districts contended over means of reducing *de facto* segregation, the situation in which schools in multiracial cities remained overwhelmingly white or minority because of residential patterns. Large-city districts still have many one-race schools for this reason, although "magnet schools" have achieved some integration. Separate treatment of students with disabilities was the target of congressional action in 1975, mandating that public schools educate them in the least restrictive situation possible.

Since the *Brown* decision, the equal protection clause has been applied to a wide variety of government services. In *Hawkins v. Town of Shaw, Mississippi* (1971), the Fifth Federal Circuit Court of Appeals ruled that a city may not discriminate by the racial makeup of neighborhoods in providing such essential municipal facilities and services as street paving, sewers, and drainage. In *Shapiro v. Thompson* (1969) the Supreme Court forbade a state to discriminate in granting welfare benefits between those who had lived in the state more than one year and those with less than a year's residence.

However, equal protection is not the same as equality in every case. Some groups—children and persons with disabilities—are targeted by public programs for custodial treatment or protection, and these programs have been upheld as serving a legitimate public purpose. Age, gender, race, and ethnicity have been treated more ambiguously; the Supreme Court in the 1980s was less inclined to accept favored treatment of such groups unless it specifically corrected instances of past discrimination against them. In many public services, simple equality is administratively unworkable. Police protection in a high-crime area can never be "equal" to that in a less troubled neighborhood if one measures it by the actual number of crimes committed. A major crime reduction effort is likely to require more police officers where danger of crime is greatest, thus reducing the level of protection in more secure areas.

Remedies of Violations of Rights   The third issue in public rights is the use of action by a public agency to remedy violations of rights within the private sector or by other government agencies. The Civil Rights Acts of 1964 and 1965 empowered the Justice Department to investigate and prosecute violations of equal access to public accommodations, employment, voting, and programs receiving federal grant assistance. Similar legislation in the states over succeeding years also outlawed discrimination in education, housing, medical care, and many other services on grounds of race, ethnicity, gender, physical disability, marital status, and age. Enforcement agencies were also established to investigate complaints and take administrative and judicial action to remedy offenses.

Official enforcement of these legally defined rights is hampered in several ways. Individuals who suffer discrimination must usually initiate action with a formal complaint. Then that complaint has to be investigated by the proper agency, and its backlog of cases may be so large that this may take a long time. Most commonly, action begins with negotiation with the alleged discriminator in an effort to reach voluntary resolution of the dispute. Only if that fails does the agency go to court, and a definitive ruling may take years to emerge, particularly if there are appeals to a higher court. The "administrative distance" that a person must travel before relief is granted is even greater when a federal agency must first deal with a state or local government and the latter resists such pressure.

Protection of Property, Beliefs, and Way of Life   The fourth area of rights relevant to administration is that which precludes government infringement upon a person's property, beliefs, and way of life. We have gradually defined a right of privacy, building on the First Amendment (particularly the guarantees of free exercise of religion and freedom of expression and association) and the first clause of the Fourth Amendment. These bar intrusions on personal life unless an overriding public interest is involved, and administrators must follow due process in carrying out such intrusions.

The historic freedoms identified in the First Amendment—religion, speech, press, and assembly—are relatively well defined in Supreme Court rulings. For example, there are limits on government aid to religious institutions that provide social and educational services. Aid must serve a secular purpose and not primarily promote the religion, and it must not create "excessive entanglements" between government and religion (*Lemon v. Kurtzman,* 1971). Public aid to religious organizations, such as Catholic Charities and the

Salvation Army, for social services they perform for the general public is not barred, nor is a state prohibited from funding "secular" aspects of the curriculum of a religious school.

In recent years Congress and the courts have extended the scope of many religious rights. A state cannot deny unemployment compensation to a person who was fired from a job simply for refusing to work on his religion's holy day, as in *Sherbert v. Verner* (1963), where the plaintiff was a Seventh Day Adventist, for whom Saturday is the day of rest. Congress passed the Religious Freedom Restoration Act in 1993, stipulating that governments can interfere with religious beliefs or practices only to serve a "compelling state interest" and then are limited to the least restrictive means. This could, for example, prevent cities from keeping places of worship from locating in residential areas, a recurring source of political controversy.

Pornography, Privacy, and AIDS: Emerging Controversies

As for the other First Amendment freedoms, the Supreme Court has held in various ways that they can be restricted only when their exercise presents the clear prospect of public harm or disorder. Government may impose "prior restraint" (advance censorship) on speech or print only for the most compelling reasons, such as in banning pornography involving children. A city may restrict the location of adult entertainment businesses but may not ban them altogether. In general, these rulings interpret the Constitution very strictly in favor of individual liberty, and although such rights are violated at times, lower courts usually have clear guidelines by which to rule.

Privacy issues are more complex, with new controversies emerging. In some matters clear legal principles have been established. Businesses and factories may be subject to unannounced health and safety inspections if they are covered by a specific regulatory statute. Welfare officials can pay spontaneous visits to homes of benefit recipients under programs such as Aid to Families with Dependent Children, which prior to 1988 presumed that there was no male wage earner in the family. If the inspector is refused entry, benefits can be terminated (*Wyman v. James,* 1971). In *Griswold v. Connecticut* (1965), the Supreme Court ruled that government cannot ban the use of contraceptives, again upholding privacy in personal relationships. Yet the Court later sent a contrary signal by holding that states may ban homosexual acts in private between consenting adults (*Bowers v. Hardwick,* 1986). Understandably, officials prefer to stay out of situations involving sexual behavior unless a minor is involved or there is violence or coercion.

Many other issues are demanding reinterpretations of the Fourth Amendment, from pornography and drug use to police sur-

Box 8.5

How Far Shall Government Go to Protect Public Housing Residents?

No place in the nation is more dangerous today than a big-city public housing project. Gunshots are frequent and killings routine in such Chicago dwellings as the Robert Taylor Homes. Gang violence, turf wars between rival drug dealers, and random drive-by shootings have terrorized residents, who appeal vainly to police for protection.

President Clinton proposed, in the spring of 1994, to give police sweeping powers to enter project apartments without a warrant to confiscate drugs and illegal weapons. Federal courts had previously blocked efforts to do this, citing the Fourth Amendment. It could be legal if tenants, when they signed their leases, consented to it, he claimed. This would be part of a larger effort to increase security in public housing by patrolling high-crime areas and frisking suspicious persons.

The clash in government's roles here is obvious. There is a constitutional right to privacy; there is also an inherent right to safety and security. Must public housing tenants, who are poor and often of color, give up their privacy to gain their security? Housing authorities argue that they cannot manage the buildings properly in a violent setting without additional powers. Civil liberties advocates respond that the social status of public housing residents is in effect costing them the rights that are protected for more affluent persons.

---

veillance of suspected criminals and parental discipline of children. Box 8.5 highlights a conflict between privacy in one's home and the need to keep that living environment safe. On one side, it is argued that fewer restraints on administrators and law enforcement officers would free them to take stronger action against drug trafficking and child abuse. Civil libertarians warn that government intrusion in personal lives has no natural stopping point and could spawn the very tyranny that the writers of the Bill of Rights feared.

The AIDS epidemic has raised many difficult issues in privacy debates. Some states require reporting of all HIV virus carriers, whereas others call only for AIDS victims to be registered. Public health officials in some states have authority to quarantine AIDS carriers under certain circumstances to minimize spread, which immediately alerts others. Even if victims were forbidden to engage in behavior likely to transmit the disease, enforcement of that ban would be impossible unless the persons were in custody. Public health officials discern an equally poignant dilemma in regard to permitting health professionals who have the HIV virus to continue practicing. To bar them may be unjust if there is no danger of their transmitting the disease, but for even one patient to become infected would be unacceptable. In the absence of any definitive Supreme Court ruling on this problem, the debate will continue, and administrators must fall back on such statutes, lower court decisions, and precedents as they judge to apply in individual situations, as unsatisfactory as they may be.

Political Issues in Administrative/ Citizen Relations

People have often asked, "Can modern organizations be compassionate? Can they 'care'?" (Thompson, 1975, p. 8). For a government organization to show personal regard for those it serves, regulates, or otherwise deals with, its employees must be caring and have the opportunity to show it. Yet the logic of bureaucracy, having rightly enshrined impartiality, consistency, and conformity to law and rules, can prevent those individuals from expressing compassion. Citizens are indeed entitled to fair and respectful treatment, and when they do not receive it, they can turn it into a political issue. When they expect special favors, the conflict can be even sharper.

Conflict and Equity in Administrative Choices

Conflict commonly arises when a policy affects segments of the public that have different interests. The typical regulatory agency serves the general public in keeping food safe to eat, utility prices at a fair level, and nuclear power plants from leaking radioactivity. But when the Food and Drug Administration considered protecting consumers by banning the use of a chemical (Alar) that improves the appearance of apples, it encountered resistance from the producers and sellers of the chemical and the apple growers who use it. One group may view a given regulation as oppressive, another as beneficial, and a third with mixed feelings. Although resolving conflicts does not have to be a zero-sum game in which one party's gain exactly matches another's loss, the most likely compromise is one that fails to please anyone.

A second problem is that agency actions toward a legally recognized clientele may have unintended and negative consequences for other groups of people. The "occasional victim" often appears in this connection. For example, in the urban freeway programs of the past four decades, the intended beneficiaries were the motorists and businesses benefiting from safer and more rapid access. However, many residents and merchants were uprooted from the neighborhoods that were destroyed to make way for the roads. Property owners were compensated, but renters of homes and business spaces had to leave also, and Congress mandated relocation aid for them only after much harm had been done. Since the freeways made mass transit less viable, those who continued to rely on it often had to pay higher fares for poorer service. Most government programs designed to benefit specific constituencies encounter similar problems because their direct and indirect effects reverberate through an interdependent society. It is essential that planners take significant side effects into consideration.

As a third issue, various clienteles of the government provide feedback to agencies on their performance and influence future policy and implementation. This grows out of the "structure of influence" described in Chapter 2 and is a central function of interest groups. They also provide essential political support to the agencies, which must compete with many others for funds and authority. It is common for federal agencies to create advisory committees representing the business groups they serve or regulate. In 1984 there were 928 officially recognized advisory bodies attached to federal departments and agencies and focused on matters ranging from vocational education to weapons systems. Many observers are concerned that these advisory groups constitute channels for unfair influence and conflicts of interest, since many of those represented in the groups benefit from federal contracts or subsidies (Seidman & Gilmour, 1986, pp. 293–300).

A fourth concern is the effect on citizens of the actions of public employees whose jobs permit considerable discretion but who work in locations that cannot be directly supervised by higher administrators. Such **street-level bureaucrats** include law enforcement officers, social workers, health and safety inspectors, doctors and nurses in government hospitals, and teachers. Their jobs may be well defined by the law and agency rules, yet much of their official conduct may be shaped by the degree of compliance or belligerence they encounter from the client. Besides, the employees' personalities enter the picture as they use their discretion in various situations (Lipsky, 1979). Since their work is not subject to immediate supervision, disputes over whether a police officer used brutality in an arrest or a teacher was biased against a child may be difficult to investigate, let alone resolve.

Rationing and Bias in Service Provision

In addition to the administrative conflicts and problems already discussed, public agencies may inadvertently ration the services they provide or show biases among recipients. This may happen in several ways. Free services to which people are legally entitled may have "costs" of various sorts attached. There is a psychological cost or stigma in depending on a "poor people's service." When applying for aid, the person must supply information about family, finances, and living conditions that is otherwise considered private. Next, there is a cost in time, because of, for example, the lengthy application process and delays in processing and providing the aid. The necessity of traveling to an office in order to apply may impose a particular hardship. Further, the client may have difficulty obtaining information about the benefit and how to apply for it. Those who

Box 8.6

How Does the Welfare System Treat Its Clients?

Barbara Sabol had a big question. Sabol, who heads New York City's immense Human Resources Administration, wanted to determine how her agency was treating the more than one million persons who depend on its benefits. She got her answer by putting on disguises and posing as a welfare applicant herself over a span of 8 months in 1992.

In her journeys from one office to another, Sabol encountered many indignities. She was sent to wrong offices, waited in long lines, and had a clerk lose a set of her important documents. She claimed she was searching for a job and needed temporary assistance until she found one. It took 6 to 8 weeks to get on the assistance rolls because, she was told, she had not supplied enough documentation. She repeatedly asked for work but was given only a part-time post as a clerk for the city. In all, she learned what it was really like to be on public assistance through the condescending and occasionally rude treatment she experienced. While she afterward praised most of her employees, she lamented the culture of the system as a whole. "I ceased to be," she concluded of her experience (Mitchell, 1993).

---

are illiterate, do not understand English, or have disabilities are especially disadvantaged when agencies do not communicate well. Overall, the "decision not to market public services strikes at clients who are isolated from informal networks. This probably affects the elderly most heavily; it certainly has a greater impact on the rural than on the urban poor" (Prottas, 1981, p. 532). Barbara Sabol's experience, described in Box 8.6, dramatizes these costs.

This bias also stems from the middle-class background and perceptions of most public administrators (Sjoberg, Brymer, & Farris, 1966). They routinely deal with one another in an impersonal, rule-oriented manner. However, most lower-class clients, because of lack of education, confidence, or communications skills, are more comfortable with relationships that are based on friendship. They are less likely to be familiar with the written and unwritten rules by which welfare agencies, schools, and the police operate. When they misunderstand what is happening, this leads to distrust that blocks further communication. These barriers prevent people from receiving the quantity and quality of service they are entitled to.

To attend to the needs of the disadvantaged, some governments have programs that target the needs of one social group and exclude others. Several cities are experimenting with special public schools for African American males, reasoning that standard educational programs fail to serve them and provide positive role models that counteract the negative environment of the streets. Chicago has subsidized housing developments specifically for low-income people with hearing impairments and the elderly of Japanese, Chinese, and

Korean origins. Although no one disputes that the needs exist, disagreements arise over how exclusive these services should be and whether there is equal opportunity for "nontargeted" people to obtain the same services.

It is essential that governments and businesses have some private, personal information about citizens, but we lack comprehensive public policies that determine the kind and degree of information that should be collected and retained or the conditions under which it should be transmitted to others. One dilemma is that the data necessary to provide equal protection of the laws—a child's test scores that confirm a learning disability or a Hispanic person's employment history—can be misused and lead to greater injustice as well. A second problem is that data privacy laws conflict with the "open government" ideal that public records should be available for public inspection to prevent governments from taking secret actions that would be contrary to the public interest. Practically speaking, there are now so many public and private computer databases in the nation, and uncounted linkages among them, that any overall regulation would be difficult to impose. New information technologies constantly come on the market, but laws or court decisions covering them do not appear until years later.

Toward a Customer Orientation in Government

We have seen that people can be regarded by their governments as constituents, clients, and victims. The latest addition to this list is "customers," popularized by Osborne and Gaebler (1992), among others. This category is intended to spark a new attitude of public service among bureaucrats, similar to that of a business that must compete for markets by offering patrons more or better service. It fits the public culture of the 1990s as well, with its widespread dissatisfaction with government and increased consumer consciousness. To regard a person as a customer is to assume that he or she has a choice between sellers and buys where the bargain is best. This model had not formerly been thought relevant to most parts of government, since government does not compete in the marketplace.

The surprise is that even government agencies with no competition have discovered that a "customer consciousness" opens up opportunities and enhances their public image. Osborne and Gaebler (pp. 170–171) offer examples such as a school district offering extended day care for latch-key children and a motor vehicle agency using computer terminals to renew drivers' licenses. Even the U.S. Internal Revenue Service, a monopoly agency if there ever was one, has issued customer service standards, cited in Box 8.7.

Agencies can listen to public voices through many channels, including surveys of patrons and the community at large, customer

---

Box 8.7

Can the Internal Revenue Service Be User-Friendly?

As part of the National Performance Review (1993, p. 60), the IRS published the following customer service standards. Since it has a well-deserved reputation as one of Washington's least user-friendly agencies, these standards will be revolutionary if the IRS consistently follows them.

- If you file a paper return, your refund due will be mailed within 40 days.
- If you file an electronic return, your refund due will be sent within 14 days when you specify direct deposit, within 21 days when you request a check.
- Our goal is to resolve your account inquiry with one contact; repeat problems will be han-

dled by a Problem Resolution Office in an average of 21 days.
- When you give our tax assistors sufficient and accurate information and they give you the wrong answers, we will cancel related penalties.
- With your feedback, by 1995 IRS forms and instructions will be so clear that 90 percent of individual tax returns will be error-free.

It will take a substantial change in organizational culture, investment in employee training, and probably an increase in personnel doing client service to accomplish these goals. Since income tax collection depends heavily on voluntary compliance, better "customer relations" might actually increase revenues.

---

councils and focus groups, electronic mail, test marketing of new services, quality guarantees, complaint tracking systems, and toll-free 800 telephone numbers to receive questions and concerns. These have been most extensively used by state and local authorities, probably because of their closer political proximity to citizens.

When customers are in the "driver's seat," Osborne and Gaebler assert (pp. 181–185), several benefits come to citizens and government alike. First, agencies become more accountable to those they serve. Second, political pressures become less important when service providers are chosen. Third, agencies are more likely to innovate when they see ways in which they can serve customers faster or better. A fourth advantage is that customer-driven services offer people more choices, as can be seen particularly in education, where charter schools and other alternatives have arisen. Further, agencies are driven to be more efficient, because they learn how to match their efforts more closely to public needs. This point was also emphasized by the National Performance Review in its 1993 report. Finally, customer orientation is likely to increase equity, by improving service to people of low income and color, who are ordinarily the most discriminated against.

We should approach the enthusiasm for customer consciousness with caution. It is most appropriate when government plays a well-defined benefactor role, from public libraries to job training, and it is necessary when citizens must deal directly with an agency (and would prefer not to) such as the Internal Revenue Service. But in many instances customers' wants are inappropriate or even illegal. A public school principal should listen carefully to parents but cannot accede to their every wish. Those who have been placed in a custodial relationship with government have been judged unable to make their own choices outside certain limits.

A further problem appears when "customers" express conflicting wants. The U.S. Food and Drug Administration relates to several publics: pharmaceutical companies, medical professionals, and drug consumers, to name just three. It must make careful judgments when deciding whether to approve a new medicine, recognizing pressures both to speed up and to practice even more caution. Each public has important political influence on its side, including the ability to sue the agency. Essentially, this customer approach adds an important dimension to government/public relations, but it must be adapted with care to each situation.

American Administration and International Publics

The publics defined in this chapter, whatever their differences, are all located within the boundaries of the United States. But other publics affected by actions of American governments not only have almost no ability to influence those actions, but also are often nearly invisible to us. These are the citizens of other nations whose lives may be caught up in the outflow of American public policy, and they deserve attention in this study of implementation. Their well-being and ours are linked, sometimes very closely.

An abundance of services to citizens of other nations marks our foreign relations, from nutrition, health, and educational aid, to public works projects. Much of this has gone to nations that support our strategic military policies, such as Israel, Egypt, Taiwan, and Pakistan. However, aid has frequently enriched the already-wealthy in some of those countries and propped up military dictatorships, while little has trickled down to those with the greatest need, thus widening the economic gaps between rich and poor.

Consider the impoverished farmer in Peru or Bolivia who finds in the coca leaf a crop that pays well enough to feed his family. The U.S. authorities, in order to dry up the source of that raw material for cocaine, would like to induce the farmer to grow something else. But can we accomplish that goal without locking thousands of rural families in poverty? We probably create untold "victims" around the world with programs designed to benefit our own citizens. Our obligations to victims are not legal but moral, and there is no accepted standard for compensating them.

That "foreign" problems return to our shores is illustrated by the fact that pesticides banned for use in American agriculture can be sold abroad and contaminate the produce we import from the countries that use them. In the mid-1980s, the U.S. government forbade the use of chlordane and heptachlor, suspected of causing cancer. A loophole in the law permitted foreign sales, and many countries do not regulate use of these chemicals at all. Their citizens, particularly farm workers, are heavily exposed to them, and no one knows what health effects they have had. In 1988 it was revealed that 42,000 pounds of beef with significant traces of those chemicals entered this country from Honduras and passed into our markets before the Food and Drug Administration detected it (Schmickle, 1990). Again, the effects are unknown.

The fortunes of all the world's publics are enmeshed with those of the United States. There is no doubt that the concerns of this chapter will become increasingly multinational in years to come.

Summary

Administrators must be sensitive to their multiple relationships with individual citizens and the private groups that represent them. We can discern three "publics": individuals in their direct contacts with government agencies, geographic communities of those similarly affected by one or more policies according to where they reside or work, and people with a common interest that is relevant to public policy and who are affected alike in that relationship.

Governments play six major roles in their relationships to these publics: (1) benefactor, providing desired and needed services and goods; (2) regulator, requiring or prohibiting some form of behavior; (3) custodian, making choices for those who are unable to take full responsibility for themselves; (4) mediator or advocate, intervening with a third party on behalf of clients; (5) employer, providing a job or pension through government directly; and (6) victimizer, causing harm or disadvantage through unintentional actions or inaction. Clients vary widely in their ability to influence government roles in their own interests.

Citizen participation denotes a formal role played by a person who is not an elected or appointed government official in advising or making decisions on implementing public policies. Many means have been developed to enable such people to take part in administrative decisions, with wide variations in effectiveness.

Administration can promote or violate the constitutional rights and liberties of Americans in four specific areas: guaranteeing due process of law in all official relationships, providing equal protection of the laws in all services and regulations, protecting the public from violations of rights by units of government or private entities, and refraining from acting in certain ways in order to respect a person's right not to be interfered with by government.

Political conflicts often arise because of differing role expectations of publics affected by a policy: unintended consequences for one public of a policy designed for another public; influence of organized clients on agency decisions; choices and actions of "street-level bureaucrats," who are not under direct supervision by higher administrators; rationing and bias in service provision according to the social characteristics of clients; favoritism toward certain groups; and the existence in data banks of personal information about citizens that threatens their privacy.

American administration also affects foreign publics in many ways, intentionally and unintentionally. Not only is the well-being of billions of the world's population affected, but there are indirect effects on Americans as well.

Discussion Questions

1. What differences should there be in the services that a nation provides to its citizens and to resident aliens? Should the services to aliens, whether "legal" or "illegal," depend on their ability to work and pay taxes?

2. What potential conflicts are there between the government-to-citizen roles outlined in this chapter? For example, can one program effectively play both a benefactor and a regulator role?

3. What practical limits are there to citizen participation in administrative decisions and processes?

4. What specific difficulties do public agencies encounter in providing "equal protection of the laws" to their many publics?

5. What conflicts between the interests of American publics and clients and those of foreign nations are most relevant to public administration?

Analytical Exercises

1. Governor Wilson of California has proposed that every resident of his state be required to obtain an official identity card and show it when applying for a job, entering school, and seeking health service. This would, among other advantages, distinguish between persons who are in the United States legally and those who are undocumented. One could imagine a future world in which the identity card also carries health data, credit standing, and a criminal record on a chip that could be read by a computer. Proponents argue that the card could reduce fraud and protect persons who are behaving legally. Opponents fear the intrusion into personal privacy and misuse of this information. Argue a case pro or con, with any modifications you care to make in the proposal.

2. Many local communities provide opportunities for citizens to be involved in public decision making alongside the formally elected officers. Planning commissions were mentioned in this chapter, but other bodies are often concerned with parks and recreation, economic development, and human relations. Make a survey of such opportunities in the city or county in which you reside or attend school and determine the extent of the influence the members can exert.

For Further Reading

Hadden, S. G. (1989). *A Citizen's Right to Know: Risk Communication and Public Policy.* Boulder, CO: Westview Press. Explores government and industry disclosure to nearby residents and local officials of hazards to life and health in plants and storage areas.

Levine, A. G. (1982). *Love Canal: Science, Politics, and People.* Lexington, MA: D. C. Heath. Comprehensive case study of the discovery of and initial efforts to remedy the nation's first well-publicized toxic waste crisis and its effects on the victimized residents of that Niagara Falls neighborhood.

Lewis, E. (1977). *American Politics in a Bureaucratic Age: Citizens, Constituents, Clients, and Victims.* Cambridge, MA: Winthrop. Surveys the many ways in which government agencies relate to people who depend on political resources to exert power; develops the "victim" concept with examples.

Lipsky, M. (1979). *Street-Level Bureaucracy.* New York: Basic Books. The first major discussion of this crucial layer of administrators who have the most direct contact with citizens.

Piven, F. F., & Cloward, R. A. (1993). *Regulating the Poor: The Functions of Public Welfare.* New York: Random House. Classic study of the welfare system as a response to economic downturns and social disorders and the problems of implementing it.

Rosenbloom, D. H., & Carroll, J. D. (1990). *Toward Constitutional Competence: A Casebook for Public Administrators.* Englewood Cliffs, NJ: Prentice Hall. Overview of court decisions interpreting the constitutional rights of citizens in their relations with administrative agencies.

9

Administrative Leadership and Management

Learning Objectives

After reading this chapter, you should be able to do the following:
1. Identify the categories of executives in government, defined by formal responsibilities and means of selection.
2. Identify the basic functions of executives common to all organizations.
3. Define the specific powers, responsibilities, and resources of government executives at the national, state, and local levels.
4. Contrast the authoritarian, democratic, and laissez-faire styles of leadership.
5. Identify the key factors to success in organizational leadership.

Most government executives, the public seems to believe, simply want to keep the status quo. They fear any change that would disrupt their comfortable routines. Although some doubtless fit this description, more and more executives at all levels strive to be change agents. Certainly this label belongs to Ada Deer, who became the first Native American female head of the U.S. Bureau of Indian Affairs (BIA) in August 1993. A Menominee from Wisconsin, she became the first member of her tribe to earn a graduate degree. She had first encountered the BIA three decades earlier, when she was a young social worker eager to bring about change on behalf of her fellow Native Americans. She failed then but now has another chance.

The BIA has long been regarded as Washington's most inept agency. Its relations with most tribal leaders have been prickly, and rank-and-file Native Americans do not trust it at all. Moreover, it has an abominable record of spending money and accounting for it. Its task is complicated by the fact that Congress has not determined what kind of relationships it wants with the tribes—nor do the tribal leaders agree among themselves. Deer pledged not only to reform the BIA internally—to train its employees and remove those who don't produce—but to rework the nation's policies toward Native Americans. Neither task was easy for her in her first year, and she was not immune to criticism (Adams, 1994).

Deer aims to be a change agent rather than a maintainer. In the current jargon, she intends to "reinvent" her part of the government. That term has come to carry many different meanings, but for her the demand is to make the BIA more responsive to her people. This suggests an emerging demand for all who head public agencies: to regard their clients or constituents as "their people" and to orient the organization accordingly.

The Ambivalent Position of Government Executives

Government's position in American society is ambivalent: supplying benefits and imposing costs, prohibiting some activities and requiring others. In reality it is our public officials who occupy this ambivalent position. We entrust them with the management of far more money than we could handle ourselves and with our lives, health, jobs, and homes. Before we do so, we give them such titles as president, governor, secretary, mayor, and superintendent. Those who run for election to their posts are expected to promise voters more benefits at less cost, and certainly more than the opponent can deliver. But the political and legal systems have woven a net of checks and balances around these executives: limited terms of office, constitutional and legal mandates and proscriptions, vigilant interest groups, political parties hungry for votes, and information media alert to every lapse and misdeed, all wrapped within the general popular suspicion that no one can be trusted with much power for long.

The ambivalence with which Americans view executives was apparent among the framers of the Constitution as they chose the powers and checks to incorporate into the new office of president. Their dilemma has echoed down the years through the greatly changing demands on public executives. In 1788 Alexander Hamilton wrote in *The Federalist* No. 71, "The republican principle demands that the deliberate sense of the community should govern the conduct of those to whom they intrust the management of their affairs; but it does not require an unqualified complaisance to every sudden breeze of passion, or to every transient impulse which the people may receive" (Hamilton, Jay, & Madison, n.d.). A republican president, responsible to the whole people, was a radical innovation in its time, and there were no known means for keeping such a person both accountable and effective.

Each official works within a system of accountability to higher executives, legislators, courts, and citizens. But that official also requires, according to Hamilton, the autonomy to act according to his or her best judgment to serve the public purposes within the law and not be harassed by constant interference over matters of means and detail. For example, a president generally has been free to pursue consistent policies toward foreign nations despite events that may spur some citizens to demand changes. Where that balance should be found has been decided repeatedly by political rather than legal or administrative criteria.

Each administrator has a formally assigned post within a bureaucratic structure to exert the control necessary to accomplish its legal objectives. But the structure of interests identified in Chapter 2 pays close attention to how they accomplish those objectives and applies power and influence that supplement (and at times contradict) the directives from higher executives. For the director of the Occupational Safety and Health Administration (OSHA), charged with oversight of workplaces, one line of control comes from the president through the secretary of labor. Another is from Congress, particularly the committees that specialize in labor legislation, as it passes laws and appropriations that apply to OSHA. Outside pressures originate in the many employers and trade associations that feel the direct effect of the rules and inspections, and from the labor unions, which usually argue that the agency is not protective enough. Judges rule on disputes that individuals raise with the agency or employers. None can be ignored, but a director has room to shift the balances between these competing demands. The challenge is to do this diplomatically while implementing the laws.

The Levels of Government Executives

Box 9.1 identifies government executives in four levels. The fourth group is the largest but least clearly defined. Its members are appointed to their posts because of their expertise and experience. Often they have risen through the ranks in the civil service system and enjoy more job security than those in groups 2 and 3. Whether the job is technical director of a naval weapons laboratory or superintendent of a state prison, the line separating its holder from "nonexecutives" is not sharp, since the demands gradually narrow as one moves down the ladder of authority. A department head with 1,000 workers usually qualifies as an executive, but an office manager with ten subordinates does not typically encounter the challenges on which this chapter focuses.

Box 9.1

Government Executives

1. Elected chief executive:

   President of the United States
   Governor of a state
   Mayor of a city or county with administrative role

2. Chief executive appointed by legislative body:

   City or county manager
   Superintendent of schools
   Special district administrator

3. Executive appointed by chief executive:

   Cabinet secretary and assistant, national and state
   Bureau and agency head, national and state
   Head of city or county department
   Commissioner of regulatory agency, national and state
   Administrator of government corporation

4. High-level administrator appointed by professional selection or through merit system:

   Immediate subordinate of those in groups 2 and 3

Since the agencies and units of government they head are often interdependent, these executives rely on others for information, material support, and sometimes political backing. OSHA works closely with its counterpart agencies in the states to enforce its rules and uses research by the Environmental Protection Agency, Public Health Service, and other units for analyses of hazardous chemicals used in the workplace. How well this works often depends on the climate for cooperation that the executives promote.

The Presidency and Its Power Each executive functions amid a complex of powers and limits to those powers. The legal position of the presidency is impressive, often reinforced in the public's mind by the news media and election campaigns. But these *powers* are no guarantee of *power* as it is understood in the political sense of the ability to enforce one's will despite opposition. The national government is so fragmented that other executive branch administrators can avoid doing a president's bidding. Members of Congress and judges have a constitutional license to resist. The president must therefore "induce them to believe that what he wants of them is what their own appraisal of their own responsibilities requires them to do in their interest, not his" (Neustadt, 1980, p. 35). Presidential power is thus the power to persuade, through a continuous process of bargaining in which the incumbent's legal powers are vital but must be augmented by incentives and sanctions, popular support, and a strong reputation for accomplishing what he wants.

The national executive branch is not a Weberian pyramid of unquestioned authority but an alliance of department and agency heads with personal goals, organizational purposes, and external interests to serve. "Each member will find it necessary at times to act contrary to the interests of the alliance when compelled to do so to protect his own vital interests. Unless a president is able to convince his departmental allies that they need him as much as he needs them, they will inevitably gravitate to another power base" (Seidman & Gilmour, 1986, p. 79). Ada Deer at the BIA has found that the change she seeks brings her into occasional conflict with her superiors and colleagues who view relations with Native Americans differently.

Lower-Level Executives   Other executives face similar difficulties in translating "powers" into *power*. The very federal executive branch officials who can frustrate the president are themselves subject to checks from all sides. Deer has a major challenge in Congress's habit of micromanaging the BIA and tacking minor mandates and restrictions onto its annual appropriations. State governors and big-city mayors must cope with similar networks of more or less autonomous officials. Those in subordinate appointed posts at state and local levels continuously interact with higher and lower officials and with equals as well.

Thus, executives who may appear from a distance to be all-powerful are actually hedged in by checks and procedural restraints on all sides. "From the inside, the leader feels like a lonely, constrained, even isolated figure . . . who cannot get his or her staff, bureaucracy, constituencies, or neighboring institutions to work together and stop fighting with one another" (Yates, 1985, p. 11). Amid such constraints, a public executive has many incentives to pursue a conserving course, protecting the status quo as preferable to changes with unknown results. Yet the demands on governments at all levels are escalating, not only to remedy problems in existing programs but to respond to new challenges in health care, energy, employment, and other fields.

Transactional and Transforming Leaders

Leaders in government and throughout society can act in two distinct roles: transactional and transforming (Burns, 1978). The transactional leader initiates exchanges with other powerful persons of items they both value. Each party serves its own purposes thereby, and there is no higher end to reach in the bargain. The transforming leader is oriented to fulfilling higher moral needs, in a relationship that enriches both leaders and followers. This leader recognizes the essential needs and interests of the public, expresses them, and secures mutual action to fulfill them.

Transactional leaders are common in all parts of government. They depend on one another and on their subordinates, as we have already seen. Agencies protect the status quo, in which they do certain jobs with certain routines and make only minor adjustments. After all, a municipal street department can only build and repair streets, and its head will interact with other city officials in deciding which streets will be improved, when, and with what work rules.

The transforming leader is much less common. Franklin Delano Roosevelt is an example of such a leader. He not only used the power and finances of the national government to respond to the Depression of the 1930s but spoke inspiringly ("the only thing we have to fear is fear itself," for example) and initiated new programs to stimulate employment that brought major changes in both our public policies and our means of implementing them. Some governors, mayors, and school superintendents have been agents of change within their more limited realms as crises over civil rights or urban decay appeared. Despite the best of efforts, the risks are high that people won't be transformed and will turn their leaders out in the next election. President Carter sought major changes in the American public's attitude toward energy consumption, but his 1980 defeat put an end to planning for conservation and alternative fuels.

Public officials have the best potential for moral leadership in times of great crisis or rising popular concern. Dr. C. Everett Koop, the U.S. surgeon general during much of the 1980s, gained much visibility as he strove to shape the nation's awareness of AIDS and the hazards of smoking. He used the news media skillfully to address deeply felt health concerns. However, he had limited powers in his office, a unit of the Department of Health and Human Services, to initiate new efforts without approval of the department's secretary, the president, and key congressional committees.

Functions of Public Executives

This list of executives' functions and duties does not consist of just six (or ten or 100) discrete demands that can be checked off each day. They are so closely linked that fulfillment of any one depends on several others. A weakness at any point can reduce overall effectiveness.

Let us consider six major functions, built on the concept of organization as a system of cooperative activity to accomplish common goals (Barnard, 1938). The central function of the head of this

Box 9.2

Major Functions of Public Executives

1. Define and articulate the mission of the organization and the part that each member plays in it.
2. Maintain exchange with the organization's external environment to obtain its essential services and resources.
3. Secure, retain, and motivate the persons whose skills are essential to the agency's mission and assign them places in which they can make their best contributions.
4. Maintain a system of communication upward and downward through the organization to support authority over subordinates and provide feedback on the results.
5. Order and manage internal conflict, harnessing specific disputes to serve the mission and keep them from destroying either the agency or its members.
6. Initiate and facilitate innovation as necessary to achieve the agency's mission in a changing environment.

system is to maintain the kind and level of cooperation necessary to fulfill its goals within its unique social, technological, and political environment. Summarized in Box 9.2, these complement the discussion in Chapter 3 of the imperatives for organizational management.

Define and Articulate the Mission

The first function of the executive is to define and articulate the mission of the organization as a whole and the part each member plays in it. This mission is "given" in the law and the agency's history, yet each new executive must renew it in the light of its current challenges. It is not sufficient to post on a bulletin board a description of the legal mission of the U.S. Consumer Product Safety Commission or the Los Angeles County Health Department. Rather, the top leaders must express the mission continually in their words and actions so that it can become more than a formality. Along with the many personal motives that employees hold, there should be a parallel commitment to the common purpose.

Many agencies define their missions broadly enough to leave room for initiative by their executives. A county child protection office has the power to remove children from their homes when those children are judged to be abused or neglected. A broader and more inspiring mission (if also more demanding and less achievable) is that of building healthy families and cultivating beneficial self-images on the part of the children it works with. "Paperwork or people" may be too simplistic a dichotomy, but a leader can induce members to consider the holistic needs and potentials of clients at the same time the members are processing a ten-page form. In so doing, the leader identifies the agency itself with its public purposes and invests it with a value beyond a mere place to earn a living (Selznick, 1957). Thus, schools become more than places to keep children off the streets for part of the day or to provide stable employment for teachers and custodians. Agencies best fulfill their public purposes when their personnel see the organization and themselves as creators of opportunity for all parts of the population, making a critical difference in the lives of the least advantaged members of the population.

Obtain Resources and Services

The second function of the executive is to maintain a dialogue with the organization's external environment to obtain essential services and resources. This is the imperative of equilibrium described in Chapter 3, which keeps the organization in existence and producing the goods and services for which it was established. The organization maintains this by performing "critical tasks" essential to this exchange (Wilson, 1989, p. 25). For example, the Centers for Disease Control in the U.S. Public Health Service maintain constant innovation at the frontiers of medical technology, and a municipal public works department keeps the water pure and the traffic flowing.

Government organizations are unlike those in the private sector in that they need not ordinarily be concerned with "going out of business." As long as they perform what legislators and constituents consider an essential function, a balance of some sort will continue. This renders the equilibrium problem one of power and extent of service rather than of survival. Yet NASA's budget has been steadily reduced, funding a lower and lower level of activity, since its executives have not, for numerous reasons, obtained funds for their more ambitious vision of space exploration. Municipal service agencies have also lost business to private contractors in some localities, as explained in Chapter 7; this also is an equilibrium issue.

An effective administrator, in this context, is one who can make a compelling case for the agency's mission and the means to fulfill it and then order its internal operations to fulfill that goal to the satisfaction of its "market." For example, to avoid privatization of first-class mail delivery, the director of the Postal Service must continually upgrade the efficiency of its operations. Similarly, national, state, and local health departments have no choice but to respond to concerns about AIDS, as Surgeon General Koop realized; however, the lack of a known cure prevents them from satisfying their customers fully.

The "market" in which public agencies compete is populated by other agencies that compete with equal vigor for the limited supply of funds. Thus, an administrator must convince legislators and chief executives that his or her agency deserves those resources more than a rival and must mobilize allies to help persuade them.

Obtain and Develop Human Resources

The third function of the public executive is to secure, retain, and motivate people with skills essential to the agency's mission and assign them to areas where they can make their best contributions. Highly skilled people usually work in a seller's market, so the agency must offer competitive terms. Civil service rules often limit salaries, and there may be other disincentives to government employment, such as the greater public scrutiny that focuses on the job.

Presidents fill by personal appointment about 500 high policy-making and -implementing posts in the departments, independent agencies, corporations, and regulatory commissions. They often seek people who occupy correspondingly high positions in major private organizations, assuming that their administrative talents can be transferred to government. However, the salary of even a cabinet secretary is well below what a corporation executive makes. Therefore, the president must persuade prospective appointees that the prestige and influence of public service will compensate for the lost income. Most governors and large-city mayors face similar difficulties in choosing top associates.

The executive must create an organizational image and climate that attract the most desirable people, hold their loyalty, and reward their service. This has to be supplemented with specific programs that reach each individual with personally important incentives, particularly in a large agency with employees at different skill levels and specialties. The manager must motivate law enforcement officers differently from social workers. People such as Ada Deer, who wanted to change BIA while a subordinate, will not usually stay in an organization committed to the status quo.

Placing personnel in the most mutually advantageous positions requires a sensitive evaluation of how well each person has done in current and past placements and what potential she has to grow in the new one. The standards of performance can vary. Technical competence, personal and political loyalty, acceptance and support by subordinates and peers, and backing by legislators and outside interests are most common. Whatever other assets a person may have, political and personal loyalty are essential in posts close to presidents and governors. When President Reagan needed someone of proven integrity and loyalty to himself to help the Central Intelligence Agency recover from the Iran–Contra scandal in 1986, he transferred William Webster from the Federal Bureau of Investigation to head the CIA.

Keep Communication Lines Open

A fourth function of the executive is to maintain a system of communication upward and downward through the organization to express authority over subordinates and to provide feedback on the results. This is partly based on the activity of communicating itself: talking, writing, and using nonverbal language to convey values, expectations, and specific assignments. The way in which top people conduct themselves sets examples for subordinates. Failure to communicate honestly and fully lets lower-echelon officials know that such communication is not expected of them either. When a secretary of housing and urban development appears to be uninterested in what is happening in lower levels of the department, as was the case during much of the 1980s, no one has a reason to call him to task (and he may be chastised by the *Washington Post* or a congressional investigating committee instead).

Much of the communication process is beyond the reach of a given executive, who must be careful that messages flow freely through an efficient system. This too requires incentives: positive ones for sharing information in a correct and timely manner, negative ones for falsehoods and the failure to transmit needed messages. When an Air Force weapons system is overrunning the costs specified in its contract, someone must report it to higher authorities so that action can be taken. When such "whistle-blowers" are fired or transferred in retaliation for their honesty, the feedback that executives need so vitally is choked off.

Manage Conflict

The fifth function of the executive is to order and manage internal conflict. The ambitions and traits that people bring to organizations inevitably lead them into conflict, whether over public goals or private ends. Highly talented and motivated people often seek confrontations as a means of expressing themselves and pursuing their visions. Only an organization with very routine functions could avoid significant conflict. The task of the executive is not to prevent or end all conflict but to use specific disputes to promote constructive change while keeping them from destroying either the agency or its members.

Internal interest groups are common in large organizations, and leaders must not ignore them when their struggle will affect the internal balance of power. (Indeed, the leaders themselves may be divided.) In 1993 employees in several federal environmental agencies, including the Forest Service, formed the Public Employees for Environmental Responsibility. Its members have criticized agency management of timber sales in national forests and of livestock grazing on federal grasslands. Their targets range from congressionally set policy to the choices of their own superiors. This sparks internal conflict that does not stay within the agencies, and so becomes a larger challenge for managers. In responding to such groups, executives do well not only to allow them to represent their members and thus win the groups' cooperation but also to keep them working toward the organization's basic commitments. There is no universal formula for how to do this, but one can typically find a middle course between suppression of conflict and complete toleration of it. If that conflict is to yield positive change, the contestants must find solutions that serve the agency's mission and provide gains for all parties as well.

Promote Innovation

Finally, executives should initiate and facilitate innovation as necessary to achieve the agency's mission in a changing environment. When the usual organizational incentives guard the status quo, leaders must introduce new ones that stimulate group members to take other paths and support the leadership despite the risks. Change may be imposed on an agency, as when a court rules that it must begin to provide a service to those with disabilities. Or the initiative can come from within. (For example, a city housing authority may undertake a program to convert old industrial buildings to low-income housing.) Change may also occur in the process of the work. (Computerization of records, for example, disturbed the status quo of countless agencies.) An entirely new task is more difficult to adapt to. (Social welfare departments, for example, must now develop employment programs for aid recipients. Monitoring their performance has been added to the traditional problem of determining eligibility for payments.)

More serious change can occur in the basic ethos of the agency and its perception of its mission. The Federal Trade Commission, hitherto a staid regulatory body, launched vigorous new measures of consumer protection and curbs on advertising during the Carter administration. Its chair, Michael Pertschuk, had been a vigorous consumer advocate and sought to use augmented legal powers to remake the agency. In the end it appeared that his staff and the other commissioners, as well as key members of Congress, did not want to move as fast as he did, and he had not prepared them adequately to do so (Heymann, 1987). Change of this nature seems to have a natural speed limit for even the most determined and able administrators, as BIA commissioner Deer is discovering. Yet there is much room for initiative under that limit for those who can exploit favorable political conditions.

The Executive at Work

Executives have many resources for carrying out their functions and must select the right ones for each task. Often they use several. There is no definitive rulebook on this, and the "right answer" must often be discovered anew for each situation.

The Executive's Sources of Authority

First, public executives have **legitimacy**, which is the standing conferred by law or the legal actions of a superior. Subordinates recognize that these executives have the right to issue orders and monitor actions. "The boss may not always be right, but he is always the boss" reflects a deeply held social and legal norm.

Legitimacy enables executives to grant rewards to or withhold them from subordinates. They can promote, dismiss, provide extra compensation (where permitted by law), change job assignments, and express verbal praise or criticism. The wider the range of their powers, the greater the potential for leadership. The potential for exercising these options in public service, particularly under strict rules of the merit system, is limited, although there has been movement aimed at broadening the possibilities.

A second source of authority is the recognized expertise of the executive in the agency's specialized field. The post of surgeon general of the United States is filled by a medical doctor of some repute whose judgments and leadership have wide credibility outside the Public Health Service and within it. A specialist farther down the ladder of authority can greatly influence the top leadership through his or her expertise. The case of the swine flu immunizations of 1976, in which Dr. David Sencer, director of the Centers for Disease Control, and other medical professionals urged quick action to prevent an epidemic, illustrates this well. (Recall it from Chapter 5.) President Gerald R. Ford and Secretary David Matthews of the Department of Health, Education and Welfare, despite their unquestioned legal authority, had little choice but to support their subordinates' urgent plans (Neustadt & Fineberg, 1983).

A leader's personality, a third source of authority, can draw others to follow and give support. This "referent power" is usually based on such intangible traits as speaking ability, physical image, and past accomplishments. A person may have and be able to articulate a special vision for the agency or the professionals in it. Hyman G. Rickover, long a navy admiral, was the initiator and passionate advocate of the nuclear-powered submarine and inspired a long line of officers, members of Congress, and others to join his quest. People with such compelling personalities are sometimes called charismatic, particularly when followers are drawn to them by the force of their character.

Box 9.3

Are Some Executive Jobs Impossible to Succeed In?

We should not assume that a manager who has all the right tools and uses them with reasonable energy is guaranteed success. It is a fact of administrative life that jobs are not of equal difficulty. In fact, there may well be "impossible jobs" in public management (Hargrove & Glidewell, 1990).

Consider the positions of chief of police, director of a corrections agency, superintendent of a big-city school system, public health commissioner, and mental health executive. They have certain features in common that not only make their jobs unpopular but also limit their accomplishments. First, they serve or hold custody of what many would consider "less than desirable" people: lawbreakers, convicted offenders, persons with chronic mental illness, and so on. These positions not only have little or no political influence but their clients' needs are also complex and hard to meet. Second,

there is often intense conflict over the agency's goals and methods, as, for example, custody versus rehabilitation in the case of corrections; whichever approach is adopted, an important constituency disagrees with it. Third, the agency and its professionals have low status in the public eye. They are not accorded the respect and deference typically given to medical and scientific specialists. "Success" is, by definition, hard to attain; victims of AIDS and many sufferers of mental illness will never be cured, and many hard-core offenders will return to prison after committing new crimes. A big-city school system is not likely to display reading and math scores equal to those of its suburban neighboring systems.

Thus these executives should be judged—and should judge themselves—by realistic standards. One can still be hopeful, and certainly there are areas for accomplishment open to any position.

The most effective executives combine these traits and, equally important, know which to call on in a given situation. Presidents and governors typically lack only the specialized expertise but can compensate by drawing on the skills of others. These traits are most sorely tested in agencies with inherently difficult missions. As Box 9.3 illustrates, their executives find "success" a very elusive outcome.

Leadership Styles

Many styles of leadership can develop from these sources of authority. First, in using **authoritarian leadership**, the executive imposes decisions on the organization with little or no discussion or opportunity for feedback from subordinates. In government this approach is most used when the law clearly calls for one action or approach or when the organization is divided and paralyzed and some action has to be taken. It may also be dictatorial if the leader fails to listen to subordinates or rejects their legitimate concerns and suggestions. Although this is not the best approach in most situations, it may be necessary and even beneficial when an urgent task or situation warrants.

Democratic leadership creates opportunities for subordinates to participate in choices of the agency's tasks and means of performing them. The executive decides only after full consideration of their views. This form requires not only occasional meetings but a regular interchange of information and feedback that gives incentives for conscientious involvement. Even when executives must decide contrary to the majority's view, they explain the reasons and so retain the confidence of their subordinates.

This form of leadership is most beneficial in innovative and problem-solving situations. For example, a child protection agency may be confronted with a sharp rise in abuse, and everyone may realize that current methods of dealing with these cases must be changed. The director may have little more expertise than some of the staff and may lack conclusive answers. This requires a collective effort to design and implement new approaches and review the results. In many cases, an executive's greatest challenge is to make sure that decisions are made when needed, when others prefer delay out of uncertainty or disagreement.

The third type of leadership, **laissez-faire**, is an extreme form of delegation. Rather than make decisions, the executive allows and encourages subordinates to make them by their own criteria. Some may consider this an abdication of leadership, and when there are choices that should be centrally made, it is. However, executives also recognize circumstances in which they must defer to subordinates who have a high degree of expertise or when they must ignore some issues in order to concentrate on others. The president, who attends only to the most important decisions, must practice a good deal of laissez-faire leadership in delegating others. His challenge is to discern which matters require his active leadership and which he can safely entrust to others.

Limits to Control

Whichever leadership style is applied, there are inherent limits to the extent to which a large public organization can be directed from a central point. Anthony Downs (1967, pp. 140–143) proposed three basic principles of organizational control. First, "No one can fully control the behavior of a large organization." Second, "The larger any organization becomes, the weaker is the control over its actions exercised by those at the top." Third, a direct corollary, "The larger any organization becomes, the poorer is the coordination among its actions."

Authority Leakage   The limits to control typically appear at several critical points in the executive's control process. The first comes in issuing orders, directives, or regulations designed to alter the behavior of subordinates. Reading these, staff members must understand what is intended and acknowledge that they should comply. Often communications from the executive must be translated into more detailed orders and procedures by subordinates and passed farther down the line. In these activities the organization is likely to experience authority leakage (Downs, 1967, p. 134): "Because individual officials have varying goals, and each uses his discretion in translating orders from above into commands going downward, the purposes the superior had in mind will not be the precise ones his subordinates' orders convey to people farther down the hierarchy." The discrepancy can result from misperceptions, deliberate distortion of orders, and/or incompetence.

Communication Blocks   A second control problem occurs in monitoring compliance with those directives. Lower-level managers, close to where the work is performed, usually track this better than those at the top. We noted in Chapter 3 the hindrances to communication that organizations generate. Often the harder an executive tries to control the behavior of subordinates, the greater the effort they make to evade or counteract such control. Typically, this comes in the failure to send messages upward that accurately and completely describe what they are doing. Governments often employ separate monitoring officials, such as inspectors and auditors, to learn "what is really going on," but this may only aggravate the evasion problem. Such surveillance may frustrate efforts to administer the agency by democratic means and create deadlock or resistance.

Internal Conflict   An executive's efforts at control can be weakened by organizational dissension, regardless of its cause. Even vigorous action may fail to correct this situation. The air traffic controllers demonstrated this in their unsuccessful 1981 strike for higher pay and less stressful working conditions. The government won that contest by firing the strikers, but the control system was weakened for a time, and its present status still arouses concern about how well the Federal Aviation Administration staffs and manages it.

New executives can avoid the personal animosities that may have built up under their predecessors but must act differently so that the situation does not recur. The Environmental Protection Agency recovered in 1983–84 from a serious internal crisis that had developed under its former head, Anne Gorsuch. Following President Reagan's pro-business philosophy, she sharply curtailed its research and enforcement activity and allowed her relations with senior staff members to deteriorate. William Ruckelshaus, who turned the agency around in both policy and management after he succeeded her, exerted enough control to remedy the worst of these problems (Heymann, 1987).

Powers and *Power* of Federal Government Executives

Successful management and control are closely linked to their context. Consequently, we must examine specific executive posts in American public administration. It is logical to begin with the presidency because it is the best known and is subject to the widest demands and most intense public scrutiny. However, generalizing about the presidency is difficult because the office has been held by relatively few men and by ones who have been very diverse. One should also remember that a president is a policy-making leader and a globally oriented diplomat. These roles often overshadow his executive responsibilities and consume much of his attention. Thus, this survey focuses on only a portion of the whole presidency.

The Formal Powers of the Presidency

The formal powers of the office, stated in the Constitution and later augmented by Congress, are not extensive. The president is to "take care that the laws be faithfully executed" (Article II, Section 3) but is not granted in that document many of the means that a modern executive would find necessary to discharge that responsibility. Thus, he or she must vigorously employ the powers that are there and make full use of political and personality resources to fulfill the mandate.

Selection of Subordinates   First, the president appoints (with the consent of the Senate) and may remove key subordinates. The selection criteria encompass some combination of administrative competence, personal loyalty, agreement with the president's major policies, and acceptability to Congress. Appointments are also influenced by outside constituencies that suggest or oppose particular candidates. For example, no person would be seriously considered for secretary of agriculture without wide backing from farmer and agribusiness groups and farm-state members of Congress. Carelessness in key choices can cripple an administration in dealing with critical issues and thus its public image. President Reagan maintained firm central control over the selection of his Cabinet officers and staff members when he came to Washington in 1981 so that he could begin his administration with a loyal cadre (Benda & Levine, 1988). However, President Clinton was embarrassed early in his administration when he nominated two candidates for attorney general who were politically disqualified for failure to pay social security taxes on hired caregivers for their children. This reflected not on their qualifications but on the White House's failure to detect their offenses.

Budget Preparation   Second, the president, with the aid of the Office of Management and Budget, proposes the annual federal budget for Congress's consideration. This process of preparing budget figures for each department also is an opportunity to monitor and evaluate departmental performance over the previous year. The president's budget figures offer Congress a starting point for deliberations and, in isolated cases (notably President Reagan's fiscal success in 1981), a nearly final budget as well. More often, though, the president must continuously bargain with the lawmakers to secure appropriations that come close to his original request. This process is explored more fully in Chapter 12.

Legislative Action   Third, the president plays a legislative role, from the proposal of bills to the final signature or veto. Recent presidents have regularly intervened in Congress's deliberations to secure the most desired policies to implement. This directly influences presidential administrative power, since Congress uses legislation not only to establish broad policies but to control many details of their implementation. President Carter's congressional liaison people were not skilled in promoting his agenda on Capitol Hill, whereas Reagan and Bush benefited from more effective contacts. President Clinton's staff can boast of such successes as the approval of the North American Free Trade Agreement and the 1994 crime bill, but it failed to convince Congress to pass the administration's health care reform program.

Executive Orders   A fourth power is to issue **executive orders**, which are directives to part or all of the executive branch and have the force of law on matters over which the chief executive has constitutional authority or a congressional grant of power (Cooper, 1986). More than 12,000 such orders have been issued since the presidency of Abraham Lincoln. They remain in effect as long as the issuing president and his successors enforce them. President Reagan used a series of executive orders, beginning with Executive Order 12291 in his first month in office, to centralize oversight of the regulatory process in the Office of Management and Budget, as discussed in Chapter 6. These orders mandated that cost/benefit analysis be applied to proposed regulations to learn whether they would be worth their costs to the government, the regulated business, and consumers. Although these orders focused on the processes of decision making, they had major impact on the number and substance of the rules issued during the Reagan administration.

The president augments these formal powers with political tactics for gaining support from the public and those government officials who either are not under his authority or can resist his directives. He must enhance his "power to persuade" by building a strong professional reputation for decisiveness and competence among the Washington community of bureaucrats, legislators, and nongovernment influentials who can grant or withhold the cooperation he seeks. This in turn depends partly on his prestige with the public outside Washington, as demonstrated not only in the opinion polls but also in communications from influential constituents (Neustadt, 1980). President Reagan used both of these to great advantage in his first term, but his two successors have struggled against adverse images in the media. Box 9.4 explores the circumstances that require a president to develop expertise in persuasion.

Support from Staff and Appointees   Another resource on which presidents depend heavily is the White House staff and their political appointees in the agencies (see Figure 2.2 on the Executive Office of the President). Foremost of these is the chief of staff, who is closest to the president and who, more than anyone else, controls access to his time and attention. These officials are vital in two respects. "Ideally, they provide a cadre of loyal lieutenants who will identify with the president's priorities and work unstintingly for his legislative program. They also hopefully provide a core group with sufficient bureaucratic and political acuity to seize the state apparatus and make it yield the desired outcomes on schedule" (Campbell, 1986, p. 254). This dependence can be harmful, though, when a staffer betrays this trust or fails to keep the president from making a serious mistake.

Bureaucracy as a Limit to Presidential Power

The most stringent limit on the extent to which any president can be a chief executive lies in the nature of bureaucratic leadership. The highest subordinate executives are presidential appointees, whereas those below them typically reached their posts after many years of climbing the ladder of the merit system in their agencies. The former are temporary, for it is unusual for a cabinet secretary or a head of an independent agency to stay in office four years. Moreover, they are "outsiders," since a career civil servant is rarely given a presidential appointment. It is not necessary to have special competence as a manager; a more important role is to be a liaison with the White House and promote the department's policies with Congress and important constituent groups.

One must descend two or three steps on the ladder to find the crucial administrative power. The most powerful figures in the federal bureaucracy are the bureau chiefs (the actual titles vary),

(continued on p. 264)

Box 9.4

The President: Leader or Clerk?

Richard Neustadt first published his classic study of the presidency in 1960, as the country looked toward a new chief executive to succeed Dwight Eisenhower. He warned that the office has some clear limits to its power, and that presidents must both understand them and find means to overcome them.

In the early summer of 1952, before the heat of the campaign, President Truman used to contemplate the problems of the General-become-President should Eisenhower win the forthcoming election. "He'll sit here," Truman would remark (tapping his desk for emphasis), "and he'll say, 'Do this! Do that!' *And nothing will happen.* Poor Ike—it won't be a bit like the Army. He'll find it very frustrating."

Eisenhower evidently found it so. "In the face of the continuing dissidence and disunity, the President sometimes simply exploded with exasperation," wrote Robert Donovan in comment on the early months of Eisenhower's first term. "What was the use, he demanded to know, of his trying to lead the Republican Party. . . ." And this reaction was not limited to early months alone, or to his party only. "The President still feels," an Eisenhower aide remarked to me in 1958, "that when he's decided something, that *ought* to be the end of it . . . and when it bounces back undone or done wrong, he tends to react with shocked surprise."

Truman knew whereof he spoke. With "resignation" in the place of "shocked surprise," the aide's description would have fitted Truman. The former senator may have been less shocked than the former general, but he was no less subjected to that painful and repetitive experience: "Do this, do that, and nothing will happen." Long before he came to talk of Eisenhower he had put his own experience in other words: "I sit here all day trying to persuade people to do the things they ought to have sense enough to do without my persuading them. . . . That's all the powers of the President amount to."

In these words of a President, spoken on the job, one finds the essence of the problem now before us: "powers" are no guarantee of power; clerkship is no guarantee of leadership. The President of the United States has an extraordinary range of formal powers, of authority in statute law and in the Constitution. Here is testimony that despite his "powers" he does not obtain results by giving orders—or not, at any rate, merely by giving orders. He also has extraordinary status, *ex officio,* according to the customs of our government and politics. Here is testimony that despite his status he does not get action without argument. Presidential *power* is the power to persuade. . . .

The separateness of institutions and the sharing of authority prescribe the terms on which a President persuades. When one man shares authority with another, but does not gain or lose his job upon the other's whim, his willingness to act upon the urging of the other turns on whether he conceives the action right for him. The essence of a President's persuasive task is to convince such men that what the White House wants of them is what they ought to do for their sake and on their authority.

Persuasive power, thus defined, amounts to more than charm or reasoned argument. These have their uses for a President, but these are not the whole of his resources. For the men he would induce to do what he wants done on their own responsibility will need or fear some acts by him on his responsibility. If they share his authority, he has some share in theirs. Presidential "powers" may be inconclusive when a President commands, but always remain relevant as he persuades. The status and authority inherent in his office reinforce his logic and his charm. . . .

A President's authority and status give him great advantages in dealing with the men he would persuade. Each "power" is a vantage point for him in the degree that other men have use for his authority. From the veto to appointments, from publicity to budgeting, and so down a long list, the White House now controls the most encompassing array of vantage points in the American political system. With hardly an exception, the men who share in governing this country are aware that at some time, in some degree, the doing of *their* jobs, the furthering of *their* ambitions, may depend upon the President of the United States. Their need for presidential action, or their fear of it, is bound to be recurrent if not actually continuous. Their need or fear is his advantage.

A President's advantages are greater than mere listing of his "powers" might suggest. The men with whom he deals must deal with him until the last day of his term. Because they have continuing relationships with him, his future, while it lasts, supports his present influence. Even though there is no need or fear of him today, what he could do tomorrow may supply today's advantage. Continuing relationships may convert any "power," any aspect of his status, into vantage points in almost any case. When he induces other men to do what he wants done, a President can trade on their dependence now *and* later.

The President's advantages are checked by the advantages of others. Continuing relationships will pull in both directions. These are relationships of mutual dependence. A President depends upon the men he would persuade; he has to reckon with his need or fear of them. They too will possess status, or authority, or both, else they would be of little use to him. Their vantage points confront his own; their power tempers his. . . .

The essence of a President's persuasive task, with congressmen and everybody else, *is to induce them to believe that what he wants of them is what their own appraisal of their own responsibilities requires them to do in their interest, not his.* Because men may differ in their views on public policy, because differences in outlook stem from differences in duty—duty to one's office, one's constituents, oneself—that task is bound to be more like collective bargaining than like a reasoned argument among philosopher kings. Overtly or implicitly, hard bargaining has characterized all illustrations offered up to now. This is the reason why: persuasion deals in the coin of self-interest with men who have some freedom to reject what they find counterfeit.

—Richard Neustadt, *Presidential Power,*
pp. 9–10, 27–28, 35

---

who in many subtle ways can frustrate the president's purposes when theirs are different. They cultivate ties with the private groups whose interests the organization serves and with the congressional committees that provide money and authority. The president can easily lose sight of his responsibility to oversee these bureaus because they are so remote from him (Koenig, 1986, p. 177). The Bureau of Indian Affairs provides a good example of such an agency, although it has been more neglected than most.

Bureau chiefs are close enough to the implementation of policy to control it and to ensure that the services important constituents expect are delivered. They gather intelligence about their own organizations and the external environment affecting it and choose how to use the data. Frequently they testify before congressional committees and take care to return phone calls from those lawmakers and their staffs. They inform the news media and the public on the agency's accomplishments and if necessary explain any mistakes or shortcomings. Like Ada Deer of the Bureau of Indian Affairs, chiefs take both glory and heat, and the president or secretary can fire them for any reason.

The bureau chiefs' interests can differ from the president's, even when they hold the same policy views and personal outlook. They seek to protect their own organizations' integrity and morale and thereby resist abrupt changes in mission and methods. The agencies' most relevant priorities are embodied in laws and budgets, which come from Capitol Hill, not the White House. They know also that Congress listens to the major constituents of each bureau when it enacts those laws and budgets. When, early in 1994, the lawmakers created a separate Office of AIDS Research within the Public Health Service, they were responding to strong pleas to step up the search for a cure for that disease.

It is no wonder, then, that all presidents control their administrations tenuously. The "management" they practice is of the selected functions to which they and their staffs (particularly in the Office of Management and Budget) pay close attention, and this cannot be a large number. As indicated earlier, the Reagan White House did make a conscientious effort to alter the course of the Environmental Protection Agency and other regulatory bodies of which the business community had complained most strongly. But even in those cases, congressional and constituent pressures built up so that the president had to retreat from his goals.

Limits Imposed by Congress

Congress also deserves mention in a discussion of federal executives. The laws it passes and the executive branch implements frequently include detailed administrative mandates for the president and subordinate executives. Furthermore, by appropriating money to fund these actions and restricting how it is to be spent, Congress delves deeply into what is normally, in the private business realm, an executive function. The Senate can also use its formal and informal roles in the appointment process to deny the president a preferred nominee. The central figures in exercising these quasi-administrative powers are the chairs of the key committees and subcommittees, acting within their own policy realms. The chairs of the Armed Services committees and Defense Appropriations subcommittees in each house exert a major influence over the aspects of Defense Department management in which they are interested. When the presidential and congressional leaders can agree on their purposes and strategies, they can give coherent direction to the implementation of policy, but some tension between them is equally likely.

State and Local Executives

The responsibilities and resources of governors, mayors, city managers, school superintendents, and other state and local executives are as different as the governments they head. Some have substantial legal and political power; others are barely more than clerks. Yet all have a range of options and may be stronger or weaker according to their own choices.

Gubernatorial Power

The role of governors within their states is similar to that of the president within the nation. They are also expected to be policy-making leaders and to take responsibility for their state's relations with other states and with national authorities. Their formal powers vary with the constitutions and laws of each state, although they have expanded markedly over the past two decades. Most have power to appoint their major administrative subordinates, and nearly all control the preparation of the budget submitted to the legislature. The survey of state administrative structures in Chapter 2 revealed that they are at least as fragmented as those in Washington, which places important constraints on governors. Like the president, therefore, state executives must have the political skill to translate their powers into effective leadership, particularly in view of growing challenges to innovate social and economic policies.

The states are equally subject, politically and administratively, to outside influences. These influences come both from Washington (as discussed in Chapter 4) and from local governments. State governors and department heads depend upon county, city, and special district officials to carry out many state programs in education and social services. In turn, the latter exert influence in their state capitals by themselves and through related interest and constituency groups.

A study of state department heads found that governors do not generally dominate their administrative branches (Abney & Lauth, 1986). A majority (53 percent) of the 778 respondents judged that the state legislature exerted more influence than the governor on their programs and objectives. Many also mentioned the federal government, state-level interest groups, and local officials and administrators. In the large states of California and New York, which most closely approach the national government in size and complexity, only 60 percent and 69 percent, respectively, rated their governors as the most influential. In general, governors have been managers, who seek to avoid conflict, rather than major innovators, who seek to transform the missions and ethos of the agencies (Abney & Lauth, 1983). The fact that state budgets must be balanced each year or biennium further discourages major policy initiatives. However, since the national government withdrew during the 1980s from many of the social welfare programs that it had begun in previous decades, governors faced demands to devise creative and efficient replacements. Thus, their leadership role has expanded out of necessity.

Subordinate state executives, like their counterparts in Washington, must balance the duty of internal management with cultivation of good external relations. They are probably more autonomous than their federal counterparts, however, given the less dominant role played by many governors and the low public visibility in which they operate. Nevertheless, state corrections, health, and social services administrators face intense scrutiny when the media publicize lapses and mistakes.

Elected Local Executives

Elected local government executives occupy positions similar to those of presidents and governors. They enjoy formal independence in controlling their executive branches, but the city council intervenes in the government process and extragovernmental groups influence it. "Strong" mayors in large cities like New York and Chicago can easily empathize with higher officials. (Recall the internal structures of local governments in Chapter 2.) Their legal powers are similar, though variable, from city to city: appointment of department heads (though not necessarily their removal), preparation of the budget for action by the council, directives to the departments, and (usually) veto of council legislation. Because they are subject to election, they enjoy greater public visibility and thus greater potential for popular backing than nonelected executives. "Weak" mayors with few or no administrative powers lack these pressures.

Like most governors and presidents, mayors do not typically come to office with administrative experience. They are strongest at legislative and public relations and are not inclined to delve into the details of how the departments are run unless a problem gets a headline in the local newspaper. Wasteful or corrupt management can reflect negatively on them, though, and they find it necessary to prevent that.

Appointed Local Executives

Appointed chief executives are widely found in medium-sized and smaller cities, all school districts, and the larger special districts. In cities and some counties the manager is usually a full-time professional. A graduate degree in public or business administration is a common requirement, as is successful experience elsewhere. Technical competence is the primary criterion, although the candidate must also show skills at public relations and policy formulation, as the experience of Camille Barnett in Box 9.5 illustrates. These man-

Box 9.5

The City Manager: Leader or Clerk?

Camille Barnett is a recent city manager of Austin, Texas, a city of about 400,000 people. But she did not fit the traditional model of a manager once taught as orthodoxy in public administration schools. That "model" manager is politically neutral, quietly translating the will of the council into reality with maximum efficiency and a minimum of publicity. Leadership outside of City Hall was not in the job description.

But Ms. Barnett learned in her career, which included positions in four cities before Austin, that cities need political leadership to attain policy success. After taking office in 1989, she averaged at least three public speeches a week and was a monthly guest on a radio call-in show. She sought to be well known in the city and to have a reputation for competence and honesty.

The single role that best fit her was that of "broker." She stood between the groups that compete for power in Austin—environmentalists, feminists, neighborhood leaders, Hispanic and African American organizations, large and small business groups—and worked out day-to-day settlements. Each one required persuasive skills, leavened with a good deal of patience. She also played diplomat with the U.S. Department of Housing and Urban Development in a dispute over spending funds from the Community Development Block Grant (Ehrenhalt, 1990). However, that role did not protect her from controversy. She left the post in 1994 after a public dispute with the city council over revenues from the city's hospital.

Many managers serve Sunbelt cities and metropolitan suburbs that have grown rapidly in population, as Austin has. With that growth has come greater social diversity and the resulting conflicts over politics and services. These communities no longer have the low-keyed politics that allows the manager to be merely a clerk. A person with solid professional credentials as an administrator can build on these skills, as Ms. Barnett did, to act as a trustworthy broker and so perform a service that few elected officials may be able to do as well. Yet he or she may have to expect a shorter tenure in any one city because of the controversies that result.

agers have full appointment, supervisory, and removal powers over the personnel under them and almost always prepare the annual budget. Their own tenure is often undefined, and the council is free to remove them for any cause.

Power Resources of Local Officials

Municipal executives appear to have greater influence within their realm than do state governors in theirs. In a survey of 185 mayor/council cities, 76 percent of the department heads ranked the mayor as first in impact on their programs and objectives, well above the council. In 312 council/manager cities, the corresponding figure was 70 percent (Abney & Lauth, 1986). This strength is due in part to the steady centralization of control within municipal governments during the twentieth century. It may also be due to the more vigorous leadership styles expected by and supplied to the public in an era when local responsibilities and the potential to fulfill them have been greatly expanded by federal aid and by public and private partnerships.

School superintendents and special district executives are chosen for their expertise. Education professionals usually dominate citizen school boards for this reason. Members of these elected boards are typically part-time and lack the oversight resources of Congress and state legislatures. School superintendents in large and diverse districts face increased pressures from parents and interest groups to maximize opportunity for disadvantaged students while being constrained by stable or declining budgets. As a result, their tenure is often cut short by resignation under pressure or outright dismissal.

External Influences on the Local Administrator   Local governments are subject to external influences, and their executives must respond to them and use them to advantage. Like their counterparts in the state capitals, they must deal regularly with federal agencies on matters of aid, regulation, and mutual support. Mayors have boasted of the federal dollars they secured in their term as a prime reason for their reelection. Local officials have extensive contact with state administrators for such matters as highways, welfare, natural resources, and health. They depend on the legislature for an important portion of their budgets and for all of their revenue-raising powers. They must lobby state legislators for both dollars and legal authority.

Sources of Support   Another portion of the local administrator's world consists of other governments and private sources of support. The complexity sketched in Chapters 2, 4, and 7 suggests that these contacts are extensive. Camille Barnett learned to use her relations with other governments, the business community, and the competing power groups to promote Austin's purposes. There is no formal prescription for this role; she had to create it herself. Since she could not dictate these arrangements, she had to employ all her bargaining skills to overcome the fragmentation that characterizes governance of a large metropolitan area.

Finally, administrators must satisfy many constituent groups. Surveys of municipal department heads identified neighborhood groups, business associations and individual business leaders, the news media, and public employee organizations as most influential on their operations (Abney & Lauth, 1986). The personal nature of local politics makes even middle-level managers readily accessible to citizens, and when a regulation or service becomes controversial, they can find themselves in the middle of an emotional dispute. But by satisfying the citizenry they strengthen their own base of support.

Politics and Administration in Tension

Executives at all levels of government feel the conflict between the administrative and the political demands of their posts. As administrators they must focus not only on efficiency, productivity, and promptness in rendering services, but also on fairness and clarity in imposing regulations. Delivering mail, inspecting restaurants, and picking up garbage are probably the most typical aspects of this "businesslike" side of government.

As executives subject to political forces they must also respond to the demands of diverse groups. For example, the environmental protection administrator deciding which chemicals to keep out of the workplace and the county social service director establishing a "workfare" program for the able-bodied unemployed move in groups with conflicting standards. The environment of many public agencies is "chaotic" in the sense that the pressures and constraints they experience fluctuate unpredictably. They cannot always maximize both efficiency in operations and responsiveness to change simultaneously.

Leading and Managing for Success

Given this complex blend of internal conditions and external constraints, the public executive is likely to be frustrated in making and following successful strategies. There is no "one best way," to be sure, but some guidance is available. Kenneth Gold (1982) surveyed five organizations in the public sector and five in business that had a reputation for productivity and good management and found them similar. (Four of the government units were the U.S. Forest Service, the Customs Service, the State Department's Passport Service, and the city of Charlotte, North Carolina.) In each case, he found that the organizations possessed the characteristics of the management detailed in Box 9.6.

In one sense, the public agencies in this survey appeared to be at a disadvantage, for they lacked the clear and consistent missions available to private-sector managers. Public officials usually expressed their goals and products in broad terms, such as providing high-quality services to their constituents most efficiently and effectively (Gold, 1982). Although the Passport Service has only one function, to issue passports after determining the eligibility of applicants, most agencies have more complex missions. The Forest Service must implement several policies, from protecting forests from fire and illegal cutting to providing commercial timber and recreational access. To balance these deliberately presents a challenge to even a high-morale organization. One can hardly expect a child protection agency, with several nearly impossible goals and inadequate personnel and funding, to rank with the Hewlett-Packard Corporation on Gold's honor roll.

(continued on p. 272)

Box 9.6

Principles of Management in Successful Organizations

Although productivity has been receiving a great deal of attention recently, most treatments of the subject have attempted to address the causes of low productivity in the United States and to describe the various techniques that have been used in efforts to improve productivity. While there is much to be learned from many of the more innovative styles of management, it may also be useful to examine the profiles of highly successful organizations for certain less easily perceptible traits, like culture and pride. This study has found a number of such characteristics, many of which cross the line between the private and public sectors. Following is a compendium of the basic management principles, or proverbs, that characterize the successful organizations examined in this study.

1. Delegation of Authority and Responsibility
- Delegate authority and responsibility to the lowest possible level.
- Trust that the worker performing the job has the most knowledge about that specific job.
- Get the best people you can find; get agreement on objectives; then turn them loose to do their job.
- Have confidence in your own people, and have the courage to stand back and let them make mistakes.

2. Decision Making
- Spread decision making around. Give people the chance, and they will figure out ways to do things better.
- Design organizations to force decisions down the chain as far as possible.
- Avoid dictating to people: they will lose their initiative and become accustomed to waiting around for you to tell them what to do.

3. Participation and Involvement
- Allow subordinates the chance to participate. People need to feel that they are a part of the organization.

- Involve people by keeping them informed.
- Give people a job to do, but don't bury them with details.
- Establish overall goals, but give people the chance to make mistakes. People must be able to see both their successes and failures.
- Learn to communicate; and especially, learn to listen.
- Recognize that ultimately you have to get the work done through people.

4. Trust and Integrity
- Trust your own people. Treat people with respect and dignity, the way you yourself would like to be treated.
- Be honest with employees.
- Demonstrate a sense of awareness and concern for others.
- Be consistent, and set an example in everything you do.

5. Objectives and Mission
- Ensure that organizational objectives are realistic, clearly understood by everyone, and in keeping with the organization's basic character and personality.
- Communicate to employees that their organization has a mission and that they are helping to accomplish that mission.
- Help people understand what is expected of them.
- Make sure that they have the tools, guidance, and freedom to do their jobs.
- Set goals high, but be sure that they are attainable.

6. Challenge and Enthusiasm
- Operate with a lean staff. People need to be challenged with plenty of work.
- Offer people new challenges and experiences whenever possible.
- Ensure that their jobs are as interesting as possible.

- Generate enthusiasm at all levels. Inspire people.
- Be willing to take risks.

7. Employee Development

- Make a commitment to train and develop people. They are your most important resource.
- Help people to recognize their own capabilities.
- Promote from within whenever possible. When you hire from the outside, you know only a candidate's strengths. When you have worked with a candidate, you know his or her weaknesses as well.

8. Individual Performance

- Provide continuous feedback to people, as promptly as possible. Recognize good performers.
- Raise poor performance issues immediately. There is a natural tendency to avoid conflict, but confronting an individual only after initial instances of poor performance have been ignored will be much more difficult.

- Be hard-nosed with poor performers. Don't beat around the bush. More often than not, poor performance can be improved if it is confronted and diagnosed.
- Don't concentrate all your efforts on the 5 percent of employees who are weak. If you do, you will never realize the potential of the other 95 percent.

9. Openness and Informality

- Keep your organization informal and open, and be accessible. Pomp and ceremony only serve to get in the way of getting the job done.
- Avoid status symbols, dress codes, and formality; they encumber an organization and are extraneous to the organization's true mission.
- Don't underestimate the importance of having fun.

—Kenneth A. Gold, "Managing for Success: A Comparison of the Private and Public Sectors," *Public Administration Review,* November/December 1982

Nevertheless, Gold's principles of good management remain valid. If an agency has well-trained and motivated social workers, for example, they should be given authority to make on-the-spot decisions about removing a child from the home.

Participation in agency rule making by all qualified members is another essential. The political process can intrude on such good intentions, however. An employee's mistake can be magnified in the local newspaper to such a degree that the manager will be forced to remove him or her. Or a legislative action can cripple the funding or counteract many hours of participative decision making. Business managers do not often encounter such problems.

Is there a place for creative innovators in the public sector? The history of private business is filled with these figures, from Eli Whitney and Henry Ford to Lee Iacocca and Bill Gates. The limits the political system puts on its executives seems to prevent such figures from emerging. Yet there has been a place for the "public entrepreneur," whom Lewis (1980, p. 9) defined as one who "creates or profoundly elaborates a public organization so as to alter greatly the existing pattern of allocation of scarce public resources." By initiating new programs or acquiring new identities for their agencies, they had major impacts on their organizations and well beyond.

Lewis describes three such entrepreneurs of note: J. Edgar Hoover, of the Federal Bureau of Investigation; Admiral Hyman Rickover, of the U.S. Navy; and Robert Moses, an urban planner in New York. The first created what amounted to a national police force; the second spearheaded the development of the nuclear-powered submarine as a major element in the nation's defense force; and the third promoted the construction of extensive parks, freeways, bridges, tunnels, and urban renewal projects in the New York metropolitan area. All three had unique opportunities in their positions, but more important, they had a clear vision of what they wanted to achieve and used both strong arguments and effective political methods to overcome opposition. They not only dominated their own organizations but extended that power to other areas in their environment that had the resources they needed or that could hinder their efforts.

We must distinguish the success of these entrepreneurs and their agencies from the public interest, however. Many would question Hoover's service to the nation in view of his alleged violations of civil rights. For example, he could not view Dr. Martin Luther King, Jr., as a bona fide leader of peaceful change, so he had his agents seek evidence that King was a Communist. Similarly, Robert Moses's biases against the poor led him to construct the parkways leading to the Long Island state parks with overpasses so low that buses could not go under them. He wanted to serve only middle-class people who owned automobiles. Strong political leaders are likely to make enemies and trample some worthy interests, and we must be ready to judge whether their accomplishments are worth the price paid for them.

Summary

Government executives occupy an ambivalent position in their agencies and in society because of the many demands made of them for service and their limited powers for meeting those demands. Elected executives range from the president of the United States to state governors to city mayors. Top appointed executives include heads of cabinet departments at all levels; managers of cities, counties, and special districts; and superintendents of schools. They must operate within a political and a legal environment that empowers them for some purposes yet requires them to bargain and compromise with others to accomplish their purposes.

Public executives have six major functions: to define and articulate the mission of their organization and the part each member plays in it; to communicate with the organization's external environment and thereby obtain its essential services and resources; to secure, retain, and motivate those with skills essential to the mission and assign them places in which they can best contribute to it; to maintain a system of communication; to order and manage internal conflict; and to initiate and facilitate innovation.

Leaders can operate in either of two roles. A transactional leader initiates exchanges with other powerful people of items they both value. In a transforming role, the leader secures mutual action that serves the higher moral needs of other leaders and their followers. Occasions for major transformations are relatively scarce, although creative leaders can generate smaller-scale opportunities.

A set of formal *powers* is inherent in the offices of public executives. However, they must learn how to apply those powers to accomplish their goals against opposition and inertia. In doing so, they can draw upon the resources of legitimacy, expertise, and personal qualities to induce others to cooperate with them. They must develop appropriate styles of leadership for the context, which can be authoritarian, democratic, or laissez-faire. To control large organizations they must overcome several kinds of limits, such as authority leakage caused by the resistance of subordinates, communication blocks that deadlock organizational directives, and management of internal conflicts and employee sanctions.

Each national, state, and local government post has a unique set of tasks and powers, together with political resources and constraints, that incumbents must learn. Their executives must develop diplomatic skills for interaction across governmental boundaries.

Managerial success in the public and private sectors is regularly associated with certain principles. There is also "political space" for entrepreneurship in government posts. Where urgent needs call for radical change, leaders have the greatest potential for either success or failure.

Discussion Questions

1. What accounts for the ambivalent position of government executives in the public mind? How did the dispute about scholarships for minority students affect that ambivalence?

2. How is the *power* of public executives different from their powers?

3. What mistakes can executives run into in choosing their top subordinates? To what extent do those choices reflect on their own competence?

4. In what situations are authoritarian, democratic, and laissez-faire forms of leadership most appropriate? What happens if a leadership style is used where it is unsuitable?

5. In what areas of government or policy issues is innovative leadership most needed today? What skills do those leaders most need to be successful?

Analytical Exercises

1. Suppose that candidates for president or governor were required to take a personality test before being allowed to run. Formulate several questions that should go into this test that identify the specific characteristics, good or bad, you would want to know about before making your choice. Explain how they are related to the person's performance in office as a chief executive.

2. Survey the news reports of President Clinton's major administrative appointments. Generalize on the characteristics and backgrounds of those he chose as top advisers, cabinet secretaries, and occupants of other high posts. You might also note who had to leave an office, such as Agriculture Secretary Mike Espy or Surgeon General Joycelynn Elders, and why.

For Further Reading

Barnard, C. (1938). *The Functions of the Executive.* Cambridge, MA: Harvard University Press. See note in Chapter 3.

Bryson, J. M., & Crosby, B. C. (1992). *Leadership for the Common Good: Tackling Public Problems in a Shared-Power World.* San Francisco: Jossey-Bass. How one can be a change agent in settings in which no person or organization has complete control.

Burns, J. M. (1978). *Leadership.* New York: Harper & Row. Sweeping study of this massive issue from historical and contemporary perspectives, with emphasis on governmental leadership.

Caro, R. A. (1974). *The Power Broker: Robert Moses and the Fall of New York.* New York: Random House. Critical biography of the man who physically reshaped the New York City metropolitan area from the 1920s to the 1960s, and the tactics he used to overcome opponents.

Denhardt, R. B. (1993). *The Pursuit of Significance: Strategies for Managerial Success in Public Organizations.* Belmont, CA: Wadsworth. Innovative visions and techniques by which government executives have changed their agencies.

Doig, J. W., & Hargrove, E. C. (Ed.). (1990). *Leadership and Innovation: Entrepreneurs in Government.* Baltimore: Johns Hopkins University Press. Case studies of government executives who have made a mark during the twentieth century.

Hargrove, E. C., & Glidewell, J. D. (Eds.). (1990). *Impossible Jobs in Public Management.* Lawrence, KS: University Press of Kansas. Explores what is "impossible" about executive posts in police, corrections, social welfare, and mental health departments, in comparison with other administrative roles.

Mackenzie, G. C. (Ed.). (1987). *The In-and-Outers: Presidential Appointees and Transient Govern-*

ment in Washington. Baltimore, MD: Johns Hopkins University Press. The characteristics, values, and career paths of top federal administrators and the effects of their high turnover on the government.

Neustadt, R. E. (1980). *Presidential Power: The Politics of Leadership from FDR to Carter*. New York: John Wiley. See note in Chapter 2.

Osborne, D., & Gaebler, T. (1992). *Reinventing Government*. Reading, MA: Addison-Wesley. The widely read collection of experiences that touched off the "reinvention movement" toward more entrepreneurial administration.

Selznick, P. (1957). *Leadership in Administration*. New York: Harper & Row. Concise statement on the ideal mission and purpose of leaders in public and private organizations.

10

Planning and Decision Making in Public Agencies

Learning Objectives

After reading this chapter, you should be able to do the following:

1. Define administrative decisions and explain how they differ from the policy-making choices in Chapter 5.
2. Define the rational method of decision making and describe its basic procedure.
3. Describe the incremental method of decision making and the conditions in which it is most likely to be used.
4. Describe the organizational-process, governmental-politics, and garbage-can models of decision making.
5. Explain the purposes, methods, and limits of intelligence gathering and forecasting in government.
6. Define planning and explain how it is done in its various forms.
7. Identify the major constraints on planning and decision making posed by political conflicts and the uncertainties of modern governing.

Americans living near the Mississippi River remember vividly the great floods of 1993. Many found that the control structures put in place at high cost over the years failed to keep the water out of their homes and fields. Although such a flood is typically called a "100-year event," there is no assurance that a century will elapse before such rains return. Responsibility for planning for the next flood rests with the U.S. government, and it is about to choose a mode of response very different from earlier plans.

A group with the mouth-filling title of the Interagency Flood Plain Management Review Committee recommended in mid-1994 to shift from relying on levees along riverbanks to vacating flood-prone areas and controlling water upstream where runoff begins. The committee represented the Army Corps of Engineers (which has the primary responsibility for navigation and flood control on the nation's rivers), the Federal Emergency Management Agency, the Environmental Protection Agency (EPA), and the departments of Interior and Agriculture. The Army Corps recognized that floodplain management was very fragmented, involving not only federal agencies but thousands of state and local governments with land use and water control powers.

A spokeswoman for the report stated,

> Our ideal flood [control] plan of the 21st century is to have some levees for a town, but with vulnerable populations moved out of the plain, and then use upland watershed treatment. This includes things like conservation reserves of farmland with no-tillage agriculture, and wetlands that act as sponges to absorb water and then slowly release it. (Holmstrom, 1994b)

The plan she outlined entails more complex decision making than the present policy of restraining flood waters, which will require countless interactions among federal, state, and local officials and the meshing of thousands of plans. From protecting wetlands in Crow Wing County, Minnesota, to planting trees along Nebraska's banks of the Missouri River, to moving Valmeyer, Illinois, to a higher location, this is a task of system guidance that challenges anyone's imagination.

Floodplain management is only one complex decision-making challenge facing government today. Reconfiguring the nation's medical care system is an even greater one, and crime control is another. Even rebuilding the family structure could be such a challenge. Public decisions are getting bigger faster than the system can control or make sense of them. This bigness can be measured in dollars spent, number of people affected, or information required. There is no possibility of centralized control by Washington bureaucrats, yet they must ensure that some form of collaboration takes place.

The Realm of Administrative Decision Making

Implementing public policies, like life itself, is a constant process of making choices amid uncertainty. Since government is society's principal tool for coping with the unknown, its choices aim to reduce the uncertainties and risks of modern life. Decisions about health, employment, education, and safety are produced continuously in bundles and streams, never in isolation, and rarely by one person deciding alone. Yet our attempt to understand such decisions requires us to distinguish one from another and to analyze the motives and methods that produce them.

Chapter 5 surveyed the making of public policies, which become the goals and tasks of government agencies. The earlier stages, from agenda setting to the assessment of policy alternatives, are constantly influenced by administrators as they evaluate the outcomes and impacts of existing policies. Their involvement leads to the making of statutory law, as legislators enact the policy alternatives they select.

Administrators move to the center of the last two stages, from implementation of the policies, in which they make further decisions that apply policies to specific situations, to the monitoring and evaluation of the results with an eye toward revising the policies. A **decision** in this context is a goal-oriented selection of one course of action from two or more alternatives. The choice may be not to act at all. This simple definition masks the complexity that underlies many actual choice situations. The goals of public policy are many, and the means of achieving them are equally numerous. Connections between the goals and the choices are always somewhat uncertain: Will action A indeed produce intended outcome B? Will it not lead to unwanted outcome C? Will it conform to the intent of the law? Can it be implemented with the funds and other resources available?

Administrators follow a decision-making cycle of their own that parallels the cycle that produces public policy generally. They must search for needed information, forecast conditions and events, assess the outcomes of possible actions, and plan for alternative futures. This cycle is irregular and unpredictable in real life, with halts, reverses, and "fast-forwards" to respond to demands and opportunities. Decisions often involve more than one agency or unit of government and require communication and bargaining to reach agreement. In addition to decisions that directly affect the public, many choices must be made on internal matters, for example, personnel, finance, and procedures.

These arenas of choice are normally smaller than those of legislatures, contained as they are within boundaries defined by legal powers of agencies, technical specialists in the subject under consideration, and the economic interests affected by the choice. Flood control in the Mississippi Valley, for example, entails specific locations and heights of levees, construction of reservoirs on tributaries, and preservation of swamps and ponds that collect and hold runoff. Such decisions may not be less difficult or controversial than those of legislatures, but they have a narrower scope in terms of persons affected and range of choices available.

Many of these administrative decisions contribute to policy made by legislatures, in the manner described in Chapter 5. A city manager may offer the council a draft ordinance that regulates the location of adult entertainment businesses. A great deal of research is likely to be invested in that draft, as well as a choice of the specific controls to be imposed and forecasts of their effects on surrounding neighborhoods and the city's law enforcement. Although lawmakers are free to make their own choices, they depend heavily on accurate and thorough staff work.

Methods of Decision Making

There are several major approaches to decision making but no one best way. These apply not just to governments but to a wide range of organizations. Each method entails certain types of goals, available information, time scale, and number of decision makers.

Rational Decision Making

The **rational decision-making** model requires that one clearly specify the goals, consider all evidence and alternatives that pertain to achieving them, and select the one that offers the best margin of benefits over costs. It is regarded by some scholars as an ideal that one should approach as closely as possible (Simon, 1957). Strongly influenced by the discipline of economics, it posits an "economic man," who, being fully informed of all relevant conditions, selects the most effective means to achieve his ends without distraction by extraneous influences. We can use the rational method, as we did Max Weber's model of bureaucracy in Chapter 3, to highlight common features of decision-making behavior that aid in the study of how to make real-life decisions. This method is sometimes referred to as "root" decision making, since it penetrates to the depth of the available information and makes full use of it.

Rational decision making involves several deliberate steps. First, the analyst identifies the goals that the choice is to achieve. If there are several, they should be ranked or weighted to clarify priorities. The more specifically they are stated, the more precise the rest of the process can be. Numerical goals are most useful, as when traffic planners aim to reduce delays on a highway by 20 percent by using a new control scheme.

Second, all alternative means of reaching the goals are defined. The number of these alternatives is potentially large, and omitting any could result in the loss of important opportunities. Traffic delays could be reduced by measures as simple as altering traffic signal intervals or as expensive as construction of overpasses.

Third, the analyst states the full consequences of pursuing each alternative: its benefits, its costs, and the risks of incurring unwanted results. Also, an estimate must be made of the likelihood that the alternative will achieve the stated objective. The consequences may affect people's personal health or well-being, the natural environment, the economic system, or future technological development. This analysis requires the largest amount of information, calling for research where it is not already in hand.

Fourth, the alternatives are compared with each other to determine which offers the greatest probability of achieving the established goals at an acceptable cost. To do this, the data must be comparable, calculated in dollars, deaths prevented, time saved, or similar objective terms. Traffic analysts use complex computer models to assess the costs and benefits of possible solutions.

Fifth, the decision makers choose the optimum alternative solely on the basis of whether or not it best serves the initial goals. If none will fulfill the goals perfectly, they must identify combinations and trade-offs. This excludes judgments of personal or political benefit to the decision maker or any other special interest.

Finally, the decision is applied in the programs, budgets, and schedules and is implemented precisely as decided. The implementation process must not be allowed to deviate from the path mapped out unless new information or conditions alter the calculations made in the first three steps.

How applicable in real situations is this mode of decision making? Much depends on the context of the decision. State traffic planners would not have trouble following these steps, nor would a federal agency have difficulty setting up procedures for mailing benefit checks. But the procedure is difficult to apply in many other choice situations. It is more realistic to view this rational method as one end of a continuum of procedures, with less formal (although not necessarily "irrational") methods at successively distant points from it.

One less formal procedure has been called the **incremental model of decision making** (Lindblom, 1959). It is a means of proceeding when the goals are not precise, the evidence and alternatives are incomplete, and political controversy will inevitably shape the final decisions. We will examine the main features of this incremental process, following the same stages as in the rational method, just discussed.

First, an analyst using the incremental method perceives the goals as imprecise, open to political dispute, and varying among observers. As Chapter 5 showed, an issue does not ordinarily become political unless its very definitions come into question. A "goal" is often defined by the possible solutions. Where there is more than one goal or solution, they are not expected to be fully compatible. In oversimplified terms, the floodplain planners are torn between keeping floodwater away from people or people away from the water.

Second, there are not enough resources or time to identify all possible solutions. Most of these are probably not acceptable to the participants anyway. Decision makers work with commonly accepted solutions unless the problem is totally new or the current ones are totally inadequate, both of which are unlikely. To obtain complete analyses of benefits, costs, and risks is impossible and unnecessary. A person who has sufficient experience with an issue to be in a decision-making post will already have formed many judgments on the most likely solutions.

In the third through fifth stages, many subjective factors influence the comparison of alternatives. Benefits, costs, and risks are judged differently by each group interested in the outcome, even when there is a reliable set of numbers to consider. The one on which the contending parties can agree has the best chance of being chosen, even though it may be less desirable to most parties than another alternative. Participants know too that the decision is not necessarily final and can be renegotiated at a later date if the situation and the balance of political power change.

Last, the plans as implemented can vary from what was chosen, particularly if those who actually do the work hold different priorities or encounter new conditions and demands from constituents. These variations are to be expected and will provide feedback into subsequent decisions.

The incremental approach has a short time horizon. No effort is made to commit the government for many years to come; the future is seen as too uncertain for that. Rather, the intent is to act in the light of today's understanding and after observing results for a year or a similarly short period, to return, and to adjust the program accordingly. If the participants agree on developing it further, they take the next incremental step. Otherwise they pause or move in another direction. Here too they "satisfice," making a choice that is "good enough" for the situation (Simon, 1957).

The rational decision method assumes that the goal is fixed, like a guiding star, and that the decision maker continually strives toward it. Incremental methods perceive goals as evolving, depending on what can be achieved in the foreseeable future or what influential groups demand. If a goal is achieved or proves unattainable, another replaces it. Although broad objectives may remain, specific goals can be as experimental as the means. The EPA, in setting and following its pollution control priorities, must be realistic. Scientists know enough about the importance of the ozone layer to the world's ecosystem to sustain a long-term commitment to keeping harmful chemicals out of it. Yet it cannot avoid short-term pressures from Congress to act on this or that crisis and must remain open to new scientific evidence that would rearrange those priorities.

The incremental method is also a democratic way of attaining consensus among persons who do not fully agree on the goals or on the means of putting them into effect. The method is openly pluralistic and assumes it is both necessary and desirable to preserve multiple centers of power while making the decisions the public requires. Rational methods imply a single decision maker or a unitary perspective, and this is rarely attainable when major public choices are on the table. Certainly, the interest groups affected by the EPA's definition of environmental hazards would not tolerate a closed "scientific" planning process. There is so much pluralism, even in the scientific community, that full unity on most environmental issues is not attainable.

The Organizational-Process Model

Three variations of the incremental method have been identified. In the **organizational-process model of decision making**, a choice is not so much the product of rational thought as it is the output of a large organization behaving in its accustomed fashion. "The behavior of these organizations—and consequently of the government—relevant to an issue in any particular instance is, therefore, determined primarily by routines established in these organizations prior to that instance" (Allison, 1971, p. 68). Since each agency has an established mission and procedures, it will "naturally" make certain choices under normal circumstances. The Social Security Administration, which provides income and health benefits for millions of clients, uses routines to simplify choices about who gets how much. Each routine may have been rationally selected at first, but following it need not take much thought. The agency seeks to minimize the time and effort it invests and to avoid the need to bargain.

The Governmental-Politics Model

The model that views decisions as the product of bargaining that takes place among many influential participants is called the **governmental-politics model of decision making**. It focuses on the "perceptions, motivations, positions, power, and maneuvers of the players," who differ in ability to shape the outcome (Allison, 1971, p. 6). It is as much a way of deciding who governs in a highly competitive environment as it is of settling substantive issues. An example of this is the current drive to control medical costs, spurred not only by the federal and state governments but by employers, health maintenance organizations, and insurance companies. The trend is toward tight reins on payments for each procedure, but the specific criteria are emerging piecemeal as the various power centers come to agreement on each one.

The Garbage-Can Model

What may be the opposite extreme of the rational process is the **garbage-can model of decision making** (Cohen, March, & Olsen,

1972). Choices emerge from a highly diverse network of decision makers that could be called "organized anarchy." Its members are many and changing, its processes are not well grasped even by its regular participants, and they do not hold agreed-upon or consistent preferences. This model lacks all the qualities needed to sustain the rational process, outlined earlier. The "garbage can" itself represents a large collection of ideas about problems and solutions from which participants can draw, depending on their interests and opportunities.

The current antidrug campaigns offer an example of garbage-can decision making in many governments. There are many views of what should be of highest priority: cutting off foreign production, stopping drug importation at our borders, arresting sellers, preventing individuals from beginning to use drugs, and rehabilitating current addicts. Each is a goal and a means to achieve other goals. Each assumes a distinct central problem linked with solutions to other problems. Since every state government and most municipal governments and school districts join with several federal agencies in picking ideas out of the "garbage can," one can see why multiple and conflicting decisions can emerge.

Governmental Intelligence

Decision makers are voracious consumers of information. Uncertainty and confusion about problems and circumstances are always enemies of confident decisions, and government agencies must be able to gather the necessary **intelligence** (in the military sense of strategically useful information) to identify the problems, future conditions, alternatives for choice, and impacts of their actions.

Obtaining Intelligence

Obtaining this intelligence is a prerequisite to decision making in any of the modes discussed in the previous section. At first glance, this may not appear difficult. Information flows to public agencies from many sources: employees, the news media, constituents, interest groups, legislators, researchers, and other parts of government. Most of this is unsolicited, and much may be "wasted," in that it is not examined fully for its relevance to the agency's mission. Planners thus have to be continuously alert to data that will help in making future choices and catalog them so they can be found later by others. For example, new developments in medical technology continually alter the demands on such public health care programs as Medicare and Medicaid. Because a new treatment for cancer or heart disease could extend the lives of many or multiply the costs of their care, planners for future expenditures in these programs must monitor these potential developments and anticipate costs accordingly.

Intelligence also involves creating needed information. Amid forecasts of global warming and rising ocean levels, governments need much more specific knowledge about expected shoreline erosion to make land-use plans: Should they prevent oceanfront building? Can they protect what is already there? How far inland should they locate roads, sewers, and other public facilities that will ensure their lasting for fifty or more years?

Information searches are never random. A person begins with an image of the problem that requires a decision and the data that are relevant to it. The open-minded decision maker will broaden the search to include whatever proves to be relevant. But no one can survey everything; the quest will always be bounded by the time available for it, the information sources at hand, the costs of the search, and the inquirer's expertise and perceptions. To return to the shoreline example, an engineer who is committed to guarding what is already threatened by the waves will primarily seek data on seawalls and other protective devices. Another planner, who has concluded that such protection is ultimately futile, will begin to study how far from the current shore to set back new developments.

The process of **external scanning** is increasingly used by government agencies for systematic information searches to aid planning (Pflaum & Delmont, 1987). It consists of three phases: the scanning itself, which involves surveying the environment of the agency to identify emerging opportunities and threats; analysis of the data obtained and the choices they pose for the agency; and dissemination of the analyzed information in forms that can be useful to those who must make decisions. Specialists survey selected areas most relevant to the agency and pool their insights in the analyses. Properly done, external scanning can provide early warning on such emerging problems as shoreline erosion so that plans can be made and political support for solutions obtained before a crisis strikes—when there is no time for learning or planning. A flexible tool, external scanning can be shaped to each agency's own mission and circumstances, its wide information base can provide credibility, and it can be used for public and legislative education.

When should the search end? In many situations one can never get "enough" information, and an ongoing external scanning process can build the data resources steadily. Nevertheless, decision deadlines make cutoffs inevitable. Budget schedules and elections also force decisions at preset times. Administrators must decide when the essential knowledge is at hand and an adequate solution is available. They know they can make different choices in the future if they have better intelligence then.

The searchers should make their investigations as inclusive as possible. Specialists are prone to have "tunnel vision" and acquire data only within the fields with which they are familiar. But many public decisions are so closely interrelated that a "wide-angle" research method is necessary. This is clearly true for the issue of immigration, for example. The flood of legal and illegal migrants across the U.S. borders has far-ranging effects, touching but not limited to employment, education, social services, crime, drug abuse, and health issues, that show up at many points in national, state, and local budgets. A Mexican immigrant settling in San Diego or a Russian in Chicago has an impact on many public agencies, and it is a major challenge to choose proper responses. If the nation intends to continue welcoming immigrants, administrators must foresee the policy and budgetary choices this will involve, as well as efficient divisions of responsibility to carry them out.

Forecasts: A Product of Intelligence Gathering

One product of searches and scans is the **forecast**: a description of a possible future event or condition with an estimate of its likelihood. A forecast can identify "probable futures," which are very likely to come about, given present trends and choices, and it may discern "possible futures," which have a small chance of occurring but whose likelihood could be increased by different choices.

Forecasts typically assume a baseline—that which could be expected if trends and forces continue at a known rate without deliberate intervention. That is, one may forecast what the rate of immigration into the United States would be if all present policies were continued and world conditions did not change. A contingency forecast would project how immigration would change under specified conditions, perhaps if the Border Patrol became more successful in excluding undocumented persons or if Mexico experienced a violent political upheaval.

Governments rely on forecasts of many kinds: trade, population, income, employment, and natural resources, to name a few. Each is only as reliable as the assumptions and data on which it rests, and analysts must choose these according to some criteria. Forecasts of employment emerge from complex computer models that incorporate masses of data weighted according to economists' judgments of their influence. Analysts study trends extended into the future for the pictures they suggest of what is to come, based on the assumption that they will continue or change in predictable ways. In general, the shorter the time period that the forecasts cover, the more reliable they are. Nevertheless, well-informed specialists often differ in their forecasts even when using the same data. The Office of Management and Budget and the Congressional Budget Office have produced conflicting outlooks for the nation's economy. Different political interests can account for at least some of this divergence.

For forecasts in which informed judgment can play a larger role than data analysis, the Delphi technique is sometimes used.

Typically, it begins with a question posed to a panel of experts—for example, "What are the most important emerging forces and conditions to affect public health in our city in the next 25 years?" The panel might include health professionals, social workers, community group leaders, clergy, educators, and others familiar with conditions that affect illness. Their answers are compiled into a list, ranked by the number of mentions each received. Then the panel is asked to refine that ranking, describing the expected impacts of those forces and indicating when in the future they are likely to occur. Panelists may also be asked to explain their judgments, particularly if they are different from the average. An extensive Delphi will go through several such rounds to refine expectations in depth. Ideally, public health agencies can use these judgments as raw material for their own planning and policies.

Since forecasts can steer policies in one direction or another, they are politically sensitive. An EPA administrator who was convinced that global warming was a major threat and wanted Congress to appropriate funds and enact regulations to combat it would be strongly tempted to publicize scientific projections of drastic climatic changes that would result from current trends. On the other hand, a group opposing this stand could find equally credible scientific data minimizing the threat and made a contrasting forecast. Thus, forecasts can be used as a drunk uses a lamppost—for support rather than illumination.

Cost/Benefit Analysis

Another technique to clarify choices and their consequences is cost/benefit analysis, a systematic comparison of the anticipated benefits and costs to accrue from a given choice. It is used in the second and third steps in the external scanning process, described earlier. Chapter 5 presented its basic steps, and Box 10.1 summarizes them.

Administrators generally draw on cost/benefit analysis for more specific choices than lawmakers. We can illustrate this with a choice that a metropolitan area must make about future mass transit services. There are several ways to move people in groups: buses, commuter vans, car pools, and light- and heavy-rail rapid transit. Assuming the major objective is to move the maximum number of people at a given net cost or achieve the highest ridership-to-cost ratio, an analyst can project the construction and operating costs of the rail line and the number of riders in a future period and compare these with similar figures for the cheaper alternatives. If an improved bus system produces the best cost/benefit ratio, then it will be the rational choice rather than the rail line. Transit planning is made more complex when an additional objective is to reduce the congestion and air pollution motor vehicles cause. One

Box 10.1

Cost/Benefit Analysis

1. Identify the objective(s) of the decision—the benefits sought from the choice under consideration.
2. Select the criteria by which the alternatives are to be compared and evaluated, such as dollar costs or number of persons benefited.
3. Identify each alternative course of action that could reach the objective(s).

4. Measure the extent of the benefits each alternative would produce and the costs it would entail, and calculate the cost/benefit ratio.
5. Select the alternative that best achieves the objectives and has the largest positive difference between costs and benefits.

must then attach dollar and health values to these goals and add them to the cost/benefit calculations. Legislators typically depend on the staff of a transit or metropolitan planning agency for this analysis.

It is often difficult to measure the costs and benefits confidently. The EPA has the task of implementing the Clean Air Act, which Congress passed in 1990. Many of the enforcement standards it imposes will rest on cost/benefit estimates—the costs of removing sulfur dioxide from power plant emissions versus the gains in personal health, for example. But estimates of both costs and benefits vary widely, and the EPA may have little reason to settle on one figure rather than another. One of its air pollution specialists admitted that he lacks a reliable price tag for cities' compliance with the ozone limits specified in the act, either its benefits or its costs (Starobin, 1990).

Assessing Impacts and Risks

Impact assessments also supply raw materials for decisions by projecting the likely and possible consequences of an action. These came to be used widely in the 1970s, stemming from the concerns of interest groups that government was undertaking many ventures with little thought of their consequences.

Environmental Impact Statements   When a unit of government or a private corporation proposes a development such as a dam, highway, or shopping center that would have serious impact on the natural environment, it must study that impact in depth. Box 10.2 summarizes the requirements for these reports, as stated in the Na-

Box 10.2

Environmental Impact Statements

Section 102(C) of the National Environmental Policy Act of 1969 states that all agencies of the federal government shall "include in every recommendation or report on proposals for legislation and other major Federal actions significantly affecting the quality of the human environment, a detailed statement by the responsible officials on—

(i) the environmental impact of the proposed action,

(ii) any adverse environmental effects which cannot be avoided should the proposal be implemented,

(iii) alternatives to the proposed action,

(iv) the relationship between local short-term uses of man's environment and the maintenance and enhancement of long-term productivity, and

(v) any irreversible and irretrievable commitments of resources which would be involved in the proposed action should it be implemented.

Prior to making any detailed statement, the responsible Federal official shall consult with and obtain the comments of any Federal agency which has jurisdiction by law or special expertise with respect to any environmental impact involved. Copies of such statement and the comments and views of the appropriate Federal, state, and local agencies, which are authorized to develop and enforce environmental standards, shall be made available to the President, the Council on Environmental Quality and to the public . . . , and shall accompany the proposal through the existing agency review processes."

tional Environmental Policy Act of 1969, which first required environmental impact statements.

As environmental impact statements have evolved, they have generally (1) described existing conditions at the location to be affected and the nature of the project; (2) stated the anticipated effects on the natural environment, including soil, water, vegetation, and pollution levels; and (3) showed how the project was designed to minimize the resulting harm. Many states followed suit in requiring such studies not only for their own projects, but also for those of private developers.

The assessment of environmental impacts was a major addition to the processes of planning and decision making. It "not only forces knowledge into policy processes where it has been hitherto either selectively employed or neglected and rejected; it also reveals the insufficiency of the information upon which society and its governments often act" (Caldwell, 1988, p. 83). In practice, the very process of preparing the statement and securing reviews by the public and other agencies usually delays project approval and provides time and information to opponents. A common outcome of these statements has been the cancellation or modification of the project. A striking example of this is the failure of the U.S. Department of

Energy to win approval of sites for the disposal of highly dangerous nuclear wastes after working through a long environmental impact assessment process.

Technology Assessment The systematic examination of the effects on society that may occur when a technology is introduced, extended, or modified, with special emphasis on those consequences that are unintended, indirect, or delayed, is known as technology assessment (TA). In 1972 Congress created the Office of Technology Assessment to do such studies at its request, and the many reports it has produced are available to the public.

A typical TA study performs three major functions. The study (1) describes in detail the specific technology (perhaps a new life-sustaining instrument or a method of computerized manufacturing) and explains how it interacts with related technologies; (2) identifies areas of society likely to feel its impacts and indicates what those impacts will be; and (3) describes alternative responses by which society and government can gain the most benefit from those impacts and minimize their harms. The ultimate purpose is to increase the options that decision makers can examine intelligently. The analyst does not make the decision directly but supplies the evidence that shapes it. Of course, choices about the development and applications of new technologies are also influenced by many political considerations, not the least of which are the interests of those who stand to profit from making, selling, and using them.

Social Impact Assessment Similar to environmental and technological forecasting but broader in scope is social impact assessment. Using this method, analysts examine the social, economic, and cultural effects of a proposed project, including those that cannot be measured readily in dollars. One such study by the Army Corps of Engineers asked how the dredging of the Yaquina Bay and Yaquina River in Oregon would affect the adjacent cities of Newport and Toledo. For example, if a larger fishing fleet were to use the bay, it was important to learn how it would affect the need for social services, the number of tourists, population movements, and alterations in the cities' political power structure (White, 1981).

Risk Assessment Administrators also analyze the many uncertainties of life by using risk assessment. In this technique the probability and magnitude of undesired and harmful outcomes of possible courses of action is forecasted (Fischhoff et al., 1984). It is most commonly used in the regulatory process, responding to public demands to limit risks to life and health from a host of technologies. Popular fears are often highly subjective, downplaying some risks while elevating others, and analysts seek to provide some realistic

Box 10.3

Risk Assessment Procedures

The risk assessment system normally consists of a four-step sequence (Breyer, 1993, pp. 9–10):

1. Identify the potential hazard in its context. For example, it may be benzene, which is believed to cause cancer, widely used as a solvent in workplaces.

2. Determine the dose and response level—the effects of a given dose or concentration over a given time period on those exposed to it. To continue the example, benzene exposure at a given level during a person's working life may be judged responsible for a certain rate of cancer deaths.

3. Estimate the actual exposure of people to the risk situation. This requires calculation of contacts with benzene in many workplaces under many different conditions.

4. Determine the resulting risk and the level of hazard experienced. Data accumulated on benzene may support a conclusion that it probably does contribute to cancer under the conditions examined.

---

guides for government decisions. Box 10.3 outlines typical procedures that risk analysts follow. In their research they gather data from many sources and often conduct studies of their own. As information accumulates, they seek to integrate and interpret it so that future analysts can decide how to use it.

Risk assessment is far from an exact science, although analysts claim that their methods and data are improving. However, the causes of a disease like cancer are not fully known, and certainly one cannot calculate the influence of a single substance such as benzene with a high level of confidence. If a worker in a plant that uses benzene is stricken with cancer, one cannot be sure of the cause. Viewing this uncertainty, critics hold that many regulatory policies have no solid justification. A further concern is that decision makers pay more attention to risks to which they can attach numbers than to those that are more serious but harder to measure. Despite these limits, risk analysis is an essential tool for decision makers who seek to raise the level of rationality.

The toughest problems government has to solve are also, not surprisingly, the least amenable to systematic forecasting. Human behavior, whether in spending money, using illegal drugs, or raising children, is subject to many conditions (including government's own policies) that we do not fully understand. If the use of marijuana and cocaine were legalized, would their use decline? The stakes in that choice are very high, but because information that use would decline is not available, policymakers choose to continue banning them and penalizing those who trade in them. The methods for gaining information on this kind of problem must probe into motives and relationships that do not lend themselves to numerical analysis.

Planning: Controlling the Future from the Present

Governments are constantly trying to control future conditions through decisions made in the present. This is the essence of **planning** and an integral part of policymaking, since choosing goals and devising steps to reach them over a given span of time are interdependent activities. If the federal government sought to end the nation's dependence on imported oil (the future condition), it would take certain steps now (such as giving industries incentives to develop sustainable sources). Planning is that explicit linkage between current choices and anticipated results. It is not simply "plan making," as if a design for the future could be inscribed in stone, valid for all time to come. Rather, planning must be a continuous process, for each change in the "present" calls for a matching change in the "future" and finding the means of achieving it.

Strategic Planning

Many governments practice strategic planning to broaden the range of factors they consider and link their plans more directly to the actions they require (Bryson & Roering, 1987). Box 10.4 summarizes its basic steps. Initially developed by private corporations, this technique has been adapted to local and state agency situations. Strategic planning typically begins with a commitment by top management to develop a plan and carry it out. Second, the organization identifies its mandates (the legal requirements that it must fulfill) and its values (the broader purposes it has set for itself). Every public agency has certain "stakeholders" with interests in those mandates and purposes, such as employees, constituents, legislators, and taxpayers, whose desires or demands have to be considered at this point.

The third step in strategic planning is to identify external opportunities and threats that would either increase or reduce the organization's ability to meet its goals. This requires extensive intelligence about trends, forces, and possible outcomes. The Department of Energy, for example, would greatly benefit from a technological breakthrough making nuclear fusion or solar energy conversion economical. While examining this goal, it must also assess its internal strengths and weaknesses, to learn whether it has adequate funding, people with the necessary skills, or the organizational clarity to develop the plan further. If the secretary of energy learns that her staff lacks specialists in alternative energy forms who can guide future research in that field, this must also be addressed.

Next, the organization must define its strategic issues: basic questions posed by all the information gained thus far. One could

---

Box 10.4

Elements of Strategic Planning

- Top management commits itself to support the planning effort and to implement the plans developed.
- The planning staff identifies the organization's mandates and values with which its planning must be consistent.
- The staff discerns its external opportunities and threats to which it must respond and which may either aid or hinder its goal achievement.
- The staff assesses the organization's internal strengths and weaknesses to learn whether it has adequate funding, persons with neces-

sary skills, and enough organizational clarity to achieve its goals.
- From the above data, planners define the strategic issues, the basic questions posed, and the tentative answers to them.
- Management devises actions that target those strategic issues, including means of removing barriers to action and remedying internal weaknesses.
- The organization continues this effort on a continuing or recurring schedule to take account of new circumstances.

---

be that its legal mandate is insufficient to deal with crucial problems or that its methods of operation are inefficient. The Department of Energy became strongly oriented to fossil fuels and nuclear energy during the Reagan and Bush administrations. Secretary Hazel O'Leary, President Clinton's appointee, was given the strategic challenge of shifting its values toward alternatives to those politically sensitive energy sources, but received little external support for it.

The final step in this planning process is to devise actions that target strategic issues, including means of removing barriers to action and remedying internal weaknesses. A schedule for actions will give guidance so that managers know what must be done first, then second, and so on. Contingency plans should be available in case a proposed action becomes impossible or fails to produce the expected results. In energy development this may entail requirements or incentives for industry to reduce fossil fuel use or shift to alternative sources. Large corporations' responses, whether in support or opposition, could also lead the Department of Energy to alter its strategies.

Effective strategic planning is not easy or cheap. Each of the preceding steps consumes much of the administrators' and specialists' time and requires an information system that can supply current and adequate data. Furthermore, planning cannot be a one-time event but must be continuously sensitive to new circumstances. An organization may routinely go through this cycle each year to keep plans up to date. Where the agency's external environment is unstable, as in the Energy Department, plans may have a short life expectancy. Recurring planning is even more necessary for that reason, when the only alternative is to drift haphazardly while hastily improvising for each day.

Land-Use Control: Government Planning at the State and Local Levels

A principal purpose of planning by government below the federal level is control of the use of land. Such land-use choices are normally made by individual and corporate landowners, but states, counties, and cities place restrictions upon them designed to ensure an environment that meets their citizens' standards of a desirable community. Urban land-use planning is intended to allow for residential, commercial, and public facilities that will meet a community's needs and provide for its well-being, yet avoid conflicts among its users. Zoning is a regulatory tool that implements the plan on a current basis. Limits are especially important in areas undergoing change from one use to another, particularly from rural to urban. The controls must be effective at the time that changes are proposed; once a shopping center has been built in an area intended for residences or a wetland is drained to make room for a factory, there is no reversing that action.

Land-use planning is also crucial when cities contemplate redevelopment of older areas. In the 1950s and 1960s federal funds enabled cities to embark on massive urban renewal schemes. They demolished old structures on many blocks in order to provide new housing and business opportunities. Typically, this was done with the cooperation of private investors, who acquired much of the land after it was cleared. Although urban renewal is no longer financed by Washington, D.C., partnerships for it are still active, as in New York City's long-delayed plans to redevelop its theater district around Times Square. In contrast to zoning, which simply requires legal authority to prevent an action, developmental planning also calls for the financial resources to carry it out.

Turning Plans into Reality: The Chances for Success

The official who prepares a plan is often not the one who puts it into effect. Thus, the implementation of a plan is a separate step and is more subject to political influence. Levin and Sanger (1994, p. 40) distinguish between *point* and *line* decisions. The former is a choice taken at one point in time among several alternatives. Line decisions run in a series, in which many people act consistently in one direction to follow through from the beginning point.

The adoption of a plan is a point decision, but it envisions a chain of actions, confirmed and implemented year by year through line decisions. Failure to act at one point can invalidate a plan. Many land use and public facilities plans for cities and metropolitan areas gather dust on shelves while development proceeds in other directions. One of the most ambitious of the American city designs was prepared in 1909 by the eminent planner Daniel Burnham for Chicago and its suburbs. If followed, it would have given the city broad boulevards and palatial public buildings in the European style. However, the city's politicians and business leaders (who commissioned Burnham to do the plan) acted only on parts of it and it remains a relic of the "City Beautiful" movement. The main causes of the abandonment of plans have been their lack of realism, failure to gain wide popular acceptance of their major features, and changes in the values of later decision makers and the political pressures on them.

Planning offers the most promise in situations where major changes are possible and predictable, the desired direction is agreed upon, and tools are available to control the course of change. But because it is always done amid uncertainty as to outcomes, there is risk that a given plan will fail to achieve its objectives.

> The planning process is like rolling a pair of dice—one of which is loaded. There is a higher than random probability of success, but a certain degree of risk remains. The most that any planner can hope for—and this, in fact, is a great deal—is that the anticipated outcome of a plan can be approximated with minimal deviations due to unforeseen developments. (Eaton, 1980, p. 27)

Minimizing risks requires the intelligence gathering described in the previous section, for it portrays the changing world into which one's choices must fit. The time frame for governmental planning can vary widely, but one to ten years is most common. Beyond that length of time, there are too many uncertainties for there to be a reasonable confidence level. To be sure, the consequences of decisions may last for many decades.

Effective plans should also be modified as time passes and circumstances and values change. The Interstate Highway System, created by law in 1956 but planned well before then, has grown over the years from its original network. Metropolitan-area freeways have been added, but local citizen resistance has forced the Federal Highway Administration to drop plans for some inner-city roads. Periodic updates in the light of new data and altered public preferences are essential. Box 10.5 describes the most recent effort of planning for surface transportation, which alters both the procedures used for it and the modes of transportation used.

Each decision is made in a unique political environment composed of three basic elements: its goals and purposes, the resources available to inform and implement it, and the persons and institutions

The Political Environment of Decision Making

Box 10.5

In How Many Ways Can We Plan for Transportation?

A notable shift has begun in the nation's planning for surface transportation. Since the first national highway act was passed in 1916, the emphasis has been on road development. Even in urban areas, in which there has been some aid to mass transit systems, the bulk of spending has been on freeways. The Intermodal Surface Transportation Efficiency Act (ISTEA), which became law in 1991, envisions two major changes, particularly for metropolitan areas.

First, the act deemphasizes roadbuilding in favor of new technologies to make existing roads more efficient and the air above them cleaner. Recognizing that each urban region has different mobility needs, it allows flexibility in choices for mass transit, car pool lanes, bicycle access, and congestion reduction. Cities with serious smog problems can institute means to reduce ozone, hydrocarbons, and other vehicle-borne pollutants.

Second, ISTEA transfers some of the authority to use federal funds to metropolitan planning organizations. These agencies are intended to represent a broad spectrum of interests and local governments in their region, which presumably will know best how to meet their unique transportation needs. The New York City area, which depends heavily on mass transit, must be viewed differently from Houston and Phoenix, which are highly decentralized and rely more on private cars.

ISTEA, if these expectations become reality, will make the planning process more pluralistic than ever. Highway planning has been concentrated in federal and state transportation departments, with minimal input from other officials. It will be difficult to reconcile the many transportation-related interests in a major metropolitan area, and intense political struggles are likely.

---

participating in it. No decision is isolated from all others so that one can focus attention on it apart from anything else that happens at the time. Rather, each decision has a history of preceding choices that set the conditions for it, and each has a context of related choices that are on the agenda at the same time and provide either opportunities or limits. Any Energy Department decisions to reduce oil consumption must be harmonized with such other policy choices as motor vehicle fuel efficiency, disposal of radioactive wastes from nuclear power plants, and clean-air legislation.

Degrees of Difficulty: Convergent and Divergent Problems

The environment of broad public goals and the problems to be solved are crucial. In the late 1960s, people asked, "If we can put a man on the moon, why can't we solve the problems of the urban ghettos?" The chain of decisions that placed Neil Armstrong on the moon in 1969 was perhaps the closest thing to a large-scale rational process we have seen. The problem itself was *convergent* in the sense that all lines of thinking began at one purpose and led logically to only one solution. The National Aeronautics and Space Administration (NASA) had abundant funds for research and development of hardware and the time to investigate all promising avenues. One set of techniques proved to be superior to all others in the eyes of the few experts who ran the program.

Why couldn't the problems of the urban ghettos be solved in the same way? Basically, they were *divergent* problems that had many potential definitions and solutions, not all of them compatible with one another. No single goal united urban policymakers, unlike that of reaching the moon. No known technique would cut the tangled web of unemployment, inadequate housing, discrimination, disease, substance abuse, family instability, and illiteracy, and no amount of research and development would provide more than partial answers. People with conflicting political ideologies define "success" differently, and only rarely will an outcome meet with everyone's approval.

Some programs require large-scale, long-term commitments. We can distinguish between "big" decisions, which are unique, are of high impact, and involve large commitments of resources, and "little" ones, which are marginal and easily fit in with previous ones (Krieger, 1986). To build an urban rapid transit network is a big decision, because a usable system is not created with mere pieces of routes here and there. The Washington, D.C., Metro was first conceived in the 1960s and is still not complete, although it is heavily used. A "megaproject" like the Metro cannot be designed incrementally, although it can be modified to some extent while under construction. A rational decision method must be applied in its overall design to ensure that it is coherent and each step of its development takes place in a proper sequence. On the other hand, development of a bus transit network can be done through incremental decisions, since its routes and equipment can be easily altered to meet changes in demand.

The fact that most legislation fails to state precise and consistent goals for programs adds to the difficulty of pursuing a rational method on a large scale. Although it is possible to design a specific job training program by using a systematic procedure, a large and complex area such as urban policy is too broad and open to dispute to permit this. Some legislative goals are stated in ideal terms (e.g., "full employment") with no prospect of achievement by any known methods. Administrators can aim at some fraction of this goal, perhaps reduction of the unemployment rate by one percentage point, but even such a limited goal is subject to disagreement.

Among the resources needed for decision making and implementation are information, time to process it, and funds and skills to carry out choices. Information of sufficient quantity and quality does not usually fall into an administrator's lap or data base. It must be sought out at some cost. A major factor hampering the nation's (and states') toxic waste cleanup efforts is ignorance of which sites are most hazardous, what chemicals they contain, and what technologies are most appropriate to clean them up. To learn who is liable for the waste and to investigate the health impacts on surrounding residents takes additional time. Research to study all these factors delays action and costs money that would otherwise pay for the cleanup itself. Under such pressures, administrators often "satisfice," settling for a lower level of information than may be needed to do the best job.

Timing Decisions

The timing of decisions also shapes the methods used. The moon landing was to be accomplished in the decade of the 1960s, a span of eight years after President Kennedy made his momentous pledge. This allowed the technical choices to be made in a long, orderly sequence after the necessary research and experimentation. But most public policy choices are intensely studied only after the problem has become urgent and immediate action is imperative. When pressure for a quick decision is high, officials will consider only a small number of alternatives. Those that they have thought out in advance or that are promoted most zealously will have the advantage. Further, decision makers sometimes restrict the number of participants and impose secrecy on the process (Downs, 1967, p. 183).

The incremental method, always building on recent experience and assuming that decisions can be changed based on new information, is suited to conditions of high uncertainty. One can argue that administrators ought to be more farsighted, and they would agree. If they practice strategic planning, they can project their analysis further into the future than otherwise. But as a fact of life, top decision makers rarely get far ahead of the urgencies of the week and generally study information resources only when they must make an immediate choice.

The Circle of Decision Makers

Finally, the number, identity, and placement of the decision makers is another crucial factor. Rational decision making assumes that one or a very few qualified persons make the choices, with no distraction or dissent from outside sources. NASA was given a great deal of technical autonomy, and although many skilled scientists and engineers contributed their knowledge, the top management made the final commitments.

We have seen, however, that most decisions are made in situations where many share power. Incrementalism is uniquely suited to pluralistic, competitive politics, in which interpersonal agreement is integral to basic decisions and every participant claims some part in the action. Even major investment choices often require this interchange. When the Portland, Oregon, metropolitan area chose to construct a light-rail transit line, it first had to assemble an intergovernmental decision-making system. The participants consisted of federal, state, regional, and municipal officials who had to clear away financial, legal, and technical obstacles. The choice of a route to the city's northeast side was a by-product of many policies: federal support of mass transit with highway funds, Portland's overall transportation plans, and the relative power to be wielded by the state, cities, and regional agencies over public investments (Edner, 1984). Many officials weave a broad net of responsibility, not only to spread the costs and stresses but also to accumulate support and neutralize opponents. Thus, the "buck" may not stop anywhere but keep revolving around the circle of participants.

The personalities, ambitions, and interests of the individual decision makers and their interpersonal dynamics also shape choices. At times, the group process itself generates choices that no individual might produce alone or in a different group. "Groupthink" is a way of reaching decisions within a cohesive group, in which the "members' strivings for unanimity override their motivation to realistically appraise alternative courses of action." It is a "deterioration of mental efficiency, reality testing, and moral judgments that results from in-group pressures" (Janis, 1972, p. 9). The group or its leaders may have strong shared values and biases that incline the members to favor or oppose certain courses of action without deeply examining them. Members, even if they have misgivings about a decision, tend to subordinate their own judgment to that of the consensus. Much of the evidence for groupthink's influence comes from American foreign policy disasters of the past 50 years, but the concept can be applied as well to domestic choices.

The collective blindness of groupthink can be prevented if the leaders of the decision-making team avoid stating their own views at the outset, make deliberate efforts to reward the critical thinking of all members and ensure that their views are fully expressed, and from time to time subject the group's thinking to outside criticism. Sensitive guidance is called for, for if the group goes too far in the other direction and lacks mutual trust and cohesion, it cannot function well.

Open and Closed Decision Systems

All these factors—the difficulty of the matter to be decided, the timing of the choice, and the number, interests, and interactions of the participants—shape the degree of openness of the decision-making system. Early in this chapter it was stated that administrative decision making tends to be more "closed" than that of legislative bodies and to be characterized by minimal publicity and dominance by specialists. Administrators often seek to restrict the scope of decision-making processes to save time and minimize controversy. Yet choices reached by such methods may not be in the public's best interest. During the 1970s many decisions on toxic waste management were initially "closed" and frequently produced no action to clean up pollution sites. The Love Canal incident (at Niagara Falls, N.Y.; recall Box 8.2 on page 223) in the late 1970s revealed how inadequate that system was, when local and state officials at first did nothing about the chemical contamination in that residential community. Citizen groups have since opened the process, not only changing outcomes but also forcing many new hazardous sites onto the agenda for cleanup (O'Brien et al., 1984).

The Costs of Decisions

All decision making entails costs. One cost is the time spent in meetings sharing information and deliberating on choices. Individuals consume time in researching, analyzing, and presenting information. Books, documents, tapes, computers, and other sources and means of processing information represent major investments. Many decisions "cost" or "gain" political support or reduce consensus and harmony within an agency. Costs can appear in the forms of personal stress, career disruptions, and lost elections. Decision makers naturally seek to minimize these costs.

What is the relationship between the cost of a decision and its quality? If twice as much money, time, talent, or information is invested in a given choice, will its quality be doubled? No one can say. Poor decisions have been made in both haste and leisure. If there are too few participants, this may contribute to "tunnel vision," but other decisions have been blunted or stalled by the involvement of too many. So many variables affect the quality of choices that "costs" alone cannot be a reliable determinant.

Summary

Decision making is a central demand on administrators. Some of their choices contribute to public policymaking by legislators, whereas many others become part of administrative law, putting flesh on the bones of statutory law in the process of implementing it. A decision is a goal-oriented selection of one course of action from two or more alternatives. It is always made amid uncertainty and in the hope that the means indeed serve the ends.

Several models of decision making are widely used, distinguished by the assumptions and methods that underlie them. The rational model is the most systematic, and it is useful when goals are clearly defined and all factors affecting the decision are known. The incremental, organizational process, governmental politics, and "garbage-can" methods are less rigorous but are used frequently when the dimensions of the choice are not well known or are in dispute.

Administrators require an intelligence process to search for and obtain information and to generate forecasts of probable and possible futures. They employ such techniques as external scanning of new developments, Delphi forecasting, cost/benefit analysis, and impact assessments to foresee effects of environmental changes, new technologies, and risky courses of action. Forecasting is extremely difficult and subject to conflicting interpretations when it examines the motives and behavior that underlie major social problems.

Planning is the effort to control future conditions by decisions made in the present. It is most successful when the desired change is known and tools are available to steer its direction and pace. Governments rely on planning to guide their choices on such matters as national energy management and local land use. Of increasing importance is strategic planning, the means by which organizations link their goals, strengths, and weaknesses with the conditions in the external environment in which they seek to act. Planners and managers must remain flexible to recognize new opportunities and situations and modify their plans accordingly.

The political environment of decision making is shaped by the goals involved in a particular decision, the resources available to inform and implement it, the time frame in which it is to emerge, and the persons and institutions participating in it. When goals are narrow and precise, adequate resources are on hand, and the decision makers are few and in general agreement, the rational method is practical. However, when these conditions are not present, more subjective means are needed to reach even partial and temporary consensus. It sometimes happens when members of a group must make a collective choice that they fall into "groupthink," in which their desire for harmony and agreement leads them to suppress doubts and uncertainties that may require more serious consideration.

Discussion Questions

1. What are the major obstacles to intelligent assessment of the likely impacts of technological or environmental projects? How can they be minimized?

2. Why is the rational method of decision making so often considered superior to the other forms described in this chapter? What are its central advantages?

3. What types of policy issues are hardest to forecast with confidence? Why?

4. What are the major hindrances to effective planning, strategic or otherwise? To what extent are they internal to the organization, and to what extent are they external?

5. How does "groupthink," when it pervades an organization, affect the plans and decisions made by the organization? Is it always detrimental?

Analytical Exercises

1. Obtain and examine a copy of the land-use plan for the city or county in which you live or attend school. Determine the criteria used for the major designations— why one parcel of land is reserved for industrial use, another for commercial, and still others for single-family homes. If changes in the plan have recently been made, find out why. Learn whether there are any current conflicts over specific choices.

2. Assume that Congress has set a goal that the nation will reduce by 50 percent over the next 10 years its consumption of fossil fuels. This goal reflects widespread concern about the growth in the amount of carbon dioxide in the atmosphere, because this is believed to cause climatic warming. Outline the planning that must take place to achieve this goal, including restrictions that will be needed, development of energy alternatives, and incentives for change and efficiency. Arrange these in a series of progressive steps for each year.

For Further Reading

Allison, G. T. (1971). *Essence of Decision: Explaining the Cuban Missile Crisis.* Boston: Little, Brown. A classic on the making of decisions, with implications for the domestic as well as the foreign policy realm.

Bryson, J. M., & Einsweiler, R. C. (Eds.). (1988). *Strategic Planning: Threats and Opportunities for Planners.* Chicago: American Planners Association. Fourteen articles survey the methods and current applications of strategic planning and management at all levels of government.

Derthick, M. (1990). *Agency under Stress: The Social Security Administration in American Government.* Washington, DC: Brookings Institution. Analysis of the SSA's responses to pressures on its decisions on who is and is not eligible for benefits.

Lindblom, C. E. (1965). *The Intelligence of Democracy.* New York: Free Press. Analysis of the incremental methods of decision making and justification for them as most appropriate to a democratic political system.

Meyerson, M., & Banfield, E. C. (1957). *Politics, Planning, and the Public Interest.* New York: Free Press. Account of how politics encountered and defeated planning in Chicago housing policy.

Simon, H. J. (1957). *Administrative Behavior,* 2nd ed. New York: Free Press. See note in "For Further Reading" section of Chapter 1.

11

Public Personnel Management

Learning Objectives

After reading this chapter, you should be able to do the following:
1. Identify the categories of civilian public employees in terms of how they are chosen.
2. Describe the six major historical concepts of public personnel.
3. Describe the organization of personnel administration in the national government.
4. Identify the key public policies for recruitment, selection, promotion, compensation, and termination of public employees.
5. Describe the collective-bargaining process and the policies for union organization of public employees.
6. Describe means for identifying and dealing with conflicts of interest by public employees.
7. Summarize the problems currently facing the public service system and potential courses of action to deal with them.

T he Clinton administration had several thousand executive branch jobs to fill after election day in 1992. But filling them did not prove to be easy, either for the recruiters or for those selected. With each appointment goes a process called vetting, a British term for the background investigating that determines whether a person is "fit" for the job. This procedure has become much more demanding over the years, largely because presidents have been acutely embarrassed when past misdeeds of their subordinates became public.

   Consider the case of one nominee. A White House lawyer began by spending over an hour asking him questions. This was followed by more than 60 hours spent filling in six sets of forms that detailed his personal and financial history, past affiliations, and criminal record (if any). He gave his fingerprints and allowed the Federal Bureau of Investigation and Internal Revenue Service to probe their records on him, which for a "normal" nominee takes 3 to 5 weeks.

However, it is not enough for appointees simply to be vetted. As a group, nominees must reflect diversity of race, gender, and home states. It is said that the president rejected all eleven of Agriculture Secretary Mike Espy's preferred appointees for posts in his department because all were men. President Clinton (and Hillary Clinton) were closely involved in each selection, and this resulted in many delays in filling the top positions (Solomon, 1993).

There is a paradox here: In a time when bureaucrats appear to be held in lower public esteem than ever, the process of selecting them is becoming ever more rigorous. This is understandable to a point, but if the appointees are indeed purer, more competent, and more representative of America, what explains their continued low image? Many such questions surround the people who do the work of government.

Public Personnel and the Public Purposes

The public purposes introduced in Chapter 1 place many demands on government employees. The diversity of those purposes, from inspecting coal mines and shutting off the cocaine trade to researching plant genetics and counseling pregnant teenagers, requires a much broader range of skills than is required of any private corporation. Governments must find persons who can do these jobs and fit their abilities and motives to the positions and constituencies they serve.

Public employees must also have a keen sense of responsibility to the citizens who employ them. To be sure, employees in private enterprises are accountable in their own spheres, but these are narrower. For example, urban planners are hired by private land developers to design projects that will yield profits. But government planners for a locality must consider whether proposed projects fit the community's plans and ordinances.

These public responsibilities pose several dilemmas for government managers of personnel. First, should they make it a top priority to provide career opportunities for people from a wide variety of social, racial, ethnic, and linguistic backgrounds? Or should they aim to hire the most clearly competent candidates, even if this leads to an all-male or all-white staff? The meanings of both *equal opportunity* and *competence* are open to debate.

A second dilemma concerns motivating and rewarding people according to their performance. Private employers often link salary, promotions, and perquisites with good work. But government personnel systems usually give equal treatment to all employees, reinforced by a detailed body of rules to avoid favoritism or discrimination by supervisors. Is it possible to compensate public servants for high-quality work without showing social, political, or personal bias?

The third dilemma involves the potentially conflicting loyalties and commitments of public servants. How should an economist in the Department of Agriculture reconcile her responsibilities to the government with her loyalty to the dairy industry, which formerly employed her (and to which she may someday return)? All public employees may encounter conflicts of interest between their public duties and personal benefit that raise questions about honesty and fairness.

In 1992 about 18.745 million people were employed by all units of government in the United States (*Statistical Abstract of the United States,* 1994, Table 493). Slightly more than 3 million civilians worked for the federal government, 4.6 million were employed by the fifty states, and local governments had just over 11 million employees. The number of federal employees began to dip slightly in 1994. President Clinton had pledged in his 1992 campaign to reduce the workforce, and he and Congress later agreed on a cut of 272,800 jobs by the year 1999. A report late in 1994 showed that 103,000 had left the system, many with the incentive of "early retirement" buyouts.

Figure 11.1 classifies state and local employees according to their service functions. The total federal, state, and local payroll for October of that year was $32.4 billion–$388.6 billion when projected over the entire year. The general workforce trend at this level is upward, particularly in the social service and health agencies that meet the needs of the growing number of those near or below the poverty line.

Figure 11.1, portraying the categories of state and local employees, begins to suggest the complexity of the personnel management task. These employees are more diverse in their skills than those at the federal level. Additionally, there are seven different categories of civilian employees in the public service. Five of these categories are formal and have specific methods for recruitment, selection, evaluation, and advancement. The remaining two categories include workers who are not actually in the employ of governments yet contribute to their operations (see Figure 11.2).

A Profile of Public Servants

Top-Level Appointees

The first category, small in employee numbers but large in visibility and influence, consists of top-level appointed executives and policy advisers. This category includes the federal cabinet secretaries and

(continued on p. 308)

Figure 11.1

Distribution of State and Local Government Employees by Type of Government and Function, 1989

Note: October 1989 figures. The charts show the functional areas that employ at least 4 percent of the workers at each level of government. The number of workers is calculated on a full-time equivalent basis. Data from U.S. Census Bureau.
Source: Dale Glasgow and Associates, *Governing*, pp. 70–171, February 1991.

The expansion in responsibilities being placed on counties and states continues to show up in their workforce numbers. Counties, with an increase of 3.2 percent, registered the largest proportional rise among general-purpose governments in the year ending October 1989. State government employment grew by 2.9 percent, municipal and township jobs by only 0.8 percent each. Over the 10-year period beginning in October 1979, municipal employment grew the least, at 3.6 percent; township by 6 percent; state by 14.5 percent; and county by 17 percent. The major job areas in each jurisdiction are shown in the graphic.

Figure 11.2

Categories of Public Servants

Type of Position	Typical Examples
1. Appointed employees	Executives, Cabinet secretaries, and agency heads High policy advisers Regulatory commissioners Executive staff advisers and assistants
2. Merit system employees	Members of federal Senior Executive Service Most clerical and subprofessional personnel Postal service workers
3. Professional employees	Medical and scientific personnel Attorneys, accountants, engineers Law enforcement officers Educators at all levels Social workers
4. Patronage employees	Clerical and technical posts filled by political criteria
5. Wage employees	Persons in skilled and semiskilled trades organized in unions
6. Contract employees	Persons employed by private organizations under contract to government: custodians, consultants. social service workers
7. Volunteers	Persons who provide a public service without compensation: firefighters, school aides, police auxiliaries

These categories of public servants differ in their legal positions, methods of selection, compensation, and job rights. Contract employees and volunteers are included here, even though they are not official government employees, because they provide important public services.

assistant secretaries, other agency heads and their deputies, regulatory commissioners, top personnel in the Office of Management and Budget, and key diplomats—all presidential appointees. Governors and local executives have employees who are counterparts, from a director of a state transportation department to a chief of police. Although many of these appointments must be confirmed by a legislative body, the elected executives who make them have considerable leeway to choose individuals whose views are personally and politically compatible with their own.

Such people are recruited from the ranks of business, universities, the professions, and government itself. Immediately after President Clinton's election in November 1992, he established a transition team of more than 100, consisting mostly of lawyers, to advise on the appointments he would make and investigate the candidates. They had to fill more than 2,000 positions that required Senate confirmation, plus many others, as for the White House staff, that did not. These choices were also influenced by Democratic members of Congress and party activists around the country, who covet these posts as "spoils" to reward those who win the national election. Since appointees were to govern as a team, the president had to choose people who were not only competent but able to work with one another.

The justification for this personnel stratum is that chief executives are entitled to have people of their own choosing in the posts most crucial for implementing their programs. These appointees have broad discretionary powers and are subject only to the will of the one who is accountable to the people for the administration—the president or governor. Such a concept assumes a definable line separating the top levels of each agency's personnel pyramid. Above this line, the staffing is properly done by the chief executive. Below the line, policymaking discretion is sufficiently low that posts can be filled by merit-based criteria. In the federal government the "cap" of the pyramid that contains political appointees grew during the 1980s and early 1990s to include posts that previously were occupied by career civil servants.

Although the obvious challenge is to obtain the best-qualified people who are also politically acceptable, it may be difficult to persuade a preferred choice to take an offered job. Those who can meet these standards are already employed in responsible posts, and if they are in business or a private profession, they are likely to be drawing salaries well in excess of what a cabinet position pays. Presidents Bush and Clinton had to leave many positions unfilled in the first year of their administrations partly because of the refusal of many to take them.

At the federal level the average tenure in a high-level post is just under 2 years (Fisher, 1987). Some of the turnover consists of people moving between government posts, but most departures are to the private sector. This movement is normally voluntary, but people may also be removed by the one who appointed them. Appointees are expected to offer their resignations to a new chief executive. Heclo (1977) referred to them as "birds of passage" and characterized the peaks of the federal bureaucracy as "a government of strangers." Short tenure also appears to be prevalent among state and local administrators, although some acquire such stature and/or expertise as to survive many changes of governor or mayor.

Political factors inevitably influence appointments. A prudent president consults with party leaders, members of Congress, and constituent groups for each cabinet and subcabinet appointment, and strong opposition to a candidate induces him to drop that person from consideration. African Americans, women, and Hispanics claim a share of high federal and state appointments, as do the various factions of the political party. A key appointee to a police or public works post can cement the political relationship between a mayor and the ethnic group or union the person represents. We can view such appointments as an exchange of political assets: the chief executive gains political and policy support, while prestige and benefits flow to the appointees and the groups with which they are affiliated (Lowi, 1964).

The Merit Sector

The second category of government employees is the largest in number: the civilian career or **merit sector** of public employment. These workers are selected on the basis of having demonstrated competence for the job through experience, examination, or education. In the first category the focus is on the individual officeholder, but this selection process begins by defining each position to be filled, its necessary qualifications, and its level of pay. The post may be that of an entry-level word processing clerk, with dozens of similar openings to be filled. A competitive process identifies the best-qualified applicants, and the choice is made by the immediate supervisor of the post, typically among the three to five highest-rated candidates. As long as performance is satisfactory, the person cannot be removed.

Most federal agencies are covered by the comprehensive civil service system known as the General Schedule, but government corporations such as the Postal Service have a separate structure. All state and most local governments have a merit structure with the preceding general characteristics, although they vary in the positions covered.

This general merit system has the advantages of wide coverage and internal consistency. Thus, a word-processing clerk with the Border Patrol in San Diego meets the same standards as one with those duties in the Pentagon. Federal employees under the General Schedule can transfer between agencies and locations and progress up the steps of the pay scale. Because of its generality, however, the General Schedule is not as well suited to highly specialized personnel needs, where positions cannot be easily standardized and unique individual qualifications are paramount.

The **Senior Executive Service** was established by Congress in 1978 and was intended to be a pool of people in the merit system who had executive experience and skills and could occupy the agency posts just below those reserved for the politically appointed executives and communicate effectively with them. A further intent of Congress was to provide status and financial incentives so that these employees would remain with the government rather than shift to the private sector. They are ranked on a separate salary schedule (see Table 11.1) and can be rewarded for exceptional per-

Table 11.1

Federal Executive Branch Civilian Employees by Agency, 1992

Department of Defense	983,000
Postal Service	791,992
Department of Veterans Affairs	260,205
Department of the Treasury	161,951
Department of Health and Human Services	131,191
Department of Agriculture	128,324
Department of Justice	96,927
Department of the Interior	85,260
Department of Transportation	70,558
Department of Commerce	38,086
Department of State	25,734
National Aeronautics and Space Administration	25,425
Federal Deposit Insurance Corporation	22,467
Department of Energy	20,962
General Services Administration	20,770
Environmental Protection Agency	18,196
Department of Labor	17,889
Department of Housing and Urban Development	13,701
Department of Education	5,113

Source: Statistical Abstract of the United States, 1994, Table 527.

Executive branch employees vastly outnumber those of the legislative and judicial branches, and workers in just two organizations—Defense and the Postal Service—make up more than 60 percent of executive branch employees.

formance. Up to 10 percent of the pool can be made up of the president's political appointees, while the rest are selected from those in the merit system. As of 1990 there were 7,359 people in this service.

Experience with the Senior Executive Service has fallen short of its designers' hopes. Turnover has been high (as much as 10 percent a year), as personnel encountered frequent unwanted reassignments between agencies, limits to the performance bonuses they had expected, and strong political pressures to conform to the prevailing White House philosophy. There are no well-defined career ladders that aspiring newcomers can set their eyes on. Thus, this service lacks a clear identity and esprit de corps to attract talented individuals (Huddleston, 1988–89).

Professional Personnel

The professional personnel system, the third category of government employees, follows the merit principles but focuses on specialized qualifications for a post. These ranks encompass state university faculty and administrators, doctors in public hospitals, scientists in the National Institutes of Health, and engineers with public works agencies. The means of selection and evaluation are separate from those for general-merit employees and reflect instead the professionals' unique characteristics. Agencies recruiting them must operate similarly to private employers and offer competitive salaries and perquisites.

Patronage Employees

Patronage employees are hired because of their connections to a political party or because they are favored by elected executives. Unlike the first category of executive appointees, however, they are in posts with lower levels of responsibility. Patronage was the dominant system during most of the nineteenth century, when positions were filled with political supporters of the appointer. This category included customs collectors, mail carriers, janitors, and even some public school teachers. Any competence (or lack of it) they displayed on the job was less relevant than their political affiliation. Holders of these positions supported their patrons by voting correctly (when much voting was not by secret ballot), turning out the votes of others, and contributing a share of their pay to the party treasury. If they did not perform their political duties or if their patron lost an election, they were usually ousted.

Patronage is still practiced in some state and local governments where partisan politics is deeply rooted. It even survives under the guise of merit procedures, when employees may be repeatedly hired for "temporary" positions, which do not carry the same tenure rights as those with permanent status. The practice was sharply curtailed after 1976, when several U.S. Supreme Court rulings over a period of 14 years held that lower- and medium-level employees cannot be selected, promoted, demoted, or fired for reasons related to their party affiliations. However, patronage need not be based solely on partisan criteria. Family, friendship, and business associations also influence decisions to hire one person rather than another. Patronage can also affect the selection of contractors, and the favored vendor will show its gratitude in the politically expected ways.

The Wage System

Many public employees in the skilled and semiskilled trades are in the fifth category, a wage system. They range from plumbers at a naval air station to municipal bus drivers. Most of these workers belong to unions, which represent them in relations with their employers. Like employees in the merit system, they must demonstrate their qualifications and can retain their positions through changes in administrations. They are also placed in salary grades and may advance through the system. Their wages, however, are set differently, as is noted later in this chapter.

Contract Employees

Although technically not government personnel, contract employees are paid with public funds and perform public services. Chapter 7 indicated that governments increasingly are buying services from businesses and nonprofit organizations. Although complete figures are unavailable, it is likely that more people work for private firms under contract to the national government than are employed directly. These employees provide flexibility, since the contract specifies when and how they will be used and they have no merit system protection. At the end of the contract period, a new agreement can be made that releases any or all of them. The contractor determines compensation and working conditions, except that it must pay workers at least the prevailing union-scale wage when they are employed on a federal project.

Volunteers

The last group of public servants consists of volunteers who are not organized in any personnel system but provide important public services with little or no material compensation under the **coproduction** concept introduced in Chapter 7. The total number of volunteers is unknown, but they include those who donate their time to hospitals, schools, social service agencies, correctional institutions, and crime prevention activities. Best known in smaller cities and rural areas are volunteer firefighters, who provide most or all of the staffing of about 90 percent of the fire departments in the nation (Savas, 1987, pp. 80–81).

As public purposes have expanded, government has grown by hiring more and more employees. However, the type of employee it has usually sought has changed with the political circumstances and the tasks to be done. We can discern six distinct types, each corresponding to a historical period yet still valid today as criteria for selecting at least some public servants (Mosher, 1968).

Evolution of the American Public Personnel System

Government by Gentlemen: Aristocrats

President George Washington established the precedent for government by gentlemen, which characterized executive appointments for the first 40 years of the history of our country. He declared his intent to make "fitness of character" his primary object in evaluating such persons (White, 1948, p. 258). In fact, he found such fitness among those from socially prominent families, with the most formal education, in the more prestigious occupations, and among those who had already held leadership positions in their own communities and states. The demands of government were not complex and did not call for narrowly trained specialists. Rather, it was necessary for the new national government to win popular respect by the efficient and honest performance of its duties. The young nation's "gentlemen" were not sharply distinguished from the less-favored classes but had a strong, self-defined mission to govern.

Government by the Average: Democrats

The westward movement of the frontier that created states and communities with no traditional ruling class brought forth the concept of government by the common man. This second and more democratic concept of public service thus came to dominate after 1830. The duties of government remained simple, usually calling for no more than a modest degree of literacy and arithmetic skills. By this time a new party system (Democrats and Whigs) with vigorous grass-roots organizations appealed to the growing numbers of voters. Executives came to regard public jobs as prizes, or "spoils," for their political supporters; thus, this was called the *spoils system.* If any Democrat could collect customs levies or run a post office as well as any Whig, why shouldn't a Democratic president appoint a man of his own party?

President Andrew Jackson also made a case for frequent rotation in office.

> There are, perhaps, few men who can for any great length of time enjoy office and power without being more or less under the influence of feelings unfavorable to the faithful discharge of their public duties. . . . The duties of all public officers are, or least admit of being made, so plain and simple that men of intelligence may readily qualify themselves for their performance; . . . more is lost by the long continuance of men in office than is generally to be gained by their experience. [cited by White, 1954, p. 318]

He believed that the employee's political ties to his patron (thus the term *patronage*) would supplement frequent turnover as a deterrent to corruption.

Government by the Good: Meritocrats

Experiences with the spoils system were not the happiest. Incompetence, nepotism, and bribery became widespread at all levels of administration as many employees put party concerns or self-interest first. These abuses, together with the rising demands on governments for social and technical services, spurred the call for reform. The turning point was the assassination in 1881 of President James Garfield by an unsuccessful job seeker. Congress responded 2 years later with passage of the Pendleton Act, establishing a system for hiring and retaining federal employees solely on the basis of demonstrated qualifications for their positions. It originally applied only to about 10 percent of jobs, although the president could expand its coverage by executive order (Van Riper, 1958, p. 105). State and local governments gradually followed in setting up merit systems, as their dominant political figures supported or permitted it.

This new concept of government by the good supplemented rather than replaced the first two systems. As it was gradually implemented at all levels of government, it stressed three principles. First, employees were to be personally honest, in sharp contrast to the venality of the patronage system, and their morality was to set an example of the nation's highest ideals. Second, they were to demonstrate specific qualifications for the posts they assumed, either by test or experience. If there were several applicants for a post, the one who scored highest (or among the highest) was to be hired and could count on retaining the job as long as his performance met the standards. The third merit principle was political neutrality. Although employees could vote and express partisan preferences, they were obligated to serve executives of both parties with equal faithfulness. Only in this way could a person pursue a stable career through many administrations and gain the skills that experience produces.

Government by the Efficient: Managers

The fourth personnel concept—government by the efficient— emerged after the turn of the twentieth century. The concept of administration as a science had taken hold, thanks to Frederick Taylor and his disciples. Its ideal was maximum output for a given level of input. This was most relevant to municipal government with its routine tasks, such as street paving and water supply. The private New York Bureau of Municipal Research was founded in 1906 to advise city officials on efficient management in the faith that there was "one best way" to operate.

Government by Executives: Administrators

As government agencies continued to grow in size and responsibilities, especially during the 1930s, the fifth concept emerged: government by administrators. Executives in the U.S. Department of Agriculture or a state highway department needed more than honesty, efficiency, and political neutrality; they had to control large organizations, each with its own financing, personnel, planning, and supervisory tasks. New agencies to distribute benefits, create jobs, and regulate corporate behavior required the ability to learn and change. As we saw in Chapter 3, bureaucracies are based on vertical authority relationships, and the capacity to relate effectively both "upward" and "downward" is essential.

Thus, the field of administrative management emerged at that time within both the profession and the discipline, as described in Chapter 1. This paralleled developments in private business, and management was seen as a generic skill that was transferable not only among government agencies but also between business and government. Because the pool of qualified persons was relatively small, government had to use more individualized personal and performance criteria, such as prior performance, to supplement the merit-based standards.

Government by Specialists: Professionals

Since World War II, government's responsibilities have steadily expanded into realms requiring a high degree of specialization, and the concept of government by professionals has emerged in response to that need. The professions themselves have burgeoned throughout society, and scarcely one of them is unrepresented in some agency of government. However, the qualifications for employment are typically set outside government by such groups as the medical, engineering, and bar associations. Geologists, psychiatrists, and accountants bring into their public posts the competencies and standards in which they were educated and often have distinct identities within the public service. As a group, they are less amenable to being "managed" in the traditional sense and more insistent on using their own discretion within their specialties than nonprofessional employees.

In this adding on of public personnel concepts, none has been discarded. The aristocratic tradition continues informally in the dominance of graduates of such prestigious universities as Harvard, Yale, and Stanford in high positions, although affirmative action efforts have opened many doors to graduates of less eminent schools. The "average person" concept has gained new urgency in equal employment opportunity programs since the 1960s. Honesty, efficiency, and broad administrative competence are of even higher priority at this time when public servants are regularly bad-mouthed by politicians, the media, and many citizens.

An important landmark in the continued professionalization of the federal personnel system was the Civil Service Reform Act of 1978. It codified the central principles of the merit system, specified the rights and responsibilities of employees, delegated additional authority to agencies for managing and evaluating their personnel, clarified the process for discharging workers, established a framework for relations with employee organizations, and created the Senior Executive Service, referred to earlier. A further innovation was to replace the Civil Service Commission (which both advised managers on personnel issues and protected the rights of employees, which are obviously conflicting roles) with an Office of Personnel Management (OPM) and a Merit Systems Protection Board, which were to handle those functions separately. In general, Congress and the Carter administration sought to supply incentives and remove barriers to higher productivity. As we shall see, this change has had many effects, although not necessarily the ones intended.

The general merit, professional, and wage systems in the federal government described earlier are governed by an extensive body of rules. The National Performance Review (1993, p. 19) reported that there are 850 pages of personnel law, supplemented by 1,300 pages of regulations on how to implement that law, and another 10,000 pages of guidelines, and that 54,000 people work in personnel management positions throughout the system. There is general consensus that the system is too complex to understand, let alone work efficiently.

Organization for Personnel Management

Personnel responsibilities are divided along several lines. The managers of the agencies in which the employees work are responsible for defining the positions available, selecting people to fill them (within defined limits), and evaluating their performance. Managers' control over employees, however, is circumscribed by many legal provisions and outside influences.

Cooperating with these managers at the federal level is the Office of Personnel Management, an independent agency under the president's control. It makes the regulations under which the departments supervise and evaluate their personnel and it recruits and tests candidates for positions that are common throughout the government. This system also includes the Federal Labor Relations Authority and Federal Mediation and Conciliation Service, which oversee labor–management relations of federal employees and resolve disputes in the collective-bargaining process. The Merit Systems Protection Board is an autonomous agency that can investigate and intervene in suspected violations of personnel policies and employee rights and hear appeals from agency managers' decisions. Moreover, the president has power to issue executive orders affecting the management of the personnel of federal agencies.

The typical state and larger local government has a personnel department that is responsible to the chief executive and conducts or oversees the definition of jobs and recruitment of people to fill them. Furthermore, it makes the rules by which the operating agencies evaluate and promote their personnel. Sometimes, a semi-independent personnel board or civil service commission makes regulations with the intent of excluding political biases from the choices. These governments usually have a larger proportion of employees who belong to unions or other bargaining agencies than does the federal government and require specialized agencies for conducting negotiations and resolving impasses (Klingner, 1983).

Personnel managers in state and local agencies are subject to influence from outside their hierarchies (Lee, 1982). These sources include (1) unions that have organized (or hope to organize) government employees; (2) groups that represent minorities, women, veterans, and people with disabilities and seek equal opportunity and affirmative action policies; (3) professional organizations, such as the American Bar Association and National Society for Professional Engineers, that are concerned with standards of conduct and their profession's image; (4) local and state officials' associations, representing many public employers; and (5) groups interested in government pensions, civil liberties for employees, and economy in government. When these groups' demands conflict, major controversies can appear, as, for example, in the issue of racial quotas for hiring and promoting firefighters and police officers.

Legislators, being sensitive to large blocs of public employees in their states and districts, are also vitally interested in personnel matters. Compensation is one of the most controversial issues legislators deal with, but they must also decide on benefits, work rules, employee rights, and collective bargaining.

The Personnel Management Process

The personnel process for merit-based systems has four basic stages, corresponding to their major tasks: (1) recruitment, selection, and initial placement of employees; (2) evaluation, promotion, and training; (3) compensation; and (4) discipline and termination. Whether at the national, state, or local level, each is covered by specific rules intended to guarantee both competence and fairness.

Recruitment, Selection, and Placement of Employees

In most cases a "job" originates as a defined position with certain duties and requirements for qualification such as a college degree, two years of relevant experience, or a 70 percent score on a competence examination. The agency advertises the job publicly using various media, and indicates the means by which a person can apply for it. After the closing date, the supervisor of the position or the personnel agency reviews the applications and selects as many of the best-qualified persons as there are posts to be filled.

Box 11.1

State of Minnesota Policies on Equal Employment Opportunity and Affirmative Action

Affirmative action begins with an understanding of two related concepts: nondiscrimination and equal employment opportunity.

Discrimination means unfair treatment, whether intentional or unintentional, based on protected characteristics. Under the Minnesota Human Rights Act, the following characteristics are protected under some circumstances: race, color, creed, religion, national origin, sex, marital status, status with regard to public assistance, disability, and age.

Equal employment opportunity is a nondiscrimination policy, the policy of basing all personnel decisions solely on individual merit of applicants and employees related to the specific job requirements, and without regard to protected characteristics.

Affirmative action emphasizes the positive, active steps needed to bring about change rather than a passive attitude of simple nondiscrimination. Affirmative action can be defined as the removal of all barriers to employment opportunity that are not based on specific job requirements and the provision of employment and advancement opportunities to people in protected groups that were formerly underrepresented in an agency's workforce.

—Department of Employee Relations,
State of Minnesota

This formal and seemingly straightforward process presents managers with choices that are often political as much as administrative. On the one hand, the agency seeks the person best prepared for each position. Only a few are suited to become air traffic controllers or narcotics investigators, and less-demanding posts also require a specific set of skills. However, the opportunity for public employment is of great significance to social groups whose members have been excluded in the past. Whereas only white males were once considered suitable to hold many posts, this eligibility has been extended to women, racial minorities, and the disabled. Governments must practice **equal employment opportunity**: complete fairness to all employees and applicants without discrimination on the basis of race, ethnic background, gender, age, or physical disability. Moreover, to compensate for past discrimination, an agency is obligated to take **affirmative action**: special efforts to invite members of disadvantaged groups to apply for employment and to hire them for positions for which they meet the basic qualifications. (See Box 11.1 for a typical policy of a state government.)

These two perspectives often clash in practice. Written (and sometimes performance) examinations have been the standard means for measuring qualifications for most positions. They may test general knowledge, job-specific knowledge and skills, leadership potential, physical ability, and personality traits. African Americans and Hispanics have tended to score low on tests requiring general knowledge and literacy and have thus failed to qualify for many jobs. Women have been refused police and firefighting openings because of high physical strength requirements. Now, as the result of legislation and court rulings, such tests of knowledge or physical performance can be used only if closely related to the demands of the job. A candidate for a welfare agency position, for example, would have to demonstrate the ability to understand and apply eligibility rules in the manual. What constitutes a "high enough" score is, however, still a matter for judgment.

The federal government used the Professional and Administrative Career Examination (PACE) for a decade prior to 1982 to test candidates for entry-level career positions in many categories. It was suspended after it was found that disproportionately few persons of color passed it, and for several years a variety of means were used to examine applicants' qualifications. Not until 1990 was a new professional and administrative test devised, entitled Administrative Careers with America (ACWA), which focuses on the specific issues a person would encounter in a typical job.

The alleged conflict between "competence" and "opportunity" also intrudes into the process of selecting specific people. Those who pass a test are ranked by score on a list of eligibles from which an agency may choose. The rule may require that the person with the highest score be chosen or may permit a selection from the highest three (at the federal level). Strict adherence to such a rule has often excluded those with educational deficiencies. Although this practice theoretically identifies the best-qualified people, there is no assurance that a slightly higher score signals superior competence.

In the effort to combat discrimination, whether it was intended or not, some governments instituted racial or gender quotas. In 1972 the Alabama State Police, then all white, was ordered by a federal court to hire one black person for every white until 25 percent of the entire force was black. This mandate is understandably controversial, not simply as an issue of competence versus equality but also because such "reverse discrimination" may be as demeaning to minorities who are hired as to whites who are rejected.

The courts have struggled for 20 years to reach consensus on the extent to which public agencies can take an employee's race or gender into consideration in personnel decisions. By 1989 a series of U.S. Supreme Court rulings had held that affirmative action programs can be used by governments and private employers to remedy discrimination against identifiable victims. However, the greater their negative impact on specific nonminorities, the less likely judges are to approve them. In practice, the employer must first justify considering an applicant's race, which may be done when a person has been discriminated against in the past or belongs to a minority group that has been routinely excluded. Second, it has to take care that an affirmative action plan does not unduly harm non-minority people (Nalbandian, 1989). Rigid quotas based on race or gender are hard to justify before the courts today, but flexible "hiring goals" have been more acceptable. There is no obvious balance point between the rights of competing groups, but courts have accepted a variety of methods that fit different circumstances.

Evaluation, Promotion, and Training of Employees

Evaluation of employee performance presents equally sensitive problems. Often a newly hired person is placed on probation for a few weeks to several years, varying with the position and the individual's qualifications. During this time, the supervisor is to evaluate the work, and a person whose performance is unsatisfactory can readily be dismissed. Those who have passed the probationary period are still evaluated periodically, although their status is more secure.

For all government employees, performance evaluation can serve several purposes. First, it can help a supervisor decide whether to retain a probationary employee; this has been most common in state and local governments. Second, it can guide in the allocation of new duties. Third, evaluation contributes to promotion decisions if the appraisal suggests that the person has the ability to fill a more responsible position. Fourth, it may be used in choosing which people to lay off because of employment cutbacks (although a simple seniority rule, which ignores a person's actual performance, is most commonly used). When high-level employees are evaluated, political judgments often mingle with appraisals of their efficiency.

Promotion choices parallel the dilemmas in the initial selection: how to find qualified persons and provide maximum opportunities. Formally, when a vacancy in a position exists, those below it on the hierarchy who are qualified may apply for promotion. The principle of merit dictates the choice of the most qualified person. However, the higher the post on the ladder of responsibility, the more subjective are the key factors that must be considered. With many governments reducing their staffs and management positions, promotion opportunities are ever more scarce, increasing both the competition for them and the demands for equal opportunity practices.

Legal mandates for equal opportunity and affirmative action apply to promotions as well, although they may be easier to avoid. Even when programs have succeeded in increasing the number of disadvantaged people in entry-level positions, few of them may make it to higher posts. The U.S. Office of Personnel Management reported in 1994 that whereas more than half of all positions in GS (General Schedule) grades 1 and 2 are held by persons of color, the proportion steadily decreases at higher grades. Only 8 percent of the Senior Executive Service consists of minorities. When a supervisory post requires leadership ability, a still-common executive mind-set views males and whites as more qualified and acceptable than females and people of color.

Progress often comes only after employees challenge discriminatory practices. In 1994 African American employees of the Immigration and Naturalization Service sued the agency, claiming that they were systematically denied promotion because of their race. Only one black person then held a senior post—ironically, the Equal Employment Opportunity director. In addition, many of these employees asserted that a prevailing climate of racism caused them to be demeaned and harassed. Director Doris Meissner had committed the agency to fair promotion but had not been in office long enough to make a real change in its culture. Since the class action suit involves more than 800 officers, a settlement could be costly (Sontag, 1994).

Governments at all levels find it necessary to develop and upgrade employees' skills to enhance both performance in current positions and promotion potential. Part of this training focuses on improving employee understanding of the substantive policies of government and the context in which they operate. Thus, county social workers may attend a seminar on AIDS and its effects on victims. Another kind of training is pointed toward specialized skill development, perhaps the operation of a computer system or leadership principles for new managers. Such training is particularly important in helping members of disadvantaged groups to qualify for promotion. Today's rapid changes in information technology and methods of service delivery mandate effective training programs for personnel to work most effectively.

Programs for training and education vary widely according to the level of government and the position. Relatively little training is provided at the lowest skill levels, whereas extensive leadership development programs benefit professionals and top managers. Universities and professional organizations offer continuing education, and the employees' agencies often pay the costs of participation. The Federal Executive Institute in Charlottesville, Virginia, has long helped prepare people for promotion. By a recent estimate, the federal government (not including the Postal Service) spends about $550 million annually for training its employees, a mere 0.8 percent of the total payroll. In contrast, the private firms in the Fortune List of 500 Largest Industrial Corporations spend somewhat more than 3 percent of their payrolls on employee development (National Commission on the Public Service, Task Force on Education and Training, 1989).

State and local governments increasingly recognize the need to train people, even at the entry level. They forecast major growth in their need for engineers, health and social service workers, computer analysts, and corrections officers even while the number of young people who finish school ready to enter such careers is dropping. The New York State government has initiated programs to upgrade the skills of new job recruits, particularly persons of color, and further develop them for administrative posts as they demonstrate their competence. This will require major additions to training budgets, not a likely prospect for states and localities facing financial stress (Katz, 1990).

Compensation

Salaries and benefits must be high enough to attract and retain competent people who have other career choices outside of public service. A government's internal compensation scales relate closely to the defined responsibilities of each position. In comparison to salaries for comparable private positions, most government personnel are less well paid, although this disparity varies with the position and region of the country. Each classified position within the merit system occupies a rank on the pay scale. Such rankings depend on the job's knowledge and skill requirements, responsibilities, number of persons supervised, physical demands, and working conditions.

Top-level federal executives are paid on an Executive Schedule (as are judges and members of Congress). A cabinet secretary earned $138,900 in 1995, for example. The Senior Executive Service has a separate section of this schedule. The independent Commission on Executive, Legislative and Judicial Salaries meets every 4 years to recommend salary adjustments. The president can modify them if he wishes and then transmits them to Congress; the new amounts take effect in 30 days unless both Houses reject them. Since top federal salaries are politically controversial, this procedure is meant to reduce direct conflict over them. In 1990 sharp increases in top executive salaries were approved, with the aim of closing the gap between federal pay and comparable positions in nonprofit organizations and other governments. Some states have a similar schedule for their appointed executives.

Most federal white-collar merit positions are on the General Schedule, which has eighteen steps and ten longevity points within each step. Thus, those who occupy a clerical post graded at GS-3 and have a given amount of experience receive a specific salary, although there is some variation for the cost of living in different parts of the country. The overall schedule of salaries is set by Congress and is increased regularly (most commonly in election years) to compensate for rises in living costs. State governments and all but the smallest local units have similar pay ranks. An employee can get a pay raise through longevity, promotion to a higher rank, or an increase in the entire schedule.

Separate compensation scales exist for professional employees not on the General Schedule. These scales reflect the fact that the positions involved are more individualized, and there may be more competition for these employees' services. This is the "rank-in-person" concept rather than the "rank-in-grade," on which the General Schedule is based. It is used, for example, by the Department of Veterans Affairs for its medical, dental, and nursing positions. Many municipal governments use this type of scale in setting salaries for professional employees as well.

About 400,000 federal blue-collar workers on the wage system are paid according to the prevailing rate for comparable private employees in their metropolitan area or region. Their unions and an employee advisory board recommend changes to local-area wage boards, and the Office of Personnel Management makes the final decision. Thus, an electrician in the Capitol in Washington, D.C., may earn more than one with the same qualifications and duties at an Air Force base in the rural South. State and local wages are commonly set by direct collective bargaining with the union involved.

Compensation also includes benefits such as health insurance, retirement plans, and paid leave. In many cases these benefits have been more generous than in the private sector, which helps to make up for lower salaries. Like private employers, however, governments face steeply rising costs for health benefits, and some have sought to economize by increasing the contribution that employees must make or by reducing the level of benefits.

Controversial questions surround the use of merit pay in public compensation. Private corporations are free to reward their employees for superior performance with bonuses and other perquisites. Nearly all governments prohibit this, fearing the favoritism and corruption that might accompany it. However, members of the Senior Executive Service are eligible for annual bonuses of up to 20 percent of their salaries. In 1987 a total of 2,006 of them received an average of $5,894 each (National Commission on the Public Service, Task Force on Recruitment and Retention, 1989). Pay scales for comparable posts in the federal merit system may vary between localities, as permitted by a 1990 act of Congress. State and local governments have also experimented with merit pay. For example, the top staff members of Michigan's public employees' pension fund were rewarded in cash when the fund's investment growth exceeded the standard set at the beginning of the year (Witt, 1989). However, "exceptional performance" is much harder to identify for most employees, whose accomplishments cannot be measured in numbers.

The issue of equity in compensation was one of the most debated of the 1980s. In previous decades the issue concerned the relative pay of public and private employees doing the same types of work, state and local comparability with federal salaries, and the relative compensation for clerks as contrasted with secretaries, and engineers with managers. In 1963 Congress mandated the standard of "equal pay for equal work" for federal employees in the Equal

Pay Act, and the Civil Rights Act a year later extended that to all employers.

Despite legislation, jobs predominantly held by women and persons of color have continued to feature lower pay levels than those with similar demands that are typically held by white males. When it was simply a matter of paying female custodians less than men for the same work, this was easily corrected. More difficult are situations in which the jobs are different but have similar levels of qualifications. For example, librarians, who are typically women, have often been paid less than plumbers, who are most often male, even though the two positions require equal amounts of experience and the librarian must have a college degree.

The campaign for **comparable worth** was initiated by women's and civil rights organizations to remedy this disparity, and many state and local governments responded. As mandated by the Minnesota legislature for the state and its local governments, this agenda entails an evaluation of the skills, effort, responsibility, and working conditions of each position without regard to who currently holds it. Those rated at an equal level are to be compensated equally. The state provided additional funds to raise the compensation of the underpaid, and it is the only state to penalize local governments (with a reduction in state aid) for noncompliance. As of 1994, only 87 out of 1,640 local units had not complied.

Comparable worth has been at the center of many political disputes, similar to those over affirmative action. Those in "overrated" positions fear that their pay will be cut to allow for others' increases, a realistic prospect where no extra funds are available. The intangible aspects of job evaluations are another source of concern; the physical dangers in law enforcement and firefighting are obviously greater than those in counseling and data processing. There is also fear that making "women's jobs" more expensive will result in cutbacks in such positions. Yet politically strong groups that define this as an issue of rights are increasingly successful.

Discipline and Termination

Every employer must have means to remove those who do not contribute to its mission. But adverse actions against employees are politically sensitive when a government is the employer. A 1912 federal act provides that an employee "may be removed or suspended without pay only for such cause as will promote the efficiency of the service," and many states and localities have similar provisions. Such protection against arbitrary dismissal is at the heart of the merit system. Box 11.2 outlines the federal procedure for demotion and termination.

Box 11.2

Basic Procedure for Demoting or Removing a Federal Employee

1. An employee whose performance is unsatisfactory must be notified in writing of the standards to be followed and told how he or she falls short. Supervisors take informal steps to help him or her improve.

2. If performance remains unacceptable, employee is again informed of this in writing, given a period of time in which to improve, and told of the consequences of failure to improve.

3. If performance still remains unacceptable, he or she is given 30 days' advance written notice of demotion or removal and the reasons for it.

4. The employee is given a reasonable time to reply to the notice orally and/or in writing and may be represented by legal counsel.

5. A written decision of demotion or removal is issued within 30 days of expiration of the notice period, which again specifies instances of unacceptable performance. An official at a higher level than the immediate supervisor must concur.

6. The employee may appeal the demotion or removal to the Merit Systems Protection Board or proceed through a grievance procedure stipulated by a collective-bargaining agreement.

—U.S. Office of Personnel Management

Employees may be transferred or terminated when there is a reduction in force without negative judgment against them personally. Or, demotion or termination may occur when the employee has proved to be incompetent or has seriously violated regulations. A transfer to another position is another common means of discipline, although the employee may not necessarily be reduced in grade with the move. In all adverse actions employees have legal rights of appeal; a federal agency action can be reviewed by the Merit Systems Protection Board and may be taken to the courts by the employee as well. Discrimination by race can appear in such actions also. A 1995 report by the U.S. Office of Personnel Management indicated that African American federal employees were more than twice as likely to be dismissed as those of other groups.

State and local personnel systems may also provide for arbitration under the terms of a collective-bargaining agreement. In general, public employers must provide convincing evidence of an employee's inadequate performance through lengthy proceedings before he or she can be removed. It was recently reported that the public sector discharge rate is less 1 percent a year, whereas among private companies it varies from 2 percent for industrial employees to 10 percent for service workers (Walters, 1994a). Allowing for wide differences among governments and supervisors, it is neither easy nor impossible to fire public servants.

Governments deal with their employees not only individually but also as organized in various unions and associations. These groups are concerned, as in the private sector, with compensation, working conditions, employee rights, and performance standards. Their basic aim is to exercise power in the management process through **collective bargaining**: negotiations leading to a contract that states the terms of their relationship.

Public Employee Organizations

The History of Public Employee Organizations

Employee organizations in the public service emerged somewhat later than those in the private sector. Congress, in 1912, recognized the right of federal employees to join unions but did not endorse collective bargaining with them. State and local authorities rarely recognized them as legitimate bargaining units, and their employees occasionally resorted to strikes to gain recognition and members. The Boston police strike of 1919, suppressed by Governor Calvin Coolidge, was a failure in the short run but stimulated the formation of police associations around the country.

The turning point in federal relations with unions was President Kennedy's Executive Order 10988 in 1962, which supported the right to organize and engage in collective bargaining. In the following decade both General Schedule and wage system employees organized rapidly. By 1993 about 60 percent of civilian federal employees belonged to exclusive bargaining units, affiliated with more than 125 unions (National Performance Review, 1993, p. 134). The major federal unions are the National Federation of Federal Employees, the American Federation of Government Employees, the National Treasury Employees Union, various trade and craft unions, and several organizations of postal workers.

Although some state and local governments began collective bargaining with employees before 1960 (mainly with teachers, police officers, and firefighters), this practice grew dramatically afterward. By 1988 a total of twenty-six states and the District of Columbia had comprehensive collective-bargaining policies for their employees. Nearly half of their employees belonged to an employee organization, and about 35 percent were covered by a contractual agreement. About 37 percent of all government employees were union members, and an additional 7 percent were represented by a union. In addition to teachers and safety employees, organization was also common among health, transit, and sanitation workers and the skilled trades generally. The American Federation of State, County and Municipal Employees had 1.167 million members in 1993 and is one of the fastest growing of all unions. Specialized groups represent teachers (the National Education Association and the American Federation of Teachers) and police.

The Collective-Bargaining Process

The typical collective-bargaining process begins with the formation and recognition of the bargaining unit. A majority of employees in a workplace, such as a hospital or school district, can elect to be represented by a union, which becomes their bargaining agent. The second step is the designation by the union local and employer of their bargaining teams; the former may use employees, but professional negotiators are also common.

The bargaining process itself is the third step. There are wide differences among governments in what is subject to negotiation. At the federal level, compensation and working hours are excluded, as is the legal specification of employee rights and work standards. State and local governments may include these, as their lawmakers have determined. The two parties may settle readily or take months to come to an agreement, and employees may threaten to strike. If they cannot agree, they may resort to mediation by a neutral person, which aims for a voluntary settlement, or arbitration, which is a compulsory settlement determined by a third party, to which both sides agree in advance.

Once the terms have been accepted by the negotiators, ratification is the next step. If a majority of the union's members reject a contract, the parties return to the bargaining table. Management does not ordinarily encounter internal dissension over a settlement unless a city council or school board decides that a wage increase exceeds its budget. Finally, implementation of the contract completes the cycle. Each side has to be vigilant that the other complies with it, and differing interpretations have to be ironed out by their representatives. The problems that arise can be topics for the next bargaining cycle.

Effects of Public Employee Unionization

The ultimate weapon of employee organizations is the work stoppage. Strikes have been fairly common at the state and local level since the 1960s, but among federal employees only the postal workers in 1970 and the air traffic controllers in 1981 have walked out. Several states permit strikes by nonessential employees (safety and health workers are excluded). In most governments, however, they are illegal, and jail terms and fines for strikers and their union leaders are the prescribed penalties. Extensive means for mediation and arbitration stand ready to settle strikes once they occur. A chief executive may personally intervene in urgent situations; the late mayor Richard J. Daley of Chicago used his renowned clout several times to head off walkouts by city employees and teachers.

Nearly all observers believe that collective bargaining has increased the costs of government. Salaries and benefits have increased with each contract settlement, although no one can say what the increases would have been had employees not been organized. In addition, public employee unions won substantial gains in health and retirement benefits. The unions' success has certainly reduced the financial discretion of state and local budgeteers, since they must anticipate new wage settlements and other costs imposed by the agreements. In response, unions plausibly argue that these gains have helped to keep public employment attractive to competent people who would otherwise work in the private sector.

Public employee unions have the reputation, partially deserved, of protecting members' jobs and income by blocking needed improvements in government efficiency. This has been one of the reasons for the privatization moves described in Chapter 7. However, current union leaders have begun to participate with administrators in designing programs to downsize agencies or reassign employees. In Philadelphia and Indianapolis, in Ohio and Illinois, unions have supported efforts to make agencies more responsive to citizens and reduce wasteful procedures and staffing (Walters, 1994b).

Conflicts of Interest

A further problem in public personnel management springs from the potential conflicts of interest that lurk in many positions. Public servants are expected to be impartial toward their clients and to make decisions based on the public interest and not their own benefit or that of a special group. The challenge is to identify potential conflicts and to choose the best ways to avoid them.

A **conflict of interest** arises from a personal association, investment, or belief that may inhibit a public employee from performing in conformity with the law and the public good. Federal rules define it as any situation in which employees' private benefits, usually economic, conflict with their public duties. These rules prohibit taking official actions that might result in, or create the appearance of, personal gain. Simply getting into a situation from which one could benefit can violate a conflict-of-interest law (Warren, 1988, chap. 5).

Sources of Conflicts of Interest

It can be difficult to determine just when these standards have been violated. The dilemmas are most pressing with political appointees, who typically come from private-sector positions in business and the professions and soon return to them. One aspect of the problem is former employment. For example, a question arose in 1985 about Thomas Roberts, a member of the Nuclear Regulatory Commission who was previously with a company making reactor equipment. When a commission decision involved that company, he cast a vote, although observers argued that he should have abstained (Burnham, 1985). The very fact that most of the regulators came from the regulated industry in the first place raises larger ethical questions, although the evidence does not show strong pro-industry biases (Quirk, 1981).

A person's future employment ambitions may also introduce conflicts of interest. Frequently, those with technical expertise leave government service for more lucrative posts in business. A Defense Department procurement specialist who sought future employment with a particular weapons contractor might favor that company with awards and information, in essence "buying" the position with public resources. If, once in the private position, this person returned to do business with the former agency, the knowledge and acquaintances gained there might improperly favor his company.

More broadly, an employee may reap financial or personal gain from an official choice. A municipal public works director may decide to extend a sewer line to serve some vacant land he owns and wishes to develop. Or a state human services commissioner may contract for service with a firm owned by a personal friend. Such abuses are hard to control, given the broad discretion and myriad interests many officials have.

Another kind of interest conflict occurs in the political and partisan realms. It may appear when a local building inspector overlooks safety violations in an apartment house owned by a major contributor to his party or when a contract is awarded by a federal agency to a company owned by a prominent member of the president's party (and because of that party identity). Such favoritism was widespread in the Department of Housing and Urban Development (DHUD) during the Reagan administration. Subsidies and favorable loan arrangements for housing construction were awarded to prominent Republicans despite negative recommendations on the projects by department staff. Although the misdeeds in DHUD were blatant, the pervasiveness of partisanship at many government levels makes it hard to draw the line between proper and improper behavior.

Procedural Controls and Legislative Standards

There are many partial remedies for conflicts of interest. Codes of ethics and standards adopted by agencies and professional associations to define unacceptable behavior have become stricter over the years. Since compliance with these codes of ethics depends upon members' dedication to the public interest or their desire to uphold the image of the profession, the actual influence that such codes and standards have on behavior is not clear. Only a few professional associations, such as those in medicine and law, have legal sanctions to back up their codes of conduct.

As the opening story of this chapter indicated, intensive background checks screen potential appointees to high federal positions. Yet the government still depends on the honesty of the nominee and informants in providing information, and some problems slip through this screen. Applicants for lower-level posts may be given little or no scrutiny, particularly since former employers are increasingly reluctant to provide derogatory information.

Statutes define prohibited behavior and penalties that apply to both the public official and any person who seeks to induce an illegal act. Congress passed the Ethics in Government Act in 1978 to deal with the problems of previous and subsequent employment of high-level federal executives, discussed earlier. It is illegal for former executives to try to influence decisions in an agency with which they were personally and substantially involved. Furthermore, under certain conditions they may not return to that agency to lobby for one or two years after leaving its employ. The act also mandated disclosure of financial interests for all persons appointed at the GS-16 level and above. The act is riddled with exceptions and has been hard to enforce, although Michael Deaver, former aide to President Reagan, was convicted of violations under this act in 1988.

Congress tightened federal restrictions in 1989 in the Ethics Reform Act. Employees are not allowed to accept fees for writing articles or making speeches that are related to their official duties. Former high political appointees are barred from lobbying anyone in the executive branch for a year after leaving their positions. Some employees resented this limit on their activities, while others who were subject to the stronger lobbying ban resigned before January 1, 1991, when the act went into effect. President Clinton announced stricter guidelines for his senior appointees shortly after his election, notably a 5-year ban on lobbying their former agencies after their departure.

Some states and municipalities have enacted similar ethics laws. New York City requires people with major decision-making responsibilities to disclose their investments and outside sources of income. Regulations formulated in 1990 bar former employees from lobbying the agency in which they worked for 1 year afterward, although they may at no time influence city action on matters in which they personally participated. At all levels, enforcement of these ethics rules has been difficult and politically sensitive. When the rules are effective, it is due more to employees' voluntarily complying with them than to legal prosecution of violators.

The federal government's major legal tool for dealing with partisan political biases is the Hatch Act. It was passed in 1939 after Congress learned that the Works Progress Administration, a New Deal job-creation agency, had coerced employees into making political contributions to retain their jobs. It bars merit employees from holding posts in political parties, running for election to a partisan office, making campaign speeches, circulating nominating petitions, and collecting political contributions from others. No supervisor may try to persuade subordinates to support a political candidate in any way. State and local employees in programs that are financed in whole or part by federal funds are also covered, except for those in educational institutions, who are exempt. Some state and local governments have laws that are variants of the Hatch Act that cover other personnel.

Employees generally follow these restrictions, although some resent being "Hatched." Urged by leaders of federal employee unions, Congress passed a bill in 1990 allowing federal civil servants greater freedom to participate in party politics, but the bill's supporters were not able to override President Bush's veto. The White House argued that the federal service must be politically neutral, and there did not appear to be widespread demands by civil servants themselves to ease the restrictions.

Public Employee Rights, Responsibilities, and Empowerment

Public servants are citizens, just as nonemployees are, but their rights were more narrowly defined in the past. Before the 1950s, public employment was, under the law, a privilege to which a person had no inherent right. A government could impose any requirement it saw fit for obtaining and holding a position. At times civil rights were denied to government employees who read the "wrong" literature, favored racial integration, or did not attend church (Rosenbloom, 1983). For them the Bill of Rights had only limited value.

The rights of public employees have been extended considerably in recent decades. Freedom of speech is now broadly protected and may be curtailed only when its use violates the Hatch Act on partisan activity, breaches confidentiality, or otherwise interferes with the performance of the person's duties. Those who "blow the whistle" on illegal or wasteful activities within their agencies are protected from official retaliation. The equal protection guarantee of the Fourteenth Amendment has been defined, as we have already seen, to bar discrimination on grounds of race, gender, age, or marital status. Sexual harassment of federal employees was defined and banned in 1980 by the Equal Employment Opportunity Commission, but specific complaints have posed many difficulties in interpretation. Because some state constitutions define equality more strictly, public employees in those states enjoy a wider range of rights in such matters as privacy, freedom of speech, and equal protection (Friesen, 1988). However, employees may be required to undergo tests for use of illegal drugs if their jobs are crucial to public safety.

Other rights pertain to job tenure. Legislative and court decisions provide for due process in disciplinary and termination actions. At the federal level and in many state and local governments, an employee has the right to a public hearing conducted by a neutral examiner before removal or demotion. In the national government, the Merit Systems Protection Board conducts such hearings and may order corrective action in case of agency misconduct.

The federal government, however, has not been a model employer in protecting the procedural rights outlined in this chapter. About 15,000 employees each year file complaints that they have suffered from some form of discrimination, usually based on gender or race. The Equal Employment Opportunity Commission (EEOC), which investigates these complaints and seeks to resolve them, was less than diligent in the performance of its duty, according to a 1991 study by the General Accounting Office. It took an average of 418 days for the EEOC to resolve a complaint, and some departments and agencies required more than 3 years to conclude a case. Resistance to equal employment action in many agencies has been quiet but effective (Newlin, 1991).

The responsibilities of public employees fall into three categories. Most generally, they are obligated to the members of the public who are affected by their performance. "The ethical identity of the public administrator, then, should be that of the citizen who is employed *as* one of us to work *for* us; a kind of professional citizen ordained to do that work which we in a complex large-scale political community are unable to undertake ourselves. Administrators are to be those 'especially responsible citizens' who are fiduciaries for the citizenry as a whole" (Cooper, 1984, p. 307). This is a very general role, yet for those employees who are in regular and close contact with those they serve, such as police officers and social workers, it may in practice contradict their other responsibilities.

The second responsibility, to obey superiors in the bureaucratic chain of command, is much more specific and is often elaborated in rules. Any hierarchy depends on this principle, and no organization that aims to operate in a consistent and impartial manner can tolerate widespread violation of it. For those at low levels of responsibility, the will of their superiors is ordinarily clear. But persons in higher posts may not find it as easy to know the wishes of their superiors. The head of a state health department may have to guess how the governor wants a sensitive case regarding AIDS resolved and to proceed without a clear directive.

Employees also have a responsibility to carry out the duties and maintain the values unique to the positions they hold. Some responsibilities are professionally defined; a doctor in the county health department follows the guidelines of the medical and public health communities. Other responsibilities depend on a person's inner values and convictions, such as a city planner's devotion to a concept of civic beauty and order or a Treasury agent's anger toward drug dealers. Concepts of duty vary as widely as the people employed, although agencies tend to attract and hold those who have similar commitments.

As much as a government may try to encase these principles in codes and procedures, managers must remember that a variety of people fill the posts, and they can at times be emotional, ambitious, contentious, lazy, idealistic, and so on. There is no guarantee that the personality of an individual will fit perfectly into the tasks and human environment of a position. Thus, personnel management must also be an "art form," particularly when dealing with employees in roles that call for initiative, discretion, and teamwork. The proper balance between employee rights and responsibilities in a given workplace or unit of government may be largely determined by mission and political context.

A third word has been added in the 1990s to supplement "rights" and "responsibilities": *empowerment.* At all levels of the public service, the theme runs, employees are under so many restrictions that they cannot use their intelligence and talents to the fullest. This was a strong message of the National Performance Review (1993). As that and other documents explain, empowering public employees is partly a matter of lifting unnecessary supervision. The federal government averages one manager or supervisor for every seven employees, whereas private organizations typically have a much higher ratio. It is also necessary to give employees the training, equipment, and incentives to do their jobs at a high level of quality. For example, developments in information technology are so rapid that all organizations must invest large sums in both hardware and training to keep current—and governments that lag behind lose efficiency. Box 11.3 on the transformation of New York City's Bureau of Motor Equipment illustrates the potential for such changes.

Prospects for the Public Service

A "quiet crisis" for the public service was identified in 1989 by well-informed observers and has not yet been resolved in the mid-1990s. The National Commission on the Public Service was a privately sponsored study group of eminent individuals led by Paul Volcker, former chairman of the Board of Governors of the Federal Reserve System. The commission's report identified several disturbing trends in the federal workforce that, if not reversed, will lead to serious deterioration of the government's ability to meet its current and emerging responsibilities. Volcker (1988) stated, "Government in general, and the federal government in particular, is increasingly unable to attract, retain, and motivate the kinds of people it will need to do the essential work of the republic" in years to come.

Box 11.3

How Can the City of New York Reinvigorate Its Bureau of Motor Equipment?

One of the seemingly mundane duties of a city government is to keep its motor vehicles running. For a bureau that must supply vehicles to collect trash and garbage on a regular schedule, the condition of its trucks is of vital importance. And in the late 1970s, they were not running well. At least half of New York's 6,500 sanitation vehicles were out of service at a given time. The bureau had to pay its employees overtime for night work on the vehicles that were operating. It was no secret why this was happening. Employees' morale was low and there was a wide gulf of misunderstanding between them and bureau management.

Ron Contino was appointed head of the motor equipment bureau at that low point and realized that drastic changes were needed. His main move was to establish a joint labor/management team that had genuine power to change conditions. The union representatives who agreed to serve were commissioned to survey their members on ways to improve working conditions and the quality of work done. The committee implemented the best suggestions they received.

The bureau became a different place as a result. Employees' attitudes changed as they saw that their participation made a difference. After 4 years, the average workday saw 80 percent of the trucks ready for service. And this was accomplished on a smaller budget for materials and operating expenses. Contino's sharing of power at the highest level was the key to this change (Denhardt, 1993, pp. 144–147).

The commission's first concern was that salaries of federal personnel at all but the lowest levels of responsibility are significantly below those for comparable posts in the private sector. The roots of this problem are both budgetary and political. Members of Congress are reluctant to elevate pay for the executive branch much above their own, yet they do not want to antagonize constituents with major increases for themselves. The raises in executive pay approved in 1990 fell short of closing the gap. Within the General Schedule, it is difficult to recruit the most talented attorneys, accountants, and engineers, even at entry levels, because salaries are often half of what these professionals could earn elsewhere.

Second, the commission reported that the president's increased placement of political appointees rather than career executives in high department posts limits advancement prospects for the most talented administrators. Having reached the promotion ceiling in their agencies, they often leave for comparable (and better-paying) positions in the private sector. This trend will not soon be reversed, given the need of presidents to exert control over the bureaucracy, which results in reduced opportunities for top-level managerial talent within the merit structure. This trend contradicts the high hopes of the creators of the Senior Executive Service.

A "loss of excitement" in working for the government was also noted by the commission. This is a harder problem to measure but was so often cited by civil servants that it cannot be ignored. The downsizing of many federal programs during the 1970s and 1980s reduced the demand for innovative people. Simply maintaining or improving the efficiency of existing programs is inherently less challenging than developing new ones. These factors weakened the external image of the federal service as viewed by young college students, most of whom reported in a commission survey that they would not seriously consider a career there (National Commission on the Public Service, *Leadership for America: Rebuilding the Public Service,* 1989, p. 26).

To remedy this situation, the commission offered twelve recommendations in 1989 (see Box 11.4). Outside the nation's capital, most of these have long been recognized as necessary and practical reforms. Neither the White House nor Congress took them seriously, however, and provided no money or legal authority to support them. Amid the many claimants for federal attention, "bureaucrats" rank near the bottom. In the prevailing Washington view, the civil service is taken for granted and it is assumed that there will always be someone to work. Many also believe that the nation's real sources of change in the 1990s are in the private sector, which can pay for the talent it needs. As Paul Volcker responded, with the many foreign and domestic challenges that this country faces, due to growing governmental responsibilities, future presidents and Congresses will need all the help they can get.

Do state and local governments also face a personnel crisis? In general, yes, concluded the National Commission on the State and Local Public Service (1993). The picture is too complex for easy generalizations, but these governments also face the challenges that the Volcker Commission identified. Political resistance to change and recurring budget crises also limit needed pay increases. However, many state and local governments are free to set the salaries of selected executives high enough to attract the most competent candidates. A city looking for a manager or a school district seeking a superintendent with proven competence compete in a seller's market that can escalate salary offers.

There is no comprehensive evidence on the trends in politicization of top executive posts in state and local governments. The level of professionalism in their administrative personnel has steadily risen over the decades as the practice of political patronage has declined. This has attracted some former federal employees and some new graduates who might otherwise have considered federal employment. Some states, however, experience a drive by governors similar to that of presidents to extend their control into the departments through appointees of their choosing.

Box 11.4

Recommendations for Rebuilding the Public Service

First, Presidents, their chief lieutenants, and Congress must articulate early and often the necessary and honorable role that public servants play in the democratic process, at the same time making clear they will demand the highest standards of ethics and performance possible from those who hold the public trust. . . .

Second, within program guidelines from the President, cabinet officers and agency heads should be given greater flexibility to administer their organizations, including greater freedom to hire and fire personnel, provided there are appropriate review procedures within the Administration and oversight from Congress.

Third, the President should highlight the important role of the Office of Personnel Management (OPM) by establishing and maintaining contact with its Director and by ensuring participation by the Director in cabinet level discussions on human resource management issues.

Fourth, the growth in recent years in the number of presidential appointees, whether those subject to Senate confirmation, noncareer senior executives, or personal and confidential assistants, should be curtailed. Although a reduction in the total number of presidential appointees must be based on a position-by-position assessment, the Commission is confident that a substantial cut is possible, and believes a cut from the current 3,000 to no more than 2,000 is a reasonable target. . . .

Fifth, the President and Congress must ensure that federal managers receive the added training they will need to perform effectively. . . .

Sixth, the nation should recognize the importance of civic education as a part of social studies and history in the nation's primary and secondary school curricula. . . .

Seventh, America should take advantage of the natural idealism of its youth by expanding and encouraging national volunteer service. . . .

Eighth, the President and Congress should establish a Presidential Public Service Scholarship Program targeted to 1,000 college or college-bound students each year, with careful attention to the recruitment of minority students. . . .

Ninth, the President should work with Congress to give high priority to restoring the depleted purchasing power of executive, judicial, and legislative salaries. . . .

Tenth, if Congress is unable to act on its own salaries, the Commission recommends that the President make separate recommendations for judges and top level executives and that the Congress promptly act upon them. . . .

Eleventh, the President and Congress should give a higher budget priority to civil service pay in the General Schedule pay system. . . . The Commission therefore recommends a new civil service pay-setting process that recognizes the objective fact that pay differs by occupation and by localities characterized by widely different living costs and labor market pressures.

Twelfth, the President and Congress should establish a permanent independent advisory council, composed of members from the public and private sector, both to monitor the ongoing state of the public service and to make such recommendations for improvements as they think desirable. . . .

—National Commission on the Public Service,
Leadership for America:
Rebuilding the Public Service, 1989

The more innovative state and local governments have also been more successful than the federal government in attracting creative personnel. Most new policy developments are now found at

(continued on p. 340)

Box 11.5

Is Japan More Successful in Attracting High-Quality Civil Servants?

Japan's public service system offers a sharp contrast to that of the U.S. Much higher prestige accompanies government employment there, and the result is clear to many bright university graduates. The Japanese sense of an "elite" civil service is foreign to the American tradition and probably could not be transplanted across the Pacific, as some framers of the Senior Executive Service hoped. Japan has a long history of a merit-based bureaucracy, rooted in the Confucian ideal of government by the wise and ethical.

The pay is mediocre, the hours long and vacations short. Working conditions? A squat building in downtown Tokyo with dingy corridors, pockmarked tile floors and cheap metal desks that wouldn't look out of place in Bucharest. Despite such drab surroundings, Japan's highly respected Ministry of International Trade & Industry continues to attract the country's finest college graduates.

One such is Kazumasa Kusaka, now 42, who heads MITI's nuclear energy industry division. Kusaka joined MITI 20 years ago, just after he graduated from Tokyo University, Japan's most elite institution of higher learning. During job interviews in his senior year, Kusaka received offers from big private companies such as Nippon Steel and Sumitomo Bank, but he chose to enter MITI. Says he, "The choice was to endure 20 to 30 years in a large company dreaming that one could become a board member and get power and money, or get two-thirds of the salary in MITI but have challenges and responsibilities even in the first ten years."

It is not uncommon, for example, for MITI bureaucrats in their late 20s to be drafting legislation for parliament or meeting with board members of major companies who are 30 years their senior. Says Kusaka, "There is a sense of running the country. Perhaps it's an illusion, but that mind-set really motivates officials to work hard without financial incentives."

In Japan, government ministries promote from within, and one climbs the ladder, rung by rung. Unlike in the U.S., there is no danger that a conscientious bureaucrat will one day find himself taking orders from an inexperienced political appointee suddenly moved in over him.

Kusaka is on the fast track. The best bureaucrats at MITI distinguish themselves by being assigned to challenging jobs, such as monitoring big industries like autos and computers, or negotiating hot issues like trade relations with the U.S. and the European Community. Kusaka, for example, was transferred in 1971 to the textile products department when it was in the final stages of negotiating Japan's first major trade dispute with the U.S. He moved to autos in the late 1970s as conflict with the U.S. erupted. In 1987 he went to MITI's trade policy planning division to help develop a new strategy for negotiations with the U.S.

Does such a world-beater feel stuck heading the nuclear power department? No. In Japan, nuclear power remains a hot issue. Dependence on energy imports is one of the Japanese economy's biggest weaknesses. Recently an antinuclear movement made up of housewives, farmers and left-wing extremists has been trying to block construction of new plants. Hence, the personable and unflappable Kusaka was called in to set up town meetings in local strongholds of antinuclear advocates.

Kusaka is an Osaka native whose father was executive vice president of Norinchukin, a large agricultural bank. Like all of Japan's elite bureaucrats, he entered MITI after passing the rigorous civil service examination. Last year only about 4% of the 12,000 test takers passed. MITI usually takes 26 or 27 generalist college graduates a year—80% of them from Tokyo University and almost all of them men.

Seniority at MITI is so strict that bureaucrats talk of colleagues being in classes. Kusaka, for example, is considered a member of the class of 1970, because that's the year he entered

MITI. In MITI's rigid hierarchy, classmates become good friends: They drink and play golf and tennis together. This creates a team spirit and sense of pride. Generalists, the MITI men move up by seniority for 13 or 14 years, rotating every 2 years into a broad variety of jobs in MITI's four main areas: industry, trade, energy and technology.

Kusaka's starting salary was $1,000 a year. Today MITI's starting pay is much better—$20,000, rising to $33,000 after 10 years of experience and $57,000 after 20 years. This is about a third less than starting pay for top graduates who go to work for private companies.

Hours? Nine-thirty a.m. to 10:30 p.m. is standard; in hot spots like the Americas desk, where Kusaka has served, the day often ends at 3 a.m.

At the age of 35 or 36, MITI class members face their first weeding out process, when the fast-trackers are moved into the more important positions, though titles remain similar. Higher up, the work becomes more managerial and policy-oriented, and the bureaucrats spend more time meeting with politicians, business executives, academics, the press and the public.

The second weeding out stage is after 25 years, at age 47. Those who do not make the fast track by then are quietly advised to take early retirement. "You're tapped on the shoulder and told it's time for you to start thinking about your future," explains Kusaka. MITI helps place the early retirees in other government agencies or in the private sector, where they can win a substantial pay increase.

Several class members fade away each year for the next three or four years until the penultimate winnowing date, when only four or five are promoted to director-general positions. The director-generals compete for about four years for the grand prize, elevation to administrative vice minister, the top career spot in MITI and a position of enormous prestige. When a class member is promoted to vice minister, his remaining classmates are expected to resign.

The vice minister, who usually serves only one year, automatically becomes leader of the class and is expected to help his departing classmates find useful employment in the private sector. The Japanese call this move from government to private industry *amakudari,* "descent from heaven." A former MITI director-general or vice minister is almost assured a board position at a major corporation, which can pay at least $200,000 a year. Jokes Kusaka, "An ex-MITI official is useful as an adviser, but they're not so useful in running a company."

Kusaka has a leg up on some of his colleagues in that he was selected in 1975 to study abroad, as were 5 other of his 18 classmates. He received a master's degree from Princeton's Woodrow Wilson School of Public & International Affairs in 1977. Three years later he married his wife, who also worked in MITI. While abroad, MITI bureaucrats are expected to learn English and to gain a better understanding of Americans, because almost all of the bureaucrats will be engaged in trade talks with the U.S. at some point in their careers. . . .

What qualities put Kusaka on the fast track? For a clue, look at the reasons Kusaka was selected to combat the swelling movement against nuclear power. Besides being fully capable of grasping the technological aspects of nuclear power, Kusaka is quick on his feet, and he comes across as sincere, persuasive, reasonable and diplomatic.

None of this is to say that the U.S. civil service does not attract a good number of smart and qualified people, but the fact is that the most aggressive young Americans opt for the private sector, where there is fatter pay, faster advancement and, to be honest about it, much more prestige. Our system and theirs are products of extremely different cultures, but there is no denying that Japan's top-notch civil service sometimes gives it an edge these days.

—Andrew Tanzer, "There Is a Sense of Running the Country," *Forbes,* April 30, 1990 that level, from housing and economic development to consumer protection and human services. Therefore, state and local agencies can sometimes provide employees with a greater opportunity than the federal government to make changes and gain a sense of accomplishment. This sense of "making a difference" is a powerful motivator in many career choices. Box 11.5 on the Japanese civil servants reinforces this point. Their American counterparts may well envy them. It is clear, however, that our democratic culture is reluctant to grant as much power to the occupants of our bureaucratic niches.

Summary

Personnel management in government differs from that in the private sector because of its accountability to the public purposes. Management is thus faced with several contradictions that must be resolved in providing democratic opportunity while obtaining competence.

Public servants fall into seven categories: top-level appointed executives and those in major policymaking and advisory posts, merit system employees (including the Senior Executive Service), professionals, patronage employees, wage employees, contract personnel, and volunteers. Each category has distinct selection and managerial standards.

Public employment has developed six distinct images in the American experience: aristocratic, democratic, meritocratic, managerial, administrative, and professional. Each of these remains valid in representing an aspect of the public service ideal.

The administration of personnel systems is divided between staff support and line management. Personnel managers must deal with (1) recruitment, selection, and placement of employees; (2) training, evaluation, and promotion; (3) compensation; and (4) discipline and termination. These functions are covered by rules and procedures intended to maximize both quality of personnel and fairness of treatment.

Public employees are widely represented in unions and associations, many of which bargain collectively with state and local governments over pay and work conditions. There is a growing sense of employee rights that restrains governments in their management practices. Personnel managers must protect the integrity of the public service by preventing or minimizing conflicts of interest—associations and involvements that inhibit employees from conforming to the law and serving the public good.

Major concerns have been expressed about the quality of the public service in view of its poor public image and low salaries. These must be addressed in future years. In contrast, Japan's government is consistently able to draw high-ranking university graduates into its service, where they can expect to have responsibilities equal to their talents.

Discussion Questions

1. Do the stricter ethics regulations in the government service today really lead to more competent and public-spirited employees, or simply to those with fewer conflicts of interest?

2. What are the advantages and disadvantages of having political appointees rather than experienced career persons in the top administrative posts?

3. How important do you think it is for public employees to reflect the racial, ethnic, and gender proportions of the population? Explain your position.

4. Is it possible to avoid all conflicts of interest in the public service? If not, what is the maximum level that we can tolerate if it is necessary to obtain competent and experienced personnel?

5. Compared to a career in business, are there any intrinsic rewards to working for government at any level? Is there a "public service ethic" that gives such employment a unique quality?

Analytical Exercises

1. One of the aims of the National Commission on the Public Service (and of its state and local counterpart) was to encourage competent students to consider and seek careers in government. Commissioners urged removal of the bureaucratic barriers to learning about openings and applying for them that so often discouraged those who had such an interest. To test whether any real change has taken place, find the telephone number of the nearest federal employment information center and call it. Evaluate the spoken information and any written material that is sent to you: Is it clear and attractive? Does it provide a good sense of the opportunities available? Do you understand the process of applying and qualifying for a position? (Alternatively, you could do this for your state, county, or city employment office.)

2. Interview an official in a local or state government position to learn how he or she perceives the abstract concept of "public service." To what extent is this person merely filling a job, and to what extent is there a calling of social or professional significance? If the interviewee feels such a calling, ask how well he or she is able to fulfill it under current working conditions.

For Further Reading

Ingraham, P. W., & Kettl, D. F. (1992). *Agenda for Excellence: Public Service in America.* Chatham, NJ: Chatham House. Collection of articles that highlight key issues and prospects for the federal personnel system.

Lipsky, M. (1979). *Street-Level Bureaucracy: Dilemmas of the Individual in Public Services.* New York: Russell Sage/Basic Books. See note in Chapter 8.

Mackenzie, G. C. (Ed.). (1987). *The In-and-Outers: Presidential Appointees and Transient Government in Washington.* Baltimore: Johns Hopkins University Press. See note in Chapter 9.

Mosher, F. C. (1968). *Democracy and the Public Service.* New York: Oxford University Press. Classic study of the evolution of the federal service and the concepts it followed in seeking certain types of employees.

National Commission on the Public Service. (1989). *Leadership for America: Rebuilding the Public Service.* Washington, DC: U.S. Government Printing Office. Significant report on the shortcomings of the federal personnel system, with recommendations for upgrading its substance and image.

The Administration of Public Money

Learning Objectives

After reading this chapter, you should be able to do the following:
1. Describe the types of budgets used by governments and the purpose of each.
2. Trace the budget-making process of the federal government through the executive and legislative branches.
3. Identify the fiscal and political factors that constrain budget making at all levels of government.
4. Describe the process of managing, controlling, and reviewing government expenditures.
5. Describe the policy choices and administrative processes in collecting government revenue.
6. Identify the means by which governments incur and manage debt.
7. Identify the current sources of stress in federal, state, and local finance and alternative responses to it.

T he deep public concern about crime and safety has created a paradox. Both the public and the politicians who serve them are much more willing to spend money on police and prisons to deal with crimes after they have been committed than they are to spend for programs that have some chance of preventing crime, such as those that provide urban juveniles with educational, vocational, and sports opportunities. Although agreement on a method to control crime is difficult to reach, there is no disagreement that spending on crime—its prevention, detection, prosecution, and punishment—is one of the fastest-growing items in national, state, and local budgets.

According to the U.S. Department of Justice, more than 1

343

million people were locked in federal and state prisons by the beginning of 1995, and that number will probably exceed 2 million in another decade. In 1992 each inmate cost $50.22 per day in direct spending, a figure that since then has risen by more than a dollar per year. With new get-tough state and federal legislation that requires longer sentences, more prison time per sentence, and life imprisonment for third-offense felonies, the cost per inmate will rise as fast as the number of those locked up.

It is difficult to total the huge costs for police, prosecution, courts, and imprisonment, not to mention those to governments and private citizens for security systems, insurance, and losses due to crime. Existing penal facilities constitute a major component of these costs. Federal and state prison systems spent $21.3 billion in 1993. Construction of new prisons added $1.4 billion in 1992, and this figure is likely to double or triple in the next decade. Further cost increases are tied to the needs of the inmates. They are entitled to proper health care, according to the courts. Medical costs in general are rising, and as prisoners age and serve longer sentences, their needs multiply. The incidence of AIDS in this population is high, with all that means for costs. Finally, the number of incarcerated women is increasing rapidly; this poses the additional problem of caring for their children. The complexity of these costs obscures their size to the public and to policymakers. It is challenging even to identify all the crime-related costs in a federal or state budget.

When so much money is being spent in a specific area of government responsibility, we should always look for those who benefit from it. A "corrections/industrial complex" has arisen quietly, made up of companies that build and operate prisons and that supply goods and services to them, unions of police and corrections workers, and communities that want the jobs that prisons bring. Senator Edward Kennedy of Massachusetts, for example, won political points among local businesses when he announced in 1994 that Fort Devens, an army base soon to be closed, would become a prison for 1,600 inmates (Moore, 1994). Both public and private organizations with economic interests in security and corrections persistently lobby Congress and state legislatures to expand public spending. This is entirely aside from the question of whether such spending increases public security or prevents crime, since there is no clear connection between dollars spent and value received.

Public Money and the Public Purposes

Money is the pivotal resource for public administration. Although it cannot buy such intangible necessities as employee creativity or public compliance with laws, there is no substitute for sufficient funds to accomplish most public purposes. Money is also the central point of political controversy. Decisions on which programs to fund and how much to spend on them express government's priorities and means of serving those priorities. They also entail choices on how revenue will be raised and from whom.

The management of public money differs from that of private enterprise in four major ways. First, the aims of national, state, and general-purpose local governments are so diverse that they spark continual conflicts over limited funds. There are many worthy reasons for spending public money but no obvious criteria for resolving such conflicts. No single measuring rod can determine whether a $100 million prison is preferable to an equally funded program to combat AIDS or rehabilitate drug abusers. Administrators and legislators alike must fall back on political choices shaped by past spending habits, opinion polls, or the lobbying strengths of the competing groups.

Second, because of unforeseen conditions in society, governments must adjust to sharp changes in spending and revenue. A surge in unemployment, a natural disaster, or an epidemic like AIDS can cut expected income or suddenly require increased outlays. State and local governments that depend on a certain level of federal aid must remake their budgets if Congress eliminates a program. Good forecasting may give some advance warning of new conditions, but governments have so many open-ended commitments that they cannot adjust as quickly as most private-sector organizations.

Third, by law government budgeting and spending must be an open process, with key decisions made in the public arena. Each administrative department or interest group that contends for dollars can reinforce its pleas with publicity, persuasion, votes, or campaign contributions. Although the chief executive of the nation, state, or city prepares a unified plan for revenue and spending, final approval of the plan comes only after adjustment to the prevailing political forces. Although backroom deals are common in legislative chambers, they must pass the test of formal approval and may be reversed later.

Fourth, public money choices are also subject to constraints imposed by law and political conditions outside government. The public's willingness to pay taxes is an obvious limit, as is the interest rate that governments must pay to borrow. The national government has the greatest leeway, for it can incur any debt it chooses. State and local governments, on the other hand, must balance their operating budgets. Local units must also operate within close restrictions set by their states in both spending and revenue and by the value of the taxable property within their boundaries.

These differences create tension in governments' financial management. Like private businesses, they must seek stability, control, and efficiency to give the citizens the most service for their tax dollars. Yet this imperative conflicts with the need to cope with unpredictable events, inconsistent demands, and shifting political forces. "Each of us has particular programs that benefit us or aid someone we know, or we may view particular governmental activities as essential to the community or the nation. But the structure of the political system does not permit us to choose which programs we want and discard the rest; rather the political system works toward the exchange of benefits. To get what we want necessitates our acceptance of programs other people want" (Wildavsky, 1988, p. 31). For this reason spending programs often become agglomerations that distribute benefits to many claimants in proportion to their bargaining strengths.

Budgeting by Administrators

The central role for administrators in financial management is the preparation of a **budget**. In its simplest form the budget is a plan for future spending, built on certain income expectations and demands for public services. Properly done, it incorporates and fulfills the agency's planning described in Chapter 10.

Budget Purposes

Budgets as Policy   First, a budget is a policy document that states what the government intends to do and the resources it will devote to each activity. Chapter 5 defined public policy as government's choices of actions intended to serve the public purposes. Policy statements link law, organizations, and tasks, and a budget adds the money to make that connection tangible. Often the amount of money allocated to a task indicates its relative importance. Since the late 1980s, Congress and the president have repeatedly proclaimed their determination to combat the import and use of illegal drugs. But the modest level of funds asked and appropriated for this war indicates that its real priority was not as great as the rhetoric made it seem. On the other hand, the enormous sums provided for health and income support for the elderly point to the very high ranking of this goal.

Budgets as Management   Second, a budget is a managerial document that projects the means to implement policies. Increased spending on police and prisons at all levels of government carries out promises by legislators to get tough on crime. Although the rhetoric exceeds the reality in this instance too, it is obvious that the cost of building a new prison must be accompanied by annual funding to operate it. The budget also enables managers to control the pace and direction of spending during the fiscal year. Its line items stand as limits on the outlay for each subject. Thus, a manager cannot legally overspend on favored projects with funds drawn from others.

Budgets as Economic Choices   Third, a budget is an economic document that allocates scarce resources to meet competing needs. Demand for governmental aid always exceeds funds available. When dollars are directed to a new prison, for example, they are unavailable for crime prevention. Because large public budgets also have a major impact on private economies, they are designed with these in mind as well. Public works spending not only produces highways, prisons, and school buildings, but also creates jobs, enhances land values, and promotes business enterprise. Government health programs reorder the budgets of countless households, businesses, and medical providers.

Budgets as Politics   Fourth, a budget is a political document. It specifies which benefits and costs will be distributed to whom, temporarily settling the power struggles over these choices. Furthermore, its precise composition reflects who has been most politically successful in shaping that distribution. Each item, whether it allocates funds for additional narcotics officers for a police department or more drug rehabilitation counselors for a welfare agency, serves the aims of one or more special groups (although broader publics may also benefit).

Planning each year's budget requires that administrators and legislators consider several factors. First, they must anticipate mandatory spending, such as federal entitlement programs, interest on debt, and the federal programs that state and local governments must support, such as Medicaid and environmental protection. Second, they identify the continuing discretionary programs that have strong political support and thus little flexibility. Defense at the federal level and education at state and local levels are in this category. Third, they can consider high priorities for expansion or innovation if funds are available. Crime control and corrections, as highlighted earlier in this chapter, are most prominent in the 1990s.

Budget makers turn reluctantly to one more category: "vulnerable" programs that can be reduced or eliminated with a minimum of political or administrative conflict. In many cases increased spending in one area requires a matching cut in another. Conservative lawmakers prefer to reduce benefits to low-income households, whereas liberals take aim on defense spending and programs benefiting business. Settling these differences often requires the most time and exacts the highest political price.

Budget Types

Several types of budgets, which arrange expenditures in different ways, are widely used. Each gives administrators and legislators a unique grouping of the spending items, which in turn aids their

Box 12.1

Common Budget Types

Line-item: lists each item purchased and its cost within each department or unit.

Performance: lists expenditures in groups according to their objective within each agency or unit.

Program: groups expenditures by the broad purposes served by that unit of government, regardless of which agency spends them.

Current-expenditure: identifies funds to be spent entirely within the given fiscal year.

Capital: identifies and schedules funds to be spent over a period of years, ordinarily for construction projects that constitute the government's "investments."

decision making. Box 12.1 summarizes the most common types of budgets.

The Line-Item Budget   The first type, the **line-item budget**, simply lists the specific items that are to be bought. A small city's budget might itemize the purchase of four motor vehicles, a year's supply of gasoline, and a contract for maintenance services. This is the easiest to draft and permits scrutiny of each item, but it does not show how the purchase relates to the city's overall mission.

The Performance Budget   Organized according to the objectives of each agency and the expenditures necessary to achieve them, **performance budgets** have been adopted by many state and local governments as well as the national government (beginning in 1950). They enable managers and legislators to evaluate the efficiency of operations, which the line-item budget does not. Thus, two of the new vehicles mentioned in the previous paragraph might be listed in the police department's section of the budget, another might be listed for the public works director, and the last could be included in the section for the parks and recreation department. Grouped with them are all other expenditures that serve those agencies. Vehicle maintenance costs are also divided among them in proportion to their use. An accurate performance budget permits officials to learn how much each function is costing overall, to compare its costs with those of other city departments, and to examine comparisons of functions and costs with similar cities. It also allows them to evaluate future funding choices in the light of that comparison. A manager who finds that the city's policing costs are higher than those in comparable communities can search for the reasons while budgeting for the following year.

The Program Budget   To organize spending by the broad purposes that the government serves, regardless of which agency uses
the funds, the **program budget** is often used as a supplement to
the first two forms. It can be especially useful in larger governments
with more complex responsibilities. A state government might want
to know how much it is spending (or proposing to spend) on the
protection and enhancement of its natural environment. For this
purpose it would group together such efforts of diverse agencies as
pollution control, forest protection, flood prevention, fish and game
management, and mining regulation. This emphasizes the outputs
of government activity rather than the inputs used to produce them.

An oft-cited purpose of program budgeting is to enable analysts to study alternative means of achieving broad objectives. Should
a school policy to aid children with learning difficulties focus on
providing special education programs for those of traditional school
age? Or should the district identify children with such needs at
earlier ages and prepare them for school with programs like Head
Start? They can lay out these choices systematically and compare
them before allocating funds. Program budgets also aid comparison
of costs with results. The school district can calculate what it spends
per child on remedial education over an 8-year period, for example,
and may learn that one approach is more cost-effective than another.
However, preparing an extensive program budget consumes a great
deal of time because of the volume of data that must be analyzed.
In a busy agency this demand discourages its use.

The Current-Expenditure and Capital Budgets   On another dimension is the distinction between **current-expenditure budgets**
and **capital budgets**, also widely used in state and local governments. The former cover all items to be funded during the current
fiscal year: salaries, materials, and services necessary to the ongoing
activities. Such budgets are widely required by law to be balanced
by revenues.

Capital budgets project the costs of acquiring land, buildings,
roads, and equipment that will have a life of more than 1 year. Some
of it is paid for with current revenue or with funds accumulated
for that purpose, but major items are typically financed with long-
term bonds to be repaid during their expected period of use. These
normally are part of a planning process that sets priorities for them
over 5 to 10 years. This involves such technical judgments as which
part of a city's sewer system should be rebuilt first, but whether a
new swimming pool will precede any sewer work is a political
decision.

Although the national government does not have a separate
capital budget, many of its agencies prepare 5-year investment programs. The Army Corps of Engineers must plan for facilities that
meet its responsibilities for flood control, navigation, water supply,

and hydroelectric power on the nation's rivers and in its harbors. Each year, it selects the top-priority projects for the funds that Congress provides. Because of the local impacts that these investments have, congressional and interest group pressures on these choices are often intense. For all governments capital expenditures or the lack of them affect operating budgets as well. For example, a new dam or park requires additional operating funds, and deteriorated pipes cost money in the form of lost water.

It is easy for governments to neglect capital investments in their infrastructures, since they do not yield distinct benefits during the current fiscal year. New York City drastically reduced maintenance of its many bridges during the 1970s, and the resulting deterioration began to disrupt traffic in the late 1980s. The National Council on Public Works Improvement (1988), a study commission established by Congress, reported that spending by all governments on transportation facilities, water resources, and waste management facilities amounted to just 7 percent of their total expenditures in 1984, compared with 20 percent in 1950.

Decision Making for Budgets

Whatever the formal budget methods, the style of making decisions on each item of spending reflects its political context. In ongoing programs the major influence on both administrators and legislators is the level of previous expenditures. That is, when budget makers must choose how much to allocate to soil conservation or fire protection, it is natural to begin with what is being spent in the current year. This habit is the basis for an *incremental* approach to budgeting. Akin to the incremental style of decision making described in Chapter 10, this type of budgeting accepts the current year's spending level as a base, which is not questioned unless there is a major failing in the program or department concerned. The debate focuses instead on any proposed increases that exceed the rate of inflation or begin a new service. The larger the proposed increase, the greater the scrutiny it receives. A modest decrease is also possible if there is general pressure for reduced spending.

This incremental method avoids the necessity of reviewing every item of spending in depth every year, an obvious impossibility for a large government. Not only is there a lack of time, but the political debates and conflicts likely to erupt if everything were open to question would prevent any other work from being done. Yet this method allows programs to become entrenched and escape reexamination when conditions might call for different spending choices. The 1980s witnessed erratic changes in the federal budget that often were not incremental in this sense, particularly certain large cuts in social and regulatory programs out of favor with the Reagan administration. Even so, Congress and interest groups continued to seek predictable funding trends that would protect programs most vital to them.

Since it attempts to control a future year's spending, budgeting requires accurate foresight. A government's finances depend on many conditions that it cannot control. Budget makers must first project future revenues, given existing legal provisions. Income tax yields are particularly sensitive to the economic health of the nation or state, so this forecast actually focuses on changes in business activity and employment. Local governments examine trends in property values to determine real estate tax yields based on them. State and local units must also estimate the grants they will receive from higher-level governments, which is not easy when grant programs are in constant flux.

Budget planners must also forecast demands for government spending. Price levels increase because of inflation, but the rates of increase vary from year to year. Federal and state laws automatically commit certain funds for pensions, unemployment compensation, and health benefits, and these outlays depend on the number of eligible people. Federal environmental regulations require even small towns to build expensive water treatment facilities. Local governments must maintain the protection, education, and maintenance services on which their citizens depend and which their states mandate. A new contract with the employees' unions may increase the payroll. Thus, there is often very little leeway for innovation, and even established programs are vulnerable to cuts to meet heavy new demands.

Third, budget makers must forecast the cost of servicing their debts. A change of just one percentage point in the interest rate on new borrowing alters federal interest payments by several billion dollars. These rates are hard to predict even a year in advance. State and local officials who borrow for capital projects must also watch Wall Street, since an increase there will raise their costs of building roads and schools and may force them to cut back investment plans. They must budget for annual payment of the interest and part of the principal.

Spending projections have many sources. The Office of Management and Budget, Treasury Department, Council of Economic Advisers, and Congressional Budget Office all do forecasting for the national budget and draw upon studies by private economists as well. State budget officials also make these projections within their own realms. They devise intricate computer models to aid them, although the validity of such models depends on the basic assumptions made and the quality of data input. No single technique has been proven "best." Since economic forecasting is far from a precise science, views of the future can differ widely, and an executive may rely on political motives in selecting one from many. The forecasts of presidents and governors are often more optimistic than those of legislative or private economists, particularly in election years.

The Politics of the Budgetary Process

Budgeting is shared between the executive and legislative authorities. Appropriating funds and imposing taxes are constitutional prerogatives of legislators, from city councils to Congress. Yet preparation of a budget prior to the lawmakers' deliberations has been accepted in the twentieth century as an executive responsibility. Neither functions apart from the influence of the other. This makes them both rivals and partners, shouldering responsibility for an outcome that neither may delight in.

The chief executive is usually the key figure in budget preparation but is surrounded by a cluster of agencies, staff aides, and outside sources of influence, which vary with the size of the government. The manager of a small city may need to consult only with the heads of the operating departments about their requirements for the upcoming year and to ascertain the prospects for revenue before putting requests on paper. But the president, a governor, and the mayor of New York City must combine inputs from a great many sources.

The Making of the Federal Budget

The federal budget-making process is the most intricate of all. As Figure 12.1 shows, the fiscal year begins on October 1 and is named for the year in which it ends. Thus, fiscal year 1996 began on October 1, 1995, and ends on September 30, 1996. However, planning for that year's budget began in the spring of 1994. A key player in this process is the Office of Management and Budget. Its director, a presidential appointee who must be confirmed by the Senate, is one of the president's closest financial advisers. The OMB had a staff of 586 in 1992, most of them specialists in financial and program analysis.

Initiating the Process: OMB and the Agencies   The OMB opens the planning during the spring months by preparing the economic assumptions and forecasts described in the preceding section. These identify the broadest context that will shape both revenue and spending. From this phase come specific instructions to the executive departments and agencies as to overall spending ceilings and changes in policy emphasis. At that point, they review their own activities and begin to estimate their spending needs.

By early autumn the OMB begins to work with the estimates that the agencies have submitted. Its analysts compare the requests with the president's guidelines, among other criteria. Typically, the amounts requested add up to more than the OMB can approve and

Figure 12.1

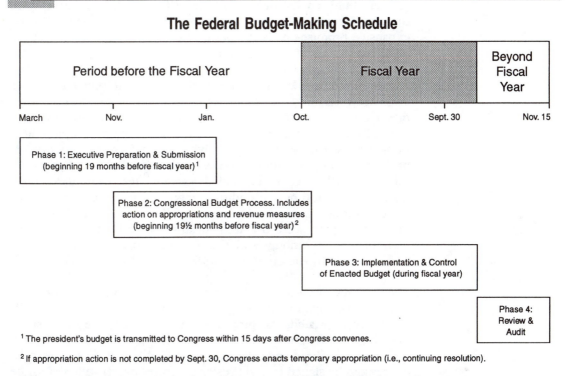

The Federal Budget-Making Schedule

Period before the Fiscal Year	Fiscal Year	Beyond Fiscal Year

March   Nov.   Jan.   Oct.   Sept. 30   Nov. 15

Phase 1: Executive Preparation & Submission (beginning 19 months before fiscal year)[1]

Phase 2: Congressional Budget Process. Includes action on appropriations and revenue measures (beginning 19½ months before fiscal year)[2]

Phase 3: Implementation & Control of Enacted Budget (during fiscal year)

Phase 4: Review & Audit

[1] The president's budget is transmitted to Congress within 15 days after Congress convenes.

[2] If appropriation action is not completed by Sept. 30, Congress enacts temporary appropriation (i.e., continuing resolution).

Source: U.S. General Accounting Office, *A Glossary of Terms Used in the Federal Budget Process* (3rd ed.), 1981.

The period in which the Executive Branch and Congress must prepare and enact the federal budget for a fiscal year is longer than the fiscal year itself, a testimony to the complexity of the task.

must be reduced. This September-to-December period witnesses some intense negotiations over specific dollar amounts. In the end the president must make it his own budget and may personally intervene to support or oppose any item he chooses. Each budget item is a potential point for bargaining between the White House and Capitol Hill, and the president stakes out his initial positions in the document.

The departments and agencies naturally seek approval for as much money as possible to support new and existing programs. In doing so, they may use what has been called the Washington Monument strategy: threatening to cut a highly visible and popular service if they are denied the requested funds. (The Department of the Interior once threatened to close that tourist mecca when OMB cut its projected budget.) As President Clinton was putting his 1995 budget in final form late in 1993, he met many times with his department heads, who protested the cuts he proposed for their departments. Defense Secretary Les Aspin not only appealed to the president over reductions in the military budget but made his displeasure public, which is rarely done (Ifill, 1993). In Clinton's case the cuts mandated by the hard fiscal realities conflicted with the expansive promises he had made in his election campaign and the policy ambitions of his appointees.

The President's Role   The president presents his budget to Congress between mid-January and early February, along with a budget message summarizing and justifying those figures. By this time, all the OMB/agency disputes over funding have been settled, although Congress reopens some of them when defenders and constituents of the agencies carry their appeals up to Capitol Hill. Congress has full power to raise, lower, and delete any item in the executive budget and to add new spending categories, not bound in any way by the president's proposals. Several of President Reagan's budgets in the mid-1980s were declared "dead on arrival" in Congress, underlining this autonomy and the legislative branch's political disagreements with the chief executive.

The Congressional Role   Congress follows an intricate procedure of authorizing expenditures and appropriating funds. Before funds can be appropriated, the programs on which they are to be spent must be formally authorized. These actions can be initiated by any standing committee and take the form of bills that must pass both houses and be signed by the president. **Appropriation** is a separate action that permits funds to be taken from the Treasury to pay for those programs. Discretionary appropriations are made through the thirteen bills into which the executive budget is traditionally divided. Each bill is assigned to a separate subcommittee of the House and Senate Appropriations Committees, which are solely responsible for such legislation. The subcommittees hold hearings in which each department and agency accounts for its past activities and defends its requests. Many appropriations are for one fiscal year only, although some can be spent over several years.

Congress has bound itself to certain procedures by means of which to enact the federal budget. By April 15 of each year it must approve a budget resolution presented to it by the Budget Committees in each house. This sets an overall spending limit, which it is committed not to exceed. It then has until June 30 to complete action on all appropriations bills. The interval between the latter date and the start of the new fiscal year, on October 1, is to allow time for the Office of Management and Budget to make sure that the appropriations do not exceed the spending limits set earlier. The committees are guided by the Congressional Budget Office, established in 1974 to produce spending and revenue forecasts. Revenue choices need not be made annually (although some changes occur every year) and are the province of still other committees: Senate Finance and House Ways and Means.

Lawmakers have not rigorously followed their timetable, which requires all financial decisions to be made by September 30. It has failed to meet that deadline in most years, usually taking an extra month or two to pass all appropriations. Political disputes and the pressure of other business often tie up both houses, and the sheer number of separate funding items in a trillion-dollar budget takes considerable time to process. If the October 1 deadline is not met, Congress enacts a continuing resolution that permits temporary funding of the agencies at some rate agreeable to both houses. Although this device does make money available, it delays administrative planning for the year until the actual number of dollars to be available is decided. After the spending bills are enacted, Congress passes supplemental appropriations during the fiscal year to meet unforeseen needs; the total of these ranged between $9 billion and $32 billion annually during the 1980s (Rubin, 1990, pp. 193–196).

The executive branch monitors the congressional budget process at each step of the way. Not only must the president sign each appropriation bill before it becomes law, but he can use the threat of a veto to influence its content before it comes down from Capitol Hill. The president and executive departments have liaison people who communicate regularly with the legislators. The director and staff of OMB also speak and bargain for the president. They can respond quickly should a proposal surface to cut a program favored by the president or add an item he opposes.

Outside Interests   Many groups outside government also have high stakes in this budget process. They range from military weapons contractors to health insurance companies to the American Association of Retired Persons. State and local governments have a major stake in the intergovernmental aid described in Chapter 4. They exert influence at all stages of decision making to protect an existing share of the budget or expand a program that would give them new benefits. Interest groups often form coalitions to lobby for a package of appropriations that benefits each partner; the various agricultural commodity producers are skilled at this.

Debt Servicing   The budgeting options of the federal government are restricted in several ways. First, Congress must make an automatic appropriation to pay the interest on the national debt, which depends on the size of the debt and the interest rate paid to bondholders. In fiscal year 1994 the net interest paid was $203.4 billion, which was about 14 percent of all federal outlays. The debt itself totaled $4.676 trillion at the end of that year (*Statistical Abstract of the United States,* 1994, Tables 504 & 509).

Entitlements   A second constraint on federal budget options comes from **entitlements,** which are legally required payments to individuals. Through the 1935 Social Security Act and its amendments, recipients are entitled to monthly payments according to their contributions. The Social Security Administration has authority to pay out whatever is necessary under the law. Congress may change this outlay only by altering the formula, and the political forces protecting retirement programs will permit no reduction. Other entitlements include Medicare, Medicaid, unemployment compensation, Aid to Families with Dependent Children, food stamps, veterans' benefits, pensions for retired government personnel, and agricultural subsidies.

Taken together, these entitlements, interest payments on the debt, and the contracts and obligations made in preceding years are labeled "relatively uncontrollable outlays" by the OMB. Their size and growth rate cannot be altered in the short run; they can only be anticipated and built into the budget. These do not pass through the congressional deliberation process, since appropriations for them are preset. Most of these are automatically increased each year to keep pace with the cost of living, and benefits for the elderly grow even more rapidly to cover the increasing size of that age group. In fiscal year 1994 the cost of these outlays totaled $1.033 trillion, nearly 70 percent of the entire federal budget (*Statistical Abstract of the United States,* 1994, Table 509).

The remaining 30 percent was the amount over which the president and Congress have discretion. Even that is hard to change from one year to another, since much of the cost involved is tied to commitments to personnel, facilities, and programs vital to the national interest and to politically influential groups. "As entitlements come to dominate much of public spending, they act so as to place the budget on automatic pilot. Far more than before, the budget is determined by prior authorizations" (Wildavsky, 1988, p. 274). A congressional commission warned in 1994 that entitlement payments were growing so rapidly that they would overwhelm the entire budget in another 30 years. Figure 12.2 provides an overall perspective on federal spending.

The Search for Spending Limits   The huge deficits of the 1980s and early 1990s have forced the president and congressional leaders into intense bargaining at the end of each annual budget cycle. Their interplay resulted in the Budget Enforcement Act of 1990, which placed separate caps on discretionary spending in defense, domestic programs, and aid to foreign countries, and prohibited shifting funds from one category to another. In allocating expenditures for domestic programs, more dollars to combat crime means reducing funds for another program by an equal amount. Additionally, entitlement benefits cannot be expanded unless taxes are increased or

Figure 12.2

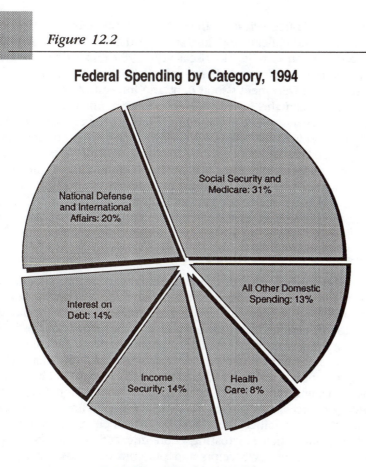

Federal Spending by Category, 1994

National Defense and International Affairs: 20%

Social Security and Medicare: 31%

Interest on Debt: 14%

All Other Domestic Spending: 13%

Income Security: 14%

Health Care: 8%

Total Spending: $1.484 Trillion

Source: *Statistical Abstract of the United States*, 1994, Table 504.

The largest category of federal expenditures in fiscal 1994 was entitlements for the fast-growing elderly segment of the nation's population.

another benefit is reduced; only cost-of-living increments are allowed. If spending is increased contrary to these rules, an across-the-board cut in programs outside the entitlements is required. In making this agreement, Congress gave up some of its power over appropriations. The winner was OMB, which gained the authority to track tax and spending bills as they move through Congress and reduce or "sequester" amounts that exceed the limits. This arrangement was continued after President Clinton took office.

Spending outside the Budget   The budget does not give a complete picture of federal spending, however. An important percentage of outlays does not appear in the budget at all. Federal agencies loan money or guarantee private loans to farmers, home buyers, financial institutions, and college students, among others. About $589 billion in credit was outstanding in fiscal year 1989 (*Statistical Abstract,* 1994, Table 515). None of these loans is budgeted for, but each is added to the government's total debt and interest obligations, since the Treasury and the Federal Reserve System finance them. However, they become a net outlay only if the borrowers default. Similarly, the hundreds of billions of dollars that bailed out the failed savings and loan institutions over the past several years were formally "off budget." However, like ordinary expenditures, they must still be financed. Congress and the president also agreed in the fall of 1990 that the costs of the Persian Gulf military operations would be outside the budget limits.

State and Local Budgeting Procedures

State budgeting follows a similar procedure. Twenty-one states enact budgets for 2-year periods; the rest prepare them annually. Legislatures operate similarly to Congress in passing spending and tax bills. Most governors have powers and staff assistance similar to the president's but on a smaller scale. Unlike the president, most governors have power to delete or reduce specific spending items while signing the bill as a whole. This **item veto** power, widely used in some states and rarely in others, allows for an additional check on spending choices. Forecasting revenues and spending is more crucial for the states, since they must balance their budgets, but it is more difficult, since fluctuating economic activity causes greater surges and dips in tax receipts and program demands. Changes in federal tax laws can both boost and cut state revenues. A state that is prospering economically is under strong pressure to increase spending or reduce tax rates. Many states create reserve funds in their budgets to insulate themselves from embarrassing shortfalls. Figure 12.3 displays the major categories of spending by state and local governments.

Trust Funds and Dedicated Revenues

Trust funds are kept as separate accounts from the government's general fund and may be drawn upon only for the uses specified by law. The largest of these at the federal level are the old-age, survivors, and disability funds, collectively known as Social Security, which together contained $374 billion at the end of fiscal year 1993. The fund dedicated to pensions for retired federal civilian employees contained $319 billion, and another $98 billion awaited military retirees. The Medicare insurance fund had $149 billion. Other funds are designated for airports, highways, and unemployment insurance. In 1993 all federal trust funds contained $1.080 trillion (*Statistical*

Figure 12.3

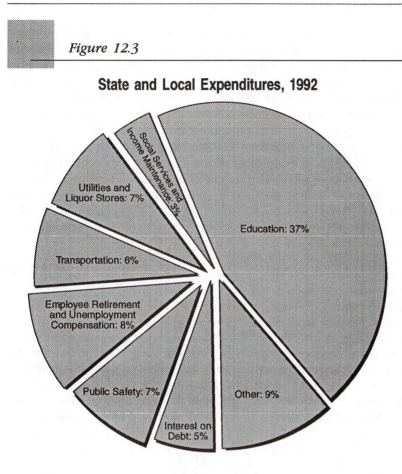

State and Local Expenditures, 1992

- Education: 37%
- Social Services and Income Maintenance: 3%
- Utilities and Liquor Stores: 7%
- Transportation: 6%
- Employee Retirement and Unemployment Compensation: 8%
- Public Safety: 7%
- Interest on Debt: 5%
- Other: 9%

Total $1.147 Trillion

Source: Statistical Abstract of the United States, 1994, Table 464.

Government spending below the federal level is dominated by human services programs, notably education and a variety of social benefit and income-support programs.

Abstract of the United States, 1994, Table 506). Many states have similar funds, primarily for public employee pensions, highways, and education. In this way a government can "bank" money for future use.

Many trust funds are fed by dedicated revenues. For example, the FICA payroll deductions are placed into the social insurance funds, and the federal gasoline tax receipts fuel the highway trust fund. Other earmarked revenues are spent in the year in which they are received. Several states devote their hunting and fishing license fees to fish and game development; others allocate the proceeds from lotteries to public schools.

The rationale for dedicated revenues and trust funds is to provide a direct link between the source and its beneficiaries. Drivers pay the gasoline tax and benefit from improved highways in proportion to the miles they travel (although the connection between lotteries and education is not as obvious). Politically powerful groups have secured dedicated revenues and trust funds to protect benefits they receive. Since the flow of money is automatic and not subject to the appropriation process, they need not fear cutbacks. The "highway lobby" in most states has a wide base of supporters who resist any reform that might subject road funding to the uncertainties of budget politics. During the past 20 years the proportion of dedicated federal revenues increased sharply, whereas those going into the general fund declined by the same amount (Cogan, Muris, & Schick, 1994, p. 21).

Local government budgeting varies with the unit and structure. Most full-time administrative mayors propose budgets and influence council action on them. In cities and special districts with a professional manager or superintendent, that executive takes the lead in budget proposals. The smaller the budget, the closer the attention a legislative body can pay to it and thus use its independent judgment. State governments specify, often within narrow limits, what revenues they can raise and how, so they have little room in which to maneuver. Because both state and local governments depend on federal aid to a significant extent, and state aid to local units is large, their budget making must be sensitive to expected intergovernmental transfers.

Budgeting Reforms

Because of these intricate procedures, legal constraints, and incessant political bargaining, the budgeting process of large governments often appears to be beyond anyone's control. Persistent complaints that the federal budget process did not permit coherent funding choices led President Lyndon Johnson in 1965 to institute the Planning-Programming-Budgeting System (PPBS). It required each agency to determine its major mission objectives, state how it would accomplish each and at what cost, and summarize and justify the agency's policies within each objective. The logic was sound: Programs evaluated and compared in this way could be altered or replaced if they were unsatisfactory. But PPBS proved difficult to practice, even for those offices that took it seriously, and required much additional staff time to collect and digest the information. Having failed to meet its goals, the system was quietly abandoned by the time Richard Nixon moved into the White House.

The failure of PPBS stemmed from the very factors that render budgeting problematic in the first place. Most multiservice agencies have such broad objectives that they find it impossible to state them clearly. Protection of public health, for example, is a subgoal of several departments and independent agencies. The means to achieve each goal are likewise diverse and not confined to a single objective, nor is it possible to justify the policies in a purely rational framework, since most are based on a political rationale rooted in the demands of particular constituency groups. The PPBS analyses were therefore easily slanted to serve such political goals or an organization's self-protection. "PPBS created an incentive to doctor information so that all programs appeared to be a smashing success, even in those cases where the agency itself knew the program was not working and would like to change or replace it" (Downs & Larkey, 1986, p. 163).

Zero-based budgeting (ZBB) was another attempt at rational fiscal planning. President Carter introduced it in 1977, having used it in Georgia when he was governor. It contradicted the incremental logic of budgeting by requiring that an agency's entire funding, not just the changes and new programs, be examined annually. If administrators could not justify an existing program in the agency's overall priorities, they were to reduce or terminate it.

As formulated by Carter, ZBB required a process of identifying "decision units," the smallest and most specific units of spending, and "decision packages," analyses of the programs and activities within each decision unit. Each decision package was to be ranked according to its efficiency. When all the data were in place, a budget maker could ideally select the most efficient means of achieving each objective and its most appropriate funding level.

ZBB was first applied in the formation of the federal budget for fiscal year 1979, presented in January 1978. But like PPBS, ZBB analyses took much time and did not make a substantial difference in the final budget figures. No significant changes in spending took place during either Carter administration, in Atlanta or Washington, as a result of the decision packages that were prepared. Agencies did the required paperwork but proceeded along the same policy and fiscal paths as before. They found themselves steered by the much stronger political forces that had initiated their programs and had acted against any proposed spending cuts (Downs & Larkey, 1986, pp. 177–78). Some state and local governments instituted PPBS and ZBB procedures, and they survive in some form for programs that are sufficiently clear-cut to permit such analyses. The performance budget, described earlier, applies many of the principles of PPBS and ZBB and has proved to be workable where agencies are committed to it and experienced in its procedures.

Both PPBS and ZBB were based on unrealistic ideals and ignored the power of the many interests within and outside of government who use the present flexible, pluralistic system to their own advantage. The reformers wanted to centralize decisions with the chief executive and with congressional majorities. But the financing system had evolved over the years to serve many interests and constituencies, and they were not to be thwarted. Moreover, neither Johnson nor Carter saw his procedural reform as worth fighting for if it meant sacrificing substantive policy goals (Grafton & Permaloff, 1983).

Managing and Reviewing Government's Expenditures

Once enacted into law, a budget becomes a tool for management to control the pace and objectives of spending. The total funding for each agency is typically divided into allotments for each quarter or month. Thus, the agency cannot spend its annual appropriation in 10 months and then pressure the legislature for an extra sum to see it through the year. This limit does not insulate budgets from political conflicts, but such conflicts focus on the timing of expenditures and how they are divided among specific projects. For example, a city may begin a housing rehabilitation program in one neighborhood before another because its planning is further along or because its alderman is president of the city council.

Administrators are typically required to spend the entire amount appropriated, although they cannot exceed it. Nevertheless, there are good reasons for money to remain in some accounts at the end of the year. For example, the authorized program might have been slow to operate, it might have been impossible to spend the amount efficiently, or the need for spending might not have been as great as expected. As another illustration, federal farm subsidies vary with market prices for the supported commodities. If the latter are higher than projected, the spending will be lower. The allocation for unspent funds typically expires at the end of the fiscal year unless it is a multiyear appropriation, as with military weapons acquisitions, which are scheduled over several years.

Spending Conflicts and Controls

A controversy arose in the early 1970s about whether a president could impound (refuse to spend) sums that Congress had appropriated. Franklin Roosevelt was the first of several presidents to disagree with an appropriation, but Richard Nixon had actually impounded about $17 billion by 1973. Congress required, in the Impoundment Control Act of 1974, that when a president chooses not to spend a given amount, he must request a rescission (cancellation of the appropriation), which takes effect if both houses approve it within 45 days. President Reagan disputed this mandate, but a federal appeals court upheld Congress in 1987. Although legal penalties are set forth for presidents who violate this mandate, both the White House and Capitol Hill prefer negotiation over such issues to open conflict. Since the early 1980s relatively small rescissions have been asked and granted with little conflict. Spending may also be deferred to a later fiscal year.

At the federal level this change must meet with congressional approval. The annual amounts deferred averaged $13 billion from 1982 to 1988 (Rubin, 1990, pp. 197-98).

Agencies may also reprogram or transfer funds from one account to another when unexpected conditions make it necessary and if Congress has given prior authorization. Many state and local executives have the discretion to reprogram on their own. Major fund shifts can be controversial when they contradict the intent of the legislative body that appropriated them. As a result of all these factors—multiyear funding, rescissions, transfers, and reprogramming—the amount spent in a given year may be different from that which lawmakers appropriated.

Accurate accounting is essential to inform administrators of how the funds are spent. Although there are accepted standards for financial accounting and reporting, many governments fall short of them because of inadequate employee training, lack of efficient technology, and occasional corruption.

Auditing

After funds have been spent, an **audit** determines what was spent for what purposes and whether the expenditures conformed to law. Audits can be tools to aid future planning and preserve financial integrity. Four different types of audits are performed, depending on the objectives. The most common is the *financial* audit, which determines whether financial records are complete and accurate and whether the funds were spent in accordance with the law. The second type is the *management* audit, which inquires into the efficiency of the spending activity. Examiners may uncover improper use of equipment or personnel or the duplication of programs. These may occur in the managers' use of their discretion and are not necessarily illegal. The third type, the *program* audit, takes a broad perspective and determines whether the overall objectives of the program are being met. Such an audit may also define alternative ways to meet objectives at a lower cost. Here examiners must use their own judgment to a greater extent and cannot rely only on numbers to answer their questions. The fourth type, and the most demanding of all, is the *performance* audit, which is directed at most or all operations of an entire agency or department. These audits are least common, because of their complexity and the sensitive political issues that may surround them. For example, a big city's housing and community development agency is likely to come under criticism from many directions for doing too much, doing too little, or not acting for the right people. An in-depth program or performance audit might give fuel to critics and create pressures for changes. Such audits are actually a form of evaluation, which is the focus of Chapter 14.

Financial and management audits are typically done by a specialized unit within each agency in large governments. In the federal and state governments, external auditing offices oversee these activities and conduct program and performance audits. The General Accounting Office (GAO), which is responsible to Congress, supervises such audits and does studies of its own when requested by Congress. It has increasingly devoted its time to analyzing the quality of the programs it reviews and recommending improvements. In recent years the GAO's performance audits have included recommendations for policy and management changes, which aroused controversy about whether it was overstepping its bounds.

Spending control in state and local governments, by contrast, is relatively simple, although waste and fraud can occur there also. Councils in small cities and counties can examine every spending item if they care to, but the larger the government, the more discretion must be given to the administrators. Many states have elected auditors who supervise this function for the state and local units; others vest this function in an auditor's office answerable to the legislature. State and federal auditing offices share the task of accounting for the more than $100 billion of intergovernmental programs, such as Medicaid and food stamps.

Collecting the Public Revenue

Raising the funds necessary to serve the public purposes also poses complex political and administrative choices. It is not simply a matter of getting enough money; rather, the "ways and means" of who pays how much under which circumstances leave deep imprints on the economy and must be planned for. Taxes on corporate profits and income earned from investments (capital gains) affect the flow of investments into those enterprises, for example, and indirectly act on the pace of the nation's economic growth. Figure 12.4 outlines the major revenue sources of the federal government.

Revenue decisions, like those for spending, are ultimately made by agreement of the legislative body and the chief executive. However, top administrators in revenue or finance departments have considerable influence on the proposals they consider. When the president or a governor submits a bill to amend the tax code, it has probably been written by the Treasury Department or the counterpart state agency, based on data and analyses generated by those revenue specialists.

Criteria for Choosing Revenue Sources

These lawmakers and executives apply two broad criteria in choosing revenue sources and the amounts to take from them: equity and ease of administration. American governments have found that no

Figure 12.4

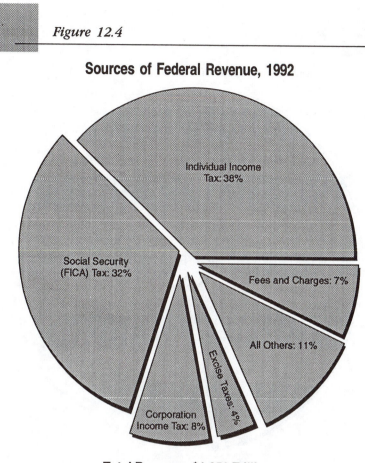

Sources of Federal Revenue, 1992

Individual Income Tax: 38%

Social Security (FICA) Tax: 32%

Fees and Charges: 7%

All Others: 11%

Excise Taxes: 4%

Corporation Income Tax: 8%

Total Revenue: $1.259 Trillion

Source: Statistical Abstract of the United States, 1994, Table 464.

Taxes on individuals provide the major share of federal revenues. As a result, when personal income levels fluctuate with economic conditions, the government's income is affected accordingly.

single revenue source is ideal by both standards. The major sources used today are taxation of the earned income of individuals and corporations, levies on sales, taxes on the value of land and buildings, and fees for services provided to consumers. The first is the mainstay of the national government and many states; the second is used by most states and a few local units and by the national government on selected items; the third is the prime source of revenue for general-purpose local governments and school districts; the fourth is used by nearly all governments to a lesser degree. The major federal revenue source of the nineteenth century, tariffs on

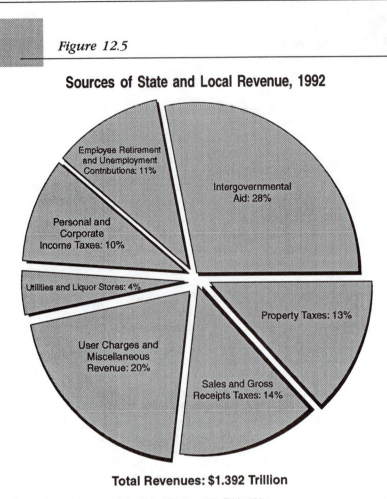

Figure 12.5

Sources of State and Local Revenue, 1992

Employee Retirement and Unemployment Contributions: 11%

Personal and Corporate Income Taxes: 10%

Utilities and Liquor Stores: 4%

User Charges and Miscellaneous Revenue: 20%

Intergovernmental Aid: 28%

Property Taxes: 13%

Sales and Gross Receipts Taxes: 14%

Total Revenues: $1.392 Trillion

Source: Statistical Abstract of the United States, 1994, Table 464.

State and local governments rely on several sources of income, no one of which dominates. Individual states and localities may vary widely from this overall summary, however.

imports, is now almost negligible at $17 billion. The main sources of state and local revenue appear in Figure 12.5.

The equity criterion has both horizontal and vertical dimensions. A tax is horizontally equitable to the extent that two taxpayers with equal ability to pay are taxed equally. This can apply to two persons with the same income, real estate values, or dollar value of purchases. Vertical equity defines a proportional relationship between tax burdens and those with different capacities to pay. In this concept, a person with a greater capacity should carry the larger burden. If the percentage of tax paid increases with income (e.g., from 10 percent at $10,000 to 20 percent at $20,000), the tax is said to be progressive. If the reverse takes place, the tax is defined as regressive. When the ratio is the same at all income levels, it is a proportional tax. The equity question is complicated by the fact that ability to pay is not necessarily matched by the benefit one receives from the government in services or income supports.

Tax Administration

The administration of revenue collection involves six steps. First, tax authorities identify sources (individual earners, merchants collecting sales taxes, and owners of taxable real estate). The second step is to determine the value represented by each taxpayer (amount of sales and income and the market value of the property). The third stage is collection, which secures the payment that is defined by law. Fourth, audits determine whether the proper amount was indeed paid. Fifth, the taxpayer is permitted to appeal an administrative decision that he or she believes to be unfair, and the amount may be adjusted. The last stage provides for enforcement of payment where there is resistance. Tax administrators are not the most popular public servants, but by acting fairly and giving the appearance of fairness, they can minimize opposition.

Income Taxes   Income taxes are relatively easy to collect if we assume that individuals and corporations honestly declare their incomes and provide other required information. Nearly all Americans accept the legitimacy of income taxes, even while they grumble. If the United States had the widespread resistance to direct taxation that France and Italy have, the Internal Revenue Service and counterpart state tax agencies could only function with expensive surveillance and inspection. There are many methods of catching cheaters, but it costs the government money to pursue each one.

To fulfill a variety of policy purposes, income taxation may be selective. For example, a portion of contributions to religious and charitable organizations can be deducted from taxable income. This is an incentive for people to support such organizations voluntarily. Tax liability is also reduced for the blind, those over 65, and those with dependents. Another major deduction is the interest paid on home mortgages. All these **tax expenditures** (the exclusions, deductions, credits, and preferential tax rates) resulted in a loss of about $385 billion in tax revenue to the national government in fiscal year 1993 (*Statistical Abstract of the United States,* 1994, Table 510).

Sales Taxes   Taxes on business transactions are relatively easy to administer, since they are collected by retailers and turned over to the government at set intervals. Cheating is usually easy to detect. Such taxation, however, raises serious questions of fairness. Sales and gross receipts taxes, which are widely used by state and local governments, impose a flat percentage on a wide range of goods and services. The poor and the wealthy pay the same tax on a given purchase. It is only when the wealthy buy more that they pay more. However, some states exempt food, clothing, and medicines from the tax to reduce the impact on lower-income people.

Local Real Estate Taxation   Local governments rely heavily on real estate taxes. The rationale is that since many local services are property related, those whose holdings are more valuable derive greater benefit from them and should thus pay more. This is most true for police and fire protection, public works, and other services that protect and enhance property values. This logic is not convincing, however, for education and other social services, which are also heavily financed by property taxes in most states. Yet because of tradition and the difficulty of increasing other forms of taxation, the property tax remains vital to these local governments.

Real estate taxation presents a complex challenge to administrators (Raphaelson, 1987). First, the market value of each structure and parcel of land must be determined by a state, county, or city assessor. This must be done often enough to keep current with changing values yet be equitable throughout a community. Second, the assessed or taxable value of the property must be calculated. Typically, different types of property are taxed at varying percentages of market value. Owner-occupied homes and farms, for example, are treated more favorably than factories and office buildings. From this one can calculate the total value of taxable property in any county, city, or special-purpose district. Third, the local unit chooses the amount of revenue to obtain from the property tax, and the collector computes the tax that must be paid on each piece of property to supply the sum required by each local government that taxes it. This assessment is based on a percentage of assessed value. For example, if a community has a $100-million-tax base and requires $1 million in a given year, property owners must pay, on average, 1 percent of the taxable value of their holdings.

The major administrative problem (which also becomes political) in real estate taxation is assessment of value. The value of an ordinary home is not hard to assess, since similar homes often sell in market transactions. But a large office building, shopping center, or industrial plant is unique, and if it has not been sold recently, its value is subject to an assessor's judgment. Political pressures and even illegal influence have distorted these judgments in some cities. Owners may contest assessors' valuations through an administrative procedure and later may take the dispute to court.

User Charges   User charges supplement these common taxes, although they produce less revenue (DiLorenzo, 1987). They are the prices that a person pays for direct services bought from a unit of government: university tuition, a postage stamp, water, wood from a national forest, a room in a public hospital, or a subway ride. A price can be charged when the product or service is provided to the payer and denied to another who does not pay. The price may be set higher than its cost and so return a surplus to the government, as is done by many municipalities that generate and sell electricity. But pricing decisions are more commonly shaped by social policies. Urban transit fares do not typically cover the entire cost of providing transportation. They are subsidized to encourage ridership on the assumption that the resulting drop in automobile traffic benefits the entire community. Other charges vary with user income. For example, a low-income person receives free medical attention in a public hospital, whereas one with a higher income is charged the standard rate, and the elderly are often charged less for services than those of preretirement working age.

Governments also use debt to finance their operations. Borrowing involves an obligation to repay the sum borrowed and to pay interest. However, the use of debt by the national government is considerably different from that by state and local units.

Managing Government's Debts

Borrowing by the Federal Government

Congress has given the national government virtually unlimited borrowing power. It sets a legal ceiling on the national debt but raises it whenever needed. When the Treasury requires additional funds to meet congressional appropriations or entitlements, it markets bonds, notes, and bills to the public (including foreign countries), to other federal agencies and trust funds, and to the Federal Reserve banks. At the end of fiscal year 1993, about one-fourth of the debt was held in federal accounts, such as the Social Security trust funds. Each debt instrument is sold for a term varying from 30 days to 30 years. When it matures the Treasury issues a new obligation to replace it. The interest level depends on the life of the instrument and the prevailing rates in the bond market when it is issued. During 1995 rates ranged from 4 percent for short-term securities to 8 percent for 30-year bonds.

State and Local Borrowing

Most state and local governments are forbidden by their laws or constitutions to incur long-term debt to finance current operations. However, they may take short-term (less than 1-year) loans in anticipation of tax revenues or federal and state aid. Bonds with a long life are used only to finance capital projects. Their repayment schedule parallels the life of the project, typically 20 to 50 years. In 1992 all units of state and local government had outstanding debts totaling $971 billion, less than one-fourth that of the federal government. The states held $372 billion; localities accounted for the remaining $599 billion (*Statistical Abstract of the United States,* 1994, Table 474).

Financing through Bonds State and local debt is issued in two kinds of instruments. "Full faith and credit," or guaranteed, bonds are backed by the total tax revenue of the issuing government, whereas revenue bonds pledge for repayment only the income generated by the project they finance. A common use for the former is public buildings, streets, and parks, which do not produce income. The nonguaranteed revenue bonds, on the other hand, have financed sports stadiums, toll roads and bridges, airports, sewer and water facilities, hospitals, and industrial development, all of which draw income from their users in the form of fees, rentals, or assessments. Because such income is not fully ensured, governments must pay a higher rate of interest on revenue bonds than they pay for those backed by the general tax base. About two-thirds of state and local debt is in the form of nonguaranteed bonds.

Interest paid to the holders of both kinds of bonds is exempt from federal income tax, and most states exempt interest on their own bonds from their income taxes. This attracts investors in the upper-income brackets who seek tax-free income. It also permits interest rates to be about 25 percent lower than on a good-quality corporate bond, which is taxable. Such exemptions amount to an indirect federal subsidy.

The rate of interest a government must pay depends partly on its credit rating. Moody's and Standard & Poor, two leading credit-rating services, examine governmental and corporate borrowers and assign grades that reflect their judgment of the bonds' security. The highest rating that Standard & Poor gives is AAA, which qualifies the bonds so rated for the lowest prevailing interest rate. A rating of BBB or below indicates a higher risk that the borrower will default. A high rating signals a low level of debt, a strong and stable tax base, and competent financial management. A change in this rating, up or down, could mean millions of dollars in interest saved or lost for a state or major city. Naturally, to gain or keep a good rating can become a political as well as an economic goal and compel officials to manage their finances conservatively.

Politics and Fiscal Responsibility The politics of incurring debt can be sensitive, which offers opportunities for irresponsibility and corruption. Public officials in the past borrowed heavily for projects that enhanced their popular standing and prospects for reelection but left the debt to be repaid by taxpayers for years afterward. For this reason many states put a ceiling on the long-term general obligation debt that a local unit can incur. Furthermore, they require that new borrowing be approved by either the legislative body or the voters in a referendum. Their vote is a judgment both on the act of borrowing and on the project to be built with the money.

New York City offers an example of irresponsible borrowing for current operations. In the early 1970s, faced with spiraling demands for social services and a revenue base that could not support them without politically unacceptable tax increases, officials increasingly covered deficits with short-term loans. Furthermore, they drew on funds borrowed for capital projects to pay current expenses. This debt accumulated to such an extent that when the city needed to refinance about $3 billion in 1975, the major banks refused to provide the money. The Securities and Exchange Commission, a federal regulatory agency, required the public disclosure of New York's precarious situation and questionable accounting practices. This made new bonds impossible to market. To default on the debt was unthinkable. Finally, New York State established alternative management of the city's debt consisting of the Municipal Assistance Corporation and the Emergency Financial Control Board. Together with the federal government, they designed a long-term program for financial discipline and recovery (Bailey, 1984). This board still has an oversight role today.

Fiscal Administration in Turbulent Times

When governments plan for their fiscal and policy futures, they must assume that present trends will continue, current revenue sources will remain, and demand for spending will not change drastically over the short run. But conditions since the late 1970s have shaken such assumptions and presented governments with choices ranging from bad to catastrophic. While the problems of American governments are not easy to resolve, they appear to be less difficult than those faced by Sweden in 1994, which are described in Box 12.2.

In 1978 California voters approved Proposition 13, a ballot initiative that put a ceiling on the state and local governments' powers to raise taxes, particularly on real estate. Massachusetts citizens voted for Proposition 2½, which limited real estate tax payments to that percentage of a property's value. Other states made major tax cuts as well. The effects of these changes varied among states and communities, but in general, governments have been forced to reduce some services and rely more on other revenue sources to maintain the services they do provide.

The Reagan administration in 1981 secured passage of a major revenue and spending reduction package that cut both federal per-

Box 12.2

How Can Sweden Adjust to New Fiscal Realities?

Swedish voters made two important decisions in the fall of 1994: to replace their relatively conservative governing coalition with the Social Democrats and to endorse membership in the European Union. These choices occur against a backdrop of growing fiscal distress for one of the continent's most prosperous nations. In power for several decades after 1932, the Social Democrats gradually established a welfare state that met a wide range of social needs. By 1990 it was devoting one-third of its gross domestic product to public social benefits (by contrast, the United States allocated only 15 percent for that use). The public, a large proportion of whom are employed by government, has come to expect these benefits as a right.

By 1994, many observers feared that Sweden could no longer afford to be so generous. As unemployment rose, so did the public debt. The nation's budget deficit in 1993 was nearly 13 percent of its gross domestic product, far exceeding the corresponding figure of 3.5 percent in the United States. To make matters worse, Sweden's productivity rate was declining, and with it the resources necessary to sustain the social benefits. Arguments that heavy taxation and public spending are crippling prospects for recovery are increasingly accepted by many voters. Now a member of the European Union, Sweden will face stiffer competition for its markets in the future.

The dilemma, which is clearly more serious than that faced by the United States, is how to cut spending on highly popular programs without creating greater social distress. Whether the Social Democratic government, or any successor after future elections, can do this is highly uncertain. But that may be easier to do sooner rather than later, when the economy could be even weaker.

sonal income taxes and grant aid to state and local governments. No longer could the latter count on steadily increasing dollars from Washington to enable them to expand services. Aid for housing and social services was cut sharply. Many states encountered unexpected deficits and were forced to increase taxes during this period.

The 1981 federal tax cut created unforeseen problems. Despite the promises of the president's advisers that the deficit would soon disappear because of vigorous economic growth, the deficit increased, which put greater pressures on Congress and the White House to restrain spending. Entitlements and interest on the debt also increased steadily, and many discretionary items were reduced. Military spending expanded as well, but considerable waste resulted as the Pentagon became careless in using its new-found treasure. By the end of the 1980s, analyses uncovered waste and corruption in many weapons programs. Spending reductions can often be an incentive to greater efficiency, but large increases are likely to have the opposite effect. The intense bargaining between President Bush and congressional leaders in the fall of 1990, described earlier, was one direct outcome of this sequence that began in 1981. The strenuous efforts by President Clinton and the Republican leadership in

Congress to cut spending further in 1995 are writing yet another chapter in this lengthy story.

State and local governments have responded to fiscal pressures in several ways. First, they have cut services. They have deferred highway and bridge maintenance, reduced frequency of refuse collection, and put libraries on shorter hours. Public pressures have put limits on these cutbacks, however, and the less popular and visible programs have been most affected.

Second, state and local governments have drawn resources from the private sector by the various means highlighted in Chapter 7. Using privately constructed and operated prisons makes large initial investments unnecessary, for example. Some local governments, school districts, and state universities have formed private foundations to support activities beyond the capacity of their public funding. Others seek additional help from charitable donors. The Annenberg Foundation announced a gift of $50 million in 1994, for example, to enable New York City to create new experimental public schools. Privately financed toll roads are yet another idea, as Box 12.3 illustrates. There is a large but unknown potential for joint-venture funding of most state and local functions. As businesses learn to succeed financially in these ventures, they are likely to become more willing to enter into them.

Third, user fees have been increased. Cities are charging more for parking, building permits, waste services, airport access, and use of recreational facilities. Some public schools charge for athletics and field trips. States have increased university tuitions and park fees. Many cities also charge impact fees on new commercial and residential developments, assessing them for the costs of the highway, utility, and park expansions necessary to serve them.

A fourth alternative is more efficient provision of services. The use of computers has enabled governments to eliminate some jobs. They have cooperated with one another to reduce duplication. For example, two or more adjacent cities may combine their police or fire departments, and a city and county may consolidate their libraries or health departments for greater economies of scale. Evaluation analyses have been stepped up to discover more efficient methods of crime prevention, care for abused children, and treatment of drug addicts (Hatry et al., 1987).

Both reductions and expansions are in the foreseeable future for government budgets, but planners must be creative. Spending on programs to combat drug abuse, provide long-term care for the elderly, and deal with toxic chemicals in the environment are due to expand even for governments with tight budgets. Given greater demands for services and popular resistance to taxes, there will be strong incentives to be both imaginative and frugal. The incremental approach can hinder creativity if one simply assumes that the future will be like the past. Although this approach has the virtue of mini-

Box 12.3

Private Toll Highways: Roads of the Future

California has always financed its highways with a combination of federal aid and state gasoline taxes. It charges tolls only on bridges that cross the arms of San Francisco Bay. But it completed in 1993 what was perhaps its last publicly constructed freeway, the Century Freeway across the southern Los Angeles basin. A sign of new times is the Foothill Tollway, under construction in suburban Orange County parallel to Interstate 5, and a set of additional lanes for State Route 91 between Santa Ana and Riverside, financed by private investors who will collect a toll from motorists. They are betting that the chronic traffic congestion on the free roads will spur drivers to pay to save time. The state expects to gain this road capacity at no cost in public funds. Other states, such as Washington, are seriously studying privately owned toll roads as well. New technologies will eliminate traffic backups at toll-booths. Each car will have a coded sticker or radio transponder that can be read by electronic monitors, and the owner will then receive periodic bills.

mizing political conflict, it does not readily respond to new demands and alternatives. For example, a school district that faces a rise in the number of at-risk children it must serve requires long-range directions for its budgets as well as short-term adaptiveness to immediate problems and resources.

Summary

Public finance differs from financial management in the private sector because it is closely linked to the public purposes, its trends are difficult to forecast, its decisions must be made in an open forum, and it is subject to legal constraints. All these factors cause it to be surrounded by intense political conflicts.

Government budgets are simultaneously policy, managerial, economic, and political documents. They can organize expenditures in line-item, performance, or program modes. They can distinguish between current-year and long-term capital spending. The dominant decision-making approach to budgeting has been incrementalism, with its orientation to small changes and implicit acceptance of spending programs of previous years. Budget makers must be competent in forecasting revenue, spending demands, and borrowing costs well in advance of the year in which these will occur.

Budget approval is shared between the executive and legislative authorities at all levels of government. The former propose revenue and spending levels, and the latter enact them into law. At the federal level, the Office of Management and Budget lays the groundwork for each fiscal year's proposed budget by providing forecasts and incorporating each agency's funding requests into a document that ultimately is reviewed and accepted by the president. Congress may make changes in the proposed budget, and it enacts appropriations bills that fund it. The president has the final word through signing the expenditure and revenue bills.

The federal budget process is constrained by so-called uncontrollable and off-budget expenditures and the use of trust funds with dedicated revenues. The current large deficits also limit the freedom of budget makers. Such fiscal-planning methods as the Planning-Programming-Budgeting System (PPBS) and zero-based budgeting (ZBB) have been tried to bring greater order and efficiency to federal spending choices, but with little success.

State and local budgets are enacted through similar executive/legislative cooperation. They are additionally constrained by the uncertainty of federal aid levels (and of state aid, for local units).

Once enacted, a budget is a means for managerial control of spending. Administrators are normally required to spend the entire amount appropriated unless changes are approved by the legislative body. Unspent funds expire at the end of the fiscal year unless specifically included in a multiyear appropriation. After the funds have been spent, financial, management, program, and/or performance audits are conducted to determine what was obtained with the money and whether applicable laws were complied with.

The major revenue sources of the federal government are taxes on individual and corporate incomes. State and local governments rely on a combination of taxes on incomes, retail sales and real estate, as well as on charges for services. Each source features a distinctive process for collection as well as advantages and disadvantages in administration.

State and local governments borrow money for capital expenditures, whereas the federal government finances part of its current spending through debt. State and local units usually borrow by selling bonds to investors and must pay the prevailing interest rate. Additionally, they are subject to legal and political checks on the debt they can incur.

The 1980s presented all governments with major fiscal turbulence, as administrators contended with shifting demands for spending and curtailed resources. They have attempted to cope with these pressures through cutbacks in public services, privatization of some functions, increased user fees, and greater efficiency in operations. Higher taxes have also been necessary in many states and localities.

Discussion Questions

1. What are the advantages of the incremental method of budgeting? What are its disadvantages?

2. How does the organization of Congress make it difficult for that institution to decide on a national budget in 8 months?

3. Why have Congress and the president allowed the "relatively uncontrollable" expenditures to take up so large a part of the federal budget?

4. Why have the national, state, and local governments chosen to rely on a variety of revenue sources rather than just one?

5. As the demands on governments change, their budgets for specific functions must expand or contract to meet them. What criteria should they rely on to help make those difficult choices?

Analytical Exercises

1. Determine what portion of the federal budget is devoted to payments to the elderly for retirement income and medical care, and the rate at which it has grown over the past decade. Look also at projections for future growth and compare them with the past growth rate. Then identify the political organizations of retired people and their lobbying efforts to preserve and extend those benefits. Reach a conclusion about the likely difficulties of reducing those benefits in the future in order to balance the budget.

2. Study a recent budget for the city, county, or school district in which you live or attend school. Determine how much of each item of expenditure is determined by local officials at their own discretion and how much is mandated by state or federal laws or programs. Try to get a sense of the trends in those expenditures so that you can forecast where the growth is likely to take place.

For Further Reading

Bailey, R. W. (1984). *The Crisis Regime: The MAC, the EFCB, and the Political Impact of the New York City Financial Crisis.* Albany, NY: State University of New York Press. How New York City got into and out of its debt crisis of the 1970s, with lessons for all financial managers.

Downs, G. W., & Larkey, P. D. (1986). *The Search for Government Efficiency.* Philadelphia: Temple University Press. Survey of federal efforts at budget and finance reform, their outcomes, and why they generally failed.

Kettl, D. F. (1992). *Deficit Politics: Public Budgeting in Its Institutional and Historical Context.* New York: Macmillan. The struggle to balance the federal budget amid disagreements over what the deficits really mean for the economy.

Makin, J. H., & Ornstein, N. J. (1994). *Debt and Taxes: How America Got into Its Budget Mess and What to Do About It.* New York: Times Books. Very readable history of public finance from colonial times to the present.

Rubin, I. S. (1990). *The Politics of Public Budgeting.* Chatham, NJ: Chatham House. Survey of the budgetary process in national, state, and local governments and the political factors that shape it.

Wildavsky, A. (1988). *The New Politics of the Budgetary Process.* Glenview, IL: Scott, Foresman. Lucid account of how the federal government makes financial decisions and why budgets become political documents.

13

Implementing Public Policy

Learning Objectives

After reading this chapter, you should be able to do the following:

1. Define implementation, output, outcome, and impact.
2. Identify the four alternative meanings of implementation success and the use of each.
3. Identify alternative fates of a problem as a result of implementing a policy designed to solve the problem.
4. Explain the nature and significance of the five implementation requirements: policy translation, resource sufficiency, orchestration of effort, political and legal support, and a supportive socioeconomic environment.
5. Explain how problem succession occurs and how government agencies can learn from implementation experiences.

After the civil rights movement matured and transformed American public policy in the 1960s, one of its agendas focused on people with physical disabilities—their opportunities for education, employment, housing, and access to public places. Access is a particular problem for many; for example, those who are confined to wheelchairs often cannot use public transportation.

A policy for maximizing access to public transportation must include some concept of how to achieve the goal and what costs are acceptable. One such policy might be *equal* (or *full*) *accessibility,* under which the disabled would use the same vehicles as everyone else once these had been modified to accommodate people with special needs. This policy assumes that the disabled have the right to access without being segregated—the same equality as is secured by their equal rights to education, health care, and other public services. The alternative is the *effective mobility* approach, which would provide needed access for people with special needs by some cost-effective means, though not necessarily the same means used by those who are not disabled. This approach permits service providers greater flexibility in choosing the means and is likely to cost less as well.

Twenty-five years of legislative and administrative history have produced major advances in access for the disabled. Congress first acted on this issue in 1970, when it declared that disabled people have the same right to use mass transit facilities and services as others and that transit providers must make "special efforts" to provide access to them. Section 504 of the Rehabilitation Act of 1973 stated that no qualified person is to be excluded from a service because of disability in any program receiving federal financial assistance, which includes urban mass transit agencies. However, legislation neither defined crucial terms (such as *special efforts*) nor set forth a clear choice between the two basic approaches.

Two federal agencies shared responsibility for action. The Urban Mass Transportation Administration (UMTA) of the Department of Transportation (DOT) lacked experience with this type of policy and took 3 years (1973–76) to develop rules that gave examples of what special efforts could be used by local transit agencies to comply with the law. The DOT implicitly accepted the effective mobility concept because of its primary concern for the cost-effectiveness of transit services and its preference for letting local agencies choose how to carry out the mandates of the law. The UMTA's brief history gave it a strong orientation to local agencies' interests, and it was not prepared to play the dictator.

However, the Department of Health, Education, and Welfare (DHEW, known after 1979 as the Department of Health and Human Services) was made responsible for coordinating all federal efforts to implement Section 504 and establish guidelines for recognizing discriminatory practices. Thus, its Office of Civil Rights drafted regulations, finally approved in 1978, that applied the full accessibility principle to urban mass transit. Naturally, it had a strong commitment to promote civil rights generally and thus to overcome state and local resistance. Conforming to the DHEW regulations, DOT changed direction and a year later issued a rule that local transit agencies must equip all new buses with wheelchair lifts and provide elevator access to rapid transit facilities. Much of this was because the new DOT secretary, Brock Adams, believed in the full accessibility principle himself. Private groups representing the disabled, which had organized to defend and extend their gains, applauded this development.

The DOT rule was opposed by local governments and the American Public Transit Association (APTA), which argued that such modifications would be very costly and would not offer more mobility than would separate special services for the disabled. The APTA sued in federal court, and in 1981 an appeals judge returned the regulation to the DOT for reconsideration. By this time the Reagan administration was in power, with its "less government is better" philosophy, and the new DOT leadership rescinded the rule. It was not until 1986 that a new rule reaffirmed local authorities' discretion on meeting the needs of people with disabilities. By that time most metropolitan areas had initiated some form of transit service for the disabled. Some was provided by public agencies and some was supplied by private organizations.

The landmark 1990 Americans with Disabilities Act strengthened this policy. It required that public transit vehicles be usable by disabled people and that cities provide demand-responsive services at a level of access comparable to that available to the nondisabled. Yet it also recognized the challenges of implementation by giving local transit agencies some flexibility in choosing the means and methods. As a result, such services are widely available, although they are not always equal. Individual mobility still depends not only on a person's physical condition and living situation, but also on the variable quality of local transit system management.

This case illustrates well how Congress, two federal departments, the federal courts, and local transit agencies struggled to agree on how to implement laws that were widely supported but that lacked agreement on how to implement them and pay for their costs. It shows how the implementation stage is a vital part of policymaking by turning enacted laws into results. This chapter illustrates many of the problems that government agencies encounter in making policy work.

Government's "Bottom Line"

If profit is the ultimate end of business, what is the corresponding objective of government? What standard can public officials and their constituents use to identify a performance goal? This question directs us to the concept of implementation, which is defined most simply as the process of making public policy work, that is, of achieving the purposes for which it was made. Such achievement is the central mission of administrative agencies, but, as we shall see, no sharp line separates it from the policymaking process.

The process of implementation deserves rigorous study for one reason: to learn how to do it better. The results of many public policies have disappointed their sponsors and clients for many reasons. Paving streets and mailing benefit checks aside, public administration is a science that cannot be practiced with a high degree of reliability. Yet both successes and failures can provide valuable lessons to policymakers and administrators. As Chapter 1 described, the nation's experience with housing policies was a cycle of new program efforts, of learning from experience, and of remaking policy accordingly. We have certainly learned much about what does not work, but as knowledge accumulates, such experience can lead to improved performance as well.

Implementation: The Lessons of History

Prior to the 1960s few students of public administration pondered the problematic character of implementation. They assumed that once a policy had been established by a legislature and assigned to a capable agency with sufficient authority and resources, carrying it out was a technical matter requiring only honesty and competence. This perspective underlay the dichotomy between "politics" and "administration," which dominated scholarly prescriptions in that period. Indeed, much of what government did (and continues to do) was routine enough to be so regarded. For example, collecting garbage and delivering mail are familiar tasks that can be achieved very successfully if done with standardized procedures.

But after 1933, when government increased its efforts in the public purposes of promoting economic growth, enhancing quality of life and personal opportunity, and protecting the environment, it undertook tasks that are not as routine. To combat poverty and racial discrimination called for new knowledge and unfamiliar methods, and implementation became uncertain. To protect consumers from unsafe products was a task as broad as the market itself—and it was very different from carrying letters.

By the early 1970s scholars were beginning to examine the results of the many new programs, and their reports were full of dismay. A landmark study of implementation was a critique of economic development efforts in Oakland, California, entitled *Implementation* and first published in 1973 (Pressman & Wildavsky, 1973) (see Box 13.1). The book's subtitle indicates the authors' frustration: "How great expectations in Washington are dashed in Oakland; or why it's amazing that federal programs work at all." Scholarly studies that followed this critique often took the same line: They examined programs that fell short of high expectations and diagnosed their failure. The news media and popular literature further fueled such criticisms by conveying an image of government as bumbling at best and often harmful to its citizens. From this some observers concluded that government ought to reduce its efforts to solve social and economic problems, either because there is little that it can do to improve the situation or because private institutions are more effective.

Box 13.1

What Prevents Public Programs from Working as They Are Intended?

One of the more ambitious federal programs of the 1960s aimed at renewing the economic health of large cities and rural regions such as Appalachia. The Economic Development Administration (EDA) was given $332 million in 1966 alone to provide loans and grants to state and local governments and private enterprises that would stimulate new jobs. Oakland, California, was targeted early for assistance because of its high unemployment rate.

The EDA and Oakland city officials undertook several projects beginning in 1966: a marine freight terminal, an industrial park at the waterfront, hangars and other improvements at the Oakland airport, and an access road to the Oakland Coliseum. Several businesses were selected for loans to create jobs. There were also to be training programs to open up jobs for the hard-core unemployed. By 1971 the marine terminal was completed and several other projects had been started, but few permanent jobs had been created, and participants were generally disappointed at the lack of results.

What went wrong? Pressman and Wildavsky (1973, p. 113) said it concisely: "None of the participants actually disagreed with the goal of providing jobs for minority unemployed, but their differing perspectives and sense of urgency made it difficult to translate broad substantive agreement into effective policy implementation." They identified fifteen distinct participants, governmental and private, that had different aims and priorities and enough legal authority or political influence to impede or redirect action. These participants had to spend much time in meetings to express their views, work out compromises, and coordinate actions, and often joint action could not be quickly arranged. For the construction of one hangar at the airport, seventy distinct agreements were required that took nearly 6 years to arbitrate among the participants. Construction of a health center for West Oakland went better: The fourteen agreements it required took only a little more than a year. While a halt or an objection at any one point would not necessarily have canceled a program, progress could be slowed enough to change the conditions or reduce someone's willingness to proceed with it—and delay, as it turned out, was the major nemesis of the EDA's ambitions for Oakland.

Recent Perspectives on Implementation

Recent studies of government administration have taken the more constructive approach of emphasizing institutional learning and error correction. Levin and Ferman (1985) examined the generally successful efforts of nine programs that trained unemployed youths for jobs. This was a difficult task, since many of the clients lacked necessary skills and work habits, and employers were reluctant to hire such high-risk people. The authors emphasized that it is impossible to design an innovative program to work perfectly the first time and that program directors need enough sensitivity and flexibility to perceive problems as they appear and correct them promptly. This approach is echoed in many such studies:

> Policy implementation . . . is a testing and feedback process. . . .
> Implementation helps us to detect errors in our ideas and de-
> signs and then correct them. It gives us the opportunity to make
> errors, which is the most realistic way to detect weaknesses in
> our policy ideas. . . . Effective implementation . . . is something
> that one ends up with after the learning process of error detec-
> tion and correction. (Levin & Ferman, 1985, p. 14)

Such an optimistic perspective has been more consistent with
a liberal agenda than with a conservative one, in that most studies
have assumed that socioeconomic policy objectives were worthy
even though outcomes fell short of intentions. However, the authors
of these studies often counsel policymakers to base their objectives
on an informed sense of what can be achieved. Others assert that
policy should not always be confined to a narrow perception of
"workability." If social change is really needed, these critics say,
policy should be targeted at the conditions that hinder its implementation (Linder & Peters, 1987).

The Levels of Implementation

We can define three levels of policy implementation (Levy,
Meltsner, & Wildavsky, 1974, pp. 1–2). An **output** is the immediate service or good provided by a program (e.g., a bus equipped
with a wheelchair lift, immunization of a low-income family's
child against measles, or regulation of a toxic chemical). It is the
easiest element of the three levels to identify and measure, and
informed observers can agree on whether it was provided and
met a valid need.

An **outcome** is an intermediate-range result of the implementation of a policy (e.g., employment of a person with a disability
because of bus access, reduced disease levels in a school resulting
from immunizations, or improved groundwater quality free of hazardous chemicals). An outcome is not always as visible as the output,
and it is subject to differing value judgments. Two observers can
disagree in their choice of criteria or of evidence to identify an
outcome. It is hard to measure the actual unemployment rate of
people with disabilities, for example, and thus to discern when a
decline occurs.

Finally, an **impact** is a long-term consequence for society of
applying the policy, often in combination with other policies that
affect the situation. We might cite as impacts a higher quality of
life for all wheelchair-bound people in a city, better school performance because children are not absent as a result of illness, or greater
recreational use of a clean body of water. Because many forces shape
economic opportunity and school performance, the study of impacts produces the least clear conclusions and is the most open to
diverging judgments.

The study of outputs dominates implementation analysis, since they are the immediate evidence of administrators' efforts. Short-run perspectives thus draw the most attention. In beginning to consider longer-range outcomes and impacts, one enters the realm of evaluation, of applying value judgments to what was or was not implemented. This aspect of implementation is too complex to permit a sharp line to be drawn between the objective survey of implementation and the more subjective evaluations based on it. The latter will be explored more fully in the next chapter.

A major source of conflict in the policy implementation process is the divergent concepts of the meaning of *success* that are held by policymakers, administrators, members of the public, and scholars. What each group assumes about the norms and purposes of the implementive process shapes the ways in which they study the process. We can discern four different perspectives, each with a logic that leads an analyst in a different direction.

The Many Meanings of Success

The Idealistic Perspective

First, one can take an idealistic view that the central purpose of implementation is to solve the problem for which the policy was devised so that it needs no further attention from policymakers—a permanent "fix." In this view there is a knowable and direct relationship between the problem and its solution. Implementation, therefore, can be a largely predictable process of applying proven techniques to familiar conditions. Implementation "failure" thus results from neglect or willful refusal to apply the correct techniques.

A secondary goal is efficiency: The solution is to be achieved at minimum cost. If a lake is being polluted by discharge of a city's raw sewage, the obvious solution is a treatment plant large enough to purify the water. If the size of the city remains unchanged, that plant should suffice for the indefinite future.

The Legalistic Perspective

The second perspective is legalistic: It calls on administrators to fulfill without deviation the explicit mandate of the policy. Agency personnel thus are formally subordinate to the dictates of the legislature, which in turn represents the people's will. This perspective resembles the idealistic approach in that it leaves administrators little discretion, but it differs in that it regards the "right" policy as the one that is framed by law rather than the one that provides the definitive solution to the problem. Like the

Box 13.2

A Public Program Is Successful If . . .

idealistic perspective it provides a permanent solution to the problem;

legalistic perspective it complies with the legislative mandate of how to solve the problem;

responsive perspective it is continually being shaped by the situations in which the policy is applied, by the wills and values of the citizens affected by it, and by the views of lower-level administrators;

experimental perspective it is shaped by the experiences and responses of administrators as they encounter problems and devise remedies.

first perspective, the legalistic view takes a "top-down" approach to implementation, in which policy and control move down a hierarchical ladder.

Financial responsibility is also an important norm in this perspective: Expenditures must conform to the budget that provides those funds. An example of this is a program to aid low-income families in securing housing. The law specifies that people below a certain income level are eligible and that no one above that limit qualifies, even if he or she has had difficulty in finding a home. The program succeeds if it aids those, and only those, who meet the legal standard. It fails when, and only when, it does not comply with its mandates.

The Responsive Perspective

The responsive or adaptive approach portrays implementation as continually being shaped by the changing circumstances in which the policy is applied and by the values and responses of those affected by it. This is a "bottom-up" perspective, unlike the first two approaches, which depend on direction from the original policymakers. In the adaptive approach the administration may properly deviate from the language of the policy (or the language may be so vague as to provide unclear direction). Administrators thus have more autonomy vis-à-vis the legislative body and top executives but are subject to greater influences from interest groups and organized constituents who want the policy to be carried out in ways most favorable to them. At times a program will even be redirected to conform to clienteles' demands or needs. The search for transit access for people with disabilities is a history of such adaptation. Since the legislators did not at first determine the methods by which public access policy was to be implemented, the federal and local agencies and courts developed the policy over the years. In this perspective a policy fails when it lacks "fit" to the given situation and is unresponsive to its clienteles' demands.

The Experimental Perspective

Finally, the experimental approach is suited to situations in which no proven solutions to the problem are available. The policy mandates may be clear or vague, but the methods must be developed by trial and error. Here, the administrators have considerable autonomy to try approaches, evaluate the results, and alter the program accordingly. However, in contrast to the responsive approach, the "right way" is determined from experience as judged by the administrators (though they do well to heed political pressures from outside the agency). This view applies the principle of Levin and Ferman's concept, cited earlier, of implementation as error correction and is also a "bottom-up" approach. The youth employment programs studied by Levin and Ferman achieved many of their goals because the program managers experimented with various methods. If one fell short, they made adjustments or turned to another. Policy failure thus results primarily from rigidity and inability to learn from experience.

Applying Different Perspectives to Implementation

Each perspective is appropriate in some circumstances. The idealistic view can be applied only in limited situations. To remedy traffic congestion at a major intersection is a task with clear boundaries and standard solutions. The legalistic approach is likewise confined to straightforward matters for which precise legal language is appropriate, such as eligibility for benefits. The last two concepts are most relevant to the many problems of public policy for which "answers" are multiple, uncertain, and open to controversy. For these problems, implementation standards must evolve over time as administrators discern the changing issues and requirements in each situation.

These perspectives are relevant to four tools for implementation described in Chapter 1: cash payments to individuals, construction and maintenance of infrastructures, provision of publicly beneficial services, and regulation of individual and corporate behavior. Using the first two tools is most amenable to the idealistic and legalistic perspectives, since implementation can be standardized to a great extent once the beneficiary or the project has been chosen (not always an easy task, admittedly). Policy statements can easily embody the requirements for Social Security payments and sewer construction, and administrative

Box 13.3

What Can Happen to the Problem at Which a Policy Is Aimed?

- It can be *eliminated* entirely by the policy as implemented and no other problems are produced.
- It can be *reduced* to such a low level that there is no further need or demand for action.

- It can be *succeeded* by another problem that has less serious effects or can be solved more easily.
- It can be *exacerbated* by the policy and/or replaced by more difficult problems, with still other problems created in addition.

judgments will focus on straightforward technical, rather than political, choices.

The third and fourth tools of implementation are not as clear-cut: Services and regulations apply to discrete and changing situations and reach those with unique needs. Administrators have a wider latitude for discretion, and accomplishment is usually harder to measure. The national government's response to the savings and loan failures of the late 1980s and the sale of those institutions' assets had to be responsive to local economic conditions, as well as experimental in methods. When legislators cannot foresee in detail all that must be done, they must leave administrators wide discretion to implement their general statements. Thus, it happens that much of the policy is actually remade while it is being implemented. What occurs during this process may depart substantially from the original intentions of the lawmakers. The necessity for discretion provides administrators with much of the power they exercise in the political system.

Success and Failure: The Fate of Problem Solving

Thinking further about the elusiveness of a public policy's success, we can ask what happens to the problem. A problem (recall the definition in Chapter 5: a gap between a current and a preferred situation) can have four different fates. Each fate represents some form of success or failure, as defined by politically influential people who have preferences about a current situation. Box 13.3 summarizes four alternative results that a policy can produce. First, the problem can be eliminated entirely by the policy as implemented, with no new problems created. Although this is the most popular and appealing concept (imagine a drug-free nation!), it is also the rarest outcome. The worldwide eradication of smallpox is an example of such a solution. However, problems very seldom disappear without a trace, and they can reappear in other forms. Indeed, solutions typically create other problems. For example, highway planners in the 1940s and 1950s believed that urban freeways were the answer to traffic congestion on city streets. While such arteries probably did ease movement in many cities, they created or compounded urban blight and air pollution—for which new solutions had to be found.

A second form of success is problem recession. A program may effectively reduce a problem's impact on the public to such a low level that there are no demands for additional action. When the economy is depressed and unemployment rises, government is virtually required to act to create jobs directly and to stimulate private investment. If this is successful (the economy responds favorably and employment figures rise), officials may turn their attention to other issues. Problem recession may also result when the public ceases to expect that any more can be done about it. Although deaths from motor vehicle accidents are still appallingly frequent, they are not considered a major national problem, because the number of fatalities has declined and no additional safety regulations are considered feasible.

A more promising outlook was suggested by Levin and Ferman (1985, p. 130), who argue that "policy progress occurs through a process of *problem succession:* Problems are not so much solved as superseded. . . . We seek . . . to move from less preferable problems to more preferable problems." Assuming that some problems can never be fully eliminated, policymakers seek to replace them with others that are more manageable or that impose less hardship or inconvenience on the public. An example of a less preferable problem is to have thousands of people with disabilities cut off from social and recreational amenities because public transportation and public buildings can't accommodate them. Administrators would prefer the problem of expanding services to the disabled when public access has allowed them to benefit from those services. When implementation makes such an advance without creating other and worse problems, one could reasonably call it a success.

The most obvious example of failure is problem exacerbation. The program may have rendered the problem worse and created still other problems. The high-rise public housing projects built in large cities during the 1950s did represent a short-term improvement in living conditions over the slums they replaced. But their design and management were such that many deteriorated quickly and became ugly and dangerous. Often the residents, who had no other options for housing, were left worse off than before, with no hope of improving their living conditions.

The Requirements for Successful Implementation

What must happen for a government program to be implemented effectively? We could liken the beginning of the implementation process to the assembly of a machine. As one author phrased it,

> [Imagine] a large machine . . . to turn out rehabilitated psychotics or healthier old people or better-educated children or more effective airplanes or safer streets. This machine must sometimes be assembled from scratch. It can sometimes be created by overhauling and reconstituting an older, or preexisting, machine. (Bardach, 1977, p. 36)

The implementation process must be better than machine-like. It must respond to its environment and alter itself in ways that its assemblers may not be able to foresee, like a living organism. No two administrative situations are exactly alike, but we can identify some basic requirements. Box 13.4 offers a glimpse of the "machinery" that cities use to recycle wastes.

Implementation Requirement 1: Policy Translation

First, the policy must provide a clear and consistent statement of its objectives and the means for achieving them. Recall from Chapter 5 the steps in the policy cycle of defining the problem and setting the objectives. Laws are usually designed to attack several problems and achieve several objectives simultaneously. Child welfare programs aim both to protect children physically and to enhance family stability and parental competence. These are not necessarily incompatible goals, but a program must be carefully designed to blend the two.

Policy Design Difficulties can appear because of faults in the policy design, which may not convey to administrators clear guidelines for what they are to do. There may be multiple or uncertain concepts of the problems and objectives, reflecting legislative conflict and compromise. For good political reasons, ambiguous statements are common in legislative policies. They enable advocates of conflicting goals to come to sufficient agreement to pass a bill, since very specific language would arouse too much opposition. Ambiguity also allows different constituencies to believe that they will receive something from the program. "Legislators can satisfy demands to 'do something' about a problem by passing a vague statute with ambiguous meaning, then letting administrative agencies hash out the more conflictual details behind the scenes" (Stone, 1988, pp. 124–125). This burdens the administrators with the harder task of giving the policy its real meaning.

Box 13.4

How Can Waste Recycling Be Successful?

Cities and counties around the nation pay close attention to old newspapers, glass bottles, and aluminum cans these days. Not only are the landfills that used to be their final resting places filling up, but the marketplace is paying good cash for these commodities. Making recycling work, however, presents officials with several dilemmas.

If "success" is diverting the waste stream to the reuse market, many communities can report progress. Portland, Oregon, boasts that 75 percent of its residents put out recyclable materials regularly. In many areas popular support for recycling is high, judging from reports from such places as Casa Grande, Arizona. This in itself is another measure of success.

If the criteria are economic, however, the judgment may be different. Many cities are find-ing that collecting, sorting, and marketing recyclables costs more than they earn from it, and often more than their old practice of dumping waste into landfills. A 1992 study calculated that the average program cost $175 per ton collected and earned only $40, leaving a net outlay of $135. Where landfill space is still available, a manager may be unable to convince the council to continue the program.

Cities are experimenting with ways to reduce costs and maximize participation. They can vary the materials picked up (different types of paper, plastic, metals, glass), the frequency of collection, the management of recycling (governmental or private), and the means of marketing the commodities. Managers must be sensitive to the wide range of local conditions and alternatives that affect their efficiency (Arrandale, 1994).

In addition, legislators may have framed the policy for symbolic purposes, not intending it to be fully implemented. They may have sought only to signify government's concern for a problem, since they had neither the means nor the funds to solve it. Or they may have wanted to endorse a politically popular ideal or to please an important constituency. This is not necessarily deception by policy-makers, although it can create unrealistic popular expectations. It also puts administrators in a no-win situation: If they do not take the policy seriously, they invite criticism for dereliction of duty; but if they do act, even their best efforts may not satisfy their critics.

Several policy design problems were present in legislators' search to provide greater public access for the disabled. By not giving clear direction on the type of accessibility to promote, Congress made it difficult for the DOT and the DHEW to develop an imple-mentive strategy. It took 3 years from the passage of Section 504 of the Rehabilitation Act of 1973 to publish the first set of rules, and it took 13 years to develop final provisions that were acceptable to the courts and local transit authorities. Two alternative concepts—effective mobility and equal accessibility for the disabled—had to be reconciled in many rounds of administrative and interest-group conferences and judicial deliberations. This evolutionary method may indeed be more effective at generating and refining some policies, but it is less open to public view and is subject to manipulation by special interests.

Problem Definition In translating policy, implementers need to define the problem clearly. An uncertain definition of the problem was present in solving the dilemma for the disabled. There are many kinds of disabilities, some of which prevent an individual from using public transit. To estimate how many people have such limitations is not easy; a 1978 report for the DOT calculated that 7.4 million urban dwellers had some problems in using mass transit and that 1.4 million could not use it at all (Katzmann, 1986, p. 4). A program to increase mobility in public places for those who need it most has to be sensitive to all the circumstances that such people face: the disability itself, their range of income, their living situations, their distance from established transit routes, and social discrimination.

Unintended Conflicts Implementation of policy can often run into unintended conflict with another policy. Government's responsibilities are closely intertwined, and one accomplishment is often a prerequisite to a second. Or to do one thing well may make it harder to achieve another. If related goals are the responsibilities of separate agencies, conflict is more likely. Urban mass transit began a period of growth in 1973, thanks to the oil price increases imposed by the Organization of Petroleum Exporting Countries. All three levels of government expanded bus and rail services, usually with increased subsidies from tax revenues. They did attract more riders, but public costs climbed with them, and by 1976 concerns about efficiency dominated the thinking of many transit officials. In this context the last thing they wanted was costly new vehicles that could carry wheelchairs. The effective mobility concept was most compatible with prevailing transit programs, since it could be realized in many ways, even with private contractors.

The Effects of Symbolism Mobility for the disabled had a symbolic character, too. Justice and compassion support better opportunities for the disadvantaged, and with legislators keenly aware of what their refusal to address the issue would mean, Section 504 passed with little discussion. But the disabled took the promise very seriously, and, perceiving their dignity and lifestyles to be at stake, they applied significant pressure on administrators to support their interpretation of the policy. By failing to state specifically how the policy was to be implemented, Congress left the DHEW, the DOT, and the local transit operators vulnerable to conflicts over both the symbols and the reality of the policy's implementation.

Implementation Requirement 2: Resource Sufficiency

Policy cannot be implemented with good intentions alone. Each implementation effort requires a unique set of facilities, skills, information, and technology. For any given level of goal achievement, a corresponding level of resources must be supplied. Homeless people cannot be housed permanently without adequate low-cost housing, nor can air traffic move safely when sufficient airport space is lacking. Cleaning up a toxic waste dump requires state-of-the-art knowledge of the chemicals' effects and technology for rendering them harmless. And each step in turn demands a given sum of money, the basic resource needed to procure nearly all the other resources.

Resource selection is a challenge to both policymakers and administrators. The former must foresee what will be required to meet their expectations when designing the program. Their natural temptation is to set high expectations before confronting the hard realities of costs. Their budgets define that supply of available funds, and they must make difficult tradeoffs in selecting what resources will be indispensable for the program's success.

Initiating Funding   Administrators play a dual role in the funding process. First, they make the initial requests for funds that the lawmakers consider, as Chapter 12 described. "The bureaucracy is hardly the passive agent of its congressional overseer; . . . it is constantly working to manipulate its master so as to achieve mutually profitable arrangements" (Wilson, 1989, p. 251). These proposals are often carefully designed to win support from key members, supplying benefits to their states or districts, and fitting their program priorities. In this process resource allocation occurs at the very heart of political conflict and coalition building. Federal and state highways, water facilities, and parks, with their benefits to specific political subdivisions, have long been allocated by such bargaining.

Allocating Resources   After enactment of the budget, administrators play the second role of preparing detailed plans for deploying their resources. There must be corresponding "budgets" for all other necessities likely to be in short supply: people with needed talents, specialized information, building space, and even the time for thinking and conferring among the program managers. For innovative programs the resource needs can be hard to foresee. Much of what government is called upon to do in implementing public policy has not been done before, and the pioneer's role is always risky. Most often the ability to innovate is acquired during the implementation through making mistakes and learning from them. Successful resource planning depends on foresight that may grow only gradually. If, at a certain step in policymaking and planning, means fall out of step with goals, planners must be quick to reconcile the two.

Those who advocated the equal accessibility approach in resolving the dilemma for the disabled seemed to give little thought to costs. Indeed, they did not have direct responsibility for raising or allocating those funds. The cost burden fell most heavily on mass transit system operators and the state and local governments that financed them, and officials at those levels sought the least expensive way to provide adequate service. Already faced with demands to serve mostly low-income people, to reduce traffic congestion and oil consumption, and to give fare breaks to students and the elderly, these officials had stretched their available funds too far.

An essential technological solution for providing equal accessibility for the disabled was a bus that would accommodate wheelchairs and that could be produced in large enough volume to replace existing vehicles within a decade. In 1972 the DOT drew up specifications for an all-purpose vehicle to bring the newest technology to city streets and contracted with three companies to produce prototypes of the bus for testing. After Section 504 was enacted in 1973, the DOT added the wheelchair access standard and named the yet-unborn vehicle *Transbus*. If successful, it would have brought the policy goal of equal accessibility closer to realization. But it proved to be technically difficult to design a low-floor bus with a wheelchair lift that was also reliable and economical. In 1979, after research and experimentation with prototypes, the *Transbus* project died a quiet death. Claiming that they could not meet the cost and performance specifications, all American bus firms declined to bid on it.

A few years later, however, once companies had time to develop the technology and find markets, a bus with a wheelchair lift became available, although at high cost. By 1988 many major cities had such buses and thousands of new ones were on order. Local chapters of Americans Disabled for Accessible Public Transportation (ADAPT) exerted strong pressure on transit agencies to acquire the buses. Federal funds covered most of the cost of installing the lift, which made the change easier.

Implementation Requirement 3: Orchestration of Effort

We can embellish upon Bardach's (1977) machine model with yet another concept, that administration is like a concert by a large orchestra. It has three essential elements: agreement by the musicians to play Beethoven's Fifth Symphony and not a work by Bach or Bartok; effective communication of the score and of each artist's part in it; and the coordination of each person's performance precisely according to the score. This is the **system perspective**, envisioning a network of interdependent parts whose actions must support one another for the policy to succeed. We have already seen that nearly all public policies involve two or more government agencies, often at least one from each level—federal, state, and local—and frequently from private organizations as well.

Many minds and hands are involved in making public policy work.

> No one, in the sense of a single institution or small, coordinated set of actors, is in charge of the implementation of domestic programs in the United States. In a very real sense, there is no single government in the United States to promote, oversee, or conduct implementation.... Rather, there are many governments and, in some cases, government is often undistinguishable from nongovernment. (Ripley & Franklin, 1986, p. 3)

In general, an agency that must share with others the administration of a program can take one of three stances: (1) It can cooperate fully with them based on agreement on the exact ends and means of implementation; (2) it can resist sharing, with the lowest input of joint effort that is legally required; (3) it can try to dominate the program or steer it in a direction different from what the other agencies prefer (Heymann, 1987, p. 100). An example of resistance occurred in El Paso, Texas, where federal, state, and local law enforcement agencies have conflicting jurisdictions over traffic across the border with Mexico. State and county police did not assist the surveillance efforts of the U.S. Drug Enforcement Administration (DEA), and mutual hostility kept the DEA from cooperating with the U.S. Customs Service. However, when there is cooperation, it is usually due to informal understandings between individual administrators, which can end when personnel change (Carter, 1980).

Communication and Cooperation The communication stream must reach to every agency to convey the whole sense of a policy and any procedures and regulations added along the way. Communication must be precise enough to explain how the new policy directives relate to what is already going on, what changes it will and will not require in administrators' conduct, and what new standards administrators are to follow. For those administrators with wide discretion, it must also define the limits within which they operate. Both the text of the Americans with Disabilities Act and the federal rules that implement it affect public and private facilities very broadly. A major effort was required to acquaint millions of people, including the disabled themselves, with those requirements, and a great deal of ignorance and misunderstanding remained 5 years after the act's passage.

Orchestration implies agreement. When administrators are well disposed to the policy and its procedures, they are more likely to carry it out conscientiously and cooperate with one another when joint action is required. This applies to whole agencies and departments, which can block policy in the absence of such dispositions.

The typical public agency has many tasks to fulfill, and some inevitably take a higher priority than others. Those that best fit the dispositions of its leadership will get the most attention.

Such agreement is vital at all levels of the public organization and those agencies that cooperate with it. In programs that regulate or serve the public directly, contact personnel—the "street-level bureaucrats" (Lipsky, 1979)—constitute the difference between success and failure. As mentioned earlier, these include police officers, public school teachers, social workers, and health professionals, all of whom work away from direct supervision by their managers but who make decisions that can deeply affect the lives of their clients. A driver of a municipal bus equipped with a wheelchair lift can make a trip comfortable or unpleasant for a person with a disability simply by a friendly attitude or a careless manner of driving.

Delivery of social services (as distinct from money) to the needy requires dedicated personnel who will "go the extra mile" when needed. This occurred in a modestly successful program in Louisville, Kentucky, for placing homeless people in jobs. In one instance the staff of the company employing a recovering drug addict looked for him immediately after he quit work and began to fall back into his drug habit; through their efforts he returned to his position (Kilborn, 1990). Difficult social problems affecting those with physical or emotional disabilities often require efforts that go beyond the formally mandated procedures. One-to-one relationships can easily make or break programs that aim to help these people.

Authority Leakage When administrators' dispositions do not support a policy, it becomes harder to implement. As noted in Chapter 3, conflicting goals or styles of operation can lead to authority leakage, which is the failure of subordinates to carry out directives from above. Although some distortion of orders is unavoidable in large organizations, it reaches major proportions when there is lack of interest in, or active opposition to, the policy in question. The agency's top management may lack the time, information, or sense of urgency to deal effectively with this leakage. Career personnel, because of their long tenure and experience, may disagree with elected executives and political appointees. Authority is even more likely to "leak" when national, state, and local agencies share responsibility. For example, a transit administrator under orders to cut the costs of a money-losing bus network has every incentive to avoid purchasing expensive new buses that will accommodate people with disabilities.

Games Administrators Play Hindering actions by those within the administering agencies often take the form of "games" (Bardach, 1977). In one kind of game administrators divert resources to benefit individual or group purposes not authorized in the policy, as when a private group secures a government grant to fulfill an official purpose but diverts the money elsewhere and devotes little or none to the official purpose. In a second game, the agency is deflected from its goal, often when it is assigned too many tasks for its capacity, and it simply jettisons those that are hardest to implement or least popular with the staff.

A third kind of game is played when massive outside resistance to the policy overwhelms an agency's ability to enforce the policy and punish those who do not comply. For example, many employers have hired illegal immigrants, in violation of federal law. The number of these illegal residents is so great that the Immigration and Naturalization Service (INS) cannot investigate even a major fraction of them. INS then faces the dilemma of how heavy-handed to be in imposing compliance on violating companies.

Last are dissipation-of-energies games. These occur, for example, when several organizations sharing responsibility seek to evade unwanted tasks or avoid blame for an impending failure by shifting the focus of effort or attention and wearing down the original momentum. A dissipation-of-energy game was played when the toxic waste stew was discovered at Love Canal in Niagara Falls, New York, in the 1970s (recall this issue from Chapter 8). Neither the local nor state government wanted the responsibility of cleaning it up. Government officials do not typically set out to play games rather than carry out their duties, but they have conflicting incentives that shape how they act in situations that call for individual judgments.

Orchestration problems abounded in the "effective mobility for the disabled" issue. Although there was no blatant occurrence of authority leakage, the agencies did engage in a variety of games to maximize their own missions. For instance, the Urban Mass Transit Administration's close orientation to local mass transit agencies and its mission to serve many groups, not just the disabled, clashed with the broader enforcement mandate given to the DHEW's Office of Civil Rights. Neither was "right" or "wrong" per se, but resolution of this conflict cost a great deal of time and frustrated both the disabled and the transit operators.

Corruption   Outright lawbreaking by public officials may be relatively rare but can be devastating to a program. Agencies ranging from the U.S. Customs Service and the Federal Bureau of Investigation to county and city law enforcement departments are plagued by huge bribes offered to their agents by drug dealers. Such a generous payoff can induce an officer to overlook a cocaine shipment, an intentional nonaction that would be hard to detect. Naturally, when such corruption is widespread within public agencies, it erodes citizen confidence in government as well as officials' trust in their own colleagues.

Orchestration of Innovation In general, orchestration is hardest when an agency is required to implement an innovative policy or adopt new methods. "All organizations by design are enemies of change, at least up to a point; government organizations are especially risk averse because they are caught up in a web of constraints so complex that any change is likely to rouse the ire of some important constituency" (Wilson, 1989, p. 69). The DOT did not oppose accommodation of disabled riders in its mass transit policies, but since they weren't among its influential constituents, it did not immediately respond to their demands. Just as orchestras need to practice a new composition before performing it publicly, agencies need time to adapt their procedures and relationships to new tasks.

Implementation Requirement 4: Political and Legal Support

The political and legal environment of administration shapes program outputs and results. This environment consists of influential people and groups inside and outside of government that can determine the degree of a program's success. This cluster varies with each policy area and may change over time. Box 13.5 describes several environmental factors that hinder efforts to increase employment of disabled people.

Opposition from Government and the Private Sector First, implementation of a new policy can be stymied or redirected by opposition from influential forces within government or in the private sector. For example, a law may have passed the legislative body by a narrow margin, or it may have been vetoed and the veto may have been overridden. The losing side in such a conflict may then transfer its opposition to the administrative arena and find allies there. Naturally, the winners seek to protect their gains and attract supporters from among the new policy's beneficiaries. The result is a political contest that resembles the legislative struggle. Intense lobbying often takes place as the opposing sides bring their political artillery to bear: informed arguments, publicity, and pressure from the chief executive, key legislators, and influential constituents. Groups that are well organized and that gain access to officials at high levels are more likely to win such administrative battles.

As we saw, the rule makers in the Urban Mass Transit Administration (UMTA) were hard-pressed by the advocates of the two rival concepts of mobility. Local mass transit operators and many elderly people argued for the effective mobility approach, whereas disabled people, including Vietnam War veterans, rejected what they considered to be segregated transit in favor of the full accessibility concept. Many local government officials opposed all federal stipulations on how to organize their transit services. Not wanting to alienate any of these important constituencies, the UMTA avoided taking

Box 13.5

Jobs for the Disabled: Why Aren't More Working?

A prime intended outcome of the Americans with Disabilities Act (and, indeed, of promoting mobility) is to increase employment opportunities for the disabled. Employers must make reasonable accommodation for otherwise qualified people who are confined to wheelchairs or have other physical limitations. However, two recent studies have revealed that the proportion of those who are defined as disabled and are in the workforce has actually declined. Whereas 33 percent of people with disabilities aged 16 to 64 were employed full or part time in 1986, 31 percent were so employed in 1994.

There are many reasons for the decline. Employers continue to be prejudiced against the disabled and are concerned about the costs of providing access; moreover, they are reluctant to add disabled people to their health insurance coverage, which may lead to higher premiums.

Some observers claim that many disabled people live in a "culture of dependency" and lack the confidence to compete for a job and adjust to unfamiliar conditions.

Perhaps more important is disabled people's reluctance to give up benefits they are already receiving. Two federal programs, Supplemental Security Income and Social Security Disability Income, provided $54 billion to the disabled in fiscal year 1994, and some states add to that aid. The rules governing these benefits are complex, and recipients and job counselors often don't understand them (Holmes, 1994). Taking a job may well mean the loss of monthly checks. This is an example of how one government program, meeting legitimate needs, can hamper the implementation of another. Such findings call for further careful study and revisions.

quick action. This problem of reconciling conflicting interests was complicated by the Department of Health, Education, and Welfare. For good reasons Congress defined this matter as affecting DHEW's civil rights responsibilities as well as the DOT's mass transportation arena. Although both departments had the will to act, they were subject to very different political influences.

Legal Challenges   Policy implementation can be further hindered or altered by legal challenges and adverse court decisions. These are usually initiated by opponents of the legislative or administrative decision that spawned the policy. The last resort for a person or group on the losing side of a conflict is a civil suit in which the complaint may range from improper procedures followed in the rule making to unconstitutionality of the policy itself. The case is first tried in the lowest federal or state trial court, depending on which level of law the charge relates to. The loser of that verdict may appeal to a federal or state appeals court, which either upholds or reverses the first ruling. A very few cases reach the U.S. Supreme Court, which accepts only those of broadest significance. If that body declines to hear the appeal, the decision rendered by the previous court is ordinarily final. A higher court may also call for a new trial to reconsider the case within altered guidelines. Since judicial proceedings can take several years in complex cases, implementation of a policy in litigation is often held up until all suits are settled.

The federal courts played a vital part in the efforts to provide transportation for people with disabilities. Their role was to interpret what Congress meant in the several applicable laws and to decide whether the actions taken by the DOT and the DHEW met that intent. Advocates for the disabled filed the first suits in the early 1970s, as they sought prompt and vigorous enforcement of Section 504 of the Rehabilitation Act of 1973, discussed earlier. They sought injunctions prohibiting local mass transit agencies from acquiring any equipment that did not meet the full accessibility standard. The DOT responded that it was meeting its legal obligations by promoting a variety of local mass transit services that met all needs of disabled people. This defense enabled it to win most of the first round of lawsuits. But a series of later decisions revealed that the judiciary was as uncertain about how to interpret the statutes as were the administrators. Later the federal courts rejected the full accessibility concept in favor of effective mobility but refused to resolve disputes about the means of providing transportation. Judges, being generalists, lack expertise in technical issues and try to avoid giving detailed orders regarding such matters. But in February 1989, a federal appeals court ordered the DOT to require all mass transit authorities to equip new buses with wheelchair lifts. This action settled a suit filed by Americans Disabled for Accessible Public Transportation that had claimed that sufficient progress was not being made.

The courts played an ambivalent role in this controversy, being "less the eager participant than an instrument used by all sides—the disabled and the transit industry—to secure desired ends. The courts have strengthened one side, then the other, and in so doing have affected the competing factions within the bureaucracy" (Katzmann, 1986, p. 14). When different state or federal district courts render inconsistent decisions on an issue, this not only increases the administrators' uncertainty but invites further litigation and causes more delay.

Support from Program Clients A third category of essential political support is that of the program's clients themselves. A policy for providing a service assumes that people want it enough to comply with the conditions necessary to receive it. In the 1988 Family Support Act, Congress mandated sweeping reform of the welfare system, notably requiring aid recipients to participate in work or training programs (recall the opening story of Chapter 4). To qualify for the maximum federal assistance, states had to enroll at least 7

Box 13.6

Can We Make Driving Safer?

Scholars and journalists alike prefer to write about the failures of government rather than its successes. However, both are necessary to grasp the dynamics of implementation. A notable success is the steady improvement in highway safety. The death rate in car and truck accidents per 100 million miles traveled dropped from 2.8 in 1982 to 1.8 in 1992. There are two ways to improve safety—improved equipment and highways and more careful driving. Both approaches have succeeded. Vehicles are safer and new highways are better engineered. Moreover, fewer people are driving while intoxicated and more are complying with state laws requiring safety belts and child seats. New equipment regulations will soon go into effect that mandate air bags, antilock braking systems, stronger roofs, and seats for children between the ages of 5 and 8.

This encouraging picture poses a dilemma for students of implementation: How much safer can we expect to make road travel? We can reasonably expect the death rate to approach 1.0 by the turn of the century, when many vehicles will have the new equipment. But what is necessary to reduce it further, how expensive will it be, and how will the driving public accept it? Public policy choices entail some judgment of what can be made to work, not only in a technical sense but also in a social and political sense. When safety depends on the choices of individuals acting alone behind their steering wheels, it is tied to the immeasurable margin of human fallibility.

---

percent of their welfare caseloads in these programs by fiscal year 1990, which had to increase to 20 percent in 5 years. Local communities running the programs had to ensure that the jobs, schooling, and child care were available. Nevertheless, the ultimate success of such efforts depends on the diligence with which clients enroll in and use the opportunities provided them (Kosterlitz, 1989). A sensitive combination of "carrots" (such as financial incentives) and "sticks" (legal regulation with a penalty for noncompliance) is necessary to motivate clients. Box 13.6 shows how such a combination has been applied to increase highway safety, as well as the likely limits to its success.

When a program imposes limits or prohibitions on clients, their voluntary compliance is especially crucial. Public programs presume widespread and willing cooperation, whether in paying income taxes, observing speed limits, or maintaining restaurant sanitation. Government is not in a position to monitor mass behavior continuously. Compliance depends on five basic factors: sufficient communication of the policy to the public, personal ability (physical or financial) to comply with it, agreement with the policy itself and its importance, acceptance of the actions necessary to comply, and the belief that the government has the authority to compel compliance (Coombs, 1980). Thus, government must create the conditions and incentives that secure this compliance, even from those who would profit from noncompliance.

Implementation Requirement 5: A Supportive Socioeconomic Environment

A final category of requirements for policy success lies in the social and economic conditions not under the control of the policy or even of government in general. Lawmakers formulate a policy to fit an assumed context, the "ecology" of administration (Gaus, 1947). They may simply project their present circumstances into the future or draw upon well-researched forecasts of changed conditions. The policy is designed to change some aspect of that expected future, yet it depends on other crucial factors staying the same. A job training program aims to prepare students for skills that are expected to be in demand, but a recession or a major plant closing in the community can frustrate that effort. The policy can thus fail solely because of an unanticipated change in the environment.

The first policy statements on mass transportation for the disabled fit the political ethos of the 1970s well. Seen as an advancement of both civil rights and urban mass transit, the issue was attractive in a period of growing federal aid to state and local governments and decreasing Vietnam War expenditures. By the early 1980s, however, after a variety of local mass transit services for the disabled had been established and governments in general were cutting back on discretionary services, the policy's goals had been achieved as far as most believed practical. Even so, the political strength of people with disabilities grew, which was reflected very decisively in the Americans with Disabilities Act.

Many factors not under government's control can promote or hinder the success of a public policy. Public opinion of people with disabilities has become much more favorable and has facilitated their increased access to jobs, housing, and education as well as mass transportation. New technologies have helped those with visual and hearing impairments to succeed in careers that were once closed to them. Equal rights for such people has thereby acquired more legal significance. Yet a recession may cause employers to lay off the disabled first and close doors to other employment, thereby making their access to public transit less meaningful.

Problem Succession and Government Learning

What is the most that governments can expect when they implement policy? What expectations can citizens hold of their governments' efforts? It depends on what view one holds of the entire enterprise of making policy work. Recall the idealistic, legalistic, responsive, and experimental perspectives discussed earlier in this chapter. Each entails a distinctive way of answering these questions.

The first portrays very high expectations: to "solve" the problem in a comprehensive, long-term manner. No performance short of this goal will suffice. Congressional action in 1970 mandated accessibility to mass transit services as a right. This implied that government was obligated to take comprehensive steps to guarantee it to those who otherwise would be unable to travel on a city bus or a subway. Thus, to the extent that disabled people continue to lack this promised mobility because of inadequate government action, the implementation has failed.

The legalistic perspective is no less demanding. The language of the policy sets forth what government's obligations are. They may or may not be adequate to solve the problem, but this is not the central consideration. If Section 504 had stated clearly that the effective mobility concept would guide all efforts, and if local agencies had provided special transit services designed for the disabled, they would have implemented the law. Even if those services failed to meet the unique needs of some or were not extended to all, implementation would have succeeded by this standard. What weakens the legalistic approach is the failure, already noted, to state the standards clearly enough to guide the administrators. When the exact solution is unknown or not agreed upon, legal statements will lack precision.

The third and fourth perspectives are more useful in judging the implementation of nonroutine programs such as expanding services to the disabled. The responsive method relies on clients and constituents not only to influence the policies but also to interpret them while they are being administered. What are the rights of a disabled person? Congress in 1970 mandated only the general principle, but groups like the Paralyzed Veterans of America and the American Coalition of Citizens with Disabilities claimed the prerogative to define their rights in practical detail (Katzmann, 1986, p. 110). A successful implementation strategy is thus one that is accepted by the various interest groups with a stake in the policy.

The experimental perspective is also useful in view of the struggle to develop the *Transbus* and the plethora of arrangements in local communities to provide effective mobility with available resources. No one could have stated in 1973 whether such a bus would be available; that had to be learned. Few communities had experience in organizing systematic mass transit service for their disabled residents, but between the federal grants and political pressures, they learned how. Success, by this perspective, is measured by how much constructive learning took place and how services improved as a result. The current availability of a variety of service programs and vehicles for disabled people supports a positive judgment.

All policies are linked with others, and success in one may lead to success or failure in another. At the very least, policies create new demands for services and actions, which government often must respond to. Since people confined to wheelchairs can get around the city at will, they have pressed for (and received) more recreational programs, continuing education opportunities, and employment training. There may be no logical limits to such expansion of services, but lawmakers must fall back on political and financial criteria for funding some and restricting others.

Summary

Implementation is the process of making public policy work, of achieving the purposes for which it was made. No two policies are ever implemented identically, nor is it usually possible to predict how a given process will go. It is always necessary to anticipate the details of implementation at the beginning of the program and to be ready to learn from experience and to adjust the program accordingly. An output is the immediate good or service provided by a program, an outcome is its intermediate-range result, and an impact is a long-term consequence of the policy in combination with others that affect the targeted situation. The exact meaning of implementation is open to dispute. The idealistic, legalistic, responsive, and experimental perspectives offer varying ways to view it. Success of a program may be defined as the elimination, recession, or succession of the targeted problem. Exacerbation of the problem is a clear signal of program failure.

Proper implementation depends on several basic requirements, which administrators must take care to plan for. These include a clear and correct policy translation into action, sufficient resources to accomplish the goals, orchestration of all participants, political and legal backing for the necessary action, and a supportive socio-economic environment.

Discussion Questions

1. How differently would opportunities for people with disabilities have developed if Congress had specifically included the disabled in the civil rights legislation it passed in the 1960s, equating them with people of color?

2. Why is it possible to define success and failure of public policies so differently? What are the political consequences of this ambiguity in defining these terms?

3. What tactics must agency heads use to orchestrate shared programs? How can

they secure needed cooperation from key executives and agencies and avoid conflict?

4. How can an administrator maintain political and legal support for a controversial or expensive program once it is in operation?

5. How can government learning best be promoted? How should what is learned be analyzed and publicized?

Analytical Exercises

1. The Americans with Disabilities Act is having many effects on public and private facilities and employment. Interview a person in a public school or library, factory, major retail store, or other large facility used by the public to learn the changes required by this act and the resulting rules. Learn as much as you can about the costs of complying with them, the time required to do so, and the amount of discretion allowed in choosing the means. Draw a conclusion about how prompt and thorough compliance is likely to be.

2. Congress passed a major bill in 1994 to combat crime. Among other provisions, it supplied funds to enable local governments to hire more police officers. In addition, many states have recently toughened the penalties for crime with longer prison terms. Study the outputs and outcomes of this effort in your local communities, perhaps by interviewing police and corrections officials and examining statistics on crime rates, arrests, prison population, and similar figures. Infer from your findings how successful this policy is.

For Further Reading

Bardach, E. (1977). *The Implementation Game: What Happens after a Bill Becomes Law.* Cambridge, MA: MIT Press. Exploration of the many impediments to policy implementation that can arise, using the example of mental health reform in California.

Katzmann, R. A. (1986). *Institutional Disability: The Saga of Transportation for the Disabled.* Washington, DC: Brookings Institution. The source of the controversy highlighted in this chapter.

Levin, M. A., & Ferman, B. (1985). *The Political Hand: Policy Implementation and Youth Employment Programs.* New York: Pergamon. Useful because it surveys successful programs for training and placing unemployed youth in jobs and identifies why the programs were successful.

Percy, S. L. (1990). *Disability, Civil Rights, and Public Policy: The Politics of Implementation.* Tuscaloosa: University of Alabama Press. Analyzes the origins and implementation of broad programs to aid people with disabilities.

Pressman, J. L., & Wildavsky, A. (1979). *Implementation.* (2nd ed.). Berkeley: University of California Press. One of the best studies of nonimplementation of policy, this book explores why economic development programs in Oakland fell far short of expectations.

Salamon, L. M. (Ed.). (1989). *Beyond Privatization: The Tools of Government Action.* Washington, DC: Urban Institute Press. Surveys the many means by which governments can implement policy and the criteria by which one can be selected over others.

14

Evaluating Public Policies and Programs

Learning Objectives

After reading this chapter, you should be able to do the following:

1. Define and state the benefits of evaluating policies and their implementation.
2. Identify the several approaches to evaluation and the types of policies and circumstances for which each is appropriate.
3. Identify the several standards used in evaluation: effectiveness, efficiency, legality, responsiveness, technical criteria, political criteria, and equity.
4. Trace the customary procedures for conducting an evaluation.
5. Recognize the obstacles and misunderstandings that can hinder evaluation.

Few federal programs have aroused as much controversy as the Superfund effort to clean up abandoned hazardous waste sites. With cost estimates to government and private parties ranging up to $100 billion, hard questions are being asked about whether the results have been worth that sum. Asking these questions are business representatives, environmentalists, state and federal officials, and members of Congress. The fate of Superfund hangs on who gives which answers.

Superfund was born in 1980, when Congress passed the Comprehensive Environmental Response, Compensation, and Liability Act, which was designed to attack the problem of inactive sites in which hazardous wastes had been dumped in the past but for which no one owner was currently responsible. Once a site was identified, it was to be cleaned up, either by the parties that had originally deposited the wastes or by the federal government. In the latter case, costs were to be covered either by the liable parties (of which there could be hundreds) or by the Superfund itself, a revolving fund financed by several sources, including taxes on chemicals and petroleum. Not only is the law complex, but the procedures developed by the Environmental Protection Agency (EPA) mandated lengthy studies of the sites, the necessary remedial action, and the sources of the waste.

In the first 12 years of Superfund's existence, the federal government spent $7.7 billion on cleanup efforts and business paid out $6.3 billion more. By January 1993 only 56 sites had been completely cleaned up, although some work had been done on 217 more sites. However, 1,289 locations had been identified as high-priority problems. Of the costs, nearly $3 billion went to legal fees, since considerable litigation was necessary to determine liability for the wastes (Feldmann, 1994).

Such a complex program has no lack of evaluators, nearly all of whom are critical. Church and Nakamura (1993) did a scholarly assessment of six specific site cleanups to examine the strategies used and their degree of success. They found that the EPA used three different strategies: *coercion,* in which it prosecuted vigorously the responsible parties to secure action or payment; *accommodation,* by which the EPA and the polluters reached agreement by negotiation; and the *public works* approach of cleaning the site quickly by the agency's own actions. Although the results were complex, the analysts observed that each strategy was workable for some kinds of situations but not for others. A most important lesson was that the agency had to choose the appropriate tool for each and be willing to change the strategy if necessary.

The Learning and Planning Process

The challenges to public policy never stop coming, and those who design and implement policies can never stop learning. Evaluation is the central process in this learning: identifying and measuring the outcomes and impacts of a policy and judging whether and how well its objectives were (or are being) met. Recall the distinction made in Chapter 13 among outputs, outcomes, and impacts: An output is the immediate good or service provided by a program; an outcome is the intermediate result of the policy for its targeted area; and the impact is the policy's broad and long-term consequence for society. Careful study of the last two of these concepts requires one to state not just what happened and whether the policy was, in fact, implemented, but also how the process and results conformed to accepted standards. Outcomes and impacts are measurements of value, ultimately rooted in the public purposes outlined in Chapter 1.

Sound analysis of policy implementation is the best means that governments have for improving both their policies and their methods. It is the last step in the policy cycle described in Chapter 5, the transition that leads to a new cycle of problem definitions, objectives, and alternatives. Thus, the evaluator is an essential participant in the policymaking process, looking forward to what could be done and backward to what has (or has not) been done. However, this potential for learning is not often fulfilled, for reasons to be discussed.

The Procedural Benefits of Evaluation

Evaluation done with intent to use what is learned can have several benefits. First, it is an essential part of the communication flow that enables elected executives, legislators, and the general public to hold administrators accountable for their actions. The Superfund's funding expired in October 1995, and its future depends on the results to that date as measured by the evaluators who are politically significant to Congress and the administration.

Second, evaluation enables administrators to change programs and outputs and to reorganize agencies when necessary. Governments must continually adapt their means of implementation to changing objectives and environments. The U.S. Department of Labor began in 1978 to fund local projects to generate jobs and train unemployed youth under the Youth Employment and Demonstration Projects Act. By that time there was experience with previous employment programs that had failed to achieve their objectives, and this program was designed to avoid such failure. Levin and Ferman (1985) studied nine of these programs and learned that they had worked quite well. More important, they learned why: The program operators had continuously corrected problems as they appeared. These local executives came to realize that their timely and sensitive intervention was crucial to bringing about a harmony of interests between the trainers and the would-be employers and to provide the incentives to all trainees to adapt their behavior to the program goals.

Third, evaluation benefits program design and budgeting. By seeing how each element of past programs worked in combination and how outside factors influenced them, it is possible to plan for the full range of conditions that will shape the success of future efforts. Often planners conceive of a program too narrowly and are unprepared to recognize and avoid the many contingencies that could defeat their efforts. A training program for unemployed youths may have disappointing results if planners have not prepared to deal with factors commonly influencing disadvantaged youth (such as substance abuse; in this instance, proper preparation would include adding counseling and rehabilitation and altering funding priorities to target such hindrances).

Sensitive evaluation can also contribute to the problem definition and goal-setting stages. It is tempting to blame youth unemployment simply on the lack of job skills or motivation to work or on
discrimination against minorities. But studies have repeatedly shown
that such people cannot be pigeonholed so easily. Obstacles like
substance abuse are often present, but they may be compounded
by low intelligence, emotional disturbances, illiteracy, a history of
criminal offenses, and physical disabilities. Learning to what extent
these conditions are present should also lead to more realistic (and
perhaps lower) expectations of what a program with a given design
and funding level can accomplish.

The Historical Development of Evaluation

Systematic evaluation came to be a major concern of policy analysts
and implementers only in the 1960s, when governments ventured
deeply into innovative social policies. Economic opportunity, criminal
justice, education, civil rights, and urban development programs were
endowed with billions of dollars and intricate new administrative relationships. As each program got under way, analysts within and outside the agencies sought evidence of how well it was working and
how they could improve it. To their dismay most evaluation studies
showed that the programs did not achieve their expectations. Analysts
also discovered that they did not even know how to identify and measure the most important outcomes, which limited the value of their
work for future policy design (Weiss, 1987).

In the past 20 years, evaluation of public programs has continued along many paths, using a variety of methods. Although analysts have accumulated an impressive stock of data and judgments,
they have often been disappointed in their lack of direct impact on
either the content of policy or its implementation. Yet they continue
to pursue and refine their craft, confident that indirect contributions are also valuable. Both administrators and their clients do well
to develop skills at various types of evaluation so that they can
maintain their vigilance over the programs for which they are responsible or on which they depend.

Approaches to Evaluation

There is no standard model for evaluation; each study must be designed to fit its specific purposes and circumstances. We can contrast the major alternatives along several dimensions (as summarized
in Box 14.1). First, evaluation may be pursued in either an intuitive
or a scientific mode. The former is relatively informal and is guided
largely by impressions and subjective judgments. This intuitive
method of evaluating constantly takes place in many contexts as
administrators and their clients reflect on what they are doing and

Box 14.1

Overview of Approaches to Evaluation

1. **Intuitive**: informal collection of information, relying for guidance on impressions and subjective judgments.

2. **Scientific**: systematic collection and analysis of data, guided by social science theory and the use of statistical methods.

3. **Passive**: relies on sources outside the program administrators to supply opinions and criticisms.

4. **Active**: information collected at the initiative of the evaluators, largely or completely by standards of their choosing.

5. **Narrow**: focuses on one program or segment thereof with intention only of improving it.

6. **Broad**: focuses on widespread program or many related programs, seeking results to apply to many similar efforts.

7. **Summative**: surveys what the program or policy accomplished in factual, measurable terms.

8. **Formative**: evaluates program outcomes and impacts to learn whether and how the program or its process should be designed or operated differently.

9. **Inside**: done by the immediate administrators or others in the agency carrying on the program.

10. **Outside**: done by anyone outside the program agency who has no involvement in its administration.

---

the results of their actions. Although necessarily subjective, this method often detects the needs that more systematic means of evaluation must later address.

Performance Measurement: The Scientific Mode

The scientific mode of evaluation entails the systematic collection and analysis of data, guided by social science theory and using statistical methods. Its results will be more valid than the intuitive mode in cases where the necessary data can be obtained and interpreted with confidence. One form is **performance measurement**, which Hatry (1989, p. 469) defines as the systematic and accurate measurement of the efficiency and effectiveness of programs and organizational performance. It bases judgments on quantification of such disparate factors as street miles paved, hospital mortality rates, student reading-test scores, and solution rates of crimes. The U.S. Bureau of Labor Statistics regularly calculates and publishes productivity indexes for most federal agencies, which are stated as the ratio of physical units of output to the employees' working time.

The Passive/Active Continuum

Second, evaluations can take place on a passive/active continuum. Passive studies rely simply on clients of the program or other observers for opinions and criticisms. Administrators often assume that a program is working well unless evidence exists to the contrary. If complaints increase, the program might require a more systematic look. In active studies, by contrast, evaluators seek data on their own initiative, largely or completely by standards of their own choosing. Volunteered information will be useful at times, but it cannot be the core of a systematic effort. A high dropout rate by those in a job training program clearly signals a problem. Some of the dropouts might willingly register their complaints and tell why they quit, but active evaluation is necessary to learn each person's reasons, particularly those that would not be expressed voluntarily.

Scope: Narrow and Broad Surveys

Third, evaluations can vary according to the scope of the survey. If it is very narrow, the survey might focus on one class of youths in one job training program in one city. It might seek data on who gained employment, for how long, and for what wages. It should also permit a judgment on whether the program made the crucial difference in clients' lives. A broad survey, by contrast, might examine the results of all such programs around the country for a 10-year span and inquire into the successes of tens of thousands of people for a significant segment of their lives. The narrow study is much easier to do and can give rapid feedback to a single program still in process. The broader the study is, the more it can rise above variations in local leadership and economic conditions. But it takes much more time and money, and its results may not be directly useful to any individual program director.

Summative and Formative Approaches

Fourth, evaluation may take a **summative** or a **formative** approach. A summative evaluation surveys what the program accomplished in factual, measurable terms. One might state, for example, that a certain percentage of the graduates of a youth employment program found jobs of specific types and at particular salary levels and that the graduates held them for specified periods of time. Any competent evaluator, given the same data, would arrive at the same conclusion. If some quantitative employment goals had previously been set, one could conclude whether or not they had been achieved.

A formative evaluation, by contrast, requires more judgment on the part of the evaluator, who seeks to learn whether and how the program should be designed or operated differently. It might focus on the outcomes and impacts of an agency or one of its programs: why the programs produced the results they did and whether they met the clients' needs. Or it could concentrate on the process by which the results were produced (e.g., key decisions, delivery

Box 14.2

Was Our Success Hidden, or Did We Really Lose Ground?

Evaluations can be used also to justify or condemn broad policies and programs. Using a variety of statistics, Schwarz (1988) and Murray (1984) each examined the host of social programs that the nation pursued during the decades of 1960 through 1980 to raise living standards of the most disadvantaged of our population. Although they had access to the same data, they came to opposite conclusions: Schwarz termed the endeavors "America's Hidden Success," whereas to Murray the disadvantaged were "Losing Ground."

Murray marshaled his evidence in arguing that "things not only got worse for the poor and disadvantaged . . . , they got much worse than they 'should have gotten' under the social and economic conditions that prevailed in the society at large" (1984, p. 135). For example, every new federal social program during this period held out the hope that it would stabilize families by increasing opportunities for jobs, housing, education, and health. But every measure indicates that family stability declined at a rapid rate despite these programs.

He attributed this worsening to the fact that the social programs gave the poor an incentive to remain poor so that they could continue to collect benefits. This judgment cannot be drawn directly from the data, of course, but it is a logical interpretation to Murray. The "ground was lost" because the programs left the poor worse off than they would have been (given the social and economic trends of the period) if the programs had never been implemented.

On the other hand, Schwarz asserts that these same programs were more successful than the public appears to believe, and certainly more than Murray portrays them. One central indicator is that by the second half of the 1970s, only 4 to 8 percent of the American public remained below the "poverty line," in contrast with 18 percent in 1960. The major difference in their income was in the amounts transferred through federal programs; economic growth in the private sector did not reach most of the very poorest. Furthermore, there were major gains in health, housing, and education statistics, which are also attributable to public programs.

The obvious conclusion from Schwarz's evaluation is that the programs should continue and be expanded if there is to be any hope of further reductions in poverty. Their success is relatively "hidden" because a large number of people continue in poverty, and the news media focus on them rather than on those whom the programs help to succeed. The cutbacks in federal social programs during the 1980s allowed more people to slip into poverty, giving up some of the gains of the earlier period.

Studies of this kind would not be used to evaluate specific administrative efforts; the data do not measure the efficiency or productivity of the U.S. Office of Economic Opportunity or Chicago community action programs. Yet they do suggest what government can and cannot do effectively and so contribute to the ongoing policy debates.

systems, and agency/client interactions). If a program were failing, this method would offer the best chance to learn why and how failures could be corrected during the life of the program. Often outcome and process evaluation are done in tandem, since data from one phase inform the other. Both require attention to the political and social contexts that support or weaken implementation. These assessments can be more controversial than summative evaluations, and equally competent evaluators can start with different assumptions and draw very different conclusions. (An example of data yielding separate conclusions on the nation's welfare programs is discussed in Box 14.2.) Such studies serve administrators best if they also mark out paths for reform.

Inside and Outside Evaluations

The evaluator is also significant to the outcome, for each individual brings a unique perspective. An inside evaluation is done by the immediate administrators or others within the agency, as in the youth employment programs mentioned earlier. Insiders have the advantage of being most familiar with the program and of having direct access to the data, and they have practical need of the results. But there is the obvious risk that they may cover up negative outcomes to avoid criticisms from outside the agency and ultimate program cuts; thus, they may produce an overly favorable report.

Outside evaluations can be done by anyone not involved in the program's administration: legislators, auditors, interest groups, news media, or scholars. Legislative investigation committees are active in this manner when they sense trouble in a program, and they often contract with outside evaluators to gather and analyze data. Such an evaluator may have no need to give a favorable appraisal but could have partisan motives to emphasize negative evidence. Republican congressional committees are understandably tempted to make a Democratic administration look less than ideally run, and vice versa. The 1989–90 investigations by a House committee into the operations of the Department of Housing and Urban Development under the Reagan administration provide a recent example of this. The budget process is an annual opportunity for legislators to conduct evaluations as they contemplate altering an agency's funding level. Auditors also provide evaluations, many of them for financial purposes. The General Accounting Office, a congressional agency, has done many evaluations of federal programs and agencies that have often been critical and have occasionally led to major reforms.

Evaluations can come from outside the permanent machinery of government as well. Temporary commissions are often appointed by presidents, governors, and mayors to investigate problems of major public concern. Although these appointments are politically motivated, some have produced useful analyses and recommendations. Among these was the Gates Commission, whose 1970 report on the military personnel system advocated that the armed forces be made up entirely of volunteers. That proposal was adopted by Congress 3 years later. Box 14.3 provides a capsule summary of the evaluations made in 1988 by the National Council on Public Works Improvement, appointed by President Reagan. This "report card" format was a unique effort to draw public attention to its conclusions.

Box 14.3

Report Card on the Nation's Public Works

Many evaluations of government programs are too detailed for the average citizen to make sense of. The National Council on Public Works Improvement sought instead to give a highly readable "report card" on the nation's efforts to maintain its means of transportation, water supply, and waste management. One might argue that this evaluation errs in the opposite direction: It groups many programs, with varying levels of success, into large categories and assigns a single rating to them. Furthermore, as with a B or C grade in a college course, the criterion of measurement may not be clear, further confusing the public it is meant to enlighten.

Subject Category	Grade	Successes/Recent Changes	Problems/Future Weaknesses
HIGHWAYS	C+	Federal and state gas tax increases have injected new capital into the system. This, along with increased operations and management (O&M) spending, has improved pavement conditions. However, quality of service in terms of congestion is declining.	Spending for system expansion has fallen short of need in high-growth urban and suburban areas. Many roadways and bridges are aging and require major work. Needs of most rural and smaller systems exceed available resources. Highway Trust Fund has a sizeable cash balance.
MASS TRANSIT	C-	Federal capital grants have helped improve quality of service in some areas, but overall productivity of the system has declined significantly. Growth of transit vehicles is double the rate of increase in ridership. Diverting people from cars is increasingly difficult.	Mass transit is overcapitalized in many smaller cities and inadequate in large, older cities. Systems rarely are linked to land-use planning and broader transportation goals. Maintenance has been erratic and inadequate, especially in older cities.
AVIATION	B-	In general, the aviation system has handled rapid increases in demand safely and effectively. However, service has begun to decline in the face of increasing airport and airspace congestion as a result of strong traffic growth. The air traffic control system is currently undergoing a $16 billion modernization.	Congestion is the system's primary problem. Despite recent increases in authorizations, sizeable cash balance remains unspent in the Airport and Airway Trust Fund. The air traffic control system needs substantial upgrading to maintain safety.
WATER RESOURCES	B-	Water Resources Act of 1986 made cost-sharing mandatory for many types of water projects. This change should improve project selection and reduce overall project costs.	Cost-sharing will improve efficiency but also increase local costs of water projects. Poorer communities may find it difficult to finance projects. Implementation is often excessively slow and cumbersome.

Subject Category	Grade	Successes/Recent Changes	Problems/Future Weaknesses
WATER SUPPLY	**B-**	While regional performance varies, water supply stands out as an effective, locally operated program. Strict new standards created by the 1986 Safe Drinking Water Act will require drastic increases in water rates over the next decade.	Many public water systems suffer from pricing below costs, inability to meet purity standards, or source contamination. Storage and distribution systems are deteriorating in some older cities, and supplies are limited in some parts of the West and several cities along the East Coast.
WASTEWATER	**C-**	Over 75 percent of U.S. population is served by secondary treatment plants. Shift from federal grants to state revolving loans may improve efficiency of plant construction. Broadened focus on nonpoint source pollution and groundwater contamination may accelerate progress toward cleaner water.	Despite $44 billion federal investment in sewage treatment since 1972, water quality has not improved significantly. This is due in part to uncontrolled sources of pollution, such as runoff from farmland and roadways. Overall productivity of secondary treatment facilities is declining, resulting in an increase in water quality violations.
SOLID WASTE	**C-**	Testing and monitoring of solid waste facilities are more rigorous as a result of tougher environmental standards. Waste-to-energy technology is growing as alternative to landfills. More aggressive waste reduction, separation, and recycling efforts are beginning at the local level. However, few states have moved boldly on these measures.	Nation faces significant costs of adequate and safe facilities. Limited data suggest trends toward fewer but safer landfills, rapid growth in resource recovery, and little progress toward waste reduction. Public opposition to siting all types of facilities is a major problem.
HAZARDOUS WASTE	**D-**	Funding for site cleanup has increased fivefold since 1986, but progress has been slower than expected. Only a small fraction of the 2 tons of waste per capita produced in America each year is being treated safely. Major challenge is still ahead of us.	Nation has forfeited much of its opportunity to reduce waste before it is produced. Waste control legislation promotes "end-of-pipe" rather than source reduction solutions. Congressional mandates and schedules may be overly optimistic, given administrative resources. A massive backlog of poisons and needed cleanup projects faces the nation.

Source: National Council on Public Works Improvement, *Fragile Foundations: A Report on America's Public Works* (p. 6), 1988, Washington, DC: U.S. Government Printing Office.

Many federal and state agencies commission studies by private consultants who have expertise in the field in which the program operates. The Manpower Demonstration Research Corporation is well known for its formative evaluations of employment programs in several states, and its findings are carefully studied in the current wave of welfare reform efforts. Such professional consulting has developed into a major growth industry that consumes hundreds of millions of dollars in public funds each year.

The clients of many programs and the interest groups that represent them constantly assess, from their individual perspectives, the programs that benefit or regulate them. The Sierra Club and the chemical industry have both evaluated the national government's pollution control programs, but no one would mistake the report of one group for that of the other. Although members of the public provide important perspectives, they too have obvious biases. Policymakers and administrators are well aware of such views and usually give more credence to those that support their own positions.

Scholars, journalists, and researchers have made useful independent evaluations. These include a dissertation by a graduate student on a city housing program, a story by a reporter looking into a highway construction scandal, and an examination by a professional writer of the regulation of the pharmaceutical industry. Church and Nakamura, who did the study of Superfund cited at the opening of this chapter, are university political scientists. The reputations of these people depend on the quality of their work as judged by the criteria of their disciplines or peers. Their conclusions also can reflect their own values: A politically liberal scholar is likely to evaluate a social welfare program differently than one with conservative views, and each may select different evidence as most relevant to his or her conclusions. Reporters and their editors are tempted to sensationalize their findings to gain readers or viewers. Users of these evaluations must therefore not automatically take them as paragons of objectivity.

Timing

It is also necessary to decide when to evaluate a given program. It is common to conduct formative studies while a program is under way to permit midstream adjustments. Yet these studies have the disadvantage of not being able to identify long-range outcomes and impacts that could lead to conclusions different from those of a short-range study. If the real evaluation is left to the end of a program, there is no possibility of correcting it, although the knowledge gained can benefit similar programs in the future.

The choice of evaluator and type of study must depend on the study's main objective. If the goal is to find and correct ongoing problems in a program, there is an advantage to research done close

Box 1.3

The Essential Tools of Implementation

Examples:

1. Cash payments to individuals

Pensions to retired and disabled persons
Support to low-income and unemployed
Subsidies to farmers
Home rental subsidies
Below-market-rate home and business loans
Food stamps (cash equivalents)

2. Construction and maintenance of infrastructures

Airports, harbors, highways, and streets
Mass transit facilities
Water and waste treatment facilities
Public schools, hospitals, prisons
Museums, libraries, sports facilities
Military bases and weapons

3. Provision of services

Teaching and counseling
Medical and nursing care
Delivering mail
Public transportation
Research and information distribution
Mediating and resolving conflicts
Promoting economic development

4. Regulation of individual and corporate behavior

Criminal apprehension and prosecution
Restricting use of harmful chemicals
Standards for professional practice
Land-use zoning and building controls
Controls on wages and workplace safety
Controls on financial transactions

5. Maintaining capacity to govern

Collecting taxes and fees
Maintaining own facilities
Internal spending controls
Hiring and managing personnel
Planning and decision making
Communication within government and to public
International diplomacy

Box 1.1

The Essential Public Purposes

Examples:

1. Protect lives, property, and rights of citizens.

   National defense
   Antidiscrimination regulations
   Public health and disease control
   Police and fire protection
   Workplace safety regulation

2. Maintain/ensure supply of essential resources.

   Protection of oil imports
   Emergency food supplies
   Energy aid for poor
   Water supply

3. Support persons unable to care for themselves.

   Pensions for retired persons
   Homes/therapy for disabled
   Foster homes for children
   Unemployment compensation

4. Promote steady and balanced economic growth.

   Interest rate regulation
   Financing for new businesses
   Stimuli to international trade
   Employment skills training
   Transportation facilities
   Labor/management negotiations

5. Promote quality of life and personal opportunity to succeed.

   Education, early childhood to adult
   Housing assistance
   Cultural amenities
   Recreational facilities

6. Protect natural environment.

   Conservation of soil and water resources
   Wildlife protection
   Pollution control
   Wastes management

7. Promote scientific and technological advancement.

   Subsidies to scientific research
   Space exploration
   Patents for inventions
   Information dissemination

Box 14.4

Standards for Evaluation of a Policy

1. **Effectiveness**: fulfillment of the program goals, the extent to which the policies are achieving the intended benefits.

2. **Efficiency**: the margin of benefits gained from a program over the resources invested in it.

3. **Legality**: conformance to law and the U.S. and state constitutions.

4. **Responsiveness**: meets the needs and demands of clients and is modified on the basis of their reactions to the program.

5. **Technical criteria**: standards set by the professional groups operating within government that define acceptable practice in their respective fields.

6. **Political criteria**: resolution of conflict and maintenance of cooperation among contending groups in the administrative department.

7. **Equity**: extent to which public programs' benefits and costs are distributed so that no group or individual receives less than a minimum benefit level or pays more than a maximum cost.

to the process. On the other hand, long-range evaluation of a controversial program is best done by one or more outsiders. When the aim is to improve administrative procedures and techniques, it may be wisest to involve several evaluators and techniques.

All evaluations, by definition, are value-laden. They must draw upon one or more standards in judging whether and how well a policy or program succeeded. In fact, a thorough evaluation must consider all the expectations that chief executives, legislators, clienteles, and the general public may hold of the program, and these may not be fully compatible. The evaluator must not only choose which criteria to use but also how to rank them in importance and relate the evidence to each one. The standards identified in Box 14.4 have several potential definitions and can overlap one another, so this selection is necessarily simplified.

Standards for Evaluation

These standards serve as frames of reference that guide the analyst to choose certain kinds of data over others for evaluation. They cause some judgments to be more credible and relevant than their alternatives. Thus, anyone reading such evaluations does well to remember where the analyst stands. If this be "bias," it is not necessarily an intent to mislead or propagandize the audience. Reputable evaluators often seek to stimulate discussion of values and standards. Indeed, "public policy in a democratic system is the product of debate; the task of the policy analyst is to raise the level of that debate and provide informed contributions to it" (Bobrow & Dryzek, 1987, p. 21).

Program Effectiveness

One widely used standard for judgment is the program's **effectiveness** in fulfilling its goals as defined by the policymakers. It is the "extent to which the policies are achieving the benefits they are supposed to achieve plus any unanticipated side benefits" (Nagel, 1986, p. 99). This is easiest to apply if the problem to be solved and the expected benefits are clearly defined, but many tasks lack these prerequisites. For example, it is unclear how many hazardous waste sites Congress expected to clean up through the Superfund program, since no full inventory has ever been made, nor is it known what action was necessary for a complete remedy, since few sites have been thoroughly surveyed. One notable example is that of Love Canal (recall its mention in Chapter 8), which has been managed as well as possible in the view of many specialists.

Efficiency

A second criterion is **efficiency**, which is understood as the margin of benefits gained from a program over the resources invested in it. This is akin to productivity, a common measure more often used in private industry. There are several ways to think of this, such as identifying maximum benefit for a given cost level, minimum cost for a given amount of benefit, or the best cost/benefit ratio for any chosen level of the two. One might compare the costs of one technique for removing wastes with those of another, for example. If one were cheaper and yielded similar results, it could be labeled the more efficient method.

Efficiency is a difficult standard to apply. Government projects are not always intended to meet narrow criteria of efficiency and will usually appear to be inefficient compared to projects of organizations with fewer goals to meet (Wilson, 1989, p. 318). If a site (another Love Canal, perhaps) were deemed especially dangerous to public health, action would be speeded up, which would reduce the efficiency level. The litigation that usually accompanies programs in which the private parties assert their legal rights clearly makes them less efficient.

Legality

A third standard is legality, which is more restricted in scope than effectiveness or efficiency and so is easier to meet. (Recall the legalistic concept of implementation success in Chapter 13.) Although a program's conformance to law and to the U.S. and state constitutions may be obvious, disputes do arise. Liability for hazardous waste on most sites had to be settled in the courts. Judges gradually build up precedents for deciding similar cases. This standard of legality is not simply a concern of the courts, however. Administrators have become sensitive to broader definitions of the legal rights of their personnel and clients for their own protection and for the success of their programs in rights-conscious environments.

Responsiveness

Fourth, responsiveness to the ongoing needs and demands (which are often not identical) of clients is a central political standard. A responsive program is not only designed to meet those needs and demands but is modified as needed on the basis of clients' reactions. A responsive program can also be effective (by this standard) if the demands conform to the real needs, but its efficiency cannot always be assured. However, the demands may not come equally from all parts of the constituency. A successfully completed Superfund project in Woburn, Massachusetts, can be traced to a vigorous neighborhood movement arising out of high rates of cancer among its citizens. There are undoubtedly equally dangerous sites that lack politically demanding clients.

Technical Criteria

Evaluation criteria that have been set by the professional groups operating within government, that define acceptable practice in their respective fields, and that have been widely accepted by the public agencies in which these groups work are defined as technical standards. In many cases the professionals resist laymen's efforts to influence their choices. This conflict is perhaps strongest in professions with highly technical methods not readily understood by outsiders, such as medicine, accounting, and engineering.

In the Superfund program the EPA drew not only on its own engineers and related specialists, but also on contractor personnel. Standards had to evolve with experience in order to detect toxic substances, determine the degree of hazard, and eliminate or neutralize the danger. At the same time attorneys were developing professional standards for determining liability and fair settlements. Both sets of standards remained open to dispute within their respective communities, however.

Political Criteria

Legislators and interest groups apply many political standards to public programs. These refer to the power relationships between contending groups in the administrative process: conflict resolution, maintenance of cooperation, and citizen participation in decisions. A breakdown in the relationship between a federal and a state agency implementing a program can nullify years of competent program design. Or altered political alignments may not yield major outcomes until years later. For example, the effort to involve neighborhood residents in planning and monitoring the Model Cities programs of the 1960s and subsequent community improvement projects was not immediately effective in most localities. However, it was a major stimulus to urban residents to organize politically, and many active neighborhood and citywide organizations emerged out of those committees and advisory boards to wield significant influence more than a decade later.

Evaluators should realize that some political criteria are narrow and self-seeking. A new dam or a highway in a congressional district (commonly known as a "pork barrel" project) boosts the political image of the representative from that district, who highly publicizes his or her "achievement" just before an election. An ambitious agency head may operate a program so as to win a promotion. These private goals shape many administrative choices, and a sensitive evaluator must watch for such hidden agendas.

Equity

The final evaluation standard is **equity** and it may be the hardest to apply, since it embodies many other standards and alternatives for making judgments. In a narrow sense, equity is the extent to which public programs' costs and benefits are distributed so that no one receives less than a minimum benefit level or pays more than a maximum cost (Nagel, 1986, p. 99). The broader meanings of *equity* blend into such concepts as fairness and justice, with all their innate ambiguities. Equity may sometimes call for equality between people and groups, but at other times it may require unequal treatment to compensate for previous inequities.

An example of public library financing illustrates several ways of defining *equity*. Assume there are two branch libraries in a city, one in a high-income neighborhood and the other in an area populated by poor people. The two neighborhoods have the same population size. Strict *market* equity dictates that the city spend equal amounts on the two branches. However, *compensatory* equity requires that more be spent on the branch in the poorer area, to encourage more reading by those who have least access to books and to improve the residents' literacy and levels of information. Another alternative is *demand* equity, in which the city awards funds in proportion to the branches' circulation rates or patrons' requests for service. This would probably benefit the high-income neighborhood branch more. An evaluator must choose which concept is to guide the analysis.

Broad discussions of justice and fairness also draw upon ideological commitments. A liberal evaluator may approach a study with the assumption that when government sets worthy goals for social or economic change that are popularly supported, it need only have well-designed programs and conscientious administration to succeed. If a program proves to be ineffective or inefficient, it can be corrected with sufficient knowledge and the will to make it work. By contrast, a traditional conservative has less confidence in government's ability to initiate even desirable social change. Such a person, when evaluating a program that has proved unsuccessful, is more likely to conclude that government cannot improve the situation and so will call for termination of the effort.

Lessons for Administrators

What guidance are administrators likely to get from evaluations conducted by any of the preceding standards? Weiss (1987, p. 44) concluded that analyses of many social programs "were not well equipped to tell how programs managed to make an impact on people's lives or what factors prevented them from doing so. They could not explain why programs worked or failed. . . . Evaluation did not yield many clues about promising directions for change." Contrary to expectations, "few evaluation reports lead to direct and immediate changes in policy or practice. . . . More often, evaluation reports are cited, referred to, used in testimony, or footnoted, to support positions already taken. More than a signal for direction, evaluation becomes ammunition in policy battles." The plurality of standards and conflicts among the involved parties is plainly one reason for this.

   Nevertheless, a study that scrutinizes the effectiveness and efficiency of administrators' efforts is most relevant to the given policy's immediate operations because it can deal with concerns of procedures, resource allocation, and agency management. However, if the policy itself is seriously flawed or encounters obstacles outside the government's structure, one needs to apply broader standards for analysis. The Church and Nakamura study of Superfund (1993) is a bridge between the two types. It does not show the engineers how to remove polychlorinated biphenyls more efficiently, nor does it enable EPA lawyers to reach settlements more quickly. But it uses comparative evaluations of three strategies to urge administrators to be more sensitive to the human and physical contexts in selecting their mode of action.

Procedures for Evaluation

Just as there are many forms of evaluation, there are many valid approaches to generating findings and conclusions. Box 14.5 presents items that moderately systematic evaluations should include and a general order in which analysis most logically occurs. Ideally, the evaluation procedure is planned when the program is imple-

Box 14.5

In Conducting an Evaluation of a Policy, the Analyst . . .

1. identifies the relevant audience and its concerns;

2. lists the goals that the program as implemented should have accomplished and the standards that are to be applied;

3. collects all relevant performance data—resource inputs and output measurements;

4. portrays the changes in the targeted situation resulting from the policy by comparing what resulted from the program with what would have happened in its absence;

5. compares the inputs with the outputs, the goals with the results, and the costs with the benefits;

6. identifies reasons for the results obtained in steps 4 and 5; and

7. recommends changes in the policy or the method of its implementation.

mented in order to obtain performance information when it is needed. Otherwise, the analysis must be added later.

Identifying the Audience

First, the evaluator should identify the relevant audience and its concerns. If a study of one waste site cleanup has been specifically requested by a supervisor who can act on it, the report should contain material that he or she needs to know and can use. Other studies may be aimed at generating data for a chief executive who must evaluate the agency head's performance, a legislative body about to enact a budget, or the general public that demands investigation of media charges about mismanagement. A news reporter surveying charges of footdragging or favoritism in cleanup projects may address the broadest audience of elected officials, voters, and community organizations, all of whom may participate in responding to the problem.

Listing the Goals

As the second step, the evaluator should list the goals the program should have accomplished. The difficulty of doing this varies with the complexity of the program itself. A city's sewer expansion project has obvious goals—for example, to lay N miles of pipe at a cost of Z dollars or less. It should be no challenge to determine whether that was done. An endeavor to promote recreational opportunities for people with physical disabilities can be judged successful if a reasonable increase occurs in those utilizing the opportunities.

Box 14.6

How Shall Minnesota Reach Its Milestones?

In 1992 Minnesota Planning, a state agency, published *Minnesota Milestones*, a long-range plan for the state. It listed twenty broad goals and seventy-nine "milestones" to measure whether progress was being made toward them. For example, the teen pregnancy rate, which in 1980 was twenty occurrences per 1,000 women below the age of 18, was targeted to drop to eleven by the year 2000 and to eight in 2020. The plan also sought improved energy efficiency: a 12 percent drop in BTUs used per person from 1990 to 2000 and a 22 percent drop by 2020. Some measures were more subjective; for a goal of reduced discrimination against persons of nonmajority cultures and ethnic backgrounds, the evidence was public survey data with fewer complaints of unfair treatment (Minnesota Planning, 1992). A "report card" with pluses and minuses on some of the milestones was issued a year later, the first of intended annual progress reports, updating the performance data and commenting on changes or lack of them. This is an example of *benchmarking,* which several states and cities have begun in response to wide public demands that governments not only become more effective but also report their achievements (or lack of them) to the citizens.

It is more difficult to state goals of large-scale projects, which contain narrow targets nested within more general ones. One approach used by several state governments is *benchmarking,* which is the setting of measurable goals to be attained by a given year (see Box 14.6).

This approach states a goal, explains the context and source of the numbers, and makes recommendations both for achievement of the goal and for improved monitoring of the situation in the future. If well publicized and used year by year as a guide to action, it can be a constructive tool for evaluation.

Collecting Data

In the third stage the analyst collects all relevant performance data. These fall into several categories. First, there are resource inputs, such as monetary costs, personnel time, and facilities. These are probably accessible for individual site cleanup projects, and probably for a whole year's series of such actions. But the larger the program, the more data there are to collect, not all of which may be available or in comparable form. At times, an analyst must fall back on general estimates of major items.

A second cluster of performance data consists of output measurements, such as the number of sites remedied, the volume of wastes processed, and the payments collected from liable parties.

These can be grouped for a particular time period or region of the country.

The analyst obtains these data from agency records, observations by trained personnel, surveys of citizens or clients, and direct physical measurements, such as chemical concentrations. Quantitative measurements are best if available, but the analyst must decide how significant each statistic is to the overall evaluation. In the field of family services, data might initially indicate that visits by social workers to troubled families increased by one-third, but the analyst should also seek to learn how long those visits lasted and what they accomplished, which are more difficult tasks. Evaluation by collecting performance data is further complicated by the need to identify the exact type and task of the given organization, as explained in Box 14.7.

Charting Changes

The fourth part of the evaluation portrays the resulting changes in the targeted situation: the real difference that the policy produced. The analyst compares what resulted from the program with what would have happened without it so as to establish a causal chain of events linking the activities of the program with the observed outcomes (Mohr, 1988). This requires a historical perspective, to determine what the situation was at the outset or at an earlier phase of the program. Thus, for example, one could compare concentrations of cancer-causing substances in a river before and after cleanup.

Sometimes "proxy" or indirect measures of changes are necessary. Citizen surveys with rigorous sampling and analysis techniques are commonly used to gather perceptions and feelings about program results. A city could poll residents in a neighborhood on their sense of safety as a result of a cleanup project. Surveys can also identify problems for further examination by other means.

Comparison and Analysis

The next stage of evaluation compares the inputs with the outputs, the goals with the results, and the benefits with the costs.

This is the heart of most evaluations, for it lays the groundwork for the judgments that make the work useful for the future. Engineers who seek improved highway safety and traffic control have experimented with formats of signs, lane widths, signals, and lighting. Over the years they have found that some combinations lead to fewer accidents or smoother vehicle flow. Unless their costs are out of line, these combinations are likely to be widely chosen. Such evolution has certainly contributed to increased highway safety.

Box 14.7

Evaluation in Four Types of Organizations

The ability of an observer to identify performance varies with the type and task of the specific agency. Wilson (1989, pp. 159–169) distinguished four such types. In production organizations, both their outputs and their outcomes are quite visible and thus present the most clear-cut evidence to evaluators. The Postal Service and the Social Security Administration—and probably also a state highway department—are of this type.

Second, procedural organizations are those in which activities can be easily observed but not their outcomes and impacts. It is difficult to tell, for example, whether the visits by an inspector from the Occupational Safety and Health Administration (OSHA) are in fact making a given workplace less hazardous.

Wilson's third type is the craft organization, in which employee activities are hard to observe and measure, but their results are well documented. Employees of the Wage and Hour Division of the U.S. Department of Labor, which enforces the Fair Labor Standards Act, spend most of their time away from the office investigating complaints and negotiating agreements with employers. The degree to which those agreements comply with the law, however, can be easily determined.

Finally, there is the coping organization, in which both the outputs and the outcomes are difficult to observe and evaluate. Police officers and public school teachers must use much discretion in dealing with unique problems among their clients, and they most often do so away from direct supervision. Yet mere arrest totals or mathematics achievement scores fail to document completely how well they have used their discretion. The message here for evaluators is to be alert to the *kind* of organization under scrutiny and the exact type of task they are examining.

Explaining the Results

In the sixth stage of evaluation the analyst identifies reasons for the results learned in the fourth and fifth steps. Like any explanation, this one is open to a range of judgments. If smoother traffic flow and greater driver satisfaction followed installation of new direction signs and traffic signals, the analyst can probably conclude that the former is the result of the latter unless there were obvious intervening factors. If one set of projects was less cost efficient than others, it should be possible to learn why.

A major hindrance to explanations of this kind is that the outcomes identified need not have resulted solely from the program being investigated. All programs have external influences and generate unintended consequences. For example, traffic congestion is growing steadily in major metropolitan areas despite new freeways and other infrastructural improvements. Frustrated planners now realize that new freeways further stimulate automobile use and intensify commercial development, which in turn attracts even more drivers—a result often not sufficiently forecasted in the freeway planning stage. Thus, an evaluator must learn how to create room for these external and unanticipated influences in future policy designs and prepare contingency plans.

A further demand on the analyst is to judge whether a given positive or negative impact was due to the design of the policy—its goals, means, and resources provided—or to the administrators' implementation of the policy. Fixing blame for misdeeds is always politically sensitive, but it must be done as constructively as possible. Giving credit is also necessary in order to offer a model for repeating successes. If a school district finds that its students' reading achievement scores increased from one year to the next, it must learn whether the change was due to its own efforts and, if so, how those efforts produced those results. This task too blends the objective and subjective in ways that only the evaluator can decide.

Recommending Changes

The last stage of evaluation is necessary if one seeks directly to influence future choices: recommending changes in the policy or its implementation. Such admonitions can range from detailed prescriptions for reducing costs and tightening supervision to comprehensive redrafting of policy goals and philosophy. Or they can simply call for pursuing the present course. If the prescriptions simply reflect the preferences of the evaluator with no real concern for feasibility, they are useless. Evaluations that broadly sketch a "best of all possible worlds" solution but detail no clear path to get there are also of limited value. On the other hand, recommendations can be very "safe," stating and justifying what those involved have already decided to do. The most useful prescriptions are those that have a real chance of making improvements but that are controversial enough to warrant serious debate.

Church and Nakamura concluded (1993, pp. 171–172) that the Superfund was more ambitious than it should have been. Since it relied on private contractors to do the cleanup work, the EPA had limited ability to control the details of any project. By insisting on very high standards and strict penalties on those found to have contributed to the waste accumulation, it actually slowed the work inordinately and reduced compliance. They concluded that a more conciliatory approach, with somewhat less exacting standards, would have done the job more quickly and more cheaply.

Validity

The validity of evaluation studies is a major concern for both analysts and users. If the evaluation of a program accurately measures what it was intended to study, it is said to have *internal validity*. That is, for our study example, it provided an accurate picture of the six Superfund cleanup sites. This internal validity is the most important aim of most evaluations. External validity is the transferability of the findings to similar settings (Sylvia, Meier, & Gunn, 1985, p. 79). That quality enables an evaluator to assume that research of the same kind would be applicable to other hazardous waste sites (or would not be for specific reasons).

Challenges to Evaluators

In-depth, constructive evaluation is not easy and is not often well done. Too often, a needed evaluation may not take place at all. Serious analysis requires time and money as well as people who are skilled and willing to carry it out. If a program is not well financed to begin with, a director is understandably reluctant to divert limited funds to a study with an unknown outcome. The director may prefer a passive approach and may rely on whatever information comes in along the way or on intuitive staff judgments. An ongoing formal evaluation could also distract from the work itself, thereby raising needless doubts among the personnel and undermining the director's authority. There is a natural human resistance to being evaluated, particularly when one's job is on the line (Zedlewski, 1986).

Additionally, many technical and process difficulties can prevent or impede evaluation (Hatry, 1989). Needed data may not be publicly available or may cost more in time or money to collect than the agency can spare. Some categories of performance may not be fully measurable. For example, the very presence of a police officer in a neighborhood may deter criminal acts to a degree that cannot be determined. Many influences that are not under the administrators' control impinge upon the success of a program. To illustrate this point, variations in weather and the choices of individual farmers—two factors that are outside the powers of the U.S. Department of Agriculture—shape the outcomes of farm commodity programs.

Finally, policy may be a "moving target," for as a program is implemented, it changes its environment or subjects so much that its goals lose their relevance. Analysts should expect these changes to occur while the evaluation is under way and realize that some changes simply will not be predictable (Wittrock & deLeon, 1986, p. 55). Thus, an evaluator faces the dual dilemma of deciding whether the policy was suitable to the original situation and whether it *remained* appropriate to the *changed* situation that it produced.

Also, the initial evaluation scheme may need revision to account for an altered situation. A city's economic development program that succeeds in attracting new employers may have to turn its attention to expanding housing supply, building access roads to the new workplaces, and enlarging its sewage treatment facilities.

These "moving policies" can easily cross boundaries between agencies and levels of government, which compounds responsibility problems.

The Challenge of Politics and Bureaucracy

Political and bureaucratic realities conflict with the assumptions and purposes of evaluation. Evaluators are potential agents of change for their organizations and so pose threats to their colleagues and working relationships. As they criticize programs and procedures, they may come to favor different objectives and clienteles from those currently being pursued. "Prepared to impose change on others, evaluators must have enough stability to stick to their own work. They must hang onto their own organization while preparing to abandon it. They must combine political feasibility with analytic purity. Only a brave individual would predict that these qualities can be found in one and the same person and organization" (Wildavsky, 1979, pp. 213–214).

Some evaluations are requested or conducted by people who openly aim either to continue the program under study (thus, they seek publicity for its positive outcomes) or to have it changed substantially or terminated. In the latter case, they may present data that show that it has failed, that it could not have been made to work, or that a very different program would have succeeded. Such hidden agendas are common, unaccompanied by any desire for what a disinterested analyst would call objectivity.

Since no in-depth evaluation of a significant program can really be neutral, and since the questions and standards chosen at the beginning inevitably shape the conclusions, political advocates stand ready to use evaluations for their own purposes. Intensive studies have been done of the numerous efforts to expand economic opportunity for the poor, and anyone can find in these analyses some evidence to support whatever position he or she advocates. Evaluation "wars" sometimes break out, and the contestants use their selected evidence like missiles to destroy the other side's arguments. Does busing schoolchildren to achieve racial integration really improve learning performance? Yes, it did in city *A*, but no, it didn't in city *B*. Such debates can obscure the deeper meanings of those cities' experiences, which might lead a more open-minded person to conclude, "Yes, if . . ." or "No, but. . . ."

Evaluation as a Campaign Device

Electorally ambitious people similarly exploit evaluations of policies and programs. An incumbent president or a governor running for reelection will feed the press evidence that the administration's bold efforts spurred economic development, reduced poverty, and made the environment cleaner. The opponent responds by documenting the incumbent's shocking waste of taxpayers' money and utter failure to improve educational performance or care for the elderly.

The political character of evaluations is well illustrated by the 1984 report of the President's Private Sector Survey on Cost Control, popularly named the Grace Commission after its chair, J. Peter Grace. After an 18-month study the commission reported that the national government could save $424.4 billion over 3 years by making the 2,478 changes it recommended. The largest categories of potential savings fell in areas that the commission labeled program waste, system failure, and personnel mismanagement. The categories ranged from excessive costs of military parts and erroneous Social Security benefits to excessive military and civil service retirement payments and maintenance of thousands of small, rural (and, according to the survey, unnecessary) post offices. The commission claimed that it had applied the tenets of business management to the government's operations but argued that its recommended improvements would not affect the substance or legislative intent of any program (President's Private Sector Survey on Cost Control, 1984).

The report of the National Performance Review, led and publicized by Vice President Gore in the first year of the Clinton administration, was no less a political document, and clearly reflected the priorities of a moderately liberal Democratic regime. Unlike the Grace Commission, the review did not advocate eliminating many programs. Rather, it proposed means to make existing ones work more efficiently. As an evaluation document, it said in essence, "Goverment is doing the right things but not very well."

The Concept of Waste

The word *waste* was often used in reports on the Grace Commission's findings, a word that automatically sends signals to the public of incompetence or corruption. But a competent evaluator realizes that the term can be used in several different ways. We can think of *waste* generally as the avoidable misuse or loss of money and other valued resources. But there is much room for judgment in this.

Illegal Waste   Illegal waste results from actions deliberately taken that are contrary to law to serve private rather than public purposes. Such actions may be committed by government personnel, as with theft of government property or failure to perform duties. Illegal waste can also consist of a citizen's receiving a benefit to which he or she is not legally entitled, whether by a false claim of need or by a clerical error. Fraud is a major category here. The General Accounting Office identified 77,211 cases at twenty-one federal agencies during a 30-month period in 1976 through 1979. These actions and the penalties for them are catalogued in law, although detecting them and those responsible is hampered by inadequate records, lack of staff competence, frequent rule changes, and widely varying client needs and situations (Young, 1983).

Mistaken Waste   Mistaken waste consists of losses that result from actions taken within the law and with good intentions. Public agencies spend millions of dollars on treatment of people addicted to drugs and alcohol with no discernible long-term success. The federal government, fearing a widespread epidemic, undertook a massive preventive effort to immunize the public against swine flu in 1976 (recall the discussion of this episode in Chapter 5), but no such epidemic occurred. Was the campaign really necessary? It was a calculated risk, in which the costs of overzealousness appeared to be smaller than the potential for tragedy. If these two examples genuinely constitute waste, they are certainly in the mistaken category. In such situations one could argue that better information and foresight could have prevented the waste. On the other hand, when government must innovate to deal with a previously insoluble problem, some such waste is virtually unavoidable. Sensitive learning from those situations is the best way of minimizing such waste in the future.

Discretionary Waste   Discretionary waste consists of intentional actions and results that appear wrong to some analysts but not to others, depending on their expectations or ideologies. The Grace Commission identified 12,469 rural post offices that serve 100 or fewer customers each and estimated that $272 million could be saved over 3 years if these offices were closed and service centralized in larger facilities. But to the people served by them, those post offices are essential. Congress had no doubt that its constituents needed them and did not regard them as wasteful. Others decry the waste of money spent on aircraft carriers, antismoking campaigns, or art exhibits—all of which are specific policy choices.

These three categories of waste illustrate the fine distinctions that evaluators must often make, a situation that renders them vulnerable to disputes over policy or ethical issues as well as administrative efficiency. No one condones illegal waste. But it is difficult to quantify the utility of a rural post office to its patrons or the inconvenience of traveling farther for service if it were closed. Those who already favored saving money through such closings doubtless welcomed the Grace Commission's report as support, whereas opponents were likely to denounce the assumptions on which the recommendation was made.

Summary

Evaluation is the process of identifying the outcomes and impacts of public policies and judging whether and how well objectives are met. It is a necessary learning process for governments that seek to be accountable to their citizens, to improve their implementation processes, and to design better policies and methods for the future.

Many approaches can be taken—from the relatively quick, informal, and superficial to the highly systematic and scientific. The methods of each evaluation project, and the persons chosen to do it, have to be suited to the chosen purposes and circumstances.

Leading standards by which an agency or a program can be evaluated include effectiveness, efficiency, legality, responsiveness to situations and clients, technical criteria set by professional organizations, political criteria relating to conflict resolution and cooperation, and equity. These standards are not necessarily compatible in their applications and interpretations and require further refinement by the evaluator.

Procedures for evaluation include identifying the relevant audience; listing program goals; collecting relevant performance data; charting changes; comparing inputs with outputs, goals with results, and benefits with costs; identifying reasons for the results; and recommending changes in the policy or its implementation.

Many obstacles prevent evaluation from being done at all or done well enough to be useful. There can be resistance from program participants for personal or institutional reasons or unwillingness to divert resources to the task. Political influences can block studies from being done or distort their findings. The terms are subject to widely differing interpretations, such as the elusive concept of *waste*.

Discussion Questions

1. What are the essential differences between evaluating a city's street maintenance program and evaluating its public school system? Which is more difficult and why?

2. Why are many kinds of information that are not completely (or even partially) quantifiable needed for evaluations?

3. What drawbacks would probably be found in an evaluation that considered only the efficiency or effectiveness of a program?

4. What standards should be used to evaluate the performance of an entire unit of government, such as a state or city? Which ones are most important to examine?

5. Evaluations get most attention when they criticize inadequate performance and recommend how it should be improved.

What value is there in identifying excellent performance, where there are no changes called for?

Analytical Exercises

1. It is easy today to find amateur evaluations of such public welfare programs as Aid to Families with Dependent Children; they abound in the popular media and talk shows. More professional evaluations are also available in publications ranging from the *New York Times* to journals on social work and public policy. Survey a selection of the latter sources to identify the writers' underlying values and judgments that they use as measuring rods in their critiques. Try to get a broad picture of the many (and often conflicting) standards that they use.

2. Critics often focus on the nation's public school systems, from Head Start to the universities, claiming that these institutions are failing to prepare the nation's youth for the twenty-first century. In general, what criteria do they have in mind for this evaluation? For your part, make a list of the standards that we ought to use to evaluate a part of the education system of your choice. Your list might include standardized test scores, graduation rates, or employment success, but add others you believe to be relevant.

For Further Reading

Church, T. W., & Nakamura, R. T. (1993). *Cleaning Up the Mess: Implementation Strategies in Superfund.* Washington, DC: Brookings Institution. Evaluation of alternative approaches to cleaning up highly toxic waste dumps, cited in this chapter.

Levin, M. A., & Ferman, B. (1985). *The Political Hand: Policy Implementation and Youth Employment Programs.* New York: Pergamon. See further reading in Chapter 13. This is also an excellent example of a scholarly evaluation study.

Meehan, E. J. (1979). *The Quality of Federal Policymaking: Programmed Failure in Public Housing.* Columbia, MO: University of Missouri Press. Evaluates the St. Louis experience with public housing, from the disaster of Pruitt-Igoe to other relatively successful projects.

Murray, C. (1984). *Losing Ground: American Social Policy, 1950–1980.* New York: Basic Books. Evidence marshaled in such a way as to show the futility of most federal social programs of the past four decades, with author's recommendations for reform.

Neustadt, R. E., & Fineberg, H. (1983). *The Epidemic That Never Was: Policy Making and the Swine Flu Affair.* New York: Vintage Books. Report by two scholars on the events and outcomes of the swine flu inoculation program of 1976.

President's Private Sector Survey on Cost Control. (1984). *War on waste.* New York: Macmillan. The report of the Grace Commission, which presents a conservative agenda for reducing the size of government from the perspective of corporate executives.

Schwarz, J. E. (1988). *America's Hidden Success: A Reassessment of Public Policy from Kennedy to Reagan* (rev. ed.). New York: W. W. Norton. Reaches the opposite conclusion from Murray's, with emphasis on different data and outcomes.

Administrative Accountability

Learning Objectives

After reading this chapter, you should be able to do the following:

1. Define accountability in the context of the American constitutional system.
2. Identify the internal/formal means of accountability: executive control, budget preparation, rule-making procedures, inspectors general and auditors, chief financial officers, and investigative commissions.
3. Identify the external/formal means of accountability: legislative oversight, budgetary review and enactment, rule making, veto, investigation, casework, audits, ratification of appointments, judicial review and takeovers, intergovernmental controls, and the electoral process.
4. Identify the external/informal means of accountability: monitoring by interest and clientele groups and professional communities, information media, and freedom-of-information laws.
5. Identify the internal/informal means of accountability: professional standards, ethical codes and values, and whistle-blowers.
6. Understand the political hindrances to accountability.

T housands of college and trade school students around the nation benefit from grant and loan programs administered by the U.S. Department of Education (DOE). Many more would like to get help but are denied it because serious mismanagement by that department allows billions of dollars annually to slip away to ineligible schools and students. Here lies a complex illustration of how a unit of government can go out of control.

Congress provides student aid in two forms. Pell grants of up to $2,300 are awarded each year to more than 4 million students from low-income families. Other students can obtain loans that must be paid back over a period of time; these averaged $13.8 billion annually in the 5 years prior to 1993. Typically, the students do not see this money, since it goes directly to the school, which then reduces its tuition charge by the amount granted or loaned. The school certifies that it has a certain number of students who qualify, and the government then supplies the funds. DOE does not require justification for the requests until later.

Because of fraud, $3 to $4 billion is lost each year. Fraud enters the system in two ways. Some institutions, most often profit-making vocational schools, recruit and certify low-income students in order to get the grants. Fictitious names also find their way onto the lists. Then school officers take the funds and divert them to their own use. Second, many students who get loans find that their training does not help them to find jobs and so default on their loans. Other students who are able to repay their loans simply delay doing so and encounter little or no pressure to meet their commitments.

The villains in this scene are not only dishonest schools and deadbeat students. DOE is lax in holding them accountable, a laxity that really originates in Congress. Such misuse of federal funds should be detected by the department's program auditors, who examine the loan and grant justifications. But DOE in 1994 had only 96 auditors to cover 7,400 schools across the nation, perhaps one-third of the number needed. The auditors get no internal training, so new employees cannot perform at their best until they gain experience. Furthermore, they lack computer systems that can alert them to possible frauds. Such weakness in the department traces back to Congress's refusal to expand DOE's budget, in spite of adding programs (many in elementary and secondary education) for it to supervise (Winerip, 1994). Clearly, the accountability process has broken down here. Among the many lessons that we can draw from this case is that when government is highly complex, the public often finds it difficult to evaluate its actions and hold it accountable for them.

The Meaning of Accountability

We can describe a unit of government, one of its agencies, or an individual public servant as being accountable when the public purpose is served in a manner that conforms both to the law and to the will of the public as interpreted by its elected representatives. When this does not occur, there are means by which the agency or person can be made to comply or suffer penalties. This process requires continuous communication between governments and their citizens and elected representatives about performance and effective steps to deter or correct any actions that fail to meet standards.

One key question is, *To whom* are administrators accountable? The ultimate answer in a democracy, of course, is "the citizens." But in a representative form of government, accountability is more specific. First, using the preceding example, the Department of Education answers to the president as chief executive. Second, its powers and funds are provided by Congress, which also holds it accountable. Third, its actions can be invalidated by the courts after a legal challenge, and judges are obliged to uphold the Constitution and laws and to determine if and when an agency has violated them. We can also identify a cluster of informal institutions that extend the people's oversight of their governments: interest groups and news media, most notably. Many people first learned of fraud in DOE programs by reading the *New York Times.*

For what are administrators accountable? There are at least four general requirements: to make laws work as intended with a minimum of waste and delay; to exercise lawful and sensible administrative discretion; to recommend new policies and changes in current ones as needed; and to enhance citizen confidence in government administration (Rosen, 1989, p. 4). These requirements are supplemented by the individual criteria of the missions mandated for each agency. To expand educational choices for low-income students is a specific task of the Education Department. The legally defined responsibilities are surrounded by the less-well-defined public purposes introduced in Chapter 1 and are wrapped in the broader yet politically vital concept of the "public interest."

To maintain this accountability, we have encased our governments in an intricate network of legal and political checks. The United States has not placed much faith in the moral character of its government leaders as a force to avoid misdeeds. Rather, we rely on elaborate rules that limit the discretion of officials. We require them to face periodic elections or to be accountable to officials who do. We have made them accountable to one another by dividing power among executive, legislative, and judicial institutions. And we have placed "watchdogs" in the system to guard one another. The National Performance Review (1993, p. 6) learned that there were about 700,000 federal employees who "manage, control, check up on, or audit others," which is about one-fourth of the total payroll. As an earlier observer noted, "Although this system made it difficult for wise and virtuous leaders to bless us with their statecraft, it also gave assurances that no evil men could ever torment us" (Moore, 1981, p. 3). Even so, procedural checks cannot fully replace individual moral character as guarantors of accountable government.

This chapter examines the means of bureaucratic accountability in a framework developed by Gilbert (1959). There is, first, the distinction between formal and informal means. Formal channels are those prescribed by the Constitution, statutory law, or administrative procedure. The president's powers to issue executive orders, Congress's budget-making role, and the courts' prerogative of judicial review are examples. Informal channels, by contrast, have their origins in public preferences, individual ethical standards, and the many competing participants in the political process.

An internal/external dichotomy draws a line between the sources of accountability initiatives. *Internal* sources originate in the executive establishment of the particular government, normally headed by a president, governor, mayor, or city manager. In a legal and bureaucratic sense, accountability is vested with the top official. *External* sources include all other involved institutions: the legislative body, the courts, higher units of government, and the larger political environment.

We can describe four categories built on these distinctions: internal/formal, external/formal, external/informal, and internal/informal. Since they are interdependent, it is impossible to separate them sharply at every point. Figure 15.1 highlights these categories.

Formal Accountability within the Executive Branch

All the internal/formal methods build on the assumption that a single chief executive who is informed of subordinates' activities can control them. The framers of the national and state constitutions created the position of a single chief executive through whom the voters could hold accountable, for example, the military establishment and taxing authorities. Cities and special districts with professional managers require these officials to account constantly for administrative outcomes and have given them extensive powers of control for that purpose. However, the clarity and unity of the executive's control steadily fade as the government's activities increase in number and diversity. The accountability potential of a suburban city manager is thus greater than that of the president of the United States or the mayor of New York City.

Executive Control by Powers of Management

Government executives are vested with legal powers to control the hierarchy beneath them, which forms the "first line" of accountability. Chapter 9 surveyed these powers as well as the practical and legal limits to such control. Executives' effectiveness in practice depends on their willingness and ability to use their legal powers, along with the political contexts in which they operate. This is also true for subordinate executives—cabinet secretaries, agency directors, field office heads, and others who have significant discretion and control over a set of activities.

Figure 15.1

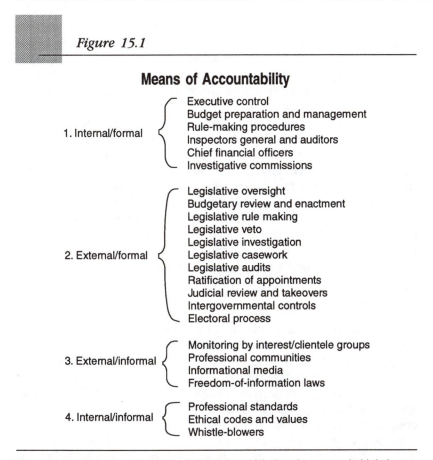

Means of Accountability

1. Internal/formal
- Executive control
- Budget preparation and management
- Rule-making procedures
- Inspectors general and auditors
- Chief financial officers
- Investigative commissions

2. External/formal
- Legislative oversight
- Budgetary review and enactment
- Legislative rule making
- Legislative veto
- Legislative investigation
- Legislative casework
- Legislative audits
- Ratification of appointments
- Judicial review and takeovers
- Intergovernmental controls
- Electoral process

3. External/informal
- Monitoring by interest/clientele groups
- Professional communities
- Informational media
- Freedom-of-information laws

4. Internal/informal
- Professional standards
- Ethical codes and values
- Whistle-blowers

There are many means, direct and indirect, by which Americans may hold their governments accountable for their performance. This often makes the choice of which means to use in a given situation more difficult, however.

Executives' management powers are tools to maintain the accountability of the administrators below them. Personnel management, issuance of orders and directives, and the ability to reorganize offices and reassign duties make up these powers. The administrative procedures that guarantee due process in making regulatory decisions or providing individual benefits further guide individual discretion and check arbitrary behavior. Preparation of the annual or biennial budget for submission to the legislature provides a regular opportunity to assess and control the actions of agency and program personnel and of outside contractors and clients. Each estimate for a spending category entails a judgment of the agency or program involved and an opportunity to alter its resources and authority. The White House and Congress could expand the Department of Education's auditing capacity with additional funds if they saw fraud reduction as a high priority.

In large and complex agencies, executives find it necessary to augment their ability to learn what is happening in their spheres of accountability and to respond to these circumstances. Many executives have expanded their own staffs for oversight and review of administrative actions. President Nixon added the management role to the Office of Management and Budget (OMB) in 1970 to link its budget-making choices with evaluation of ongoing operations. The OMB's power to review proposed regulations, described in Chapter 6, further illustrates this. Many state governments have similar offices that serve their governors. Chief executives commonly find that performance information necessary to ongoing accountability does not flow upward naturally. They must seek it out, specifically and persistently, from those who know where it is and what it means. This staff can be a hindrance, however, if executives fail to use it effectively, for it can become another barrier between themselves and those they are trying to control.

Rule-Making Procedures

Another set of accountability mechanisms encompasses the procedures for making administrative regulations. The normal course of federal rule making was described in Chapter 6 as a means of securing fair and effective decisions. Since it is extensively documented, offers opportunity for public comment and objection, and has a stipulated appeal process, it can serve the purposes of accountability as well. There is a history of why the rule was made, who and what influenced it, and the actions taken to implement it. This does not ensure that all wrongdoing comes to light, but attaching a "paper trail" increases the likelihood that it will.

Inspectors General and Auditors

By congressional mandate, every federal department and most independent agencies and regulatory commissions have an Office of Inspector General to investigate wrongdoing, initiate criminal proceedings if necessary, and recommend changes in policies and procedures. Inspectors general must report their findings twice a year to Congress and the head of the agency. For example, the inspector general and internal auditors of the National Aeronautics and Space Administration played major roles in the agency's self-searching that followed the *Challenger* disaster in 1986. In their shared opinion, management faults were spread across the entire agency and were intricately linked with the decisive chain of events that led to the failure of the O-rings on that fateful morning (Romzek & Dubnick, 1987). The highest administrators had lost contact with the working levels and needed these supplemental channels to provide additional information.

The mere presence of officers with broad investigatory powers can be a deterrent to improper behavior. However, disputes continue between Congress and the Justice Department over how much authority the inspectors general should have to conduct criminal investigations independently of other officials who have that formal responsibility. Overall, evidence from the reports of the various inspectors general indicates a mixture of successes and failures (Gormley, 1989b, pp. 122–124). From his recent study of thirty-four inspectors general, Light (1993) concluded that they have at best been backward-looking—seeking and penalizing failures to comply with rules—rather than searching for ways to increase future agency competence to implement policy. There is an obvious need for the first role, but if we think of accountability in positive terms as well, the second is equally necessary.

Chief Financial Officers

Congress further augmented the federal agencies' internal accountability system in October 1990 by requiring that twenty-three cabinet departments and independent agencies have a chief financial officer appointed by the president or, in some cases, by the agency head. The duties of this person include developing an accounting system to promptly identify fraud and abuse and reporting it to the top departmental or agency managers and OMB. This mandate, with which the White House concurred, clearly reflected Congress's concern about programs, such as the bailout of the savings and loan institutions, that could cost the government many billions of dollars in the future. In that crisis, it was difficult to foresee the huge dollar outflow because there were no reliable means of identifying and reporting on its causes (Lawrence, 1991).

Investigative Commissions

The *Challenger* tragedy was examined by another executive-initiated means of accountability: the investigative commission. Shortly after the event, President Reagan appointed former secretary of state William Rogers to head such a group, which made its report after less than 6 months of work and highlighted the managerial and technical failings associated with the disaster. The history of such presidential commissions includes the one that probed the causes of the urban riots of the 1960s (the Kerner Commission) and the one that recommended changes in the regulation of nuclear power plants after the 1979 Three Mile Island accident (the Kemeny Commission). A common purpose for forming such groups is to deflect political criticism and delay the making of hard decisions. However, both the Rogers and Kemeny Commissions made important recommendations that led to management changes. Essentially, these commissions are tools that the chief executive may use to serve the most urgent administrative and political purposes.

Despite such mechanisms, the fact remains that "making the bureaucracy accountable to the president in any comprehensive or enduring way is impossible; making it alert to his preferences is possible in those cases where presidents put loyal and competent subordinates in charge of making decisions in presidential agencies" (Wilson, 1989, p. 276). President Reagan grasped this truth well, and many of his appointments reflected the importance he placed on loyalty to his political agenda. What frustrated him, though, was that Congress did not leave direction of the executive branch solely to his discretion.

Formal Accountability to External Authorities

The separation-of-powers system, which is the centerpiece of the national and state constitutions, gives major roles to legislative and judicial bodies in holding administrators accountable. The powers of the federal government that the executive branch exercises are actually assigned to Congress (Article I, Section 8, of the Constitution lists most of these); the president has them by delegation only. Such delegation, although constitutional, must be accompanied by sufficient standards to guide their use, as the U.S. Supreme Court ruled in *United States v. Curtiss-Wright Export Co.* (1936).

Legislative Oversight of the Executive Branch

Congress, in overseeing the executive branch, is not greatly restrained by the fact that the president has formal responsibility for its operations. Rather, its powers of oversight extend into all parts of the vast executive hierarchy. **Legislative oversight** consists of "inquiries into bureaucratic performance that result in either formal or informal recommendations being made to the bureaucracy" (Gormley, 1989b, p. 198). (See Box 15.1, which describes two basic approaches to oversight.) The process begins with learning what is actually happening on the executive side of the constitutional fence and concludes by shaping the hierarchy's actions to the legislators' will. Administrators take care to respond to both actual and potential probes. Oversight is also widely practiced in state and local governments, where the task is usually easier because of their smaller size.

Budgeting as a Tool of Accountability

The most regular means by which national, state, and local legislators maintain administrative accountability is the annual or biennial budget process described in Chapter 12. It gives many committees

Box 15.1

How Does "Police-Patrol" Oversight Differ from "Fire-Alarm" Oversight?

All these concepts of legislative oversight fall into two broad forms: "police patrol" and "fire alarm" (McCubbins & Schwartz, 1984).

Police-Patrol Oversight
Analogous to the use of real police patrols, police-patrol oversight is comparatively centralized, active, and direct: at its own initiative, Congress examines a sample of executive-agency activities, with the aim of detecting and remedying any violations of legislative goals and, by its surveillance, discouraging such violations. An agency's activities might be surveyed by any of a number of means, such as reading documents, commissioning scientific studies, conducting field observations, and holding hearings to question officials and affected citizens.

Fire-Alarm Oversight
Analogous to the use of real fire alarms, fire-alarm oversight is less centralized and involves less active and direct intervention than police-patrol oversight: instead of examining a sample of administrative decisions, looking for violations of legislative goals, Congress establishes a system of rules, procedures, and informal practices that enable individual citizens and organized interest groups to examine administrative decisions (sometimes in prospect), to charge executive agencies with violating congressional goals, and to seek remedies from agencies, courts,

and Congress itself. Some of these rules, procedures, and practices afford citizens and interest groups access to information and to administrative decision-making processes. Others give them standing to challenge administrative decisions before agencies and courts, or help them bring alleged violations to congressmen's attention. Still others facilitate collective action by comparatively disorganized interest groups. Congress's role consists in creating and perfecting this decentralized system and, occasionally, intervening in response to complaints. Instead of sniffing for fires, Congress places fire-alarm boxes on street corners, builds neighborhood fire houses, and sometimes dispatches its own hook-and-ladder in response to an alarm.

—Mathew D. McCubbins and Thomas Schwartz, "Congressional Oversight Overlooked: Police Patrols versus Fire Alarms," *American Journal of Political Science*, Vol. 28, February 1984

In general, the authors conclude, Congress and state legislatures follow the fire-alarm practice most often, since it consumes less of their time and they can limit their attention to those problems that dominate the political scene. Police patrols are able to uncover mismanagement earlier than the fire-alarm method allows, but they require more sustained (and costly) efforts and may tread on politically sensitive toes.

---

the opportunity to examine the performance of agencies and programs under their jurisdiction, although they lack the time to do this in depth for all but a few. Furthermore, appropriation bills may contain detailed language on how funds can be spent. For example, in 1992 there were 2,150 directives, earmarks of funds, instructions, and prohibitions in Congress's actions pertaining to the Interior Department. Its secretary, Bruce Babbitt, found in 1993 that he was specifically ordered by Congress to maintain twenty-three positions in a field office of the anthracite reclamation program (National

Performance Review, 1993, pp. 4 & 17). Auditors, particularly in Congress's General Accounting Office, can report on compliance with those restrictions.

Rule Making by Legislatures

A second means of effecting accountability is legislative adoption of highly detailed rules for administrators to follow that sharply limit their discretion. This is most obvious in the environmental protection legislation of the 1970s, which set specific standards for pollution reduction and fixed both dates and percentages by which emissions were to be reduced (Gormley, 1989b, pp. 213–215). The Delaney amendment referred to in Chapter 6, which mandates a ban of all food additives known to cause cancer in laboratory animals, is another example. It leaves no legal discretion to declare some concentrations too small to be harmful. This activity has been condemned as "micromanagement" by some observers who are concerned that this practice violates the constitutional authority of executives. Yet legislators, aware of the political pressures that could lead executives not to carry out their intentions, often distrust administrators and so narrow agencies' discretion on politically sensitive choices.

The Legislative Veto

One aspect of this detailed lawmaking is the **legislative veto**, used both in Congress and in the state legislatures. It is a requirement in a law or an appropriation that an agency secure explicit approval from the whole legislature or one of its committees before it can take certain actions. At the national level the agency must notify Congress or a given committee of its intention to act and then wait for 30 or 60 days, as specified in the given act, while the lawmakers consider a veto. A veto by at least one of the houses is necessary to deny the action. This practice survives informally despite having been declared unconstitutional by the U.S. Supreme Court (*Immigration and Naturalization Service v. Chadha,* 1983) for its violation of the separation of powers. It is part of the normal White House/Capitol Hill bargaining over legislation, in which the former accepts built-in congressional vetoes in return for provisions it would not otherwise obtain. This is particularly evident in funding bills in which the administration must secure written approval of the House and Senate Appropriations Committees before spending for stipulated items (Tolchin, 1989). State legislatures widely practice the legislative veto process with no apparent judicial hindrance (Gormley, 1989b, pp. 209–213).

Investigation

Legislators have broad powers to investigate any operations of government they choose. Congress and state legislatures can request any information they need for lawmaking, and they commonly conduct specific probes. In the late 1980s, ten of the thirty-eight standing committees in Congress had permanent investigating subcommittees. To stay informed, committees require periodic reports from agencies on specific programs for which they have special concern. Most members rate this means of accountability very highly (Rosen, 1989, pp. 64–66). Use of this tool is controversial, however. Many administrators deplore the frequency with which they must appear before one oversight committee or another and the time they must spend in preparing answers to questions. Defenders of this practice argue that it is the lawmakers' only means of obtaining some kinds of information and that the potential for an investigation deters wrongdoing.

Legislative Casework for Citizens

Another accountability tool involves legislators still further in the details of implementation: their casework on behalf of constituents. It has long been customary for citizens to appeal to their members of Congress when they have a problem with a government agency or wish a special service. Members are happy to respond because they see in each request an opportunity to please constituents and win votes. Staff aides in the capitals and in the members' home states and districts forward these requests to the appropriate agency for response. It is widely believed that complaints and inquiries sent through this channel receive faster and more favorable action than those that citizens send directly to a given agency. Members' casework also gives Congress and state legislators another means of monitoring agency performance, since numerous complaints and high dissatisfaction levels usually indicate deeper problems that have to be attacked by other means. Rosen (1989, pp. 60–61) reports a high regard on Capitol Hill for this means of accountability.

Legislative Audits

Another means of accountability is the legislative audit. Congress established the General Accounting Office (GAO) in 1921 to oversee the auditing done within the executive branch and gave it legal powers to investigate all uses of federal funds. In 1993 the office submitted 1,115 evaluation reports that not only stated its findings but also recommended ways to improve programs. In the days before the Clinton administration took office, the GAO identified seventeen federal programs that were especially vulnerable to waste, fraud, and mismanagement, one of them the student loan program described at the opening of this chapter. The GAO director, whose title is comptroller general, urged Congress to give close attention to these trouble spots (Bowsher, 1993). Federal agencies accept most of the GAO's recommendations for change, and Congress has taken many of its suggestions for legislative action. However, a panel of the National Academy of Public Administration expressed concern in 1994 that the GAO was edging too far into the realm of policy advocacy that belongs to the members of Congress.

Most states have such audit agencies as well. Some auditors are elected by the voters and so are completely independent of other parts of the government. Others are responsible to their legislatures and, like the GAO, probe increasingly into policy implementation and performance quality as well as financial management. As state and local government programs expand and become more complex, the need for oversight grows.

Ratification of Appointments

The Senate alone has a tool for oversight in its power to ratify (and thus reject) presidential appointments to high administrative posts and regulatory commissions. Since it processes thousands of nominations every session, this tool cannot be widely used to control the administration. However, the Senate can give clear signals in selected appointments on how it wishes the agency to be run. Former senator John Tower, picked by President Bush in 1989 to be secretary of defense, was rejected after a lengthy public hearing by the Armed Services Committee, which had been concerned about both his personal behavior and his recent close ties with major military contractors. Many state senates and city councils have similar powers over executive appointments.

The Struggle for Power between the Executive and the Legislature The past 20 years have witnessed growing "custody battles" over bureaucracies within both the national and state governments. Legislators compete with chief executives, who often have different political agendas, to give direction to agencies. A president or governor of one party often faces a legislative majority of the opposite party in Congress or the legislature, and neither wants to yield control to the other. State administration has become more subject to all the formal and informal controls identified in this chapter as it takes on increased responsibilities for social and environmental programs. However, these conflicts usually confuse the lines of accountability (Gormley, 1989a). Legislators pay special attention to agencies that distribute benefits to specific geographic areas and economic groups. The Agriculture Department's crop price supports, for example, are of great interest to members representing farmers (Wilson, 1989, pp. 275–276). In the long run, executives win some and legislators win others, and most solutions represent bargains between them.

Judicial Control: Review and Takeovers

The Process of Judicial Review The judiciary also holds the executive branch accountable. The power of **judicial review** enables judges to determine the constitutionality of specific legislative and executive actions. Basically, it "enables nine justices to have the last word on what constitutional and statutory provisions really mean and to have the final say over whether governmental officials, at any level of government, are acting in a way which is consistent or inconsistent with constitutional or statutory requirements" (Warren, 1988, p. 422). The 1970s saw a major increase in the use of court rulings to control bureaucracies, particularly where citizen rights were at stake.

Judicial action can begin only with a criminal action initiated by a public prosecutor or a civil suit by a private party. Judges have no power to strike down on their own initiative a newly passed regulation. In this respect the courts play a passive role. Furthermore, major disputes can be definitively settled only by the U.S. Supreme Court, and several years are likely to pass between the initial filing of the suit and a final Court ruling. However, most Supreme Court rulings have constitutional authority and thus are the standard to be followed by lower courts and all executives and legislatures in the nation.

In many situations a court follows a ruling for the plaintiff or defense with one or more orders compelling or prohibiting certain actions, with which an official or agency must comply. Forty-two states were under court orders in 1994 to reduce overcrowding and/or to improve health care in their prisons, a response both to the states' failure to build sufficient facilities to match the growing numbers of offenders they were locking up and to the constitutional ban on "cruel and unusual punishment."

More dramatic was the order by U.S. District Court Judge Russell Clark in 1989 that the Kansas City, Missouri, school system eliminate all vestiges of racial segregation. His action was a response to a suit protesting that the system's inferior inner-city schools amounted to segregation, which violated the U.S. Supreme Court's ruling in *Brown v. Board of Education of Topeka, Kansas* (1954 and 1955). For years previously, Kansas City voters had repeatedly turned down proposals for school tax increases and bond issues. To comply with that ruling the district, with state assistance, has spent more than $1 billion to build new schools and remodel others; acquire facilities for computers, science, and sports; and massively upgrade the curriculum. Whether this enormous sum bought a better education has been vigorously argued, but in time this will offer a lesson on the impact of money on educational quality.

Courts, like legislative bodies, lack the direct means to enforce their orders. Some may require changed policies, increased expenditure of money, or reorganization of power. Missouri officials complied reluctantly with the order on Kansas City schools, knowing that the price was reduction of state aid to other school districts. However, administrators may resist and delay action on those orders that they disagree with, often with the backing of their own constituents. The slow pace of racial integration in public schools in the 1960s and 1970s illustrates this, as does the fact that prayer and Bible reading remain a part of the public school day in some communities. No one has taken legal action against such religious activities, so the courts have had no opportunity to rule on them.

Suits against Governments   Another important role of the courts is to settle suits by citizens against units of government. At one time, governments claimed absolute immunity from such suits, and the courts, looking back to the medieval English dictum that "the king could do no wrong," upheld them. Now, by contrast, a person or a corporation injured or unfairly treated by a government agency has the right to sue and collect damages under certain conditions (Wise, 1989). First, the federal government has absolute immunity from suit over the actions of its employees unless it consents to be sued. It has given consent in cases of false imprisonment, malicious prosecution, and violations of due process. Second, the president, legislative and judicial officials, and federal criminal prosecutors also cannot be sued for the performance of official actions. Third, other federal officials may be sued but are immune from liability if they can show that their actions were legal.

These conditions are spelled out in a series of Supreme Court decisions on specific disputes, however, and it is difficult to foresee how specific future suits will be settled. A 1988 decision (*Berkovitz v. United States*) held that the federal government could be sued by a boy who became paralyzed after receiving a polio vaccine from a batch that the Food and Drug Administration had approved without the required testing. This contrasted with earlier rulings that the Federal Aviation Administration is immune from negligence claims stemming from crashes of airliners that it certified.

In environmental disputes the courts have greatly expanded the liability of federal, state, and local authorities both for lapses in enforcing the laws and for their own misdeeds. Even low-level maintenance employees have been prosecuted and imprisoned by the Environmental Protection Agency and the U.S. Department of Justice for mishandling wastes. Courts have also found government employees guilty of failing to report their actions on such matters as transporting hazardous waste. The Clean Water Act of 1990 imposed complex burdens on local governments not only for their own sewage but also for all discharges into their treatment facilities. Aside from the merits of those regulations, all public agencies must pay closer attention to their rules, resources, and training of personnel responsible for environmental choices. As O'Leary (1993, p. 548) concludes, "Maintaining a reasonable level of morale and a public service ethic in such an atmosphere will become an even tougher challenge for public managers."

It is easier for citizens to sue their state and local governments than the federal government and to collect damages when their rights are violated, although this varies with the diversity of state court decisions. Authorities below the federal level have no general constitutional protection against such legal action. The key legal basis for this is Section 1983 of the U.S. Code, enacted as the Civil Rights Act of 1871, which defines officials as liable when they deprive people of their constitutional rights, privileges, and immunities. Rodney King won damages from the city of Los Angeles in 1994 after his videotaped beating by police officers. Governors lack the immunity that the president enjoys, and local officials can be held liable for damages in actions judged after the fact to have violated the law, even though they may not have understood at the time that they were violating it (Wise, 1989).

In our increasingly litigious society, such lawsuits have multiplied in number and size of claims. Between 1977 and 1983, about 3,000 suits of this nature were tried in the federal courts (Rosenbloom & Carroll, 1990, p. 30). As a result, state and local units' liability insurance has become much more costly and difficult to obtain. A further consequence, perhaps of mixed benefit, is that state and local officials are more cautious and, in some cases, refrain from certain actions that pose a higher-than-usual level of risk.

In summary, there is a clear trend in the courts toward allowing citizens to challenge administrators' decisions, even those based largely on legal discretion. Judges view such conflicts as disputes over rights of citizens (and thus of agency obligations), which must be examined by legal principles. For example, when the Environmental Protection Agency is required by law to design air quality programs, the courts have seen this as a mandate for a specific kind of program. Judges have thereby imposed detailed requirements on state and local governments and private businesses, as well as time limits for meeting them.

Control of One Government Unit by Another

Another channel for formal accountability is the power of one unit of government to supervise and check actions by another. We saw in Chapter 4 that the federal government can oversee specific actions of state and local authorities by means of regulations attached to its financial grants. In 1994 the General Accounting Office found that children's day-care centers in four states did not meet the states' own licensing standards. Congress's concern about daycare is that welfare recipients with small children need such care if they take jobs. Accordingly, congressional programs to promote recipients' employment will fail if day-care facilities are as dangerous to children's health and safety as were some of those inspected (Pear, 1994). A state or city government's deviation from a federal rule is usually not punished if it can bring sufficient political influence to bear in its defense. But the rules have considerable influence on state and local government employees, who prefer to avoid conflict.

State governments exercise primary oversight over their local units. Legally, the latter are subordinate, although state officials do not exercise general managerial supervision over them. This control is most salient in education, health, and public safety, where local lapses can affect large numbers of people. Many control efforts are linked with financial aid to general-purpose local government units and school boards. Oversight also provides for last-resort measures. For example, several states permit their education departments to take control of local school districts when they fail to meet legal standards. That became a reality for the Jersey City, New Jersey, school system in 1989 after it was charged with political corruption and academic mismanagement. The state board of education appointed a new superintendent for the system, who revised its personnel and financial practices and rewrote its curriculum. As of 1994 the results, as measured by student achievement scores, were mixed, and state officials admitted that improvement would be slow (Olmstead, 1994).

The Ombudsman

Many state and local governments employ an **ombudsman**, an official who receives citizen complaints and investigates alleged wrongdoing or unfair treatment. The office originated in Sweden in 1809 (along with the title, which means *agent*) and is now found in many industrialized nations. Although there is little demand for ombudsmen with broad powers in the United States, since legislators commonly function in this role through their casework, such officials do function in many U.S. cities. For example, Denver's Office of Citizen Response processes an average of 150 questions and 75 complaints per month. It cannot compel administrators to correct problems as the Swedish ombudsman can, but it enlists the support of the mayor and city council in case of disagreements (Rosen, 1989, pp. 95–96). Specialized offices to help the elderly and disabled exist in many states and communities, but their powers are also limited.

Box 15.2

How Do Civilian Police Review Boards Hold Law Enforcers Accountable?

Ask the typical police officer whether he or she would like to have a civilian review board to oversee the conduct of law enforcement in the city and you would probably get a strong "No!" in return. But it is a growing means of holding the police accountable: Some thirty-five of the nation's fifty largest cities have such a group that examines citizen complaints ranging from brutality to simple rudeness. They are most popular in communities of color, where police/citizen relationships are especially prickly.

Review boards' powers are not great, typically. Most can only investigate complaints against police conduct and publicize their find-

ings. A few can recommend disciplinary action where warranted, but only police officials can actually impose it. Law enforcement professionals argue that civilians do not experience the stresses and dilemmas of their work in dangerous situations and thus cannot fairly judge their conduct. The boards' impact is hard to assess overall, since we cannot know how much change in the officers' behavior has resulted or whether citizens have more confidence in them. In the long run, such boards may enable city officials to evaluate more effectively the work of their police and their supervisors (Andrews, 1993).

The Electoral Process

Finally, the electoral process itself is a formal means of accountability, the ultimate one in a nation based on popular sovereignty. It is, however, often an ineffective tool. Popularly elected executives face the voters only at scheduled intervals, and voter choices are shaped more by candidates' personalities and party ties than by judgments of performance in office. Yet incumbent governors and mayors have often been ousted as a result of voter perceptions that their policies had failed or that their administrations had been corrupt. Some states and local units also permit voters to recall (remove) elected officials before the end of their terms in special elections. A petition signed by a large (often 25 percent) proportion of registered voters is necessary to call an election. Thus, this process is not used often.

In general, these formal/external means of accountability function most often when the external institutions have the legal power and the political will to determine that wrongdoing has taken place, or is likely to do so in the absence of controls, and to decide on a clear deterrent or remedy. When administration is carried on properly, or at least does not arouse major complaints, overseers need not pay close attention to it. The powers of a legislative body are broadest in this respect, and the institutional rivalry that often prevails between it and the executive branch adds a political incentive. The courts operate within a narrower sphere of action, although their final word supersedes that of all others. The voters also have authority, but although their choices are unmistakable, the reasons for them are often less so, and the signals they send to nonelected administrators may not be easily read or quickly heeded. An additional means of citizen oversight, the civilian police review board, is described in Box 15.2.

Informal Accountability outside Government

Because so many individuals and private groups depend on government decisions and programs for their well-being, they keep close watch on the performance of selected agencies. These form the "structures of interest" first introduced in Chapter 2, which in many cases augment the means of accountability already discussed.

Interest Groups and Clienteles

Interest groups and organized clienteles of government agencies pay close attention to the implementation and outcome of public policies. Many groups have very specialized concerns, ranging from agricultural pesticides to home mortgages. Through publicity and lobbying, they hold the relevant federal, state, and local agencies accountable to their particular constituencies. Other groups have a much broader membership and must diffuse their influence over a wide range of issues; the AFL-CIO and the American Association of Retired Persons (AARP) are examples. Many groups also mobilize their members to conduct "grass-roots lobbying" of legislators and administrators and work to influence election outcomes through endorsements and campaign contributions. In addition, small citizen "watchdog" groups monitor the work of some public agencies, often those in consumer and environmental protection, and respond to performance lapses with publicity and lawsuits.

In small local governments, interest groups are easy to form and can readily learn what government is doing. A group of parents dissatisfied with their district's public schools can mobilize to press for reforms, win elections to the school board, and even oust an uncooperative superintendent. Neighborhood organizations in large cities have systematically identified lapses in housing inspection, police protection, street and sewer maintenance, and social services and have secured desired improvements.

At the federal level, however, consumer groups have a harder time being heard than do business groups. For example, if the Occupational Safety and Health Administration were to relax enforcement of a particular workplace standard, an industry trade association might applaud the move as a wise step toward greater production efficiency. The union representing the workers, however, could well denounce the change as one that would jeopardize their members' safety. Which group would have the most effect on the agency would depend in part on the prevailing political views in both the executive branch and Congress at the time. Additionally, if the affected workers were not unionized, there might be no countervailing response to OSHA's move. Whether or not an interest group is effective at the federal level often depends on an adversarial process. Without this process, corporate interests may prevail.

Professional Associations

Constituting a second locus of external/informal accountability, professional associations pay close attention to the performance of their members in the public and private sectors. Many public servants are certified members of medical, legal, educational, engineering, scientific, social work, and accounting associations. Through their education and apprenticeships, they have learned the prevailing norms and standards that apply in both the public and private sectors. Often they move between governmental and private positions during their careers. Public hospital administrators, for example, may look as much to their association for guidance on policy as to their state or county executives who are not in that profession. Review boards in medicine and law can revoke an association member's right to practice in cases of misconduct. Such associations also hold government accountable from the outside. Dr. Alice Stewart, an epidemiologist, concluded from her research in the 1970s that radiation was causing cancer among workers at the Hanford nuclear weapons plant in Washington state. Although the federal government managed to conceal that fact for many years, the persistent efforts of Stewart and her allies in the field led the secretary of energy in 1990 to open the records for examination and confirm her claim (Schneider, 1990).

Information Media

The news media and other information brokers constitute a third set of informal guardians of public accountability. When Bob Woodward and Carl Bernstein exposed the plot of President Nixon's re-election committee to burglarize Democratic Party offices in the Watergate building in 1972, they reinforced the image of the heroic American news reporter who uncovers corruption in City Hall. Many participate in this scrutiny: reporters and photographers, editors and television producers, magazine and book writers, scholars and researchers. Many organizations also profit politically and financially (while providing an essential public service) by exposing government's misdeeds. Admittedly, the media do not lack for biases. A slant toward a partisan or an ideological perspective, emphasis on news stories that are sexually explicit or involve violence, and exaggeration of dubious or scanty evidence are common sins of even respectable media sources.

By making government information public, the media promote accountability. Secrets are very hard to keep because so many can gain from their being revealed. This causes great frustration in the national security community, since whatever Americans can learn, other nations can learn. In other realms, however, the probability that a questionable action will become public knowledge is a major deterrent to sins of both commission and omission.

In many cases the news media play up information that is already in the public domain and compel the government to pay attention to it. The *New York Times* published many articles late in 1988 on the failings of the nuclear weapons production facilities under the jurisdiction of the Department of Energy. These stories highlighted the waste of funds, radiation hazards to employees and others in the plants' environs, and careless disposal of wastes, all of which were well documented by the General Accounting Office, the National Academy of Sciences, and the Energy Department itself. The data were extensive and scientifically complex, and it was necessary to compile and interpret them so that the public could understand them. These articles added to the credibility of the Stewart studies described earlier. One reporter described the lack of supervision exercised by the House and Senate Armed Services Committees over these operations and may well have caused those bodies to pay closer attention (Butterfield, 1988).

Open Government: Freedom of Information

Public Access to Information   Both interest groups and information brokers depend on a free flow of data. The federal Freedom of Information Act of 1966 stated, "Each agency, on request for identifiable records made in accordance with published rules stating the time, place, fees to the extent authorized by statute, and procedure to be followed, shall make the records promptly available to any person." Exceptions to this are many, however, and agencies are often reluctant to provide even legally accessible documents. Debates over information release continue to focus on protection of national security data, commercially usable information, and respect for personal privacy. On balance, the act has probably had a beneficial effect by enabling private groups to understand government operations better (Warren, 1988, p. 207).

Public Access to Meetings   Open decision-making processes can also promote accountability. The Government in the Sunshine Act, passed by Congress in 1976, requires that all meetings of multimember federal agencies be open to the public. They must be in a publicly accessible location and their dates and times must be announced in advance. A meeting may be closed to the public only when sensitive matters are at stake, such as personal data, military security, or privileged trade secrets. A 1988 study by the General Accounting Office concluded that agencies were complying with this ruling, although the GAO admitted that violations of the act would be hard to detect (U.S. Senate, Committee on Governmental Affairs, 1989).

Every state has similar laws for itself and its local governments, although it is unknown how widely they are followed. Minnesota law, for example, requires that all meetings of public boards, such as city councils and school boards, be held in a public place with due advance notice and that minutes be available. A meeting may be closed only to protect the privacy of those being discussed, as in employee evaluation and discipline. Moreover, this law is enforced.

How far these "open government" requirements have promoted accountability is uncertain, but it is clear that information flows more freely than it did before. Skeptics charge that these requirements have also slowed down decision making, made consensus harder to reach in difficult choices, and given members incentives to tailor their actions to the political and interest constituencies watching them (Warren, 1988, p. 211). In that they have reinforced the safeguards previously discussed, however, they probably have a positive effect. Box 15.3 describes a very different system in Japan, where information is withheld from citizens.

Informal Accountability within the Executive Branch

The final group of controls encompasses the personal commitments, loyalties, and values carried by each public servant and the sense of collective responsibility held by their working groups and organizations. A classic debate occurred in print years ago between two respected scholars of government over the issue of formal versus informal means of accountability. Carl Friedrich (1940) argued that we must rely heavily on the internal values and sense of responsibility of public officials for the quality of government. The formal checks are necessary but limited in their scope, particularly on innovative and technical matters, which demand action not spelled out in the laws. In rebuttal, Herman Finer (1941) held that these internal values are not explicit enough to be a consistent guide to administrative choice. Rather, we must place our reliance on the formal means of accountability, since only they can be widely understood and consistently applied.

This section examines the values on which Friedrich would depend more heavily. He stressed that administrators are closely involved in the formation and revision of policy, which can take

Box 15.3

Can the Japanese Break Their Wall of Secrecy?

Residents of the Tokyo suburb of Kyodo tried to break a hallowed tradition when they sought to learn why it was decided to build an elevated commuter railway through their neighborhood. The government would not tell them its reasons, since Japanese bureaucrats have a long-established practice of releasing only the information they want the public to have.

Secrecy is deeply rooted in Japanese tradition. Civil servants learn early in their careers that they must control information. Otherwise, public scrutiny would lead outsiders to second-guess them and create controversy. This extends even to the medical field, for doctors rarely tell patients what drugs they are prescribing for them.

That wall is cracking, however. The current reform movement in Japanese politics, spurred by revelations of corruption among high members of parliament, has stimulated new demands for openness. The Kyodo residents sued the city of Tokyo, and the court forced it to hand over a binder of documents evaluating the alternatives for the rail line. They learned to their surprise that it was only one part of a larger traffic plan that would deeply affect their community. It was the first time that administrators had been forced to reveal this kind of data. Civil libertarians are pressing for a national freedom of information law, similar to that of the United States. Whether or not it passes, the pressures are growing to make government in Japan more accountable to its people (Sterngold, 1994).

place even while it is being implemented. Having expertise in their policy areas, they can use their informed discretion, which the law explicitly requires in many cases. Often the necessary choice is the one sanctioned by a body of specialized knowledge, the codes of a profession, or the judgment of one with much experience in the field. At the same time, officials must be sensitive to the public's needs and demands, since administrative decisions affect them. Friedrich does not assert that the formal checks are unnecessary or harmful. Rather, he proposes that the informal standards supplement the formal means of accountability on the inevitably subjective dimensions of public policy.

Administrative Discretion and Ethical Principles

The sensitive realm of child abuse offers many instances of discretionary ethics. To whom are the social workers who visit homes and observe possible mistreatment actually accountable? In 1988 the U.S. Supreme Court ruled that the Constitution does not obligate state and local governments to protect their citizens from harm by private individuals (*DeShaney v. Winnebago County*). The plaintiff was the mother of a boy who had suffered permanent brain damage from abuse by his father. She charged that county social service officials violated his constitutional rights by not protecting him when they had reason to suspect he was in danger. Chief Justice Rehnquist stated in his majority opinion, "The most that can be said of the state functionaries in this case is that they stood by and did nothing when suspicious circumstances dictated a more active role for them." However, if they had intervened when it was unnecessary, "they would likely have been met with charges of improperly intruding into the parent-child relationship," which would have violated the due process clause of the Fourteenth Amendment, on which the suit was based. This decision, juxtaposed with the state laws that require protective action, forms the framework within which informal accountability based on the values of administrators must be effective. There are mandates to act and limits to such actions, but no precise rules on when to do what.

Serving the Public Interest   Five ethical principles are helpful to guide the exercise of administrative discretion (Warwick, 1981). First, the choice should serve the interests of the broadest relevant publics. In a choice to restrict use of a chemical found to cause cancer, the "protected public" may be much larger than the group that will lose jobs or profits from that action. Yet that balance may be complicated by the fact that the adverse effects for the latter group may be much greater than the benefits to the former. Discerning the stakes of each "public" here is an ethical challenge in itself.

Reflective Choice   The second principle is reflective choice, which is due care and specific consideration of the alternatives and consequences rather than passing them off as routine and perfunctory. It is tempting for social workers with many more cases than they can reasonably care for to make snap judgments, such as saying, "This family is just like the one I saw an hour ago." Administrators with short deadlines are often pressed for decisions, and failing to make them creates further problems. Reflection may, however, uncover factors that lead to more informed decisions.

Truthfulness   The third principle, truthfulness, is not merely a refusal to lie but a holistic presentation of information and viewpoints that enables other participants, including private citizens, to evaluate decisions and actions intelligently. This contradicts commonly used political tactics, which use, withhold, or put a particular spin on information to serve personal or special interests. Reports on the extent of child abuse in a county should present a realistic picture that enables social workers to respond sensitively and give citizens a means of evaluating the welfare department's performance.

Respect   Fourth, considerable respect should be given to established procedures, regulations, and the other ties that hold a bureaucracy together. This does not require "going by the book" when it would be senseless or harmful. Rather, it provides consistency and predictability that enable others to relate to the agency with confidence. Well-formed procedures can help prevent discrimination in treatment of clients according to race, ethnicity, or language.

Citizen Rights   Finally, a responsible official avoids using means that violate citizen rights, cause mental or physical harm, or undermine popular trust in government. Achievement of a worthy end can be frustrated by improper steps to get there. Removal of a child from a home is a drastic but occasionally necessary step and must not be done in a manner that causes the child further anguish or permanently ruptures family ties.

Administrative Ethics and Whistle-Blowing

It is impossible to ensure that all governmental employees hold these principles to a sufficient degree or retain them on the job. The temptations to both corruption and neglect of duty are many and often come from within the government itself. Therefore, it is vital that those who maintain the performance standards discussed in this chapter provide employees with every incentive to meet them. Although this may sometimes call for more rules, it can also mean giving conscientious and capable child protection workers more freedom to use their best judgment.

A practical application of these ethical norms arises when employees encounter mismanagement or wrongdoing inside their own organizations. The bureaucratically proper response is to seek correction first within the organization. The supervisors have the obligation to deal with internal wrongdoing and should be given the opportunity to do so. But when the needed correction is not made or the higher officials are part of the problem, the employee may "blow the whistle" by publicizing the problem outside the agency. This release may be to the news media, an interest group, the legislature, or another part of government. Two private organizations—the Government Accountability Project and the Coalition against Government Waste—have passed along many whistle-blowers' messages and protected their anonymity. In so doing, they help link the internal and external realms.

Whistle-blowing has been fairly widespread, though well documented only at the federal level. It has produced much useful evidence for the accountability process, and the prospect that an employee will "go public" probably has deterred some contemplated wrongdoing. It has cost honest employees much grief, however, since most have suffered retaliation from supervisors, and any vindication has come years later. Actually, only a small proportion of federal employees who know of fraud or mismanagement do anything about it, according to one survey (cited by Rosen, 1989, pp. 149–150). The major reasons given by employees who chose to ignore the wrongdoing were a belief that nothing would or could be done about it and a fear of retaliation.

Whistle-blowing is now officially sanctioned: The U.S. Code of Ethics for government employees obligates them to "expose corruption wherever uncovered" and to "put loyalty to the highest moral principles and to country above loyalty to persons, party, or Government department." To reinforce this duty and protect this channel of accountability, Congress provided protection to whistle-blowers in the 1978 Civil Service Reform Act and extended it in 1989 legislation. It provided an Office of Special Counsel in the federal personnel management structure with a mandate to delay firing or demoting workers who had filed complaints and to protect them from other forms of harrassment (Jos, Tompkins, & Hays, 1989).

It is important that administrators both avoid situations that employees would have reason to expose and reduce opportunities for errors to go undetected. Managers can provide means for taking criticism seriously, and their doors must always be open to those with grievances. Those who do come with legitimate problems related to the organization's performance must be treated with respect and not penalized in any formal or informal way, as specified by the 1989 legislation.

Whistle-blowing also has an important place in government's relations with its contractors. Chapter 7 described the great reliance at all levels on private suppliers of goods and services. The potential for fraud and mismanagement is as great in the private sector as it is in the public. Under the False Claims Act, first passed in 1863, those who bring evidence of misconduct are entitled to a portion of any money that the government recovers in a suit. A former employee of one contractor was awarded $7.5 million in 1992 after he revealed that his firm overbilled the Pentagon by more than $1 billion. There have been many such suits, which has raised concern that some are motivated more by greed than by dedication to the public good.

The many factors identified in Chapter 13 that prevent governments from implementing policies and the obstacles to evaluation noted in Chapter 14 also make it difficult to hold governments accountable. These factors are not necessarily evils to be wiped out in the next reform, however. They lie in the very nature of the public purposes or in the constitutional methods we have chosen for fulfilling them. Thus, we have to understand these obstacles and the means to maximize accountability in the face of them.

The Politics of Accountability

The controls on national, state, and local bureaucracies reviewed in this chapter can be broadly categorized as either "muscles" or "prayers" (Gormley, 1989b). The former are **coercive controls**, which use legal compulsion to secure compliance or prevent abuse and leave administrators little or no discretion. "Prayers" are **catalytic controls**, which call on administrators to address a problem but do not mandate a particular response. **Hortatory controls** fall between these two poles and apply incentives and pressures for action but leave some room for discretion. The express commands and standards given to the Food and Drug Administration for outlawing cancer-causing food additives are coercive controls, or muscles. Catalytic controls, or prayers, often come from citizens and interest groups in petitions to clean up toxic waste sites in their neighborhoods, for example. A hortatory control might be exerted in a report by an audit agency stating that action must be taken to reduce carbon monoxide levels in a city's air. Each approach has strengths and weaknesses and is useful for some situations. Coercive controls are found in the formal/internal and formal/external categories, whereas the two informal groups have exclusively catalytic means. Some catalytic controls also surround the coercive ones in the formal categories. Hortatory controls are scattered throughout both formal categories.

Conflicting Administrative Roles

Against which obstacles must these controls be effective? One cluster lies in the conflicting responsibilities of public officials. We have identified the dilemma facing conscientious public servants who find wrongdoing within their work groups or agencies. To whom do they owe primary loyalty? Choosing whether or not to blow the whistle forces them to weigh suppression of their conscience against the consequences of harming the reputations of colleagues and supervisors. Yet blowing the whistle is necessary when the organization suppresses information that should be made public.

An agency as a whole may be in a quandary when a popular governor gives it certain directions and an equally determined legislature sets different priorities. The ethical dilemma may be resolved in practice if a clear winner of the power struggle emerges, but until then the agency's accountability may be hampered. A further conflict appears in a state or local agency that receives large amounts of federal funds and must follow the rules that accompany them. Those rules, however, may be unsuited to local conditions or priorities, and the agency head must wrestle with how to meet both imperatives.

No rule can tell administrators how to resolve interagency conflict, since the rules themselves have created it. Rather, administrators at all levels must be sensitive to the legitimate justifications of each claim on loyalty and to the consequences of violating it. Frequently, they find compromises that satisfy the most important values in the situation, and in other cases the balance of political forces leads the parties to certain solutions.

Confusion of Responsibility

A second obstacle to accountability is the "many-hands" problem. As we have often seen, our nation relies on networks of organizations to serve most public purposes. Environmental, social service, and housing programs blend federal, state, and local authority in policy and administration, and many programs also involve private-sector organizations. The separation-of-powers system ensures that legislators will be closely involved in the details of implementation when it suits them, and judges' decisions regularly expand or curtail administrators' authority and mandates.

"Many hands" confuse accountability. "When citizens look for officials to call to account for a policy, they rarely find anyone who single-handedly made the policy. They often cannot even discover anyone whose own contribution to the collective outcome seems significant enough to warrant credit or blame for it" (Thompson, 1987, p. 40). This search also frustrates legislators, interest groups, and others with a stake in the situation. Martin (1948) chronicled the 1947 coal mine explosion in Centralia, Illinois, that took 111 lives, as well as the failure of that state's Department of Mines and Minerals to enforce safety regulations there. He concluded from the evidence, "As one strives to fix responsibility for the disaster, again and again one is confronted, as were the miners, not with any individual but with a host of individuals fused into a vast, unapproachable, insensate organism. . . . Certainly all those in authority were too remote from the persons whose lives they controlled."

Many of the policy issues on which polls find high popular dissatisfaction are those under "many-handed" control: drug abuse, homelessness, declining educational performance, and environmental poisoning. Even when there are serious attempts at central coordination, as with a federal "drug czar," they often have little effect. Although there is consensus that public action is needed, it evaporates when the discussion turns to specifics.

There is no single remedy for the "many-hands" problem, but its negative effects can be minimized with a combination of formal and informal, coercive and catalytic means. Statutes, administrative rules, executive orders, and contracts can portray clearly the duties of each person in the chain of command. Within these, administrators can exercise their own sense of responsibility to communicate, plan joint action, and work through the obstacles that appear. This happens every day in the many programs that do succeed with little complaint or publicity. Each mode of accountability can support the other.

Growth of Bureaucratic Controls

The more sensitive and difficult the policy issues for which governments are responsible, the greater is the pressure to multiply the means of ensuring accountability. The social legislation of the 1960s sought to accomplish many more changes in national life than ever before, and it is no surprise that the 1970s saw an upsurge in efforts to control the bureaucracies that were implementing these changes. The controls were targeted at wrongdoings of which these agencies were guilty to some extent, such as favoring influential clients, resisting needed change, and handling individual cases arbitrarily and unfairly. Thus, the number and use of both coercive and catalytic controls discussed in this chapter were multiplied at the state and national levels.

The results of this "bureau-bashing" led to new and no-less-harmful wrongdoings. The 1980s saw increased reliance on rigid procedures to avoid unfairness, avoidance of high-risk actions even when beneficial, the generation of statistics that give the outward impression of progress in meeting goals even when the reality is otherwise, and showing deference to influential legislators with oversight powers. These added to the existing offenses. From this experience Gormley concluded that prayers are preferable to muscles in most instances when control is needed. Prayers are often successful in eliciting action because they let administrators use their expertise to find the most effective ways (1989b, p. 5).

Summary

Public administrators work within a complex pattern of accountability that reflects both the complexity of government organization in a pluralistic society and the variety of duties for which they are responsible. A unit of government, one of its agencies, or an individual public servant is accountable when each serves a public purpose in a manner that conforms both to the law and to the expectations of citizens. When this does not occur, the agency or person can be compelled to comply or suffer penalties.

The basic means of maintaining this accountability can be analyzed in four categories: (1) formal means within the executive structure; (2) formal means outside the executive structure; (3) informal means outside the executive organization, undertaken by individual and organized citizens; and (4) informal means inside the executive organization.

Formal/internal means include hierarchical controls, budget preparation, internal audits, inspectors general, and investigative commissions. Much depends on the dedication of the chief executive in ensuring that these means work as intended.

Formal/external controls are imposed by legislative bodies and courts in their constitutional functions of checking and balancing the executive branches. These exist in an atmosphere of rivalry and competition for power. In intergovernmental checks a higher unit can hold a lower one accountable for actions on shared-responsibility programs.

The informal/external agents of accountability—interest groups, professional communities, and the news media—are valuable for ensuring the responsiveness of government to various constituencies and fair treatment of individuals who come to their attention. Freedom of information and open governmental decision making are essential to this.

In the fourth means, informal/internal, the individual and group values and standards that public servants themselves hold are vital. This is especially true in those matters of sensitive discretion, such as specialized medical choices, for which society must trust responsible people to do their best. Such discretionary matters are least subject to formal checks, although they can be shaped over the long run by all the other influences.

Accountability in practice involves two political dilemmas. The first is that public agencies have several responsibilities and sources of direction; to follow one completely may be to violate another. Second, the "many hands" involved in implementing public policy blur responsibility for it, since it is difficult to assess partial blame or credit for actions.

Discussion Questions

1. How can ordinary citizens know whether and how well all these means of holding government accountable are working as they should?

2. Which of these means of accountability failed most seriously as the misdeeds in the Department of Education's student loan programs multiplied?

3. Can there be too much accountability, so that administrators become overly sensitive to criticism and fail to act when necessary in controversial matters?

4. To what extent do (and should) political rivalries motivate and direct legislative bodies in their efforts to hold the executive branch accountable?

5. How useful are ethical standards for guiding the choices and behavior of government administrators? What can they accomplish and what limits do they have?

Analytical Exercises

1. Find a news article on some instance of alleged misconduct by a public official or agency, preferably a specific situation at the state or local level. (The allegation may be true, false, or exaggerated.) Learn how the reporter obtained the information, the seriousness of the charge, and who is responsible for acting on it. Then trace the response to it by the officials concerned and draw any lessons you can about government accountability.

2. The 104th Congress, under control of the Republicans, has a political incentive to uncover wrongdoing in the executive branch. Find one or more examples of congressional investigations and evaluate their findings. Learn all you can about the sources of their information, the validity of their charges, and the responses, if any, of the administration.

For Further Reading

Glazer, M. P., & Glazer, P. M. (1989). *The Whistleblowers: Exposing Corruption in Government and Industry.* New York: Basic Books. Case studies of many who blew the whistle on wrongdoing, why they did, and whether and how they were vindicated.

Gormley, W. T. (1989). *Taming the Bureaucracy: Muscles, Prayers and Other Strategies.* Princeton, NJ: Princeton University Press. Enlightening survey of the many means used to control administrative agencies, with the results of their use. Generally recommends use of prayers over muscles.

Romzek, B. S., & Dubnick, M. J. (1987, May–June). Accountability in the public sector: Lessons from the *Challenger* tragedy. *Public Administration Review, 47,* 227–238. Excellent analysis of the accountability issues that the tragedy raised, with particular relevance to government relations with contractors.

Rosen, B. (1989). *Holding Government Bureaucracies Accountable* (2nd ed.). New York: Praeger. Broad and detailed survey of the means of accountability used by national, state, and local governments.

Rosenbloom, D. H., & Carroll, J. D. (1990). *Toward Constitutional Competence: A Casebook for Public Administrators.* Englewood Cliffs, NJ: Prentice Hall. See further reading in Chapter 8.

Glossary

Accountability The process by which public officials answer to the citizens directly or indirectly for the use of their powers. 17

Adjudication A proceeding in which a regulatory agency makes a distinct ruling on each case before it. 172

Advocates Public officials who express their self-interest through loyalty to a large organization or a broad group of functions. 74

Affirmative action Special efforts to diversify workforces by inviting persons of disadvantaged groups to apply for employment and hiring them for positions for which they meet the basic qualifications. 319

Agenda A list of issues that warrants serious consideration for policymaking. 132

Appropriation A legislative action to permit funds to be taken from the Treasury to pay for authorized programs. 354

Audit The determination of what money was spent, for what purposes, and whether the expenditures conformed to law. 363

Authoritarian leadership A leadership style in which the executive imposes decisions on an organization with little or no discussion or opportunity for feedback from subordinates. 257

Authority The source of political power that inheres in an elective or appointive office. 152

Budget A plan for future spending that is built on certain income expectations. 346

Bureau Max Weber's term for a organization requiring officials, scribes, records, and rules. 63

Bureaucracy A form of organization that (a) is large enough that its top managers cannot have face-to-face relations with their subordinates, (b) is sufficiently specialized to require a precise division of labor, and (c) consists of offices arranged in a chain of command from the top executive to the lowest employee. 62

Bureaucratic ideology Beliefs or statements about how the organization involved is valuable to society and the means by which it promotes those values. 76

Cabinet departments The 14 major executive organizations of the national government; also found in state and some local governments. 37

Capital budgets Plans for the costs of acquiring land, buildings, roads, and equipment that will have a life of more than one year. 349

Catalytic controls A means of accountability in which administrators are called upon to act on a matter, but no specific action is mandated. 456

Centralization The extent to which operations in every part of an organization are controlled by its chief executive and/or detailed rules. 84

Centralized federalism An American style of government in which state policy and administration are mobilized to serve nationally defined goals. 102

Citizen participation Formal roles played by people who are not elected or appointed government officials in advising or making binding decisions on implementing public policies. 224

Climbers Self-interested public officials who primarily seek power, income, and prestige. 74

Closed system An organization with a relatively thick "shell" insulating it from external influences. 69

Coercive controls A means of accountability that uses legal compulsion to secure compliance or prevent abuse of power. 456

Collective bargaining Negotiations leading to a contract that states the terms of the employer-employee relationship. 327

Commission form A system of local government consisting of an elected body that both legislates and administers. 49

Comparable worth A principle under which jobs requiring equal skills, effort, and responsibility are paid

461

equally without regard for the race or gender of persons currently holding them. 325

Conflict of interest A personal association, investment, or belief that may inhibit a public employee from performing in conformity with the law and the public good. 329

Conglomerate A system of hierarchies united at the top by a single directorate. 86

Conservers Self-interested public officials who primarily seek to maintain their existing advantages rather than to enhance their power. 74

Contracting Government purchase of goods and services from private suppliers. 193

Cooperative federalism An American system of sharing responsibilities between national and state levels of government. 100

Coproduction Participation of private persons in providing public services. 197, 313

Coprovision Private contributions of money or expertise to provision of public services. 197

Council/manager form A system of local government that consists of an elected council that hires a professional manager to direct the administration. 49

Current-expenditure budgets Plans for funds to be expended entirely within the given fiscal year. 349

Decision A goal-oriented selection of one course of action from two or more alternatives. 279

Democratic leadership A leadership style in which the executive provides opportunities for subordinates to participate in choices about the agency's tasks and means of performing them. 258

Dual federalism A style of American government in which policy realms of the national and state governments were small and largely separate from one another. 100

Due process of law Procedures that government must follow in acting toward an individual. 231

Economic regulation Rules and rule making concerned with preserving competition in industries and maintaining fair prices for products and services. 165

Effectiveness The degree to which a program fulfills the goals defined by the policymakers. 416

Efficiency The margin of benefits gained from a program over the resources invested in it. 416

Entitlements Legally required benefit payments to individuals. 356

Equal employment opportunity Fair treatment of all applicants and employees without discrimination on the basis of race, ethnic background, gender, age, or physical disability. 319

Equilibrium The balance of intake and output that an organization maintains with its environment and that enables it to survive. 70

Equity The extent to which program benefits and costs are distributed so that no group or individual receives less than a minimum benefit or pays more than a maximum cost. 418

Executive orders Directives from a chief executive to all or part of the executive branch that have the force of law on matters within the executive's authority. 261

External scanning The process of surveying an organization's environment, analyzing the data obtained thereby, and reporting it in usable formats. 285

Federal system Combined national and state authorities and the norms that control their relations. 97

Federalism A system in which the total powers of government are divided by a constitution between one authority that governs the whole nation and several that govern its political subdivisions. 32, 96

Fiscal federalism The flow of money among national, state, and local levels of government and the intergovernmental aspects of federal taxation. 103

Forecast A statement of a possible future event or condition with an estimate of its likelihood. 286

Formal communication Messages that follow the hierarchical structure and relate to the exercise of authority and the duties of each member of the organization. 77

Formative evaluation The analysis of the outcomes and impacts of an agency or a program to learn why the results occurred and how performance can be improved. 409

Garbage-can model of decision making A model that portrays choices as emerging from a highly diverse and fluid network of decision makers and unsystematic processes. 283

General-purpose local government A form of local administration that includes counties, towns, and municipalities, which are all responsible for many governmental functions. 45

Governmental-politics model of decision making A model that portrays choices as being made by competing players, each of whom seeks power over the decision-making system. 283

Grant-in-aid The transfer of money from one level of government to another. 103

Hierarchy A system of persons holding authority over others and having the ability to command behavior and punish lack of compliance. 63

Hortatory controls A means of accountability that relies on incentives for administrators and pressures for action but leaves some room for discretion. 456

Human relations perspectives A view of organization that takes into account the social relationships in the workplace and their impact on productivity. 67

Impact The long-term consequences for society of the implementation of a policy. 382

Implementation The process of realizing public policy, thereby attempting to achieve the public purposes for which the policy was made. 146

Incremental model of decision making A model that portrays the process of making choices when goals are not precise, the evidence and alternatives are incomplete, and political controversy shapes the final decisions. 281

Independent regulatory commissions Governmental bodies of three or more members that regulate a segment of the private economy. 40

Influence The means of prevailing in a conflict without using legal sanctions or threats of deprivation. 153

Informal organization Relationships formed voluntarily among members of an organization that reflect and condition their motives and behavior. 68

Institutional agendas Items that specific government bodies or leaders rank as high priorities for action. 134

Intelligence Strategically useful information. 284

Intergovernmental relations The interactions among national, state, and local governments in making and implementing their shared policies. 97

Iron triangle Coalition of an administrative agency, one or more interest groups, and the appropriate legislative committees, all of whom cooperate to achieve common goals. 154

Issue networks Coalitions of public officials, other professionals, and private citizens who cooperate on significant public issues. 157

Item veto An action by a state executive to delete or reduce spending items in an appropriation bill while signing the bill as a whole. 358

Joint powers agreements Accords that allow local governments to purchase services from one another or share a function for which they have legal powers. 115

Judicial review The power of courts to determine the constitutionality of legislative and executive actions. 443

Laissez-faire leadership A form of delegation in which the executive allows and encourages subordinates to make decisions according to criteria of their choosing. 258

Leader/follower organization An organizational format consisting of one superior and a cluster of subordinates. 85

Legislative oversight Surveillance of bureaucratic performance to determine its conformity to law and legislative intention. 438

Legislative veto A requirement in a law or an appropriation that an agency secure explicit approval from the whole legislature or one of its committees before it can take certain actions. 440

Legitimacy The standing conferred on an executive by law or the legal actions of a superior. 256

Line-item budget A budget that lists specific items to be purchased and their costs. 348

Mandates Legal requirements for action that the national government imposes on state and local governments or that the states impose on their local units. 108

Market failure Shortcomings in the private economy's service to the public that justify government regulation in some form. 164

Mayor/Council form A system of local government that consists of an elected chief executive and a legislative body, each with distinct powers. 48

Merit sector Public employees hired on the basis of having demonstrated competence for the job through experience, examination, or education. 310

Monocratic Describing the form of bureaucracy in which each unit of the system is headed by a single individual. 66

Mosaic organization A loosely joined collection of autonomous units able to make some decisions jointly. 85

Negative externalities Costs of economic transactions that fall upon persons not participating in these transactions. 164

Ombudsman An official who receives citizen complaints and investigates alleged wrongdoing or unfair treatment. 446

Open systems Organizations that are constantly vulnerable to outside influences at all levels of the hierarchy. 69

Organization The assembly of knowledge, power, and will to accomplish certain purposes. 61

Organizational-process model of decision making A model that portrays choices as the outputs of a large organization behaving in its accustomed fashion. 283

Outcome The intermediate-range result of the implementation of a policy. 382

Output An immediate good or service provided by a program. 382

Partnerships Long-term cooperative relationships between one or more units of government and private organizations in projects for which they share resources and control. 194

Patronage The practice of appointing lower-level government employees for their connections to the political party or to elected executives in office. 312

Performance budgets Budgets that list expenditures in groups according to their objectives within each agency or unit. 348

Performance measurement The systematic measurement of the efficiency and effectiveness of programs and organizational performance. 408

Planning The process of choosing goals and devising steps to reach them over a given span of time. 292

Popular agenda Problems and issues in which the general public is most interested. 132

Power The ability to achieve one's goals in the face of opposition. 149

Power structures Groups that consistently exercise power in a social system over a period of time. 155

Private contributions Financial or in-kind support of public enterprises by private citizens or organizations. 193

Privatization, pure The complete or partial transfer of a function from government to the private sector or the sale of government-owned assets to a private holder. 193

Program budget A budget that groups expenditures according to the broad purposes served by government, regardless of which agency uses the funds. 349

Public administration The process by which government organizations supply essential goods and services, managing resources and resolving conflicts under a mandate to do so fairly and efficiently, while accounting to the public for both means and outcomes. 2, 18

Public policies Government's choices of actions that are intended to serve the public purposes. 11

Public purposes The broad tasks that the public expects government to carry out. 4

Public sector That portion of the nation's resources that are obtained and allocated by units of government. 9

Publics Groups of people with distinct relationships to some aspect of public policy. 218

Rational decision making (model) A style that portrays the process of making choices as one in which an individual specifies goals, considers all evidence and alternatives that pertain to achieving them, and selects the one that offers the best combination of benefits and costs. 280

Regulation The process by which government requires or prohibits certain actions by individuals and institutions. 163

Roles Consistent relationships and forms of behavior suited to particular settings. 219

Rule making Formulation of general regulations applicable to many similar situations. 172

Scientific management The concept that there is one best way to design and manage jobs and organizations. 18

Senior Executive Service A pool of executives in the merit sector who occupy agency posts just below those reserved for politically appointed executives. 310

Separation of powers A principle by which government is divided into legislative, executive, and judicial branches, each with powers of its own and means to check and balance the others. 32

Social regulation Rules and rule making concerned with protecting or promoting the health, safety, and opportunities of individuals who may be harmed by business practices. 166

Span of control The number of persons or units overseen by one supervisor. 84

Special-purpose local governments Units of local governments that are responsible for one or a few related functions. 47

Statesmen Public officials who express their self-interest through devotion to their individual definitions of the "general welfare." 74

Statutory law Public policy formally enacted by legislative bodies. 131

Street-level bureaucrats Public employees who work in locations not directly supervised by higher administrators and who exercise much discretion in performing services. 237

Summative evaluation A factual statement of what a program or an agency accomplished. 409

System perspective A view of a network of interdependent parts in which individual choices and actions affect the entire network. 392

Tax expenditures The exclusions, deductions, and preferential rates that reduce the income taxes paid by individuals and corporations. 367

Tools of implementation The techniques and procedures for carrying out public purposes. 15

Trust funds Accounts separate from the government's general fund and reserved for purposes specified by law. 358

Vouchers Official certificates for a stipulated good or service, which may be given to a provider in exchange for the good or service. 193

Zealots Public officials who express their self-interest through loyalty to a very specific cause. 74

References

Aaron, Henry J., ed. *Setting National Priorities.* Washington, DC: Brookings Institution, 1990.

Abney, Glenn, and Thomas P. Lauth. "The governor as chief administrator." *Public Administration Review* 43 (January–February 1983): 40–49.

___. *The Politics of State and City Administration.* Albany: State University of New York Press, 1986.

Adams, Rebecca. "An activist chief for Indian Affairs." *National Journal*, September 24, 1994, p. 2234.

Advisory Commission on Intergovernmental Relations. *Citizen Participation in the American Federal System.* Washington, DC: ACIR, 1979.

___. "Which level should do what: Criteria for decisionmaking." *Intergovernmental Perspective* 8 (Spring 1982).

___. *Regulatory Federalism: Policy, Process, Impact and Reform.* Washington, DC: ACIR, 1984.

Advisory Commission on Intergovernmental Relations. *Intergovernmental Decisionmaking for Environmental Protection and Public Works.* Washington, DC: ACIR, 1992a.

Advisory Commission on Intergovernmental Relations. *Metropolitan Organization: The Allegheny County Case.* Washington, DC: ACIR, 1992b.

Allison, Graham T. *Essence of Decision: Explaining the Cuban Missile Crisis.* Boston: Little, Brown, 1971.

Amirrezvani, Anita. "The data game." *Governing* (February 1990): 42–45.

Andrews, James H. "Civilian-review boards gain public support." *Christian Science Monitor*, November 22, 1993.

Argyris, Chris. "The individual and the organization: Some problems of mutual adjustment." *Administrative Science Quarterly* 2 (June 1957): 1–24.

Arnstein, Sherry R. "A ladder of citizen participation." *Journal of the American Institute of Planners* 35 (July 1969): 216–224.

Arrandale, Tom. "A guide to recycling: Collecting more, costing less." *Governing*, August 1994, pp. 59–75.

___. "When the poor cry NIMBY." *Governing*, September 1993, pp. 36–41.

Axelrod, Donald. *A Budget Quartet: Critical Policy and Management Issues.* New York: St. Martin's, 1989.

Bachmann, Geraldine. "Attleboro Mall: Risky business under Section 404." *Urban Land* 46 (February 1987): 2–5.

Bachrach, Peter, and Morton S. Baratz. "Decisions and nondecisions: An analytical framework." *American Political Science Review* 57 (September 1963): 632–42.

Bailey, Robert W. *The Crisis Regime: The Mac, the EFCB, and the Political Impact of the New York City Financial Crisis.* Albany: State University of New York Press, 1984.

___. "Uses and misuses of privatization." In *Prospects for Privatization*, edited by Steve H. Hanke. *Proceedings of the Academy of Political Science* 36:3 (1987): 138–152.

Bardach, Eugene. *The Implementation Game: What Happens after a Bill Becomes Law.* Cambridge, MA: MIT Press, 1977.

Barden, J. C. "Foster care system reeling, despite law meant to help." *New York Times,* September 21, 1990.

Barnard, Chester. *The Functions of the Executive.* Cambridge, MA: Harvard University Press, 1938.

Barr, Cameron. "Dual role dogs U.S. border agency." *Christian Science Monitor,* December 14, 1990.

Beam, David R. "Washington's regulation of states and localities." *Intergovernmental Perspective* 7 (Summer 1981): 8-18.

Belsie, Laurent. "Pesticide use prompts moral, scientific debate." *Christian Science Monitor,* November 22, 1989.

___. "Make a better bottle and people will beat a path . . ." *Christian Science Monitor,* April 26, 1990.

Benda, Peter M., and Charles H. Levine. "Reagan and the bureaucracy: The bequest, the promise, and the legacy." In *The Reagan Legacy: Promise and Performance,* edited by Charles O. Jones, pp. 102-142. Chatham, NJ: Chatham House, 1988.

Berger, Joseph, and Elizabeth Kolbert. "New York schools and patronage: Experience teaches hard lessons." *New York Times,* December 11, 1989.

Blair, William G. "Workers' resignations threaten quality of private social services." *New York Times,* December 20, 1987.

Bobrow, Davis B., and John S. Dryzek. *Policy Analysis by Design.* Pittsburgh: University of Pittsburgh Press, 1987.

Bosso, Christopher J. "Transforming adversaries into collaborators: Interest groups and the regulation of chemical pesticides." Paper presented to the 1986 annual meeting of the American Political Science Association, Washington, DC.

Bowman, James S., ed. *Ethical Frontiers in Public Management.* San Francisco: Jossey-Bass, 1991.

Bowsher, Charles A. *Government Management— Report on 17 High-Risk Areas* (Testimony before the Committee on Governmental Affairs, U.S. Senate) Washington, DC: General Accounting Office, 1993.

Breyer, Stephen. *Breaking the Vicious Circle: Toward Effective Risk Regulation.* Cambridge, MA: Harvard University Press, 1993.

Brown, Elizabeth A. "New U.S. standards squeeze cities, states." *Christian Science Monitor,* February 5, 1991.

Bryce, Robert. "US-Mexican border cleanup stalls in bureaucratic halls." *Christian Science Monitor,* November 28, 1994.

Bryner, Gary C. *Bureaucratic Discretion: Law and Policy in Federal Regulatory Agencies.* New York: Pergamon, 1987.

Bryson, John M., and William D. Roering. "Applying private-sector strategic planning in the public sector." *American Planning Association Journal* 53 (Winter 1987): 9-22.

Burnham, David. "Officials come and go; ethics stay." *New York Times,* August 31, 1985.

Burns, James M. *Leadership.* New York: Harper & Row, 1978.

Butterfield, Fox. "Trouble at atomic bomb plants: How lawmakers missed the signs." *New York Times,* November 28, 1988.

Caiden, Gerald E. "The vitality of administrative reform." *International Review of Administrative Sciences* 54 (September 1988): 331-357.

Caldwell, Lynton K. "Environmental impact analysis (EIA): Origins, evolution, and future directions." *Policy Studies Review* 8 (Autumn 1988): 75-83.

Campbell, Colin. *Managing the Presidency: Carter, Reagan, and the Search for Executive Harmony.* Pittsburgh: University of Pittsburgh Press, 1986.

Carson, Rachel L. *Silent Spring.* Boston: Houghton Mifflin, 1962.

Carter, Marshall. "Agency fragmentation and its effect on impact: A borderlands case." *Policy Studies Journal* 8 (Summer 1980): 862-870.

Chira, Susan. "Preschool aid for the poor: How big a head start?" *New York Times,* February 14, 1990.

Chisholm, Donald. *Coordination Without Hierarchy: Informal Structures in Multiorganizational Systems.* Berkeley: University of California Press, 1989.

Church, Thomas W., and Robert T. Nakamura. *Cleaning Up the Mess: Implementation Strategies in Superfund.* Washington, DC: Brookings Institution, 1993.

Cobb, Roger W., and Charles D. Elder. *Participation in American Politics: The Dynamics of Agenda-Building.* Boston: Allyn & Bacon, 1972.

Cogan, John F., Timothy J. Muris, & Allen Schick. *The Budget Puzzle: Understanding Federal Spending.* Palo Alto, CA: Stanford University Press, 1994.

Cohen, Michael D., James G. March, and Johan P. Olsen. "A garbage can model of organizational choice." *Administrative Science Quarterly* 17 (March 1972): 1-25.

Cohen, Noam. "Weather Service faces tough test." *New York Times,* January 13, 1991.

Congressional Quarterly. *Federal Regulatory Directory.* Washington, DC: CQ Books, 1986.

Coombs, Fred S. "The bases of noncompliance with a policy." *Policy Studies Journal* 8 (Summer 1980): 885–892.

Cooper, Joseph, and William F. West. "Presidential power and republican government: The theory and practice of OMB review of agency rules." *Journal of Politics* 50 (November 1988): 864–895.

Cooper, Philip J. "By order of the president: Administration by executive order and proclamation." *Administration and Society* 18 (August 1986): 233–262.

Cooper, Terry L. "Public administration in an age of scarcity: A citizenship role for public administrators." In *Politics and Administration,* edited by Jack Rabin and James S. Bowman. New York: Marcel Dekker, 1984.

Cothran, Dan A. "Japanese bureaucrats and policy implementation: Lessons for America?" *Policy Studies Review* 6 (February 1987): 439–458.

Cushman, John H., Jr. "President moves to loosen grip of White House on regulations." *New York Times,* October 1, 1993.

___. "Forest Service is rethinking its mission." *New York Times,* April 24, 1994.

___. "Private transportation workers to join ranks of those tested for drug use." *New York Times,* December 18, 1989.

Dahl, Robert A. *Who Governs?* New Haven: Yale University Press, 1958.

Dahl, Robert A., and Charles E. Lindblom. *Politics, Economics, and Welfare.* New York: Harper & Row, 1953.

David, Irwin T. "Privatization in America." *The Municipal Year Book,* pp. 43–55. Washington, DC: International City Management Association, 1988.

Davis, Gary, and Bruce Piasecki. "Concluding remarks: The next steps after land disposal." In *America's Future in Toxic Waste Management: Lessons from Europe,* edited by Bruce Piasecki and Gary Davis, eds., pp. 223–232. Westport, CT: Quorum Books, 1987.

de Neufville, Judith I., and Stephen E. Barton. "Myths and the definition of policy problems: An exploration of home ownership and public–private partnerships." *Policy Sciences* 20(3) (1987): 181–206.

de Tocqueville, Alexis. *Democracy in America,* edited by Phillips Bradley. (Original work published in 1835.) New York: Vintage Books, 1945.

Dearborn, Philip M. "Assessing mandate effects on state and local governments." *Intergovernmental Perspective,* Summer–Fall 1994, pp. 22-26.

Denhardt, Robert B. *The Pursuit of Significance: Strategies for Managerial Success in Public Organizations.* Belmont, CA: Wadsworth, 1993.

DeParle, Jason. "HUD and private sector unite to push development of poor areas." *New York Times,* March 22, 1994.

Desai, Uday. "Public participation in environmental policy implementation: Case of the Surface Mining Control and Reclamation Act." *American Review of Public Administration* 19 (March 1989): 49–65.

Dillin, John. "Were US motorists shocked by Clinton's ethanol action?" *Christian Science Monitor,* July 11, 1994.

DiLorenzo, Thomas J. "User charges and special districts." In *Management Policies in Local Government Finance,* 3d ed., edited by J. Richard Aronson and Eli Schwartz, pp. 260–284. Washington, DC: International City Management Association, 1987.

Downs, Anthony. *Inside Bureaucracy.* Boston: Little, Brown, 1967.

___. "Up and down with ecology—the 'issue-attention cycle.'" *The Public Interest* 28 (Summer 1972): 38–50.

Downs, George W., and Patrick D. Larkey. *The Search for Government Efficiency.* Philadelphia: Temple University Press, 1986.

Dunford, Nathaniel. "N.Y.C., true to form." *New York Times,* April 10, 1990.

Easton, David. *The Political System.* New York: Alfred Knopf, 1953.

Eaton, Joseph W. "Planners as experts in uncertainty." *World Future Society Bulletin* 14 (March–April 1980): 27–32.

Edner, Sheldon M. "The evolution of an urban intergovernmental transportation decision system: Portland's investment in light rail transit." *Journal of Urban Affairs* 6 (Winter 1984): 81–97.

Ehrenhalt, Alan. "The new city manager is (1) invisible, (2) anonymous, (3) nonpolitical, (4) none of the above." *Governing* (September 1990): 41–46.

Eisinger, Peter K. *The Rise of the Entrepreneurial State: State and Local Economic Development Policy in the United States.* Madison: University of Wisconsin Press, 1988.

Eisner, Marc Allen. *Regulatory Politics in Transition.* Baltimore: Johns Hopkins University Press, 1993.

Feldmann, Linda. "Clinton proposals will rejig Superfund." *Christian Science Monitor*, February 1, 1994.

Ferris, James, and Elizabeth Graddy. "Contracting out: For what? With whom?" *Public Administration Review* 46 (July/August 1986): 332–344.

Finer, Herman J. "Administrative responsibility in democratic government." *Public Administration Review* 1(4) (1941): 335–350.

Fischhoff, Baruch, Stephen R. Watson, and Chris Hope. "Defining risk." *Policy Sciences* 17 (October 1984): 123–139.

Fisher, Linda L. "Fifty years of presidential appointments." In *The In-and-Outers: Presidential Appointees and Transient Government in Washington*, edited by G. Calvin Mackenzie, pp. 1–29. Baltimore: Johns Hopkins University Press, 1987.

Foster, Catherine. (1990). "Slump endangers welfare reform." *Christian Science Monitor*, December 28, 1990.

Friedrich, Carl J. "Public policy and the nature of administrative responsibility." In *Public Policy: 1940*, edited by Carl J. Friedrich and Edward S. Mason, pp. 3–24. Cambridge, MA: Harvard University Press, 1940.

Friesen, Jennifer. "The public employee's role in state constitutional rights." *Annals of the American Academy of Political and Social Science* 496 (March 1988): 88–97.

Fritschler, A. Lee. *Smoking and Politics: Policymaking and the Federal Bureaucracy*, 4th ed. Englewood Cliffs, NJ: Prentice Hall, 1989.

Fulton, William, and Morris Newman. "The charge of the electric car." *Governing*, (June 1994): 40–45.

Garnett, James L., and Charles H. Levine. "State executive branch reorganization: Patterns and perspectives." *Administration and Society* 12 (November 1980): 227–276.

Gaus, John M. *Reflections on Public Administration*. Tuscaloosa, AL: University of Alabama Press, 1947.

Germani, Clara. "New agency tries to break the thick web of drug-induced problems." *Christian Science Monitor*, January 25, 1991.

Gerston, Larry N., Cynthia Fraleigh, and Robert Schwab. *The Deregulated Society*. Belmont, CA: Brooks/Cole, 1988.

Gilbert, Charles S. "The framework of administrative responsibility." *Journal of Politics* 21 (August 1959): 373–407.

Gold, Kenneth. "Managing for success: A comparison of the private and public sectors." *Public Administration Review* 42 (November/December 1982): 568–574.

Gormley, William T., Jr. (1989a). "Custody battles in state administration." In *The State of the States*, edited by Carl E. Van Horn, pp. 131–152. Washington, DC: CQ Press, 1989.

———. [1989b]. *Taming the Bureaucracy: Muscles, Prayers and Other Strategies*. Princeton, NJ: Princeton University Press, 1989.

Grafton, Carl, and Anne Permaloff. "Budgeting reforms in perspective." In *Handbook on Public Budgeting and Financial Management*, edited by Jack Rabin and Thomas D. Lynch, pp. 89–124. New York: Marcel Dekker, 1983.

Grodzins, Morton. *The American System*. Chicago: Rand McNally, 1966.

Gross, Bertram M. *The Managing of Organizations*. 2 vol. New York: Free Press, 1964.

Gulick, Luther, and L. Urwick, eds. *Papers on the Science of Administration*. New York: Institute of Public Administration, 1937.

Haas, Lawrence J. "Dodging the budget bullet." *National Journal* (October 1, 1988): 2465–2469.

Hadden, Susan G. *A Citizen's Right to Know: Risk Communication and Public Policy*. Boulder, CO: Westview, 1989.

Hale, George E., and Marian L. Palley. *The Politics of Federal Grants*. Washington, DC: CQ Press, 1981.

Halloran, Richard. "Fighting fraud on a smaller scale." *New York Times*, January 14, 1989.

Hamilton, Alexander, John Jay, and James Madison. *The Federalist*. New York: Modern Library, n.d.

Hargrove, Erwin C., and John C. Glidewell, eds. *Impossible Jobs in Public Management*. Lawrence: University Press of Kansas, 1990.

Hatry, Harry P. "Determining the effectiveness of government services." In *Handbook of Public Administration*, edited by James L. Perry. San Francisco: Jossey-Bass, 1989.

——— et al. *Program Analysis for State and Local Governments*, 2nd ed. Washington, DC: Urban Institute, 1987.

Heclo, Hugh. *A Government of Strangers: Executive Politics in Washington*. Washington, DC: Brookings Institution, 1977.

———. "Issue networks and the executive establishment." In *The New American Political System*, edited by Anthony King. Washington, DC: American Enterprise Institute, 1978.

Hey, Robert P. "Lesson from GAIN program: Realism a must." *Christian Science Monitor*, June 15, 1989.

Heymann, Philip B. *The Politics of Public Management*. New Haven: Yale University Press, 1987.

Hilts, Philip J. "A guardian of U.S. health is failing under pressures." *New York Times,* December 4, 1989.

Hinds, Michael deCourcy. "Troubles of a safety agency: A battle to keep functioning." *New York Times,* March 18, 1989.

___. "U.S. adds programs with little review of local burdens." *New York Times*, March 24, 1992.

Hirschmann, Albert O. *Exit, Voice and Loyalty: Responses to Decline in Firms, Organizations, and States.* Cambridge, MA: Harvard University Press, 1970.

Holmes, Steven A. "In 4 years, Disabilities Act hasn't improved jobs rate." *New York Times*, October 23, 1994.

Holmstrom, David. "Indians buck the bureaucracy." *Christian Science Monitor*, November 8, 1992.

___. "Major changes in flood control advanced in key federal study." *Christian Science Monitor*, July 21, 1994.

Huddleston, Mark W. "Is the SES a higher civil service?" *Policy Studies Journal* 17 (Winter 1988–89): 406–419.

Hunter, Floyd. *Community Power Structure*. Garden City, NY: Doubleday, 1953.

Huntington, Samuel P. "The marasmus of the I.C.C." *Yale Law Journal* 61(4) (1952): 467–509.

Ifill, Gwen. "White House split over budget cuts." *New York Times*, December 16, 1993.

Jacobson, Louis. "A hands-on community builder." *National Journal*, September 10, 1994.

Janis, Irving L. *Victims of Groupthink*. Boston: Houghton Mifflin, 1972.

Johnson, William C. *The Politics of Urban Planning*. New York: Paragon House, 1989.

"Joining inner-city school alliances." *National Journal*, September 3, 1988.

Jones, Bryan D. *Governing Buildings and Building Government*. Tuscaloosa: University of Alabama Press, 1984.

Jones, Bryan D., and Lynn W. Bachelor, with Carter Wilson. *The Sustaining Hand: Community Leadership and Corporate Power*. Lawrence: University Press of Kansas, 1986.

Jos, Philip H., Mark E. Tompkins, and Steven W. Hays. "In praise of difficult people: A portrait of the committed whistleblower." *Public Administration Review* 41 (November/December 1989): 552-561.

Katz, Jeffrey L. "Help wanted." *Governing* (August 1990): 68–72.

Katzmann, Robert A. *Institutional Disability: The Saga of Transportation Policy for the Disabled*. Washington, DC: Brookings Institution, 1986.

Kaufman, Herbert. *The Forest Ranger: A Study in Administrative Behavior*. Baltimore: Johns Hopkins University Press, 1960.

___. *Administrative Feedback: Monitoring Subordinates' Behavior*. Washington, DC: Brookings Institution, 1973.

Kerwin, Cornelius M. *Rulemaking: How Government Agencies Write Law and Make Policy*. Washington, DC: CQ Press, 1994.

Kettl, Donald F. *Government by Proxy: (Mis?)-Managing Federal Programs*. Washington, DC: CQ Press, 1988.

___. *Sharing Power: Public Governance and Private Markets*. Washington, DC: Brookings Institution, 1993.

Kilborn, Peter T. (1990a) "In small steps, program puts homeless into jobs." *New York Times*, January 28, 1990.

Kingdon, John W. *Agendas, Alternatives, and Public Policies*. Boston: Little, Brown, 1984.

Klingner, Donald E. "Variables affecting the design of state and local personnel systems." In *Public Personnel Administration,* edited by Steven W. Hays and Richard C. Kearney, pp. 18–26. Englewood Cliffs, NJ: Prentice Hall, 1983.

Knack, Ruth Eckdish. "Empowerment to the People." *Planning* (February 1993): 21–28.

Knott, Jack H., and Gary J. Miller. *Reforming Bureaucracy: The Politics of Institutional Choice*. Englewood Cliffs, NJ: Prentice Hall, 1987.

Koenig, Louis W. *The Chief Executive*, 5th ed. San Diego: Harcourt Brace Jovanovich, 1986.

Kosterlitz, Julie. "Devil in the details." *National Journal* (December 2, 1989): 2942–2946.

Krieger, Martin H. "Big decisions and a culture of decisionmaking." *Journal of Policy Analysis and Management* 5 (Summer 1986): 779–797.

Kweit, Mary Grisez, and Robert W. Kweit. *Implementing Citizen Participation in a Bureaucratic Society*. New York: Praeger, 1981.

Langton, Stuart. "The evolution of federal citizen involvement policy." *Policy Studies Review* 1 (November 1981): 369–378.

Lawrence, Christine C. "New chief financial officers straddle branches of power." *Congressional Quarterly* (August 17, 1991): 2286–2287.

Lee, Robert D., Jr. "Participants in the public personnel management process." *Policy Studies Journal* 11 (December 1982): 261–270.

Lemov, Penelope. "Jailhouse, Inc." *Governing* (May 1993): 44–48.

Levin, Martin A., and Mary Bryna Sanger. *Making Government Work*. San Francisco: Jossey-Bass, 1994.

Levin, Martin A., and Barbara Ferman. *The Political Hand: Policy Implementation and Youth Employment Programs*. New York: Pergamon, 1985.

Levine, Richard. "Koch argues city can't totally end fatal child abuse." *New York Times*, December 31, 1988.

Levy, Frank S., Arnold J. Meltsner, and Aaron Wildavsky. *Urban Outcomes: Schools, Streets, and Libraries*. Berkeley: University of California Press, 1974.

Lewis, Eugene. *American Politics in a Bureaucratic Age: Citizens, Constituents, Clients, and Victims*. Cambridge, MA: Winthrop, 1977.

———. *Public Entrepreneurship: Toward a Theory of Bureaucratic Political Power*. Bloomington: University of Indiana Press, 1980.

Lewis, Neil A. "Two studies rate U.S. and states on meeting children's needs." *New York Times*, January 9, 1990.

Lewis-Beck, Michael, and Tom W. Rice. "Government growth in the United States." *Journal of Politics* 47 (February 1985): 2–30.

Light, Paul C. *Monitoring Government: Inspectors General and the Search for Accountability*. Washington, DC: Brookings Institution, 1993.

Lindblom, Charles E. "The science of muddling through." *Public Administration Review* 19 (1959): 79–88.

———. *Politics and Markets: The World's Political-Economic Systems*. New York: Basic Books, 1977.

Linder, Stephen H., and B. Guy Peters. "Relativism, contingency, and the definition of success in implementation research." *Policy Studies Review* 7 (Autumn 1987): 116–127.

Linowes, David F. *Privatization: Toward More Effective Government* (Report of the President's Commission on Privatization). Urbana: University of Illinois Press, 1988.

Lipsky, Michael. *Street-Level Bureaucracy*. New York: Basic Books, 1979.

Long, Norton E. "Power and administration." *Public Administration Review* 9 (1949): 257–264.

Longley, Lawrence D., Herbert A. Terry, and Erwin G. Krasnow. "Citizen groups in broadcast regulatory policy-making." *Policy Studies Journal* 12 (December 1983): 258–270.

Lowi, Theodore J. *At the Pleasure of the Mayor: Patronage and Power in New York City, 1898–1958*. New York: Free Press, 1964.

Mahtesian, Charles (1994a). "Immigration: the symbolic crackdown." *Governing* (May 1994): 52–57.

———. (1994b) "The human services nightmare." *Governing* (December 1994): 44–48.

March, James G., and Johan P. Olson. "Organizing political life: What administrative reorganization tells us about government." *American Political Science Review* 77 (June 1983): 281–296.

Marini, Frank, ed. *Toward a New Public Administration: The Minnowbrook Perspective*. San Francisco: Chandler, 1971.

Martin, John Bartlow. "The blast in Centralia No. 5: A mine disaster no one stopped." *Harper's Magazine* (March 1948): 193–220.

McCubbins, Mathew, and Thomas Schwartz. "Congressional oversight overlooked: Police patrols versus fire alarms." *American Journal of Political Science* 28 (February 1984): 165–179.

Medoff, Peter and Holly Sklar. *Streets of Hope: The Rise and Fall of an Urban Neighborhood*. Boston: South End Press, 1994.

Meier, Kenneth J. *Regulation: Politics, Bureaucracy, and Economics*. New York: St. Martin's, 1985.

Michels, Robert. *Political Parties: A Sociological Study of the Oligarchical Tendencies of Modern Democracy*. (Originally published in 1915.) New York: Free Press, 1966.

Mikesell, John L. *Fiscal Administration: Analysis and Applications for the Public Sector*, 2nd ed. Chicago: Dorsey, 1986.

Mills, C. Wright. *The Power Elite*. New York: Oxford University Press, 1956.

Minnesota Planning. *Minnesota Milestones: A Report Card for the Future*. Saint Paul, MN, 1992.

Minnesota, State of, Department of Employee Relations. *Affirmative Action Manual*. n.d.

Mitchell, Alison. "Posing as welfare recipient, agency head finds indignity." *New York Times*, February 5, 1993.

Moharir, Vasant V. "Administration without bureaucratization: What alternatives?" *International Review of Administrative Sciences* 55 (June 1989): 165–181.

Mohr, Lawrence B. *Impact Analysis for Program Evaluation*. Pacific Grove, CA: Brooks/Cole, 1988.

Moore, Mark H. "Realms of obligation and virtue." In *Public Duties: The Moral Obligations of Government Officials,* edited by Joel L. Fleischman, Lance Liebman, and Mark H. Moore, pp. 3–31. Cambridge, MA: Harvard University Press, 1981.

Moore, W. John. "Locked in." *National Journal*, July 30, 1994, pp. 1784–1788.

___. "Mandates without money." *National Journal* (October 4, 1986): 2366–2370.

___. "Federalism renewed, with reservations." *National Journal* (January 30, 1988): 274.

Morgan, David R., and Robert E. England. "The two faces of privatization." *Public Administration Review* 48 (November/December 1988): 979–987.

Morrison, David C. "Pentagon polluters." *National Journal* (July 1, 1989): 1689–1691.

Mosher, Frederick C. *Democracy and the Public Service*. New York: Oxford University Press, 1968.

Murray, Charles. *Losing Ground: American Social Policy, 1950–1980*. New York: Basic Books, 1984.

Nagel, Stuart S. "Efficiency, effectiveness, and equity in public policy evaluation." *Policy Studies Review* 6 (August 1986): 99–120.

Nalbandian, John. "The U.S. Supreme Court's 'consensus' on affirmative action." *Public Administration Review* 49 (January/February 1989): 38–45.

National Commission on the Public Service. *Leadership for America: Rebuilding the Public Service*. Washington, DC: 1989.

National Commission on the Public Service, Task Force on Education and Training. *Investment for Leadership*. Washington, DC: The Commission, 1989.

National Commission on the Public Service, Task Force on Recruitment and Retention. *Committing to Excellence*. Washington, DC: The Commission, 1989.

National Commission on the State and Local Public Service. *Hard Truths/Tough Choices: An Agenda for State and Local Reform*. Albany: Nelson Rockefeller Institute of Government, State University of New York, 1993.

National Council on Public Works Improvement. *Fragile Foundations: A Report on America's Public Works*. Washington, DC: U.S. Government Printing Office, 1988.

National Performance Review. *Creating a Government That Works Better and Costs Less*. New York: Plume Books, 1993.

Neustadt, Richard E. *Presidential Power: The Politics of Leadership from FDR to Carter*. New York: Wiley, 1980.

Neustadt, Richard E., and Harvey Fineberg. *The Epidemic that Never Was: Policy Making and the Swine Flu Affair*. New York: Vintage Books, 1983.

Newlin, Eliza. "Doing what feds say, not what feds do." *National Journal* (June 22, 1991): 1570–1572.

O'Brien, Robert M., Michael Clarke, and Sheldon Kamieniecki. "Open and closed systems of decision making: The case of toxic waste management." *Public Administration Review* 44 (July/August 1984): 334–340.

O'Leary, Rosemary. "Five trends in government liability under environmental laws: Implications for public administration." *Public Administration Review* 53 (November/December 1993): 542–549.

Olmstead, Larry. "Deciphering state's takeover of Jersey City schools." *New York Times*, November 26, 1993.

Osborne, David, and Ted Gaebler. *Reinventing Government*. Reading, MA: Addison-Wesley, 1992.

"Panel urges privatization of U.S. services." *New York Times,* March 19, 1988.

Pear, Robert. "Suits force U.S. and states to pay more for Medicaid." *New York Times*, October 29, 1991.

___. "Auditors find many problems in day care centers." *New York Times,* February 11, 1994.

Peirce, Neal R. "Will Los Angeles choke on Pacific Rim growth?" *National Journal*, December 17, 1988.

___. "Some cities (finally) are listening up." *National Journal*, September 10, 1994, p. 2099.

Perritt, Henry H., Jr. "Negotiated rulemaking in practice." *Journal of Policy Analysis and Management* 5(3) (1986): 482–495.

Peters, Charles. "From Ougadougou to Cape Canaveral: Why the bad news doesn't travel up." *Washington Monthly* (April 1986): 27–31.

Pflaum, Ann M., and Timothy J. Delmont. "External scanning—a tool for planners." *American Planning Association Journal* 53 (Winter 1987): 58–68.

Presidential Commission on the Space Shuttle *Challenger* Accident. *Report.* Washington, DC: U.S. Government Printing Office, 1986.

President's Private Sector Survey on Cost Control. *War on Waste.* New York: Macmillan, 1984.

Pressman, Jeffrey L., and Aaron B. Wildavsky. *Implementation.* Berkeley, CA: University of California Press, 1973.

Prottas, Jeffrey. "The cost of free services." *Public Administration Review* 41 (September/October 1981): 526–534.

"Public employment growth." *Governing* (February 1991): 70–71.

Quirk, Paul. *Industry Influence on Federal Regulatory Agencies.* Princeton, NJ: Princeton University Press, 1981.

Raphaelson, Arnold H. "The property tax." In *Management Policies in Local Government Finance,* 3rd ed., J. Richard Aronson and Eli Schwartz, eds., pp. 201–228. Washington, DC: International City Management Association, 1987.

Reagan, Michael D. *Regulation: The Politics of Policy.* Boston: Little, Brown, 1987.

Reagan, Michael D., and John G. Sanzone. *The New Federalism,* 2nd ed. New York: Oxford University Press, 1981.

Renfrow, Patty D., and David J. Houston. "A comparative analysis of rulemaking provisions in state administrative procedure acts," *Policy Studies Review* 6 (May 1987): 657–665.

Rhodes, Richard. *The Making of the Atomic Bomb.* New York: Simon & Schuster, 1988.

Ripley, Randall B., and Grace A. Franklin. *Bureaucracy and Policy Implementation,* 2nd ed. Chicago: Dorsey, 1986.

Roberts, Sam. "Long after Lisa, tragedy of abuse can still happen." *New York Times,* February 8, 1988.

Romzek, Barbara S., and Melvin J. Dubnick. "Accountability in the public sector: Lessons from the *Challenger* tragedy." *Public Administration Review* 47 (May/June 1987): 227–238.

Rose, Arnold M. *The Power Structure: Political Process in American Society.* New York: Oxford University Press, 1967.

Rosen, Bernard. *Holding Government Bureaucracies Accountable,* 2nd ed. New York: Praeger, 1989.

Rosenbloom, David H. "What every personnel manager should know about the Constitution." In *Public Personnel Administration,* edited by Steven W. Hays and Richard C. Kearney, pp. 27–41. Englewood Cliffs, NJ: Prentice Hall, 1983.

Rosenbloom, David H., and James D. Carroll. *Toward Constitutional Competence: A Casebook for Public Administrators.* Englewood Cliffs, NJ: Prentice Hall, 1990.

Rubin, Irene S. *The Politics of Public Budgeting.* Chatham, NJ: Chatham House, 1990.

Salamon, Lester M. "The goals of reorganization: A framework for analysis." *Administration and Society* 12 (1981): 471–500.

___, ed. *Beyond Privatization: The Tools of Government Action.* Washington, DC: Urban Institute Press, 1989.

Savas, E. S. *Privatization: The Key to Better Government.* Chatham, NJ: Chatham House, 1987.

Scavo, Carmine. "The use of participative mechanisms by large US cities." *Journal of Urban Affairs* 15:1 (1993) pp. 93–109.

Schattschneider, E. E. *The Semi-Sovereign People.* New York: Holt, Rinehart & Winston, 1960.

Schatz, Willie. "Learning the Lingua Franca." *Washington Post National Weekly Edition,* April 30–May 6, 1990.

Schmickle, Sharon. "Exported pesticides returned in the food we ate." *Minneapolis Star Tribune,* June 6, 1990.

Schneider, Keith. "U.S. admits waste in its contracts." *New York Times,* December 2, 1992.

___. "Scientist who managed to 'shock the world' on atomic workers' health." *New York Times,* May 3, 1990.

Schneider, Mark, and Kee Ok Park. "Metropolitan counties as service delivery agents: The still forgotten governments." *Public Administration Review* 49 (July/August 1989): 345–352.

Scholz, John T. "State regulatory reform and federal regulation." *Policy Studies Review* 1 (November 1981): 347–359.

Schwarz, John E. *America's Hidden Success: A Reassessment of Public Policy from Kennedy to Reagan,* rev. ed. New York: Norton, 1988.

Seidman, Harold, and Robert Gilmour. *Politics, Position and Power: The Dynamics of Federal Organization,* 4th ed. New York: Oxford University Press, 1986.

Selznick, Philip. *Leadership in Administration.* New York: Harper & Row, 1957.

___. *TVA and the Grass Roots.* New York: Harper & Row, 1966.

Shannon, John. "The faces of fiscal federalism." *Intergovernmental Perspective* 14 (Winter 1988): 15–17.

Simon, Herbert A. *Administrative Behavior,* 2nd ed. New York: Free Press, 1957.

Simon, Herbert A., Donald Smithburg, and Victor Thompson. *Public Administration.* New York: Alfred Knopf, 1950.

Sjoberg, Gideon, Richard A. Brymer, and Buford Farris. "Bureaucracy and the lower class." *Sociology and Social Research* 50 (1966): 325–337.

Smith, Steven Rathgeb, and Michael Lipsky. *Nonprofits for Hire: The Welfare State in the Age of Contracting.* Cambridge, MA: Harvard University Press, 1993.

Solano, Paul D., and Marvin R. Brams. "Budgeting." In *Management Policies in Local Government Finance,* 3d ed., edited by J. Richard Aronson and Eli Schwartz, pp. 93–117. Washington, DC: International City Management Association, 1987.

Solomon, Burt. "The true secrets of Clintonites linger behind the 'vetting' veil." *National Journal,* March 13, 1993, pp. 644–645.

Sontag, Deborah with Stephen Engelberg. "Black officers in I.N.S. push racial boundaries." *New York Times,* October 30, 1994.

Specter, Michael. "Oregon legislators face up to the hard job of 'playing God.'" *Washington Post National Weekly Edition,* February 15–21, 1988.

Stanfield, Rochelle L. "Bridging the gap." *National Journal,* January 15, 1994.

Starobin, Paul. "Foggy forecasts." *National Journal,* May 19, 1990, pp. 1212–1215.

Starr, Paul. "The limits of privatization." In *Prospects for Privatization,* edited by Steve H. Hanke. *Proceedings of the Academy of Political Science* 36(3) (1987): 138–152.

Statistical Abstract of the United States, Washington, DC: U.S. Government Printing Office, 1994.

Steffens, Richard. "What the incubators have hatched." *Planning,* May 1992, pp. 28–30.

Steinbach, Carol F. "New corporate activism on schools." *National Journal,* April 7, 1990.

Sterngold, James. "Japanese begin to crack the wall of secrecy around official acts." *New York Times,* May 15, 1994.

Stevens, William K. "Governors take aim at U.S. strings that come without money attached." *New York Times,* February 21, 1988.

Stevenson, Richard W. "The pain of British privatizations has yielded a string of successes." *New York Times,* February 22, 1994.

___. "Competition for contracts trims costs for Pentagon." *New York Times,* March 31, 1988.

Stone, Deborah. *Policy Paradox and Political Reason.* Glenview, IL: Scott, Foresman, 1988.

Svara, James H. and Associates. *Facilitative Leadership in Local Government.* San Francisco: Jossey-Bass, 1994.

Sylvia, Ronald D., Kenneth J. Meier, and Elizabeth M. Gunn. *Program Planning and Evaluation for the Public Manager.* Monterey, CA: Brooks/Cole, 1985.

Tanzer, Andrew. "There is a sense of running the country." *Forbes* (April 30, 1990): 202–203

Taylor, Frederick. *Scientific Management.* New York: Harper & Row, 1947.

Thomas, Owen. "Citizen patrols: Self-help to an extreme?" *Christian Science Monitor,* July 5, 1988.

Thompson, Dennis F. *Political Ethics and Public Office.* Cambridge, MA: Harvard University Press, 1987.

Thompson, Victor A. *Without Sympathy or Enthusiasm: The Problem of Administrative Compassion.* Tuscaloosa: University of Alabama Press, 1975.

Tierney, John T. "Government corporations and managing the public's business." *Political Science Quarterly* 99 (Spring 1984): 73–92.

Tolchin, Martin. "Study says half of those eligible get food stamps." *New York Times,* November 15, 1988.

___. "The legislative veto, an accommodation that goes on and on." *New York Times,* March 31, 1989.

Uhlig, Mark A. "A system that couldn't save a child from lethal abuse." *New York Times,* November 6, 1987.

U.S. General Accounting Office. *A Glossary of Terms Used in the Federal Budget Process,* 3rd ed. Washington, DC: GAO, 1981.

U.S. Office of Management and Budget. *Budget of the United States Government, Fiscal Year 1991.* Washington, DC: U.S. Government Printing Office, 1990.

U.S. Office of Personnel Management. *Taking Action on the Problem Employee.* Washington, DC: U.S. Government Printing Office, 1984.

U.S. Senate Committee on Governmental Affairs. *Government in the Sunshine Act: History and Recent Issues.* Washington, DC: U.S. Government Printing Office, 1989.

U.S. Senate Committee on Governmental Affairs, Subcommittee on Federal Services, Post Office and Civil Service. *The Department of Energy's Reliance on Private Contractors to Perform the Work of Government.* Washington, DC: U.S. Government Printing Office, 1990.

Valente, Carl F., and Lydia D. Manchester. *Rethinking Local Services: Examining Alternative Delivery Approaches.* Washington, DC: International City Management Association, 1984.

Van Riper, Paul P. *History of the United States Civil Service.* New York: Harper & Row, 1958.

___. "The American administrative state: Wilson and the founders." In *A Centennial History of the American Administrative State,* edited by Ralph Clark Chandler, pp. 3-36. New York: Free Press, 1987.

Vickers, Geoffrey. "The assumptions of policy analysis." *Policy Studies Journal* 9 (Special issue #2, 1980-81): 552-58.

Volcker, Paul A. *Public Service: The Quiet Crisis.* Washington, DC: American Enterprise Institute for Public Policy Research, 1988.

Wald, Matthew L. "Recharting war on smog." *New York Times,* October 10, 1989.

Walsh, Annmarie Hauck. *The Public's Business: The Politics and Practices of Government Corporations.* Cambridge, MA: MIT Press, 1978.

Walters, Jonathan (1994a). "The fine art of firing the incompetent." *Governing,* (June 1994): 34-39.

___. (1994b). "The reinvention of the labor leader." *Governing* (November 1994): 44-48.

Warren, Kenneth E. *Administrative Law in the Political System,* 2nd ed. St. Paul: West, 1988.

Warwick, Donald P. "The ethics of administrative discretion." In *Public Duties: The Moral Obligations of Government Officials,* edited by Joel L. Fleischman, Lance Liebman, and Mark H. Moore, pp. 93-127. Cambridge, MA: Harvard University Press, 1981.

Weber, Max. *The Theory of Social and Economic Organization,* translated by A. M. Henderson and Talcott Parsons. (Originally published in 1922.) New York: Free Press, 1964.

Weiss, Carol H. "Evaluating social programs: What have we learned?" *Society* 25 (November/December 1987): 40-45.

West, William F., and Joseph Cooper. "The rise of administrative clearance." In *The Presidency and Public Policy Making,* edited by George C. Edwards et al., pp. 192-214. Pittsburgh: University of Pittsburgh Press, 1985.

White, Leonard D. *The Federalists.* New York: Macmillan, 1948.

___. *The Jacksonians.* New York: Macmillan, 1954.

White, William T. "Yaquina Bay: A case study in social impact assessment." In *Methodology of Social Impact Assessment,* 2nd ed., edited by Kurt Finsterbuch and C. P. Wolf, pp. 129-133. Stroudsburg, PA: Hutchinson Ross, 1981.

Wildavsky, Aaron. *Speaking Truth to Power: The Art and Craft of Policy Analysis.* Boston: Little, Brown, 1979.

___. *The New Politics of the Budgetary Process.* Glenview, IL: Scott, Foresman, 1988.

Wilson, James Q. *Bureaucracy: What Government Agencies Do and Why They Do It.* New York: Basic Books, 1989.

Wilson, Woodrow. "The study of administration." *Political Science Quarterly* 56 (December 1941): 486-506. [Originally published in *Political Science Quarterly* 1 (June 1887): 197-222.]

Winerip, Michael. "Billions for school are lost in fraud, waste and abuse." *New York Times,* February 2, 1994.

Wirt, Frederick M. *Power in the City: Decision Making in San Francisco.* Berkeley: University of California Press, 1974.

Wise, Charles R. "The liability of public administrators." In *Handbook of Public Administration,* edited by James L. Perry, pp. 585-601. San Francisco: Jossey-Bass, 1989.

Witt, Elder. "Sugarplums and lumps of coal." *Governing* (December 1989): 28-33.

Wittrock, Bjorn, and Peter deLeon. "Policy as a moving target: A call for conceptual realism." *Policy Studies Review* 6 (August 1986): 44-60.

Woll, Peter. *American Bureaucracy.* 2nd ed. New York: Norton, 1977.

Woolley, John T. *Monetary Politics: The Federal Reserve and the Politics of Monetary Policy.* Cambridge, UK: Cambridge University Press, 1984.

Yates, Douglas. *The Politics of Management.* San Francisco: Jossey-Bass, 1985.

Young, John D. "Reflections on the root causes of fraud, abuse, and waste in federal social programs." *Public Administration Review* 43 (July/August 1983): 362-369.

Zedlewski, Edwin W. "A short history of a recent virtue." *Policy Studies Review* 6 (August 1986): 63-70.

Index

Page references in **bold** indicate glossary terms.

Credits & Acknowledgments

Chapter 3
78 © 1990, *The Washington Post.* Reprinted with permission.

Chapter 4
109 Reprinted by permission from *The Christian Science Monitor,* © 1991, The Christian Science Publishing Society. All rights reserved.

Chapter 7
200 © 1987 by Chatham House Publishers, Inc. Reprinted by permission.

Chapter 9
263–264 Reprinted by permission of Allyn & Bacon from *Presidential Power: The Politics of Leadership from FDR to Carter* by Richard E. Neustadt, copyright © 1986. All rights reserved. 271–272 Reprinted with permission from *Public Administration Review,* © 1982 by the American Society for Public Administration. All rights reserved.

Chapter 11
306–307 Figure 11.1 Reprinted by permission of Dale Glasgow and Associates. 338–339 Reprinted by permission of *Forbes* magazine, Forbes, Inc., 1990.

Chapter 15
439 Reprinted from "Congressional Oversight: Overlooked Police Patrols versus Fire Alarms," by Mathew McCubbins and Thomas Schwartz, *American Journal of Political Science,* Vol. 28, February 1984, by permission of The University of Wisconsin Press.